II CORINTHIANS

THE NEW TESTAMENT LIBRARY
Current and Forthcoming Titles

Editorial Advisory Board

C. CLIFTON BLACK
M. EUGENE BORING
JOHN T. CARROLL

COMMENTARY SERIES

MATTHEW. BY R. ALAN CULPEPPER, MCAFEE SCHOOL OF THEOLOGY, MERCER UNIVERSITY
MARK. BY M. EUGENE BORING, BRITE DIVINITY SCHOOL, TEXAS CHRISTIAN UNIVERSITY
LUKE. BY JOHN T. CARROLL, UNION PRESBYTERIAN SEMINARY
JOHN. BY MARIANNE MEYE THOMPSON, FULLER THEOLOGICAL SEMINARY
ACTS. BY CARL R. HOLLADAY, CANDLER SCHOOL OF THEOLOGY, EMORY UNIVERSITY
ROMANS. BY BEVERLY ROBERTS GAVENTA, PRINCETON THEOLOGICAL SEMINARY
I CORINTHIANS. BY ALEXANDRA R. BROWN, WASHINGTON & LEE UNIVERSITY
II CORINTHIANS. BY FRANK J. MATERA, THE CATHOLIC UNIVERSITY OF AMERICA
GALATIANS. BY MARTINUS C. DE BOER, VU UNIVERSITY AMSTERDAM
EPHESIANS. BY STEPHEN E. FOWL, LOYOLA COLLEGE
PHILIPPIANS AND PHILEMON. BY CHARLES B. COUSAR, COLUMBIA THEOLOGICAL SEMINARY
COLOSSIANS. BY JERRY L. SUMNEY, LEXINGTON THEOLOGICAL SEMINARY
I & II THESSALONIANS. BY SUSAN EASTMAN, DUKE DIVINITY SCHOOL
I & II TIMOTHY AND TITUS. BY RAYMOND F. COLLINS, THE CATHOLIC UNIVERSITY OF AMERICA
HEBREWS. BY LUKE TIMOTHY JOHNSON, CANDLER SCHOOL OF THEOLOGY, EMORY UNIVERSITY
JAMES. BY REINHARD FELDMEIER, UNIVERSITY OF GÖTTINGEN
I & II PETER AND JUDE. BY LEWIS R. DONELSON, AUSTIN PRESBYTERIAN THEOLOGICAL SEMINARY
I, II, & III JOHN. BY JUDITH M. LIEU, UNIVERSITY OF CAMBRIDGE
REVELATION. BY BRIAN K. BLOUNT, UNION PRESBYTERIAN SEMINARY

CLASSICS

HISTORY AND THEOLOGY IN THE FOURTH GOSPEL. BY J. LOUIS MARTYN,
UNION THEOLOGICAL SEMINARY, NEW YORK
IMAGES OF THE CHURCH IN THE NEW TESTAMENT. BY PAUL S. MINEAR,
YALE DIVINITY SCHOOL
PAUL AND THE ANATOMY OF APOSTOLIC AUTHORITY. BY JOHN HOWARD SCHÜTZ,
UNIVERSITY OF NORTH CAROLINA, CHAPEL HILL
THEOLOGY AND ETHICS IN PAUL. BY VICTOR PAUL FURNISH, PERKINS SCHOOL
OF THEOLOGY, SOUTHERN METHODIST UNIVERSITY
THE WORD IN THIS WORLD: ESSAYS IN NEW TESTAMENT EXEGESIS AND THEOLOGY.
BY PAUL W. MEYER, PRINCETON THEOLOGICAL SEMINARY

GENERAL STUDIES

THE LAW AND THE PROPHETS BEAR WITNESS: THE OLD TESTAMENT IN THE NEW.
BY J. ROSS WAGNER, PRINCETON THEOLOGICAL SEMINARY
METHODS FOR NEW TESTAMENT STUDY. BY A. K. M. ADAM, UNIVERSITY OF GLASGOW
NEW TESTAMENT BACKGROUNDS. BY CARL R. HOLLADAY, CANDLER SCHOOL OF
THEOLOGY, EMORY UNIVERSITY

Frank J. Matera

II Corinthians

A Commentary

WESTMINSTER
JOHN KNOX PRESS
LOUISVILLE · KENTUCKY

© 2003 Frank J. Matera

2013 paperback edition
Originally published in hardback in the United States
by Westminster John Knox Press in 2003
Louisville, Kentucky

13 14 15 16 17 18 19 20 21 22—10 9 8 7 6 5 4 3 2 1

All rights reserved. No part of this book may be reproduced or transmitted in any form or by any means, electronic or mechanical, including photocopying, recording, or by any information storage or retrieval system, without permission in writing from the publisher. For information, address Westminster John Knox Press, 100 Witherspoon Street, Louisville, Kentucky 40202–1396. Or contact us online at www.wjkbooks.com.

Scripture quotations, unless otherwise indicated, are from the New Revised Standard Version of the Bible, copyright © 1989 by the Division of Christian Education of the National Council of the Churches of Christ in the U.S.A., and used by permission. The translations of 2 Corinthians and quotations from 2 Corinthians are the author's translation.

Book design by Jennifer K. Cox

Library of Congress Cataloging-in-Publication Data is on file at the Library of Congress, Washington, D.C.

ISBN-13: 978-0-664-22117-1 (hardback)
ISBN-10: 0-664-22117-3 (hardback)
ISBN-13: 978-0-664-23900-8 (paperback)

∞ The paper used in this publication meets the minimum requirements of the American National Standard for Information Sciences—Permanence of Paper for Printed Library Materials, ANSI Z39.48-1992.

In loving memory of my mother
Bertha Shivok Matera
1912–2003

CONTENTS

Preface		ix
Abbreviations		xi
Bibliography		xiii
Introduction		1
1	Ministry and Conflict	1
2	The Argument and Structure of 2 Corinthians	3
3	The Theology of 2 Corinthians	9
4	Between 1 and 2 Corinthians	15
5	Opposition at Corinth	20
6	One or Many Letters?	24

COMMENTARY

1:1–11		The Salutation and Benediction	35
Part 1	1:12–7:16	**The Crisis over Paul's Apostolic Integrity**	**45**
A.	1:12–2:13	Paul's Narration of Recent Events	46
	1. 1:12–14	The Letter's Theme	46
	2. 1:15–22	Paul's Reliability	50
	3. 1:23–2:4	A Change of Plans and a Harsh Letter	57
	4. 2:5–11	Forgiving the Offender	60
	5. 2:12–13	Paul's Anxiety at Troas	63
B.	2:14–7:4	The Integrity of Paul's Apostolic Ministry	65
	1. 2:14–4:6	The Ministry of a New Covenant	68
	a. 2:14–3:6	Qualified by God	68
	b. 3:7–18	The Ministries of Moses and Paul	82
	c. 4:1–6	Paul's Apostolic Integrity	97
	2. 4:7–5:10	Ministry and Apostolic Suffering	105
	a. 4:7–15	Life and Death in Apostolic Ministry	106

	b. 4:16–18	Present Transformation	113
	c. 5:1–10	Final Transformation	116
	3. 5:11–6:10	A Ministry of Reconciliation	126
	a. 5:11–21	Ambassadors for Christ	127
	b. 6:1–10	Appeal and Defense	145
	4. 6:11–7:4	Paul's Appeal for Reconciliation	156
C.	7:5–16	Paul's Narration of Recent Events Resumed	170

Part 2 8:1–9:15   An Appeal to Complete the Collection   179

A.	8:1–6	The Grace Given to the Churches of Macedonia	184
B.	8:7–15	An Appeal to Complete the Collection	188
C.	8:16–24	A Recommendation for Titus and the Two Brothers	194
D.	9:1–5	Paul's Purpose in Sending the Delegation	199
E.	9:6–9	The Relationship between Sowing and Reaping	204
F.	9:10–15	The Theological Significance of the Collection	206

Part 3 10:1–13:10   Defense and Warnings in Preparation for Paul's Third Visit   213

A.	10:1–18	Paul's Integrity and Missionary Assignment	216
	1. 10:1–11	Bold Whether Absent or Present	216
	2. 10:12–18	Paul's Assignment	228
B.	11:1–12:13	Boasting Foolishly	237
	1. 11:1–4	An Initial Appeal to Bear with Paul	239
	2. 11:5–15	Not Inferior to the Super-Apostles	244
	3. 11:16–21a	A Renewed Appeal to Bear with Paul	254
	4. 11:21b–29	Daring to Boast as a Fool	259
	5. 11:30–33	Boasting in Weakness	271
	6. 12:1–10	Boasting in Visions and Revelations	274
	7. 12:11–13	Peroration	286
C.	12:14–13:10	Preparations for Paul's Third and Final Visit	290
	1. 12:14–21	The Announcement of the Visit	291
	2. 13:1–10	The Need to Prepare for Paul's Visit	302

13:11–13   The Letter Closing   310

Index of Ancient Sources   315

Index of Authors   325

Index of Subjects   327

PREFACE

The writing of a commentary is an intensely personal endeavor. It requires concentration, discipline, and most of all, long periods of uninterrupted time. Somewhere in the midst of such a project, one begins to feel as though he or she has become a monk or hermit, cut off from the familiar social world of family and friends who are about the business of earning their daily bread. At such moments the noonday devil appears and interrogates the would-be author: "Why are you composing yet another commentary when there are so many, most of which are better than what you will write?" But if the temptation to abandon the task is resisted, and if the work is completed, the commentator finally receives his or her answer: the privilege of studying the sacred page, of asking it questions and being questioned by it, is itself sufficient reason to write yet another commentary. Thus every commentator eventually learns that even if the work falls short of one's expectations, as inevitably it will, the effort has not been in vain. Such, at least, has been my experience in writing this commentary on one of the most remarkable letters of the New Testament, a letter that challenges our understanding of ministry at nearly every turn of the page.

The research for writing this commentary began several years ago when I received an invitation from Westminster John Knox Press to write a commentary on 2 Corinthians for this series, the New Testament Library, but the actual writing was done during a sabbatical year (2001–2002). At the beginning of this project, I was, like many New Testament students, more or less persuaded of the composite nature of 2 Corinthians, and I simply assumed that I would adopt one or another of the many partition theories that have been proposed to explain the origin of this letter. But as my research progressed, I became more and more convinced that the present canonical form of this letter makes good literary, theological, and historical sense. Accordingly, I have aligned myself with a growing number of commentators who have questioned the need for partition theories and espoused the literary integrity of 2 Corinthians, for reasons that are explained in the introduction and throughout the exegetical sections of this commentary.

Now that this work has been completed, it is my pleasure to acknowledge the help and support that I have received from so many people. To Beverly

Gaventa, my editor for this volume, I owe a debt of gratitude for the care with which she read this manuscript and for the many helpful suggestions that she made. To my colleagues at Catholic University and my friends at Curley Hall, I am thankful for their constant interest in this project, which reminded me that although I worked alone I was never really alone. To my brother and sister-in-law, Joe and Lois Matera, I express my gratitude for their generous hospitality, which afforded me a quiet retreat where I often did some of my best thinking about 2 Corinthians. Finally, to the memory of my mother, who first taught me the rudiments of the faith I love so dearly, I dedicate this volume.

FRANK J. MATERA
THE CATHOLIC UNIVERSITY OF AMERICA
WASHINGTON, D.C.

ABBREVIATIONS

AB	Anchor Bible
AnBib	Analecta biblica
Ant.	*Jewish Antiquities*
BDAG	Bauer, W., F. W. Danker, W. F. Arndt, and F. W. Gingrich. *Greek-English Lexicon of the New Testament and Other Early Christian Literature*. 3d ed. Chicago: The University of Chicago Press, 1999.
BETL	Bibliotheca ephemeridum theologicarum lovaniensium
BFT	Biblical Foundations in Theology
BGBE	Beiträge zur Geschichte der biblischen Exegese
Bib	*Biblica*
Brenton	Sir Lancelot C. L. Brenton, *The Septuagint Version: Greek and English*. Grand Rapids: Zondervan, 1970.
BTB	*Biblical Theology Bulletin*
CBQ	*Catholic Biblical Quarterly*
DPL	*Dictionary of Paul and His Letters*. Edited by G. F. Hawthorne and R. P. Martin. Downers Grove, Ill.: InterVarsity Press, 1993.
Ebib	*Etudes bibliques*
EDNT	*Exegetical Dictionary of the New Testament*. Edited by H. Balz. Translated by G. Schneider. Grand Rapids: Eerdmans, 1990–1993.
ETL	*Ephemerides theologicae lovanienses*
HTR	*Harvard Theological Review*
ICC	International Critical Commentary
Int	*Interpretation*
JTS	*Journal of Theological Studies*
J.W.	*Jewish War*
JBL	*Journal of Biblical Literature*
JSNT	*Journal for the Study of the New Testament*
JSNTSup	Journal for the Study of the New Testament: Supplement Series

KJV	King James Version
LS	*Louvain Studies*
LXX	Septuagint
MT	Masoretic Text
NAB	New American Bible
NEB	New English Bible
Neot	*Neotestamentica*
NovT	*Novum Testamentum*
NRSV	New Revised Standard Version
NTG	New Testament Guides
NTS	*New Testament Studies*
RB	*Revue biblique*
REB	Revised English Bible
SBLDS	Society of Biblical Literature Dissertation Series
SBT	Studies in Biblical Theology
ScEs	*Science et esprit*
SJT	*Scottish Journal of Theology*
SMBen	Série monographique de Benedictina: Section paulinienne
SNTSMS	Society for New Testament Studies Monograph Series
TDNT	*Theological Dictionary of the New Testament.* Edited by G. Kittel and G. Friedrich. Translated by G. W. Bromiley. 10 vols. Grand Rapids: Eerdmans, 1964–1976.
TSK	*Theologische Studien und Kritiken*
WUNT	Wissenschaftliche Untersuchungen zum Neuen Testament
ZNW	*Zeitschrift für die neutestamentliche Wissenschaft und die Kunde der älteren Kirche*

BIBLIOGRAPHY

In the commentary that follows, commentaries are cited by author and page number.

1. Commentaries

Allo, E.-B. *Saint Paul Seconde Épître aux Corinthiens*. Ebib. Paris: Gabalda, 1937, 2d ed. 1956.
Barnett, Paul. *The Message of 2 Corinthians*. The Bible Speaks Today. Downers Grove, Ill.: InterVarsity Press, 1988.
———. *The Second Epistle to the Corinthians*. The New International Commentary on the New Testament. Grand Rapids: Eerdmans, 1997.
Barrett, C. K. *A Commentary on the Second Epistle to the Corinthians*. New York: Harper & Row, 1973.
Belleville, Linda L. *2 Corinthians*. The IVP New Testament Commentary Series. Downers Grove, Ill.: InterVarsity Press, 1996.
Best, Ernest. *Second Corinthians*. Interpretation: A Bible Commentary for Teaching and Preaching. Louisville, Ky.: John Knox, 1987.
Betz, Hans Dieter. *2 Corinthians 8 and 9: A Commentary on Two Administrative Letters of the Apostle Paul*. Hermeneia: A Critical and Historical Commentary on the Bible. Philadelphia: Fortress, 1985.
Bruce, F. F. *I and II Corinthians*. The New Century Bible Commentary. Grand Rapids: Eerdmans, 1971.
Bultmann, Rudolf. *The Second Letter to the Corinthians*. Original German Edition. Edited by Erich Dinkler. Translated by Roy A. Harrisville. Minneapolis: Augsburg, 1985.
Calvin, John. *2 Corinthians and Timothy, Titus, and Philemon*. Translated by T. A. Smail. Calvin's New Testament Commentaries. Grand Rapids: Eerdmans, 1996.
Carrez, Maurice. *La deuxième épître de Saint Paul aux Corinthiens*. Commentaire du Nouveau Testament deuxième série 8. Geneva: Labor et Fides, 1986.

Chrysostom, Saint John. *Homilies on the Epistles of Paul to the Corinthians.* In vol. 12 of *The Nicene and Post-Nicene Fathers.* Series 1. Edited by Philip Schaff 1896–1889. 14 vols. Repr. Peabody, Mass.: Hendrickson, 1994.

Danker, Frederick W. *II Corinthians.* Augsburg Commentary on the New Testament. Minneapolis: Augsburg, 1989.

Fallon, Frank. *2 Corinthians.* New Testament Message 11. Wilmington, Del.: Michael Glazier. 1980.

Furnish, Victor Paul. *II Corinthians.* Anchor Bible 32 A. Garden City, N.Y.: Doubleday, 1984.

Garland, David E. *2 Corinthians.* New American Commentary 29. Nashville: Broadman & Holman, 1999.

Hafemann, Scott J. *2 Corinthians.* The NIV Application Commentary. Grand Rapids: Zondervan, 2000.

Heinrici, C. F. Georg. *Der zweite Brief an die Korinther.* Kritisch-exegetischer Kommentar über das Neue Testament. Göttingen: Vandenhoeck & Ruprecht, 1900.

Héring, Jean. *The Second Epistle of Saint Paul to the Corinthians.* Translated by A. W. Heathcote and P. J. Allcock. London: Epworth, 1967.

Hughes, Philip E. *Paul's Second Letter to the Corinthians: The English Text with Introduction, Exposition and Notes.* New International Commentary. Grand Rapids: Eerdmans, 1962.

Kistemaker, S. J. *Exposition of the Second Epistle to the Corinthians.* New Testament Commentary. Grand Rapids: Baker, 1997.

Lambrecht, Jan. *Second Corinthians.* Sacra Pagina 8. Collegeville, Minn.: Liturgical Press, 1999.

Lietzmann, Hans, and Werner Georg Kümmel. *An die Korinther I & II.* Handbuch zum Neuen Testament. 5th enlarged edition. Tübingen: J. C. B. Mohr (Paul Siebeck), 1969.

Martin, Ralph P. *2 Corinthians.* Word Biblical Commentary 40. Waco, Tex.: Word Books, 1986.

McCant, Jerry W. *2 Corinthians.* Readings: A New Biblical Commentary. Sheffield: Sheffield Academic Press, 1999.

Omanson, Roger L., and John Ellington. *A Handbook on Paul's Second Letter to the Corinthians.* UBS Handbook Series. New York: United Bible Societies, 1993.

Plummer, Alfred. *A Critical and Exegetical Commentary on the Second Epistle of St. Paul to the Corinthians.* ICC. Edinburgh: T. & T. Clark, 1915.

Sampley, J. Paul. *The Second Letter to the Corinthians.* Pages 1–180 in *2 Corinthians, Galatians, Ephesians, Philippians, Colossians, 1 and 2 Thessalonians, 1 and 2 Timothy, Titus, Philemon.* Vol. 12 of *The New Interpreter's Bible: A Commentary in Twelve Volumes.* Edited by Leander E. Keck. Nashville: Abingdon, 2000.

Scott, James M. *2 Corinthians.* New International Biblical Commentary. Peabody, Mass.: Hendrickson, 1998.
Thrall, Margaret. *A Critical and Exegetical Commentary on The Second Epistle to the Corinthians.* 2 vols. ICC. Edinburgh: T. & T. Clark, 1994, 2000.
Wan, Sze-kar. *Power in Weakness: The Second Letter of Paul to the Corinthians.* The New Testament in Context. Harrisburg: Trinity Press International, 2000.
Windisch, Hans. *Der Zweite Korintherbrief.* Kritisch-exegetischer Kommentar über das Neue Testament. Göttingen: Vandenhoek & Ruprecht, 1924.
Witherington, Ben, III. *Conflict and Community in Corinth: A Socio-Rhetorical Commentary on 1 and 2 Corinthians.* Grand Rapids: Eerdmans, 1995.

2. Monographs and Articles

Amador, J. D. H. "Revisiting 2 Corinthians: Rhetoric and the Case for Unity." *NTS* 46 (2000): 92–111.
Andrews, S. B. "Too Weak Not to Lead: The Form and Function of 2 Cor 11.23b–33." *NTS* 41 (1995): 263–76.
Ascough, R. S. "The Completion of a Religious Duty: The Background of 2 Cor 8.1–15." *NTS* 42 (1996): 584–99.
Barrett, C. K. *Essays on Paul.* Philadelphia: Westminster, 1982.
Bash, Anthony. "A Psychodynamic Approach to the Interpretation of 2 Corinthians 10–13." *JSNT* 83 (2001): 51–67.
Bates, W. H. "The Integrity of II Corinthians." *NTS* 12 (1965): 139–46.
Beale, G. K. "The Old Testament Background of Reconciliation in 2 Corinthians 5–7 and Its Bearing on the Literary Problem of 2 Corinthians 6:14–7:1." *NTS* 35 (1989): 550–81.
Belleville, Linda L. "A Letter of Apologetic Self-Commendation: 2 Cor 1:8–7:16." *NovT.* 31 (1989): 142–63.
———. "Paul's Polemic and Theology of the Spirit in Second Corinthians." *CBQ* 58 (1996): 281–304.
———. *Reflections of Glory: Paul's Polemical Use of the Moses-Doxa Traditions in 2 Corinthians 3.1–18.* JSNTSup 52. Sheffield: Sheffield Academic Press, 1991.
Betz, Hans Dieter. "The Concept of the 'Inner Human Being' (*ho esō anthrōpos*) in the Anthropology of Paul." *NTS* 46 (2000): 315–41.
Bieringer, Reimund. "Der 2. Korintherbrief in den neuesten Kommentaren." *ETL* 67 (1991): 107–30.
———, ed. *The Corinthian Correspondence.* BETL 125. Leuven: Leuven University Press, 1996.
Bieringer, Reimund, and Jan Lambrecht. *Studies on 2 Corinthians.* BETL 112. Leuven: Leuven University Press, 1994.

Boers, Hendrikus. "2 Corinithians 5:14–6:2: A Fragment of Pauline Christology." *CBQ* 64 (2002): 527–47.

Bonneau, Guy. "À La Vie, À La Mort: Le conflit à Corinthe et ses enjeux théologiques en 2 Co 2,14–7,4." *ScEs* 51 (1999): 351–66.

Bornkamm, Günther. "The Authority and Integrity of the New Testament." *NTS* 8 (1962): 258–64.

Breytenbach, C. "Paul's Proclamation and God's 'Thriambos' (Notes on 2 Corinthians 2.14–16b)." *Neot* 24 (1990): 255–71.

Brown, Alexandra R. "The Gospel Takes Place: Paul's Theology of Power-in-Weakness in 2 Corinthians." *Int* 52 (1998): 271–85.

Campbell, Douglas A. "An Anchor for Pauline Chronology: Paul's Flight from 'the Ethnarch of King Aretas' (2 Corinthians 11:32–33)." *JBL* 121 (2002): 279–302.

Carrez, Maurice. "Le 'nous' en 2 Corinthians. Paul parle-t-il au nom de toute la communauté, du groupe apostolique, de l'équipe ministérielle ou en son nom personnel? Contribution à l'étude de l'apostolicité dans 2 Corinthiens." *NTS* 26 (1979–80): 474–86.

Chow, John K. *Patronage and Power: A Study of Social Networks in Corinth.* JSNTSup 75. Sheffield: JSOT Press, 1992.

Collange, J.-F. *Énigmes de la deuxième épître de Paul aux Corinthiens: Étude Éxégétique de 2 Cor. 2:12–7:4.* SNTSMS 18. Cambridge: Cambridge University Press, 1972.

Crafton, Jeffrey A. *The Agency of the Apostle: A Dramatic Analysis of Paul's Responses to Conflict in 2 Corinthians.* JSNTSup 51. Sheffield: Sheffield Academic Press, 1991.

Craig, W. L. "Paul's Dilemma in 2 Corinthians 5.1–10: A 'Catch-22'?" *NTS* 34 (1988): 145–47.

Dahl, Nils Alstrup. "A Fragment and Its Context: 2 Cor. 6:14–7:1." Pages 62–69 in *Studies in Paul: Theology for the Early Christian Mission.* Minneapolis: Augsburg, 1977.

Danker, Frederick W. "Paul's Debt to the *De Corona* of Demosthenes: A Study of Rhetorical Techniques in Second Corinthians." Pages 268–80 in *Persuasive Artistry: Studies in New Testament Rhetoric in Honor of G. A. Kennedy.* Edited by Duane F. Watson. JSNTSup 50. Sheffield: Sheffield Academic Press, 1991.

De Lorenzi, Lorenzo, ed. *Paolo: Ministro del Nuovo Testamento (2 Cor 2,14–4, 6).* SMBen. Sezione Biblico Ecumenica, 9. Rome: Benedictine Editrice, 1987.

deSilva, David. *The Credentials of an Apostle: Paul's Gospel in 2 Corinthians 1–7.* Bibal Monograph Series 4. N. Richland Hills, Tex.: Bibal Press, 1998.

———. "Measuring Penultimate against Ultimate Reality: An Investigation of the Integrity and Argumentation of 2 Corinthians." *JSNT* 52 (1993): 41–70.

Duff, Paul B. "Metaphor, Motif, and Meaning: The Rhetorical Strategy behind the Image 'Let in Triumph' in 2 Corinthians 2:14. *CBQ* 53 (1991): 79–92.

———. "The Mind of the Redactor: 2 Cor 6:14–7:1 in Its Secondary Context." *NovT* 35 (1993): 160–80.

———. "2 Corinthians 1–7: Sidestepping the Division Hypothesis Dilemma." *BTB* 24 (1994): 16–26.

Dunn, James D. G. "2 Corinthians 3:17 'The Lord Is the Spirit.'" Pages 115–25 in *The Christ and the Spirit*. Vol. 1: *Christology*. Grand Rapids: Eerdmans, 1998.

Fee, Gordon D. *God's Empowering Presence: The Holy Spirit in the Letters of Paul*. Peabody, Mass.: Hendrickson, 1994.

Fellows, Richard G. "Was Titus Timothy?" *JSNT* 81 (2001): 33–58.

Fitzgerald, John T. *Cracks in an Earthen Vessel: An Examination of the Catalogues of Hardships in the Corinthian Correspondence*. SBLDS 99. Atlanta: Scholars Press, 1988.

Fitzmyer, Joseph A. "Glory Reflected on the Face of Christ (2 Cor 3:7–4:6)." Pages 64–79 in *According to Paul: Studies in the Theology of Paul*. New York: Paulist Press, 1993.

———. "Qumran and the Interpolated Paragraph in 2 Cor 6:17–7:1." Pages 205–17 in *Essay on the Semitic Background of the New Testament*. Sources for Biblical Studies 5. Missoula, Mont.: Scholars Press, 1974.

Forbes, Christopher. "Comparison, Self-Praise, and Irony: Paul's Boasting and Hellenistic Rhetoric." *NTS* 32 (1986): 1–30.

Furnish, Victor Paul. "Paul and the Corinthians: The Letters, the Challenges of Ministry, the Gospel." *Int* 52 (1998): 229–45.

Georgi, Dieter. *The Opponents of Paul in Second Corinthians*. Translated by Harold Attridge et al. Philadelphia: Fortress, 1986.

———. *Remembering the Poor: The History of Paul's Collection for Jerusalem*. Translated by Ingrid Racz. Nashville: Abingdon, 1992.

Gillman, John. "A Thematic Comparison: 1 Cor 15:50–57 and 2 Cor 5:1–5." *JBL* 107 (1988): 439–54.

Glasson, T. F. "2 Corinthians v. 1–10 versus Platonism." *SJT* 43 (1990): 145–55.

Goulder, M. "2 Cor. 6:14–7:1 as an Integral Part of 2 Corinthians." *NovT* 36 (1994): 47–57.

Grindheim, Sigurd. "The Law Kills but the Gospel Gives Life: The Letter-Spirit Dualism in 2 Corinthians 3.5–18." *JSNT* 84 (2001): 95–115.

Hafemann, Scott J. *Paul, Moses, and the History of Israel*. Peabody, Mass.: Hendrickson, 1996.

———. "Paul's Use of the Old Testament in 2 Corinthians." *Int* 52 (1998): 246–57.

———. "'Self-Commendation' and Apostolic Legitimacy in 2 Corinthians: A Pauline Dialectic?" *NTS* 36 (1990): 66–88.

———. *Suffering and Ministry in the Spirit: Paul's Defense of His Ministry in II Corinthians 2:14–3:3*. Grand Rapids: Eerdmans, 1990.

———. *Suffering and the Spirit: An Exegetical Study of II Cor. 2:14–3:3 within the Context of the Corinthian Correspondence*. WUNT. 2 Reihe, 19. Tübingen: J. C. B. Mohr (Paul Siebeck), 1986.

Harvey, A. E. *Renewal through Suffering: A Study of 2 Corinthians*. Studies of the New Testament and Its World. Edinburgh: T. & T. Clark, 1996.

Hay, David M., ed. *Pauline Theology*. Vol. 2: *1 and 2 Corinthians*. Minneapolis: Fortress, 1993.

Hays, Richard B. *Echoes of Scripture in the Letters of Paul*. New Haven: Yale University Press, 1989.

Hester, D. A. "The Unity of 2 Corinthians: A Test Case for a Re-discovered and Re-invented Rhetoric." *Neot* 33 (1999): 411–32.

Hyldahl, Niels. "Die Frage nach der literarischen Einheit des Zweiten Korintherbriefes." *ZNW* 64 (1973): 289–306.

Kennedy, James Houghton. *The Second and Third Epistles of St. Paul to the Corinthians*. London: Methuen, 1900.

Kertelge, Karl. "Letter and Spirit in 2 Corinthians 3." Pages 117–30 in *Paul and the Mosaic Law*. Edited by James D. G. Dunn. Grand Rapids: Eerdmans, 1996.

Kim, Seyoon. "2 Cor. 5:11–21 and the Origin of Paul's Concept of Reconciliation." *NovT* 39 (1997): 360–84.

Kreitzer, Larry. *2 Corinthians*. NTG. Sheffield: Sheffield Academic Press, 1996.

Kunz, W. S. "2 Corinthians: Implied Readers and Canonical Implications." *JSNT* 62 (1996): 43–63.

Lambrecht, Jan. *Collected Studies on Pauline Literature and on the Book of Revelation*. AnBib 147. Rome: Editrice Pontifio Instituto Biblico, 2001.

———. "The Defeated Paul, Aroma of Christ: An Exegetical Study of 2 Corinthians 2:14–16b." *LS* 20 (1995): 170–86.

———. "The Fool's Speech and Its Context: Paul's Particular Way of Arguing in 2 Cor 10–13." *Bib* 82 (2001): 306–24.

———. "Paul's Appeal and the Obedience to Christ: The Line of Thought in 2 Corinthians 10,1–6." *Bib* 77 (1996): 398–416.

———. "Paul's Boasting about the Corinthians: A Study of 2 Cor 8:24–9:5." *NovT* 40 (1998): 352–68.

———. *Pauline Studies: Collected Essays*. BETL 115. Leuven: Leuven University Press, 1994.

Lohse, Eduard, ed. *Verteidigung und Begründung des apostolischen Amtes (2 Kor 10–13)*. Rome: Abtei St. Paul vor den Maruern, 1992.

Marshall, Peter. *Enmity in Corinth: Social Conventions in Paul's Relations with the Corinthians*. WUNT. 2 Reihe, 23. Tübingen: J. C. B. Mohr (Paul Siebeck), 1987.

Martyn, J. Louis. "Epistemology at the Turn of the Ages." Pages 89–110 in *Theological Issues in the Letters of Paul*. Studies of the New Testament and Its World. Edinburgh: T. & T. Clark, 1997.

Matera, Frank J. "Apostolic Suffering and Resurrection Faith: Distinguishing between Appearance and Reality." Pages 387–405 in *Resurrection in the New Testament: Festschrift J. Lambrecht*. Edited by R. Bieringer, V. Koperski, and B. Lataire. BETL 165. Leuven: Leuven University Press, 2002.

McCant, J. W. "Paul's Thorn of Rejected Apostleship." *NTS* 34 (1988): 550–72.

McKay, K. L. "Observations on the Epistolary Aorist in 2 Corinthians." *NovT* 37 (1995): 154–58.

Mitchell, Margaret M. "New Testament Envoys in the Context of Greco-Roman Diplomatic and Epistolary Conventions: The Example of Timothy and Titus." *JBL* 111 (1992): 641–62.

Morray-Jones, C. R. A. "Paradise Revisited (2 Cor 12:1–12): The Jewish Mystical Background of Paul's Apostolate. Part 2: Paul's Heavenly Ascent and Its Significance." *HTR* 86 (1993): 265–92.

Moyer, Hubbard. "Was Paul Out of His Mind? Re-Reading 2 Corinthians 5:13." *JSNT* 70 (1998): 39–64.

Murphy-O'Connor, Jerome. "Faith and Resurrection in 2 Cor 4:13–14." *RB* 95 (1988): 543–50.

———. *Paul: A Critical Life*. Oxford: Clarendon Press, 1996.

———. *The Theology of the Second Letter to the Corinthians*. New Testament Theology. Cambridge: Cambridge University Press, 1991.

Nickle, Keith F. *The Collection: A Study in Paul's Strategy*. SBT 48. Naperville, Ill.: Alec R. Allenson, 1966.

O'Mahony, Kieran J. *Pauline Persuasion: A Sounding in 2 Corinthians 8–9*. JSNTSup 199. Sheffield: Sheffield Academic Press, 2000.

Osei-Bonsu, Joseph. "Does 2 Cor. 5.1–10 Teach the Reception of the Resurrection Body at the Moment of Death?" *JSNT* 28 (1986): 81–101.

Peterson, Brian K. "Conquest, Control, and the Cross: Paul's Self-Portrayal in 2 Corinthians 10–13." *Int* 52 (1998): 258–70.

———. *Eloquence and the Proclamation of the Gospel in Corinth*. SBLDS 163. Atlanta: Scholars Press, 1998.

Pickett, Raymond. *The Cross in Corinth: The Social Significance of the Death of Jesus*. JSNTSup 143. Sheffield: Sheffield Academic Press, 1997.

Quesnel, Michel. "Circonstances de composition de la seconde épître aux Corinthiens." *NTS* 43 (1997): 256–67.

Rissi, Mathias. *Studien zum Zweiten Korintherbrief: Der alte Bund—Der Prediger—Der Tod*. Abhandlungen zur Theologie des alten und neuen Testaments 56. Zurich: Zwingli Verlag, 1969.

Rolland, P. "La structure littéraire de la Deuxième Épître aux Corinthiens." *Bib* 71 (1990): 73–84.
Savage, T. B. *Power through Weakness: Paul's Understanding of the Christian Ministry in 2 Corinthians*. Cambridge: Cambridge University Press, 1996.
Schmithals, Walter. "Die Korintherbriefe als Briefsammlung." *ZNW* 64 (1973): 263–88.
Scott, J. M. "The Triumph of God in 2 Cor 2.14: Additional Evidence of Merkabah Mysticism in Paul." *NTS* 42 (1996): 260–81.
———. "The Use of Scripture in 2 Corinthians 6:16c–18 and Paul's Restoration Theology." *JSNT* 56 (1994): 73–99.
Stockhausen, Carol Kern. *Moses' Veil and the Glory of the New Covenant: The Exegetical Substructure of II Cor. 3,1–4,6*. AnBib 116. Rome: Pontifical Biblical Institute, 1989.
Stowers, Stanley K. "PERI MEN GAR and the Integrity of 2 Cor 8 and 9." *NovT* 32 (1990): 340–48.
Strecker, G. "Die Legitimität des paulinischen Apostolates nach 2 Korinther 10–13." *NTS* 38 (1992): 566–86.
Sumney, J. L. *Identifying Paul's Opponents: The Question of Method in 2 Corinthians*. JSNTSup 40. Sheffield: JSOT Press, 1990.
Taylor, N. H. "The Composition and Chronology of Second Corinthians." *JSNT* 44 (1991): 67–87.
Watson, Frances. "2 Cor. X–XIII and Paul's Painful Letter to the Corinthians." *JTS* 35 (1984): 324–46.
Wedderburn, A. J. M. "Paul's Collection: Chronology and History." *NTS* 48 (2002): 95–110.
Welborn, L. L. "The Identification of 2 Corinthians 10–13 with the 'Letter of Tears.'" *NovT* 37 (1995): 138–53.
———. "Like Broken Pieces of a Ring: 2 Cor 1.2–2.13; 7.5–16 and Ancient Theories of Literary Unity." *NTS* 42 (1996): 559–83.
Williamson, Lamar. "Led in Triumph: Paul's Use of *Thriambeuō*." *Int* 22 (1968): 317–32.
Young, Frances, and D. F. Ford. *Meaning and Truth in Second Corinthians*. BFT. Grand Rapids: Eerdmans, 1987.
Zmijewski, Josef. *Der Stil der paulinischen "Narrenrede": Analyse der Sprachgestaltung in 2 Kor 11, 1–12,10 als Beitrag zur Methodik von Stiluntersuchungen neutestamentlicher Texte*. Bonner Biblische Beiträge 52. Cologne-Bonn: Peter Hanstein Verlag, 1978.

INTRODUCTION

1. Ministry and Conflict

Second Corinthians is perhaps the most personal and revealing of Paul's letters. In terms of content it deals with the nature and exercise of Paul's apostolic ministry, functioning as a kind of *apologia pro vita sua*. In terms of tone, it is both compassionate and defensive, reconciling and provocative, forgiving and threatening, joyful and complaining, as Paul expresses his love for as well as his disappointment with a community that has misunderstood the nature of his ministry among them.

Written in response to a situation that threatened the relationship between Paul and the community, 2 Corinthians presupposes a prior history between the apostle and his community that has all the makings of a dramatic story: intruding villains, conflict and mistrust, sexual immorality, and suggestions of monetary mismanagement. If the events that transpired between Paul and the community were plotted as a narrative, a contemporary literary critic might suggest a plot of conflict that could be summarized in this way: The father and founder of the Corinthian community, Paul, finds himself alienated from his "children," who, abetted by intruding apostles, have called into question his integrity. To resolve this conflict, Paul must engage in an extended defense of his ministry in order to show the Corinthians that they, and those who have intruded upon his missionary field, have misunderstood the essential nature of apostolic ministry and, therefore, of the gospel. In this story, Paul and his associates (Timothy and Titus) find themselves in conflict with the Corinthians and a group of intruding apostles (whom Paul sarcastically dubs "super-apostles") over the very nature of apostolic ministry. At stake in this conflict are nothing less than the nature of ministry and the shape of the gospel that will be preached at Corinth.

If this brief analysis is correct, then 2 Corinthians is of vital importance for the contemporary church, which finds itself struggling with many of the same problems and issues that Paul encountered at Corinth: conflicts between ministers and their congregations, questions about the nature and style of ministry, the financial remuneration of ministers and the issue of patronage that underlies it, the obligation of more affluent congregations to support churches that are in need, and the ever-present danger of sexual immorality.

The responses that 2 Corinthians offers to these and other questions are deeply rooted in the nature of the gospel, and it is this theological dimension of the letter, more than anything else, that makes 2 Corinthians so important for the contemporary church. For example, Paul's defense of his apostolic ministry takes the form of an extended excursus in which he grounds his ministry in the promise of a new covenant and the new creation that God has effected through Christ (2:14–7:4). His exhortation for the community to separate itself from immorality is rooted in a keen understanding of the church as a community of the new covenant that has been sanctified by God's work of reconciliation in Christ (6:14–7:1). His call for the Corinthians to complete the work of the collection is made in the context of a theology of God's grace as manifested in the self-giving of God's Son (8:1–9:15). His reasons for not accepting the financial patronage of the Corinthians derive from a desire to preach the gospel free of charge without becoming their client (11:7–11), and his biting critique of the intruding apostles explains how the power of the gospel manifests itself in weakness and suffering rather than in boasting and extraordinary displays of one's ministry (10:1–12:21). In a word, Paul does not simply rebuke and reprimand. Rather, he continues to preach the gospel by showing that the manner in which he exercises his ministry is, in fact, the working out of the gospel that he preaches.

Second Corinthians, then, is an intensely personal writing in which the apostle speaks more extensively and intimately than in any of his other letters. The casual reader might dismiss this letter as self-centered and accuse Paul of protesting too much, but a closer reading reveals a theology no less profound than that in Paul's letters to the Romans and the Galatians. Here the careful reader will discover an insightful understanding of the relationship between apostolic suffering and divine consolation. Here the attentive reader will encounter a theology of reconciliation rooted in the salvific work of Christ that effects a new creation. Here the patient reader will uncover a deeper understanding of the resurrection and the resurrection body that awaits believers. Here the observant reader will find an extensive theology of the God who raises the dead. Within this letter, the apostle provides his audience with a vision of Christ as the image of God into whose glorious image believers are being transformed daily. Within this letter is the most penetrating and extensive discussion of apostolic ministry found in the New Testament. Those who persevere in the reading of this letter will come to a new appreciation of Paul as a self-sacrificing apostle who endures apostolic suffering for the sake of the church. Here they will encounter the meek and gentle apostle who patterns himself after the gentleness and meekness of Christ. Here they will find an apostle of perfect integrity who continually lives in God's presence, deeply aware that he must stand before the judgment seat of Christ. In a word, they will discover an apostle whose very life so embodies the gospel he preaches that to imitate him is to imitate Christ.

Introduction

Second Corinthians is often overshadowed by 1 Corinthians, which is better known, more clearly structured, and generally easier to comprehend. But for those who have not yet wrestled with 2 Corinthians, there are untold treasures to be mined, treasures that will provide them with a new understanding of God, Christ, the Spirit, ministry, and the church.

2. The Argument and Structure of 2 Corinthians

Since most people "dip into" a commentary in order to study a particular passage rather than read the commentary from start to finish, it may be helpful to summarize the content and argument of 2 Corinthians, as presented in this commentary, so that those who read only parts of this work will have a sense of the whole. What follows, then, is a synopsis or digest of the historical background and the literary-theological argument that Paul presents in this letter.

Second Corinthians begins with a salutation (1:1–2) and benediction (1:3–11) which signal two of the themes that Paul develops in this letter: (1) the comfort or consolation that God has granted Paul in the midst of suffering and affliction, especially the great affliction that he suffered in Asia (1:8), and (2) Paul's understanding of God as "the God who raises the dead" (1:9). The first theme is important because the manner in which Paul conducts his ministry has become a point of contention between him and the Corinthians, many of whom did not understand the reason for, and the nature of, his apostolic sufferings. The second is a leitmotif that runs throughout the letter: the God in whom Paul believes is the God and Father of Jesus Christ, the God who raises the dead. It is because of his faith in this God who raises the dead that Paul carries the dying of Jesus in his body so that the life of Jesus might be manifested in his body (4:10). Consequently Paul is firmly convinced that just as he presently experiences the sufferings of Christ, so he will enjoy the comfort and consolation that come from God. Paul's letter, then, will be about his apostolic sufferings and afflictions and the comfort that he receives, as Christ's apostle, from the God who raises the dead.

Part 1: The first part of 2 Corinthians (1:12–7:16), the longest and most complicated, deals with a crisis over Paul's apostolic integrity. Is Paul reliable and trustworthy? Can one depend upon him and the gospel he preaches? This part of the letter contains three sections.

In the first (1:12–2:13), Paul begins a narration of the recent events that have transpired between him and the community, events that have called into question his apostolic reliability. Although the precise nature of what happened is not clear, most commentators believe that Paul found it necessary to make an emergency visit to Corinth after he had written 1 Corinthians. This visit was a painful experience for Paul, since it appears that he was insulted or injured by a member of the community, and the Corinthians did not come to his defense.

Grieved by what happened, Paul altered his travel plans and returned to Ephesus, where he wrote a harsh and reprimanding letter to the Corinthians in lieu of a further visit.

Although the Corinthians were aware of these events, they did not know Paul's version of them. Why did he change his travel plans so abruptly? Why did he send them a harsh and reprimanding letter rather than visit them again as he had promised? Paul's purpose in 1:12–2:13 is to defend his reliability by giving his version of these painful events.

In 1:12–14 Paul announces the theme of this letter. He is writing so that the Corinthians, who already understand him in part, will comprehend him fully. When they do, they will make him their boast, just as he has already made them his boast. Having stated his theme, Paul defends his reliability, despite his change of travel plans, by grounding his faithfulness in the faithfulness of Jesus Christ (1:15–22). Paul then explains that he altered his plans and sent the Corinthians a harsh letter in order to avoid another painful visit (1:23–2:4). He now wants them to forgive the person who played a leading role in the events associated with that painful visit (2:5–11). In 2:12–13 Paul tells the Corinthians how distraught he was when he came to Troas, because he did not find Titus, the one who carried the harsh letter to Corinth. Somewhat unexpectedly, however, Paul halts his narration of these events, thereby holding the Corinthians in suspense as to their outcome. Did Paul eventually find Titus? If he did, what did Titus report? And how did Paul respond to Titus's report?

In the second section of part 1 (2:14–7:4), Paul interrupts his narrative and provides the Corinthians with a profound exposition of the apostolic ministry that he exercises. This apparent excursus serves several purposes. First, it keeps the Corinthians in suspense about Paul's response to the events that have transpired between him and them. Second, it provides the Corinthians, who have questioned the nature of Paul's ministry, with a theological exposition of how he understands his apostolic ministry. Third, it presents the Corinthians with a theology of reconciliation that can serve as a foundation for complete reconciliation with Paul.

This second section, the excursus on apostolic ministry, is divided into four parts. In the first (2:14–4:6). Paul presents himself as the minister of a new covenant empowered by the Spirit of the Living God. By the gospel that he preaches, Paul enables believers to contemplate the glory of God so that they are transformed from glory to glory. Drawing a bold comparison between his new covenant ministry and the ministry of Moses, Paul argues that if the ministry of the old covenant, which was destined to be abolished, was glorious, then it is all the more certain that the ministry of the new covenant, which will not perish, is glorious. This is why Paul acts more openly than Moses, who, aware that his ministry was to be abolished, placed a veil over his face.

In the second part of this exposition (4:7–5:10), Paul explains the relationship between this glorious ministry of the new covenant and his apostolic sufferings, which appear incongruous with such a glorious ministry. Drawing upon the theme of the God who raises the dead, he presents his suffering as a process of transformation. Thus, despite appearances, his apostolic sufferings are his participation in Christ's resurrection life, a life that Paul already experiences and will fully possess when the God who raises the dead presents him with a heavenly habitation, the resurrection body.

In the third part of this exposition of his ministry (5:11–6:10), Paul turns to the theme of reconciliation. Convinced that one man, Jesus Christ, has died for all, Paul no longer views Jesus from a merely human point of view. He now understands that God was working through Christ to reconcile the world to himself. Consequently, in Christ there is a new creation, and Paul has become Christ's ambassador who calls people to be reconciled to God. In the fourth and final part of this exposition of his apostolic ministry (6:11–7:4), therefore, Paul exhorts the Corinthians to be reconciled to God, lest they receive the grace of God in vain. Reminding the Corinthians of his apostolic hardships on their behalf, he calls upon them to open their hearts to him, just as he has opened his heart to them; for one cannot be reconciled with God if one is not reconciled with Christ's ambassador.

After this extended presentation of his apostolic ministry, in 7:5–16 Paul returns to the narration that he interrupted at 2:13. Drawing upon the theme of the God who comforts him in all of his afflictions, Paul relates how God consoled him at the arrival of Titus, who brought the good news that the Corinthians had repented of their role in the circumstances that led to Paul's painful visit.

By the end of 1:12–7:16 it is clear that one crisis has been resolved: the crisis occasioned by the painful visit during which someone injured Paul, causing him to leave Corinth and write a harsh letter in lieu of the visit he had promised. Paul's powerful summons to reconciliation in 6:11–7:4, however, indicates that there are still outstanding problems at Corinth that have not been settled, problems with which he will deal in chapters 10–13.

Part 2: In the second part of 2 Corinthians (8:1–9:15), Paul takes up the question of the collection for Jerusalem. Although the Corinthians eagerly began the collection "last year" (8:10), they have not completed it, perhaps because of the crisis occasioned by the painful visit. Whatever the cause for the delay, Paul is now confident enough to exhort the community to finish what it began. Although both chapters deal with the collection, Paul never explicitly refers to money, preferring a variety of other terms instead, the most frequent being *charis* ("grace"). Thus these chapters present the collection in light of God's "favor" (*charis*), laying the groundwork for a theology of grace.

Paul begins by reminding the Corinthians, who belong to the Roman province of Achaia (southern Greece), of the grace that God bestowed upon the churches of the Roman province of Macedonia (northern Greece). God's grace effected an overflowing generosity on the part of the Macedonians, despite their profound poverty. Consequently Paul has been encouraged to ask Titus to complete the work of the collection at Corinth (8:1–6). Recalling how richly God has endowed the Corinthians with spiritual gifts, and calling to mind the generosity of Christ who became poor for their sake (8:9), Paul exhorts them to resume the collection in which they were once so eager to participate (8:7–15). Next he recommends a delegation consisting of Titus and two unnamed "brothers" he is sending to Corinth (8:16–24). Paul knows that it is not necessary for him to remind the Corinthians of the collection but, since he has already boasted to the Macedonians that the Corinthians have been ready since last year, he does not want to be embarrassed, nor does he want the Corinthians to be ashamed, should he come and find them unprepared. Consequently, he is sending this delegation to ensure that everything will be in order when he arrives (9:1–5). Next Paul employs the metaphor of sowing and reaping, to assure the Corinthians that God, who gives the seed, will provide them with the wherewithal to sustain their generosity (9:6–9). The appeal concludes with Paul explaining the deeper meaning of the collection. Not only will it assist the poor in Jerusalem, but it will establish a bond of unity between the Corinthians and the Jewish Christian believers of Jerusalem. Thus what first appears to be a simple appeal for money becomes, on closer examination, a profound reflection on the grace of God that enables believers to extend generosity to each other.

Part 3: In the third part of his letter (10:1–13:10) Paul makes a spirited defense of his apostolic integrity, warning the community to mend its ways before he returns for his third and final visit. On first reading, the altered tone of these chapters is somewhat surprising, since Paul has just expressed his joy at the repentance of the Corinthians (7:5–16) and appealed to them to complete the collection (8:1–9:15). Despite his joy and confidence, however, his call for reconciliation in 6:11–7:4 had already indicated that all was not well at Corinth. Likewise, Paul's remarks about preachers who "trade on" the word of God (2:17), who require letters of recommendation (3:1), and who boast in externals rather than in the reality of things (5:12) hinted at the presence of intruders in Corinth. Having settled the crisis of the painful visit in Part 1 (1:12–7:16), and having urged the Corinthians to complete the collection in Part 2 (8:1–9:15), in Part 3 (10:1–13:10) Paul deals with other problems that must be settled before his final visit to Corinth.

The problem with which Paul deals in the third part of this letter is double-faceted. On the one hand, intruding apostles have come to Corinth and accepted the patronage of the Corinthians, raising questions about Paul's refusal to accept the financial support of the community and the nature of his apostolic ministry. Second, certain members of the community have still not repented of their immorality, and so Paul warns them to repent; otherwise he will severely punish them.

Introduction

This third part consists of three sections. In the first (10:1–18), Paul defends himself against charges that there is a discrepancy between the boldness that he has manifested in his letters to the Corinthians, when absent, and his timid behavior when he is in their midst. For, though his letters are powerful in their threats to punish wrongdoers, his physical presence is weak and disappointing. Warning the Corinthians that he will act powerfully, if he must, he reminds them that he is the founder and father of their community. He was the first to come to Corinth with the gospel, not the intruding missionaries who are boasting in his work.

In the second and longest section (11:1–12:13), Paul regretfully engages in a contest of foolish boasting. He does not want to boast of his ministerial accomplishments, and he spends the first part of the speech looking for the proper way to broach the topic (11:1–21a). But he eventually boasts of his apostolic hardships, as well as of his visions and revelations (11:21b–12:10), in order to show the Corinthians that he is not inferior to the intruding apostles, whom he satirically dubs "super-apostles." By the end of the speech, however, Paul acknowledges that he has become a fool (12:11–13), for he has been forced to boast on his own behalf, since the Corinthians, who should have commended him, have not.

Having defended himself against the intruding apostles, in the third section (12:14–13:10) Paul announces his final visit to Corinth, warning the Corinthians to be ready lest he be forced to act harshly. Paul will not burden the community by requiring its financial support, and he hopes that he will not have to act with the authority that the Lord has given him for building up, and not for tearing down. But everything depends upon the Corinthians. If they want to avoid another painful visit, those who have sinned and not repented must repent, and all must avoid jealousy and strife.

The letter concludes with a brief exhortation, greeting, and an elegant blessing that extends the grace of Jesus Christ, the love of God, and the fellowship of the Holy Spirit to the Corinthians.

Overall, 2 Corinthians is best viewed as a letter in which Paul must defend and explain the following: (1) his change of travel plans and his decision to send a harsh letter rather than visit the community again; (2) the relationship of his hardships and afflictions to his glorious new covenant ministry; (3) his decision not to accept the patronage of the Corinthian community; and (4) the nature of his apostolic ministry in light of the criticisms of the intruding "super-apostles." The letter, however, is not merely an apology, as Paul himself notes (12:19). He writes to provide the Corinthians with something to boast about to those who boast in the outward appearance of things (5:12). He wants the Corinthians to commend him as their father, the apostolic founder of their community. The letter can be outlined as follows:

2 Corinthians 1:1–11		The Salutation and Benediction

Part 1

	2 Corinthians 1:12–7:16	*The Crisis over Paul's Apostolic Integrity*
A.	2 Corinthians 1:12–2:13	Paul's Narration of Recent Events
	1. 2 Corinthians 1:12–14	The Letter's Theme
	2. 2 Corinthians 1:15–22	Paul's Reliability
	3. 2 Corinthians 1:23–2:4	A Change of Plans and a Harsh Letter
	4. 2 Corinthians 2:5–11	Forgiving the Offender
	5. 2 Corinthians 2:12–13	Paul's Anxiety at Troas
B.	2 Corinthians 2:14–7:4	The Integrity of Paul's Apostolic Ministry
	1. 2 Corinthians 2:14–4:6	The Ministry of a New Covenant
	a. 2 Corinthians 2:14–3:6	Qualified by God
	b. 2 Corinthians 3:7–18	The Ministries of Moses and Paul
	c. 2 Corinthians 4:1–6	Paul's Apostolic Integrity
	2. 2 Corinthians 4:7–5:10	Ministry and Apostolic Suffering
	a. 2 Corinthians 4:7–15	Life and Death in Apostolic Ministry
	b. 2 Corinthians 4:16–18	Present Transformation
	c. 2 Corinthians 5:1–10	Final Transformation
	3. 2 Corinthians 5:11–6:10	A Ministry of Reconciliation
	a. 2 Corinthians 5:11–21	Ambassadors for Christ
	b. 2 Corinthians 6:1–10	Appeal and Defense
	4. 2 Corinthians 6:11–7:4	Paul's Appeal for Reconciliation
C.	2 Corinthians 7:5–16	Paul's Narration of Recent Events Resumed

Part 2

	2 Corinthians 8:1–9:15	*An Appeal to Complete the Collection*
A.	2 Corinthians 8:1–6	The Grace Given to the Churches of Macedonia
B.	2 Corinthians 8:7–15	An Appeal to Complete the Collection
C.	2 Corinthians 8:16–24	A Recommendation for Titus and the Two Brothers
D.	2 Corinthians 9:1–5	Paul's Purpose in Sending the Delegation
E.	2 Corinthians 9:6–9	The Relationship between Sowing and Reaping
F.	2 Corinthians 9:10–15	The Theological Significance of the Collection

Part 3

2 Corinthians 10:1–13:10		Defense and Warnings in Preparation for Paul's Third Visit
A.	2 Corinthians 10:1–18	Paul's Integrity and Missionary Assignment
	1. 2 Corinthians 10:1–11	Bold Whether Absent or Present
	2. 2 Corinthians 10:12–18	Paul's Assignment
B.	2 Corinthians 11:1–12:13	Boasting Foolishly
	1. 2 Corinthians 11:1–4	An Initial Appeal to Bear with Paul
	2. 2 Corinthians 11:5–15	Not Inferior to the Super-Apostles
	3. 2 Corinthians 11:16–21a	A Renewed Appeal to Bear with Paul
	4. 2 Corinthians 11:21b–29	Daring to Boast as a Fool
	5. 2 Corinthians 11:30–33	Boasting in Weakness
	6. 2 Corinthians 12:1–10	Boasting in Visions and Revelations
	7. 2 Corinthians 12:11–13	Peroration
C.	2 Corinthians 12:14–13:10	Preparations for Paul's Third and Final Visit
	1. 2 Corinthians 12:14–21	The Announcement of the Visit
	2. 2 Corinthians 13:1–10	The Need to Prepare for Paul's Visit
2 Corinthians 13:11–13		The Letter Closing

3. The Theology of 2 Corinthians

"The Theology of 2 Corinthians" is a somewhat anachronistic and misleading phrase since Paul was not a theologian in the modern sense of the term and was not writing theological treatises. Rather, he describes himself as an apostle of Christ Jesus (1:1), the minister of a new covenant (3:6), an ambassador of Christ who calls people to be reconciled to God (5:20), and the letters that he writes are occasional in nature. In this occasional correspondence, however, he reflects on the God who effected salvation in God's Son, Jesus Christ, on the power of God's Spirit that is at work within the church and in his ministry, and on the moral and ethical implications of what it means for believers to be members of the new covenant community. Accordingly, although Paul was not a theologian in the modern sense of the term, his writings are profoundly theological, and they have challenged generations of theologians.

The theology of 2 Corinthians is especially rich, providing readers with an insight to Paul's understanding of (1) the God who raises the dead, (2) Christ, the agent of God's salvation, (3) the Spirit of the Living God, (4) the ministry of the new covenant, (5) the community of the new covenant, and (6) the paradox of a gospel in which affliction leads to comfort and power is perfected in weakness.

1. *The God who raises the dead.* Paul identifies God in a variety of ways in 2 Corinthians. God is "our Father" (1:2), "the God and Father of our Lord Jesus Christ" (1:3; 11:31), "the Father of mercies and the God of all consolation" (1:3), "the Living God" (3:3), "the God who comforts the downcast" (7:6), "the God of love and peace" (13:11). The most significant manner in which Paul identifies God, however, is "the God who raises the dead" (1:9), a description that is intimately related to Paul's understanding of the gospel he preaches.

Paul came to this knowledge of God on the basis of what God did in raising Jesus Christ from the dead. Because God raised Christ, Paul is confident that "the one who raised the [Lord] Jesus" will also raise him and all who believe in Christ (4:14). Accordingly, Paul affirms that God is the one who has prepared believers for resurrection life (5:5) and that God will provide them with a resurrection body that Paul describes as a building from God, "an eternal dwelling in the heavens, not made by human hands" (5:1). Because he believes in "the God who raises the dead," Paul is confident that God, who has already rescued him from so many life-threatening dangers, will rescue him in the future (1:10). This "God who raises the dead" empowers Paul to endure his sufferings on behalf of the gospel, sufferings that he views as transformative (4:16–18). This God is "faithful" (1:18), the source of extraordinary power (4:7; 13:4), and it is fitting to render glory and thanksgiving to him (4:15; 9:11–13).

The God who raises the dead is the one who reconciled the world to himself through Christ (5:18). In order to accomplish this, God effected a divine interchange whereby his Son, the sinless Christ, assumed the sinful human situation so that sinful humanity might experience the righteousness that comes from God (5:20). Thus, in and through Christ, God has effected a renewal of creation whereby those who are in Christ are a "new creation" (5:17). Having renewed his creation and forgiven the trespasses of sinful humanity (5:19), God continues to strengthen believers in Christ, anointing and sealing them with his own Spirit, the "first installment" or "pledge" (*arrabōn*) of the fullness of salvation that is yet to come (1:21–22; 5:5).

God is the one who gave Paul the new covenant ministry of reconciliation (5:18). Accordingly, Paul views the whole of his life in relation to God. For example, his single-hearted devotion and sincerity come from God (1:12). God has made him his prisoner and now leads him in a triumphal procession in which Paul manifests the knowledge of God (2:14). It is God who has qualified Paul to be the minister of a new covenant (3:5), illuminating his heart with "the knowledge of the glory of God on the face of [Jesus] Christ" (4:6). It is God who has given Paul his apostolic assignment to come to Corinth (10:13).

The God of 2 Corinthians is the God of Israel, "the Lord Almighty" who speaks in and through the Scriptures (6:16, 17, 18). He is the God whose glory attended the giving of the old covenant (3:7–11). But in Jesus Christ, and through the power of the Spirit, Paul has come to a renewed understanding of

Israel's God that is inseparable from his knowledge and experience of Jesus Christ. This is why Paul identifies the God who raises the dead as the God and Father of Jesus Christ.

2. *Christ, the agent of God's salvation.* "Christ" (*Christos*) is a title that originally designated God's anointed one, the Messiah, and Paul undoubtedly understood its significance, though it was quickly becoming a name that was losing its titular sense among his Gentile converts. However, even Paul's Gentile converts would have realized that the one whom they called "Christ" was the one whom God had anointed with his Spirit, the same Spirit with which God anointed them when he sealed and gave them the Spirit as the pledge of their final redemption (1:21–22). Although Paul employs the simple designation "Christ" in most instances, he also refers to "Christ Jesus" (1:1), "Jesus Christ" (1:3; 4:6; 13:5), "the Lord Jesus Christ" (1:2, 3; 8:9; 13:13), and "Jesus Christ as Lord" (4:5).

Paul identifies himself as an apostle of Christ (1:1) who preaches the gospel of Christ, which is the good news whose content is Christ (2:12; 4:4; 9:13; 10:14). Having been taken prisoner by God, Paul has become the aroma of Christ, a fragrance that leads some to death and others to life (2:15–16). He views the Corinthians as a letter of Christ that he has administered (3:3).

Paul acknowledges that he once evaluated Christ from a purely human point of view (5:16), but he now understands that Christ died for all (5:14–15). That is, Christ died as a representative for all, and he died in place of all, so that they might live "for the one who died and rose for them" (5:15). This death was the means by which God reconciled the world to himself (5:18–19) when God made the sinless Christ "sin" in order to make sinful humanity "the righteousness of God" (5:21). Put another way, Jesus Christ became poor so that humanity might become rich (8:9). Paul now views himself as Christ's ambassador who calls people to reconciliation (5:20), and he is deeply aware that it is his responsibility to present the Corinthians as a chaste virgin (11:2) to their espoused, Christ, before whose judgment seat they must stand (5:10).

Jesus Christ is the faithful Son of God in whom all the promises of God find their fulfillment (1:19–20). Glorified by God at his resurrection, the glorious Christ is "the image of God" (4:4), and believers are now being transformed from glory to glory into that same image as they contemplate God's glory in Christ (3:18), thanks to Paul's new covenant ministry.

Because God exalted Christ by raising him from the dead, Christ is "Lord." Thus Paul refers to "the Lord Jesus Christ" (1:2, 3; 8:9; 13:13); "our Lord Jesus" (1:4); "the Lord Jesus" (4:14; 11:31); or, simply "the Lord" (5:6, 8; 8:5, 19, 21; 10:8; 11:17; 12:1, 8; 13:10). For Paul and his converts, "Lord" (*kyrios*) was a confessional title that pointed to the exalted status that God bestowed upon Jesus in raising him from the dead. More than any other title, *kyrios* defines the relationship between Christ and those who believe in him: Christ is their Lord and Master, the one before whose judgment seat they must appear (5:10). In turn, believers are Christ's servants or slaves, who must serve him with all their heart.

In a few instances, Paul refers to "Jesus" (4:5, 10, 11, 14; 11:4), apart from any reference to "Christ" or "Lord." Since Paul also speaks of "the Lord Jesus" (4:14), however, he is not making a distinction between "Jesus" and "Christ," as is often done when referring to the "historical Jesus" and the "risen Christ." For Paul, the crucified one is the risen one, and the risen one is the crucified one.

To summarize, Christ is the Son of God, the agent of God's salvation whereby God reconciled the world to himself. He is the exalted *kyrios*, the perfect image of God's glory, the one who died for all. It is this Christ who gives new meaning to Paul's understanding of God as the one who raises the dead.

3. *The Spirit of the Living God.* If Christ is the agent by whom God has reconciled the world to himself, the Spirit is the life-giving power that God has given believers as the "down payment" or "pledge" (*arrabōn*; 1:22; 5:5) that, at the resurrection of the dead, they will receive the fullness of salvation that God has effected in Christ. This Spirit is the very Spirit of "the Living God" (3:3), and it is the presence of this Spirit that makes Paul's ministry the ministry of a new covenant. For, whereas the old covenant was written on tablets of stone, the new covenant is written by the Spirit of the Living God. For Paul, it is this Spirit who gives life (3:6) and empowers his new covenant ministry, so that he can call his ministry "the ministry of the Spirit" (3:8).

For Paul, the Spirit is the one who removes the veil that prevents people from believing in Christ. In explaining why a "veil" still lies over the hearts of his Jewish contemporaries who have not believed in Christ, Paul makes an allusion to Exod 34:34 when he writes, "whenever he turns to the Lord, the veil is removed" (3:16). Commenting on this allusion, Paul explains that in this passage "the Lord" refers to "the Spirit" (3:17). Thus what the passage really means is that whenever anyone turns to the Spirit of the Living God the veil that conceals the meaning of Israel's Scriptures is removed. Since the Spirit has removed this veil from the members of the new covenant community, they now contemplate the glory of God and are being transformed from glory to glory into the same image (3:18), which is Christ, the perfect image of God's glory (4:4).

Paul's understanding of God, Christ, and Spirit in 2 Corinthians can be summarized in this way. By Christ, God reconciled the world to himself and gave those who believe in Christ the Spirit, the pledge of their final salvation. The presence of this life-giving Spirit removes the "veil" so that believers can contemplate the very glory of God as they hear the glorious gospel of Christ, who is the image of God. As they contemplate God's glory in Christ, through the power of the Spirit, they are being transformed from glory to glory, by the Lord who is the Spirit.

Introduction

4. *The ministry of a new covenant.* If God has reconciled the world to himself through Christ, and if the Spirit of the Living God has removed the veil so that believers can contemplate the glory of God, it is through Paul's new covenant ministry that God makes the offer of reconciliation. For this reason, Paul views himself as Christ's ambassador through whom God makes the appeal to be reconciled to God (5:20). In proclaiming the gospel of reconciliation, Paul brings to light the knowledge of the glory of God that is reflected on the face of Christ (4:6) so that when people "hear" the gospel with faith, they actually "see" the glory of God on the face of Christ.

Paul calls this ministry that he exercises the ministry of a new covenant because the powerful presence of the Spirit in his life and in the lives of his converts has convinced him that Jeremiah's prophecy of a "new covenant" (Jer 31:31) has been fulfilled in Christ. Consequently Paul boldly compares his ministry, which he describes as a ministry of the Spirit (3:8) and of righteousness (3:9), with the ministry of Moses, which he portrays as a ministry of death (3:7) and condemnation (3:9), since it lacked the life-giving power of the Spirit. Paul, however, exercises his ministry not in virtue of his own qualifications but because God has qualified him to be the minister of this new covenant (3:5–6). This is why Paul can say that he is God's coworker (6:1) and a minister of God (6:4).

Although Paul portrays his ministry as being more glorious than the ministry of Moses because it is destined to endure, whereas Moses' ministry was destined to be abolished (3:11), Paul's purpose is not to denigrate Moses or the covenant that God established with Israel at Sinai but to highlight the surpassing work of God in Christ. From Paul's point of view, the difference between these two ministries and covenants is the absence or presence of the Spirit. Moses' ministry could not endure because it was not a ministry of the Spirit and so administered a written code that was incapable of giving life, whereas Paul's new covenant ministry gives life and will endure because it is empowered by the Spirit of the Living God. The new covenant, then, can be viewed as the old covenant renewed and empowered by the Spirit that the Living God gave in reconciling the world to himself through Christ, thereby effecting a new creation (5:17).

5. *The community of the new covenant.* Paul's ministry results in a new covenant community, a community of people who have been renewed by the power of God's Spirit. Despite his difficulties with the Corinthians, Paul continues to view them as the people of a new covenant, since God has sealed and anointed them with his Spirit (1:21–22). Accordingly Paul is confident that even now they stand in the realm of the faith (1:24); for they are a letter of Christ that he administers by the Spirit of the Living God (3:3). Consequently, Paul reminds the Corinthians that they are a sanctified community, the temple of the Living God. Because they are a sanctified community, they must maintain certain boundaries between themselves and unbelievers (6:14–7:1). This is the reason that Paul is so concerned about those who continue to live an immoral life (12:21; 13:2).

Such behavior contradicts the very nature of the Spirit-filled community he has established at Corinth through his new covenant ministry. The church at Corinth enjoys a dignity that it still does not fully appreciate because it has not yet understood the nature and the results of Paul's new covenant ministry in its midst.

6. *Gospel paradoxes.* The Corinthians did not appreciate Paul's new covenant ministry and their status as a people of the new covenant, in large measure because they did not grasp the paradoxical nature of the gospel Paul preached to them. In their view, Paul's afflictions and sufferings were signs of weakness that were unworthy of an apostle of Jesus Christ. Accordingly, when other preachers arrived at Corinth who appeared more powerful and eloquent, many of the Corinthians sided with them and criticized Paul. Although the conflict between Paul and the Corinthians was undoubtedly multifaceted, it was ultimately rooted in the inability or the refusal of the Corinthians to embrace the paradoxical nature of the gospel that Paul had already discussed in 1 Cor 1–4. In 2 Corinthians Paul develops this paradox in relation to his apostolic sufferings and weaknesses.

Because Paul believes in the God who raises the dead and reconciles the world to himself through Christ, the death of Jesus plays a central role in his apostolic life and the gospel that he preaches. Accordingly, he describes himself as a fragile earthen vessel (4:7) whose outer person (what the world sees and perceives) is wasting away (4:16). He is afflicted, bewildered, persecuted, struck down (4:8–9), and he is so closely associated with the reality of Christ's death that he carries the "dying" (*nekrōsis*: 4:10) of Jesus in his body. Despite these outward afflictions and the external wasting away of his body, Paul believes that his "inner self" (what the world cannot see or perceive) is being transformed by these sufferings and afflictions (4:16). Therefore, he associates himself with the dying of Jesus through his apostolic sufferings so that the resurrection life of Jesus will be manifested in his body now (4:10) and at the resurrection of the dead (5:1–5). Affliction and suffering, then, are essential components of apostolic ministry, since they are the apostle's participation in the dying and death of Jesus, without which there can be no sharing in his resurrection. They are not to be sought in and for themselves, but they will occur in the life of those who authentically preach the gospel. Rather than conceal his apostolic hardships, Paul gladly embraces them as the marks of his apostleship (4:7–12; 6:4–10; 11:21b–33; 12:10).

According to the gospel that Paul preaches, God made the one who did not know sin to be sin (5:21); that is, Christ took on the sinful human condition. Or, as Paul says in 8:9, Christ became poor so that humanity might become rich. Because Christ took on the human condition, Paul can say of Christ that "he was crucified by reason of weakness" (13:4). In and through this weakness, God manifested his power, so that Paul can also write, "but he lives by reason of the power of God" (13:4). The fundamental paradox of weakness and power then is rooted in Christ's death, which has been made possible by the incarnation. Embracing this paradox in his life, Paul boasts in his own weaknesses (11:30; 12:9), aware that Christ's "power is made perfect in weakness" (12:9). This is not to say that power is weakness. Rather, in a manner that can be understood only in light of the paradox of the cross, power comes to its perfection in and through weakness. Because the Corinthians did not grasp this paradox, they could not appreciate Paul's apostolic ministry among them and the new covenant community that he established in their midst.

The theology of 2 Corinthians can be summarized in this way. The God who raises the dead has reconciled the world to himself by Christ and given believers the Spirit. Through Paul's new covenant ministry, which entails suffering and affliction on their behalf, the people of this new covenant, who have been empowered by the Spirit, gaze upon the glory of God shining on the face of Christ and are being transformed from glory to glory. In Christ, they have become a new creation.

4. Between 1 and 2 Corinthians

In 1 Corinthians, Paul deals with a number of issues that surface again in 2 Corinthians: divisions and factions; the nature of apostolic ministry; the problem of immorality, and his refusal to accept the financial support of the community. As he writes 1 Corinthians, even though some at Corinth have become "arrogant" and do not think that he will come to them (1 Cor 4:18), Paul appears to be confident that these issues will be resolved by his letter (1 Corinthians) and by Timothy, whom he is sending "to remind you of my ways in Christ Jesus, as I teach them everywhere in every church" (1 Cor 4:17). In 1 Cor 16, therefore, Paul instructs the Corinthians about the collection, which he hopes to receive when he arrives (vv. 1–4), and he promises to visit them after passing through Macedonia and perhaps spend the winter with them before going to his next destination, which at this point remains undetermined. For the present he will remain in Ephesus until Pentecost, suggesting that Paul is writing in the spring, perhaps of 54 or 55 C.E. In verses 10–11, Paul asks the Corinthians to receive Timothy and send him on his way in peace "for I am expecting him with the brothers."

By the time that Paul writes 2 Corinthians, there has been a dramatic change in his relationship with the Corinthians. He has made a visit to Corinth that was especially painful (2:1), after which he sent the Corinthians a letter written "with great affliction and anguish of heart" (2:4), reprimanding them for their role in the incident that made his visit so painful (2:5–11; 7:12). In addition to these events, the Corinthians have not completed the collection for Jerusalem (8:10–11), intruding apostles have come to Corinth (10:12–18; 11:4–15), and problems of division and immorality have surfaced once more (12:19–13:4). All of this raises the question, "What happened between the writing of 1 and

2 Corinthians?" Before responding to this question it will be helpful to summarize three aspects of the problem: (1) Paul's painful visit to Corinth, (2) the offender, and (3) the harsh letter.

1. *The painful visit.* In 2 Cor 2:1 Paul mentions a painful visit that he made to Corinth. Although some suppose that Paul is referring to his initial visit, when he first preached the gospel to the Corinthians (see Acts 18:1–18), this would be a strange way to describe a visit that resulted in the foundation of the church at Corinth. More importantly, in 12:14 Paul writes, "Behold, I am ready to come to you this *third time*," and in 13:1-2, "This is the *third time* that I am coming to you. . . . On my *second visit* I forewarned, and now that I am absent I am forewarning, those who previously sinned and all the rest that when I come again I will not be lenient." These references to a second visit that has already occurred and to a third that is imminent suggest that the painful visit was Paul's second visit to Corinth. Thus Paul made at least three visits to Corinth.

- An initial visit when he preached the gospel at Corinth (2 Cor 1:19; cf. Acts 18)
- A second visit that caused him great distress (2 Cor 2:1; cf. 12:14; 13:1–2)
- A third visit when he gathered the collection for Jerusalem (2 Cor 12:14; 13:1–2)

But why did Paul make a second visit to Corinth? Although it might appear that he was simply carrying out the travel plans announced in 1 Cor 16:5–9, there is an important discrepancy between those plans and what he actually did according to 2 Cor 1:15–2:4. Whereas 1 Cor 16:5–9 indicates that Paul intended to come to Corinth by way of Macedonia, from what he writes in 2 Cor 1:15–16, it appears that Paul came directly to Corinth.

Of course, Paul may have changed or modified the travel plans of 1 Cor 16:5–9.[1] Whereas he originally intended to come to Corinth by way of Macedonia and spend the winter in Corinth, he decided to come to Corinth first, visit Macedonia, and then return to Corinth once more. The plans mentioned in 2 Cor 1:15 then would be a "modification rather than a complete displacement"[2] of Paul's original plans announced in 1 Cor 16:5–9. Or Paul may have revised the travel plans of 1 Cor 16:5–9 because the situation at Corinth required his immediate attention. In this case, his second visit would have been an emergency visit.[3]

---

1. This is the suggestion of M. Thrall, *A Critical and Exegetical Commentary on The Second Epistle to the Corinthians* (2 vols.; ICC; Edinburgh: T. & T. Clark, 1994, 2000), 1:74.
2. Ibid.
3. This is the suggestion of E.-B Allo, *Saint Paul Seconde Épître aux Corinthiens* (*Ebib*; Paris: Gabalda, 1937, 2d ed. 1956), 51–52, and V. Furnish, *II Corinthians* (AB 32 A; Garden City, N.Y.: Doubleday), 143–44.

Having arrived in Corinth, Paul would have informed the community of his plans to go to Macedonia after this visit and then return to Corinth once more for a longer visit before being sent on by them to Judea (2 Cor 1:15–16). The difference in Paul's travel plans can be outlined as follows:

1 Corinthians 16:5–9	*2 Corinthians 1:15–16*
from Ephesus	from Ephesus
to Macedonia	to Corinth
to Corinth	to Macedonia
	to Corinth

Whatever happened, Paul did not carry out either set of travel plans, leading some to question his reliability. More importantly, his second visit to Corinth (sometimes called "the intermediate visit" because it occurred between the writing of 1 and 2 Corinthians) proved to be a painful visit for him and the community, requiring him to leave Corinth and return to Ephesus.

2. *The offender.* Even if Paul's second visit was not a response to a deteriorating situation at Corinth but a modification of his original plans, it is obvious that something happened during that visit that caused him to leave Corinth and recall this visit as having been particularly painful. From what he writes in 2:5–11 and 7:12, it appears that someone whom he calls "the offender" (*tou adikēsantos*; 7:12) played a central role. It is also clear that Titus had already returned from Corinth (7:5–16) and reported that although Paul's harsh letter had grieved the Corinthians, it led them to repentance (7:9–13). Indeed the Corinthians had already punished the offender, and apparently too harshly, for Paul must now ask them to forgive the offender, lest Satan take advantage of them (2:5–11).

Paul writes somewhat obliquely about the one who was injured by the offender because he is more interested in concluding this painful affair than in opening old wounds. Accordingly, in 2:5 he says, "if someone has caused grief, he has not grieved me, but to some degree—not to exaggerate—all of you." Then in 7:12 he explains, "therefore, even if I wrote to you, it was not for the sake of the offender, nor for the sake of the offended, but for the sake of revealing to you, before God, your zeal for us." Despite this oblique language, one suspects that Paul was the injured party, even though this is never explicitly stated.

Who then was the offender? The traditional answer identifies the offender as the immoral man whom Paul condemns in 1 Cor 5:1–5 for living in concubinage with his father's wife. This explanation of the offender, which was embraced by nearly all commentators of the ancient, medieval, and Reformation periods (Tertullian being an exception), as well as by many commentators up to the early twentieth century, does not reckon with an intermediate visit and identifies Paul's harsh letter with 1 Corinthians. However, there are too many discrepancies between the immoral man described in 1 Cor 5:1-5 and the offender described in of 2 Cor 2:5-11; 7:12 to sustain this interpretation.[4] For example, in 1 Cor 5:3-5 Paul pronounces judgment over the man and commands the community to hand him over to Satan for the destruction of his flesh, but in 2 Cor 2:5-11 Paul must persuade the Corinthians to forgive the man and restore him to their community lest Satan outwit them.

If the offender was not the immoral man of 1 Cor 5:1-5 but another individual, was he a member of the Corinthian community or an outsider? C. K. Barrett[5] forcefully argues that he was not a Corinthian, otherwise it is difficult to understand why Paul writes that the Corinthians proved to be innocent in the matter (7:11). He proposes that the offender was a visitor who claimed superior rights for himself, challenged Paul's position, "belittled his authority, and had thus both injured and insulted his person."[6] It is difficult, however, to reconcile this view with Paul's appeal to restore the offender to love. In other words, the discussion of 2:5-11 suggests that the offender was a member of the community. The results of this survey can be stated as follows:

- The offender was a member of the community but not the immoral man mentioned in 1 Cor 5:1-5.
- The injured party was probably Paul or someone closely associated with him, for example, Timothy.
- If Paul was the injured party, the offender may have challenged his authority or questioned his handling of the collection.
- To the extent that the community did not come to Paul's defense and sided with the offender, it was responsible for what happened.
- Even if the injured party was someone other than Paul, Paul viewed the injury as a serious matter and a challenge to his authority.
- In Paul's view, the entire community had been injured to some extent, even if it did not realize this at the time.

3. *The harsh letter.* Whatever happened at Corinth during the painful visit, it was serious enough for Paul to alter his plans yet again and return to Corinth, where he wrote a harsh letter to the Corinthians to which he refers in 2:3, 4, 9; 7:8, 12. According to 2 Corinthians, Paul composed this letter as a substitute for a visit to Corinth that he promised but did not carry out (2:3), and he wrote from deep grief and anxiety of heart so that the Corinthians might know his love for them (2:4). He also wrote to test their character and see if they would be obedient in all things (2:9). He realized that the letter saddened them, but he

---

4. See the analysis of these differences in Furnish, *II Corinthians*, 164-68.
5. C. K. Barrett, "*HO ADIKĒSAS* (2 Cor. 7.12)," in *Essays on Paul* (Philadelphia: Westminster, 1982), 108-17.
6. Ibid., 113.

Introduction

rejoiced that this sadness led them to repent (7:8). Finally, in writing about the offender and the injured party, he explained that his purpose was to reveal to the Corinthians their zeal for him (7:12), a zeal that they had now manifested by their repentance. Thus Paul wrote this letter with great anguish of heart to express his love, to test their character, and to reveal to them their zeal for him. If the letter grieved the Corinthians, it also grieved Paul.

Just as ancient, medieval, and Reformation commentators identified the offender with the immoral man and the painful visit with Paul's first visit to Corinth, so they assumed that this harsh letter was 1 Corinthians. As attractive as this solution is, it is not convincing, since the contents of 1 Corinthians do not correspond with Paul's description of the harsh letter, the more so if the immoral man of 1 Cor 5:1–5 is not the offender mentioned in 2 Corinthians. Accordingly, just as modern commentators posit an intermediate visit, so they posit an intermediate letter between 1 and 2 Corinthians to explain the historical circumstances that occasioned 2 Corinthians At this point, however, the agreement ends, since commentators also espouse a variety of theories about the composite nature of 2 Corinthians to explain its origin (see section 6, pp. 24–32). Thus, whereas some maintain that the harsh letter has been lost, others argue that it is embedded in 2 Corinthians.

Those who argue that the harsh letter is embedded in 2 Corinthians point to the strident tone of chapters 10–13 and to some extent of 2:14–7:4, in which Paul makes a vigorous defense of his apostleship—the kind of defense that one would expect from Paul if someone had called into question his apostolic integrity. On the other hand, those who argue that the letter has been lost note that there is no mention of the offender or of the painful visit in either 2:14–7:4 or 10–13, a datum that is difficult to explain, since the painful visit and the role of the offender are among the few things known about the content of the harsh letter. For this reason it seems more probable that the severe letter has been lost.

What occurred between the writing of 1 Corinthians and the writing of 2 Corinthians? Although any reconstruction of what transpired will be hypothetical, this commentary presupposes the following scenario:

- Timothy returns from Corinth with a report that old problems (immorality and community dissension) have not been resolved and that new problems have arisen. If the intruding apostles have already arrived in Corinth at this early stage, Timothy would have told Paul about them as well.
- Paul alters the travel plans outlined in 1 Cor 16:5–9 and makes an emergency visit to Corinth (the second visit).
- This emergency visit proves to be a painful experience for Paul because someone injures or insults him, perhaps by challenging his authority, and the community does not come to Paul's defense.

- Paul alters his travel plans and returns to Ephesus.[7]
- From Ephesus he sends a harsh letter to the Corinthians delivered by Titus.
- Concerned about the community and its reactions to his harsh letter, Paul leaves Ephesus and goes to Troas in search of Titus to learn of the community's response to his letter. Not finding Titus at Troas, he travels to Macedonia, even though he had found a fruitful field for evangelization in Troas.
- Paul meets Titus in Macedonia, perhaps in Philippi, and Titus reports that the community has repented of its role in the affair and punished the offender, apparently too severely in Paul's estimation. If the intruding apostles were not in Corinth at the time of the painful visit, they are probably present by this time, and Titus would tell Paul about them as well as about the continuing problems of immorality at Corinth.
- With a renewed confidence in the community, because it has repented of its role in the crisis occasioned by the painful visit, Paul writes 2 Corinthians from Macedonia (perhaps from Philippi) to give his version of what transpired (chaps. 1–7), to encourage the community to resume the collection (chaps. 8–9), and to prepare for his third and final visit by dealing with the intruding apostles and warning those who have not repented of their immorality (chaps. 10–13).

5. Opposition at Corinth

In the closing chapters of 2 Corinthians, Paul vigorously defends himself and his ministry from intruders, whom he satirically calls "super-apostles" (11:5; 12:11). His sustained defense of his ministry in the face of these super-apostles raises a number of questions. Who were they? Where did they come from? Why did they oppose Paul? Why did Paul oppose them? Generally speaking, the answers to these questions have taken one of two forms.[8] Some scholars,

---

7. At this point it is difficult to determine exactly what happened. Did Paul intend to go to Macedonia after the emergency visit and return to Corinth for a longer visit but change his plans and return to Ephesus instead? Or, as he left Corinth for Ephesus, did he promise the Corinthians a double visit (with a visit to Macedonia in between) but never carry out these plans? In either case, Paul did not visit the Corinthians as he promised, and this change of plans called into question his faithfulness and integrity.

8. For a thorough historical investigation of the way in which scholars have dealt with the question of Paul's opponents at Corinth, see R. Bieringer, "Die Gegner des Paulus im 2. Korintherbrief," in R. Bieringer and J. Lambrecht, *Studies on 2 Corinthians* (BETL 112; Leuven: Leuven University Press, 1994), 181–221, and the essay on Paul's opponents in Thrall, *II Corinthians*, 2:926–45. A popular but helpful survey is found in Larry Kreitzer, *2 Corinthians* (NTG; Sheffield: Sheffield Academic Press, 1996), 71–82.

Introduction

observing that Paul highlights the Jewish identity of these apostles and contrasts his new covenant ministry with the ministry of Moses, have proposed that the super-apostles belonged to the Judaizing movement of the early church, akin to the opposition that Paul encountered at Galatia. They argue that the opponents came from Judea, perhaps with the support of the Jerusalem apostles, preaching a law-observant gospel.

Others, noting that there is no polemic against the law or circumcision in 2 Corinthians, as there is in Galatians, maintain that the intruders, who were Christian missionaries, represented a form of Hellenistic Judaism characterized by powerful manifestations of the Spirit, esoteric knowledge, rhetorical eloquence, and ecstatic experiences.[9] Despite the many theories that have been proposed, questions about the identity, the origin, and the teaching of the intruders have not been resolved. The reason for this is the very nature of 2 Corinthians, which is an occasional writing. Since the super-apostles were in Corinth and many of the Corinthians were attracted to them, there was no need for Paul to identify them or explain their teaching to the Corinthians. For his part, Paul was more interested in defending his own apostleship and warning his converts of the danger such intruders posed. Modern readers of 2 Corinthians, however, are not in the position of the Corinthians who knew who the intruders were; consequently it will be helpful to summarize what Paul says about them.

In chapter 10, Paul makes a number of statements in which he alludes to the intruding apostles in a rather oblique manner, although he has not yet identified them as the super-apostles, as he will do in 11:5 and 12:11. At this early stage in his argument he simply refers to "some," "someone," "this one," and so forth. For example, he writes:

> I ask that when I am present I may not have to act boldly with the confidence that I have in mind for acting boldly toward *some* who consider us as walking according to the flesh. (10:2, emphasis added)

> If *someone* is convinced in his own mind that he belongs to Christ, let *him* consider again for *himself* that just as *he* belongs to Christ so do we. (10:7, emphasis added)

> Lest I appear as frightening you through letters—because *someone* says "the letters are severe and powerful, but his physical presence is weak and his speech contemptible"—let *this one* consider that, what we are in word through our letter when absent, we are in action when present. (10:10–11, emphasis added)

After defending his integrity in 10:1–11, in 10:12–18 Paul ironically admits that he is not "bold enough" to classify or compare himself with "*some* who

---

9. The most important exponent of this position is D. Georgi, *The Opponents of Paul in Second Corinthians* (Philadelphia: Fortress, 1986).

commend themselves . . . evaluating themselves with themselves and comparing themselves with themselves" (10:12). Paul asserts that, unlike these people, he has not gone beyond the missionary limits God assigned to him. In affirming that he has stayed within the limits that God has apportioned to him and reminding the Corinthians that he was the first to bring the gospel to them, Paul implies that those who have been criticizing him and commending themselves have intruded into his missionary field by coming to Corinth. Paul, however, does not identify them or refer to their teaching, since there was no need to do so. At this point in the letter, he is primarily concerned to remind the Corinthians that such apostles have intruded into his missionary field and criticized him unjustly.

Paul's most explicit statements about the intruders come in the following chapters, in the midst of his foolish boasting (11:1–12:13). It is at this point that he ironically identifies them as "super-apostles" (11:5; 12:11). Writing in a highly charged and polemical context, he presents them in a negative light, for in his view they are deceiving the Corinthians, just as the serpent deceived Eve (11:2–3). Although Paul never discloses the nature of their teaching, he implies that they preach "another Jesus" so that the Corinthians have received another spirit and a different gospel than they received from him (11:4).

Insisting that these intruders do not work on the same terms that he does, because they have accepted the financial patronage of the Corinthians, he castigates them as "false apostles" and "deceitful workers" who disguise themselves as apostles of Christ. They present themselves as "ministers of righteousness," but in fact they are Satan's ministers (11:13–15). From Paul's point of view the intruding apostles have dominated, exploited, taken advantage of, and abused the Corinthians (11:20)—a series of charges that is probably connected to the fact that, unlike Paul, the intruders have accepted (or perhaps even demanded) financial support from the community.

When Paul actually begins his foolish boasting, he makes several references to the Jewish pedigree of the intruders, assuring the Corinthians that if the super-apostles are "Hebrews," "Israelites," and "Abraham's seed," so is he (11:22). Then, in a rather remarkable statement, given his harsh words about the intruders, Paul asks, "Are they ministers of Christ?—I am speaking as if I were out of my mind—I am even more so" (11:23), seemingly contradicting what he said earlier when he identified the super-apostles as Satan's ministers (11:15). But given the polemical nature of this material, the contradiction is more apparent than real. Paul is not so much interested in presenting an objective view of the intruders as he is in defending himself from the criticisms that the super-apostles have made against him in his absence. Thus, though Paul might have acknowledged the apostolic credentials of these apostles in another setting, he refuses to do so in this setting. In his view, whether the intruders realize it or not, they have become the unwitting servants of Satan by overreaching their missionary mandate and boasting in Paul's work. Their presence, in his view, has led to false accusations against him and further dissension within the community.

In addition to these explicit comments about the intruding apostles, there are three other important texts, in the first part of 2 Corinthians, in which Paul may also be referring to the intruding apostles:

> For we are not, as so many, trading on the word of God; rather we speak before God in Christ from sincerity, as from God. (2:17)

> Are we beginning to commend ourselves again? Or, do we need—as some do—letters of recommendation to you, or from you? (3:1)

> We are not commending ourselves to you again but giving you an opportunity for boasting on behalf of us, so that you might have something to say to those who boast in appearance and not in the heart. (5:12)

If Paul is indeed referring to the super-apostles in these texts, then he views them (1) as reaping gain from the gospel they preach, (2) as requiring and presenting letters of recommendation, and (3) as boasting in their accomplishments. In contrast to them, he preaches the gospel free of charge (11:7). He does not need letters of recommendation because he was the first to bring the gospel to Corinth (10:14); thus the community has become his letter of recommendation. And unlike the intruders he has learned to boast in his weaknesses (12:9) rather than in the mere appearance of things.

In light of this brief review, three issues emerge. The first, and perhaps the most important for Paul, is the question of missionary assignment. Since he was the first to preach the gospel to the Corinthians, he interprets his initial proclamation of the gospel at Corinth as an indication that Corinth belongs to the missionary field that God has apportioned to him (10:13–18). He is the father and founder of the community which, in turn, has become his letter of recommendation (3:2). This is why he views the super-apostles as intruders who are boasting in his missionary work.

The second issue is financial support or patronage. Although Paul acknowledges the right of those who preach the gospel to be supported by the gospel (1 Cor 9:3–14), he chooses not to burden the Corinthians with supporting him, so that he can preach the gospel to them without cost. But there is a further motive underlying this decision: Paul is not willing to enter into a patron-client relationship with the Corinthians whereby some of the more affluent members of the community can view themselves as his patrons and he has to act as their client, thereby compromising his ministry. In contrast to Paul, the intruders do not appear to have viewed the situation of patronage in this way, and so they have entered into just such a relationship. In Paul's view, they have compromised the gospel.

The third issue is related to the second, and is at the heart of Paul's theology: the question of ministerial style. Whereas Paul's understanding of the paradoxical nature of the gospel has taught him that suffering, affliction, and weakness belong to the essence of a gospel that proclaims Christ crucified, neither the intruding apostles nor the Corinthians appear to grasp this aspect of the gospel as keenly as does Paul. Consequently, whereas the super-apostles boast in those things that highlight their apparent ministerial success, Paul glories in his sufferings, afflictions, and weaknesses as signs of his participation in the dying of Jesus and the power of the resurrection.

Although Paul implies that the super-apostles preach "another Jesus," he never deals with the "content" of their gospel, suggesting that the conflict between him and the super-apostles, and those at Corinth who side with them, has more to do with the way in which he and the super-apostles exercise their ministry than with actual doctrinal disputes. Whereas Paul focuses on the need to participate in the dying of Jesus in order to bear the life of Jesus (4:10), the intruders appear to emphasize the glory and power of the risen Lord to the detriment of the crucified one. Consequently Paul and the super-apostles exercise their ministries differently: Paul through suffering and hardship, the intruders through displays of power and eloquence. Steven Kraftchick captures the relationship between the messenger and the message that Paul embodied when he writes: "Not only the message but the speaker must convey the gospel, and this means that life proceeding out of death must be manifest in him. Only when the mode of speech and the presence of the speaker are consonant with the cruciform nature of the message can the word of the cross occur and so be the power of God. (1 Cor. 1:18)."[10] In this regard, more than any other, Paul and the intruders preach a different gospel.

6. One or Many Letters?

In his thorough historical investigation of the many partition theories that have been proposed to explain the composition of 2 Corinthians, Reimund Bieringer notes that until the nineteenth century most commentators assumed that the circumstances that occasioned the composition of 1 Corinthians also occasioned the writing of 2 Corinthians.[11] Consequently nearly all exegetes identified the letter to which Paul refers in 2 Cor 2:4 and 7:8 with 1 Corinthians, and the offender to whom he refers in 2 Cor 2:5–8 and 7:12 with the immoral man of 1 Cor 5:1–5. But in 1830 Friedrich Bleek[12] suggested that Paul made an "inter-

---

10. Steven J. Kraftchick, "Death in Us, Life in You: The Apostolic Medium," in *Pauline Theology*, vol. 2: *1 and 2 Corinthians* (ed. David M. Hay; Minneapolis: Fortress, 1993), 173.

11. R. Bieringer, "Teilungshypothesen zum 2. Korintherbrief. Ein Forschungsüberblick," in *Studies on 2 Corinthians*, 69.

12. F. Bleek, "Erörterungen in Beziehung auf die Briefe Pauli an die Korinther," *TSK* 3 (1830): 614–32.

mediate visit" between the writing of 1 and 2 Corinthians and wrote an "intermediate letter" between the composition of 1 and 2 Corinthians. Then in 1849 Heinrich Georg Ewald[13] proposed that an "intermediate incident" occurred between the writing of 1 Corinthians and the writing of 2 Corinthians at the time of the intermediate visit. With the concepts of the intermediate visit, the intermediate letter, and the intermediate incident in play, scholars investigated anew the particular historical circumstances that occasioned the writing of 2 Corinthians, and they asked if the intermediate letter might not be embedded in the present form of 2 Corinthians. Johann Solomo Semler[14] had already planted the seeds for such an inquiry when in 1776 he proposed that chapters 10–13 represent a separate letter that Paul sent to the Corinthians (after writing a letter composed of chapters 1–9) upon learning further details about the situation at Corinth.[15] But the major breakthrough came in 1870 when Adolf Hausrath[16] introduced "the Four Chapter Hypothesis," arguing that 2 Cor 10–13 represents the whole or a fragment of the harsh letter to which Paul refers in 2 Cor 2:4; 7:8. According to Hausrath, Paul wrote chapters 10–13 as a separate letter *before* chapters 1–9. In Great Britain, working independently of Hausrath, James Houghton Kennedy developed a similar hypothesis but in greater detail.[17] By the end of the nineteenth century, therefore, several scholars were viewing 2 Corinthians as a composite letter, that is, as a letter composed of two or more earlier letters that a later editor compiled into one.

Although the theory of an intermediate visit, letter, and incident, and the Four Chapter Hypothesis of Hausrath and Kennedy played a major role in viewing 2 Corinthians as a composite letter, there were also other factors at work. Aware that the historical circumstances which occasioned 2 Corinthians were different from those that led to the composition of 1 Corinthians, scholars began to look more closely at 2 Corinthians for clues to the historical circumstances that led to its composition. As they did, they isolated blocks of material that appeared to be fragments of earlier letters that a later editor brought together. Four of these blocks are particularly significant in the quest for the historical

---

13. H. Ewald, "Bemerkungen über die Paulusbriefe" (*Jahrbücher der biblischen Wissenschaft*, 2: 1849, Göttingen, 1850), 225–29.

14. J. S. Semler, *Paraphrasis II. epistulae ad Corinthios. Accessit Latina Vetus translatio et lectionum varietas* (Halle-Magdeburg, 1776).

15. H. D. Betz, *2 Corinthians 8 and 9: A Commentary on Two Administrative Letters of the Apostle Paul* (Hermeneia: A Critical and Historical Commentary on the Bible; Philadelphia: Fortress, 1985), 3. Betz provides a very helpful history of research (3–36) about the growth and development of partition theories in the study of 2 Corinthians.

16. A. Hausrath, *Der Vier-Capitel-Brief des Paulus an die Korinther* (Heidelberg, 1870).

17. J. H. Kennedy, *The Second and Third Epistles of St. Paul to the Corinthians* (London: Methuen, 1900). The second and third letters to which the title refers are the harsh letter (2 Cor 10–13) and the letter that followed it (2 Cor 1–9) respectively.

background and composition of 2 Corinthians: 2 Cor 10–13; 2 Cor 2:14–7:4; 2 Cor 6:14–7:1; 2 Cor 8–9.

1. *Second Corinthians 10–13*. These four chapters, in which Paul defends his apostolate from intruding missionaries and warns the Corinthians of his impending visit, are characterized by a harsh polemical tone, which many commentators have not been able to reconcile with the tone of the first nine chapters of the letter, in which Paul expresses his joy at Titus's good news that the community has repented and then exhorts the Corinthians to complete the collection. For this reason, some have suggested that these chapters are part of, or the whole of, the harsh letter that Paul wrote to the Corinthians. If so, then they must have been written before chapters 1–9. Others, however, have proposed that these chapters were written shortly after chapters 1–7 (or chapters 1–9), when Paul received a report from Corinth that intruding missionaries had arrived and were causing new problems for him in his relations with the Corinthians.

2. *Second Corinthians 2:14–7:4*. In these chapters Paul presents a profound exposition of his apostolic ministry, identifying himself as the minister of a new covenant who calls people to reconciliation. As nearly all commentators now recognize, these chapters are found between two statements in which Paul expresses his anxiety at not finding Titus at Troas (2:12–13 and 7:5–6) and only later resumes his narrative by relating how God comforted him by Titus's arrival at Macedonia. Thus, if 2:14–7:4 is removed from the narrative, there is a smooth transition from 2:12–13 to 7:5–6.

> When I came to Troas to preach the gospel of Christ and a door was opened for me by the Lord, my spirit was ill at ease because I did not find Titus, my brother. But saying farewell to them, *I* went on to Macedonia.... For, even when *we* came to Macedonia, our flesh had no relief, but we were afflicted in every way: external struggles, internal fears. But the God who comforts the downcast comforted us by the coming of Titus. (2:12–13; 7:5–6)[18]

Without Paul's exposition of his ministry (2:14–7:4), there is no interruption in the narrative of 1:12–2:13 and 7:5–16, which gives Paul's account of the recent events that have transpired between him and the community. For this reason, several commentators suggest that the harsh letter consists of 2:14–7:4 and 10–13, or that 2:14–7:4 is an earlier letter on ministry which once stood by itself.

3. *Second Corinthians 6:14–7:1*. In this block of material Paul exhorts the Corinthians not to be yoked with unbelievers. As he does so, he employs a chain of scriptural quotations in which God promises to dwell among his people. On the basis of these promises, Paul summons the Corinthians to separate them-

---

18. The transition, of course, is not quite as smooth as some claim, since Paul employs the first person singular pronoun ("I") in 2:13 and the first person plural pronoun ("we") in 7:5.

selves from every defilement. This section has puzzled interpreters for several reasons. First, many find it difficult to explain the function of this exhortation within its present literary context. Second, the material contains an unusually large number of words that occur nowhere else in Paul's writings. Third, in the view of some this material encourages a separation from unbelievers that Paul does not otherwise require of his converts. Moreover, the omission of these verses results in a smooth transition from 6:11–13 to 7:2–4.

> We have spoken candidly to you, O Corinthians. Our heart is open to you. You are not restricted by us; you are restricted by your own affections. I speak as to my own children; in exchange open your hearts to us. . . . Make room for us in your hearts! We have taken advantage of no one. I am not speaking to condemn you, for I have already said that you are in our hearts that we might die together and live together. I have spoken frankly to you, I have great confidence in you. I am filled with encouragement. In all our affliction, I am overflowing with joy. (6:11–13; 7:2–4)

Because the omission of 6:14–7:1 leads to this smooth transition, several commentators argue that a later editor interpolated these verses into 2 Corinthians. Most of those who view 2:14–7:4 as part of the harsh letter or as an earlier letter do not include 6:14–7:1.

4. *Second Corinthians 8–9*. In chapters 8–9 Paul encourages the Corinthians to complete the work of the collection for Jerusalem. In 9:1, however, he begins as if he were addressing the topic for the first time, "Concerning the ministry for the holy ones, it is superfluous for me to continue writing to you." He then refers to "the brothers" whom he is sending ahead to make advance arrangements for the collection (9:3), even though he has spoken of the brothers in 8:16–24. Because each of the chapters can be read as a separate letter, scholars have made the following proposals: (1) chapters 8 and 9 were once two separate letters, written independently of chapters 1–7; (2) chapter 8 follows chapters 1–7, and chapter 9 is an independent letter; (3) chapter 9 follows 1–7, and chapter 8 is an independent letter.[19]

How scholars interpret these four blocks of material determines their views about the literary integrity or the composite nature of 2 Corinthians. Using the names of their earliest proponents, Bieringer groups the major partition theories according to four hypotheses.

The Semler-Windisch Hypothesis. According to this hypothesis, the intermediate letter is not embedded in 2 Corinthians. Rather, Paul's letter of reconciliation consists of chapters 1–7, and chapters 10–13 were written shortly after, when Paul learned of a new crisis at Corinth. Some who espouse this hypothesis argue

---

19. R. Bieringer, "Teilungshypothesen zum 2. Korintherbrief," in *Studies on 2 Corinthians*, 67–105. See the helpful chart on 96–97 that lists the scholars who propose these hypotheses.

that chapters 8–9 belong with chapters 1–7, whereas others include only chapter 7, and still others only chapter 8. Scholars also disagree as to whether 6:14–7:1 should be included with chapters 1–7.[20]

The Hausrath-Kennedy Hypothesis. According to this hypothesis, chapters 10–13 are all or part of the harsh or intermediate letter, and they were written before chapters 1–7, which is Paul's letter of reconciliation with the community. As in the case of the Semler-Windisch hypothesis, opinions vary as to whether chapters 8–9 belong with chapters 1–7 and whether to include 6:14–7:1 with chapters 1–7.[21]

The Weiss-Bultmann Hypothesis. According to this hypothesis, the harsh letter consists of 2:14–7:4 (minus 6:14–7:1) and chapters 10–13, and 1:1–2:13 and 7:5–16 constitute Paul's letter of reconciliation. According to Bultmann, chapter 8 was probably attached to the letter of reconciliation, and chapter 9 to the harsh letter.[22]

The Bornkamm-Schmithals Hypothesis. Günther Bornkamm proposes that Paul wrote a letter to the Corinthians on the nature of ministry (2:14–7:4 minus 6:14–7:1) in the early stage of the crisis. When the crisis became more severe, he sent a harsh letter (10–13). Then, when the crisis was resolved, he wrote a letter of reconciliation (1:1–2:13 plus 7:5–16). Chapter 8 was composed as a separate letter, or it may have been attached to the letter of reconciliation. Chapter 9 was a separate letter. Walter Schmithals has proposed several elaborate hypotheses based on this outline.[23]

Evaluation. Each of these hypotheses has its strengths and weaknesses. For example, the Semler-Windisch hypothesis (10–13 were written at a stage later than 1–7) explains the change in tone between chapters 1–9 and 10–13 by arguing that the arrival of the intruding super-apostles occasioned a new crisis at Corinth that necessitated a further letter (10–13). But this reconstruction suggests that Titus, who had recently been at Corinth, had somehow misjudged the seriousness of the crisis at Corinth and said nothing to Paul about it or the intruding apostles in his initial report (7:5–16). Furthermore, it does not take into account the earlier indications of this crisis found in chapters 1–7, where Paul is already defending the style of his apostolic ministry and calling the Corinthians to reconciliation.

---

20. Among the commentators who espouse some form of this hypothesis are C. K. Barrett, F. F. Bruce, R. Martin, M. Thrall, V. Furnish, and J. Murphy-O'Connor.

21. Among the commentators who espouse some form of this hypothesis are A. Plummer and J. Héring.

22. This hypothesis has not been embraced to the extent that other partition theories have, and it does not have a major proponent among the commentators on 2 Corinthians in the world of British or American scholarship.

23. Among the commentators who espouse this hypothesis are F. Fallon, H. D. Betz, and J.-F. Collange.

The Hausrath-Kennedy Hypothesis (10–13 precedes 1–7) explains the change in tone between chapters 1–9 and 10–13 by viewing chapters 10–13 as the harsh letter, and so composed before chapters 1–9. But chapters 10–13 make no reference to Paul's painful visit or to the offender, two data that one would expect to find in the harsh letter.

The Weiss-Bultmann Hypothesis (the harsh letter consists of 2:14–7:4 plus 10–13 and the letter of reconciliation consists of 1:1–2:13 plus 7:5–16) goes further in explaining the change in tone between chapters 1–9 and 10–13 by proposing that 2:14–7:4 and 10–13 make up the harsh letter. The remaining material is then viewed as the letter of reconciliation (1:1–2:13 plus 7:5–16). The Bornkamm-Schmithals Hypothesis resolves the tension between chapters 1–9 and 10–13 in a similar way by designating 2:14–7:4 as an independent letter on ministry, 10–13 the harsh letter, and the remaining material, 1:1–2:13 plus 7:5–16 as Paul's letter of reconciliation. Both solutions achieve their goal by a massive rearrangement of the text that groups together like material, supposing that Paul operated with contemporary patterns of academic logic. As a result, neither hypothesis leaves room for the rhetorical devices that otherwise characterize Paul's epistolary style, especially the use of the "ring pattern" whereby he introduces one topic (the narrative of 1:1–2:13), then interrupts it with another (an exposition of his ministry 2:14–7:4), only to return to the original topic (7:5–16).

The Literary Integrity of 2 Corinthians. Although many New Testament scholars continue to favor some form of the partition theory as the best way to explain the present literary structure of 2 Corinthians, as well as the historical circumstances that gave rise to the letter, this commentary argues for the literary integrity of 2 Corinthians.[24] In doing so, it does not dispute (1) that Paul made an intermediate visit to Corinth (the so-called painful visit), (2) that he wrote an intermediate letter (the so-called harsh letter), and (3) that something occurred at the time of this visit (the intermediate incident) which occasioned the writing of this letter. As noted in section 4 ("Between 1 and 2 Corinthians"), these proposals are the best way to explain the literary and historical data

---

24. The recent commentaries of P. Barnett (1997), F. Danker (1989), D. E. Garland (1999), S. J. Hafemann (2000), J. Lambrecht (1999), J. W. McCant (1999), J. M. Scott (1998), and B. Witherington III (1995) also proceed on the assumption of the letter's literary integrity. In addition to these commentators, the literary integrity of 2 Corinthians has been defended in the following recent studies: J. D. H. Amador, "Revisiting 2 Corinthians: Rhetoric and the Case for Unity," *NTS* 46 (2000): 92–111; F. W. Danker, "Paul's Debt to the *De Corona* of Demosthenes: A Study of Rhetorical Techniques in Second Corinthians," in *Persuasive Artistry: Studies in New Testament Rhetoric in Honor of G. A. Kennedy* (ed. D. F. Watson; JSNTSup 50; Sheffield: Sheffield Academic Press, 1991), 268–80; D. A. Hester, "The Unity of 2 Corinthians: A Test Case for a Re-discovered and Re-invented Rhetoric," *Neot* 33 (1999): 411–32; Frances Young and D. F. Ford, *Meaning and Truth in Second Corinthians* (BFT; Grand Rapids: Eerdmans, 1987), 27–59.

of 2 Corinthians. But for reasons that will be presented in the exegesis of this letter, this commentary does not view chapters 10–13 as a separate letter written before or after the composition of chapters 1–9. Nor does it treat 2:14–7:4 as an independent letter or as part of the harsh letter. Likewise, it prefers to view chapters 8–9 as a single, sustained exhortation to complete the collection. Finally, it maintains that even if 6:14–7:1 comes from another source, Paul is the one who introduced it into 2 Corinthians. In a word, this commentary maintains that the present form of 2 Corinthians is essentially the same letter that Paul sent to the Corinthians after the events of the painful visit and the harsh letter. Although the detailed exegetical arguments for this position are made in the commentary that follows, it will be helpful to summarize them here.

First, this commentary acknowledges that there is a change in tone between chapters 1–9 and chapters 10–13, where Paul deals with the intruding missionaries who have come to Corinth. It recognizes the vigorous manner in which Paul approaches his topic in chapters 10–13 comes somewhat unexpectedly, since he has just expressed his joy at the community's repentance (7:5–16) and appealed to the Corinthians to complete the work of the collection (8:1–9:15). The juxtaposition of these two parts of the letter, however, is not as incompatible as one might suppose if one keeps Paul's rhetorical goals in view.

Although Paul has expressed his joy that the community has repented over the incident that occurred at the time of the painful visit (7:5–16), his strong appeal for reconciliation in 6:11–7:4 suggests that, despite his joy at Titus's good report, not all of the problems have been resolved. Indeed the presence of Paul's appeal for reconciliation (6:11–7:4), immediately preceding Titus's report that the community has repented (7:5–16), causes a certain tension within chapters 1–7. Thus it is not surprising that the Weiss-Bultmann and the Bornkamm-Schmithals Hypotheses argue that 2:14–7:4 belongs to the harsh letter or is an earlier letter. But there is no need to follow these suggestions, since the following explanation accounts for the data.

In chapters 1–7 Paul is dealing with *two crises*, one that has *already* been resolved (the crisis of the painful visit and the offender) and another that has *not yet* been resolved (the crisis occasioned by the presence of intruding apostles and the continuing problem of immorality) but that Paul hopes to settle by appealing to the goodwill generated by the repentance of the Corinthians for their role in the first crisis.[25] Indications of the second crisis, which has not yet been resolved, are already present in chapters 1–7, where there are strong intimations that Paul is being criticized (by the Corinthians and/or by the super-apostles) for lacking letters of recommendation (3:1), for preaching a gospel

---

25. This is the basic argument for the literary integrity of 2 Corinthians that is put forth by R. Bieringer in his essay, "Plädoyer für die Einheitlichkeit des 2. Korintherbriefes. Literarkritische und inhaltliche Argumente," in *Studies on 2 Corinthians*, 131–79.

that is veiled (4:1–6), for commending himself (5:11), and for being beside himself (5:13). Because there are such misgivings about his apostolic ministry, Paul appeals to the Corinthians to open their hearts to him as he has to them (6:11–13; 7:2–4). And because some of them have still not repented of their immorality (12:21; 13:1–2), he exhorts them to cleanse themselves from "every defilement of flesh and spirit" (7:1; also see 6:14–18). Thus, even though the Corinthians have punished the offender (2:5–11) and repented of their role in the incident of the intermediate visit (7:8–12), there are serious problems at Corinth with which Paul must deal.

From a rhetorical point of view, Paul's purpose in chapters 1–7 is to consolidate his position with the Corinthians by expressing his joy at their repentance regarding the events of the painful visit, thereby laying the groundwork for his assault on the intruding apostles and those who have not repented of their immorality (12:21; 13:1–2). Accordingly in 1:12–2:13 he gives his account of the events surrounding the first crisis, and in 7:5–16 he expresses his joy at the repentance of the Corinthians over their role in this particular crisis. In 2:14–7:4 he provides the Corinthians with a profound meditation on the nature of his apostolic ministry, which lays the groundwork for dealing with the intruders in chapters 10–13; in 6:1–7:4 he makes an appeal to the Corinthians to be reconciled to him and shun all immorality, foreshadowing what he will say in chapters 10–13. Put another way, in chapters 1–7 Paul prepares for chapters 10–13, where he will finally deal with the intruders and warn the community to mend its ways before he arrives.

Second, although Paul's exposition of his apostolic ministry in 2:14–7:4 "interrupts" his narration of the events that have transpired since the painful visit, this ring pattern—whereby he begins one line of thought, interrupts it, and then completes it—is not uncommon in Paul's writings. The parade example of such a "ring pattern" is Paul's discussion in 1 Corinthians of participation in banquets where the food has been sacrificed to idols. In 1 Cor 8:1–13 Paul begins with the question about such banquets and their relation to idolatry. He then appears to interrupt this line of thought with a discussion of his apostolic ministry in 1 Cor 9:1–27. However, he returns to the discussion of food sacrificed to idols and idolatry in 1 Cor 10:1–11:1. But as most commentators now recognize, Paul interpolates the discussion of his apostolic ministry in chapter 9 in order to provide the Corinthians with an example of how to alter their behavior and solve the problem of the strong participating at such banquets to the detriment of the weak. By this pattern, whereby he interrupts his narrative at the precise moment when he is most distraught at not finding Titus at Troas (2:13), Paul accomplishes two things. First, he holds the Corinthians in suspense before telling them what they most want to hear: his reaction to their repentance (7:5–16). Second, he provides an exposition of apostolic ministry (2:14–7:4) that explains what he means when he writes, "But the God who comforts the downcast comforted us by the coming of Titus" (7:6). Hardship and affliction are integral parts of Paul's glorious new covenant ministry. The distress that he experienced at not finding Titus and the comfort that God afforded him at Titus's arrival are concrete examples of what he means.

In a similar vein Paul's brief exhortation in 6:11–7:4, even if he inherited it from another source, is an example of Paul's use of a ring pattern. In this case, the middle section (6:14–7:1) exemplifies what the Corinthians must do in order to open their hearts to Paul (6:11–13; 7:2–4); they must separate themselves from every defilement because they are the temple of the Living God.

Third, while it is true that chapter 9 appears to take up the topic of the collection anew, as if Paul had not dealt with it in chapter 8, a closer reading indicates that Paul is not so much beginning the topic anew as he is explaining why he is sending the Corinthians a delegation headed by Titus (8:16–24); namely, so that neither Paul nor the Corinthians will be embarrassed when he arrives. Indeed Paul's reference to the "brothers" in 9:3 presupposes what he has already written in 8:16–24 about Titus and the two brothers. Thus the flow of the argument can be summarized in this way. Having told the Corinthians of the extraordinary generosity of the Macedonians (8:1–6), Paul appeals to the Corinthians to complete the collection (8:7–15). To assist them, he is sending Titus and two brothers (8:16–24) who will assure that the collection is ready (9:1–5). Therefore, the Corinthians should be generous (9:6–9), because God is the source of their generosity (9:10–15). There is no need to treat these chapters as separate letters.

If these arguments are correct, Paul wrote 2 Corinthians for the following reasons: (1) to bring to a close the crisis over the painful visit; (2) to encourage the Corinthians to resume the collection; (3) to resolve, on the model of the first crisis, a second crisis caused by the intruding apostles and the unrepentant. In terms of his rhetoric, Paul begins by recounting his version of the first crisis, in the midst of which he provides the Corinthians with a rich exposition of his apostolic ministry (chaps. 1–7). Confident that the first crisis has been resolved, he asks the community to complete the collection (chapters 8–9). On the basis of this goodwill, he undertakes to resolve the serious and outstanding crisis of the intruding missionaries and the unrepentant so that his third visit will not be a painful visit.[26]

---

26. When all is said and done, it is probably impossible to present a conclusive argument that will convince everyone of a particular partition theory or of the literary integrity of 2 Corinthians. But even if one grants that 2 Corinthians is a composite letter, it is still necessary to deal with the fact that someone brought the supposed fragments of this letter together, thereby giving 2 Corinthians its canonical form and viewing it as a literary unity.

COMMENTARY

The Salutation and Benediction
2 Corinthians 1:1–11

Second Corinthians consists of three parts: an opening salutation and benediction (1:1–11), the main body of the letter (1:12–13:10), and the letter's conclusion (13:11–13). The second part, as one would expect, is the longest and most detailed portion of the letter, for it is here that Paul explains and defends the substance and style of his apostolic ministry to the Corinthians.

The letter opening, however, is not insignificant; for, as he often does in his correspondence, Paul employs these introductory verses to signal important themes that he will develop in the body of the letter. For example, in the letter salutation he immediately identifies himself as "an apostle of Christ Jesus through the will of God" (v. 1), thereby foreshadowing a major theological theme of this letter: the nature of his apostolic ministry. In the opening benediction, he introduces other themes to which he will repeatedly return in order to explain and defend the nature of this apostolic ministry. Among these are the consolation that "the God who raises the dead" (v. 9) brings to the afflicted, Paul's participation in the sufferings of Christ (v. 5), and the significance of his own sufferings and afflictions for the Corinthian community (v. 6). These initial verses then play an important role, inasmuch as they foreshadow themes that Paul will develop as he explains and defends the style and nature of his ministry. Authentic apostolic ministry, he will argue, involves participation in the sufferings of Christ, which are the afflictions that necessarily accompany apostolic service. Authentic apostolic ministers, however, are not discouraged by these afflictions, because they know that "the God who raises the dead" (v. 9) comforts and consoles them.

> 1:1 Paul, an apostle of Christ Jesus through the will of God, and brother Timothy,[a] to the church of God in Corinth, with all the sanctified throughout Achaia. 2 Grace and peace to you from God our Father and the Lord Jesus Christ.
>
> 3 Blessed be the God and Father of our Lord Jesus Christ,[b] the Father of mercies and God of all consolation, 4 who consoles us in our every affliction so that we can console those in every affliction through the consolation by which we ourselves are consoled by God. 5 Because as the sufferings of Christ abound in us, so, through Christ, even our consolation abounds. 6 If we are afflicted, it is for your consolation, and salvation. If we are consoled, it is for your consolation, which becomes

effective[c] by endurance of the same sufferings that even we suffer. 7 Our hope on your behalf is firmly established, since we know that just as you share[d] in the sufferings, so you will share[e] in the consolation.

8 We do not want you to be unaware, brothers and sisters,[f] about our affliction that occurred in Asia; because we were burdened far beyond our strength so that we despaired even of life. 9 Indeed, we bore within ourselves the sentence of death in order that we would not rely on ourselves but on the God who raises the dead. 10 He rescued us from such great dangers[g] and will rescue us. In him, we have hoped.[h] And he will rescue us yet again 11 as you assist by your prayer on our behalf so that thanks may be given by many persons for the favor bestowed upon us through the help of many persons.

a. The Greek employs a definite article, *ho adelphos* ("the brother"), highlighting Timothy's place within the Christian community, which is a new family of brothers and sisters in Christ. It may also point to Timothy's status as Paul's missionary colleague (Thrall, 1: 82).

b. The Greek could be construed as an indicative statement, "Blessed is God . . . ," but the liturgical nature of the benediction suggests that the phrase is an exclamatory prayer.

c. The participle *energoumenēs*, which could be construed as a passive, is here translated as a middle voice.

d. The noun *koinōnoi* ("participants") is rendered as a verb.

e. A verb must be supplied at this point.

f. *Adelphoi* ("brothers") has all the members of the community in view, women as well as men.

g. Several witnesses (ℵ, A, B, C, D[gr], G[gr]) read the singular, *tēlikoutou thanatou* ("so great a death."), but P[46], a very significant manuscript, reads the plural *tēlikoutōn thanatōn* ("such great deaths"). The more difficult reading of P[46] is adopted here, although it is not to be taken literally, as the translation indicates.

h. Some manuscripts (ℵ, A, C, D[2]) read *hoti* at this point, providing a reason for Paul's hope: "*because* he will rescue us again." This translation follows P[46], which does not contain *hoti*. As a result, a period is placed after "we have hoped," and a new sentence begins with "And he will rescue us yet again," concluding with v. 11.

These opening verses consist of two sections: a salutation (vv. 1–2) and a benediction (vv. 3–11). Like other Pauline greetings, this one identifies the writer and the recipients of the letter, to whom Paul wishes grace and peace. Readers of the Greek text will note how "Christ Jesus . . . Jesus Christ" (*Christou Iēsou . . . Iēsou Christou*) enclose the greeting.

The opening exclamatory statement ("Blessed be the God and Father of our Lord Jesus Christ," v. 3) of the benediction echoes the final words of the greeting ("from God our Father and the Lord Jesus Christ," v. 2), thereby relating the two sections of the letter opening to each other. This benediction consists of two

The Salutation and Benediction

units. In the first (vv. 3–7), Paul praises the God who consoles the afflicted, explaining how his apostolic sufferings and afflictions benefit the Corinthians, whom he associates with himself as participants in Christ's sufferings and therefore as beneficiaries of God's consolation. Paul begins the second unit (vv. 8–11) with a disclosure formula ("We do not want you to be unaware . . .") and mentions a particular affliction he endured in Asia that led him to trust in "the God who raises the dead" (v. 9) rather than in himself. Thus, though some commentators would identify verses 8–11 as the beginning of the letter body because of the disclosure formula in verse 8, these verses belong to the benediction, providing a particular example of how God rescued Paul from affliction.

Throughout this unit Paul employs the first person plural ("we"), as he does throughout much of this letter. Although the plural could refer to Paul and Timothy, the letter's cosenders, the use of "we" in v. 8, which clearly has Paul's affliction in Asia in view, strongly suggests that the use of "we" in this unit is a literary plural that refers to Paul.

[1:1–2] Paul begins with a greeting in which the senders (Paul and Timothy) identify themselves to the recipients (the Corinthians and other believers in the province of Achaia), to whom they wish grace and peace. Although the basic form of the greeting (sender to receiver, grace and peace) remains essentially the same in all of the Pauline letters, there are slight variations from letter to letter. For example, though Paul calls himself as an apostle in some letters, he identifies himself as a "slave" (*doulos*) or "prisoner" (*desmios*) of Jesus Christ in others. Moreover, although he names Timothy as a cosender of this letter (which does not necessarily imply coauthorship), he mentions Sosthenes and Silvanus as cosenders in other letters. There are, however, no cosenders named in Romans, Galatians, Ephesians, Colossians, and the Pastorals. Most importantly, Paul varies the way in which he identifies himself in his letters, either in light of his circumstances or of his purpose for writing. In Philemon, for example, he identifies himself as a prisoner for Christ Jesus, since he writes from prison. In Philippians he presents himself a "servant" or "slave" of Christ Jesus because he calls the community to a life of unity based on the example of Christ's self-emptying servant love. Here and in Romans, 1 Corinthians, Galatians (as well as Ephesians, Colossians, and the Pastorals), he identifies himself as an apostle because his apostleship has been called into question.[1]

The letter's opening, "Paul, an apostle of Christ Jesus through the will of God," anticipates Paul's theme, the nature of his apostolic ministry. Before embarking upon his theme, Paul asserts, as he does in other letters, that his apostleship is

---

1. This commentary distinguishes between the Pauline letters whose authorship is not disputed (Romans, 1 and 2 Corinthians, Galatians, Philippians, 1 Thessalonians, and Philemon) and those letters whose Pauline authorship is disputed (Ephesians, Colossians, 2 Thessalonians, 1 and 2 Timothy, and Titus). There are important arguments, however, for the Pauline authorship of Colossians and 2 Thessalonians, and perhaps for 2 Timothy.

grounded in the will of God (*thelēmatos theou*), an expression that occurs frequently in his letters, as well as in the deuteropaulines (see Rom 1:10; 12:2; 1 Cor 1:1; 2 Cor 8:5; Gal 1:4; Eph 1:1; Col 1:1; 4:12; 1 Thess 4:3; 5:18; 2 Tim 1:1). Since the will of God is what God intends to bring about, it also discloses God's plan, and it is not surprising that Ephesians speaks of the mystery or secret purpose of God's will (Eph 1:9). By identifying the origin of his apostleship with the will of God, Paul secures the high ground from which he will defend himself against those who call into question the nature and manner of his apostleship.

Although Paul was firmly convinced of his apostolic call, he found it necessary to defend his status as an apostle (see 1 Cor 9:1–2), as well as the divine origin of his call (see Gal 1:1). It is not surprising, then, that in the greetings of Romans, 1 and 2 Corinthians, and Galatians he identifies himself as an apostle who has been called and set apart for the gospel. In doing so, he reminds his converts of his call and conversion when God revealed his Son to him and called him to be an apostle to the Gentiles (see Gal 1:15–17).

Although the concept of "apostle" is related to the Jewish notion of the *saliah* who acted as the representative of the one who sent him,[2] it has clearly taken on a fuller meaning in early Christianity, especially in Paul's letters, where it refers to one who has seen and been commissioned by the risen Lord. For a complete understanding of what *Paul* means by apostleship, however, it is necessary to read what he claims for his apostleship, especially in Galatians and 2 Corinthians.

Paul identifies Timothy as a cosender of this letter, just as he identified Sosthenes as the cosender of 1 Corinthians (1 Cor 1:1). Timothy is also identified as a cosender of Philippians and Colossians, as well as 1 and 2 Thessalonians, which name Silvanus as a cosender as well. In listing Timothy as a cosender, Paul does not necessarily mean that Timothy was the letter's coauthor, despite the numerous occasions that Paul makes use of the first person plural in this letter. Rather, Paul probably mentions Timothy because he had sent him to Corinth about the time that he was writing 1 Corinthians (1 Cor 4:17; 16:10), leading Chrysostom (*Homily* 1:2) to note that Paul associates Timothy with the writing of this letter because he had recently been restored to him. If Timothy had already returned, it would have been appropriate to name him as the cosender of this letter, which deals with issues with which he would have been familiar.

The Acts of the Apostles describes Timothy as a disciple, the son of a Jewish mother and a Greek father, whom Paul circumcised (16:1–3). According to Acts, he accompanied Paul on his second missionary journey. He and Silas (probably to be identified with Silvanus) remained in Beroea when Paul was no longer welcome there and so went on to Athens (17:14). While in Athens, Paul summoned Timothy and Silas (17:15), and they eventually joined him at

---

2. See Paul W. Barnett, "Apostle," *DPL*, 45–51.

Corinth, where he was already preaching (18:5). Thus, as Paul notes in 2 Cor 1:19, Timothy and Silvanus (whom Acts calls Silas) were present at Corinth during Paul's first visit, when he established the church there. Acts also notes that Paul sent Timothy and Erastus to Macedonia, while he remained in the province of Asia (19:22).

Paul describes Timothy as his coworker (Rom 16:21), his beloved child who is faithful in the Lord (1 Cor 4:17), and in Phil 1:1 he associates Timothy with himself as a slave of Christ Jesus. In 1 Thess 3:2, he calls him "our brother and co-worker for God in proclaiming the gospel of Christ." Paul, or someone writing in his name, also addressed two letters to Timothy, who had assumed a leadership role in the church at Ephesus (1 Tim 1:2), and he exhorts him, "Share in suffering like a good soldier of Christ Jesus" (2 Tim 2:3), because the time of his (Paul's) death is at hand (2 Tim 4:6). Despite the high regard in which Paul holds Timothy, he never identifies him as an apostle. Timothy belongs to the community of believers and holds a special position as one of Paul's coworkers, but he is not an apostle, presumably because he has not seen the Lord and been commissioned by him as was Paul.

In sending this letter "to the church of God in Corinth, with all the sanctified throughout Achaia," Paul acknowledges the special dignity of the Corinthian congregation, even though the Corinthians are still at odds with him over some points. Although Paul usually has the local congregation in mind when he refers to the "church" (*ekklēsia*), in this instance he employs an expression that probably originally referred to the earliest Jerusalem congregation, "the church of God" (*hē ekklēsia tou theou*) that Paul persecuted (1 Cor 15:9; Gal 1:13). By identifying the Corinthian congregation as "the church of God," Paul now gives the Corinthians the same title of honor he gives the church of Jerusalem. Second Corinthians does not develop the concept of the church as universal or cosmic, as do Ephesians and Colossians, but this expression ("the church of God") moves in the direction of viewing the churches of God (Rom 16:4) as united in, and manifestations of, the church of God (1 Cor 1:2; 10:32).[3]

In addition to identifying the Corinthians as the church of God, Paul calls them—and other believers in the Roman senatorial province of Achaia—"the

---

3. This statement supposes that Ephesians and Colossians belong to the deuteropauline correspondence, that is, that they were written by someone else in Paul's name. The changed perspective in the ecclesiology of Ephesians and Colossians, when compared with the nondisputed Pauline letters, is one of the reasons scholars argue against the Pauline authorship of letters such as Colossians and Ephesians. Whereas the nondisputed Pauline letters tend to view the church as the local congregation at Rome, Galatia, Philippi, etc. Ephesians and Colossians view the church in a way that transcends (though it still includes) the local congregation. The church is now viewed as Christ's body and Christ as the head of the body. Since the Christology of these letters is cosmic in scope, the church is viewed as universal because it is the body of the cosmic Christ. See Eph 1:22; 4:12; Col 1:18, 24.

sanctified" (*hoi hagioi*). This sanctification, however, should not be confused with personal holiness, a notion that is often conveyed by the translation "saints." Rather, believers are holy or sanctified because of what God has done for them in Jesus Christ. In the words of 1 Cor 1:30, Christ Jesus is their "wisdom from God, and righteousness and sanctification (*hagiasmos*) and redemption." Believers are sanctified because Christ became sin on their behalf so that they might become the righteousness of God (2 Cor 5:21). Accordingly, like Israel of old, they must maintain a certain distance between themselves and unbelievers, because they are the temple of God (6:14–7:1). If they do not, and if certain people do not repent before Paul's impending third visit, he will punish them severely (13:1–14).

Paul concludes his greeting by wishing the Corinthians the "grace and peace" that come from God who is "Father" and Jesus Christ who is "Lord." Except for 1 and 2 Timothy, which expand the greeting to read "grace, mercy, and peace," this same greeting occurs in all of the Pauline letters and evokes the *charis* ("grace"), the gracious act of God in Jesus Christ whereby God reconciled humanity to himself (5:18–21) so that the justified are at "peace" (*eirēnē*) with God (see Rom 5:1–2). By associating Jesus with God as the source of grace and peace, Paul points to the unique relationship that the risen Lord has with God because he is God's Son (1:19), the perfect reflection of God's glory (4:4). Paul is careful to maintain the distinction between "God" (*theos*), who alone is Father, and Jesus Christ, whom God has established as "Lord" (*kyrios*, see Phil 2:11).

[3–7] In most of Paul's letters a brief prayer of thanksgiving follows the greeting, but in 2 Corinthians Paul makes use of a benediction rather than a thanksgiving in order to praise God. Although both thanksgivings and benedictions are prayers, the benediction has a more liturgical tone, akin to that found in Jewish benedictions such as the *Shemoneh Esreh*, also known as the Eighteen Benedictions, which begins, "Blessed are thou, O Lord, our God and God of our fathers."[4] The canticle of Zechariah (Luke 1:68–79) provides yet another example of a benediction, as do Eph 1:3–14 and 1 Pet 1:3–12, both of which employ the opening phrase found here, "Blessed be the God and Father of our Lord Jesus Christ" (Eph 1:3; 1 Pet 1:3).

Paul's decision to use a benediction rather than a thanksgiving is related to the personal nature of this letter, in which he explains and defends the style of his apostolic ministry. Whereas the letter of thanksgiving tends to offer a prayer of thanks for what God has done for the community, Paul employs a benediction to praise the God who has consoled him in his apostolic afflictions. In doing so, he provides the Corinthians with a compelling reason to align themselves

---

4. For the full text of this prayer, see Martin McNamara, *Intertestamental Literature* (Wilmington: Michael Glazier, 1983), 200–203.

The Salutation and Benediction

with him and to join others who are already giving thanks for his deliverance. Chrysostom (*Homily* 1:3) also suggests that Paul employs this benediction to respond to those who found fault with him for postponing his promised visit. According to Chrysostom, then, Paul points to the many afflictions he endured on their behalf and thereby gains their sympathy. The repeated use of words such as "comfort" (*paraklēsis*), "to comfort" (*parakaleō*), "affliction" (*thlipsis*), "to afflict" (*thlibō*), and "suffering" (*pathēma*) in this benediction (vv. 3–11) signals major themes that Paul will develop in the rest of the letter.

Paul begins his benediction by praising God, who consoles him in all of his afflictions (vv. 3–4). It is "the God and Father of the Lord Jesus Christ," already noted in the greeting, whom Paul further identifies as "the Father of mercies" (cf. Exod 34:6; Pss 25:6; 69:16) and "the God of all consolation" (cf. Isa 40:1; 49:13). In the second half of the benediction (vv. 8–11), Paul will identify this God as "the God who raises the dead" (1:9). From the outset of the letter, then, it is clear that the primary actor in the story that Paul presupposes is "God" (*ho theos*).[5] Bultmann (21) notes that Paul often uses a genitive to characterize God. For example, he speaks of "the God of steadfastness and encouragement" (Rom 15:5), "the God of hope" (Rom 15:13), "the God of peace" (Rom 16:20; 1 Thess 5:23), and "the Lord of peace" (2 Thess 3:16). This God is the faithful God who made promises to Israel that have been fulfilled in his Son, Jesus Christ (2 Cor 1:18, 20). This is the God who has "anointed" and "sealed" believers and given them the Spirit (1:21–22), the God who leads Paul in a triumphal procession (2:14), the God who reconciled the world to himself (5:18–19), the God of love and peace (13:11).

In praising God as the Father of mercies and God of all consolation, Paul affirms that God is the source of the mercy and consolation he has experienced in his apostolic ministry, despite his afflictions. These afflictions encompass the physical suffering and mental anguish that he endures because of his apostolic ministry, especially as described in the hardship lists of 4:8–11; 6:4–10; 11:23–29; 12:10, the first two of which mention "affliction" (*thlipsis*) at the beginning of their lists (4:8; 6:4). Though some at Corinth view Paul's afflictions as a sign of weakness that calls into question his apostolic ministry, Paul affirms that God consoles him in his afflictions so that he can comfort others by means of the consolation with which God has consoled him (1:4). Apostolic affliction, then, leads to divine consolation, so that apostolic ministers can console the afflicted with the very consolation they have received from God. What

---

5. There are seventy-eight references to *ho theos* ("God") in 2 Corinthians, compared to forty-seven references to "Christ," nineteen to "Jesus," and twenty-nine to "Lord." The multiple occurrence of "*ho theos*" is even more striking if one notes that "Jesus," "Christ," and "Lord" are often used in combination with each other in 2 Corinthians. For a suggestive study of the notion of God in 2 Corinthians, see Frances Young and D. F. Ford, *Meaning and Truth in Second Corinthians* (BFT; Grand Rapids: Eerdmans, 1987), 235–61.

this consolation entails will become clearer in 4:16–18, where Paul describes how believers are transformed daily as they wait to be clothed with their heavenly habitation, the resurrection body (5:1–10). Put another way, God's consolation is the sure hope of resurrection life that believers paradoxically experience in the midst of affliction.

Having blessed the God who consoles him (vv. 3–4), Paul develops the relationship between affliction and consolation (vv. 5–7) further by introducing a new concept, "the sufferings of Christ" (*ta pathēmata tou Christou*; v. 5) and by drawing the Corinthians into the equation for the first time. Although *ta pathēmata tou Christou* could refer to the sufferings that Jesus endured (see 1 Pet 1:11), the immediate context equates "the sufferings of Christ" with afflictions, suggesting that afflictions endured on behalf of the gospel are a direct participation in Christ's sufferings much as Christ's sufferings were a participation in humanity's sufferings (see Bultmann, 24). For Paul, then, there is an intimate relation between the sufferings of Christ and the consolation believers experience; for when the former abounds (*perisseuei*), so does the latter.[6]

The establishment of this relationship between apostolic affliction and the sufferings of Christ allows Paul to make a bold move. Aware that Christ suffered "for" (*hyper*) others, and having related his own afflictions to these sufferings, Paul now views his own afflictions as sufferings "for" (*hyper*) others. Accordingly, he writes that if he is afflicted, it is "for" their "consolation and salvation" (v. 6), and if he is consoled, it is "for" their consolation. His affliction and consolation are for their consolation. For when he is consoled by God through Christ, the Corinthians will also find consolation from the assurance that if they endure the sufferings of Christ, then they will share in the consolation Paul himself has received. But what does Paul mean when he says that his affliction is *for their salvation*? He certainly does not mean that he is the one who saves them. Rather, when they participate in the sufferings of Christ as he does, then they will understand the paradoxical message of the gospel that God is at work in weakness (12:9). Thus Paul's own example and preaching become an aroma of life for them (2:15). If they do not understand this, then the paradoxical word of the gospel will become an aroma of death for them (2:15). The relationship between affliction and comfort, then, becomes yet another way for Paul to state the paradox of the gospel. For the God who raises the dead is the God who comforts the afflicted.

---

6. Young and Ford (*Meaning and Truth in 2 Corinthians*, 166–85) provide an insightful discussion of Paul's use of the metaphor of the economy of God in 2 Corinthians. In a world that thought in terms of limited goods and services, Paul presents a divine economy of abundance in which God's goodness, blessings, and consolation are limitless and beyond measure. Thus in the present instance there is no limit to the consolation that God affords through Christ; it always overflows in ever greater abundance. This theme of God's abundant economy also occurs in chapters 3–4 in reference to the new covenant that overflows with glory and in chapters 8–9 in reference to the collection for the saints. See 3:9; 4:15; 8:2, 7; 9:8, 12, where the verb "abound" (*perisseuō*) occurs.

[8–11] Some commentators view these verses as the beginning of the body of the letter because of the disclosure formula, "We do not want you to be unaware" (v. 8). This phrase, however, does not necessarily indicate the beginning of the letter body (see Rom 1:13; 11:25; 1 Cor 10:1; 12:1; 1 Thess 4:13, where the same phrase occurs but not as the opening of the letter body). Rather, these verses are closely related to the first part of the benediction, and they are best viewed as a part of the benediction. Having explained in a general way how God consoled him in his afflictions, Paul now brings forth a specific example that deeply affected his understanding of God and of his ministry.[7] Commentators have often tried to relate what Paul says here to his remark in 1 Cor 15:32 that he "fought with wild animals at Ephesus" and to the episode in Acts that narrates how his life was threatened at Ephesus (Acts 19:23–41). However, since Acts 19 does not report that Paul was arrested and given a sentence of death, and since 1 Cor 15:32 is brief and enigmatic, both texts are problematic. If the Corinthians knew the event to which Paul was referring, then there was no need for him to explain it further. But even if they did not, as is the case with contemporary readers, the point that Paul makes is not lost. Something extraordinary happened to him in Asia, and he despaired of his life.

The verb that Paul employs (*exaporeō*) to describe the state of his mind at this crisis occurs only once in the Septuagint (LXX Ps 87:16) and only twice in the New Testament (2 Cor 1:8; 4:8). In LXX Ps 87:16 (= MT 88:15) it describes the emotions of the psalmist who, having been exalted by God, is now utterly humbled and "perplexed." In 2 Cor 4:8, Paul writes that he is "bewildered but not in doubt" (*aporoumenoi all' ouk exaporoumenoi*). Here (v. 8) he portrays himself as so extraordinarily burdened that he even "despaired" (*exaporēthēnai*) of life. The difference between Paul's attitude then (when he despaired of life) and his state of mind as described in 4:8 suggests that the incident in Asia resulted in a renewed understanding of his apostolic sufferings just as the appearance of the risen Christ altered his understanding of the crucified Christ.

Paul goes further. He now understands that there was a divine purpose to this "sentence of death" (*apokrima tou thanatou*), for it taught him to rely on "the God who raises the dead" (1:9) rather than on himself. If Paul was indeed imprisoned at Ephesus—there is no firsthand evidence that he was—then the sentence of death should probably be taken literally: a fearsome prospect for Paul, who hoped to be alive at the Lord's parousia (see 1 Thess 4:17). The phrase, however, could also be taken metaphorically, perhaps as referring to an illness that brought Paul to the point of death. Whatever happened, this affliction taught him to rely on "the God who raises the dead" (1:9) rather than on

---

7. See the helpful study of A. E. Harvey, *Renewal through Suffering: A Study of 2 Corinthians* (Studies of the New Testament and Its World; Edinburgh: T. & T. Clark, 1996). This study views Paul's experience in Asia as a major turning point in his understanding of suffering in his ministry.

himself, and it evidently deepened, if not altered, his understanding of his apostolic afflictions.

Paul's description of God as the one who raises the dead is the climax of his benediction, and this understanding of God underlies all that he writes in 2 Corinthians. Although there is a similar description of God in the second of the Eighteen Benedictions as "sustaining the living, resurrecting the dead," the phrase clearly has a special meaning for Paul because of Christ's resurrection (see 4:14). Having been rescued from this great danger, Paul is confident that the God who raises the dead will continue to rescue him from whatever dangers lie ahead. Thus he concludes his benediction by calling upon the Corinthians to join with others in giving thanks for the gifts bestowed upon him, thereby uniting them with a chorus of people who are already thanking God for rescuing the apostle. In doing this, Paul shrewdly provides the Corinthians, many of whom have criticized him, with yet another opportunity to align themselves with him rather than criticize him.

In summary, the opening benediction focuses the attention of the Corinthians on God, the Father of mercy and the God of all consolation, the God who raises the dead and rescues his apostle. In light of this understanding of God, Paul will now explain the nature of his apostolic ministry in terms of suffering, weakness, and affliction.

Part 1

The Crisis over Paul's Apostolic Integrity
2 Corinthians 1:12–7:16

Second Corinthians 1:12–7:16 is the first part of the body of Paul's letter, the other two parts being 8:1–9:15 (Paul's appeal to the Corinthians to complete the collection) and 10:1–13:10 (Paul's final defense of his apostolic ministry and his warning to the community as he prepares for his third and final visit to Corinth). This part of the letter consists of three sections. In the first (1:12–2:13) Paul gives his account of the recent events that have transpired between him and the community, explaining why it was necessary for him to change his travel plans and why he decided to send the Corinthians a harsh letter rather than visit them again in painful circumstances. In the second section (2:14–7:4) Paul will interrupt this account in order to reflect upon the nature of the new covenant ministry he exercises amid his apostolic sufferings as he calls people to reconciliation. Then, in the third section (7:5–16) Paul will return to the narration he interrupted in 2:13 and recount Titus's report that the harsh letter has led the Corinthians to repent of the incident that occurred on the occasion of Paul' second, painful visit to Corinth.

The purpose of Part 1 (1:12–7:16) is to bring to a closure the rupture that occurred between Paul and the Corinthians because of the painful visit. With this episode resolved, in Part 2 (8:1–9:15) Paul will be able to take up the question of the collection for Jerusalem that the Corinthians had already begun but not yet completed. Building upon the goodwill and reconciliation that has already been effected, in Part 3 (10:1–13:10) Paul will deal with the problem of preachers (whom he dubs "super-apostles") who have intruded upon his missionary assignment, and he will call upon those Corinthians who have not yet repented of their immoral behavior to do so before he arrives for his third and final visit.

A. Paul's Narration of Recent Events
2 Corinthians 1:12–2:13

Second Corinthians 1:12–2:13 begins a section in which Paul gives his account of the recent and painful events that have transpired between him and the community since the writing of 1 Corinthians. Thus it can be viewed as a narrative of past events. Inasmuch as it is Paul's account of the events, it is also his response to criticisms leveled against him because he canceled a promised visit to Corinth and wrote a severe letter instead. This account of these events will be interrupted by an extended discussion of Paul's apostolic ministry (2:14–7:4), after which Paul will resume his narrative by recounting his meeting with Titus and express his joy at Titus's report that the community has repented of its role in the painful visit (7:5–16).

The account begins with a unit (1:12–14) that announces the letter's theme; namely, Paul's apostolic integrity provides the Corinthians with a reason to boast in him just as he boasts in them. In defense of his apostolic integrity and reliability, he will explain that his altered travel plans are not to be interpreted as duplicity or vacillation on his part, since his reliability is rooted in the faithfulness of Jesus Christ, the Son of the faithful God (1:15–22). Rather, he postponed his promised visit in order to spare the community further sadness, and he wrote a severe letter so that the Corinthians might know his love for them (1:23–2:4). Now that they have punished the offender who caused sorrow to all of them, it is time to forgive the offender lest Satan outwit them (2:5–11). For his part, Paul was so concerned for their welfare that he left a fruitful mission in Troas and went to Macedonia in search of Titus so that he could learn of their welfare (2:12–13). Could there be any greater indication of his integrity and love for them?

1. The Letter's Theme (1:12–14)

1:12 This is our boast, the testimony of our conscience: that we have conducted ourselves in the world with single-hearted devotion[a] and God-given sincerity, not by worldly wisdom[b] but by the grace of God—especially toward you. **13** For we do not write anything to you except what you can read and understand.[c] I hope that you will comprehend fully,[d] **14** even as you have understood us partially, because we are your boast even as you will be ours on the day of our[e] Lord Jesus.

A. Paul's Narration of Recent Events

a. Several good witnesses, including P[46], read *hagioteti* ("holiness") instead of *haploteti* ("single-hearted devotion"), and it is difficult to choose between the two on the basis of the external evidence. *Haplotes* fits the context better since Paul is defending himself from charges of being duplicitous, and it also occurs in 2 Cor 8:2; 9:11, 13; 11:3, whereas the only other occurrence of *hagiotes* in the New Testament is Heb 12:10.

b. Literally, "fleshly wisdom" (*en sophia sarkikē*), a wisdom apart from God, rooted in what is merely mortal and so destined to perish. Paul criticizes this kind of wisdom in 1 Cor 1–4.

c. The wordplay (*anaginoskete . . . epiginōskete*) is not apparent in the English translation. A translation such as "know" and "ac*know*ledge" captures some of the wordplay.

d. The context suggests that *heōs telous* be translated "fully," but it is possible to render it "to the end." If it is translated in this way, Paul hopes that the Corinthians will understand what he has written until, or at the day of, the Lord's parousia.

e. A few manuscripts, including P[46], omit "our."

Verses 12–14 function as an exordium that announces the orator's theme, inasmuch as they explain why Paul writes this letter: He intends to show the Corinthians that, just as they are his boast and will be his boast on the day of the Lord's parousia, so they should boast in his apostolic work because he is the apostle and father of their congregation.[1] Although this should have been obvious to the Corinthians, it was not. The Corinthians did not commend Paul as they should have (12:11) when intruding apostles, whom Paul dubs "super-apostles" (11:5; 12:11), came to Corinth criticizing the manner in which he exercises his ministry. As a result of these criticisms, some of the Corinthians questioned the conduct of Paul's apostolic ministry, especially his refusal to accept their patronage. Consequently, instead of boasting about Paul's ministry among them, the Corinthians compared his ministry to that of the super-apostles, whose ministry they viewed as superior to Paul's (see Paul's remarks in 11:5; 12:11). In response to this situation Paul writes 2 Corinthians, providing the Corinthians with an opportunity to boast in him so that they will be able to respond to those who prize appearances rather than what comes from the heart (see 5:12). In doing so, he defends and explains the nature of his apostolic ministry, which paradoxically manifests God's power and consolation in and through weakness and affliction, a theme he has already broached in the benediction.

This unit (1:12–14) consists of three parts. In the first (v.12) Paul calls upon his conscience as a witness to his integrity. In the second (vv. 13–14a) he indicates that he is writing so that the community will completely understand him. In the third (14b) he provides a supporting reason for his hope that they will

1. John T. Fitzgerald (*Cracks in an Earthen Vessel: An Examination of the Catalogues of Hardships in the Corinthian Correspondence* [SBLDS 99; Atlanta: Scholars Press, 1988], 157–58) notes that these verses function "in the same way as an exhortium does in a speech." They announce the subject and the purpose of the letter.

fully understand him: they are his boast, and he wants them to view him as their boast. Thus two references to boasting enclose this unit: Paul's affirmation that his "boast" (*kauchēsis*) is the testimony of his conscience (v. 12a) and his statement that he is, or should be, a cause of "boasting" (*kauchēma*) for the Corinthians, just as they will be his boast at the Lord's parousia (v. 14b). Although Paul employs the plural ("we," "our") throughout this section, it is probably to be construed as a literary plural, that is, a reference to Paul, since it is his behavior that is in view as the following sections show.

[1:12] Paul's boast is the testimony of his conscience. Boasting plays an important role in Paul's writings, especially in 2 Corinthians, and it will be explained in greater detail in the exegesis of chapters 10–13. For the moment, it is sufficient to note that the verb "to boast" (*kauchaomai*) occurs thirty-six times in the Pauline letters (thirty-seven times in the New Testament), twenty of which occur in 2 Corinthians. The noun "boasting" (*kauchēsis*) occurs ten times in the Pauline writings (eleven in the New Testament), six of which occur in 2 Corinthians. Finally, the related noun "boast" (*kauchēma*) occurs ten times in the Pauline letters (eleven times in the New Testament), three of which occur in 2 Corinthians. Overall, Paul views boasting as something to be avoided and insists that those who boast should boast in the Lord (1 Cor 1:31; 2 Cor 10:17) or in the cross of the Lord Jesus Christ (Gal 6:14). In 2 Cor 12:5, as Paul recounts his visions and revelations, he asserts that if he must boast, he will boast in his weakness. Here in verse 12 Paul speaks of the testimony that his "conscience" renders as his reason for pride or "boasting" (*kauchēsis*). In writing this, he is not implying that he is blameless before God. For, as he notes in 1 Cor 4:4, although he is not "conscious" (*synoida*) of having done anything wrong, he is not thereby acquitted since it is the Lord who will judge him. The testimony of Paul's conscience, therefore, is not to be equated with an act of self-justification. Rather, for Paul "conscience" (*syneidēsis*) functions as "the inner tribunal that determines whether one's behavior agrees with the moral norms and requirements affirmed by the mind" (Scott, 35). Therefore, whether their conscience is "weak" or "strong" (see Paul's teaching in 1 Cor 8:1–11:1), believers must abide by its independent judgment, which either accuses or excuses them of wrongdoing (Rom 2:15). Understood in this way, Paul is saying that in the tribunal of his conscience he is not aware of anything that accuses him of conducting himself in a duplicitous manner toward the Corinthian community.

Paul affirms that he acted with a "single-hearted devotion" (*haplotēs*) and "sincerity" (*eilikrineia*) that derive from God. To explain what he means, he contrasts two kinds of behavior: conduct according to "worldly wisdom" (literally "fleshly wisdom") and conduct according to "the grace of God." Paul has already criticized behavior according to a wisdom that is merely human, and therefore mortal, in 1 Cor 1–4. What he means by conduct according to "the grace of God" is more difficult to determine, since he employs *charis* ("grace")

A. Paul's Narration of Recent Events

in so many ways, especially in this letter.[2] The contrasts with "worldly wisdom," however, suggests a pattern of behavior that relies and depends upon God's graciousness. Put another way, Paul is not his own master but lives under and according to God's grace. This is why he describes his single-hearted devotion and sincerity as coming from God. This testimony of his conscience will be crucial to his argument since some of the Corinthians have depicted him as vacillating and unreliable for altering his travel plans (1:15–22). Paul, however, insists that he is "single-hearted" and "sincere" in his behavior toward the Corinthians. In writing this, he may also have in mind his decision to support himself so as not to burden the Corinthians financially, an aspect of his ministry that was a cause of tension between him and the community, since each side interpreted this decision differently (see 11:7–15; 12:13–18).[3]

[13–14a] In addition to defending his conduct toward the Corinthians, Paul must explain the style of his letter writing, since the two are interrelated. Although the present tense of *graphomen* ("we write") might suggest that Paul has only this letter in mind, it is more likely that he is referring to his letters in general and, perhaps in a particular way, to the severe letter "written in tears" that he will discuss in the next chapter (2:3–4). For example, in 1 Cor 5:9 he refers to a misunderstanding between himself and the Corinthians concerning what he said in a letter that he apparently wrote before 1 Corinthians. Moreover in 4:3–4, a passage closely related to this unit, Paul defends his conduct, as he does here, and responds to a criticism that his "gospel is veiled." Thus, even though Paul's critics acknowledged that his letters are "severe and powerful" (10:10), some have also criticized him for preaching a gospel that is veiled and obscure, and for being untrustworthy, an issue that he will address in the next unit. From the outset of this letter then, Paul affirms the integral relationship between his conduct and what he writes, between his person and his letters, a point that his opponents have challenged (10:10). Just as his own conduct is single-minded and sincere, so is the content of what he writes.

[14b] Having affirmed his conduct and the content of what he writes, Paul expresses his hope that the Corinthians will understand him fully, which is the goal and purpose of his letter. The Corinthians already know Paul partially, but he hopes that they will understand him fully, because he is their reason for boasting, just as they will be his reason for boasting on the day of the Lord. Two points need to be made here. First, Paul acknowledges that the Corinthians already understand him, and so his gospel, in part. Thus he will acknowledge that they

---

2. *Charis* ("grace") occurs frequently in 2 Corinthians (1:2, 12, 15; 2:14; 4:15; 6:1; 8:1, 4, 6, 7, 9, 16, 19; 9:8, 14, 15; 12:9; 13:13), but its meaning is not univocal and must always be determined by the context. The exegesis of chapters 8–9 provides a discussion of this term.

3. Although Paul presented his decision not to accept the community's financial support as a decision not to burden the community because he loved them, the Corinthians interpreted it as a rejection of their friendship.

already stand firm in the faith (1:24), and there has already been an initial reconciliation between him and them over the events that occurred at the time of the painful visit (7:1–16). The reconciliation between Paul and the Corinthians, however, is not complete, since intruding apostles have called into question his apostolic ministry and some members of the community have not yet repented of their immorality (12:21; 13:2). This is why Paul calls the community to reconciliation in 6:11–7:4, even though he speaks of the community as reconciled to him in subsequent verses (7:5–16). Second Corinthians then is about a double reconciliation, one that has already taken place and one that is yet to be consummated.[4] When the Corinthians understand Paul completely, that is, when they boast in and accept his apostolic ministry, which is distinguished by its participation in the sufferings of Christ, then the second reconciliation will occur.

The second point is related to the first. When the Corinthians comprehend Paul completely, then they will understand that he, not the intruding apostles, is their reason for boasting. To understand Paul completely, however, the Corinthians must comprehend the paradoxical nature of his ministry, a theme that he introduced in the benediction, namely, that his apostolic afflictions are for their consolation and salvation (1:6). Therefore, they must learn that affliction and suffering are an integral part of an authentic apostolic ministry. When they do, then they will no longer view the sufferings and afflictions of their founding apostle with shame and disdain but as reasons for boasting in him. Paul himself already has great confidence in the Corinthians (7:4, 14) about whom he has boasted to others (8:24; 9:3). In effect, then, Paul writes 2 Corinthians to provide the Corinthians with an opportunity to boast in him (5:12), as he already boasts in them, so that there may be a mutual boasting on the day of the Lord's appearance (see 1 Thess 2:19, in which Paul says that the Thessalonians will be his "crown of boasting" [*stephanos kauchēseōs*] at the Lord's parousia). To accomplish this, he must explain the authentic nature of apostolic ministry.

2. Paul's Reliability (1:15–22)

15 With this confidence, I intended to come to you first[a] so that you might enjoy a second favor[b] 16 and to pass through you to Macedonia and again to come to you from Macedonia, and be sent on by you to Judea. 17 In planning this, therefore, was I vacillating?[c] Or, what I intend, do I intend in a merely human way, so that with me it is both "yes, yes" and "no, no"?[d]

18 But as God is faithful[e] our word to you is not both "yes" and "no."

---

4. This is the thesis of R. Bieringer, "Plädoyer für die Einheitlichkeit des 2. Korintherbriefes," in R. Bieringer and J. Lambrecht, *Studies on 2 Corinthians* (BETL 112; Leuven: Leuven University Press, 1994), 131–79. See the introduction to this commentary for a fuller explanation.

A. Paul's Narration of Recent Events

19 For the Son of God, Jesus Christ, the one preached among you through us (through me, and Silvanus, and Timothy) was not "yes" and "no" but in him it was "yes!" 20 For, as many as are the promises of God, in him they find their "yes," wherefore our[f] "Amen" for the glory of God is through him. 21 The one strengthening us with you in Christ, and who has anointed[g] us, is God, 22 who has even[h] sealed us and given the first installment of the Spirit in our hearts.

a. A few commentators (Thrall, 1:136–37) take the adverb *proteron* ("first") with the verb *eboulomēn* ("I intended") rather than with the infinitive *elthein* ("to come"): "I first intended . . ." But the mention of a second grace (a second visit) suggests that "first" should be taken with the infinitive "to come."

b. Some manuscripts (ℵ[c], B, L, P) read *charan* ("joy"), but the more difficult reading (supported by ℵ*, A, C, D) is *charin* ("grace"). Paul employs *charis* several times, in a variety of ways in 2 Corinthians, especially in chaps. 8–9.

c. Literally, "was I acting with *the* fickleness" (*tē elaphria*). The definite article might suggest that Paul is responding to an accusation of fickleness that the Corinthians have lodged against him. Thus it might be paraphrased in this way, "*the* fickleness of which you accuse me."

d. P[46] simply reads "both yes and no." Compare Matt 5:37 and Jas 5:12. The reading of P[46] may be an attempt to bring v. 17 into line with v. 18, where there is not a double "yes" and "no" as there is here.

e. The text could also be translated as a simple declarative sentence, "God is faithful," but Paul seems to be using the phrase as an exclamatory statement rather than as a simple declarative sentence.

f. "Our" is a translation of *di'hēmōn*, literally, "the Amen to God unto glory through us."

g. Paul plays on the words "anointed" (*chrisas*) and "Christ" (*Christon*). God has anointed believers just as he anointed his Christ (*Christos* means "anointed one").

h. *Kai* has been translated as "even" to indicate that the last two participles ("sealed" . . . "given") are further explanations of "anointed."

Having announced the theme of this letter—his apostolic integrity, which should lead the Corinthians to boast in him—Paul reviews the events that have led some at Corinth to doubt his faithfulness and the reliability of the gospel that he preaches. Although most commentators view 1:15–2:13 as comprising a discrete section, they do not agree on its structure. For example, Lambrecht (33) and this commentary view 1:15–22 as a unit, whereas Thrall (1:136) extends the unit to include verse 24, and Furnish (132) extends it even further, to 2:2. The text, of course, is more fluid than these divisions suggest, but the oath formula in 1:23 seems to begin a new unit in which Paul gives a specific reason why he did not return to Corinth.

The first part of the unit (vv. 15–17) raises the issue of Paul's altered travel plans concluding with two rhetorical questions about his integrity (v.17). The second part (vv. 18–22) anchors Paul's faithfulness in the faithfulness of God and Jesus Christ and is related to the first part by the words "yes" (*nai*) and "no" (*ou*), which are present in both parts. The opening verse of the second part (v. 18) acts as a transitional statement and affirms that as God is reliable, so is Paul's word. In verses 19–20 Paul turns to the faithfulness of Jesus Christ to undergird his integrity, and then in verses 21–22 he returns to God, whom he describes with four participles, translated as "sustaining," "anointed," "sealed," and "given." Thus Paul surrounds the central verses that deal with Christ (vv. 19–20) with two descriptions of God (vv. 18 and 22). In this way he grounds his apostolic integrity in the faithfulness of God and his Son, Jesus Christ.

[1:15–17] Paul connects this unit to what has proceded by writing that "with this confidence I intended to come to you first." "This confidence" (*tautē tē pepoithesēi*) refers to what Paul has just said in 1:12–14, especially about his conviction that he is the boast of the Corinthians as they will be his boast on the day of the Lord. The travel plans to which Paul refers here represent a change from his original plans as outlined in 1 Cor 16. This change appears to have played a major role in the crisis between him and the Corinthians, leading to the accusation that he (and perhaps his gospel) is not trustworthy. To understand what Paul writes here, it is necessary to review his travel plans.

At the end of 1 Corinthians, Paul indicated his desire to visit Corinth and perhaps spend the winter there.

> And when I arrive, I will send any whom you approve with letters to take your gift to Jerusalem. If it seems advisable that I should go also, they will accompany me. I will visit you after passing through Macedonia—for I intend to pass through Macedonia—and perhaps I will stay with you or even spend the winter, so that you may send me on my way, wherever I go. I do not want to see you now just in passing, for I hope to spend some time with you, if the Lord permits. But I will stay in Ephesus until Pentecost, for a wide door for effective work has opened to me, and there are many adversaries. (1 Cor 16:3–9)

According to these plans Paul, who is still in Ephesus, will visit Corinth after he has passed through the Roman senatorial province of Macedonia (where the churches of Thessalonica and Philippi were situated), which lies to the north of the province of Achaia, of which Corinth was the capital. When he wrote 1 Corinthians, however, his plans were somewhat vague, since it had not yet been determined if he should accompany those who would bring the collection to Jerusalem (1 Cor 16:4). Consequently, it is not clear where he intended to go after visiting the Corinthians (1 Cor 16:6). It is clear, however, that he plans to come to Corinth *after* passing through Macedonia and that he hopes to spend a good amount of time with the Corinthians.

In 2 Corinthians Paul appears to have altered the travel plans of 1 Cor 16, for according to 2 Cor 1:15 he intended to come to them *first*, then go north to the

A. Paul's Narration of Recent Events

Macedonian churches, and finally return to Corinth by way of Macedonia, before being sent on by the Corinthian church to Judea to the church at Jerusalem. The difference between the two travel plans can be outlined in this way:

1 Corinthians 16	2 Corinthians 1
Ephesus to Macedonia	Ephesus to Corinth
Macedonia to Corinth	Corinth to Macedonia
	Macedonia to Corinth
Corinth to wherever Paul will go	Corinth to Judea

Not only are the travel plans in 2 Cor 1 different from those proposed in 1 Cor 16; it appears that Paul did not carry out the plans of 2 Cor 1 as he promised. Thus, after he visited Corinth, he seems to have returned to Ephesus instead of going to Macedonia and returning to Corinth. This change of plans, which deprived the Corinthians of the promised return visit, led some at Corinth to criticize Paul for being unreliable (1:17), a charge which suggested that if he was not reliable in these matters, then neither was the word of the gospel that he preached to them.[5]

Although we can no longer know with assurance what happened at Corinth that led Paul to alter his revised travel plans, one thing is clear. Certain members of the Corinthian church took the opportunity of Paul's failure to carry out his travel plans—which he had now altered for a second time—to call into question his reliability, as well as the reliability of the gospel he preached. This is why Paul must review and interpret what happened since the writing of 1 Corinthians. But why does he do this if the Corinthians have already repented

---

5. Since the travel plans of 1 Cor 16 and 2 Cor 1 are so different, it is unlikely that they can be reconciled with each other. Most commentators propose that something occurred between the writing of 1 Corinthians and the writing of 2 Corinthians that made it necessary for Paul to alter the travel plans of 1 Cor 16 and visit Corinth ahead of schedule, crossing over from Ephesus to Corinth by ship rather than coming by land through Macedonia (for a full discussion of these plans see the detailed excursuses of Allo, 63–68 and Thrall, 1:69–74). For example, Paul may have learned from Corinthian messengers or from Timothy, whom he had already sent to Corinth (1 Cor 4:17; 16:10–11), that the moral situation in the Corinthian church had deteriorated and this required him to make an emergency visit (note Paul's fears about the church in 2 Cor 12:20 as he prepares for his third and final visit). Once in Corinth, Paul may have proposed the revised travel plans of 2 Cor 1, namely, after spending time in Corinth, he would visit the churches in Macedonia to the north, then return from Macedonia to Corinth, with the hope of being sent on to Judea with the collection for the church of Jerusalem. This emergency or intermediate visit, however, did not go well, and it caused Paul a great deal of grief. Consequently he seems to have returned to Ephesus rather than go on to Macedonia and return to Corinth. Once at Ephesus, he wrote a severe letter out of much anguish of heart (2:3–4) reprimanding the community for its conduct. Although several scholars identify the whole or part of this severe letter with the final four chapters of 2 Corinthians (the so-called Four Chapter Hypothesis of Adolf Hausrath and James H. Kennedy), this commentary proposes that the severe letter has been lost.

of the events that occurred during his second and painful visit (see Titus's report in 7:5–16)? The answer can be summarized in this way: Although the severe letter led the Corinthians to repentance, Paul still needs to interpret and explain what happened so that the Corinthians will fully grasp the integrity of his apostolic ministry. Furthermore, since the situation of the intruding apostles has not yet been resolved, Paul narrates these events in order to prepare for his all-out assault on the super-apostles in chapters 10–13.

In verses 15–17, then, Paul explains that the purpose of the revised travel plans was to provide the Corinthians with "a second grace" (*deuteran charin*), by which he means the favor of a second visit during which he would undoubtedly strengthen and encourage them in their faith (though Martin [24] takes the phrase to mean a second opportunity for the Corinthians to be gracious to Paul). In effect, Paul is implying that he intended to extend to the Corinthians a special favor that he did not grant the churches of Macedonia, a double visit, thereby dispelling any suggestion that he was neglecting them (see Barrett, 75). However, the fact remains that he did not make this return visit, and so he now asks two interrelated rhetorical questions, each of which expects a negative answer: Did he act deceitfully with "the levity" (*tē elaphria*) of which they accused him? Did he make his plans in "a merely human way" (*kata sarka*, see 5:16; 10:2, 3; 11:18 for other occurrences of the same expression), so that one cannot trust him when he says yes or no? In each case, Paul expects the Corinthians to respond with a resounding, "Of course not!" But before explaining why he did not make the promised return visit (1:23–2:4), Paul seeks to establish his trustworthiness on firm theological ground.

[18–22] These verses are often characterized as an excursus or digression that moves from Paul's travel plans to a discussion of the faithfulness of God and Christ, only to return to a discussion of the travel plans in 1:23–2:4, thereby establishing an interlocking a b a' pattern.[6] Though it is true that these verses briefly interrupt Paul's discussion about the postponement of his visit, they are the theological foundation of his defense, inasmuch as they establish his apostolic reliability on the basis of the faithfulness of God and God's Son, Jesus Christ. Put another way, instead of providing the Corinthians with the kind of

---

6. This pattern occurs frequently in Paul's writings. After beginning one topic, Paul often turns to another, only to return to the original topic. This is especially apparent in his discussion of food sacrificed to idols in 1 Cor 8:1–11:1. This technique allows Paul to compare two topics with each other, for example, his own behavior and the behavior of the "weak" and the "strong." In 2 Corinthians he interrupts his narration of the events that have occurred between him and the community with a discussion of his apostolic ministry in 2:14–7:4. Far from being irrelevant to his narration of the recent events, the discussion of his apostolic ministry reinforces what he says about his integrity in his narration of these recent events, and vice versa. As will be noted, this pattern even occurs in smaller units of this letter. The sections of Jan Lambrecht's commentary entitled "Structure and Line of Thought" are especially helpful in isolating such "ring patterns."

A. Paul's Narration of Recent Events

practical excuse that they might have expected, Paul establishes his apostolic integrity on a firm foundation that cannot be assailed: the faithfulness of God and of God's Son.

Paul responds to his own rhetorical questions by rooting the reliability of his "word" (*logos*) in the faithfulness of God. As God is "faithful" (*pistos*), so is Paul's word. This "word" can be taken in two ways. First, it refers to what Paul says. When he says yes, he means yes; and when he says no, he means no. Of this there should be no doubt. Second, and more importantly, this "word" refers to the gospel that Paul preaches. The reliability of this gospel is rooted in Paul's apostolic integrity, which is grounded in the faithfulness of God, a concept that is found in several other places in Paul's writings (1 Cor 1:9; 10:13; 1 Thess 5:24; 2 Thess 3:3), as well as in Israel's Scriptures (Deut 7:9).

For Paul the faithfulness of God finds its clearest expression in the faithfulness of Jesus Christ, the Son of God, whom Paul, Silvanus, and Timothy preached to the Corinthians. Paul responds to the criticism leveled against him—that he cannot be trusted when he says yes or no, because he is ultimately unreliable—by insisting that just as there was no ambivalence in Christ's obedience to his Father, so it is with his own word. Jesus Christ is the perfectly obedient Son of God, whereby the Christian community makes its yes ("Amen") for God's glory,[7] and so God's promises find their fulfillment in Christ. And because Christ was faithful, so is Paul. In effect, Paul forges a chain of faithfulness that extends from God to Christ, from Christ to Paul, and from Paul to the Christian community. The faithfulness of God is manifested in the faithfulness of Christ, in whom Paul's apostolic ministry is rooted. This is why the community can, should, and must trust him.

Having explained that Jesus Christ is the manifestation of God's faithfulness, who allows believers to glorify God (vv. 19–20), Paul once more turns his attention to God (vv. 21–22) in order to remind the Corinthians of what God is doing and has done for them. Fee calls this section "one of the most God-centered, God-focused paragraphs in the Pauline corpus."[8] And indeed it is. The passage contains four participles. The first is a present participle (*bebaiōn*) that describes what God is doing: "strengthening us, with you, in Christ." The remaining participles are aorists, pointing to something that God has already done: "anointed" (*chrisas*), "sealed" (*sphragisamenos*), and "given" (*dous*) the Spirit. Whereas

---

7. Although Paul tends to use "Christ" "Christ Jesus," "Jesus Christ," and "Lord" most frequently in referring to Jesus, "Son of God" plays a prominent role in his Christology, even though it does not occur as frequently as these titles. Whereas "Lord" establishes the relation between Christ and the believer, "Son of God" expresses Jesus' relation to God. For other occurrences of "Son of God," see Gal 2:20; 3:26. For "his Son," see Rom 1:3, 9; 5:10; 8:3, 29, 32; 1 Cor 1:19; Gal 1:16; 4:4, 6; 1 Thess 1:10.

8. *God's Empowering Presence: The Holy Spirit in the Letters of Paul* (Peabody: Hendrickson, 1994), 289.

"us" (*hēmōn*) refers to Paul and his coworkers (v. 21), since Paul is defending his apostolic integrity at this point, the accompanying phrase "with you"(*syn hymin*) includes the Corinthians as the beneficiaries of God's action.

The first of these participles (*bebaiōn*) points to something God is doing: God is "confirming" and "strengthening" Paul and with him the Corinthians in their Christian life (see 1 Cor 1:7–8, where Paul employs the same verb to describe Christ as strengthening or sustaining believers to the end). The second participle (*chrisas*), which plays on the word "Christ," indicates something that God has already done: "anointed" believers. Thus, just as God anointed his "Anointed" (*Christos*) with the Spirit, so God has anointed believers with the same Spirit, thereby making them sons and daughters who are conformed to his Son. The last two aorist participles (*sphragisamenos*; *dous*), both of which are taken from the commercial language of Paul's day, further specify this anointing. Just as owners set a seal upon their goods to indicate ownership, and just as people make a down payment to guarantee future payment and delivery, so God has "set his seal"—his own Spirit—upon believers to indicate ownership and "given" them the first installment of redemption—his own Spirit—that will be "paid in full" at the parousia and the resurrection of the dead. (For other uses of "seal," see Eph 1:13; 4:30. For other uses of "first installment," see 2 Cor 5:5; Eph 1:14.)

Paul's description of himself (and the Corinthians) as anointed and sealed with the Spirit is significant because of what he will say about his apostolic ministry in 2 Cor 3. In that chapter, Paul will again turn to the Spirit when he (a) describes the Corinthian community as his "letter of recommendation" written by "the Spirit of the Living God" (3:1–3), (b) portrays himself as the minister of a new covenant (3:4–6), (c) contrasts the dispensation of the Spirit with the dispensation of death (3:7–11), and (d) compares his Spirit-empowered ministry with the ministry of Moses (3:12–18). This occurrence of "God," "Jesus Christ," "the Son of God," and the "Spirit" here within a few verses brings together essential elements of later Trinitarian theology, as does the remarkable ending of this letter, "The grace of the Lord Jesus Christ, and the love of God, and the fellowship of the Holy Spirit be with all of you" (13:14). To be sure, Paul had not yet formulated the doctrine of the Trinity that would be the subject of later conciliar debates, but passages such as this clearly provided the church with the building blocks needed for that theology. For Paul, God is the primary actor in the drama of salvation; Jesus Christ is the agent by whom God effects the plan of salvation; and God's Spirit is the empowering force of the present age.

Before turning to the next unit, it is necessary to ask a final question: namely, does this description of anointing, sealing, and giving the Spirit have the baptism of believers in view? Although the language of anointing and sealing quickly became associated with baptism in the early church, it is unlikely that

A. Paul's Narration of Recent Events

it is in the foreground of these verses, since here Paul is primarily concerned with God as the one who sustains Paul's apostolic integrity with the gift of the Spirit. Rather it is the Spirit that is in the foreground.[9]

3. A Change of Plans and a Harsh Letter (1:23–2:4)

1:23 I call upon God as my witness—staking my life on this[a]—that it was to spare you that I did not come to Corinth. 24 Not that we exercise authority over your faith, rather, we are coworkers for your joy, for you stand firm in the faith.[b]

2:1 For I determined not to come to you in painful circumstances again.[c] 2 For if I grieve you, then[d] who is there to gladden me but the one saddened by me? 3 And I wrote this very thing,[e] lest, when I come, I might be saddened by those who should make me rejoice, confident in all of you that my joy is the joy of all of you. 4 For I wrote to you out of a sense of great affliction and anguish of heart, with many tears, not to grieve you but that you might know the love that I have, especially for you.

a. This is a translation of *epi tēn emēn psychēn* (literally, "against/upon my soul"). The sense is that if Paul is speaking falsely, then let God take his life.

b. The phrase *tē pistei* could be taken as a dative of instrument, "by the faith," but most commentators take it in a local sense, in the realm of faith.

c. "Again" (*palin*) modifies "in painful circumstances" as well as the verb "to come" since Paul is referring to the painful visit he made to Corinth.

d. *Kai* is translated as "then" (so Héring, 14).

e. The verb *egrapsa* ("I wrote") is an aorist but not an epistolary aorist. Paul is referring to a letter that he has already sent (the severe letter). The phrase which follows, "this very thing" (*touto auto*), could refer to what he has just written or how he has written (if the verb is taken as an epistolary aorist). It is more likely, however, that the phrase refers to the letter Paul previously sent to the Corinthians and less likely to a specific passage within that letter.

Having provided the theological grounding for his apostolic integrity in the previous unit, Paul finally gives a specific reason for not returning to Corinth. As Calvin (25) writes, "Now at last he begins to explain why he has changed his plans." Chrysostom (*Homily* 4:1), however, is puzzled by this passage, since he interprets Paul's statement in 1:17 to mean that it is the Spirit, not Paul himself, who directs and guides the apostle's journeys. Because of this interpretation, Chrysostom asks why Paul now affirms that he (rather than the Spirit) decided that he should not go to Corinth.

---

9. Fee, *God's Empowering Presence*, 294–96.

The unit can be divided into two parts. In the first (1:23–24), Paul explains that he did not visit the Corinthians again because he wanted to spare them (v. 23). Then, lest this be misunderstood as threatening them, he insists that this does not mean that he exercises authority over their faith; rather, he acknowledges their faith (v. 24).

In the second part (2:1–4), Paul explains that he sent a letter instead of visiting them because his decision was intended to avoid further sadness for himself and the community. A number of key words unify the unit: "joy" (*chara*, 1:24; 2:3), "to come" (*erchomai*, vv. 1:23, 2:1, 3), and the frequently used "grief" or "sorrow" (*lypē*, 2:1, 3) and "to grieve" or "to sadden" (*lypeō*, 2:2, 4) in the second part of the unit and in the next unit (2:5, 7), thereby anticipating what will follow.

[1:23–24] Paul has already spoken of God on several occasions. In the letter's benediction, he praised the God of mercy and consolation (1:3), the God who raises the dead (1:9). He then identified God as the faithful God (1:18), the God who sustains believers, having anointed, sealed, and given them the Spirit as a down payment of what is yet to come. As he begins this unit, Paul calls upon God once more, but this time as his "witness" (*martys*; see Rom 1:9 and 1 Thess 2:5, 10, where he does the same). Thus Paul has invoked two witnesses on his behalf: his "conscience" (1:12) and "God" (1:23). But now he puts himself under an oath upon which he stakes his life in order to emphasize and assure the truthfulness of what he is about to say (see Gal 1:20, " In what I am writing to you, before God, I do not lie"). Later, in his criticism of the super-apostles, Paul will again call upon God to guarantee the truthfulness of what he is about to say ("The God and Father of our Lord Jesus Christ—the one who is blessed forever—knows that I am not lying" [11:31]). And at the end of this letter, he will clarify what he has been saying all along when he writes, "All this time you have been thinking that we are defending ourselves to you. We were speaking before God, in Christ. Everything, beloved, is for your edification" (12:19). In effect, Paul writes this letter in the presence of God.

In calling upon God as his witness, Paul says that it was to "spare" (*pheidomai*) the Corinthians that he did not return to Corinth (the planned visit mentioned in 1:15). The same verb occurs in 12:6, in reference to his decision to refrain from boasting, and more significantly in 13:2, where he writes: "On my second visit I forewarned, and now that I am absent I am forewarning, those who previously sinned and all the rest that when I come again I will not be lenient (*ou pheisomai*)."[10] This text is helpful for understanding what Paul says here, for in 12:14–13:10 he is anticipating his third and final visit to Corinth

---

10. Those who view chapters 10–13 as the severe letters (the so-called Four Chapter Hypothesis) point to 13:2 as evidence for their position, arguing that 1:23 sounds as if Paul is reminding the Corinthians of something that he wrote in the severe letter (Plummer, xxii–xxxvi and 44). The argument, however, can also be reversed. What Paul says in 13:2 is an echo of what he is saying here.

A. Paul's Narration of Recent Events

(see 12:14; 13:1). As he prepares for that visit, he recalls his second and painful visit, eager to avoid another painful experience at Corinth; for he fears that there may still be rivalries and jealousies among the Corinthians and that certain people have not repented of their immorality (12:20–21). Accordingly, he reminds them how on his second visit he warned the unrepentant that he would not "spare" them if he came again. If they want proof that Christ speaks through him (12:3), he will provide it by punishing them.

In this unit Paul is looking back on that painful visit without reference to the prospect of his third and final visit. Consequently, he views the painful visit from another vantage point, without averting to the problem of dissension and immorality that he will mention in 12:1–13:4. For, having written the severe letter, he is trying to explain his actions in a manner that will finalize the reconciliation between him and the community on the matter of the offender, which will be discussed in the next unit. This part of the letter, then, is more conciliatory in tone, and Paul insists that he is not trying to dominate and subject the Corinthians to himself. He readily acknowledges that they are established in the realm of faith. This affirmation is significant because it indicates that the problem at Corinth is not primarily dogmatic or creedal in nature but, as the rest of the letter will show, disciplinary and moral (see Allo, 32; Thrall, 1:162). The shift from the first person singular in verse 23 ("*I* call upon God") to the first person plural in verse 24 ("not that *we* exercise authority . . . *we* are coworkers") suggests that Paul includes Silvanus and Timothy (1:19) in this statement (Furnish, 152). Thus Paul's apostolic "team" seeks the "joy" of the community, a joy that has been disturbed by these recent events. Such joy is integral to the gospel they preach because it comes from the Holy Spirit (Rom 14:17; Gal 5:22; 1 Thess 1:6) and from God (Rom 15:13). This is why Paul can unabashedly say that his joy is their joy (2:3); for he is speaking not of a merely human emotion but of the joy that comes from God's Spirit.

[2:1–4] The mention of joy provides Paul with a transition to the second part of the unit (2:1–4), in which he employs the dialectic of rejoicing and sadness to describe his unique relationship to the community. Since the Corinthians are his dear children and he is their founding father (1 Cor 4:14–15), there should be a mutual exchange of joy between the community and its apostle, and this is what Paul hoped his apostolic visit would effect. Since his second visit to Corinth resulted in grief for him and the community, however, he decided against making the promised return visit to Corinth, lest grief be added to grief. After all, if the apostle saddened his children by a further visit, how could they—saddened by him—give him joy? Consequently, instead of visiting them again, Paul returned to Ephesus and wrote a letter out of "a sense of great affliction and anguish of heart, with many tears." The reference to "affliction" (*thlipsis*) recalls what Paul has already written about this topic in his benediction. But there is no mention of godly consolation, which must wait until Titus's report (7:6).

Although he will eventually acknowledge that his letter grieved them (7:8), here he says that he wrote so that they might know his love, "especially for you" (*perissoterōs eis hymas*), a phrase that echoes what he has already said about the sincerity of his conduct, "especially toward you" (1:12). In the next unit, he will expand upon this and say that he wrote to know their character, if they would be obedient in all things (2:9). Still later, he will explain that he wrote for the sake of revealing to them their zeal for him (7:12). In effect, Paul gives multiple—but not necessarily contradicting—reasons for the severe letter. In terms of the argument that he presents on behalf of his apostolic reliability, Paul is assuring the Corinthians that his altered travel plans and his severe letter, which he substituted for his promised visit, were for their benefit. It was to spare them further sorrow that he did not return to Corinth, and it was so that they might know his love for them that he wrote as he did.

In this section, then, Paul explains that he altered his travel plans to spare them and to avoid further sadness between himself and the community. In sending a letter rather than visiting them, he was showing them his love for them. For other references to Paul's love for the community, see 11:11 and 12:15.

4. Forgiving the Offender (2:5–11)

2:5 If someone has caused grief, he has not grieved me, but to some degree ᵃ —not to exaggerateᵇ—all of you. 6 This punishment by the majority of you is sufficient for such a one. 7 So, on the contrary, you should rather forgive and comfort, so that he is not overwhelmed by excessive grief. 8 For this reason, I urge you to reaffirm him in love. 9 For this is why I wrote,ᶜ so that I might know your character: whether you are obedient in all things. 10 Whomever you forgive, I forgive. For what I have forgiven—if I have forgiven anything—is for your sake in the presence of Christ,ᵈ 11 lest we be outwitted by Satan; for we are not unaware of his designs.

a. If the phrase *alla apo merous* ("but to some degree") is taken with *ouk eme lelypēken* ("he has not grieved me"), Paul is downplaying the grief he suffered lest he overburden the congregation with sorrow. Thus the KJV translates the verse, "But if any have caused grief, he has not grieved me, but in part: that I may not overcharge you all." Most commentators, however, take *alla apo merous* with the grief of the Corinthians: all of them were saddened, "to some degree," by the offender. This interpretation is better suited to Paul's rhetorical strategy, which seeks to show how he and the congregation share in each other's joy and sorrow.

b. The usual meaning of *epibarō* is "to burden" or "to weigh down," as in 1 Thess 2:9 and 2 Thess 3:8, but such a meaning makes little sense here. Accordingly, most commentators translate the verb in the metaphorical sense that the context seems to require: "to exaggerate," "to say too much by burdening with words." See Allo, 38.

A. Paul's Narration of Recent Events

c. As in 2:3, 4, this is not an epistolary aorist, since Paul is referring to the severe letter he has already sent to the Corinthians.

d. Although it is possible to translate *en prosōpō Christou* "in the person of Christ," it is more likely that Paul means that he forgives the person in Christ's presence, that is, with Christ witnessing or watching what he does.

Having mentioned the severe letter for the first time (2:3–4), Paul now explains why he wrote that letter: he was testing their character to see if they would be obedient in all things. The unit can be divided into two parts. In the first (2:5–8), Paul exhorts the community to forgive the offender, lest he be swallowed up in grief. In the second (2:9–11), he says that he wrote in order to test their character, assuring them that he forgives whomever they forgive, and warning them that Satan will outwit them if they do not forgive the offender (v. 11). Chrysostom (*Homily* 4:5) and Calvin (28–31) are especially sensitive to Paul's rhetorical strategy in this unit, highlighting the manner in which he shows that he and the community share in the grief caused by the offender, and the manner in which Paul beseeches rather than commands the community to forgive the offender, thereby making them partners in the work of forgiveness.

[2:5–8] In the previous unit Paul mentioned a letter that he wrote in affliction and anguish of heart, to which commentators assign names such as "the harsh letter," "the severe letter," "the letter written in tears." But to this point there has been no indication of the letter's content, since the Corinthians were familiar with the letter. It is apparent from this unit, however, and from what Paul writes in 7:8–13 that the letter dealt with an offender who grieved Paul and the community by his behavior; see 7:12, where Paul speaks of him as "the offender" (*tou adikēsantos*). Furthermore, this unit and chapter 7 indicate that the severe letter had a favorable outcome: the community repented and punished the offender. The offender, however, has not yet been restored to the community.

Because Paul writes after these events have transpired and been resolved in his favor, there is no need for him to identify the offender; so he refers to the man as "such a one" (*tō toitoutō*), "this one" (*ho toioutos*), "him" (*auton*), and so on. Indeed it would be counterproductive to do otherwise, since Paul seeks to restore the offender to the community. Likewise there is no need to describe what happened, lest old wounds be opened again. What Paul must do, even though the issue has been resolved favorably in his favor, is provide the Corinthians with a persuasive statement of his purpose in writing, so that they will forgive the offender. Furthermore, since the purpose of this letter is to give the Corinthians a reason for boasting in his ministry rather than in the super-apostles (1:12–14; 5:12), he seeks to show them that however severe his letter might have been, it was for their good and for the good of the offender, whom they should now forgive.

Instead of focusing on the sorrow that he experienced, then, Paul points to the injury that was inflicted on the community. The action of the offender did not harm only Paul; it injured them too, because, as Paul taught in 1 Corinthians, they are members of one body (1 Cor 12:12–26), so that if one member suffers, all suffer (1 Cor 12:26). Consequently the incident was not just about Paul; it was about all of them; for he is their father, and they are his dear children (1 Cor 4:14–15). Although the Corinthians did not understand it, at the time that the incident took place, they shared in Paul's grief, and Paul's severe letter seems to have impressed upon them the seriousness of the matter. For by the time that he writes this letter, they have severely punished the offender, perhaps by excluding him from their assembly (cf. the action prescribed in 1 Cor 5:5). Paul apparently believes that the punishment by the majority is in danger of consuming the man with grief. Thus the one who has caused such grief is about to be destroyed by grief! Consequently Paul "encourages" (*diō parakalō*; 2:8) them to forgive the offender and restore him to the fellowship of love. Whether there was a minority that disagreed with this majority opinion and thought that the punishment was not severe enough (Plummer, 58) or too severe (Barnett, 125) cannot be determined and is probably beside the point. What is important for Paul—who views himself as Christ's ambassador calling people to be reconciled to God (5:20)—is that the man should be forgiven, a course of action that is in line with Pauline teaching elsewhere (Gal 6:1; Eph 4:32; Col 3:13). Paul, who has already disclaimed any intention to exercise authority over their faith (1:24), implores them rather than commands them. He employs a similar approach in his letter to Philemon, especially in verses 8–9.

[9–11] Having urged the community to forgive the offender, Paul explains why he wrote the severe letter: to test their character, which will be proven by their obedience in all things. In writing this, Paul is providing the Corinthians with another reason to forgive the offender. For if they do not forgive him, they will not prove themselves obedient in all things—even though Paul has urged rather than commanded such forgiveness. Moreover, if they are disobedient in this matter, Satan will have outwitted them by using their refusal to forgive as an occasion to snatch a member from their midst. Thus Paul's reason for writing the harsh letter (to test their obedience) provides further motivation to forgive the offender, since their obedience must be ongoing.

In order to encourage them to forgive the offender, Paul assures them that he will forgive whomever they forgive. Indeed he has already forgiven the person. In the Greek text, however, the reference to the community's forgiveness precedes Paul's ("whomever you forgive, I will forgive"), leading Chrysostom (*Homily* 4:5) to note how Paul "assigns the second part to himself, showing them as beginning, himself as following." This shrewd observation highlights Paul's rhetorical strategy, which avoids lording it over their faith and encourages them to do what is in accord with the gospel so that they may be obedient in all things. Thus though there is a sense in which he has already forgiven the offender, he still waits for their forgiveness so that he can ratify it with his own; for he is their apostle. What he does, he does for their sake, lest Satan outwit them.

A. Paul's Narration of Recent Events

Satan (11:14; 12:7), also called "the god of this age" (4:4), "Beliar" (6:15), "the Serpent" (11:3), plays a significant role in 2 Corinthians, primarily as a deceiver and opponent of the gospel. As the god of this age he blinds the minds of unbelievers so that they will not see "the light of the gospel of the glory of Christ" (4:4). As Beliar he stands opposed to Christ (6:15). Because he is a liar, he disguises himself as an angel of light, just as his servants (the "super-apostles") disguise themselves as ministers of righteousness (11:15), thereby deceiving the community as the Serpent deceived Eve (11:3). It is a messenger of Satan that harasses Paul with the enigmatic "thorn for the flesh" (12:7). Consequently, when Paul writes that "we are not unaware of his designs," he reminds the Corinthians that Satan is continually devising plans to destroy their community, for example, by providing the Corinthians with seemingly good excuses for not forgiving the offender. These references to Satan indicate how real the power of evil was for Paul. Although modern readers may find it difficult to conceive of Satan in such a personal manner as does Paul, they must reckon with the biblical witness that so clearly names and identifies the adversary of God's people.

To conclude, Paul shows his concern for the offender and encourages the community to forgive him, lest Satan take advantage of them. Such forgiveness will manifest their obedience to him.

5. Paul's Anxiety at Troas (2:12–13)

2:12 When I came to Troas[a] to preach the gospel of Christ[b] and a door was opened for me by the Lord,[c] 13 my spirit was ill at ease because I did not find Titus, my brother.[d] But saying farewell to them, I went on to Macedonia.

a. There is an article in Greek before Troas (*tēn Trōada*), not represented in this translation, which may indicate that Paul is referring to the region of Troas, the Troad, rather than to the city of Troas. Some commentators argue that even if Paul intends the region, it is likely that he arranged to meet Titus in the port city of Troas (Plummer, 64; Martin, 41), especially if he expected Titus to return by ship from Corinth. Others (Thrall, 1:183, as well as BDAG, s.v. *Trōas*) urge that Paul has in mind the mission field provided by the region of Troas.

b. Literally "for Christ's gospel" or "the gospel about Christ." In either case, he came to Troas, or the region of Troas, to preach the gospel.

c. Either by "God" or by "Christ" since Paul can use *kyrios* for both. Paul, however, tends to use *kyrios* for Christ, except in scriptural quotations where *kyrios* normally refers to God. But the use of a similar expression in Col 4:3 and Acts 14:27, where "God" is the subject, might favor "God" in this instance as well.

d. Paul calls Titus his brother because Titus is his coworker for the gospel.

These verses end the first part of Paul's narrative about what has happened since the painful visit (1:12–2:13). After this unit Paul will undertake an extended discussion of his apostolic ministry (2:14–7:4). He will then conclude this narrative with an account of Timothy's report that the Corinthians have repented (7:5–16). The manner in which 7:5–16 picks up the narrative line of 1:12–13 has led many to speculate that the intervening material (2:14–7:4) belongs to another letter on apostolic ministry (Bornkamm) or to the severe letter (Bultmann). In the view of others (Allo, Furnish, Lambrecht, Martin, Thrall), Paul is purposely enclosing the discussion of his apostolic ministry by the narrative of the events that transpired between him and the community. His reasons for doing this will be discussed at the beginning of the next section.

This particular unit is the capstone of the narrative Paul has recounted thus far. Its purpose is to show the Corinthians that his love for them (2:4) was so great that he curtailed a fruitful mission in Troas (or the region thereabout) in order to go to Macedonia, where he hoped to meet Titus and learn how the Corinthians had received the severe letter. Though brief, the unit consists of three parts: a temporal clause about the fruitful mission that God granted him in Troas (v. 12); the main clause, in which Paul says that he was ill at ease because he did not find Titus (v. 13a); a concluding statement of Paul's decision to go to Macedonia (13b).

[2:12] Although the episode at Corinth caused Paul sadness and grief, it did not prevent him from preaching the gospel. Consequently, after sending a severe letter to the Corinthians, he went north to evangelize in Troas. There his mission was extraordinarily fruitful because "the Lord opened a door for me," that is, because Christ (or God) made the hearts of those to whom he preached receptive to his word (for similar statements, see 1 Cor 16:9; Col 4:3; Acts 14:27). Although Paul seems to have gone to Troas primarily to preach, it is apparent that he hoped to find Titus there with news about the Corinthian situation. This suggests that Paul had sent Titus to Corinth with the harsh letter. Even if Titus was not the bearer of that letter, it is evident from what Paul writes in 7:5–16 that Titus had been in Corinth dealing with the events that Paul has described thus far. Consequently not finding Titus at Troas was a great disappointment to Paul, leading him to curtail his preaching and go to Macedonia in hope of finding Titus.

Titus plays a prominent role in 2 Corinthians, especially in regard to these events (7:6, 13, 14) and the collection (8:6, 16, 23). His name, however, does not appear in Acts or any other Pauline letter except Galatians, where he is identified as one of Paul's Gentile converts (Gal 2:1, 3), and the Pastoral letter that bears his name. In 2 Cor 8:23 Paul identifies him as "my partner and coworker for you" (*koinōnos emos kai eis hymas synergos*) on behalf of the Corinthians, and in 12:18 he reminds the Corinthians of Titus's integrity, "Titus did not defraud you, did he? Did we not walk in the same spirit? Did we not walk in the same footsteps?"

[13] In writing that he was "ill at ease because I did not find Titus, my brother," Paul is telling the Corinthians that he was ill at ease *for their sake* since he was still concerned about the situation at Corinth. Not finding Titus at Troas meant that there would be no news about the community. Thus Paul went to Macedonia to find Titus and learn what was happening at Corinth. When Paul finally narrates his meeting with Titus, Paul is comforted "not only by his [Titus's] coming but by the comfort by which he was comforted by you, as he reported to us your longing, your grieving, your zeal on my behalf so that I rejoice all the more" (7:7). The rhetorical purpose of the unit then is to show the Corinthians his continuing love and concern for them, even after the events of the painful visit and the harsh letter.

In retrospect, it is apparent that Paul's rhetorical strategy has come to a climax in this unit. In 1:12–14, he announced that his purpose is to help the Corinthians comprehend what they understand only in part, so that they will boast in him as their apostle. In 1:15–22, he explains that the change in his travel plans was not due to vacillation on his part. He is reliable because his gospel is rooted in the faithfulness of Jesus Christ, the Son of the faithful God. The reason that he altered his plans was to spare the Corinthians further sorrow (1:23). He wrote the harsh letter to show his love for them (2:4) and to see if they would be obedient in all things (2:9). Although Paul did not make his promised return visit, and although he wrote a severe letter, his anxiety at not finding Titus at Troas and his decision to leave a fruitful mission field demonstrate his continued love and concern for the Corinthians. As Chrysostom shrewdly notes (*Homily* 5:1), the anxiety he experienced at Troas is another example of the affliction he endures as an apostle. Though Paul interrupts his narrative with a description of his ministry, he will soon explain "how the God who comforts the downcast" (7:6) comforted him. But he must first explain what it means to be an apostolic minister of a new covenant who calls people to reconciliation (2:14–7:4).

B. The Integrity of Paul's Apostolic Ministry 2 Corinthians 2:14–7:4

Paul sets aside his account of the recent events that have transpired between him and the Corinthian community and somewhat unexpectedly embarks upon the most profound discussion of apostolic ministry found in the New Testament. Although some commentators view this section of the letter (2:14–7:4) as a digression, or as a fragment from another letter, it is in fact an integral part of Paul's argument in chapters 1–7, and it lays the groundwork for his critique of the super-apostles in chapters 10–13. Thus it is not surprising that Paul will write:

Therefore, knowing the fear of the Lord, we persuade people, but we are known to God, and I hope to be known even to your consciences. We are not commending ourselves to you again but giving you an opportunity for boasting on behalf of us, so that you might have something to say to those who boast in appearance and not in the heart. (5:11–12)

By providing the Corinthians with a profoundly theological reflection on the nature of his apostolic ministry, Paul is offering them a compelling reason to boast in him as their apostle rather than to criticize and compare him unfavorably with the intruding apostles who have come to Corinth, with whom he will deal in chapters 10–13.

These chapters are the heart and soul of 2 Corinthians, the fortress from which Paul makes his apologia. For, even though he will speak about apostolic ministry again in chapters 10–13, he will do so in a way that presupposes what he writes here. Put another way, whereas Paul writes *polemically* in chapters 10–13, here he writes *apologetically*, carefully explaining the theological underpinnings of the ministry he exercises. Though both sections of the letter contribute to an understanding of his ministry, Paul could not have written as he did in chapters 10–13 had he not laid the theological foundation that he does here. Thus the change in mood that occurs between chapters 1–9 and 10–13 might be explained in this way. In chapters 1–7, Paul is explaining and defending the nature of his apostolic ministry so that the Corinthians will make him their boast and resume the work of the collection (chapters 8–9), but in chapters 10–13, having shown them that *he* is their boast, he finally deals with the intruding apostles with whom some of the Corinthians have aligned themselves.

This section of the letter (2:14–7:4) can be divided into four parts. In the first (2:14–4:6), Paul presents himself as the minister of a new covenant energized by the Spirit of the Living God and the Corinthians as his letter of recommendation. Because God has qualified him to be the minister of a new covenant, Paul's ministry is more glorious than the glorious ministry of Moses, leading Paul to act more openly and to commend himself to everyone's conscience. In the second part (4:7–5:10), Paul returns to the theme of suffering and affliction that he introduced in the benediction (1:3–11) and explains how the God who raises the dead is transforming him in the midst of affliction as he awaits the final glory of resurrection life. In the third part (5:11–6:10) Paul presents his ministry in terms of reconciliation and himself as an ambassador for Christ, who calls people to be reconciled with the God who has reconciled the world to himself through Christ. Finally, having presented himself as an ambassador of reconciliation, in the fourth part (6:11–7:4) Paul calls the Corinthians to reconciliation. Thus Paul portrays himself in three ways: (1) he is the minister of a new covenant; (2) he exercises his ministry in the midst of suffering and affliction, which paradoxically manifest the power of the resurrection; (3) he is an ambassador for Christ, calling people to reconciliation.

B. The Integrity of Paul's Apostolic Ministry

But why does Paul call the Corinthians to reconciliation when immediately after this section he will recount Titus's good news that the community has repented (7:5–16)? This tension between calling the community to reconciliation, on the one hand, and Titus's report that the community has repented, on the other, seems to support the position of those who argue that this part of the letter (2:14–7:4) should be viewed as a fragment from an earlier letter. As has already been suggested, however, Paul is responding to two problems, one of which has already been resolved (the episode of the painful visit), and one of which remains (the intruding apostles). In effect, Paul is saying to the Corinthians: Just as you have repented of the incident involving the offender, so be reconciled to me in the matter of the intruding apostles before I make my third visit. Boast in your founding apostle and father rather than in the intruding apostles.

This section of the letter (2:14–7:4) also raises an important contextual question: Why does Paul introduce this reflection on his apostolic ministry in the midst of a narrative about his recent relations with the Corinthian community that has not yet been concluded? This question must be addressed *even if* 2:14–7:4 is a fragment from another Pauline letter, unless one wishes to argue that the editor who supposedly inserted the material at this point did so in a haphazard and gratuitous manner. However, given Paul's penchant for employing ring or chiastic patterns, whereby he begins one topic (a), moves to a second (b), and then resumes the first topic (a'), it is probable that Paul purposely interrupted the narrative of his dealings with the Corinthians and introduced this reflection on his apostolic ministry.

Although Paul's discussion of apostolic ministry may surprise readers who encounter it for the first time, the placement of this material is neither haphazard nor gratuitous. For by placing this defense of his ministry within a framework of apostolic suffering (2:12–13 and 7:5–7) Paul highlights the authentic nature of his apostolic ministry (Scott, 89–90). Before he rejoices in the comfort that he received from God at the arrival of Titus (7:6–18), he explains that he is the minister of a new covenant that paradoxically manifests God's glory in apostolic suffering endured for the crucified Christ. To accomplish this, Paul situates his discussion of apostolic ministry between two statements that describe his disturbed spirit and the afflictions he endured during his stay at Troas and his journey to Macedonia in search of Titus for news about the Corinthian community.

> When I came to Troas to preach the gospel of Christ and a door was opened for me by the Lord, *my spirit was ill at ease* because I did not find Titus, my brother. But saying farewell to them, I went on to Macedonia. (2:12–13, emphasis added)
>
> [exposition of apostolic ministry, 2:14–7:4]
>
> For, even when we came to Macedonia, our flesh had no relief, but we were *afflicted in every way: external struggles, internal fears*. (7:5, emphasis added)

Paul's statements that his spirit was ill at ease and his flesh had no rest, so that he was afflicted in every way, now bracket his extended reflection on apostolic ministry and highlight the point he makes throughout this section: he exercises his glorious new covenant ministry amid sufferings and afflictions that discredit him before those who do not understand the paradoxical nature of the gospel whereby the resurrection life of the apostolic minister is manifested through suffering and death. This structure of the material can be summarized as follows:

2:12–13	Paul's suffering on behalf of the Corinthians when he did not find Titus at Troas
2:14–7:4	Paul's new covenant ministry on behalf of the Corinthians that paradoxically manifests resurrection life through suffering and death
7:5–16	Paul's afflictions on behalf of the Corinthians and the comfort God granted him at the arrival of Titus

1. The Ministry of a New Covenant (2:14–4:6)

The material of this section is divided into three units that are closely related to each other in the development of Paul's argument (so Lambrecht, 43–45 and Thrall, 1:189–90). In the first (2:14–3:6) Paul presents his qualifications to be the minister of a new covenant empowered by God's Spirit. In the second (3:7–18) he explains that his ministry is more glorious than the ministry of Moses, and so he acts more openly than Moses. In the third (4:1–6), Paul defends his ministry from accusations that his gospel is veiled. Thus, as Lambrecht has convincingly shown, the material can be arranged as a chiasm or ring pattern:[11]

a	2:14–3:6	Paul qualified by God
b	3:7–18	The ministries of Moses and Paul
a'	4:1–6	Paul's apostolic integrity

a. Qualified by God (2:14–3:6)

2:14 But thanks be to God[a] who, in Christ,[b] is always leading us in a triumphant procession, manifesting the fragrance[c] of the knowledge of him[d] in every place through us. **15** Because we are the fragrant aroma[e] of Christ

---

11. Jan Lambrecht, "Structure and Line of Thought in 2 Cor 2,14–4,6," in *Studies on Second Corinthians*, 257–94, notes several linguistic contacts between 2:14–3:6 and 4:1–6. See esp. 261–62.

B. The Integrity of Paul's Apostolic Ministry

to God among those who are being saved and among those who are perishing. 16 To the latter we are a fragrance from[f] death to death, but to the former a fragrance from[f] life to life. Who is qualified for these things? 17 For we are not, as are so many, trading on the word of God; rather we speak before God in Christ from sincerity, as from God.

3:1 Are we beginning to commend ourselves again?[g] Or do we need[h]—as some do—letters of recommendation to you, or from you? 2 You yourselves are our letter, written in our[i] hearts, known and read by all, 3 showing that you are a letter from Christ administered by us, written not with ink but by the Spirit of the Living God, not on stone tablets but on tablets that are human hearts.[j]

4 We have such confidence through Christ before God. 5 Not that we are qualified of ourselves to reckon something as coming from ourselves; rather our qualification comes from God, 6 who has even qualified us as ministers of a new covenant, not of letter but of Spirit; for the letter kills but the Spirit gives life.

a. In the Greek text "to God" is in an emphatic position at the beginning of the verse.

b. *en tō Christō* could be taken as a dative of means (it is by means of Christ that God leads Paul in his triumphant procession) or a dative of place (God leads Paul inasmuch as Paul now dwells in the sphere of Christ). Although both make sense of the text, the imagery of the procession suggests that Paul has the sphere or realm of Christ in view. Accordingly the dative is construed as a dative of place or sphere.

c. *osmē* ("fragrance") can be either a pleasant or an unpleasant odor. Here it is the former. The same noun will be used in v. 16, where the fragrance will be a sweet perfume to some and a stench of death to others.

d. *autou* ("him") could refer to Christ. Here it is taken as referring to God. The fragrance *is* the knowledge of God.

e. *euōdia* ("aroma") is always a pleasing aroma, thus the phrase "fragrant aroma," which is construed as a subjective genitive, Christ's fragrance, which may be an allusion to the fragrant aroma of his sacrificial death.

f. Some manuscripts omit *ek* ("from"), thereby avoiding the exegetical problem the preposition presents: What is the origin or starting point of this life or death?

g. "Again" (*palin*) could be taken with "commend" or with "beginning." There is little difference in meaning.

h. The particle *mē* indicates that a negative answer is expected.

i. The manuscript evidence favors *hēmōn* ("our"). Although *hymōn* ("your," attested by ℵ) is preferred by a number of commentators (Barrett, Bultmann, Martin, Thrall), the majority of commentators support the better attested reading *hēmōn*.

j. "Hearts" is awkward and some manuscripts omit "hearts" so that "fleshly tablets" parallels "stone tablets." Others change the plural of "hearts" to the genitive singular, giving the reading "fleshly tablets of the heart." In this translation "which are" has been supplied to indicate that "tablets" and "human hearts" (literally "fleshly hearts" *sarkinais*) are in apposition to each other.

With this unit Paul begins an exposition and defense of his apostolic ministry. The unit, which is part of a larger chiasm, manifests a chiastic structure, moving from a discussion of Paul's ministry (2:14–17) to a discussion of the Corinthian community (3:1–3) and back to a discussion of Paul's ministry (3:4–6). In the first member of the chiasm (2:14–17) Paul raises the question of competency for apostolic ministry (2:16), which he answers in the third member of chiasm (3:4–6) in terms of a new covenant ministry. Because God has made him the minister of a new covenant, in the second member of the chiasm Paul can argue that the Corinthian community is his letter of recommendation (3:1–3). The material of this unit then consists of three subunits:

> a 2:14–17   Who is qualified for apostolic ministry?
> b 3:1–3   The Corinthian community is Paul's letter of recommendation.
> a' 3:4–6   God has qualified Paul for a new covenant ministry.

[2:14] This verse, along with verses 15–17, comprises the first of the three subunits noted above. With it Paul begins the defense and exposition of his apostolic ministry with a cry of thanksgiving: "but thanks be to God." The same formula occurs in Rom 7:24–25a and 1 Cor 15:57, and in each case it is a response to a threatening situation.

> Wretched man that I am! Who will rescue me from this body of death? *Thanks be to God* through Jesus Christ our Lord! (Rom 7;24–25a, emphasis added)

> The sting of death is sin, and the power of sin is the law. *But thanks be to God*, who gives us the victory through our Lord Jesus Christ. (1 Cor 15:56–57, emphasis added)

A similar pattern occurs here. Having explained how profoundly disturbed he was at not finding Titus at Troas (2:12–13), Paul suddenly bursts into a cry of thanksgiving that approaches a victory shout. This thanksgiving, which is a response to the discouragement that he experienced at Troas and which anticipates the consolation he eventually experienced at Macedonia (7:6–7), also marks the beginning of a new section. For the God to whom he gives thanks is the God who is leading him[12] in a triumphal procession so that Paul is the fragrance, which is the knowledge of God and the aroma of Christ, leading some to death and others to life. Overwhelmed, Paul asks if anyone is qualified for such a ministry that results in death for some and life for others. He then

---

12. Throughout this section Paul employs the first person pronoun "we," raising the question, To whom is he referring? Although the plural can, and does at times, include other apostolic ministers, Paul seems to have himself primarily in view when he employs the plural ("we," "us"). Thus this commentary tends to refer to Paul, even when he employs such plurals, unless otherwise noted.

B. The Integrity of Paul's Apostolic Ministry

explains that he does not exercise this ministry in the questionable way that so many others do, and he suggests that he is qualified to exercise this ministry. Two powerful metaphors stand at the heart of this unit: the triumphal procession and the fragrant aroma arising from incense or perhaps from a sacrificial offering.

The first metaphor derives from the Roman practice of staging a triumphal procession after a military victory in order (a) to offer sacrifices in thanksgiving to the gods, (b) to honor the conquering general, (c) to display the spoils of war, and (d) to shame, humiliate, and eventually execute some or all of the prisoners who were being led in triumph as a sign of Roman might.[13] The Jewish historian Josephus described just such a procession when he recounted the triumphal procession that took place in Roman after the Romans defeated the Jews (*J.W.* 7.116–62). Here Paul employs the triumphal procession as a metaphor to explain how he views his apostolic ministry. In Paul's metaphor, however, God plays the role of the victorious general who leads Paul "in triumph in Christ" (*thriambeuonti hēmas en tō Christō*). Although Paul uses the triumphal procession as a metaphor for his ministry, it is difficult to determine how far he wishes to extend it. On the one hand it is evident that he is portraying God as a victorious general who has conquered his enemies, but on the other it is not immediately apparent how Paul views himself and other apostolic ministers.[14] Are they triumphal participants in the procession as were the officers of the Roman general? Or are they captives and slaves of the victorious general, who is God? If they are God's captives and slaves, are they destined for public humiliation, shame, and even death? If they are not God's slaves and captives, why does Paul portray God as treating him and other apostolic ministers in this way? Calvin was keenly aware of the problem that this metaphor presented when he wrote:

> If you take the verb literally it will mean, "who triumphs over us" but Paul means something different from the common meaning of this phrase in Latin. Prisoners are said to be led in triumph when to disgrace them they are bound in chains and dragged before the chariot of the conqueror. But Paul means that he had a share in the triumph that God was celebrating because it was through his work that it

---

13. For a detailed explanation of this background, see Scott Hafemann, *Suffering and Ministry in the Spirit: Paul's Defense of His Apostolic Ministry in 2:14–3:3* (Grand Rapids: Eerdmans, 1990), 12–34.

14. There have been a number of varying proposals for understanding this metaphor. For an overall view of these proposals, see Scott Hafemann, *Suffering and Ministry in the Spirit*, 16–34; Thrall, *II Corinthians*, 1:191–94. Also consult Lamar Williamson Jr., "Led in Triumph: Paul's Use of *Thriambeuō*," *Int* 22 (1968): 317–32; Paul B. Duff, "Metaphor, Motif, and Meaning: The Rhetorical Strategy behind the Image 'Led in Triumph' in 2 Corinthians 2:14," *CBQ* 53 (1991): 79–92; J. M. Scott, "The Triumph of God in 2 Cor 2:14: Additional Evidence of Merkabah Mysticism in Paul," *NTS* 42 (1996): 260–81.

was won, just as the chief lieutenants share the general's triumph by riding on horseback beside his chariot. Thus since all ministers of the Gospel fight under God's banner and win for Him the victory and the honour of a triumph, He honours each of them with a share in His triumph according to his rank in the army and the efforts he has made. Thus they hold a triumph, but it is not their own but God's. (*2 Corinthians,* 33–34)

The KJV follows this line of thought when it translates the text, "Now thanks be unto God which always *causeth us to triumph* in Christ." But when the verb *thriambeuō* is used with a direct object, as it is here ("us"), its usual meaning is to lead someone, such as a conquered enemy, in triumph (Thrall, 1:191). For example, in the only other occurrence of this verb in the New Testament, Col 2:15 portrays God as triumphing over his enemies.

And when you were dead in trespasses and the uncircumcision of your flesh, God made you alive together with him, when he forgave us all our trespasses, erasing the record that stood against us with its legal demands. He set this aside, nailing it to the cross. He disarmed the rulers and authorities and made a public example of them, triumphing over them (*thriambeusas autous*) in it. (Col 2:13–15)

Following this line of thought, the REB translates the text of 2 Corinthians in this way, "But thanks be to God who continually *leads us as captives in Christ's triumphal procession.*" Others (Dauzenberg, EDNT, s.v. *thriambeuō*), however, argue for a meaning such as "to make known" or "to display," the idea being that God makes the apostles known in their relationship to Christ. Chrysostom (*Homily* 5:1) interpreted the phrase in a similar way, "Who *maketh us renowned* unto all. For what seemeth to be a matter of disgrace, being persecuted from every quarter, this appeareth to us to be a matter of very great honor." Though there is no unanimity among commentators on the precise meaning of the metaphor, Margaret Thrall (2:195) provides a prudent judgment when she writes, "Whatever the exegetical difficulties, it is surely right to understand the verb in its usual, attested sense when followed by a direct object, 'lead (as a conquered prisoner) in a triumphal procession,' and to see the image as derived from the Roman triumph."

If *thriambeuō* normally means to lead someone in a triumphant procession as a captive, then Paul is presenting himself as God's captive, whom God conquered in order to be his apostle and ambassador. Paul himself is deeply aware that he was God's enemy (1 Cor 15:9) and that he is now under a divine obligation to preach the gospel. Thus when he explains why he has not made use of his rights as an apostle, as others have done, he notes, "If I proclaim the gospel, this gives me no ground for boasting, for an obligation (*anankē*) is laid upon me, and woe to me if I do not proclaim the gospel" (1 Cor 9:16). God placed this "obligation" on Paul when he "captured" the former persecutor and made

B. The Integrity of Paul's Apostolic Ministry

him his apostle and slave. Because he understands his ministry in this way, Paul preaches the gospel free of charge as an expression of the inner freedom he enjoys as Christ's slave (1 Cor 9:15–18).

To summarize, by employing the metaphor of the triumphal procession, Paul presents God as the conquering general and himself as God's prisoner. Like a captive in a triumphal procession, Paul faces suffering and perhaps even death because of the ministry he exercises. But unlike the captives in a triumphal procession, he willingly follows as apostle, slave, and captive. This is why Paul boasts in his sufferings and tells the Corinthians, "For I think that God has exhibited us apostles as last of all, as though sentenced to death, because we have become a spectacle to the world, to angels and to mortals" (1 Cor 4:9). As he will show, his sufferings in the exercise of his apostolic office paradoxically reveal the gospel that he preaches.

In the second metaphor Paul presents himself as the fragrance which *is* the knowledge of God (*tēn osmēn tēs gnōseōs autou*) and the fragrant aroma of Christ (*Christou euōdia*) to God. Although some commentators (Barrett, 98) interpret this metaphor in light of the triumphal procession (Paul is like the incense offered to the gods during the procession), others (Allo, 465) argue that the metaphor should be understood in light of the sacrificial imagery of the Old Testament since "fragrance"(*osmē*) and "odor" (*euōdia*) are frequently combined in the Greek Old Testament to describe the sweet-smelling fragrance of sacrifice, for example, Gen 8:21; Exod 29:18; Lev 1:9, 13, 17; Num 15:3, 7, 10. In a similar fashion, both words occur in Phil 4:18 and Eph 5:2, and in both instances they are related to the notion of sacrifice.

> I am fully satisfied, now that I have received from Epaphroditus the gifts you sent, a fragrant offering (*osmēn euōdias*), a sacrifice acceptable (*thysian dektēn*) and pleasing to God. (Phil 4:18)

> as Christ loved us and gave himself up for us, a fragrant offering (*osmēn euōdias*) and sacrifice (*thysian*) to God. (Eph 5:2)

Although Paul does not combine the words here, he may still be viewing them in light of such sacrificial imagery. Thus he is the "fragrance" (*osmēn*) of the knowledge of God because the gospel he preaches (the knowledge of God) is like the fragrance of sweet-smelling sacrifice that spreads forth everywhere. Paul is also the aroma (*euōdia*) of Christ to God. The odor is the fragrance of Christ's own sacrifice offered on the cross to God, which Paul exudes through his ministry. Thus Paul employs both metaphors (the triumphal procession and the fragrant aroma of sacrificial offering) to clarify the paradoxical nature of his ministry. Although he appears as a defeated and humiliated prisoner to the world, he is in fact exuding the sweet-smelling fragrance of Christ's sacrificial death by the gospel (the knowledge of God) he preaches and the ministry he exercises. Little wonder, then, that he will describe himself as always bearing the dying (*nekrōsis*) of Jesus (4:10).

[15–16] Although Paul's ministry is a fragrant aroma to God because it proclaims the death of God's Son, people perceive this "fragrant aroma" (*osmēn*) in different ways. On the one hand, it is a foul odor from death to death to those who are perishing. On the other, it is a fragrant odor from life to life to those who are being saved. Paul's use of the prepositions "from" (*ek*) and "to" (*eis*) could be interpreted as a movement from one point (*ek*) to another (*eis*). Thus, if the starting point is construed as the death of Christ, Paul is saying that those who view this death apart from its saving effect are moving from this understanding of Christ's death to eternal death, whereas those who believe that this death is the source of resurrection life are moving from an understanding of death as life to eternal life. Or Paul may simply be using the prepositions to convey emphasis through repetition (Hughes, 80–81). In either case, he intends to say that his ministry, like the gospel he preaches, is paradoxical in nature and results in a profound division among people. If his gospel is veiled, as some accuse it of being, it is veiled only "to those who are perishing" (4:3). "For the message about the cross is foolishness to those *who are perishing*, but to us *who are being saved* it is the power of God" (1 Cor 1:18).

Profoundly aware that an encounter with his ministry results in death or life—there is no middle ground—Paul asks who is qualified (*hikanos*) for such a ministry? In doing so, he may be recalling Moses' humble response to God at the time of his call, "I am not qualified" (*ouch hikanos eimi*; LXX Exod 4:10, author's translation), since he will soon compare his new covenant ministry with Moses' ministry (3:7–11). Like Moses, Paul is aware that he has no competency of his own for such a ministry (3:5). Even though Paul does not explicitly answer his own question at this point, in 3:6 he will clearly affirm that God has made him "competent" (*hikanōsen*) to be the minister of a new covenant. Moreover, the contrast that he establishes between himself and "the many" (*hoi polloi*) who "trade on" (*kapēleuontes*) the word of God (v. 17) suggests that he is qualified for this ministry in a way that they are not, but which he is yet to explain.

[17] Paul concludes this subunit with a contrast between himself and "the many" who trade on the word of God. Since the Corinthians undoubtedly knew whom he intended, there was no need for Paul to identify "the many." For the contemporary reader, however, their identity is a problem that cannot be resolved. If 2 Corinthians is a literary unity, as this commentary proposes, then Paul may have in view the intruding apostles with whom he will deal in chapters 10–13. However, if chapters 10–13 represent a separate letter that addresses a different situation, "the many" could represent yet another group. Whatever the historical situation, Paul establishes a clear contrast between himself and them. They "trade on" the word of God, but Paul speaks before God in Christ, "from sincerity" (*ex eilikrineias*), as if authorized "from God" (*ek theou*).

B. The Integrity of Paul's Apostolic Ministry

Paul	The Many
speaks before God in Christ	trade on God's Word
from sincerity	[lack of sincerity]
authorized by God	[not authorized by God]

The exegetical problem here concerns the meaning of *kapēleuontes ton logon tou theou* ("trading on the word of God"). The interpretative tradition has moved in two directions. First, since the verb *kapēleuō* refers to the activity of small merchants or retailers, some construe it as peddling or trading on "the word of God," that is, preaching the gospel for the sake of money (see 4:2–3, where Paul equates "the word of God" with "the gospel" he preaches). Second, others point to the reputation for dishonesty among such small merchants; for example, in LXX Isa 1:22 the "merchants" (*kapēloi*) dilute the wine they sell. Accordingly, commentators argue that "the many" "dilute" or "adulterate" the word of God. In 2 Corinthians, however, Paul appears more concerned about an aberrant kind of ministry than about watering down doctrine (though the two are related). Thus he may be criticizing "the many" for the manner in which they carry out their ministry, *as if* they were petty merchants hawking or trading their goods. In contrast to them, he speaks with the "sincerity" (*eilikrineia*) that is the hallmark of his ministry (see 1:12). He speaks in Christ and in God's presence (see 12:19 for a similar expression), out of a God-given authority. Paul is not so much highlighting a doctrinal issue, then, or questioning the right of the apostolic minister to be supported by the gospel (a right he affirms in 1 Cor 9:3–12) so much as he is criticizing a manner of apostolic ministry different from his own (see the extended treatment of Hafemann, *Suffering and Ministry*, 98–179).

To summarize, in this first subunit (2:14–17) Paul presents his ministry with two powerful metaphors: the triumphal procession and the fragrant aroma of incense. Led in triumph as God's prisoner and exuding the aroma of the knowledge of God, to some his ministry of suffering gives off the stench of death, to others the fragrance of life. Raising the question of apostolic competence, Paul distinguishes himself from "the many" who trade on the word of God.

[3:1] Since the Corinthians might misconstrue what Paul has just said as boasting or self-commendation, in the second subunit (vv. 1–3) Paul takes up the questions of self-commendation and letters of recommendation. Anticipating what they might say or be saying, in this verse he poses a rhetorical question that anticipates a negative answer: I do not need letters of recommendation, to or from you, do I? Paul's question, however, does not mean that he lacks a letter of recommendation. Rather, his letter is different from what the Corinthians expect; for they are his letter of recommendation, known and read by all. Altering the metaphor slightly, in verse 3 Paul describes the community as a "letter from Christ" (*epistolē Christou*) that he has administered, written not in ink but by the Spirit of the Living God on tablets that are human hearts.

Although verses 1–3 may be responding to a real or hypothetical objection against Paul, they also lay the groundwork for what he will say about that new covenant and the comparison that he will make between his new covenant ministry and the ministry of Moses. By employing vocabulary such as "heart," "ministry," "the Spirit of the Living God," and "tablets of stone," he presages arguments that he will make as well as scriptural texts and allusions from Exodus, Jeremiah, and Ezekiel, upon which he will draw.

Letters of recommendation played an important role in the early church, since they were the means by which one community introduced and recommended evangelists, missionaries, and preachers to another (see Acts 18:27), thereby assuring the legitimacy and integrity of such people. Accordingly Paul recommends Phoebe, a deaconess of Cenchreae, to the church at Rome (Rom 16:1). Likewise, although he does not explicitly use the language of recommendation, he uses 1 Corinthians to pave the way for Timothy (1 Cor 4:17; 16:10) and 2 Corinthians to prepare for the visit of Titus and the two unnamed brothers (2 Cor 8:18–23). Whether Paul ever sought such letters of recommendation for himself is another matter, since, unlike the intruding apostles whom he criticizes (10:15), he evangelized where the gospel had not yet been preached. In any case, it is evident that Paul did not come to Corinth with letters of recommendation or seek them from the community when he departed. His question here, however, suggests that he is now under some pressure from the Corinthians to produce such letters, perhaps because intruding apostles have arrived with letters of recommendation and flattered the Corinthians by asking them for such letters.

Because of the situation noted above, the language of recommendation (*synistēmi*) plays a more prominent role in 2 Corinthians than in any other Pauline letter. For example, although Paul protests that he is not recommending himself to the Corinthians (3:1), in 4:2 he commends himself in God's presence to everyone's conscience. But in 5:12 he again protests that he is not commending himself to the Corinthians but is providing them with an opportunity to boast in him. Shortly after this, he commends himself as God's servant (6:4), and in 10:12 he criticizes the super-apostles for commending themselves, concluding that it is not those who commend themselves who are acceptable but those whom the Lord commends (10:18). Although Paul seems to alternate between protesting that he does not commend himself and commending himself, the general pattern of his thought is clear enough. He knows that he has been commended to the Corinthians by God, as he will soon explain. To that extent, he need not commend himself to them as if he enjoyed some special competency of his own. But he does commend himself to everyone's conscience in God's sight, and he commends himself as God's servant on the basis of his apostolic afflictions (6:4), because of his apostolic integrity, to which his own conscience bears witness (1:12).

B. The Integrity of Paul's Apostolic Ministry

[2] When Paul asks if he is commending himself again, he expects a negative answer. Unlike the super-apostles (10:12) he does not and need not commend himself to the Corinthians. Indeed he has not commended himself to them, except to their consciences (4:2) and on the basis of his apostolic affliction (6:4), because God commends him (10:18). Nor does he need a letter of recommendation to or from the community, since he is the founding father of their congregation. With this understanding, Paul can now say that the community is his letter of recommendation written "on our hearts"(*en tais kardiais hēmōn*). Some commentators argue that the alternate reading ("your hearts") makes better sense of the context, since the Corinthian community would be a letter that all can see, whereas a letter on Paul's heart would be hidden. There is, however, a logic to the more difficult and better attested reading, "our hearts." First, since a letter of recommendation must be carried by the bearer, Paul carries his letter of recommendation in his heart. Second, since Paul is the minister of a new covenant written on human hearts by the Spirit of the Living God, his letter of recommendation is written by the Spirit on his heart. Third, his letter can be known and read by all because his apostolic integrity (the theme of this letter) makes him apparent to all. To summarize, Paul's work as the apostolic founder of the Corinthian congregation is his letter to and from the community, written by the Spirit on his heart, because he is the minister of a new covenant.

[3] Refocusing his metaphor, Paul now writes that the community is "a letter of Christ" (*epistolē Christou*) "administered" (*diakonētheisa*) by Paul. Here Paul employs a metaphor, not an allegory that needs to be decoded. In calling the community a letter of Christ, Paul could mean that the community now embodies Christ, "as having the Law of God written in them" (Chrysostom, *Homily* 6: 2). More likely, Paul means that the letter has its origin in Christ. In either case, Paul plays a necessary but intermediary role, since the origin and source of the church is Christ rather than the apostle. In founding the church at Corinth, Paul was in fact bringing into being Christ's own letter, which is now written on the apostle's heart. Accordingly, Paul's letter of recommendation, the Corinthian community, is Christ's letter.

Having spoken of the community as his letter of recommendation and as a letter from Christ, Paul completes his metaphor with two contrasts, the last of which recalls the stone tablets on which the Mosaic law was written. Beginning with a negative statement and moving to a positive one, he writes that this letter was written "not" (*ouk*) in ink or on stone tablets, "but" (*all'*) by the Spirit of the Living God on "tablets which are human hearts" (*en plaxin kardiais sarkinais*).

not	*but*
in ink	by the Spirit of the Living God
on stone tablets	on tablets of hearts of flesh

In writing this, Paul calls to mind the stone tablets (*en plaxin lithinais*) on which the Mosaic law was written (Exod 34:1, 4, 28, 29), as well as a number of prophetic texts that looked to a day when the law, given on stone tablets, would be written on people's hearts through the power of God's Spirit.

> I will give them one heart, and put a *new spirit* within them; I will remove the heart of stone from their flesh and give them a *heart of flesh*. (Ezek 11:19, emphasis added)
>
> Cast away from you all the transgressions that you have committed against me, and get yourselves *a new heart* and *a new spirit*! (Ezek 18:31, emphasis added)
>
> A new heart I will give you, and a *new spirit* I will put within you; and I will remove from your body the heart of stone and give you a *heart of flesh*. I will put *my spirit* within you, and make you follow my statutes and be careful to observe my ordinances. (Ezek 36:26–27, emphasis added)
>
> But this is the covenant that I will make with the house of Israel after those days, says the LORD: I will put my law within them, and *I will write it on their hearts*; and I will be their God, and they shall be my people. (Jer 31:33 = LXX 38:33, emphasis added)

Although Paul has not yet mentioned the new covenant (3:6), he is clearly preparing the ground for it; for even though the community is Paul's letter of recommendation written on *his* heart, the community is also Christ's letter written on *their* hearts by the Spirit of the Living God, whose temple they are (see 6:16).

To summarize, in this second subunit (3:1–3), Paul presents the Corinthian community as his apostolic letter of recommendation. The community is a letter from Christ administered by Paul and written by the Spirit of the Living God. With this reference to the Spirit, Paul anticipates what he will say in the next subunit (3:4–6) about his new covenant ministry.

[4–5] These verses begin the third subunit that comprises verses 4–6. In this unit, Paul presents himself for the first time as the minister of a new covenant empowered by the Spirit. The subunit returns to the question that Paul raised at the beginning of this unit, "Who is qualified (*hikanos*) for these things?" (2:16). Using *hikanos* as a hook word and employing a literary plural "we," Paul affirms that of himself he is not "qualified" (*hikanoi*). Rather, his "qualification" (*hikanotēs*) comes from God, who has "qualified" (*hikanōsen*) him as the minister of a new covenant of God's life-giving Spirit. This introduction of Paul's new covenant ministry sets the stage for the comparison that he will draw between the glorious ministry of Moses and his own ministry, which is more glorious still (vv. 7–11), allowing him to act with an openness that Moses did not have (vv. 12–18).

B. The Integrity of Paul's Apostolic Ministry

Paul begins with a statement of confidence based on what he has just said in verses 1–3: the Corinthians are his letter of recommendation, a letter of Christ that he administers. Paul employs a similar statement of confidence at the beginning of this letter (1:15), and he will speak of his confidence again in 10:2. This confidence, however, is not self-confidence. Rather he exercises his confidence in God's presence through the mediation of Christ. Lest there be any doubt about what he is saying, in both verse 5 and verse 6 Paul employs a negative clause followed by an adversative clause. It is "not" (*ouch*) that he is qualified "but" (*alla*) that God has qualified him as a minister of a new covenant (v. 5), "not" (*ou*) of letter "but" (*alla*) of Spirit (v. 6). Paul's confidence then comes from God. As the minister of a new covenant, he administered a letter of Christ when he founded the Corinthian community, and the community has become his letter of recommendation to and from them.

[6] The final verse of the subunit introduces the concept of "a new covenant." The concept of a new covenant derives from Jer 31:31–34 (=LXX 38:31–34) where the phrase "a new covenant" (*diathēke kainē*) occurs for the first and only time in the Old Testament.[15]

> The days are surely coming, says the LORD, when I will make a new covenant (*diathēke kainē*) with the house of Israel and the house of Judah. It will not be like the covenant that I made with their ancestors when I took them by the hand to bring them out of the land of Egypt—a covenant that they broke, though I was their husband, says the LORD. But this is the covenant that I will make with the house of Israel after those days, says the LORD: I will put my law within them, and I will write it on their hearts; and I will be their God, and they shall be my people. No longer shall they teach one another, or say to each other, "Know the LORD," for they shall all know me, from the least of them to the greatest, says the LORD; for I will forgive their iniquity, and remember their sin no more.

Within the New Testament, the only other occurrences of "new covenant" are in the Eucharist narratives of Luke 22:20 and 1 Cor 11:25, and in the Epistle to the Hebrews, which also draws upon Jer 31 (LXX 38) to present Jesus as the mediator of a "new covenant" (Heb 8:8; 9:15; 12:24 [*diathēkēs neas*]). In Heb 13:20 there is also a reference to an "eternal covenant" (*diathēkēs aiōniou*) which echoes Jer 32:40 (LXX 39:40). The phrase "new covenant," moreover, is also found in other writings such as the Damascus Document, which speaks of the members of the new covenant in the land of Damascus (CD 6:19; 8:21).

Although the Spirit plays an integral part in Paul's understanding of this new covenant, there is no reference to the Spirit in Jeremiah's prophecy of the new or eternal covenant that God promises to make with his people by placing his

---

15. In addition to this text, one should note the text of Jer 32:37–41 (=LXX 39:37–41), which speaks of an "everlasting covenant" (*diathēkēn aiōnian*).

law in their hearts (Jer 31:31–34; 32:37–41). But the Spirit does play a prominent role in the texts of Ezekiel noted above, in which God promises to give the people "a new spirit" and "a new heart," though there is no mention of a new covenant in these texts from Ezekiel. Accordingly, Carol Stockhausen has suggested that Paul has made use of the Jewish exegetical principle *gezerh shawah* to relate the texts of Jeremiah and Ezekiel to each other for the purpose of mutual interpretation.[16] In this case, Paul relates the text of Jer 31:31–34 to the texts of Ezek 11:19; 18:31; 36:26–27 on the basis of the word "heart" (*kardia*), which is found in both sets of texts. By doing this, Paul can now expand upon the idea of a new covenant found in Jeremiah by introducing the notion of the Spirit found in Ezekiel. Moreover, since the texts of Jeremiah and Ezekiel share a number of other concepts (such as [a] the failure of the people to observe the law in the past, [b] the promise that God will place his law and ordinances in their hearts, [c] the assurance of the forgiveness of transgressions so that they will be his people and he will be their God), Paul can draw upon these concepts for his new covenant theology, which can be summarized in this way: The people of Israel have transgressed God's law because they possessed hearts of stone. But the days are coming when God will make a new covenant with the people of Israel by giving them a new spirit and putting his law in their hearts of flesh so that they will obey God's ordinances from their hearts. On that day their sin will be forgiven, and God will be their God, and they will be God's people.

For Paul that day has arrived with the appearance of the gospel of Jesus Christ that empowers Paul's new covenant ministry. In the proclamation of that gospel the Spirit of the Living God has been poured into the hearts of the Corinthians, who are Paul's letter of recommendation. The Corinthians are the people of a new covenant of the Spirit, which gives life, and not of the letter, which kills.

Paul's statement that "the letter kills but the Spirit gives life" (*to gar gramma apoktennei, to de pneuma zōopoiei*) is as enigmatic as it is brief.[17] It should be clear, however, that the Spirit of which Paul speaks here is the life-giving Spirit of God mentioned in 3:3, the very Spirit who wrote the letter of Christ that the Corinthians are and that Paul has administered. In referring to this Spirit, therefore, Paul surely has in mind the promise of Ezekiel that God would grant Israel "a new heart" and "a new spirit" (Ezek 36:26–27). Exactly what Paul means by *to gramma* ("the letter") is more difficult to determine. But since he will describe the Mosaic covenant as "engraved in letters" (*en grammasin entety-*

---

16. Carol Kern Stockhausen, *Moses' Veil and the Glory of the New Covenant: The Exegetical Substructure of II Cor. 3, 1–4,6* (AnBib 116; Rome: Pontifical Biblical Institute, 1989).

17. Origen introduced a "hermeneutical understanding" of this text that has played an important role in the history of exegesis; namely, whereas "the letter" stands for a purely literal reading of Scripture, "the Spirit" points to a more profound, spiritual reading of the text that illumines its inner meaning. With the Reformation, this interpretation gave way to a salvation historical interpretation according to which "the letter" stands for the Mosaic law and "the spirit" for the gospel.

B. The Integrity of Paul's Apostolic Ministry

pōmenē) in the very next verse (3:7), and since he has already drawn a contrast between the tablets of stones (on which the law was written) and tablets that are hearts of flesh (on which Christ's letter is written), it is evident that *to gramma* is somehow related to the Mosaic law, though not simply to be equated with it. Accordingly Paul is not establishing a contrast between law and Spirit or between law and gospel, otherwise he would have written, "the law kills, but the Spirit gives life." A first, albeit negative, conclusion is this: Paul is *not* saying that the law kills.

Romans is helpful, though not decisive, for understanding what Paul means, since it uses a similar contrast. In Rom 2:29 Paul writes, "Rather a person is a Jew who is one inwardly (*ho en tō kryptō Ioudaios*), and real circumcision is a matter of the heart —it is spiritual and not literal (*en pneumati ou grammati*)." Here Paul is not denigrating circumcision but drawing upon the image of the circumcised heart (Deut 30:6; Jer 4:4) to emphasize that one must internalize circumcision and the law it presupposes, rather than boast in the external sign of circumcision and the external code of the law (Rom 2:17–24). In a similar fashion, in Rom 7:6 Paul writes that believers have been discharged from the law so that they now serve "the new life of the Spirit" (*en kainotēti pneumatos*) rather than "under the old written code" (*palaiotēti grammatos*). Again Paul is not denigrating the law, which is "holy" (7:12) and "spiritual" (7:14) and whose just requirements Christ has fulfilled (8:1–4). He is talking about the need to fulfill the law through the power of God's Spirit, rather than boast about a written code that commands but does not empower one to obey it. This leads to a second conclusion: Living in the new life of the Spirit results in an internalization of circumcision and the law that is not possible for those who know the law only as an external code of written letters, apart from the Spirit.

The text of Ezek 37:1–14 is also helpful for understanding Paul's statement that the Spirit gives life (Stockhausen, *Moses' Veil*, 67–71, 78–82). In this text, which recounts the restoration of Israel through the gift of God's Spirit, God promises to give his Spirit to the people who are like dry bones in a desert, and they will live.

kai dōsō pneuma mou eis hymas, kai zēsesthe
I will give my Spirit to you, and you will live. (Ezek 37:6, 14, author's trans.)

kai eisēlthen eis autous to pneuma, kai ezēsan
and the Spirit entered them, and they lived. (Ezek 37:10, author's trans.)

Together, the texts of Ezek 36:26–27 and 37:1–14 suggest that the new covenant promised in Jer 31:31–34 will be characterized by the life that God will give the people when God grants his Spirit. Conversely, one can deduce that where there is no Spirit, there is no life (see Stockhausen, *Moses' Veil*, 79). Thus Paul says that the letter kills, not because the letter is the law, but because the letter represents the law without the power of God's life-giving Spirit. Paul's statement that the letter kills and the Spirit gives life, then, is not an indictment of the law. Rather, he uses this brief expression to explain his new covenant ministry. His ministry brings life because it is empowered by God's Spirit; in contrast to his ministry, the Mosaic ministry (to which he will soon turn) brought death and condemnation because it administered the law as a written code. Thus it could not place the law in the hearts of God's people.

Paul's line of argument in 2:14–3:6 can be summarized in this way: The one whom God leads as captive in his triumphal procession is, paradoxically, the minister of a new covenant that finds concrete expression in the community Paul has established at Corinth. Those who question Paul's apostolic ministry have not understood that it is God who qualified Paul for this eschatological ministry.

b. The Ministries of Moses and Paul (3:7–18)

3:7 If the ministry[a] of death carved in letters on stones came in glory so that the people of Israel[b] could not gaze upon the face of Moses on account of the glory of his face, which (glory) was in the process of being abolished,[c] 8 it is all the more certain that[d] the ministry of the Spirit will[e] be in glory. 9 For if there was glory to the ministry of condemnation, it is all the more certain that the ministry of righteousness abounds in glory. 10 For what was glorious is not glorious in this respect on account of the surpassing glory. 11 For if what was being abolished[f] came[g] through glory, it is all the more certain that that which remains came[g] in glory.

12 Therefore, having such hope, we act with openness 13 and not like Moses, who put a veil on his face so that the people of Israel would not gaze upon the end[h] of what was being abolished.[i] 14 But their minds were hardened. For to this very day, at the reading of the old covenant, the same veil remains not unveiled,[j] because only in Christ is it abolished.[k] 15 But to this day, whenever Moses[l] is read, a veil lies over their heart. 16 But whenever he[m] turns to the Lord,[n] the veil is removed. 17 The "Lord"[o] is the Spirit, and where the Spirit of the Lord is, there is freedom. 18 All of us, with faces unveiled, contemplating—as in a mirror[p]—the glory of the Lord are being transformed from glory to glory into the same image as from the Lord who is the Spirit.[q]

a. *Diakonia* refers to a service or office that is intermediary in nature (see BDAG). It is sometimes translated as "dispensation" since Paul seems to have the whole Mosaic dispensation in view (covenant and law). The word has a slightly different meaning from *diakonos*, which refers to the one who serves as an agent or intermediary, and which Paul uses in v. 6. However, since Paul has in view the intermediary roles that he and Moses exercise in regard to their respective covenants, *diakonia* has been translated as

B. The Integrity of Paul's Apostolic Ministry

"ministry" in order to maintain the connection with v. 6. Paul will again employ *diakonia* in 4:1 and will refer to his *diakonia* of reconciliation in 5:18. In 6:4 he uses *diakonos* in reference to himself and in 11:15, 23 in reference to the intruding apostles.

b. Literally, "the children of Israel," which means the people of Israel, the Israelites.

c. Many translations render *katargoumenēn* as "fading," but this is hardly correct, since Paul regularly uses *katargeō* in the sense of nullifying something, rendering it ineffective or abolishing it. In this verse, the feminine participle indicates that it is the glory upon Moses' face that is in the process of being abolished. The passive participle does not indicate who or what is abolishing this glory. The exegesis suggests that it is being abolished by the proclamation of the gospel through the new covenant ministry of the Spirit.

d. The purpose of this translation ("it is all the more certain that") here, as well as in vv. 9, 11, is to highlight the *a fortiori* argument that Paul is employing. Most translators, however, render *pōs ouchi mallon* ("how much more") as a question. If the ministry of death . . . then how much more . . . ?

e. Although Paul uses the future tense, he is not implying that the ministry of the Spirit has not yet come in glory. Rather, the future indicates that the ministry of death preceded the ministry of the Spirit in time.

f. In v. 7, Paul used the feminine participle of *katargeō* because he was speaking of the glory on Moses' face that was being abolished (*doxa* being feminine). Here the neuter participle ("what was being abolished") indicates that Paul has something more in view. Since Paul has just spoken of "what was glorious" (*to dedoxasmenon*, neuter) in v. 10, *to katargoumenon* must refer to the dispensation of the old covenant to which the glory on Moses' face pointed.

g. A verb must be supplied here.

h. *Telos* ("end") could refer to the termination of what was being abolished, or to the goal of what was being abolished. The question is discussed in the exegesis.

i. What was being abolished is expressed by the participle *tou katargoumenou*, which, like the neuter participle in v. 11, refers to the old dispensation that Moses' ministry mediated.

j. The words *mē anakalyptomenon* ("not unveiled") can be taken as the predicate of the verb "remains," as in this translation, or they can be taken with the *hoti* clause that follows, giving the translation, "the same veil remains at the reading of the old covenant, *it is not unveiled* that (or because) only in Christ is it abolished."

The old covenant refers to the Sinai covenant that Paul has called the ministry of death and condemnation. Its precepts are embodied in Israel's Scriptures, especially the Torah. The old covenant, however, is not to be identified with the writings that Christians call "the Old Testament." See Belleville, *Reflections of Glory*, 232.

k. The subject of *katargeitai* is not specified. Although "the old covenant" is the nearest noun, the subject could also be "the veil." The question is discussed in the exegesis.

l. "Moses" refers to the Scriptures that embody the stipulations of the old covenant mentioned in v. 14. See Acts 15:21 for a similar usage.

m. The unexpressed subject of the verb *epistrephē* ("turns") could refer to Moses, since Paul is alluding to Exod 34:34, a text in which Moses is the subject. But the subject could also refer to Israel, since Paul has just spoken about Israel. Or it could be taken in a more general sense, "one" or "anyone."

n. Lord (*kyrios*) could refer to God or to Christ. The problem is discussed in the exegesis.

o. Lord is put in quotation marks to indicate that Paul is referring to the *kyrios* mentioned in Exod 34:34.

p. *katoptrizō* can mean "to reflect something" or "to gaze as if looking in a mirror." The latter meaning is adopted here. Believers contemplate the glory of God.

q. Literally, "from (the) Lord (the) Spirit." The Greek has been translated in several different ways as Furnish (216) notes: "the Lord of the Spirit," "the Spirit of the Lord," "the Lord who is the Spirit," " "the Lord who is Spirit," "the Lord, the Spirit," "the Spirit who is Lord." Since Paul identifies "the Lord" as "the Spirit" in v. 17, the translation "the Lord who is the Spirit" has been adopted here.

The text of 3:7–18 is the central portion of a ring pattern or chiasm.[18] Whereas the verses that bracket this material (2:14–3:6 and 4:1–6) deal with Paul and his qualification for ministry, these verses compare the ministry and conduct of Moses and Paul, as well as the effects of their respective ministries. The material is closely tied to what precedes and follows by numerous hook words that allow Paul to develop themes he announced in 2:14–3:6 and to lay the groundwork for themes that he will discuss in 4:1–6.[19] Prominent hook words in 2:14–3:6 are "death" and "life" (2:16; 3:6), "tablets of stone" (3:3), "ministers of a new covenant," "Spirit," and "kills" (3:6). In 3:7–18, Paul builds upon these concepts as he speaks of a "ministry of death" carved in letters "on stone" (3:7), "the ministry of the Spirit" (3:8), "the ministry of condemnation," "the ministry of righteousness" (3:9), "the old covenant" (3:14), "the Spirit" (3:17), and "the Lord who is the Spirit" (3:18). This material, in turn, provides a new set of hook words for what follows in 4:1–6. Thus "glory" (*doxa*), "to glorify" (*doxazō*) appear in 3:7, 8, 9, 10, 11, 18 and reappear in 4:4 where Paul speaks of the glory of Christ. "Veil" (*kalymma*) appears in verses 13, 14, 15, 16, and "to unveil" (*anakalyptomenon, periaireitai to kalymma*) in verses 14, 16. These are then taken up in 4:3 when Paul responds to the accusation that his gospel is "veiled" (*kekalymmenon*). Finally, "mind" (*noēmata*) occurs in 3:14 and 4:4, first in reference to Israel and then in reference to the unbelievers of this age. Accordingly the comparison between the two covenants in 3:7–11 builds on the theme of a new covenant ministry that gives life (2:14–3:6), whereas the theme

---

18. These verses have been the focus of intense scholarly discussion. In addition to the standard commentaries, one should consult the following: Linda L. Belleville, *Reflections of Glory: Paul's Polemical Use of the Moses-Doxa Traditions in 2 Corinthians 3.1–18* (JSNTSup 52; Sheffield: Sheffield Academic Press, 1991); Scott J. Hafemann, *Paul, Moses, and the History of Israel* (Peabody, Mass.: Hendrickson, 1996); Lorenzo De Lorenzi, ed., *Paolo: Ministro del Nuovo Testamento (2 Cor 2,14–4,6)* (SMBen, Sezione Biblico Ecumenica, 9; Rome: Benedictine Editrice, 1987); Carol Kern Stockhausen, *Moses' Veil and the Glory of the New Covenant*.

19. See Vanhoye, "L'Interprétation d'Ex 34," in *Paolo: Ministro del Nuovo Testamento*, 162–80.

B. The Integrity of Paul's Apostolic Ministry

of Moses' veil in 3:12–18 prepares for Paul's argument that his gospel is veiled only to those whose minds are blind (4:1–6).

In terms of structure, the material of this unit can be divided into two subunits: 3:7–11, in which the vocabulary of "glory" and "ministry" occurs most frequently, and 3:12–18, in which the vocabulary of "veil," "unveiling," and "the Spirit" predominates. The first subunit consists of a threefold comparison between the glory of two ministries constructed along the lines of an *a fortiori* argument: if such and such is true for the lesser, it is all the more true for what is greater. Throughout verses 7–11, Paul speaks somewhat impersonally, employing the third person singular (Vanhoye, "L'Interprétation d'Ex 34," 161).

The second subunit is more personal, making use of the first person plural. It is also more complicated, consisting of three members: (1) a contrast between the conduct of Moses and Paul (3:12–14); (2) a discussion of how the wilderness generation prefigured the Israel of Paul's day that does not believe in Christ (3:15–16); (3) an explanation of what happens when people (Jews or Gentiles) turn to the Lord, whom Paul identifies as the Spirit. The material can be outlined in this way:

3:7–11   The glory of two ministries
   vv. 7–8   Death contrasted with Spirit
   v. 9   Condemnation contrasted with righteousness
   vv. 10–11   What is being abolished contrasted with what remains
3:12–18 The veiling and unveiling of glory
   vv. 12–13   The behavior of Moses and the behavior of Paul
   vv. 14–15   Israel of old and Israel of Paul's day
   vv. 16–18   The Spirit and the unveiling of glory

[3:7–11] Having argued that he does not need letters of recommendation to or from the Corinthian community because the community is his letter of recommendation and he is the minister of a new covenant, Paul now employs an argument from the lesser to the greater to show that if the ministry of the old covenant came in glory, then it is all the more certain that the ministry of the new covenant is glorious as well. The form of this argument, called *qal wahomer* in rabbinic exegesis and *a fortiori* among Latin writers, moves from the lesser to the greater in order to show that if something is true for the lesser, it is certainly true for what is greater. For example, if the moon, which is a reflection of the sun, gives light, then the sun certainly gives light. Though such an argument makes an implicit comparison, it is not necessarily the purpose of the argument to denigrate the lesser member of the comparison. Rather, the primary purpose of the argument is to establish that the greater certainly has what the lesser possesses (Stockhausen, *Moses' Veil*, 109–11). Thus, Paul does not seek to denigrate the old covenant ministry that Moses exercised but to show that if that ministry came in glory, it is all the more certain that there is glory to the new covenant ministry of the Spirit he exercises. Paul uses a similar form of argument in Rom 5, see especially Rom 5:10, 15, 17. The present form of his argument, however, is somewhat obscured because of the comments Paul makes in verses 7 and 9. Without these comments, the form of the argument is very clear:

> If the ministry of death . . . came *in glory* . . .
> *a fortiori* the ministry of the Spirit will be *in glory*.
> For if there was *glory* to the ministry of condemnation,
> *a fortiori* the ministry of righteousness abounds *in glory*.
> For if what was being abolished came *through glory*,
> *a fortiori* that which remains came *in glory*.

As the structure shows, Paul is comparing two ministries or dispensations. The first is a ministry of death and of condemnation; it is in the process of being abolished. The second is a ministry of the Spirit and of righteousness; it remains forever. Despite the difference between the two ministries, there is glory attached to each of them. Indeed it is the *same* glory, since it is God's glory. Thus it is not Paul's purpose to denigrate the ministry of Moses, even though he uses the language of death and condemnation to describe it. Rather the primary purpose of his argument is to show that if there was glory attached to the ministry of death and condemnation, then there is all the more reason for confidence about the ministry of the Spirit and of righteousness that he exercises. Thus Chrysostom (*Homily* 7:2) insists that Paul is not disparaging the old covenant, for comparisons are made between things of the same kind, and these are not of the same kind.

The starting point for this comparison is the cryptic comment that Paul makes at the end of the preceding unit: the letter kills but the Spirit gives life (v. 6). The ministry of death and condemnation, which Paul associates with the "old covenant" (v. 14), belongs to the realm of "letter" since, in Paul's view, it was deprived of God's life-giving Spirit. Thus it could not effect life or righteousness but only death and condemnation. In contrast to this, the ministry of the Spirit and of righteousness, which Paul has already identified with the new covenant, brings life and righteousness because it is empowered by God's Spirit. Consequently, whereas the former is in the process of being abolished, the latter is destined to endure.

[7–8] One might have expected that the first comparison would be between a ministry of death and a ministry of life (rather than Spirit), since life is the opposite of death. But since Paul has already identified the Spirit as the source of life (v. 6), he refers to the ministry that he exercises as "the ministry of the Spirit," which is to be equated with the new covenant of which he is a minister (v. 6). By describing the ministry of death as carved in letters on stone, Paul

B. The Integrity of Paul's Apostolic Ministry

alludes to what he has already written about the letter that kills, recalling the stone tablets (v. 3) on which the old covenant was written (Exod 31:18; 32:15). This ministry came in glory "so that" (*hōste*) the people of Israel could not gaze or look intently at Moses' face on account of the radiant glory (*doxa*) on his face. The reference to the glory on Moses' face is the first of many allusions that Paul will make to the text of Exod 34:27-35. According to the Greek version of that text, the appearance of the skin of Moses' face was glorified (*ēn dedoxasmenē hē opsis tou chrōmatos tou prosōpou autou*; Exod 34:30) when he came down from Mount Sinai bearing the tablets of the law. Although the text does not say why this occurred, one can presume that it was the result of Moses' being in the presence of God's shining and radiant glory. However, whereas the text of Exodus says that Aaron and all the elders of Israel were afraid to draw near to Moses (Exod 34:30), Paul goes further and writes that they could not "look intently" (*atenisai*) on Moses' face because of the glory upon it—an assumption one might draw on the basis of the text from Exodus. It is at this point that Paul makes an important comment, identifying the glory on Moses' face as "the glory that was being abolished" (*tēn doxan . . . tēn katargoumenēn*). Since the text of Exodus makes no such comment, this is clearly an interpretive remark that Paul introduces on the basis of what he knows from his new covenant ministry.

The precise meaning of *katargoumenēn*, which has been translated as "being abolished," is disputed. *Katargoumenen* is the present, feminine, passive participle of *katargeō*, to which BDAG assigns these meanings: (1) "to cause something to be unproductive"; (2) "to cause something to lose its power or effectiveness," thus to invalidate something or make it powerless; (3) "to cause something to come to an end or to be no longer in existence," thus to abolish it, wipe it out, or set it aside; (4) "to cause the release of someone from an obligation." The word is used twenty-seven times in the New Testament; apart from Luke 13:7 and Heb 2:14, all occurrences are in letters attributed to Paul.[20] In most instances, Paul uses *katargeō* in the second or third sense noted above. For example, he asks if the unfaithfulness of some will "nullify" (*katargēsei*) God's faithfulness (Rom 3:3), or if he is "overthrowing" (*katargoumen*) the law (Rom 3:31). He asserts that the law does not do away with or "annul" (*katargēsai*) the promise (Gal 3:17), and he protests that if he is still preaching circumcision, then the scandal of the cross "has been removed" (*katērgētai*; Gal 5:11). In 1 Cor 13:8 he writes that knowledge "will come to an end" (*katargēthēsetai*). Likewise, when the perfect comes, the imperfect "will come to an end" (*katargēthēsetai*;

---

20. Rom 3:3, 31; 4:14; 6:6; 7:2, 6; 1 Cor 1:28; 2:6; 6:13; 13:8; 13:10, 11; 15:24, 26; 2 Cor 3:7, 11, 13, 14; Gal 3:17; 5:4, 11; Eph 2:15; 2 Thess 2:8; 2 Tim 1:10. See Hafemann *Paul, Moses, and the History of Israel*, 301-13, for a thorough examination of the use of *katargeō* outside of 2 Corinthians. He concludes, "*Katargeō* becomes for Paul a *theological* designation in which the turn of the ages is expressed in terms of what the gospel does and does not abolish and what does and does not continue to be effective or operate as a result" (309).

1 Cor 13:10). These examples, and Paul's usage apart from 2 Corinthians, suggest that even though many commentators and translators render the participial forms of *katargeō* in 2 Cor 3:7, 11, 13 as "fade," there is no lexical support for this translation, apart from the texts for 2 Corinthians. In describing the glory on Moses' face as *katargoumenēn*, then, Paul means that it was in the process of being set aside, abolished, or rendered ineffective. But by whom or what? Although Paul never explicitly says, the structure of his argument suggests that as the gospel is being preached, one ministry is replacing another, a point that will become clearer in verse 10 and as the argument develops.

It is tempting to introduce what Paul writes about the law in Romans, 1 Corinthians, and Galatians in order to explain what he means by a ministry of death. For example, Galatians insists that the law was not meant to give life (Gal 3:21), and Romans and 1 Corinthians note that the commandment that promised life resulted in death because of the power of sin (Rom 7:7–12; 1 Cor 15:56). Thus Paul can call the Mosaic ministry a ministry of death because, even though its prescriptions embodied God's will, they were frustrated by the power of sin, which used them to bring people to death. Although this is true, it should be noted that Paul is not making a comparison between the law and the Spirit here but between two ministries, *both* of which ultimately have God's law in view. The difference between them is that Paul's new covenant ministry brings life, because it is vivified by the Spirit, who writes the law on the hearts of God's people, whereas the Mosaic ministry of the old covenant cannot bring life, because the law it announces is written in letters on tablets of stone. In effect, Paul defines the Mosaic covenant in light of the new covenant; if the new covenant gives life, then the old must have brought death.

[9–10] Paul's second comparison is between the ministry of condemnation and the ministry of righteousness. The Greek word for "condemnation" (*katakrisis*) refers to a judicial judgment that involves a penalty, and it occurs only one other time in the New Testament (2 Cor 7:3). However, Paul does employ the verb "to condemn" (*katakrinō*) and, more importantly, the noun "condemnation" (*katakrima*) to note that whereas Adam's trespass brought condemnation (Rom 5:16, 18), there is no condemnation for those in Christ Jesus (Rom 8:1). Opposed to condemnation is the justification that the law could not effect. See Rom 3:20 and Gal 2:16. Although this background surely informs Paul's thought here, he is comparing two ministries rather than law and faith or law and righteousness, as in Romans and Galatians. In Paul's view, the ministry of the new covenant is a ministry of righteousness because the Spirit vivifies it; conversely the old covenant must be a ministry of condemnation because it did not grant God's life-giving Spirit, which makes people righteous. If one insists upon bringing Romans and Galatians into the argument, the proper starting point is Rom 8 and Gal 3:1–6, where Paul relates righteousness and justification to the gift of God's Spirit.

B. The Integrity of Paul's Apostolic Ministry

Paul's statement that his new covenant ministry is a ministry of righteousness is important for what he will say when he writes that God made Christ sin so that we might become the righteousness of God (5:21), and for his description of himself as wielding the weapons of righteousness (6:7). In affirming that he exercises a ministry of righteousness, Paul is preparing for his critique in chapters 10–13 of the intruding apostles, who apparently view themselves as "ministers of righteousness" (11:15) and "ministers of Christ" (11:23).

With verse 10 Paul interrupts his comparison in order to introduce a further reflection on the glory of these two ministries. Employing a paradoxical turn of phrase, he says that "what was glorified" (*to dedoxasmenon*)—the ministry of death and condemnation—"is not glorified" (*ou dedoxastai*). Then, qualifying himself, he explains why: because of the "surpassing glory" (*hyperballousēs doxēs*), that is, the glory of the ministry of the Spirit and righteousness. In saying this, Paul goes beyond what one expects from the *qal wahomer* form of argument; for he now assigns a surpassing glory to the new covenant. In doing so, however, he is not saying that God's glory in the new covenant is somehow more glorious than God's glory in the old covenant, as the third and final comparison will show.

[11] In his third comparison Paul merely speaks of what is being abolished (*to katargoumenon*) and what remains (*to menon*), arguing that if the first came through glory then the second must certainly be glorious. Although Paul does not employ the noun "ministry" (*diakonia*) in this comparison, as he did in the first two comparisons, it is clear that what is being abolished is the ministry of death and condemnation whereas what remains or endures is the ministry of the new covenant. In arguing for the glory of his new covenant ministry, Paul introduces a further comparison between the ministry of the new covenant and the ministry of death and condemnation. Whereas the former is destined to endure, the latter is being abolished, a motif that Paul will develop in the following verses when he discusses Moses' action of veiling his face in greater detail.

Lest the reader lose sight of the forest because of the trees, it will be helpful to summarize what Paul has said and what he has not said in this passage. First, the purpose of this passage is to establish the glory of the new covenant. Second, this passage is a comparison between two kinds of ministry; it is not a comparison between law and gospel or law and Spirit. Third, Paul affirms that the old covenant ministry was glorious. Indeed, he must affirm this if he wishes to make his argument. Fourth, Paul does not denigrate Moses, his old covenant ministry, or the glory that attended it. Fifth, Paul states that the ministry of death and condemnation, symbolized by the glory on Moses' face, is in the process of being abolished, of being set aside; thus it is passing away. Later, Paul will suggest that as people turn to the Lord, who is the Spirit (v. 16), the ministry of the Spirit is replacing the ministry of the Mosaic covenant. When this occurs, the old covenant attains its true meaning, because it is vivified by the Spirit that enables believers to fulfill the law of the old covenant which is now written on their hearts. Put another way, the new covenant *is* the old covenant made alive by God's Spirit. To that extent, there is one enduring covenant.

*****

[12–18] Having argued that if the ministry of death and condemnation came in glory, then it is all the more certain that there is a glory to his new covenant ministry, Paul draws a comparison between his conduct and that of Moses, who veiled his face from the Israelites of his day. This theme of veiling allows Paul to explain why the Israel of his day continues to read "Moses" as it does, whereas those whose faces are unveiled are being transformed from glory to glory. These verses then are about the veiling and unveiling of God's glory in light of old and new covenant ministries.

[12–13] Paul begins by drawing a conclusion from what he has just written. The conclusion, however, is not so much based upon the glory that attends his new covenant ministry as it is upon the enduring quality of that glory. Otherwise it would be difficult to explain why Moses and Paul act so differently, inasmuch as glory attends the ministry of each of them. The ground of Paul's hope, then, is the confidence that the new covenant and its glory will not be abolished—as is presently happening to the ministry of death and condemnation—but that it will remain and endure. Filled with this hope, Paul acts with *parrēsia*. According to BDAG *parrēsia* can refer to the courage, confidence, and boldness that one exhibits, especially in the presence of others whose rank or status is greater (see Acts 4:13, where the leaders of the Sanhedrin are amazed at the "boldness" of the uneducated apostles Peter and John). Or it can refer to outspoken and frank speech that conceals nothing (see Mark 8:32; John 7:26; 16:29 where Jesus speaks "openly" and conceals nothing). Although many argue vigorously for translating *parrēsia* as "boldness" (Hafemann, *Paul, Moses, and the History of Israel*, 339–47), the context seems to demand the sense of plain, frank, and outspoken speech (Belleville, *Reflections of Glory*, 192–98), since Paul is contrasting his behavior with that of Moses, who covered his face with a veil, and because he is combating accusations that the gospel he preaches is veiled (4:3). Accordingly, the confident hope that his new covenant ministry will endure allows Paul to speak openly and forthrightly. Moses, by contrast, put a veil over his face, suggesting that he was concealing something. With this reference to Moses' veil, Paul returns to the story of Moses narrated in Exod 34:27–35, to which he alluded in verse 7.

> The LORD said to Moses: Write these words; in accordance with these words I have made a covenant with you and with Israel. He was there with the LORD forty days and forty nights; he neither ate bread nor drank water. And he wrote on the tablets the words of the covenant, the ten commandments.
>
> Moses came down from Mount Sinai. As he came down from the mountain with the two tablets of the covenant in his hand, Moses did not know that the skin

B. The Integrity of Paul's Apostolic Ministry

of his face shone because he had been talking with God. When Aaron and all the Israelites saw Moses, the skin of his face was shining, and they were afraid to come near him. But Moses called to them; and Aaron and all the leaders of the congregation returned to him, and Moses spoke with them. Afterward all the Israelites came near, and he gave them in commandment all that the LORD had spoken with him on Mount Sinai. When Moses had finished speaking with them, he put a veil on his face; but whenever Moses went in before the LORD to speak with him, he would take the veil off, until he came out; and when he came out, and told the Israelites what he had been commanded, the Israelites would see the face of Moses, that the skin of his face was shining; and Moses would put the veil on his face again, until he went in to speak with him. (Exod 34:27–35)

When Paul alludes to this episode, it is clear that he is not merely recounting specific facts just as they are told in the Exodus account. Rather, he is commenting on them, and as he does so, he is interpreting the story in light of his new covenant ministry. Thus it is not surprising that a host of commentators, following the suggestion made by Hans Windisch in his classic commentary, have viewed the text of 2 Cor 3:7–18 as a midrash on Exod 34. In doing so, they have proposed a number of hypotheses to explain its origin and purpose.[21]

Exodus 34 never explicitly says why Moses put a veil over his face, though the reaction of Aaron and the Israelites in verse 30 indicates that they were afraid to approach him when they saw how his face had been glorified after speaking with God.[22] Nonetheless, Moses summons Aaron and the Israelites and speaks to them. Then, *after* he has finished speaking with them, Moses puts a veil on his face (Exod 34:33). This is the first reference to the veil, and it appears somewhat unexpectedly, since Moses has already spoken with his face unveiled to the people. Exodus 34:35, however, recounts what Moses did on a more regular basis, reporting that whenever he went in before the Lord, he would take the veil off until he came out to address the Israelites. Thus the last part of the narrative suggests that the veil became a permanent fixture. It is this part of the story that interests Paul, who now attributes a motive to Moses: Moses put a veil on his face so that the Israelites would not see "the end of what was being abolished" (*to telos tou katargoumenou*).

---

21. Hafemann, *Paul, Moses, and the History of Israel*, 255–63, summarizes the intricate history of this text. He, Stockhausen, and Belleville have shown that the text is an integral part of Paul's argument. If the present text is a midrash, Paul is responsible for it. The point is also made by J. A. Fitzmyer, "Glory Reflected on the Face of Christ (2 Cor 3:7–4:6)," in *According to Paul: Studies in the Theology of Paul* (New York: Paulist Press, 1993), 64–79. It is unlikely that it is a midrash from Paul's opponents, as some would argue.

22. Although Paul speaks of the "glory" (*doxa*) on Moses' face, the Septuagint uses the verb "to glorify" (*doxazein*) rather than the noun *doxa* in speaking of the appearance of the skin of Moses' face as being glorified (*kai ēn dedoxasmenē hē opsis tou chrōmatos tou prosōpou autou*; Exod 34:30).

The neuter participle "what was being abolished" (*tou katargoumenou*) is the same participle that Paul uses in verse 11, although it is now in the genitive case, suggesting that what was being abolished, nullified, or set aside was the ministry of death and condemnation, as is the case in verse 11. But how does Paul know this? How does Paul know that Moses knew this? And if Moses knew this, why does he conceal it from the Israelites? Paul, of course, knows that the ministry of death and condemnation is in the process of being annulled because the new covenant promised by Jeremiah has made its appearance in his ministry and the gospel that he preaches. *On the basis of this knowledge*, rather than any historical evidence, Paul can now impute a motive to Moses that the text of Exodus did not. Moreover, since the old was always anticipating the new, Paul can suppose that Moses knew that his ministry was to be abolished. On the basis of this understanding, Paul can take yet another step. Moses must have known that his ministry was destined to be abolished when the new finally appeared. Therefore, his purpose in veiling his face was to prevent the Israelites from gazing on the *telos* of what was being abolished. In saying this, Paul is not necessarily accusing Moses of being deceptive or trying to deceive Israel, as the next verse will show. Rather, Moses seeks to prevent the Israelites from gazing on the "end" (*telos*) of what is being abolished. Otherwise they will gaze on veiled glory (as the Israel of Paul's day is doing) rather than on the unveiled glory of the gospel (Barrett, 120; Belleville, *Reflections of Glory*, 198–225).

But what does Paul mean by the *telos* of what was being abolished? Since *telos* can mean the termination of something or its goal, there are two lines of interpretation here. First, Paul could be saying Moses put a veil on his face so that the Israelites would not see the true "goal" of what was being abolished; for example, the glory of Christ (Thrall, 1:277). Or Paul could be saying that Moses put a veil on his face so that the Israelites would not see the "end" of what was being abolished, the ministry of death and condemnation (Furnish, 207; Lambrecht, 52). Since Paul has already contrasted Moses' ministry and his own in terms of what is passing away and what remains (v. 11), the second meaning seems to cohere best with the context, even though it is somewhat tautological. The flow of Paul's thought can be summarized in this way:

- Paul's new covenant ministry of the gospel assures him that the old covenant ministry is passing away.
- Moses must have known that his ministry would be abolished when a new covenant in the Spirit made its appearance.
- Therefore, Moses must have placed the veil on his face so that Israel would not stubbornly gaze on what was destined to be abolished with the coming of a new covenant for which God has qualified him.

Although this kind of reasoning may be strange and unconvincing to contemporary readers, it coheres with Paul's logic that a new covenant has made its

B. The Integrity of Paul's Apostolic Ministry

appearance in Christ. More importantly, Paul's reasoning rests on his own profound experience of the Spirit. Given the arrival of God's eschatological salvation in the gospel, Paul now understands the full meaning of the old. Because he does, he can attribute motives to Israel's greatest representative.

[14–15] In these verses, Paul moves from the veiling of Moses' face to the veiling of the minds and hearts of the Israelites of Moses' day and his own. The material begins with a strong adversative clause ("but their minds were hardened," v. 14a). Paul then explains that the hardening of Israel's minds that characterized the Israel of Moses' day persists "to this very day," since *the very same veil* remains "at" or "over" (*epi*) the reading of "the old covenant" (v. 14b). Introducing a second adversative clause with yet another reference to "this very day," in verse 15 Paul repeats what he has just said but in a slightly different way. He notes that *a* veil (rather than "the very same veil") lies over their heart (rather than "their minds") to this very day whenever "Moses" (rather than "old covenant") is read. The comparison of verses 14 and 15 that follows shows the relationship between these two verses.

> But their minds were hardened (v. 14a)
> lies over their heart (v. 15d)
>
> For to this very day (v. 14b)
> But to this day (v.15a)
>
> at the reading of the old covenant (v. 14c)
> whenever Moses is read (v. 15b)
>
> the same veil (v. 14d)
> a veil (v. 15c)

Although Paul speaks of both the Israel of Moses' time and the Israel of his own time, he is clearly more interested in explaining the unbelief of his contemporaries. To this end, he employs the metaphor of the veil to show how a veil that lies over the heart of his contemporaries is related to Israel's response to Moses.

The strong adversative clause that opens these verses, "But their minds were hardened" (v. 14), has always been somewhat puzzling to commentators. Those who argue that Moses was concealing something from Israel (the passing glory of his face) tend to view this adversative clause as Paul's way of highlighting the responsibility of the people and downplaying Moses' behavior of veiling his face. Thus, although he veiled the glory of his face to them, the real problem was the hardness of their minds. But if the line of interpretation that this commentary has adopted is correct, then the adversative clause can be interpreted in another way: Moses put a veil on his face so that Israel would not gaze on what was destined to be abolished; *but* Israel's mind was hardened, and Israel persisted nonetheless in gazing upon Moses' veiled face, even though his glorious ministry was already in the process of being abolished because of what was to come (so Belleville, *Reflections of Glory*, 217–25).

If this line of interpretation is correct, what follows also falls into place. Paul can now say that the very same veil "remains" (*menei*, the verb used to express the permanence of the new covenant!) at the reading of the "old covenant" (*palaias diathēkēs*). Although this is the only use of the phrase "old covenant" in the Old or New Testament, it makes perfect sense in light of Paul's earlier description of his ministry as the ministry of a new covenant (3:6). By saying that the same veil remains at the reading of the old covenant, Paul draws a relationship between the Israel of his day and the Israel of Moses' day. Just as the wilderness generation persisted in looking at the veil that covered Moses' glorious face, so Paul's contemporaries persist in looking at the same veil (understood metaphorically) when they read the old covenant. As a result, just as the wilderness generation did not understand that the ministry of death and condemnation was in the process of being abolished, so Paul's contemporaries do not understand that the old covenant is in the process of being nullified as the new makes its appearance in the proclamation of the gospel.

In the final part of verse 14 Paul explains that Moses' veil remains "not unveiled" (*mē anakalyptomenon*) at the reading of the old covenant because only in Christ is it "abolished" (*katargeitai*). As the translation notes explain, the subject of *katargeitai* is not expressed. Thus Paul may be saying that in Christ the old covenant is abolished or in Christ the veil is abolished. Although the verb *katargeō* would be more appropriate for abolishing a covenant than a veil (see v. 16 where Paul uses a *periaireō* when he speaks of the veil being removed), the context suggests that Paul has the veil in view. For having said that the same veil remains as an impediment to the reading of the old covenant, he must now explain how that veil is removed; and so he responds that it is removed "in Christ." When it is, Israel reads the old covenant as it ought.

The veil, however, has not yet been removed for Paul's contemporaries. Consequently he introduces yet another adversative clause in verse 15 to explain why the Israel of his day persists in unbelief. At first, it may appear that Paul is merely repeating what he has already said but in slightly different words: "Moses" in place of "the old covenant," "a veil" in place of "the same veil," their "heart" in place of their "minds," "lies over" in place of "remains." These slight changes, however, do more than intensify what Paul has already said. They suggest that Paul's contemporaries have fallen into an ever deepening stupor because of a history of unbelief and rebellion (Belleville, *Reflections of Glory*, 237–47). Hardness of "minds" (*noēmata*) has given way to the more serious problem of hardness of "heart" (*kardia*), and the veil of Moses is now presented as "a veil," a kind of spiritual blindness that lies over the heart. In this way Paul explains why his contemporaries have not believed in the gospel he preaches: namely, just as their ancestors persisted in looking at the veiled face of Moses, so his contemporaries continue to read Moses (the old covenant)

B. The Integrity of Paul's Apostolic Ministry

with a veiled heart. This persistent gazing upon what is veiled has in turn resulted in a continued veiling of their hearts that can be abolished only in Christ.

[16] With this verse, Paul returns to the text of Exod 34 in order to explain how those who belong to the new covenant are being transformed from glory to glory as they look upon the glory of the Lord with their faces unveiled. The text establishes a contrast between the Israel of Paul's day and those who belong to the new covenant, as well as a favorable comparison between the members of the new covenant and Moses, both of whom stand in the divine presence with face unveiled. The text begins with a strong allusion to Exod 34:34, which reads as follows in the Septuagint:

> And whenever Moses went in before the Lord to speak to him, he took off the veil till he went out, and he went forth and spoke to all the children of Israel whatsoever the Lord commanded him (*hēnika d'an eiseporeueto Mōusēs enanti kyriou lalein autō periēreito to kalymma heōs tou ekporeuesthai. kai exelthōn elalei pasin tois huios Israēl hosa eneteilato autō kyrios*). (trans. Brenton)

In alluding to this verse, Paul makes two important changes. First, he no longer explicitly identifies Moses as the subject of the verb. Second, he substitutes the verb "turns" (*epistrephē*) for "went in" (*eiseporeueto*). Thus Paul is not merely quoting from Exod 34:34. He is interpreting and contemporizing the text of Exodus for his own day so that his use of Exodus is an exhortation and call to conversion: "Whenever he turns to the Lord, the veil is lifted." Because the subject of the verb is unexpressed in the Greek text, the phrase can now apply to anyone who turns to the Lord, and since Paul has just spoken of the veil that lies over the heart of his contemporaries, he surely has them in view. If Paul's contemporaries—or indeed if anyone—turns to the Lord, the veil is lifted. When the veil is lifted, then one sees the glory of the Lord as did Moses when he entered the tent of meeting with his face unveiled. The act of turning to the Lord, then, is an act of conversion. But to whom is Paul referring when he speaks of "the Lord" (v. 15)?

In Paul's writings "the Lord" (*ho kyrios*) normally refers to Christ. Consequently the exegetical tradition tends to interpret this passage christologically: whenever one turns to Christ, the veil is lifted. Indeed this even coheres with what Paul has already written, that it is only in Christ that it (the veil) is abolished (v. 14). Furthermore one might argue that this christological sense is how most Christians would normally understand the passage. When Paul quotes from Israel's Scriptures, however, *ho kyrios* usually—though there are exceptions—refers to YHWH.[23] If this is so, the *kyrios* of verse 16 could also be the Lord God, as in the text of Exodus and as the next verse suggests.

---

23. See the arguments of James D. G. Dunn, "2 Corinthians 3:17 'The Lord Is the Spirit,'" in *The Christ and the Spirit* (Grand Rapids: Eerdmans, 1998), 1:115–25; and Thrall, *II Corinthians*, 1:278–83.

[17] In this verse Paul writes, "The Lord is the Spirit." Although this has led some to identify Christ and the Spirit, and although some patristic writers understood the text to mean that the Spirit is the Lord, and so divine, Paul seems to be making a pesher-like comment (as he does in Rom 10:6–8) to explain who *ho kyrios* is in the text of Exodus. If this is so, then the text can be amplified in this way, "Now in this passage from Exodus, to which I have just alluded, *ho kyrios* stands for the Spirit of the new covenant about which I have been speaking." Thus, Paul is not identifying Christ and the Spirit, nor is he trying to show that the Spirit is God. Rather, he is continuing the theological and pneumatological focus that has characterized this chapter from its beginning: the Lord is the Spirit; that is, the Lord is the Spirit of God that energizes Paul's new covenant ministry. Accordingly the text of Exodus means that whenever anyone turns to the Spirit, the veil is lifted.

Paul then writes that where "the Spirit of the Lord" (*to pneuma kyriou*) is, there is freedom. "Freedom" (*eleutheria*) plays a major role in Paul's theology, especially in Romans and Galatians. For example, in Galatians he describes two covenants, one that results in slavery and another that results in freedom (Gal 4:21–31), and argues that the justified belong to the lineage of the freed woman and the covenant she represents. Shortly after this, he insists that it was for freedom that Christ set the justified free (Gal 5:1). Then in Romans he writes that believers have been set free from sin and become slaves of righteousness (Rom 6:18). Although notions of freedom from the law, sin, and death undoubtedly lie in the background of Paul's thought, here they are not in the foreground. Rather, Paul seems to have in mind freedom from the veil that lies over the heart of his contemporaries as they read "Moses." Such freedom allows the people of a new covenant to gaze on the glory of the Lord rather than on the veiled face of Moses.

[18] With this verse, Paul comes to the climax of his argument: the new covenant allows people to contemplate the glory of the Lord with face unveiled, as did Moses. Although Paul resumes the use of the literary plural here ("we all") the addition of "all" suggests that he is referring to all the members of the new covenant community and not just to its ministers, even if some of its ministers, such as Paul, have been granted the grace of seeing God's Son (Gal 1:16), who is the very image of God (2 Cor 4:4). But by including all the members of the new covenant, Paul is able to show the difference between the two ministries he has been comparing: whereas those who adhere to the Mosaic ministry are veiled from the glory of the Lord, those who adhere to the ministry of a new covenant are not.

If this interpretation is correct, then all the members of the new covenant are "contemplating" (*katoptrizomenoi*) the glory of the Lord, which is to say, God's glory. Although the verb *katoptrizō* can mean "to reflect" (thus to reflect God's glory on one's face), the context argues for contemplating God's glory, since Paul is contrasting the members of the new covenant with Israel, which "looked

B. The Integrity of Paul's Apostolic Ministry

intently" (*atenizō*) on Moses' face but could not see the glory of the Lord because of the veil. Moreover, the notion of transformation seems to require the sense of contemplation, since it is easier to understand how one is transformed by contemplating God's glory than by reflecting it.[24]

The act of contemplating, then, results in "being transformed" (*metamorphoumetha*) into "the same image." Although the introduction of "image" (*eikōn*) is somewhat unexpected, "the same image" likely refers to Christ, "who is the image of God" (4:4), inasmuch as he is the perfect reflection of God's glory. Consequently, when members of the new covenant contemplate the glory of God, they are transformed into the same image of God's glory, which is Christ. The process of transformation, as Paul will explain, does not occur instantaneously, as if by magic; and so Paul writes, "from glory to glory." The final phrase, "as from the Lord who is the Spirit" echoes the point that Paul made in verse 17, where he identified "the Lord" in the text from Exodus as "the Spirit."

To summarize, when people turn to the Spirit, the veil that prevented Israel from seeing God's glory is lifted from them. Consequently they contemplate the glory of God as did Moses. In doing so, they are gradually being transformed into the very image of God's Son—by the power of God's Spirit—from glory to glory. In 4:7–5:10 Paul will explain how this is worked out in practice as he discusses the paradoxical role of suffering in his apostolic ministry.

c. Paul's Apostolic Integrity (4:1–6)

4:1 Therefore, since we have this ministry to the degree that we have received mercy, we are not discouraged.[a] 2 Rather, we have renounced hidden deeds of which one is ashamed,[b] not acting cunningly,[c] nor falsifying the word of God, but in full disclosure of the truth,[d] commending ourselves before God to everyone's conscience. 3 And if our gospel is veiled, it is veiled to those who are perishing, 4 in whose case[e] the god of this age has blinded the minds of the unbelieving lest they see[f] the light of the gospel of the glory of Christ,[g] who is the image of God. 5 For we do not preach ourselves but Jesus Christ as Lord,[h] and ourselves as your slaves for Jesus' sake, 6 because the God who said, "Light will shine out of darkness," has shone[i] in our hearts to bring to light[j] the knowledge of the glory of God[k] on the face of [Jesus] Christ.

a. The verb *enkakeō* could mean "to be discouraged" or "to be fearful," according to BDAG. Thrall (1:298–99), following Liddell and Scott, interprets it as "to be remiss,"

---

24. Margaret Thrall, "Conversion to the Lord: The Interpretation of Exodus 34 in II Cor 3:14b–18," in *Paolo: Ministro del Nuovo Testamento*, 222.

"to be lax," "to be reluctant." The context, however, suggests that Paul is not discouraged despite his many hardships. The same is true for 4:16, where the verb appears again.

b. The Greek, *ta krypta tēs aischynēs* (literally "the hidden things of shame or dishonor") can be translated in a variety of ways, depending upon how one construes the genitive and how one translates *aischynēs* ("shame" or "disgrace"). See Thrall, 1:303, who gives five possible translations. In this translation, "hidden things" and "of which one is ashamed" are taken as being in apposition to each other.

c. Literally, "not walking in cunning." Paul regularly employs walking (*peripateō*) as a metaphor for behavior or conduct, as does the Old Testament (Gal 5:16; 1 Thess 4:1). To walk in a particular way is to behave or conduct oneself in a particular way.

d. The genitive could also be construed as "the full disclosure that is the truth," or "the full disclosure that comes from the truth."

e. This translates *en hois*, "among whom." Translated literally, these words suggest that the unbelieving are a subclass of those who are perishing. Paul, however, is not making such a distinction, thus the translation "in whose case,"

f. "See" translates *augasai* which, if taken intransitively, can mean "shine forth." The presence of *autois* in some manuscripts indicates that they understood the verb in this way, giving the translation, "lest the light of the gospel . . . shine forth on them." But since this translation requires an indirect object such as *autois* (only found in inferior manuscripts), most commentators render *augasai* as "see."

g. This is a literal translation of several genitives that could be construed in different ways, for example, "the light from the gospel of the glory of Christ," "the light that is the glorious gospel of Christ."

h. Literally, "Jesus Christ Lord." Paul's gospel proclaims that Jesus Christ is Lord because God has exalted him (Phil 2:11).

i. The Greek has *hōs* ("he") before the verb "shone." It is not translated because its function is to remind the reader of the subject ("the God who said"), which has already been introduced but is now separated from its verb by the scriptural allusion.

j. Literally "for the light."

k. This is another literal translation of a series of genitives that could be construed in many ways, for example, "the light of the glorious knowledge of God," "light that is the glorious knowledge of God," "the light that comes from the glorious knowledge of God."

Having compared his new covenant ministry that reveals God's glory with the ministry of Moses that concealed that glory (so that the Israelites would not gaze on a ministry that was in the process of being abolished), Paul returns to the theme of his apostolic integrity, which he introduced in 2:14–3:6. In doing so, he completes the chiasm or ring pattern begun in those verses. The bracketing units of Paul's ring composition, 2:14–3:6 and 4:1–6, are related to each other inasmuch as both focus on Paul's integrity and the God-given gospel he preaches. They also share a number of linguistic contacts. For example, in 4:1 Paul writes that having received his ministry as a result of God's mercy, he is *not discouraged*; in 3:4–6 he speaks of his *confidence* as the minister of a new covenant. In 4:2 he writes that he *does not falsify the word of God* but *commends himself* to everyone's conscience before God; in 2:17 he accuses the

B. The Integrity of Paul's Apostolic Ministry

many of *trading on the word of God,* whereas he acts sincerely before God, and in 3:1 he asks if he is *commending himself* again. In 4:3 he refers to those who are *perishing*; in 2:15 he employs the same language. In 4:6 he declares that God has enlightened his *heart*; in 3:2 he claims that the Corinthians are his letter of recommendation written on his *heart*. Finally in 4:6 he speaks of the light of the *knowledge of the glory of God*; in 2:14 he says that he manifests the aroma of *God's knowledge* in God's triumphal procession.

In addition to these linguistic contacts with 2:14–3:6, this unit has a number of linguistic contacts with the middle member of the ring pattern (3:7–18). Among the most important are the following: the reference to Paul's *ministry* (4:1), which recalls the comparison between the *ministries* of Moses and Paul (3:7–11); the accusation that Paul's gospel is veiled (4:3), which echoes the discussion of Moses' *veil* and the *veil* over Israel that the gospel lifts (3:12–18); the description of Christ as *the image of God* (4:4), which recalls Paul's claim that members of the new covenant are being transformed into *the same image* (3:18); and the references to *glory* (4:4, 6), which echo the frequent use of this term throughout 3:7–18.

Although these linguistic contacts might lead one to assume that Paul is merely repeating what he has already said, especially in 2:14–3:6, this unit develops Paul's argument further. Having argued that God has qualified him to be the minister of a new covenant (2:14–3:6), and having compared the ministries of old and new covenant (3:7–18), Paul can finally explain how his ministry discloses God's glory: by the light that comes from the gospel of the glory of Christ that he preaches. He first saw that glory on the face of the risen Christ, the very image of God, and ever since he has communicated that glorious knowledge of God by the gospel he preaches.

The unit can be divided into three parts. In the first (vv. 1–2) Paul explains why he is not discouraged, asserting that he has rejected what is hidden and acted in full disclosure of the truth. In the second (vv. 3–4) he deals with the accusation that his gospel is hidden by saying that it is concealed only from those whom the god of this age (Satan) has blinded. Finally, in the third part (vv. 5–6) Paul describes how God has enlightened his heart, thereby drawing a contrast with the blindness that Satan has brought to those on the way to destruction. The material can be outlined as follows:

vv. 1–2   Courageous and open behavior
vv. 3–4   The god of this age who blinds unbelievers
vv. 5–6   The creator God who enlightens Paul

[4:1–2] Paul begins by explaining why he is not discouraged: he possesses his new covenant ministry as a result of God's mercy. Accordingly, he has renounced what is hidden and shameful, and he openly commends himself to everyone's conscience. Paul's use of several adversatives ("rather," "but") and negatives ("not," "nor") and a series of participles allows him to defend his apostolic integrity once more. He is *not* discouraged, *rather* he has renounced hidden things, *not acting* cunningly, *nor falsifying* God's word, *but commending* himself to everyone's conscience. Although Paul does not explicitly contrast his behavior with others, as he does in 2:17, one suspects that he may have such people in mind.

If the correct translation of *ouk enkakoumen* is "we are not discouraged," rather than "we are not remiss" (as Thrall argues), Paul means that he is not discouraged by the hardships of his apostolic ministry, to which he has already adverted in the letter's benediction (1:3–11) and to which he alludes in the metaphor of himself as God's prisoner (2:14). These apostolic sufferings will come to the forefront of Paul's description of apostolic ministry in 4:7–5:10, in the midst of which he will again affirm that he does not become "discouraged" (4:16, *dio ouk enkakoumen*). The ground for this confidence is Paul's assurance that his new covenant ministry derives from the mercy that God first extended to him at the moment of his call/conversion (see 1 Cor 7:25 and 1 Tim 1:13,16, which also use the language of mercy in relation to Paul's call). At that moment God qualified Paul to be the minister of a new covenant (3:6).

In affirming that he has renounced hidden deeds, Paul is not implying that previous to his call/conversion he indulged in hidden deeds of which he is now ashamed. Although he freely acknowledges that he persecuted the church of God (1 Cor 15:9), he also boasts of his righteous conduct under the law (Phil 3:8). This affirmation, therefore, is not so much a description of the life he once lived as it is an indication of his determination not to engage in hidden conduct of which one is ultimately ashamed. Rather, as he has already said in comparing himself with Moses, he acts "openly" (*parrēsia*) or, as he affirms in these verses, "in full disclosure of the truth." Three participles explain what he means. First, he does "not act cunningly" (*mē peripatountes en panourgia*), which anticipates the charge of 12:16 that he is "cunning" (*panourgos*). Second, he does "not falsify" (*mēde dolountes*) the word of God, recalling the many who trade on the word of God (2:17). Third, he "commends" (*synistanontes*) himself to every one's conscience. But whereas he refused to commend himself in 3:1, here he commends himself in full disclosure of the truth to everyone's moral consciousness, as he will also do in 5:11. And whereas earlier he called upon the witness of his own conscience (1:12), now he commends himself to the conscience of others. Thus, if they allow their moral consciousness to bear witness, it will acknowledge his apostolic integrity.

[3–4] Having affirmed his integrity, Paul turns to the charge that his gospel is veiled. In doing so, he takes up the question of unbelief with which he has already dealt in 3:14–16 in reference to Israel. The content and origin of this charge, however, is itself veiled from the contemporary reader! Although some attribute the charge to the intruding missionaries at Corinth and/or to the

Corinthians themselves, others argue that it may have arisen from the Jewish population in Corinth with whom the Corinthians had to contend. Given Paul's emphasis on the paradoxical nature of the gospel and its wisdom, which is manifested in the folly and weakness of the cross (1 Cor 1:10–4:24), any one of the groups mentioned above could have accused Paul of preaching a message that is veiled and obscure. For if God manifested himself in the folly and weakness of the cross (1 Cor 1:18–25), how does the ministry of the new covenant reveal the glory of God? Is this knowledge of God's glory the possession of only a few, as Paul's discussion in 1 Cor 2:6–16 might suggest?

Making use of the theme of the veil, which he has already employed to his advantage in 3:12–18 to establish that members of the new covenant contemplate God's glory with unveiled faces, and recalling what he has already said about those on the way to destruction (2:15; also see 1 Cor 1:18), Paul affirms that his gospel is veiled only to those who are perishing.[25] This gospel, of course, is not his own, even though he calls it "our gospel." Rather, it is "the gospel" (8:18), "the gospel of Christ" (2:12; 9:13; 10:14), "God's good news" (11:7), which is always capable of being perverted into "another gospel," as the intruding apostles have seemingly done by preaching "another Jesus" (11:4).

For Paul, the ultimate cause of unbelief is "the god of this age." This expression, which occurs only here in the New Testament, has always caused difficulty for interpreters; for, if it refers to Satan, it attributes to Satan a designation, *ho theos,* that properly belongs to God. Accordingly, during the patristic period, when the authors of that time had to deal with systems such as Gnosticism and Manichaeism, many of them read "of this age" with "unbelievers," giving the translation "in whose case God has blinded the minds of the *unbelievers of this age.*" But since this is not the natural way of reading the Greek text, in which the two phrases are separated by several words, most commentators (but see Scott, 85) identify "the god of this age" as Satan. In this instance, Paul's emphasis is clearly on the apocalyptic expression "this age" (Rom 12:2; 1 Cor 1:20; 2:6, 8; 3:18; Eph 1:21), which he distinguishes from the age that has made its appearance with Christ's death and resurrection, so that believers are living at the point where these two ages meet (1 Cor 10:11). Satan is the "god" of "this age" in the sense that he rules over it, though God's enemies are presently being defeated, and God will be all in all when the last

---

25. J. Louis Martyn ("Epistemology at the Turn of the Ages," in *Theological Issues in the Letters of Paul* [Studies of the New Testament and Its World; Edinburgh, 1997], 89–110) argues that there is "an inextricable connection between eschatology and epistemology" (92) in Paul's thought so that those who stand at the turn of the ages are granted a new means of perception. In terms of 2 Corinthians this means that those who have embraced Paul's apocalyptic gospel see and understand in a manner that those who oppose the gospel cannot. Though Paul's gospel is veiled to the latter, so that they are on the way to destruction, it is clear and apparent to the former, who are on the way to salvation.

enemy—death—is destroyed (1 Cor 15:24–28). The Johannine description of Satan as the "ruler of this world" (John 12:31; 14:30; 16:11) provides a helpful insight to what Paul intends here.

As the "god" of this age, Satan has the power to blind people's minds—in this case the unbelieving—so that they cannot perceive the truth of the gospel that Paul preaches (see 1 Thess 2:18, where Paul says that Satan prevented him from visiting the Thessalonians). Given Paul's use of "unbelievers" (*apistoi*) in 1 Corinthians, where it refers to Gentile unbelievers (6:6; 7:12, 13, 14, 15; 10:27; 14:22, 23, 24), Paul probably has a similar group in view here, since he has already dealt with the blindness of his Israelite contemporaries in 3:14–15. More important than the identity of the *apistoi*, however, is the object of their blindness: the light of the gospel of the glory of Christ. Although this piling up of genitives can be construed in different ways, Paul clearly equates "the light" (*ton phōtismon*) with the gospel. This gospel is either the glorious gospel of Christ or, more likely, the gospel that proclaims Christ's glory. Since Paul has already described himself as the aroma of the knowledge of God that is spread abroad in every place (2:14), one may conclude that the gospel of Christ's glory is also knowledge of God, since, as Paul adds, Christ is the "image of God" (*eikōn tou theou*). By this description of Christ as the image of God, Paul clarifies what he wrote in 3:18, for it is now apparent that the "same image" into which believers are being transformed is Christ, the image of God.

Paul's description of Christ as the image of God draws upon the background of wisdom, which is described as "a pure emanation of the glory of the Almighty" (Wis 7:25), "a reflection of eternal light, a spotless mirror of the working of God," and "an image of his goodness" (Wis 7:26). This background is also apparent in the hymn of Col 1:15–20, which describes Christ as the image of the unseen God, and the opening verses of Hebrews, which name him "the reflection of God's glory" (*apaugasma tēs doxēs*; Heb 1:3). In addition to the background of Wisdom, Paul also has in view the description of humankind as created in God's image (Gen 1:26). In its sinful rebellion, however, humankind exchanged the glory of God for the image of something mortal and human (Rom 1:23). Consequently all have sinned and fallen short of God's glory (Rom 3:23). But now that the obedient Christ has reversed the sin of the disobedient Adam (Rom 5:12–21), Paul views Christ as the new or last Adam, who restores the glory of the image that humankind lost through its disobedience. Therefore, as humankind bore the image of the first Adam, so it will bear the image of the last Adam (1 Cor 15:49); for those whom God foreknew, God "predestined to be conformed to the image of his Son" (Rom 8:29).

To summarize, what Satan prevents unbelievers from "seeing" is the gospel that proclaims the glory of Christ, which is God's glory, because the Son is the image of the God of glory. To "hear" the gospel with faith is to "see" the glory of God reflected on the face of Christ (v. 6), who is the image of God.

B. The Integrity of Paul's Apostolic Ministry

[5–6] Having explained why his gospel is veiled to some, Paul returns to the theme of his apostolic ministry. He begins with a clause that substantiates what he has just said: His gospel is veiled only to the unbelieving "because" (*gar*) he does not preach himself but Jesus Christ. Then he explains why he preaches Christ, "because" (*hoti*) the light of God has shone in his heart. In these verses, then, Paul returns to the theme that he introduced at the beginning of this unit: the mercy that he has received, presumably when he was called/converted. It was at that moment that God's light entered his heart so that he saw the glory of God on the face of Christ: the content of the gospel of glory that he preaches so openly.

Paul begins by summarizing the gospel that he preaches. Its content is Jesus Christ, whom Paul proclaims as *kyrios* (Rom 10:9; 1 Cor 12:3; 2 Cor 4:5), the very name of honor that God gave to Jesus when he exalted him (Phil 2:11). Standing in the sharpest possible contrast to this title is Paul's description of himself as the "slave" (*doulos*) of the Corinthians, the only time that he portrays himself in this way in relation to the Corinthians or any other community, though he frequently refers to himself as Christ's slave (Rom 1:1; Gal 1:10; Phil 1:1). He qualifies what he says, however, by adding "for Jesus' sake." Thus, just as Christ emptied himself and took the form of a slave (Phil 2:7), so Paul becomes the Corinthians' slave for Jesus' sake. The use of this striking imagery reinforces Paul's earlier remark that he does not "rule over" (*kyrieuomen*) the faith of the Corinthians (1:24) and recalls his statement in 1 Cor 3:5 that he and Apollos are "servants" (*diakonoi*) through whom the Corinthians believe.

Having stated that he preaches the lordship of Jesus Christ, Paul now explains why: because the God who called forth light has shone in his heart[26] to reveal the knowledge of God's glory on the face of Jesus Christ. Thus, Paul establishes a sharp contrast between the god of this world who blinds people to the knowledge of the gospel of the glory of Christ and the Creator God who called forth light. The contrast is illustrated by comparing the various parts of verses 4 and 6 with each other.

v. 4a The god of this age has blinded the thoughts of the unbelieving
v. 6a The God who said, "Light will shine out of darkness," has shone in our hearts
v. 4b lest they see
v. 6b to bring to light

---

26. The Greek text, of course, employs the plural "in our hearts" (*en tais kardiais hēmōn*; v. 6), which seems strange if Paul is alluding to *his* conversion. Paul, however, has been employing a literary plural throughout this section (2:14–4:6). For example, see the use of the plural in 2:14–3:6, where it is quite apparent that he has his ministry in view. Thus it is probable, though not all will agree, that he is employing a literary plural here as well. The nature of the material, however, is such that what Paul says of himself can also be applied in large measure to other believers as well.

v. 4c   the light of the gospel of the glory of Christ, who is the image of God.

v. 6c   the knowledge of the glory of God on the face of Christ.

Paul identifies the God who has shone in his heart as the God who said, "Light will shine out of darkness." These words recall the text of Gen 1:3, "Let there be light" (*genēthētō phōs*), but they are not a direct quotation. Accordingly commentators suggest a number of other texts that may have influenced Paul, texts that refer to "darkness" (*skotos*) as well as to light.

> O people walking in darkness . . . a light shall shine upon you (*phōs lampsei ep' hymas*). (LXX Isa 9:1; trans. Brenton)

> To the upright, light has sprung up in darkness (*exaneteilen en skotei phōs*). (LXX Ps 111:4; trans. Brenton)

> We know that God has disposed his works, having made light out of darkness (*phōs poiēsas ek skotous*). (LXX Job 37:15; trans. Brenton)

Although no single text explains the origin of Paul's words (though a combination of several texts may), his intent is clear: The God of light to whom the Scriptures testify dispelled the darkness of his heart for the sake of the gospel. In writing this, it is likely that Paul refers to that occasion when God "was pleased to reveal his Son to me" (*en emoi,* Gal 1:16). At that moment of his call/conversion, Paul realized that the crucified Jesus whom he persecuted was none other than the Son of God; for he now saw the risen Jesus bathed in God's glory or, as he writes here, he saw the glory of God on the face of Christ.

Although some have contested this interpretation (Furnish, 250–51), it coheres with Paul's own account of his call/conversion, which has been deeply indebted to the call of the servant in Isa 49:1–6.[27] Just as God called the servant before he was born to be a light to the nations so that God's salvation might reach to the ends of the earth (Isa 49:1, 6), so God called Paul before he was born to preach among the nations (Gal 1:16). Here, as in Isa 49:6, Paul explains that God's light shone in his heart "for the sake of the light" (*pros phōtismon*), which is knowledge of God's glory, a glory that shines on the face of Christ, the image of God.

To summarize, Paul is not discouraged, because he received his new covenant ministry by God's mercy when God shone into his heart so that he might reveal the knowledge of God's glory in Christ. This gospel is veiled only to those whom Satan has blinded lest they see the light of the gospel.

---

27. In addition to Isa 49, Seyoon Kim ("Isaiah 42 and Paul's Call," in *Paul and the New Perspective: Second Thoughts on the Origin of Paul's Gospel* [Grand Rapids: Eerdmans, 2002], 101–27) points to the influence of Isa 42 on Paul's understanding of his call.

B. The Integrity of Paul's Apostolic Ministry

The main line of Paul's thought in 2:14–3:6 can be stated in this way: To those blinded by the god of this age, Paul's ministry is veiled, and it seems to be an exercise in failure and defeat. Accordingly, the suffering and afflicted apostle paradoxically presents himself as God's prisoner, being led in a triumphant procession. But Paul knows that his ministry has life-and-death consequences for those with whom he comes in contact and that he does not need letters of recommendation, because God has qualified him to be the minister of a new covenant empowered by the Spirit. This new covenant ministry comes in glory, as did the ministry of Moses. But whereas Moses' ministry veiled God's glory, lest the Israelites persist in gazing on what was destined to be abolished, Paul acts confidently and openly to reveal the glory of God on the face of Christ, who is the image of God. Therefore, Paul is not discouraged, for as people "hear" the gospel of the glory of Christ, they "see" God's glory on the face of Christ, a glory that is in the process of transforming them from glory to glory. Exactly how this glory is manifested in Paul's ministry will be explained in the second part of his discussion on apostolic ministry (4:7–5:10).

2. Ministry and Apostolic Suffering (4:7–5:10)

These verses are the second section of Paul's exposition and defense of his apostolic ministry. Having explained that he is the minister of a new covenant of the Spirit, in which the glory of God is revealed on the face of Christ through the preaching of the gospel, Paul now turns to the question of suffering and weakness in the apostolic minister. If Paul is truly the minister of a new covenant that reveals the glory of God, where is the glory? Why is his ministry characterized by affliction and weakness? Aware of objections such as these, Paul must show the Corinthians the intimate relationship between his suffering and affliction and his new covenant ministry. He will argue that his apostolic sufferings on behalf of the Corinthians paradoxically reveal the eschatological power of Christ's resurrection life in his mortal body (4:7–15). This is not to say that he and other apostolic ministers already experience the full power of the resurrection. Rather, he is affirming that God's eschatological future is already making itself felt in the present. Consequently, while the world sees Paul's "outer self," which is in the process of decaying, his "inner self," which cannot be seen, is in the process of being renewed day by day as it prepares to assume an eternal weight of glory (4:16–18). Therefore, Paul is confident that when his tent-like dwelling, his earthly body, is destroyed, God will provide him with an eternal dwelling, the resurrection body. Accordingly he lives as one who must stand before the judgment seat of Christ (5:1–10).

Throughout this section, Paul employs the first person plural, once more raising the question, To whom is he referring? To himself? To all apostolic ministers? To the entire Christian community? Since Paul is defending his apostolic ministry from charges and accusation leveled against him, it is likely that he is employing a literary plural here with himself as the primary referent. In using the literary plural, however, he undoubtedly also has in view other apostolic ministers who are aligned with him. Furthermore, what Paul says about resurrection and transformation, especially in 4:16–5:10, certainly applies to all believers (Lambrecht, 76). To summarize, when Paul employs "we" here, he is the primary referent. Other apostolic ministers, however, are in the background, and much of what he says can be applied to believers in general.

Although the material of this section is tightly woven together, one can distinguish three movements. In the first (4:7–15) Paul provides an initial description of his hardships and their relationship to the death and life of Jesus. In the second (4:16–18) he discusses these afflictions in terms of his inner and outer self, affirming that the inner self is already being transformed. In the third (5:1–10) he turns his attention to the future and discusses the heavenly habitation he hopes to attain when the process of transformation is complete.

a. Life and Death in Apostolic Ministry (4:7–15)

4:7 We have this treasure in earthen vessels so that it may be evident[a] that the extraordinary power is from God and not from us. 8 In every way, we are afflicted but not constrained,[b] bewildered but not in doubt,[c] 9 persecuted but not forsaken, struck down but not destroyed, 10 always bearing the dying[d] of Jesus in our body so that the life of Jesus might be manifested in our body. 11 For we the living are continually being handed over[e] to death on account of Jesus, so that the life of Jesus[f] might be manifested in our mortal flesh. 12 Consequently, death is at work in us but life in you.

13 Because we have the same spirit of faith,[g] corresponding to what is written, "I believed, therefore, I spoke," even we believe, therefore even we speak, 14 since we know that the one who raised the [Lord][h] Jesus will also raise us with[i] Jesus and present us with you.

15 For everything is for your sake, so that grace, ever increasing through more and more converts,[j] might increase thanksgiving to God's glory.[k]

a. The words "it may be evident" have been supplied to clarify why the treasure is in earthen vessels.

b. The two Greek words in this phrase (*thlibomenoi . . . stenochōroumenoi*) are closely related; the first means "to be pressed or crowded," the second "to be confined or restricted." A translation such as "hard pressed but not crushed" would be appropriate. This translation employs "afflicted" in order to relate this passage more clearly to other passages in the letter where "affliction" plays a prominent role.

c. There is a play on the sound of these words in the Greek that cannot be reproduced in English (*aporoumenoi . . . exaporoumenoi*).

B. The Integrity of Paul's Apostolic Ministry

d. The Greek word *nekrōsis* could mean the state of death or the process of dying. Since Paul seems to be speaking of something that continually occurs in his life, the second alternative has been adopted here.

e. The verb *paradidometha* is taken as a passive, but Fitzgerald (*Cracks in an Earthen Vessel*, 180) construes it as a middle: "we the living are handing ourselves over to death." However, since Paul seems to be speaking of afflictions that happen to him, the passive is more appropriate.

f. The "life of Jesus" refers to the power of the resurrection that is already at work in the life of Paul.

g. The "spirit of faith" could refer to the Holy Spirit, the source of faith, or to the disposition of faith. Commentators are divided on this point, with Barrett, Barnett, Collange, Furnish, and Hafemann supporting the former position, and Allo, Bultmann, Hughes, Plummer, and Thrall arguing for the latter. If Paul were referring to the Holy Spirit, however, one might have expected him to write *pistis tou pneumatou* ("the faith that comes from or belongs to the Spirit") rather than *pneuma tēs pisteōs*, which suggests the spirit that is faith, the spirit that comes from faith, or the spirit that has faith as its object.

h. There is strong manuscript evidence for and against the presence of *kyrios*. But since it is easier to understand why *kyrios* may have been introduced than it is to explain its omission, it is placed in brackets.

i. Since the preposition *syn* ("with") raises the problem of believers being raised with Jesus, who has already been raised, some manuscripts read *dia* ("through"), but "with" (supported by P^{46}, $\aleph^*$, B, C, D*) is the correct reading.

j. This word "converts" has been supplied to clarify what Paul means by *dia tōn pleionōn* ("through more and more").

k. The latter part of this verse can be rendered in several ways, since *dia tōn pleionōn* ("through more and more") can be taken with *pleonasasa* ("ever increasing") or with *perisseusē* ("might increase"). These words can be taken transitively or intransitively. In this translation *dia tōn pleionōn* is taken with *pleonasasa*, which, like *perisseusē*, is taken transitively.

These verses contain the first of three extended hardship lists in 2 Corinthians (see 6:4–10 and 11:23–33 for the other two). Paul employs this particular list of his sufferings and afflictions to show the paradoxical relationship between life and death in his apostolic ministry. The material can be divided into three subunits. In the first, Paul associates his sufferings with the death and dying of Jesus (vv. 7–12). In the second, he points to his faith in the resurrection of the dead (vv. 13–14) as the basis for his apostolic confidence. In the third, he indicates the ultimate purpose of his apostolic suffering (v. 15). The first and longest of these subunits (vv. 7–12) has three parts: a thematic statement in which Paul compares himself to an earthen vessel (v. 7), a hardship list consisting of eight artfully arranged participles (vv. 8–9), and Paul's explanation of his hardships in terms of the death and the life of Jesus (vv. 10–12).

[4:7] The opening verse of this unit (vv. 7–12) announces the theme of the entire section (4:7–5:10):The new covenant ministry that Paul has received is held in an earthen vessel so that it will be apparent that the surpassing power of the gospel he preaches comes from God and not from him. This earthen vessel is Paul's present bodily existence, which he describes in terms of the "outer self" (4:16) and his "earthly tent-like dwelling" (5:1). Thus, even though Paul will explicitly refer to his body (4:10) and to his mortal flesh (4:11), the metaphor of the earthen vessel designates his entire being: the weak and suffering apostle whom people see and disparage.

Paul's metaphor is open to several interpretations, since an earthen vessel is of its very nature inferior (2 Tim 2:20), ignoble (Lam 4:2), and disposable (Lev 6:28; 11:33), as well as fragile and easily broken (LXX Ps 30:13 = MT 31:12; Isa 30:14). For example, the contrast between the treasure and the earthen vessel points to the superiority of the former and the inferiority of the latter, whereas the description of Paul's apostolic sufferings in verses 8–9 suggests the notions of fragility and brokenness. Whatever the precise meaning of the metaphor, it is clear that Paul wants to establish a contrast between the vessel and the treasure that it holds, in order to show that power manifested through his ministry does not come from him but from God, thereby substantiating his earlier statement that it is God who has qualified him as the minister of a new covenant (3:6).

Although the immediate context points to "the knowledge of the glory of God on the face of [Jesus] Christ" (4:6) as the treasure that Paul bears, Paul communicates this treasure by "the light of the gospel of the glory of God" that he preaches (4:4), which is inseparable from the ministry that God has mercifully granted him (4:1). Accordingly, as with the metaphor of the earthen vessel, it is not necessary to be more precise about the treasure than is Paul himself (Furnish, 279). As the minister of a new covenant he presents himself as an inferior and fragile vessel that contains the treasure of the gospel through the new covenant ministry he exercises.

[8–9] Although Paul is a fragile earthen vessel of inferior quality (as are other apostolic ministers associated with him), the earthen vessel that he is has not been broken. To illustrate this, he rehearses a list of hardships that he has endured as an apostle of Christ. Skillfully constructed, this list consists of eight present passive participles that can be arranged in four strophes. In each pair, the first participle describes Paul's hardship (afflicted, bewildered, persecuted, struck down), and the second shows that the hardship has not overwhelmed him (not constrained, not in doubt, not forsaken, not destroyed). On first reading, it may appear that the list presents Paul in Stoic-like terms as someone who bravely endures the sufferings his ministry brings. However, Paul's thematic statement, "so that it may be evident that the extraordinary power is from God and not from us," and what he will say in verses 10–12 clearly indicate that his purpose is to show that his hardships paradoxically manifest the power of God.

B. The Integrity of Paul's Apostolic Ministry

In every way
we are afflicted but not constrained
bewildered but not in doubt
persecuted but not forsaken
struck down but not destroyed

The initial participle "afflicted" (*thlibomenoi*; v. 8a) is the most important and echoes the benediction of this letter, where Paul praises the God of all consolation, who comforts him in every affliction (1:3–7), the very God who rescued him from his great affliction in Asia (1:8–11). The concept of affliction also heads the longer hardship list of 6:4–10, describes Paul's state of mind when he arrived in Macedonia in search of Titus (7:5), and can be viewed as a general term for the many hardships of Paul's ministry.

The second strophe focuses on Paul's state of mind as "bewildered" (*aporoumenoi*; v. 8b), employing a word that he once used when he was utterly bewildered by the changed attitude of the Galatians toward him (Gal 4:20). Playing on this Greek word, he affirms that such bewilderment does not lead to embarrassment or "doubt" (*exaporoumenoi*; v. 8b). In the third strophe, Paul turns to the external hardships that come from being "persecuted" (*diōkomenoi*; v. 9a) and affirms that God has not "abandoned" (*enkataleipomenoi*) him. This word occurs frequently in the Old Testament, where God promises never to abandon his people (Gen 28:15; Deut 31:6, 8; 1 Chr 28:20; LXX Pss 15:10 = MT 16:10; 36:25; Sir 2:10). It is the same Greek word found in Jesus' great cry from the cross (Matt 27:46; Mark 15:34). Paul's hardship list, however, comes to its climax in the fourth and final strophe, where he portrays himself as struck down but not "destroyed" (*apollymenoi*; v. 9b). He has already employed this word to describe those who are on the way to destruction (2:15; 4:3) because they have not heeded the gospel, but here it takes on a more physical sense. Although Paul has been struck down, he is not "dead." Thus the list moves from a general concept of affliction to descriptions of internal and external hardships that culminate in the threat of death. Despite these afflictions, and as fragile as he is, Paul, the earthen vessel, is not broken.[28]

[10–12] Having presented a list of his hardships in verses 8–9, Paul now interprets these hardships in relation to himself (vv. 10–11) and in relation to the Corinthians (v. 12). In regard to himself, he affirms that he bears "the dying of Jesus" (*tēn nekrōsin tou Iēsou*) in his body so that "the life of Jesus" (*hē zōē tou*

---

28. The remark of John T. Fitzgerald (*Cracks in an Earthen Vessel*, 176) is apropos: "Viewed as a whole, then, the hardships that Paul lists in his catalogue have, as it were, caused cracks in him as an earthen vessel, but the vessel itself remains intact. The vessel is held together by the power of the divine adhesive, and the light that shines (4:5–6) through these cracks is none other than the light of the life of Jesus (4:10–11)."

Iēsou) might be manifested in his body (v. 10). Then in verse 11, employing a clause that begins with *gar* ("for"), he explains that he is being handed over "to death" (*eis thanaton*) in order that "the life of Jesus" (*hē zōē tou Iēsou*) might be manifested in his mortal flesh. Finally, in verse 12 Paul points to the result ("consequently," *hōste*) of his suffering for the Corinthians: while "death" (*ho thanatos*) is at work in him, "life" (*hē zōē*) is at work in them. The comparisons and contrasts that Paul establishes are best seen by arranging the material schematically:

v. 10 *always*
    bearing the DYING OF JESUS in our body
        so that
    the LIFE OF JESUS might be manifested in our body.
v. 11 *For continually*
    we, the living, are being handed over TO DEATH on account of Jesus,
        so that
    the LIFE OF JESUS might be manifested in our mortal flesh.
v. 12 *Consequently,*
    DEATH is at work in us but
    LIFE in you.

These verses indicate that Paul views the apostolic hardships listed in verses 8–9 in terms of Christ's death and resurrection or, as he writes, "the dying of Jesus" and "the life of Jesus." His sufferings are more than personal afflictions; they are a participation in the death and rising of Jesus. Despite them, or more accurately, *because of them*, the life of Jesus is manifested in Paul's body (*en tō sōmati hēmōn*; v. 10b), which he equates with his mortal flesh (*en tē thnētē sarki hēmōn*; v. 11b). The result of this process is that Paul's hardships effect "life" in the Corinthians, recalling what he said in the opening benediction, "If we are afflicted, it is *for* your consolation and salvation" (1:6).

Paul's opening statement, that he always bears "the dying" (*tēn nekrōsin*) of Jesus in his body so that the life of Jesus might be made manifest in his body, has always presented a problem for interpreters, since the only other use of *nekrōsis* in the New Testament is found in Rom 4:19 (the deadness of Sarah's womb) and in a variant reading of Mark 3:5 (the deadness of the hearts of Jesus' opponents). Although some commentators argue for this sense of deadness or mortification here as well, Paul's list of ongoing hardships suggests that he has purposely chosen this word to emphasize the ongoing process of dying that he experiences in his apostolic ministry through the hardships that he endures. By being afflicted, bewildered, persecuted, and struck down, he reflects in his person (his body) the kinds of sufferings that Jesus endured in his passion.[29] Such

---

29. On this point, see T. B. Savage, *Power through Weakness: Paul's Understanding of the Christian Ministry in 2 Corinthians* (SNTSMS 86; Cambridge: Cambridge University Press, 1996), 174–75.

B. The Integrity of Paul's Apostolic Ministry

suffering, however, is not an end in itself. Paul affirms that he bears the dying of Jesus, "so that" (*hina*) the life of Jesus might be manifested in the same body that bears the dying of Jesus. What he claims here can be understood only in light of the paradox of Christ's death and resurrection, which Paul clearly states in 13:4: "he was crucified by reason of weakness, but he lives by reason of the power of God." Put another way, Paul cannot manifest the life of Jesus apart from bearing the *nekrōsis* of Jesus, since it is precisely in weakness that God manifests power.[30]

The use of "Jesus" (four times in vv. 10–11) echoes a similar usage in 4:5. However, the manner in which Paul speaks of "the life of Jesus" as well as "the dying of Jesus" indicates that he is not drawing a distinction between "Jesus" and "Christ," as if "Jesus" represented the earthly figure and "Christ" the risen Lord.[31] Rather, he uses "Jesus" in order to draw attention to the sufferings of Jesus on the cross that resulted in life for Jesus as, Paul hopes, they will for himself.

Having stated that he always bears the *nekrōsis* of Jesus, Paul now writes that he is "continually" (*aei*) being "handed over to death" (*eis thanaton paradidometha*) on account of Jesus so that the life of Jesus might be made manifest in his mortal flesh (v. 11). The vocabulary of "being handed over" is the same language that the Synoptic Gospels employ, especially in their passion predictions, to describe the fate of Jesus (Mark 9:31; 10:33–34). Paul also employs this language when speaking of Jesus being handed over to death (Rom 4:25; 8:32; 1 Cor 11:23). The use of this vocabulary here, in reference to Paul, indicates that he is once more associating his fate with the fate of Jesus who died on the cross. But whereas he employed *nekrōsis* in verse 10, here he uses the more familiar Greek term for death, *thanatos*, since he has in view his final fate, rather than the daily dying that he endures by his hardships. He is being handed over so that the life of Jesus might be manifested in his "mortal flesh." The flesh, like the body, is the whole person, "the outer self" that one can see. The description of this flesh as "mortal," however, highlights its fragility in the face of death, the last and greatest enemy.

Paul's final statement (v. 12) draws out the consequences of his apostolic suffering: death is at work in him and life in them. The implication of this terse statement is that it is Paul's apostolic sufferings that effect life for the community. In claiming this, Paul is not substituting himself or his sufferings for Christ; for he is keenly aware that it was Christ who suffered and died for humanity, but he is making a rather striking claim for his apostolic ministry, indicating

---

30. Steven J. Kraftchick writes, "Paul argues not only that the treasure can be found in earthen vessels but that it must be. To be a message about this event and therefore to properly present it, the gospel requires a form consonant with its content, whether in the type of speech employed or in the one speaking" ("Death in Us, Life in You: The Apostolic Medium," in *Pauline Theology*, Vol. 2: *1 and 2 Corinthians* [ed. David M. Hay; Minneapolis: Fortress, 1993], 172).

31. The point is made by Savage, *Power through Weakness*, 172.

that the relationship between the community and its apostolic minister is not merely reciprocal (Hafemann, 186). As the minister of a new covenant, his ministry makes the life of Jesus present to the community by the hardships he endures (cf. 4:5). When the community fully understands the hardships that its apostle endures on its behalf, then it will see and participate in the life of Jesus that these sufferings manifest. This life is the life that Jesus already enjoys in virtue of his resurrection and that is making its appearance in the life of apostolic ministers and believers who are being transformed day by day (vv. 16–18).

[13–14] Having presented a list of his apostolic hardships (vv. 8–9) and explained their significance for him and the Corinthians, in verses 13–14 Paul explicitly refers to the resurrection, in order to indicate that his faith in the God who raises the dead undergirds his preaching of the gospel. Just as the psalmist spoke because he believed, so Paul speaks (preaches) because he believes that the God who raised Jesus will raise him with Jesus and present him, with the Corinthians, before God. His faith in the resurrection of the dead, then, allows Paul to die every day, as he notes in 1 Cor 15:30–31.

Paul's quotation comes from the opening words of Ps 115 (LXX), "I believed, therefore, I spoke," which is different from its Hebrew counterpart, Ps 116:10, "I kept my faith," but also more amenable to what Paul wants to say here.[32] Psalms 114 and 115 in the Septuagint describe the thanksgiving of a righteous sufferer whom the Lord has rescued. Although the righteous sufferer was surrounded by death (LXX Ps 114:3), the Lord delivered his soul from death (LXX Ps 114:8). The righteous sufferer now offers a sacrifice of praise to God who delivered him (LXX Ps 115:8). Although Paul quotes only the opening words of LXX Ps 115, the whole of the psalm can be viewed as a description of Paul's own experience of suffering. Like the righteous sufferer of the psalm, he has come to the abyss of death, but time and again God has delivered him (LXX Ps 115:1).

Although the righteous sufferer of the psalm does not explicitly say what he believed, Paul does, suggesting that he and the psalmist share a common faith in the God who raises the dead. This is why Paul writes that he has "the same spirit of faith, corresponding to what is written, 'I believed, therefore, I spoke.'" If "the same spirit" refers to the Spirit of God, whom Paul has mentioned throughout chapter 3, then Paul means that his faith is generated by the same Spirit that generated the faith of the psalmist. But if Paul intends the disposition of faith, then he means that he has the same kind of faith as the psalmist. The preference of this commentary is for the latter interpretation, but the first cannot be excluded.

---

32. In the Septuagint the Hebrew text of Ps 116 is divided into two psalms: Ps 114 and Ps 115. LXX Ps 114:1–9 corresponds to MT Ps 116:1–9; and LXX Ps 115:1–10 corresponds to the MT Psalm 116:10–19. Accordingly, LXX Ps 115:1 corresponds to the MT Ps 116:10.

B. The Integrity of Paul's Apostolic Ministry

Although some have tried to argue for a more existential interpretation of resurrection at this point—God will raise Paul up from his present humiliating circumstances and present him to the community—it is more likely that Paul has in view the general resurrection of the dead,[33] a topic that he has already addressed in 1 Cor 15, and which he will discuss in 2 Cor 5:1–10 from a different perspective. The one who raised Jesus from the dead is the God who raises the dead (1:9), and he will raise us "with Jesus and present us with you." In writing that God will "raise us with Jesus," Paul does not mean that Jesus has not yet been raised from the dead. Rather, as God raised Jesus from the dead, so God will raise Paul (and other believers) to be with the risen Christ. At the moment of resurrection, God will also bring forth Paul, with the Corinthians, presumably for judgment (see 5:10, where all must appear before the judgment seat of Christ).

[15] Having explained how his faith in the resurrection undergirds his apostolic preaching, Paul returns to a theme that he introduced in verse 12, where he explained how life is at work in the Corinthians because death is at work in him. Now he writes that everything is for their sake (v. 15a). Thus Paul reinforces what he wrote in 4:5: that he preaches Jesus Christ as Lord and himself as their slave. The ultimate purpose of serving the Corinthians, however, is God's glory (v. 15b). As the grace of God overflows through an ever-increasing number of people turning to the Lord by Paul's apostolic ministry, grace will effect even greater thanksgiving for God's glory. Thus Paul views his apostolic hardships within the full scope of salvation history. The sufferings are his share in the dying of Jesus and already manifest Jesus' resurrection life. When properly understood, they produce life in those who hear the gospel. As more and more people receive the gospel, thanks to Paul's ministry, God's grace leads to greater thanksgiving and glory for God. Paul, however, has not yet explained how such suffering can coexist with glory in the life of the apostolic minister. To this topic he now turns.

b. Present Transformation (4:16–18)

4:16 Therefore, we are not discouraged. But even if our outer person is decaying, our inner person[a] is being renewed day by day.[b] 17 For our present slight affliction is producing for us an eternal fullness[c] of glory

---

33. Lambrecht ("The Nekrōsis of Jesus: Ministry and Suffering in 2 Cor 4,7-15," and "The Eschatological Outlook in 2 Corinthians 4,7–15," in *Studies on 2 Corinthians* [BETL 112; Leuven: Leuven University Press, 1994], 309–33 and 335–49) argues persuasively on behalf of an eschatological outlook, against the positions of E. Güttgemanns, N. Baumert, and J. Murphy-O'Connor, who in different ways argue for a more existential interpretation of the resurrection at this point. For texts that refer to God raising Jesus from the dead, see Rom 8:11; 10:9; 1 Cor 6:14; 15:15, 20; 2 Cor 13:4; Gal 1:1. For texts that refer to believers being raised with Christ, see Rom 6:5; 8:11; 1 Cor 6:14.

beyond all measure[d] 18 as we fix our attention[e] not on what is seen but on what is not seen; for what is seen is transitory; what is not seen is eternal.

a. "Person" is supplied since a literal reading of the Greek would be "our inward" (*ho esō hēmōn*).
b. Literally, "day and day" (*hēmera kai hēmera*).
c. The literal meaning of the Greek is "weight" (*baros*). Paul may be employing the word here because the notion of God's "glory" (*doxa*; *kabod*) is related to weight or heaviness. The sense here, however, is "fullness."
d. The Greek phrase is cumbersome. Rendered literally it means "through excess for excess" (*kath' hyperbolēn eis hyperbolēn*). The phrase suggests an ever-increasing abundance of glory.
e. This phrase translates a genitive absolute (*skopountōn hēmōn*) that indicates what believers are doing as they are being transformed: fixing their attention on what is eternal.

These verses are transitional in nature (Thrall, 1:347). On the one hand, they draw a conclusion from what Paul has said in 4:7–15, as the opening phrase indicates: "therefore, we are not discouraged" (*dio ouk enkakoumen*). On the other hand, they are the basis for the argument that will follow in 5:1–10, as the first words of that unit indicate, "for we know" (*oidamen gar*). Consequently, it is not surprising that whereas some commentators view 4:7–18 (Barrett) as a single unit, others see 4:16–5:5 (Furnish) or 4:16–5:10 (Lambrecht) as a unit. This commentary treats these verses as a discrete unit because 4:16–18 describes *the present transformation* that Paul is already experiencing, whereas 4:7–15 focuses on his *daily apostolic sufferings* and 5:1–10 on *the final transformation* that he will enjoy when he is clothed with a heavenly habitation.

These three verses contain a number of contrasts. In verse 16 there is a contrast between "the outer person" and "the inner person" that is related to Paul's description of his hardships in verses 8–9. In verse 17 there is a contrast between "affliction" and "glory" that echoes what Paul has said about these terms in 3:18 and 4:8. Finally, in verse 18 there is a contrast between "what is seen" and "what is not seen" that prepares for Paul's discussion of the "earthly tent-like dwelling" and the "eternal building" in 5:1–5.

In terms of structure, verse 16 states the theme of the unit: the inner person is already being renewed. Verses 17–18 provide substantiating arguments for the theme.

[4:16] Although Paul claims that he (and all believers) are being transformed from glory to glory (3:18), he has not yet explained how this is happening in his life or the life of believers. Moreover, his discussion of apostolic suffering in 4:7–15 seems to have exacerbated the problem; for, if his ministry is one of constant hardship, where is the glory of his new covenant ministry that he so boldly announced in chapter 3? Apparently aware of this, Paul explains that as

B. The Integrity of Paul's Apostolic Ministry

his "outer person" is wasting away, his "inner person" is being renewed daily.

The first term, "our outer person" (*ho exō hēmōn anthrōpos*), is the only occurrence of this expression in Paul's writings, but in light of what he has just said in 4:7–15, and in light of what he writes here, his meaning should be clear. The outer person is what the world sees, "the earthen vessel" that is "afflicted," "bewildered," "persecuted," and "struck down" (4:8–9). The "outer person" is one's being and personality, in all of its weakness and grandeur, as externally present to the world (Allo, 135). In terms of Pauline anthropology, the "outer person" is the human being as "body" (*sōma*). Although the human being as "outer self" often participates in the being of "the old human" (*ho palaios anthrōpos*; see Rom 6:6; Eph 4:22; Col 3:9 for occurrences of this term), the two concepts are not interchangeable. Whereas Paul employs "the old human" to speak of humanity under the power of sin, there is no such moral connotation in his use of "the outer person." All human beings have an "outer self," because they are embodied beings.

Paul's concept of the "inner person" is more difficult to clarify, even though it occurs elsewhere (Rom 7:22; Eph 3:16), because he is speaking of a reality that cannot be seen.[34] The contrast that he establishes between the outer and inner person, however, indicates that the inner person refers to the whole person but from another perspective. The inner person is the embodied person as viewed from God's point of view, from the perspective of faith. The inner person is the unseen reality of the embodied person that has the possibility of being renewed. The inner person, however, is not fully coterminous with "the new person" (*kainos/neos anthrōpos*; Eph 2:15; 4:24; Col 3:10) or the "new creation" (*kainē ktisis*; 2 Cor 5:17; Gal 6:15). For whereas the inner person delights in God's law (Rom 7:22), the inner person still experiences inner conflict (Rom 7:23–24). Nevertheless, the two concepts are related, inasmuch as "the new human" is one whose "inner person" has been renewed.

In light of these concepts, Paul writes that even though the world sees his embodied self as wasting away, the self that cannot be seen and is inseparable from the body is being renewed each day. How?

[17–18] Paul's answer to the question raised above comes in these verses. Employing the kind of paradoxical language distinctive of his theology, he asserts it is precisely his afflictions that are producing "an eternal fullness of glory beyond all measure" (v. 17). The paradox that he employs here is similar to the paradox found in 4:10–11, where he affirms that he bears the dying of

---

34. A similar term appears in Plato's *Republic* (9:588), *ho entos anthrōpos* ("the inner person"), which is opposed to the *to exō elytron* ("the outer covering"). Scholars are in general agreement that Paul is indebted to Hellenistic thought for this terminology, though he seems to have given it his own meaning. It is not clear, however, how he became acquainted with this terminology. On this point, see Hans Dieter Betz, "The Concept of the 'Inner Human Being' (*ho esō anthrōpos*) in the Anthropology of Paul," *NTS* 46 (2000): 315–41, as well as the very helpful excursus by Allo, 134–37.

Jesus in order to manifest the life of Jesus, and that he is being handed over to death in order that the life of Jesus might be manifested in his mortal flesh. Given the paradoxical nature of apostolic ministry, as Paul views it, those who view affliction as unworthy of the apostolic minister or the Christian life cannot participate in the glory of the new covenant, a glory that is as inseparably wedded to affliction as is life to death.

Although Paul has his own apostolic hardships in view, what he writes here is applicable to all members of the new covenant community. When Paul says that believers are being transformed "from glory to glory" (3:18), the locus of this transformation is the "inner person." Consequently one does not see the external glory of authentic apostolic ministers or of the members of the new covenant community apart from the suffering and afflictions they endure. For Paul this glory is so real that the hardships he presently endures are insignificant and transitory in view of the glory that is already transforming his inner person.

Paul's argument finds its climax in the aphorism that "what is seen is transitory; what is not seen is eternal" (v. 18). The aphorism, of course, is an argument based not on reason or logic but on faith in the resurrection. For those who accept the Pauline view of reality, it serves as the clinching argument: what is not seen and what will endure is the inner person who is being transformed by God's glory; what is seen and will pass away is the outer person that is being sorely afflicted. Paul's thought is best summarized by outlining the contrasts that he establishes:

The Outer Person	*The Inner Person*
wasting away	renewed day by day
present affliction	eternal glory
seen	not seen
transitory	eternal

c. Final Transformation (5:1–10)

5:1 For we know that when our earthly tent-like dwelling[a] is destroyed we have a building from God, an eternal dwelling in the heavens, not made by human hands.[b] 2 For in this body[c] we sigh as we long to be clothed over[d] with our heavenly dwelling. 3 And if indeed we are clothed[e] we will not be found naked. 4 For while in this[f] tent we sigh, being oppressed, because we do not want to be unclothed but clothed over, so that what is mortal may be swallowed up by life. 5 The one who has prepared us for this very thing is God,[g] who has given us the Spirit as a pledge.[h]

6 Therefore, we are always confident and know that while at home in the body we are away[i] from the Lord, 7 for we live by faith and not by

B. The Integrity of Paul's Apostolic Ministry

what is seen.[j] 8 But we are confident and prefer to be away from the body and at home to the Lord.

9 Therefore, we aspire to be pleasing to him whether at home or away.[k] 10 For all of us must appear[l] before the judgment seat[m] of Christ, so that each may receive a recompense,[n] corresponding to what he has done in life,[o] whether good or worthless.[p]

a. The Greek is somewhat convoluted, "our earthly dwelling of the tent." The sense is that our earthly dwelling is as fragile as a tent. See 1 Chr 9:23 for a similar phrase.

b. The Greek word *acheiropoiētos* ("not made by hands") is relatively rare in the New Testament (but see its use in Mark 14:58 and Col 2:11). The sense is that what is not made by human hands comes from God (see v. 5). In this case, the reference is to the resurrection body.

c. A word needs to be supplied here. Since Paul is contrasting the earthly and heavenly body, "body" is appropriate. Some commentators (Bultmann, 133), however, take *en toutō* to mean "therefore," "for this reason."

d. The meaning of the Greek word *ependyomai*, according to BDAG, is to put a garment over an existing garment; in this case, the resurrection body over the earthly body.

e. While the text of D* reads *ekdysamenoi* ("unclothed"), the texts of P^{46}, ℵ, B, C, D^2 read *endysamenoi* ("clothed"). Although this second reading is somewhat tautological (if we are clothed, we will not be naked), it has the stronger manuscript evidence in its favor. The other reading may have arisen to avoid this tautology (if we are unclothed, we will not be naked because we will be clothed with the resurrection body). See the discussion in Metzger, *A Textual Commentary on the Greek New Testament* (United Bible Societies, 1971), 579–80.

f. A word needs to be supplied. "This" is supplied by some manuscripts (D, F, G) but it is probably not the best reading.

g. The phrase could be translated, "God is the one. . . ." This translation puts "God" at the end of the phrase for the sake of emphasis, as does the Greek.

h. The Greek reads "the pledge of the Spirit" (*ton arrabōn tou pneumatos*). The sense is that the Spirit is the "down payment" or "installment" of the fullness of salvation.

i. The Greek word *ekdēmeō* ("to be away") originally referred to leaving one's country to take a long journey (BDAG). Paradoxically, then, being at home in the body means being away from one's true home, which is with the Lord.

j. The Greek word *eidos* usually means "form" or "outward appearance." In an active sense it may mean "sight" or "seeing." Thrall (1:389) argues persuasively for the first sense, which would then refer to the form of the exalted, glorious Christ.

k. To be "at home" is to be alive in the body; to be "away" is to have left one's earthly body.

l. The Greek verb *phanerōthēnai* can also be translated "be revealed." Thus one's life will be revealed at the moment of judgment.

m. The Greek word *bēma* refers to a tribunal or judicial bench, usually set on a dais.

n. A literal reading of the Greek would be "so that each one may receive the things according to what he did through the body." The sense of the phrase seems to imply a "recompense" for what a person did in life.

o. The Greek reads *dia tou sōmatos* ("through the body").

p. The reading *phaulon* ("worthless" or "base") is found in ℵ, C. The reading one might expect, *kakon* ("bad"), is found in P⁴⁶, B, D, F, G.

Verses 1–10 may well be the most thoroughly studied text of 2 Corinthians. Despite the abundant commentary on these verses, there is little agreement among commentators about their precise meaning.[35] The basic problem concerns the relationship of these verses to 1 Cor 15, the chapter in which Paul provides the Corinthians with his most extensive teaching on the resurrection of the dead. In that passage, Paul coordinates the time of the general resurrection of the dead with the time of Christ's parousia: when Christ returns, those who have died in him will be raised and clothed with a resurrection body, and those who are still alive at the parousia will be changed and similarly clothed (1 Cor 15:51–57). If Paul is referring to the resurrection body in 2 Cor 5, as most commentators maintain, a number of questions arise. Does his teaching in 2 Cor 5 agree with what he has written in 1 Cor 15, or has there been a change in his understanding of what happens to believers after death? If Paul's teaching in 2 Cor 5 coheres with that of 1 Cor 15, why does he use the new metaphor of the building from God to describe the resurrection body? If it does not cohere with 1 Cor 15, why has he changed his view, and what is his new perspective on the resurrection of the dead? Is Paul saying that believers receive the resurrection body immediately after death, or is he implying that there is an intermediate state between death and the general resurrection during which believers are disembodied but somehow with the Lord?

This commentary argues that there has not been a major shift in Paul's thinking about the resurrection of the dead and the fate of believers between the writing of 1 Corinthians and the writing of 2 Corinthians. But since Paul is now responding to a new situation—the wasting away of his earthly body on account

---

35. In an excursus that still remains valuable, Allo (137–54) summarizes six major theories about the meaning of these verses: (1) they express Paul's weariness of the present life; (2) they express Paul's fear of being found naked, i.e., without a resurrection body; (3) they express Paul's hope for an immediate parousia so that he will not be found "naked"; (4) they express Paul's belief in the immediate possession of the glorious body after death; (5) they develop Paul's thought about an intermediate state between death and the final resurrection; (6) they play down the interval between now and the final resurrection because of Paul's great ardor to be with Christ. In a more recent article John Gillman ("A Thematic Comparison: 1 Cor 15:50–57 and 2 Cor 5:1–5," *JBL* 107 [1988]: 439–54) summarizes current approaches under three headings: (1) interpretations that see a major shift in Paul's thought between 1 Cor 15 and 2 Cor 5; (2) interpretations that argue for a consistency in Paul's thought between 1 Cor 15 and 2 Cor 5; (3) interpretations that argue that there is a difference in subject matter between 1 Cor 15 and 2 Cor 5. For a detailed study of different approaches to these verses, see F. G. Lang, *2 Korinther 5,1–10 in der neueren Forschung* (BGBE 16; Tübingen: Mohr-Siebeck, 1973). The background material in the commentaries of Furnish and Thrall is also helpful for the study of this text.

B. The Integrity of Paul's Apostolic Ministry

of his apostolic suffering—he employs a different metaphor to speak about the resurrection body.[36] It is important, then, as most commentators caution, to read these verses in light of their context and not in isolation from that context, as if Paul were simply discoursing about the resurrection of the dead (Furnish, 291).

In terms of context, 5:1–10 is the third movement in Paul's discussion about his apostolic suffering (4:7–15 and 4:16–18 being the first two), and it is related to that material in several ways. First, the opening statement of 5:1 ("For we know that") indicates that Paul is providing a further reason why he is not discouraged by his afflictions (4:16). Second, the metaphor of his body as an "earthly tent-like dwelling" (5:1) corresponds to the metaphor of his body as an "earthen vessel" (4:7) and to the description of his "outer person" (4:16) as wasting away. Third, Paul's hope that what is mortal will "be swallowed up by life" (5:4) develops the theme of death and life at work in his mortal flesh (4:10–11), as well as his conviction that his "present slight affliction" is producing "an eternal fullness of glory" (4:16–18). Fourth, Paul's confidence that God has already given him the Spirit as a pledge of future glory (5:5) is a more explicit statement of what he has already said about his inner person being renewed day by day as affliction paradoxically produces glory (4:16–17). Fifth, Paul's affirmation that he walks by faith and not by what is seen (5:7) echoes what he says about what is seen and what is not seen (4:18). Finally, Paul's longing to be clothed with a resurrection body (5:2–4) and his conviction that all must appear before the judgment seat of Christ (5:10) develop the statement of 4:14 that "the one who raised the [Lord] Jesus will also raise us with Jesus and present us with you." To summarize, the contacts between this material and what precedes show that what Paul says here is intimately related to his reflection on apostolic suffering and should not be interpreted apart from that material.

In terms of structure, this unit consists of two parts. The first (vv. 1–5) deals most directly with the issue of the resurrection body for which the believer sighs. It can be divided into a number of subunits: a thematic statement that contrasts the present body with the resurrection body (v. 1), a description of Paul's longing to be clothed with the resurrection body (vv. 2–4), and an affirmation that God has prepared this resurrection body for the believer (v. 5). The second part of the unit (vv. 6–10) describes the situation of believers as they long to be with the Lord, aware that they must stand before his judgment seat. It can also be divided into two subunits: the present situation of not yet being at home with the Lord (vv. 6–8); and the judgment that everyone must face (vv. 9–10).

---

36. In 1 Cor 15, Paul must address the following questions: Will the dead rise (15:12)? How will they rise, and what kind of bodies will they have (15:35)? In responding to these questions, he provides the Corinthians with a cosmic description of the end-time events that coordinates the general resurrection of the dead with Christ's parousia. In 2 Corinthians, Paul can presuppose that the Corinthians know this teaching and, in light of it, he explains his hope and confidence despite the sufferings that his ministry brings.

[5:1] This verse serves as the thematic statement for what follows, establishing a contrast between the "earthly tent-like dwelling" that is always in danger of being destroyed and "a building from God, an eternal dwelling in the heavens, not made by human hands." Although the contrast is clear (what is transitory and what is permanent), the precise meaning of the metaphor is disputed. On the one hand, commentators are in general agreement that the "earthly tent-like dwelling" refers to the human person (and here specifically to Paul) in his or her present bodily existence. Accordingly, it should be related to what Paul has already said about himself as "an earthen vessel" (4:7) and about his "outer person" that is wasting away (4:16). The tent metaphor clearly points to the fragility of human existence that can be destroyed and collapsed like a tent at any moment (see the use of the metaphor in Wis 9:15 and 2 Pet 1:13–14). On the other hand, the significance of the "building from God, an eternal dwelling, not made by hands," is more problematic. Although most commentators take it as a metaphor of permanence that refers to the glorious resurrection body, others argue that it refers to God's heavenly eschatological temple or to the body of the risen Christ into whom believers will be incorporated at death.[37] The adjective "not made by human hands" (*acheiropoiētos*) occurs in Mark 14:58 in reference to God's eschatological temple, but the broader context suggests that Paul has the glorious resurrection body in view, since he has just articulated his faith in the resurrection of the dead (4:14), and since the transformation of the inner self (4:16–17) anticipates what will be completed at the resurrection of the dead. Accordingly the metaphors of the fragile tent and the permanent heavenly dwelling are best taken as referring to the earthly embodied self, on the one hand, and the gloriously resurrected body-self, on the other.

In 1 Cor 15:21–23 Paul coordinates the general resurrection of the dead with the parousia of Christ: when Christ returns, then the dead will be raised (see 1 Thess 4:16). Here the present tense of the verb "we have" (*echomen*) could suggest that the resurrection body is *already* prepared and waiting for the believer, so that believers will receive their resurrection body at death. If this is the case, then Paul has altered his understanding of the resurrection of the dead as described in 1 Cor 15. This seems unlikely, however, since one would expect Paul to articulate such an important change in a more explicit manner. It is more likely that the present tense emphasizes Paul's firm conviction in what God has in store for him at the general resurrection of the dead. If his present bodily existence is destroyed—and it surely will be, since the outer self is wasting

---

37. So J.-F. Collange, *Énigmes de la deuxième épître de Paul aux Corinthiens: Étude Exegetique de 2 Cor. 2:14–7:4* (SNTSMS 18; Cambridge: Cambridge University Press, 1972), 181–93; E. E. Ellis, "II Corinthians V.1–10 in Pauline Eschatology," *NTS* 6 (1959–60): 211–24; Furnish, *II Corinthians*, 293–95; Harvey, *Renewal through Suffering*, 66–69.

B. The Integrity of Paul's Apostolic Ministry

away—he knows that God has prepared a permanent form of bodily existence for him: the resurrection body that will be disclosed at the general resurrection of the dead.

[2–4] In these verses Paul expresses his longing and desire to be "clothed over" with the heavenly dwelling that is the resurrection body. The new metaphor of being "clothed over" (*ependysasthai*) is the same metaphor he employs in 1 Cor 15:53–54, where he speaks of what is corruptible and mortal (one's present bodily existence) "putting" on (*endysasthai*) what is incorruptible and immortal (one's resurrection bodily existence), another indication that Paul is speaking here of the resurrection body. The introduction of this metaphor results in a mixed metaphor: being clothed over with a building. Nonetheless it serves Paul's purpose by pointing to the continuity between the fragile tent, which is not simply set aside but "covered over," and the permanent vesture, which is the building from God: the resurrection body.[38]

In terms of structure, these three verses form a chiasm with the central verse (v. 3) being the most problematic. In verses 2 and 4 Paul "sighs" (*stenazomen*) to be "clothed over" (*ependysasthai*) with his resurrection body, and in verse 3 he affirms that if he is "clothed over" (see the notes for the textual problem), he will not be found "naked" (*gymnoi*). The progression of Paul's thought can be outlined in this way:

v. 2 Paul *sighs* to be *clothed over* with his heavenly dwelling.
    v. 3 If *clothed over*, he will *not* be found *naked*.
v. 4 Paul *sighs* to be *clothed over*, oppressed as he is.
    He does not want to be *unclothed* but *clothed over*
    so that what is mortal may be swallowed up by life.

As the outline shows, the basic contrast is between being "clothed over" and being "unclothed," which v. 3 expresses as being found "naked." From what has already been said, it should be apparent that the state of "being clothed" refers to what occurs with the coming of the resurrection body. What is not so apparent is what Paul means by being "unclothed" or "naked." Some interpret "nakedness" in a moral sense as being without the righteousness with which one must be clothed before the tribunal of Christ (Calvin, 67), but others argue that Paul is fearful of being found "naked," that is, without a body, being in a disembodied state, should he die before the parousia and the general resurrection of the dead. Although the first interpretation coheres with what Paul writes

---

38. John Gillman, "A Thematic Comparison: 1 Cor 15:50–57 and 2 Cor 5:1–5," argues that by employing this clothing imagery in 2 Cor 5:3–4 Paul is elaborating upon the transformation imagery found in 1 Cor 15:50–57. In other words, the imagery of "being clothed over" expresses the notion of the earthly body being changed or transformed at the general resurrection of the dead.

in verse 10 about all standing before the tribunal of Christ, it does not cohere with the contrast Paul establishes in verses 1–5 between present bodily existence and the glorious resurrection body. And although the second interpretation coheres better with verses 1–5, it reads something into the text that is not explicitly there: the fate of those who die before the parousia.[39]

In light of what Paul has already said about his apostolic sufferings (4:7–15) and his inner person wasting away (4:16–18), the "nakedness" to which he refers here is best understood in terms of death, which is the ultimate destruction of the "earthen vessel" and the "outer person." In the face of this threat Paul affirms that he will not be found "naked," for he will be "covered over" with the resurrection body. In affirming this, Paul is not so much making a statement about what happens to people "between" the moment of death and resurrection, as he is affirming his hope in the resurrection (4:14) that God will not leave him naked (conquered by death), because God has prepared him for this heavenly building, his resurrection body.

Paul's thought in these verses can be summarized in this manner. In verse 2 he points to his sighing to be clothed over or transformed by the resurrection body as yet another reason why he looks to what is not seen rather than to what is seen (4:18). In verse 3 he introduces a parenthetical comment to substantiate what he has just said: the fact that he will be clothed over with the resurrection body is his assurance that he will not be found naked, overcome by death, when his outer person wastes away (4:16). Finally, in verse 4, Paul elaborates on verses 2 and 3. While oppressed, he sighs. In doing so, he still longs for the resurrection body because when he receives that body, everything that is mortal in his present existence will be swallowed up by life. The final words of this verse (v. 4c) relate what Paul writes here to what he wrote in 1 Cor 15:54, "When the perishable body puts on imperishability, and this mortal body puts on immortality, then the saying that is written will be fulfilled: '*Death has been swallowed up in victory*'"[40] (emphasis added). But whereas in 1 Cor 15:54 "death" is swallowed up in "victory," here "what is mortal" is swallowed up by "life." In light of what Paul writes in 4:10–12, he clearly means that the mortal aspects of human existence will be swallowed up by the resurrection life of Christ. Because of his confidence that resurrection life will be victorious, he longs for the resurrection body that will "cover over" his mortal body, thereby transforming all that is mortal.

[5] Paul brings the first half of this unit to a conclusion by affirming the central role of God in the work of raising the dead, thereby recalling his earlier

---

39. Paul alludes to this question in 1 Thess 4:13–18, where he discusses the fate of those who have died before the parousia, but he does not describe the state of the dead between their death and Christ's parousia.

40. On this text, see the important study of Lambrecht, "La vie engloutit ce qui est mortel. Commentaire de 2 Corinthiens 5:4c," *Studies on 2 Corinthians*, 351–61.

B. The Integrity of Paul's Apostolic Ministry

description of God as "the God who raises the dead" (1:9). He notes that it is God who has prepared us[41] for "this very thing" (being clothed over with the heavenly habitation) by giving us the Spirit as a pledge. In writing that God has "prepared us" and "given us," Paul employs the aorist tense, which points to a definitive action in the past—the event of Christ's death and resurrection. Thus God "prepared" (*katergasamenos*) believers for the general resurrection of the dead when he "gave" (*dous*) them the gift of the Spirit that Paul describes as a "pledge" (*arrabōna*), the same concept he employed in 1:22.

By saying that God has prepared believers for resurrection life by giving them the Spirit as a "pledge," Paul means that the presence of the Spirit in the life of believers is the first installment or down payment of the fullness of life that will come with the resurrection of the dead. Paul makes a similar point in Rom 8:22–23, where he writes, "We know that the whole creation has been groaning (*systenazei*) in labor pains until now; and not only the creation, but we ourselves, who have the first fruits (*aparchēn*) of the Spirit, groan (*stenazomen*) inwardly while we wait for adoption, the redemption (*apolytrōsin*) of our bodies."[42] Although Paul does not explicitly use resurrection language here, "the redemption of our bodies" clearly points to the resurrection of the dead, when the body of the believer will be fully redeemed because it will have been changed and transformed by the power of God's Spirit. In the meantime, the believer enjoys the gift of the Spirit, which is the "first fruit" of the full harvest.[43] In Rom 8:11 Paul writes, "If the Spirit of him who raised Jesus from the dead dwells in you, he who raised Christ from the dead will give life to your mortal bodies also through his Spirit that dwells in you." Though Paul wrote Romans after 2 Corinthians, Romans clearly shows his thinking about the relationship between God's Spirit and the resurrection of the dead: God will raise from the dead those in whom the Spirit dwells.

What Paul says about the Spirit here, however, must also be read in light of what he has already written about his new covenant ministry of the Spirit. Because he is the minister of a new covenant, the resurrection of the dead is an integral part of his gospel; and because the people of this new covenant have turned to the Lord who is the Spirit (3:16–17), they are being transformed from

---

41. Throughout vv. 1–10, Paul constantly employs the first person plural: "we," "us." Although he is still defending his apostolic ministry, his subject (the resurrection of the dead) suggests that he has all believers in view.

42. Paul uses the same language of "sighing" here that he employs in vv. 2 and 4. This is another indication that he has the resurrection of the dead in view, since the sighing in Romans does have the resurrection in view.

43. Although Paul employs the metaphor of the "first fruits" in Romans, it serves the same function as the metaphor of the "pledge" in 2 Corinthians: the first fruits is the promise of the future harvest, the resurrection of the dead, just as the "pledge" of the Spirit is the "down payment" for full delivery, the resurrection of the dead.

glory to glory (3:18). In effect, God has prepared believers for "this very thing" (the resurrection) by Paul's new covenant ministry, which proclaims the gospel of the glory of Christ (4:4).

[6–8] With these verses, Paul draws a conclusion grounded in his hope of being clothed over with the resurrection body. He is always confident, even though he is presently "in the body" and not yet at home with the Lord, because his hope in the resurrection assures him that he will be with the Lord. As with verses 3–4, there is a chiastic structure to these verses. Whereas verses 6 and 8 use the language of "being at home" (*endēmeō*) and "being away" (*ekdēmeō*), verse 7 interprets them in terms of walking by faith rather than by what is seen. The material can be outlined in this way:

v. 6 *We are confident and know*
    at home in the body   *away from* the Lord
v. 7 *We live by faith*   not by what is seen
v. 8 *We are confident and prefer*
    to be *away from* the body   *at home* with the Lord

As the outline shows, there is a strong contrast between being "at home in the body" and being "away from the Lord." In verse 6 Paul speaks of being at home in the body and away from the Lord, but in verse 8 he reverses this language and speaks of his preference to be away from the body and at home with the Lord. This corresponds with contrasts that he developed in the first part of this unit between his "earthly tent-like dwelling" and the "eternal dwelling not made by human hands" (5:1). Paul knows that as long as he dwells in his present earthly form of existence, he will be in exile from the Lord. And so, given a choice, he would prefer to reverse this situation and be exiled from the body and at home with the Lord. However, Paul realizes that he does not have the power to effect this change, since he cannot simply decide to leave the body and be with the Lord. Consequently, he explains the nature of his present circumstances as living by faith rather than by what is seen, thereby recalling what he wrote in 4:18 about fixing his attention on what is not seen rather than on what is seen. "What is not seen" is not only the "inner person" but the resurrection body and the "form" (*eidous*; v. 7) of the risen Christ.

For some commentators verses 6–8 are an indication that Paul is thinking of some sort of intermediate state before the general resurrection of the dead, when the Christian is with the Lord in what can only be called a disembodied state. If so, Paul would be expressing his preference to be with the Lord, even if it means being in a disembodied state prior to the resurrection of the dead. Although this is possible, given what Paul says about his desire to be with the Lord in Phil 1:23, it is hardly the plain sense of the text, which focuses on Paul's present state of existence and his desire to be with the Lord. In other words,

B. The Integrity of Paul's Apostolic Ministry

Paul is simply expressing his awareness of his present earthly experience, in all its ambiguity, as he has been doing since the beginning of this section when he first described himself as an earthen vessel (4:7).

In saying that this present bodily existence involves being away from the Lord, Paul does not mean that he is completely separated from the Lord. After all, he lives "in Christ," and Christ lives in him (see Gal 2:20). Moreover, he already enjoys the gift of the Spirit as the "pledge" of what is yet to come. Rather, he means by being away from the Lord that he is not yet in the presence of the risen Lord as he will be at the resurrection of the dead. Though it is possible that Paul may have reckoned with being in an intermediate state of being with the Lord if he should die before the parousia, it does not appear that this intermediate state is the explicit object of this text.

[9–10] These verses bring Paul's discussion of his resurrection hope to its climax and function as a transition to the next section, in which he will speak of "the fear of the Lord" (5:11). Because Paul knows that he is not yet at home to the Lord (Christ), he aspires to please the Lord, fully aware that all must stand before the judgment seat of Christ. Verse 9 repeats the language of verses 6 and 8, "being at home" and "being away." But now, Paul applies this language to the moral life of the believer. Aware that the choice between being in the body and being with the Lord is not his to make, he aspires to please the Lord whether "at home" (his present earthly existence) or "away" (when he will be present to the Lord). The first part of Paul's statement is clear and expected: he strives to please the Lord in his present bodily existence. The meaning of the second part, however, is not so apparent, since it seems to imply some sort of continuing moral choice after death. Plummer (155) suggests that the meaning of the verse is that Paul aims to win the Lord's approval "whether at His Coming He finds us in the body or already out of it," but Lambrecht (86) is probably closer to the mark when he notes that it is best "to assume less careful writing on the part of Paul or a free rhetorical language that should not be pressed." Thus Paul employs the two possible states of being to express his complete and utter desire to be pleasing to the Lord (cf. Eph 5:10).

Having expressed his desire to please the Lord in whose presence he longs to stand, in verse 10 Paul explains why: everyone must stand before the judgment seat of Christ. Thus Paul's discussion of the resurrection concludes with an eschatological vision, as is the case in 1 Cor 15:51–57. Earlier in this section Paul affirmed his faith that God would raise him and bring him, with the Corinthians, into God's presence (4:14). In Rom 14:10, he writes that all will stand before the "judgment seat" (*bēma*) of God. But here Paul states that all will appear before "the judgment seat of Christ," indicating that Paul can speak of judgment before God and before Christ. Since Paul has already expressed his intense desire to be at home with the Lord and to please the Lord, it is not surprising that here he speaks of the judgment seat of Christ who acts as judge in God's stead. Christ's judgment will be rendered on the basis of what each one has done in his or her bodily life ("through the body," *dia tou sōmatos*), echoing all that Paul has said about the body in this section (4:7–5:10). Thus bodily existence is not something to be despised or to escape from, even if it means being in exile from the Lord. The body is the place of moral action, and the Lord takes utterly seriously what people do with their bodily existence. This is why the end of the intruding apostles will correspond to their deeds (11:15). This judgment on the basis of what one has done, however, does not contradict what Paul writes in Romans and Galatians about justification on the basis of faith rather than on the basis of the works of the law. For, although God acquits those who entrust themselves to what he has done in Christ, the justified will be judged on the basis of what they have done (compare Rom 2:12–16). And although what the justified have done will not justify them, it will be the basis for the recompense they receive.

Paul's line of argument in 4:7–5:10 can be summarized in this way: He is the minister of a new covenant, but he carries the treasure of the gospel and exercises this ministry in "an earthen vessel" that is always in danger of being destroyed. The dying of Jesus, however, which he daily carries in his body by enduring his apostolic hardships, paradoxically manifests the life of Jesus. Thus he is full of confidence because of his faith in the resurrection; for while the outer person is in the process of decaying, the inner person is already being prepared for the fullness of glory. This fullness of glory will come when Paul's earthly tent-like existence is covered over by the eternal heavenly dwelling that God will provide, the resurrection body. Filled with this confidence, Paul strives to please the Lord before whose judgment seat he must stand. The glory of Paul's new covenant ministry, then, is concealed in his apostolic sufferings, but these sufferings are slowly transforming him from glory to glory until he finally attains the resurrection of the dead. Having explained the hidden glory of his new covenant ministry, Paul will now discuss his ministry in terms of reconciliation.

3. A Ministry of Reconciliation (5:11–6:10)

Thus far Paul has described his ministry in two ways. First, he is the minister of a new covenant energized by the power of God's Spirit (2:14–3:6). Second, his apostolic sufferings, which are his share in the dying of Jesus, paradoxically manifest the resurrection life of Jesus. Accordingly, although his outer person is wasting away, his apostolic sufferings are preparing him for the final transformation of glory that will occur when the resurrection body "clothes over" his frail, mortal flesh (4:7–5:10). In this section (5:11–6:10), Paul introduces a third and final element in his description of apostolic ministry. As the minister of a new covenant, he is Christ's ambassador, who proclaims the gospel message that God has reconciled the world to himself. Accordingly he appeals to

B. The Integrity of Paul's Apostolic Ministry

people to be reconciled to God. Avoiding anything that might give offense and so fault "the ministry," he commends himself as a minister of God by the apostolic sufferings that he endures in preaching the gospel of reconciliation. In the next section (6:11–7:4) Paul will make a personal appeal to the Corinthians to open their hearts to him, just as he has opened his heart to them. But before he does this, he describes the ministry of reconciliation that is at the heart of this new covenant ministry.

The material of 5:11–6:10 consists of two units, each of which contains a defense of Paul's integrity and an appeal for reconciliation with God that inevitably requires full and complete reconciliation with Christ's ambassador. In the first unit (5:11–21) Paul defends his apostolic integrity (5:11–13), which rests on his conviction that Christ has died for all (5:14–17). Christ's saving death has given Paul the ministry of reconciliation, making him an ambassador for Christ who summons people to reconciliation (5:18–21). In the second unit (6:1–10), Paul draws out the consequences of what he writes in the first. Appealing to the Corinthians not to receive this grace of reconciliation in vain (6:1–2), he again points to his apostolic integrity (6:3–4a), which he defends on the basis of the many hardships he has suffered for the sake of the gospel (6:4b–10). Accordingly, just as there is a defense of Paul's integrity in the first unit (5:11–13), so there is a defense of his integrity in the second (6:3–10). And just as there is an appeal to be reconciled to God in the first unit (5:20), so there is an appeal not to receive the grace of God in vain in the second (6:1–2). The controlling theme of the entire section is the death of Christ, by which God reconciled the world to himself (5:14–21). In terms of soteriology and Christology, this is one of the most theologically charged passages of any Pauline letter. It explains the meaning of Christ's saving death for those who hear and receive the gospel, thereby clarifying the content for Paul's new covenant ministry.

a. Ambassadors for Christ (5:11–21)

5:11 Therefore, knowing the fear of the Lord, we persuade[a] people, but we are known to God, and I hope to be known even to your consciences. 12 We are not commending ourselves to you again but giving you an opportunity for boasting on behalf of us,[b] so that you might have something to say[c] to those who boast in appearance[d] and not in the heart. 13 For, if we are beside ourselves, it is for God; and if we are sober-minded, it is for you. 14 For the love of Christ[e] directs[f] us since we have come to this conclusion: one died for[g] all, therefore all died. 15 He died for[g] all, in order that the living might live no longer for themselves but for the one who died and rose for[g] them. 16 So we no longer know anyone from a merely human point of view;[h] and, even if we once knew Christ from a merely human point of view,[h] we no longer know him in this way. 17 So, if anyone is in Christ, such a one is a new creation.ⁱ The old has passed away. Behold, the new has appeared! 18 Everything comes from God, who reconciled us to himself through Christ and gave us the ministry of reconciliation, 19 that is,ʲ in Christᵏ God was reconciling the world to himself, not counting their trespasses against them and entrusting to us the message of reconciliation.ˡ 20 Therefore, we are ambassadors forᵐ Christ, as if God were appealing through us: we implore you on behalf of Christ be reconciled to God. 21 For us, he made the one who did not know sin to be sinⁿ so that in him we might become the righteousness of God.°

a. Some manuscripts, among them P⁴⁶, read the verb as a subjunctive *peithōmen* ("let us persuade") but the indicative (*peithomen*) is the better reading. The verb may also be taken as a conative present, "we try to persuade."

b. Some significant manuscripts (P⁴⁶, ℵ, B) read *hymōn* ("you"), perhaps to deflect attention from Paul, but the context suggests that Paul is providing them with reasons to boast about himself to others.

c. The words "something to say" have been supplied to clarify the meaning of the Greek.

d. The Greek reads *prosōpō* ("face"), which functions as an idiom for what is seen.

e. The genitive could be objective ("love for Christ") or subjective ("Christ's love"). The latter makes the best sense of Paul's thought.

f. The verb *synechei* could also be translated as "urges" or "impels," but the context suggests "directs" or "controls," as is explained in the exegesis.

g. "For" translates *hyper*. Christ's death is "for," or "on behalf of" others. The word is significant for Paul's soteriology.

h. "Human point of view" translates *kata sarka*. The phrase can be taken in an adverbial or adjectival sense, as is explained in the exegesis.

i. Something needs to be supplied, since the Greek simply reads "new creation." One could translate the phrase, "there is a new creation," or "such a one is a new creation." Since Paul has already referred to the individual ("anyone;" *tis*), the second translation has been chosen here, though there are clearly cosmic and apocalyptic dimensions to Paul's thought in this section.

j. "That is" translates the difficult phrase *hōs hoti*. It can also be translated "because," or it can be viewed as the introduction to a quotation, "as it is said." The options are discussed in the exegesis.

k. "In Christ" can be taken adverbially, "God was reconciling the world *by* Christ," or locally, "God was *in* Christ." The exegesis explains the reason for taking it adverbially.

l. "The message of reconciliation" is the gospel. Thus it is not surprising that P⁴⁶ reads "the gospel" in place of "the message."

m. "For" translates *hyper*. The sense could be "on behalf of" or "in the place of" Christ.

n. It is difficult to translate the Greek in a literal manner that also communicates the meaning of the text. The sense is that God placed Christ in the sinful human condition so that humanity might experience the righteous condition that comes with God's righteousness.

B. The Integrity of Paul's Apostolic Ministry

o. "The righteousness of God" is best taken as a genitive of origin: the righteousness that comes from God. This righteousness is the new relationship that humanity enjoys with God because of God's act of justification and the change this relationship effects.

The theme of judgment, introduced at the end of the last unit (5:9–10), provides a starting point for this unit. Because he is aware that he "must appear before the judgment seat of Christ" (5:10), the "fear of the Lord" guides Paul's apostolic work as he tries to persuade people of the gospel he preaches. The two units are also related to each other by the repeated use of the verb "to appear, to be made known" (*phaneroō*), which occurs once in 5:10 and twice in 5:11. Thus, just as every one must "appear" or "be made known" before the judgment seat of Christ (5:10), so Paul is already "known" by God and hopes to be "known" by the Corinthians (5:11).

The material of the unit, as noted above, can be divided into three subunits. In the first (vv. 11–13) Paul defends his personal integrity. In the second (vv. 14–17), he explains how the death of Christ undergirds his ministry. These verses fall into two parts: verses 14–15, which appear to be indebted to traditional material about the significance of Christ's death, and verses 16–17, each of which begins with *hōste* ("so"), thereby providing supporting arguments for what Paul says in verses 14–15. In the third subunit (vv. 18–21) Paul introduces the theme of reconciliation, which provides him with yet another way to describe his ministry: as the minister of a new covenant, his ministry is one of reconciliation. These verses can also be divided into two parts. In the first (vv. 18–19) there is a remarkable focus on the role of God in reconciling humanity to himself through Christ. In the second (vv. 20–21) Paul presents himself as Christ's ambassador, who calls people to the reconciliation that God has initiated (v. 20), and concludes with a remarkable description of the divine interchange that God has effected in Christ (v. 21). Thus the whole unit moves from an affirmation of Paul's apostolic integrity to a description of him as Christ's ambassador, who exercises the ministry of reconciliation. The material can be outlined as follows:

vv. 11–13   Paul's integrity
vv. 14–17   Christ's death and Paul's ministry
  vv. 14–15   Christ's death for all
  vv. 16–17   consequences of Christ's death
vv. 18–21   The work of reconciliation
  vv. 18–19   God and Christ
  vv. 20–21   Paul as Christ's ambassador

Although Paul employs the first person plural at several points in this unit as he defends and explains his apostolic ministry, the soteriological statements he makes about Christ and the reconciliation God has effected through Christ apply to all believers.

[5:11–13] These verses are apologetic in tone, suggesting that Paul is responding to one or more accusations about the way in which he carries out his apostolic ministry. It is difficult, however, to determine the precise nature of the charges and more difficult to discern who is making them. Are some of the Corinthians accusing Paul of being a religious charlatan who tries to "persuade" people by his slick rhetoric? Is he being faulted for self-promotion because he "commends" himself to the communities that he evangelizes? Are some accusing him of being "beside himself" in the sense of "being out of his mind" because of the exaggerated claims that he makes about himself, the gospel he preaches, his religious experiences, or his encounter with the risen Lord? Or, is the accusation more subtle; namely, Paul does not enjoy the ecstatic experiences that others such as the "super-apostles" do? Finally, who is making these accusations? A particular anti-Pauline faction at Corinth? The intruding missionaries? The non-Christian Jewish populace at Corinth? Before hazarding a tentative reply to these questions, it is important to uncover Paul's line of thought in these verses.

Relating what he is about to say to what he has already said ("Therefore"), Paul affirms that he knows "the fear of the Lord." This expression, which occurs several times in the Old Testament, refers to the sense of "awe," "respect," and "reverence" that mortals should have before God. "The fear of the LORD is the beginning of knowledge" (Prov 1:7). "The fear of the Lord delights the heart, and gives gladness and joy and long life" (Sir 1:12). Paul exhibits such "fear," understood as reverence and awe, because he knows that he must stand before "the judgment seat of Christ" to give an account for all that he has done (5:10; see 1 Pet 1:17, which calls upon believers to live in "reverent fear" during the time of their exile in this life). Although "the Lord" in this Old Testament expression refers to "God," and although Paul exhorts the Corinthians in 7:1 to bring "holiness to completion by fear of God," here "the Lord" probably refers to Christ, before whose judgment seat all must stand, though some commentators (Furnish, 306) maintain that "the Lord" refers to God. This deep sense of referential fear before Christ, who will be his judge, leads Paul "to persuade" people, a statement that he immediately qualifies by affirming that even as he "persuades" people, he is "known" or "manifest" to God—as he will be known to Christ at the moment of judgment. And although he is not yet fully "known" to the Corinthians, he hopes that he will be.

Because the Greek verb *peithō* ("to persuade") can also connote a sense of cajoling or misleading someone by a devious use of rhetoric (see Gal 1:10), some commentators argue that Paul is responding to an accusation of his opponents (Bultmann, 147; Furnish, 306). But even if he is responding to such an accusation, the work of "persuading" is an integral aspect of preaching the gospel (Barnett, 279; Lambrecht, 92). By his apostolic preaching he tries to bring people to the gospel by persuading them of its truth (cf. Acts 13:43; 18:4;

B. The Integrity of Paul's Apostolic Ministry

26:28, where the verb is used in this way). This is apparent to God, but it is not yet fully apparent to the Corinthians, many of whom are mistrustful of Paul. For this reason, he seeks to become as transparent to the "consciences" of the Corinthians as he already is to God, thereby recalling what he wrote in 4:2 about commending himself before God to everyone's conscience by a full disclosure of the truth.

Since Paul's claims might be construed as self-promotion or self-commendation, he again affirms that he is not commending himself (see 3:1). In writing this, he undoubtedly has in mind the kind of self-commendation that characterizes the ministerial style of his detractors (10:12, 18) who commend themselves to the Corinthians on the basis of external appearances. In contrast to them, he commends himself to the consciences of the Corinthians (4:2) so that their moral consciousness will reveal his integrity to them. In a similar fashion, he commends himself as God's minister, whose integrity is manifested in the apostolic sufferings he endures (6:4–10).

If the Corinthians understand and embrace Paul's defense of his integrity here and throughout the letter, they will realize that he is not commending himself, as are the intruding apostles, but providing them with an opportunity for boasting on his behalf to those who boast in appearance rather than reality. In this reference to boasting, Paul recalls the thematic statement of this letter (1:12–14), in which he expresses his hope that as the Corinthians have understood him in part, so they will understand him completely. For just as they will be his boast on the day of the Lord, so he will be their boast. The Corinthians, however, have not yet understood, and in 12:10 Paul complains that it is they who should have commended him. Second Corinthians 5:12, then, is a crucial text for understanding the purpose of this letter: Paul writes so that the Corinthians will be able to boast in, and commend, him.

But who are those who trust in appearance rather than reality (the "face" rather than the "heart"; see LXX 1 Kgdms 16:7 (=1 Sam 16:7) for a similar expression)? Although there is no agreement on this point, Paul may have the intruding apostles in mind, especially if 2 Corinthians is a unity, as this commentary maintains. If so, he is trying to provide the Corinthians with something to say to the intruding apostles, whose eloquent ministerial style has called into question the weakness and suffering of his own ministry.

In the final verse of this subunit (v. 13), Paul draws a contrast between two kinds of behavior: one directed toward God, the other toward the Corinthians. He writes that if he is "beside himself," then it is for God, and if he is "soberminded," then it is for the sake of the Corinthians. The manner in which he introduces this contrast, "for" (*gar*), indicates that what he says here is meant to substantiate, in some way, what he has said in verses 11–12 about persuading others and giving the Corinthians an opportunity to boast in him. It is not immediately apparent, however, what Paul means by this contrast, since this is the only occurrence of the verb *existēmi* in his writings. Used intransitively, the general sense of the verb according to BDAG is "to be out of one's normal state of mind," either because one is out of one's senses or because one is totally amazed and astonished. Thus Paul is referring to some kind of abnormal behavior that causes him to be, or to appear to be, "beside himself." But what is this behavior? Speaking in tongues, as described in 1 Cor 14? Visionary experiences, as related in 2 Cor 12? Is Paul affirming that he enjoys such experiences, or is he responding to those who accuse him of *not* experiencing them (so Bultmann, 150; Furnish, 324; Thrall, 1:402)? Or is the expression a slur, such as that leveled against Jesus in Mark 3:21, that Paul is out of his mind?

Since Paul will be forced into boasting about visions and revelations (12:1–10), perhaps he has these ecstatic experiences in view. If this is the case, he would be saying that he has had such experiences, but they are not the concern of the Corinthians; they are a matter between him and God. But if they are a matter between him and God, why introduce them in 12:1–10, unless others have accused him of not having such ecstatic experiences? Viewing the matter from another vantage point, Lambrecht (94) suggests that Paul may be referring to an objection that his ministerial behavior is abnormal or excessive. Lambrecht asks if Paul is not pointing to his own "vehement, exaggerated reactions" that could have been misinterpreted as self-commendation. If so, Paul responds that if it seems so to the Corinthians, they should understand that such behavior is ultimately for the sake of God and is apparent to God. Toward them his behavior is sober-minded as he persuades them of the gospel.

To summarize, Paul may be responding to certain charges on the part of the intruding apostles or certain factions within the Corinthian community that his preaching is devious and his behavior abnormal, or that he does not enjoy ecstatic experiences. He responds that he acts in the "fear of the Lord," as someone fully aware that he must stand before the judgment seat of Christ. His behavior toward them is open and manifest. It is an occasion for them to boast in him.

[14–15] These verses and verses 16–17 comprise a subunit in which Paul affirms that Christ's love, manifested in his saving death, undergirds Paul's personal integrity. Making use of what appears to be an earlier tradition about Christ's death, Paul points to the all-embracing significance of that death in verses 14–15. In verses 16–17 he will draw out two consequences from this, one stated negatively, the other positively.

Having insisted that he is not commending himself but acting in a sober-minded way toward the Corinthians as he persuades them of the gospel he preaches, Paul affirms that the love of Christ controls or directs his ministry. Although "the love of Christ" (*hē agapē tou Christou*) could refer to Paul's love *for* Christ, if taken as an objective genitive, it is more likely that Paul has in view Christ's own love for him (subjective genitive), which Christ manifested in his saving death. (For other examples of the subjective genitive in regard to

B. The Integrity of Paul's Apostolic Ministry

the love of Christ or the love of God, see Rom 5:5, 8; 8:35; 2 Cor 13:13.) The verb that Paul employs here, *synechō*, is usually translated in one of two ways: (1) "to urge" or "to impel," (2) "to direct" or "to control." In the first instance, Paul would be saying that Christ's love for him provides the inner impulse or motivation for his activity; in the second, Christ's love guides or directs his activity, constraining or holding him within certain bounds. Although the Vulgate (*urget*) and recent translations such as the NRSV ("urges") and the NAB ("impels") adopt the former, the latter translation fits the context better, especially if Paul has been accused of "being beside himself." Thus he would be saying that Christ's love for him "controls" or "directs" all that he does, even if his behavior may appear to be abnormal to others.

Paul's awareness of Christ's love is grounded in his understanding of the significance of Christ's death, which he explains in the following verses:

v. 14b   one died for all (*hyper pantōn*)
    therefore
    all died
v. 15   He died for all (*hyper pantōn*)
    in order that
    the living might live no longer for themselves
        but
            for the one
            who died and rose for them (*tō hyper autōn*)

Paul's statement has two parts. In the first (v. 14b) he makes a basic affirmation about Christ's death and its consequence: Christ died for all. As a result, all died. In the second (v. 15) he reaffirms the basic statement ("he died for all") and then introduces a purpose clause to explain why Christ died for all: "in order that the living might live no longer for themselves but for the one who died and rose for them." The purpose clause adds an element not present in the first statement ("and rose for them"), which indicates that Christ's saving death and resurrection cannot be separated. In addition to pointing to the soteriological significance of Christ's death and resurrection for all, Paul discloses the implication of this event for the moral life of believers: "to live for Christ."

The basic statements that Paul makes here ("one died *for* all," "he died *for* all," "the one who died and rose *for* them") employ the same preposition (*hyper*; "for") found in a number of other Pauline letters.

Rom 5:6 "Christ died *for* the ungodly"
Rom 5:8 "Christ died *for* us"
Rom 8:32 "but [God] gave him up *for* all of us"
Rom 14:15 "of the one *for* whom Christ died"

1 Cor 11:24 "this is my body that is *for* you"
1 Cor 15:3 "that Christ died *for* our sins"
2 Cor 5:21 "*for* us he [God] made him the one who did not know sin to be sin"
Gal 1:4 "who gave himself *for* our sins"
Gal 2:20 "who loved me and gave himself *for* me"
Gal 3:13 "redeemed us from the curse of the law by becoming a curse *for* us"
1 Tim 2:6 "who gave himself a ransom *for* all"

In all of these statements, the preposition "for" (*hyper*) indicates that Christ's death was in the interest of humanity. But in what sense? On the one hand, Christ's death is substitutionary, since he took the place of humanity. This is especially apparent in the statement of Gal 3:13 that Christ became "a curse" to free humanity from the curse of the law, as well as the affirmation of 2 Cor 5:21 that God made Christ sin so that humanity could become the righteousness of God. On the other hand, Christ is the representative of humanity, the new Adam who obediently does God's will. As such, he represents humanity before God so that what God accomplishes in Christ becomes effective for all humanity. In this sense, Christ's death is "on behalf of" and "for the sake of" humanity. Accordingly, as Adam, the representative of the old humanity, led humanity into sin and death by his disobedience, so Christ, the eschatological representative of humanity, leads humanity into grace and life by his obedience (Rom 5:12–21).

Paul's initial statement about Christ's death (v. 14b) may on first reading seem puzzling, since one might have expected him to write, "one died for all, therefore *all live*." Paul's view of Christ's death, however, is not purely substitutionary; as if Christ's death means that "all" will not face death. Rather, viewing Christ as a representative, Paul affirms that humanity somehow died with its representative. It should be clear that Paul is not referring to physical death here. Although it is difficult to say precisely what he means (see Thrall, 1:409–11, for a listing of interpretations), there are other texts that shed light on his intent here. For example, in Rom 6:3–4 he reminds believers that they have been baptized "into his [Christ's] death" and "buried with him by baptism into death." He then goes on to say that if believers are united with Christ "in a death like his," they will be united in a resurrection like his (Rom 6:5). Paul then exhorts his readers to consider themselves "dead to sin and alive to God in Christ Jesus" (Rom 6:11). In Galatians, his language is stronger and more personal. He writes, "I have been crucified with Christ; and it is no longer I who live, but it is Christ who lives in me" (Gal 2:19b–20a). In saying that "all died," then, Paul views humanity as incorporated into its new representative. Consequently, when the representative died, humanity died *in* the representative, thereby dying to the powers of sin, death, and law that the representative overcame.

B. The Integrity of Paul's Apostolic Ministry

The soteriological effect of Christ's death has important consequence: Christ has died "in order that the living might live no longer for themselves but for the one who died and rose for them" (v. 15). Again, one might have expected Paul to write "in order that the living might live no longer for themselves but *for others.*" Paul's reasoning, however, is christological. The purpose of life is to live *for* the one who died and rose *for* all (cf. Rom 14:7–9). Such a life necessarily includes living for others, since Christ has died for all. But instead of beginning with humanity, Paul starts with humanity's representative, so that life *for* Christ becomes the most profound kind of service to others.

But who are "the living"? Is Paul referring to all who are alive (Plummer, 175; Thrall, 1:412)? Or does he have in view believers who have died in Christ and already enjoy the beginnings of resurrection life (Furnish, 311)? In the first instance, Paul's statement would be pointing to the moral goal of all humanity, in the second, to the moral goal of believers. Although both interpretations make good sense, Paul's use of a similar expression in 4:11 suggests that he has the first in mind.

To summarize, Paul grounds his apostolic integrity in the love Christ manifested in his saving death for all. Christ's own love controls and directs what Paul says and does as he "persuades" others to embrace the gospel.

[16–17] These verses draw out the consequences of Paul's statement in verses 14–15 that Christ died for all, and all died with him. On the basis of this conviction, Paul writes that he no longer views anyone from a merely human point of view, and if someone is in Christ, that person is a new creation. Both verses begin with *hōste* ("so"). But whereas verse 16 makes its points in a negative manner, verse 17 does so in a positive way. Yet each verse testifies to the same truth (so Allo, 167), namely, that the Christ event has radically altered Paul's perception of the human person. Though Paul may be employing a literary plural here, what he writes surely applies to all believers.

Verse 16 has two parts: a general statement that Paul no longer regards anyone *kata sarka* and a conditional sentence that, if he once knew Christ in this way, he no longer does.[44] Translated literally, *kata sarka* means "according to the flesh" and usually carries a negative connotation in Paul's writings. For example, though Paul acknowledges that he lives "in the flesh," he strongly objects to charges that he behaves "according to the flesh" (10:2–3); he declares that his moral behavior is not determined by what is fleeting and mortal and so destined to perish. In verse 16 the phrase occurs twice, and in each instance it

---

44. For a stimulating essay on the significance of the phrase *kata sarka* in this passage, see Martyn, "Epistemology at the Turn of the Ages," in *Theological Issues in the Letters of Paul,* 89–110. Martyn argues that in using this phrase Paul invites the Corinthians, especially the enthusiasts among them, "to join him in recognizing the *end* of that way of knowing" (106). "That way of knowing," which belongs to the old age, has been supplanted by the way of knowing that comes with the new creation that God has inaugurated in Christ.

is best taken as modifying the verbs "know" and "knew." Thus Paul means that his understanding of the Christ event has led to a new comprehension of humanity and its representative, the Christ. As regards humanity, Paul no longer knows, assesses, or regards human beings from a merely human or mortal point of view, since such an understanding is determined by what is carnal and so destined to perish. As regards Christ, even if he once knew Christ *kata sarka*, he no longer does.

Paul's final comment, "even if we once knew Christ *kata sarka*," raises the following question: if the conditional clause is a "real condition," in what sense did Paul once know Christ *kata sarka*? Is he referring to a period before his call and conversion, when he knew the earthly Jesus? Or is he referring to that period when he persecuted the church, because he evaluated "the crucified Messiah" from a purely human point of view as a false messiah condemned by the law? It is, of course, possible that Paul came into contact with the earthly Jesus during the period of Jesus' Jerusalem ministry or that he heard of the Galilean, but it is more likely that Paul is referring to the manner in which he once judged or understood Jesus when he persecuted the church, before God revealed to him that the crucified one is God's Son (Gal 1:16). After that revelation, Paul no longer viewed Christ, or those for whom he died, from a merely human point of view. Thus the phrase, "from now on" (*apo tou nyn*), refers to an event of cosmic proportions that has occurred in Christ, namely, the turn of the ages[45] that Paul experienced in his call and conversion.

Having stated the consequence of Christ's death in a negative fashion, Paul proceeds to develop his thesis more positively. He no longer looks upon anyone from a merely human point of view, because those who are "in Christ" are a "new creation." This leads Paul to two further statements: (1) the old has passed away, and (2) the new has appeared.

Paul's language of "a new creation," which also appears in Gal 6:15, is probably indebted to the book of Isaiah, especially Isa 65:17, which is also quoted in 2 Pet 3:13.

> For I am about to create *new heavens* and a *new earth*;
> the *former things* shall not be remembered.
> (Isa 65:17, emphasis added)

> See, the *former things* have come to pass,
> and *new things* I now declare.
> (Isa 42:9, emphasis added)

---

45. Martyn, ibid., 94, emphasizes this dimension of the phrase *apo tou nyn* when he writes, "As the second half of v. 17 shows, it is an event of cosmic, apocalyptic proportions, and Paul describes it in a manner worthy of an Enthusiast: 'New Creation!' 'Everything old has passed away!' 'Look! Everything has become new!'"

B. The Integrity of Paul's Apostolic Ministry

> Do not remember the *former things*,
> or consider the *things of old*.
> I am about to do *a new thing*.
> (Isa 43:18–19, emphasis added)

> From this time forward I make you hear *new things*,
> *hidden things* that you have not known.
> (Isa 48:6, emphasis added)

Whereas Isaiah points to a cosmic renewal that will envelop the whole creation, here and in Gal 6:15 Paul identifies this new creation with the believer who is "in Christ." According to Romans the whole creation longs for "the revealing of the children of God," since creation itself will be set free when God's children are glorified (Rom 8:18–21). Although creation has not yet been set free, the believer in Christ is a new creation, the first fruits of a cosmic renewal yet to come. Ephesians 2:15 and 4:24, which speak of a "new humanity" (*kainos anthrōpos*), are also helpful for grasping Paul's thought, since they describe the human person who has been renewed "in Christ."

As in verses 14–15, here Paul's understanding of Christ as the new Adam is once more close at hand. Christ, the representative who died for all, is the new Adam, the new creation. Consequently those who have been incorporated into him are a new creation. Conversely Adam, the representative of disobedient humanity, stands for what is old and passing away. Therefore, as if revealing a mystery, in verse 17 Paul employs the same word *idou* ("behold," "see") that is found in Isa 42:9; 43:19; 65:17–18; and 1 Cor 15:51: "Behold (*idou*), the new has appeared"; the new is Christ and those incorporated into him, "the new creation."

[18–19] These verses with verses 20–21 form the third subunit of 5:11–21. Whereas the preceding subunit (vv. 14–17) is primarily concerned with Christ's redemptive death, which has become the motivation that undergirds Paul's apostolic integrity, the focus of this subunit is God's work of reconciliation, which is the foundation for Paul's ministry of reconciliation. Within the four verses of this subunit, the noun for "reconciliation" (*katallagē*) occurs twice and the verb "to reconcile" (*katallassō*) three times. It is not surprising, then, that these verses are among the most important in all of Paul's writings for understanding his thinking on reconciliation. Other significant passages are Rom 5:1–11; 11:13–16; Eph 2:11–22; and Col 1:15–23.[46]

---

46. In Rom 5:1–11 Paul draws a close relationship between "justification" and "reconciliation." Those who have been justified are now at peace with God (5:1), which is to say, they have been reconciled. Having been justified when they were sinners and reconciled when they were God's enemies, it is all the more certain that they will be saved now that they have been justified and reconciled (5:8–11). The entire passage indicates more clearly than 2 Cor 5 the situation of enmity in which humanity found itself before God reconciled humanity to himself. In Rom 11:13–16, Paul

Verse 18 functions as a thesis statement about God's work of reconciliation, identifying Paul's ministry in terms of reconciliation. Verse 19 expands upon and explains the theme of reconciliation and the ministry it entails. These statements about God's work of reconciliation and Paul's ministry will become the foundation for Paul's call to reconciliation in verses 20–21, which will be discussed below.

Having spoken of Christ's death "for all" and the "new creation" this death effects, Paul introduces "God" as the primary actor in this drama of salvation and identifies the work of God in terms of reconciliation. Everything that occurred in the Christ event was ultimately the work of God, who was reconciling "us" (humanity) to himself "through Christ" (*dia Christou*), giving "us"—Paul and his coworkers—"the ministry of reconciliation."

The New Testament vocabulary for "reconciliation" consists of a number of compound words (*katallagē, katallassō, apokatallassō*) that indicate a change in the social relationship of people previously at enmity with each other. Accordingly people who have been reconciled with each other "exchange" a relationship of enmity and hostility for one of friendship and peace.[47] In ordinary social relationships, either party can initiate the process of reconciliation, although both parties must eventually be reconciled. In Pauline usage, however, the process of reconciliation between God and humanity always begins with God, who reconciles humanity to himself, since there is no need for God to be reconciled to humanity. The Pauline notion of reconciliation, then, is different from the concept found in 2 Macc 1:5, where the author prays, "May he [God] hear your prayers and be reconciled to you [the Jews], and may he not forsake

---

warns the Gentiles that if Israel's rejection has resulted in "the reconciliation of the world," then Israel's acceptance will surely mean "life from the dead." Here Paul's language about "the reconciliation of the world" is reminiscent of that in 2 Cor 5:19. Colossians and Ephesians, which most treat as deuteropauline writings, portray the work of reconciliation in new ways. In Col 1:15–23 Christ's work of reconciliation is cosmic in scope as God works through Christ "to reconcile to himself all things, whether on earth or in heaven, by making peace through the blood of his [Christ's] cross" (Col 1:20). Thus those who were estranged and hostile to God have been reconciled "in his fleshly body through death" (Col 1:21–22). The most distinctive presentation of reconciliation comes in Eph 2:11–21, which presents Christ as the agent of reconciliation, reconciling Gentile and Jew "in one body through the cross, thus putting to death that hostility through it" (Eph 2:16). Common to all of these texts are a situation of hostility that existed before God's work of reconciliation and the centrality of Christ's death on the cross for ending this hostility.

47. For an overview of the language of reconciliation, see the article by H. Merkel in *EDNT*, s.v. *katallagē*; J. Fitzmyer, "Reconciliation in Pauline Theology," in *To Advance the Gospel: New Testament Studies* (New York: Crossroad, 1981), 162–85; R. Martin, *Reconciliation: A Study of Paul's Theology* (Atlanta: John Knox Press, 1981); and R. Bieringer and J. Lambrecht, "'Reconcile yourselves . . .': A Reading of 2 Corinthians 5,11–21"; "Paul's Understanding of *Diakonia* in 2 Corinthians 5,18"; "2 Korinther 5,19a und die Versöhnung der Welt"; and "Sünde und Gerechtigkeit Gottes in 2 Korinther 5,21," in *Studies on 2 Corinthians*, 363–515.

B. The Integrity of Paul's Apostolic Ministry

you in time of evil" (also see 2 Macc 5:20; 7:33). The text of Maccabees seems to suppose that God is estranged from his people and can be reconciled to them by prayer.[48] For Paul, however, humanity is in a sinful situation from which it cannot extricate itself (Rom 1:18–3:20). It is not God who needs to be reconciled to humanity, but humanity that needs to be reconciled to God. For this reason, "Everything comes from God," because it is God and only God who can reconcile humanity to God.

God's work of reconciliation occurs "through Christ" (*dia Christou*). That is, if God is the primary actor in the drama of salvation, then Christ is the agent by and through whom God reconciles sinful humanity to himself. In writing that God reconciles "us" *dia Christou*, Paul is referring to Christ's representative death that he discussed in the previous unit. Since Christ is the representative of a "new creation," his death "for all" was the way in which God reconciled "us" to himself; for in surrendering his life "for all," Christ did what humanity could not do for itself.

Within the context of this statement on reconciliation Paul turns to the ministry of reconciliation, having already spoken of "the ministry of the Spirit" (3:8) and "the ministry of righteousness" (3:9), a ministry that is permanent and enduring (3:11) because it is the ministry of "a new covenant" (3:6). Now Paul affirms that God has also granted him a share in "the ministry of reconciliation." This ministry, of course, is not a new ministry that is somehow different from "the ministry of the Spirit" and "the ministry of reconciliation." Rather, the concept of reconciliation allows Paul to clarify further his understanding of the ministry of the Spirit and the ministry of righteousness. The *content* of the new covenant ministry that God has given to Paul is the reconciling work of Christ's death "for all," which requires Paul to proclaim the reconciliation God has effected in Christ.

Having stated his thesis about God's work of reconciliation in verse 18, in verse 19 Paul repeats the theme of reconciliation in order to develop and clarify what he has said.

v. 18 Everything comes from God
who *reconciled us* to himself through (*dia*) Christ
    and gave us *the ministry of reconciliation.*
v. 19 that is (*hōs hoti*)
in (*en*) Christ God was *reconciling the world* to himself
    not counting their trespasses against them
    and entrusting to us *the message of reconciliation.*

---

48. These are the only occurrences of reconciliation in the Old Testament. Josephus, however, writes about God being reconciled to those who confess and repent in *J.W.* 5.415: "and the Deity is easily reconciled to such as confess and repent." Also see *Ant.* 3.315 and 6.144–56.

As the arrangement of these verses shows, Paul alters his language even as he repeats his theme. Thus in verse 19 he expands upon verse 18 and speaks of God reconciling "the world" "in Christ," and he explains that reconciliation involves the forgiveness of sins ("not counting their trespasses"). Finally, he describes the "ministry of reconciliation" as being entrusted with "the message of reconciliation."

As indicated in the notes, verse 19 presents a number of translation problems, all of which have implications for interpreting the text. First, the opening words, *hōs hoti*, are clearly intended to relate this verse to what has preceded.[49] But how? If the relationship is causal, the phrase should be translated "since." If Paul is quoting a piece of tradition that the Corinthians already know, *hōs hoti* may be the equivalent of quotation marks, "as it is said." In the translation adopted here, *hōs hoti* is taken in a declarative sense ("that is") because Paul is restating and developing what he has just said in verse 18.

Second, the Greek phrase *theos ēn en Christō kosmon katalassōn* could be translated in several ways.[50] For example, "God was in Christ reconciling the world." Here the preposition "in" is construed locally and "reconciling" is taken as a participle, emphasizing the divine presence of God *in* Christ, a sense that coheres with the doctrine of the incarnation (so Calvin, 77; Allo, 170; Collange, 271).[51] But if the verb "was" and the participle "reconciling" are taken as an imperfect periphrastic ("was reconciling"), and if "in Christ" is taken adverbially ("by means of Christ"), then the Greek would be translated, "in (or by) Christ God was reconciling the world to himself," giving the sense that it was *by the agency of Christ* that God was reconciling the world to himself (so Chrysostom and most modern commentators).There is, however, a third possibility which stands midway between these two positions. It would take "God" as the predicate of the verb "was" and translate the phrase, "it was God, in Christ, who was reconciling the world to himself." Although this translation maintains the adverbial sense of *en Christō*, it emphasizes that it was God who was at work in Christ. Of these possibilities the second is probably the best, since the adverbial sense of "in Christ" coheres best with "through Christ" found in verse 18, and the periphrastic translation "was reconciling" highlights the ongoing work of reconciliation that God was effecting in Christ.

---

49. For a full discussion, see the commentaries of Furnish and Thrall and the essay of R. Bieringer, "2 Korinther 5,19a und die Versöhnung der Welt," in *Studies on 2 Corinthians*, 429–59, esp. 433–37.

50. Again, see the commentaries of Furnish and Thrall, as well as the study of Bieringer noted above, esp. 437–45.

51. Allo (170) says that this translation is more pleasing to him not only because it is doctrinally richer, implicitly affirming the incarnation, but because it is essentially concerned with the death of Christ with which Paul has been concerned since v. 14. Although this is a rich reading, one should not make an exegetical decision on this basis alone.

B. The Integrity of Paul's Apostolic Ministry

But what is the "world" (*kosmos*) that God was reconciling to himself by Christ? Although *kosmos* often refers to the "universe" (1 Cor 8:4; Phil 2:15), Paul's statements that God was reconciling "us" to himself (v. 18) and that God was "not counting their trespasses against them" (v. 19) suggest that he is primarily referring to the world of human beings. That is, by means of Christ, God was reconciling humanity to himself. The mention of "their trespasses" (*ta paraptōmata autōn*) helps to explain why this reconciliation was necessary: because humanity had sinned against God by trespassing God's commandments. Accordingly, as Paul writes in Rom 4:25, Christ was put to death "for our trespasses and raised for our justification" (see Rom 5:15, 17, 20 for references to Adam's "trespass," which led to death for all and increased under the rule of the law). In writing that God was not "counting" or "reckoning" (*logizomenos*) humanity's trespasses, Paul affirms that the result of reconciliation is the forgiveness of sins. This vocabulary of "reckoning" will play a prominent role in Paul's discussion of Abraham's faith in Rom 4 and the righteousness that God "reckoned" to him. Its presence here helps to draw a relationship between reconciliation and justification (Barrett, 177), a theme to which Paul will turn in verse 21.

As in verse 18, Paul concludes with yet another reference to the ministry he exercises, affirming that God entrusted "the message of reconciliation" to us (that is, to Paul and his coworkers). Although the phrase essentially repeats what Paul said about "the ministry of reconciliation," the change from "ministry" to "message" (*logon*) underlines the work of proclamation that this ministry entails and that Paul will now embark upon as he calls upon the Corinthians to be reconciled with God.

[20–21] These two verses complete the third subunit, which began with verses 18–19. As in those verses, the theme of reconciliation holds center stage. Whereas Paul spoke of God's work of reconciliation and his own ministry of reconciliation in those verses, here he exercises his ministry of reconciliation by summoning the Corinthians to be reconciled to God (v. 20) because of the divine interchange that God has effected in Christ: Christ became "sin" so that "we" might become "the righteousness of God" (v. 21). The appeal to reconciliation that Paul makes here will be followed by other appeals not to receive the grace of God in vain (6:1–2) and to be reconciled with God's apostle (6:11–13; 7:2–4).

Having identified himself as a "minister of a new covenant" (3:6), Paul now presents himself as an "ambassador for Christ" through whom God appeals, as he once appealed through Christ. The metaphor Paul chooses here is significant, since an ambassador or envoy does not represent himself but the one who sends him. Accordingly the ambassador's message is not his own but belongs to the one whom he represents. In this case Paul presents himself as an ambassador "for" (*hyper*) Christ, which can be construed as "on behalf of" Christ or "in place of" Christ, who no longer conducts his earthly ministry of reconciliation. In either case, Paul does not represent himself but the one who sent him.

Just as God once made an appeal for reconciliation through Christ, so God continues to make an appeal through Christ's ambassador: "on behalf of Christ, be reconciled to God" (v. 20). The appeal is significant for two reasons. First, it is made "on behalf of Christ." Thus it is not Paul's personal appeal but an appeal he makes "for" or "in place of" Christ. God makes the gospel of reconciliation known through him, just as he once made it known through Christ. Second, the summons to "be reconciled to God" points to the need for a response that is appropriate to God's work of reconciliation. For, although only God can initiate the work of reconciliation, this work requires a response on the part of those whom God reconciles to himself.

This summons to reconciliation, however, raises a question. If Paul has preached the gospel to the Corinthians, have they not already been reconciled to God? Yes, the Corinthians have been reconciled to God, inasmuch as God's work of reconciliation has taken place through Christ. The human response to God's work of reconciliation, however, is ongoing, and in the present instance it needs reaffirmation because the Corinthians are not yet fully reconciled with "Christ's ambassador." Paul's appeal to be reconciled to God, therefore, can be understood as the beginning of his appeal to the Corinthians to be reconciled with him (6:11–7:5); for they cannot be reconciled to God if they are at enmity with Christ's ambassador.

With verse 21 Paul provides the Corinthians with a profound reason to appropriate the reconciliation God offers them: God made the sinless Christ "sin" so that they might become "the righteousness of God." In this striking statement, Paul points to the "divine interchange" that occurred in the Christ event. In accordance with God's will, Christ assumes the sinful condition of humanity so that humanity might assume Christ's righteousness before God.

For us			
he made	the one who did not know sin	sin	
	so that in him		
	we might become		the righteousness of God

This example of divine interchange is similar to what Paul writes in Gal 3:13–14 about Christ appropriating the "curse" of the law by his shameful death on the cross so that the Gentiles might appropriate the blessing of Abraham: "Christ redeemed us from the curse of the law by becoming a curse for us—for it is written, 'Cursed is everyone who hangs on a tree'—in order that in Christ Jesus the blessing of Abraham might come to the Gentiles, so that we might receive the promise of the Spirit through faith." Paul's language here is also similar to what he writes in Rom 8:3–4 about God sending his Son "in the like-

B. The Integrity of Paul's Apostolic Ministry

ness of sinful flesh" in order to deal with sin "so that the just requirement of the law might be fulfilled in us, who walk not according to the flesh but according to the Spirit." In all of these instances, Christ takes the place of sinful humanity so that humanity can stand in the correct and proper relationship to God. All of these texts, however, present the same problem. What does Paul mean when he writes that God made Christ "to be sin," or God sent Christ "in the likeness of sinful flesh," or Christ became "a curse for us"?

Paul begins by affirming the sinlessness of Christ: God made "the one who did not know sin to be sin." This language might suggest that Paul is speaking of the sinless preexistent Christ who did not yet have an experience of human sinfulness before the incarnation, but once he entered the realm of the flesh he did (see the discussion in Windisch, 197–98). However, given the importance that Paul attributes to the perfect obedience of Christ, the new Adam, in Rom 5:12–21, he surely has in view the incarnate Christ who was the agent of reconciliation precisely because he was perfectly obedient to God.[52] What then does Paul mean when he writes that God made the sinless Christ sin for us?

In responding to this question, the history of exegesis has moved in one of two directions: (1) that God made Christ a "sin offering" for us; (2) that Christ took the place of sinful humanity so that the punishment for sin was inflicted on Christ in humanity's stead. The first position, supported by Augustine, Ambrose, Cyril of Alexandria, Thomas Aquinas, and Calvin (see Allo, 171), is attractive since it avoids any suggestion that Christ committed sin. Moreover, Paul does employ sacrificial imagery in Rom 3:25 ("a sacrifice of atonement") and 1 Cor 5:7 ("our paschal lamb, Christ, has been sacrificed"). Likewise, the phrase *peri hamartias* in Rom 8:3 could be translated, "as an offering for sin." But here it seems unlikely that *hyper hēmōn hamartian epoiēsen* means that God made Christ a sin offering for us. First, since Paul has just spoken of "the one who did not know sin," it is more likely that *hamartia* means "sin" rather than "an offering for sin." Second, in explaining the divine interchange that occurs in the Christ event, Paul establishes a contrast between "sin" and "the righteousness of God" rather than between a "sin offering" and "the righteousness of God."

In writing that God made Christ "sin," therefore, Paul means that God put Christ in humanity's place so that humanity might stand in Christ's place before God. Thus Chrysostom (*Homily* 11: 5) explains that Christ "suffered as a sinner to be condemned, as one cursed to die." And Bultmann (165) notes that "just as believers are 'just' because God regards ('reckons') them as such, though they are sinners, so Christ is regarded and treated by God as a sinner . . . though he is sinless." Although this commentary interprets the righteousness of the justified differently than does Bultmann, it agrees with the latter part of his statement. By

---

52. For other references and allusions to the "sinlessness" of Christ in the New Testament, see John 7:18; 8:46; Heb 4:15; 1 Pet 2:22; 3:18; 1 John 3:5.

writing that God made the sinless Christ "sin," Paul means that Christ absorbed the punishment for humanity's sinfulness (though Christ remained sinless). Thus Christ becomes the object of God's wrath for sin in humanity's stead.[53] In this sense the representative death of Christ described in verses 14–15 can also be viewed in terms of substitution: the sinless one takes the place of the sinner.

God's purpose in making Christ "sin" was to make "us" "the righteousness of God." In referring to "us" Paul is no longer using a literary plural to identify himself or his apostolic coworkers. Rather, with this pronoun he clearly includes the Corinthians. More importantly, he has the whole of humanity in view, since Christ died "for all" (vv. 14–15). But what does Paul mean when he writes "so that in him we might become the righteousness of God"?

Paul has already described the ministry he exercises as "the ministry of righteousness," and in 11:15 he will portray the intruding apostles at Corinth as disguising themselves as "servants of righteousness." Here, however, he refers to "the righteousness of God," which could be construed as a subjective genitive, "God's righteousness," God's faithfulness and dependability by which God saves his people. Or it could be interpreted as an objective genitive, "the righteousness that comes from God," the righteousness that God grants in Christ resulting in acquittal and justification for humanity. Although Paul probably refers to God's own saving righteousness in Rom 1:17; 3:5, 21, 23, the righteousness that comes from God seems more appropriate here (as in Rom 10:3; Phil 3:9) since Paul is establishing a contrast between the condition of Christ and the condition of humanity. Thus humanity stands in the condition of a God-given righteousness because Christ has stood in the sinful human condition before God. Put another way, God made Christ "sin" in order "to justify" humanity.[54]

Protestant and Catholic commentators, however, have tended to view this righteousness differently, the former emphasizing that righteousness is not a "quality" or "habit" but something "imputed" to the sinner, the latter emphasizing that this righteousness is something received and transforming.[55] On the one hand, the immediate context favors an "imputed" righteousness. For, just as God viewed Christ *as if* he were a sinner, though he was sinless, so God views humanity *as if* it were righteous, though it is sinful, since God "imputes"

---

53. The "wrath of God" (Rom 1:18) is not to be understood as an emotion of God, as though God were "angry" with humanity. Rather, God's wrath is God's just and necessary reaction to sin. Thus, in becoming the object of God's wrath, Christ experiences the punishment for humanity's sin by his death on the cross.

54. In asking why the concept of justification is expressed in this rather strange way, Thrall (1:443) writes, "the simplest answer is probably the best: *dikaiosynē* is written for the sake of literary symmetry."

55. Calvin (81) writes, "Here righteousness means not a quality or habit but something imputed to us, since we are said to have received the righteousness of Christ." Somewhat surprisingly, Windisch (199) describes this righteousness as something that penetrates our being, creating a new reality, an observation with which Bultmann (166) disagrees.

B. The Integrity of Paul's Apostolic Ministry

his own righteousness to humanity. On the other hand, Paul has already spoken of those who are "in Christ" as being a "new creation" (v. 17), suggesting that something transformative has happened to them in Christ. Clearly, then, Paul's thought stands somewhere between these extremes.[56] First, something happens to humanity when God bestows the gift of righteousness, for it becomes a "new creation." Second, being a new creation does not mean that the justified are already morally perfect. Rather, those who have received the righteousness that comes from God have been transformed because they are a new creation in Christ. This transformation, however, will not be complete until the parousia, when the justified are finally saved.[57]

Paul's line of thought in 5:11–21 begins with a defense of his apostolic ministry (vv. 11–13) and concludes with a discussion of Christ's death "for all" (vv. 14–17) and God's work of reconciliation (vv. 18–21) that provides Paul with an opportunity to call the community to reconciliation once more. What he writes can be summarized in this way: Although some may accuse Paul of "persuading" people in devious ways, or of "being beside himself," God knows Paul's motives. Although Paul may appear to be commending himself to the Corinthians, his purpose is to provide them with an opportunity to boast in him. As for himself, he is controlled and directed by the love of God manifested in Christ's death "for all." Because of Christ's death, Paul no longer views anyone, and certainly not Christ, from a merely human point of view. In Christ all have been renewed. God is the author of this reconciliation, the God who entrusted Paul with "the ministry of reconciliation." Therefore, as Christ's ambassador, Paul summons the Corinthians to be reconciled to God (and therefore to Paul), since God justified sinners by putting Christ in their stead.

b. Appeal and Defense (6:1–10)

6:1 As God's coworkers,[a] we also[b] appeal to you[c] not to receive the grace of God in vain; 2 for he[d] says, "At a favorable time I heard you, and on the day of salvation I helped you." Behold! Now is the favorable[e]

---

56. Since Catholic and Protestant positions on justification were forged in the midst of a heated polemic, it has been difficult for either side to appropriate the language of the other. Dialogue on this topic needs to find new language to express the reality about which both sides agree. Such language can be found in the *Joint Declaration on the Doctrine of Justification: The Lutheran World Federation and The Roman Catholic Church* (Grand Rapids: Eerdmans, 2000).

57. What Paul writes here about righteousness suggests that he sees a close relationship between justification and reconciliation. The precise relationship between the two concepts, however, is disputed. Is the Pauline notion of reconciliation subordinated to justification, or is it a broader concept than justification? Fitzmyer ("Reconciliation in Pauline Theology") suggests "that justification takes place in view of something, viz., reconciliation, so that reconciliation does not 'sharpen and point up the doctrine of justification' in Pauline thought. It is rather the other way around" (172–73). Understood in this way, reconciliation is a major Pauline category, even though it does not appear as frequently as justification.

time. Behold! Now is the day of salvation. 3 We give no occasion for offense whatsoever,[f] lest the[g] ministry be faulted, 4 but in every way, as ministers of God,[h] we commend ourselves in[i] great endurance, in afflictions, in troubles, in calamities, 5 in beatings, in imprisonments, in riots, in labors,[j] in sleepless nights, in going hungry,[k] 6 in sincerity, in knowledge, in patience, in kindness, in the Holy Spirit,[l] in genuine love, 7 in the word of truth,[m] in the power of God, through[n] weapons of righteousness[o] in the right hand and the left, 8 through honor and dishonor, through ill repute and good repute, as[p] deceitful and we are truthful, 9 as unknown and we are known, as dying and behold we live, as punished and we are not put to death, 10 as grieving but we are always rejoicing, as poor but enriching many, as having nothing and yet we possess everything.

a. "As God's coworkers" translates the participle *synergountes* ("working together"). Since the Greek does not identify with whom Paul works, something must be supplied, such as "the Corinthians," "other apostolic ministers," "God." The reason for choosing "God" is discussed in the exegesis.

b. "Also" translates *kai*, which is used to intensify what Paul says here (Thrall, 1:451). Plummer (189) suggests that *de kai* has the sense "But there is more to be said than this."

c. The Greek text emphasizes "you" by placing it at the end of the verse.

d. Since the subject of *legei* is not expressed, the verb could be translated "it says." But since Paul has just spoken of "God's grace," the unexpressed subject must be "God" (Thrall, 1:452).

e. "Favorable" translates *euprosdektos*, an intensive form of the Greek word for "favorable" (*dektos*) found in the Scripture text that Paul quotes. Lambrecht (109) argues that the emphasis has changed so that here "favorable" means a time "acceptable" to the Corinthians, whereas in the quotation it means a time "acceptable" to God.

f. The Greek (*mēdemian en mēdeni didontes proskopēn*) could be construed, "We give no occasion for offense *to anyone*," as does the Vulgate, if *mēdeni* is taken as masculine rather than as neuter.

g. Some manuscripts (D F G) add "our" (*hēmōn*). Although the resulting translation ("our ministry") is smoother, Paul is not merely speaking of *his* ministry but "*the* apostolic ministry of reconciliation" he has described in 5:18–21.

h. It is in his capacity as a minister of God that Paul commends himself to the Corinthians. He is not commending himself as a minister of God, as the Vulgate suggests when it renders the Greek, *exhibentes nosmetipsos sicut Dei ministros*.

i. Paul begins a list of eighteen items, each of which begins with *en* ("in").

j. The word *kopos* could be rendered "troubles" or "difficulties," but the context seems to require "labors."

k. The Greek *nēsteia* is the usual word for "fasting." It is translated as "going hungry," since Paul is probably referring to voluntary fasting occasioned by his apostolic work rather than to explicitly religious fasting (Plummer, 195).

B. The Integrity of Paul's Apostolic Ministry 147

l. The phrase *en pneumati hagiō* could refer to the human spirit ("in a holy spirit") or to the Spirit of God. The reason for choosing the latter is explained below.

m. The Greek *en logō alētheias* could refer to Paul's own words, which are true ("in a truthful word"), or to the gospel, which is "the word of truth," as in Eph 1:13 and Col 1: 5. The latter position is adopted here.

n. Paul begins a series of three items, each introduced by *dia* ("through").

o. Understood as a subjective genitive, "the weapons of righteousness" are the weapons that "righteousness" bestows, but the context suggests a genitive of apposition, "the weapons that are righteousness."

p. Paul begins a series of seven antitheses that begin with *hōs* ("as").

In the previous unit (5:11–21) Paul defended his apostolic ministry by explaining how his understanding of Christ's death "for all" has altered his perception of humanity and of Christ. Affirming that God has given him "the ministry of reconciliation" (5:18), so that he is Christ's ambassador through whom God appeals to people to be reconciled to God (5:20), Paul makes a more specific appeal to the Corinthians not to receive the grace of God in vain (6:1–2). Insisting that he does not give any occasion for offense, lest the ministry of reconciliation be criticized (6:3–4a), Paul employs an extensive "hardship list" in order to establish this claim and undergird his appeal (6:4b–10).[58]

The material of this unit is related to what Paul has already said in several ways. First, the appeal not to receive the grace of God in vain (6:1–2) echoes the appeal that Paul makes as Christ's ambassador (5:20). Second, "the ministry" to which Paul refers in 6:3 is "the ministry of reconciliation" that God has given to Paul (5:18). Third, the list of hardships (6:4b–10) that Paul endures for the sake of the gospel, lest the ministry of reconciliation be faulted (6:3), provides the Corinthians with "something to say to those who boast in appearance and not in the heart" (5:12).

The appeal that Paul makes in this unit provides a concrete example of his ambassadorial work on behalf of Christ, indicating that not all is well at Corinth. For even though Titus has brought Paul good news about the community (see 7:5–16), it is evident that the community has not yet been fully reconciled to its apostle (see 6:11–7:4). Nor will it be, until the issue of the intruding apostles, which Paul will discuss in chapters 10–13, is settled. In appealing to the Corinthians not to receive the grace of God in vain, then, Paul points to the need for the community to be reconciled to its apostle, since the grace of reconciliation includes reconciliation with Christ's ambassador.

---

58. Although 6:4b–10 is called a "hardship" list, not all of the items in these verses are "hardships." For example, in vv. 6–7 Paul enumerates the "virtues" and "divine powers" that enable him to bear such hardships. Given the unity of these verses, however, they can be viewed as an extended hardship list that includes items that explain how Paul endures his hardships. See Fitzgerald, *Cracks in an Earthen Vessel*, 184–201. Fitzgerald is especially interested in drawing comparisons between Paul's lists of hardships and the hardship lists found in the writings of Hellenistic philosophers.

The material can be divided into three subunits:[59] Paul's appeal to the Corinthians (6:1-2); Paul's claim that he gives no offense lest the ministry of reconciliation be faulted (6:3-4a); and the hardship list that undergirds Paul's appeal and gives the Corinthians reason to boast in their apostle (6:4b-10).

The third of these subunits, the hardship list (6:4b-10) is one of the most perfectly structured passages in Paul's writings, and there is general agreement among commentators about its structure (Thrall, 1:453). It begins with eighteen items, each introduced by the preposition *en* ("in"). The first of these items ("in great endurance") functions as a general introduction to the entire list and is followed by three groups of three hardships (4b-5). There follow two groups, each with four items, which explain how Paul endures these hardships (6-7a). Next there are three contrasts (7b-8a) introduced by *dia* ("through"). The list concludes with seven antitheses (8b-10) introduced by *hōs* ("as") which point to the paradoxical nature of Paul's ministry. The material can be outlined in this way:

> *three triads introduced by "great endurance"* (vv. 4b-5)
>   in great endurance
> in afflictions, in troubles, in calamities
> in beatings, in imprisonments, in riots
> in labors, in sleepless nights, in going hungry
>
> *two groups of four* (vv. 6-7a)
> sincerity, knowledge, patience, kindness
> Holy Spirit, genuine love, word of truth, power of God
>
> *three contrasts* (vv. 7b-8a)
> through weapons of righteousness in the right hand
>   and the left
> through honor and dishonor
> through ill repute and good repute
>
> *seven antitheses* (vv. 8b-10)
> as deceitful and we are truthful
> as unknown and we are known
> as dying and behold we live
> as punished and we are not put to death

---

59. Although the material can be divided into three subunits on the basis of content, vv. 3-10 consist of a series of participles rather than finite verbs. Accordingly these verses are dependent on the main verb of v. 1 "we appeal" (*parakaloumen*). Apart from v. 2, the entire section is a single sentence, though it is not translated as such. On the structure of this section, see Lambrecht, "The Favorable Time: A Study of 2 Corinthians 6:2a in Its Context," in *Studies on 2 Corinthians*, 515-29.

B. The Integrity of Paul's Apostolic Ministry 149

as grieving but we are always rejoicing
as poor but enriching many
as having nothing and yet we possess everything

[6:1–2] At the end of the previous unit, Paul presented himself as Christ's ambassador through whom God "appeals" to humanity to be reconciled to God, that is, to accept the reconciliation that God offers through Christ's saving death (5:20). In these two verses Paul resumes that appeal. But whereas in 5:20 God made the appeal through the apostle, here Paul makes the appeal in his capacity as one who "works with" God, that is, as God's "coworker." Paul roots this appeal in a passage from the prophet Isaiah that he interprets christologically: the eschatological day of salvation that the prophet foresaw has arrived with Christ. Commenting on this, he twice employs the adverb "now" in order to remind the Corinthians of the urgency of his appeal.

Paul makes this appeal as one "working together with" (*synergountes*) "God." Although "God" is not explicitly identified in the Greek text as the one with whom Paul works, and although it is possible that Paul has in mind as his coworkers the Corinthians (so Chrysostom, *Homily* 12:1; and Allo, 173) or perhaps other apostolic ministers, the context suggests that Paul is presenting himself as working together "with God," since God gave Paul the ministry of reconciliation (5:18), and God makes his appeal through the apostle (5:20). Thus, even though the concept of working together with God ("coworker") is liable to misinterpretation, Paul is fully aware that although he and other apostolic ministers are God's coworkers (see 1 Cor 3:9, where this is stated explicitly), it is God who gives the growth (1 Cor 3:7). In writing that he works together with God, then, Paul is simply echoing what he has already said about the ministry of reconciliation, a ministry in which God appeals through him.

Paul appeals to the Corinthians "not to receive the grace of God in vain" (v. 1). The concept of "grace" (*charis*) plays an important role in the New Testament, especially in Paul's letters. According to BDAG *charis* is a "beneficent disposition towards someone"; thus it is "favor," "grace," "graciousness," "good will" on the part of one party toward another. The *charis* with which Paul is concerned is "the grace of God," by which Paul means the gracious act of God in Christ whereby God reconciled humanity to himself. Deeply aware that he was called as a result of God's graciousness (Gal 1:15) and that he is who he is by "the grace of God," Paul emphatically notes that God's grace toward him has not been in vain (1 Cor 15:10). But why does Paul appeal to the Corinthians "not to receive the grace of God in vain"?

Paul's initial proclamation of the gospel at Corinth undoubtedly stressed the gospel of reconciliation, and one can assume that the Corinthians responded favorably to this message, as the thanksgiving of 1 Cor 1:3–9 indicates. But since the Corinthians have called into question the apostolic integrity of the one who exercises this new covenant ministry of reconciliation among them, they will have received the grace of God in vain if they are not fully reconciled with Christ's ambassador; for one cannot be at enmity with the ambassador through whom God makes the appeal for reconciliation and still be reconciled with God. The appeal "not to receive the grace of God in vain," then, is an appeal to be reconciled with Christ's ambassador.

Paul grounds this appeal in a quotation from Isa 49:8 that reproduces the text of the Septuagint exactly. The text is part of the Servant Song (Isa 49:1–13) in which God calls the servant (vv. 1–7) and then announces the salvation that the servant will effect (vv. 8–11). Paul, however, interprets the text christologically and eschatologically. The "favorable time" and "the day of salvation" have occurred in the Christ event, by which God has reconciled humanity to himself (5:14–21). Consequently in commenting on this text Paul emphatically writes "now" is the favorable time and "now" is the day of salvation. Since God's eschatological act of salvation has occurred in Christ, in whom God's new creation has made its appearance, the Corinthians must respond to Christ's ambassador "now"; otherwise they will have received the grace of God in vain.

[3–4a] Having appealed to the Corinthians not to receive the grace of God in vain, Paul asserts that he conducts himself in such a way that nobody can fault the ministry he exercises. The argument proceeds in two steps: a strong negative clause (v. 3) begun with alliteration (*mēdemian en mēdeni*) and a positive adversative clause (v. 4a) in which Paul commends himself. In the first clause, Paul relates his conduct to the ministry that he exercises by explaining that he does not provide others with an occasion for taking offense "lest" (*hina mē*) they point to his conduct as an excuse for finding fault with "the ministry." The ministry to which Paul refers is the ministry of "a new covenant" (3:6), "the ministry of righteousness" (3:9), "the ministry of reconciliation" (5:18). Here he calls it simply "the ministry" (not "our ministry," as do some manuscripts), indicating that "the ministry" is prior to and more important than the one who exercises it. Although certain people at Corinth have undoubtedly impugned the ministry Paul exercises by their criticism of him, as will become evident in chapters 10–13, Paul implies that his conduct is such that, when understood properly, this criticism is ill founded. The ministry he exercises cannot legitimately be criticized on the basis of his conduct, as the list of hardships that follows will show.

In the second clause (4b), Paul says that in his capacity as God's minister he commends himself in every way, once more raising the question of self-commendation (3:1; 4:2; 5:12). In writing this, Paul is not commending himself as a minister of God, as if he somehow had to present the Corinthians with letters of recommendation. Indeed, even if he wanted to commend or present himself as a minister of God, he could not, unless God had first "given" him the ministry that he exercises. Rather, as one who is already God's minister, he commends himself in every way, as the list of hardships will show.

B. The Integrity of Paul's Apostolic Ministry

To understand what Paul writes here, it is important to recall what he said in 5:12: "We are not commending ourselves to you again but giving you an opportunity for boasting on behalf of us." In 5:12 Paul affirms that his purpose in speaking about himself is to provide the Corinthians with something to say to those who criticize him. Here (6:4) Paul commends himself to the Corinthians by the list of hardships that follows. In doing so, he provides them with something to say to those who criticize him. Thus, when Paul speaks about himself, it is not to promote himself but to assist the Corinthians in their struggle with those who criticize him and the ministry he exercises.

[4b–5] Having made his appeal, and having based that appeal on his conduct, Paul employs an extensive "hardship list" (vv. 4b–10) to undergird his appeal and provide the Corinthians with "something to say to those who boast in appearance and not in the heart" (5:12). Paul begins by commending himself "in great endurance," which functions as the theme for all that follows. He then presents three groups of hardships, each containing three hardships. The first group is somewhat general in nature, describing the hardships that attend his ministry. The second details the kinds of hardships that others have imposed upon him, whereas the third enumerates the hardships that he has imposed upon himself for the sake of the ministry.

Since all of his hardships require endurance, "great endurance" (*en hypomonē pollē*) heads the list. *Hypomonē* is the capacity to hold out in the face of difficulty (BDAG). The word occurs rather frequently in Paul's writings (Rom 5:3, 4; 8:25; 15:4, 5; 2 Cor 12:12; 1 Thess 1:3; 2 Thess 3:5). In Rom 5:3–4 it is coupled with "affliction" (the next item on this list), which, Paul says, produces "endurance." In Rom 8:25 and 1 Thess 1:3 Paul relates it to "hope." This capacity to sustain hardship in the hope of what is yet to come is what characterizes Paul's ministry.

Having commended himself "in great endurance," Paul introduces his first group of three hardships (v. 4b): "afflictions" (*thlipsis*), "troubles" (*anankē*), "calamities" (*stenachōria*). The three words characterize in a general way the difficulties Paul must endure as God's minister. *Thlipsis* occurs frequently in 2 Corinthians (1:4, 8; 2:4; 4:17; 7:4; 8:2, 13), and the participial form of the verb heads the hardship list of 4:7–12. Its placement at the beginning of that list and at the head of this triad suggests that it best characterizes the hardships that Paul endures. *Anankē* indicates "a state of distress or trouble" (BDAG) and *stenochōria* "a set of stressful circumstances" from which there seems to be no escape (BDAG). Both words are found in the brief hardship list of 12:10. Taken together, these three terms provide a general portrait of Paul's apostolic suffering. As God's minister he is under constant duress and pressure, hemmed in on every side by stressful and distressing circumstances.

Paul's second group of three is more specific, detailing how others have afflicted him (v. 5a): "beatings" (*plēgē*), "imprisonments" (*phylakē*), "riots" (*akatastasia*). The first two items also occur in the hardship list of 11:23–32;

see verse 23. In the Acts of the Apostles, Luke often portrays Paul as enduring beatings, being the victim of mob violence, and being imprisoned (Acts 13:50; 14:19; 16:22–23; 17:5; 18:12; 19:29–30). In 11:23–32, Paul provides an even more precise list of such sufferings. What he says here, however, is sufficient to show that his ministry regularly resulted in afflictions imposed by others.

In his third group of three, Paul moves from afflictions that others have imposed upon him to those that he has imposed upon himself in order to carry out his ministry (v. 5b): "labors" (*kopos*), "sleepless nights" (*agrypnia*), "going hungry" (*nēsteia*), all three of which occur in the hardship list of 11:23–32; see verses 23, 27. Although *kopos* can also be construed as "trouble" or "difficulty," Paul is probably referring to the burdensome work and toil that he has endured in order to support himself, resulting in "sleepless nights" and "going hungry," as he labored by day at his trade and preached whenever possible.

Taken as a whole, these three groups, introduced by Paul's endurance, present a portrait of the apostle as afflicted by internal and external circumstances, oppressed by others and compelled to endure great affliction for the sake of the gospel.

[6–7a] Paul now introduces two groups, each containing four items, that characterize the moral quality of his conduct and explain how he endures the many afflictions he has just detailed. Although these eight items are often identified as "virtues," the designation is more appropriate for the first group of four than for the second, which highlights the divine assistance Paul has received. Thus any designation of these two groups as "virtues" should take into consideration this "divine assistance" that makes such a virtuous life possible.

The first group of four (v. 6a) consists of "sincerity" (*agnotēs*), "knowledge" (*gnōsis*), "patience" (*makrothymia*), and "kindness" (*chrēstotēs*). *Agnotēs* denotes "integrity," "purity" (Bultmann, 171). In 11:2–3 Paul speaks of presenting the Corinthians as a "pure bride" (*parthenon hagnēn*) to Christ, and he expresses his fear that they are being led astray from "pure devotion" (*hagnotētos*) to Christ. Here the word points to the integrity of Paul's character, which is sincere and pure in its devotion to the gospel. *Gnōsis* plays a major role in the Corinthian correspondence. More than human knowledge, it is a gift of God's Spirit (1 Cor 12:8; 13:2, 8). In 2:14 Paul has already spoken of himself as manifesting "the fragrance of the knowledge" of God, as God leads him in his triumphal procession, and in 4:6 he has spoken of "the knowledge of the glory of God on the face of [Jesus] Christ." The knowledge, then, to which Paul refers is a God-given knowledge that Paul proclaims in the gospel; it is his understanding of God's purpose. In Gal 5:22, Paul lists *makrothymia* and *chrēstotēs* among the "fruit of the Spirit." The first is a quality of "patience" and "forbearance," often predicated of God (Rom 2:4; 9:22; 1 Pet 3:20) or Christ (1 Tim 1:16; 2 Pet 3:15). The second is a quality of "goodness," "kindness," "generosity," also predicated of God (Rom 2:4; 11:22; Eph 2:7; Tit 3:4) as well

B. The Integrity of Paul's Apostolic Ministry

as of humans. Paul portrays himself, then, as a man of complete integrity who understands the purpose of God and conducts his life with Godlike forbearance and kindness. Although these are "virtues," they are the result of God's power as the next group of four will show.

Paul's second grouping of four (v. 6b) consists of "the Holy Spirit" (*pneuma hagion*), "genuine love" (*agapē anypokrita*), "the word of truth" (*logos alētheias*), and "the power of God" (*dynamis theou*). What is striking in this group is the introduction of "the Holy Spirit," leading one commentator to write, "It is scarcely credible that St. Paul would place the Holy Spirit in a list of human virtues and in a subordinate place, neither first to lead, not last to sum up all the rest" (Plummer, 196). This observation would be correct if this were "a list of human virtues." It is already apparent from the first group of four, however, that Paul has in view "virtues" empowered by God. The presence of "the Holy Spirit" here, then, is hardly out of place, especially since Paul refers to "the power of God" at the end of the list. The Spirit is the source of Paul's "knowledge," "patience," and "kindness." Moreover, "love" heads Paul's list of "the fruit of the Spirit" in Gal 5:22, and "genuine love" heads yet another list in Rom 12:9–21, in the midst of which Paul explicitly refers to the Spirit (Rom 12:11). The presence of the Spirit at the beginning of this group, which is the midpoint of the two groups, suggests that the Spirit directs Paul's virtuous life. Thus the third item, "the word of truth," does not refer merely to the truthful character of Paul's speech but to the gospel that is the "message" (*logos*) of God's truth (see Eph 1:13; Col 1:5) Paul preaches in "the power of God."

With this second group of four, Paul completes his self-description of the "virtuous life" that he leads and that enables him to endure his afflictions. His love is unfeigned and devoid of hypocrisy because it is "the fruit" of the Spirit. What he speaks is true because it is the word of the gospel. All that he does is accomplished by the power of God, which is the Spirit.

[7b–8a] Having listed eighteen items, all of them introduced by the preposition *en* ("in"), Paul provides his audience with a rhetorical respite by introducing three phrases (vv. 7b–8a), each beginning with the preposition *dia* ("through"). Once more, it is difficult to find a single word that accurately characterizes all three phrases. For, although the second and third might be viewed as "contrasts," "antitheses," or "vicissitudes," the first does not fit any of these categories. Perhaps, then, it is best to view the first phrase ("through weapons of righteousness in the right hand and the left") as a thematic statement with the second and third phrases subordinated to it. In this case, Paul would be saying that through "honor and dishonor," through "ill repute and good repute," he conducts himself with the "the weapons of righteousness."

Although "the weapons of righteousness" could be construed as the weapons with which "righteousness" provides Paul, it is more likely that Paul means the weapons that *are* righteousness. And in this case, since Paul is defending his integrity, righteousness is best understood in terms of right conduct, conduct in accordance with God's will. Paul, of course, is not reverting to some kind of "works righteousness," as if he were trying to conduct himself on the basis of his own power. For 2 Corinthians has already made it abundantly clear that Paul carries out a new covenant ministry of righteousness for which God has qualified him (3:6). Moreover, Paul has just said that God made Christ "sin" so that "we" might become "the righteousness of God" (5:21). What Paul means, then, is that his right conduct manifests the God-given righteousness of the gospel. Like a soldier with shield in his left hand and javelin in his right, Paul has been completely outfitted for battle by God. Paul employs similar imagery in Rom 6:13, where he writes, "No longer present your members to sin as *weapons* (NRSV margin) of wickedness, but present yourselves to God as those who have been brought from death to life, and present yourselves to God as *weapons* (NRSV margin) *of righteousness*" (emphasis added; for other military imagery see Rom 13:12; Eph 6:13–17; 1 Thess 5:8). In 10:4, when he begins his critique of the intruding apostles, Paul will insist that the weapons with which he wages war do not derive from the flesh but from the power of God.

The second and third phrases portray the contrasting situations in which Paul inevitably finds himself as God's minister (v. 8a):

| honor | and | dishonor |
| ill repute | and | repute |

The four items point to the constantly changing circumstances of Paul's life and ministry. For although there are moments when he is held in honor and repute, he also finds himself held in dishonor and ill repute, often by the very people who once held him in honor and repute. Such was the case at Galatia (Gal 4:12–20), and it is possible that this is now the situation at Corinth. Aware that human beings are fickle, and that he will inevitably face dishonor and slander as well as the praise of others, Paul affirms that he always conducts himself with "the weapons of righteousness." That is, while others may praise or slander him, his righteous conduct remains constant. Indeed it is precisely this righteousness that sustains him, despite the changing opinions of others.

[8b–10] Paul completes his list of hardships with a series of seven antithetical-like phrases, each of which begins with *hōs* ("as"). The first part of each phrase lists one aspect of Paul's life that one would normally view as negative ("as deceitful," "as unknown" "as dying," "as punished," "as grieving," "as poor," "as having nothing"), and the second states its opposite ("we are truthful," "we are known," "we live," "we are not put to death," "we are always rejoicing," "enriching many," "we possess everything"). The contrast that Paul establishes points to the paradoxical nature of his apostolic sufferings. For whereas the first part of each phrase portrays his actual circumstances, or how

B. The Integrity of Paul's Apostolic Ministry

people perceive those circumstances, the second describes the deeper reality of Paul's life, which others do not perceive or simply deny.

The first of the antitheses falls under the category of a slander against Paul: he is viewed as if he were a deceiver (v. 8b). Though the charge does not occur elsewhere in Paul's letters, it represents the kind of accusation leveled against Paul in the Acts of the Apostles (see Acts 21:21). More importantly, in 12:16–18 Paul will have to deal with accusations that he took advantage of the Corinthians, a suggestion that he deceived them in monetary matters. The reality, however, is Paul's truthfulness or integrity, which he has sought to establish throughout this letter. As Paul will say toward the end of this letter, "For we cannot do anything against the truth but only for the truth" (13:8).

The second antithesis points to the obscure nature of Paul's life and ministry, especially when viewed in the context of society as a whole (v. 9a). Within the Roman world he and his associates would have been of little account in the eyes of the public figures of the day. Thus Paul says of himself in 1 Cor 4:9, 13, "For I think that God has exhibited us apostles as last of all, as though sentenced to death. . . . We have become like the rubbish of the world, the dregs of all things, to this very day." Paul, however, is known to God and the communities he (Paul) has established. Indeed he has already affirmed that the Corinthians know him in part, hoping that this letter will allow them to know him completely (1:13).

In the third antithesis (v. 9b), Paul returns to the theme he developed in the hardship catalogue of 4:7–12, where he describes how he bears "the dying of Jesus" in his body so that "the life of Jesus" might be manifested in his body. That theme is repeated here; for although he is dying daily because of his apostolic afflictions (see 1 Cor 15:31), the truth is that he lives. What Paul says here is an allusion to Ps 118:17, "I shall not die, but I shall live, and recount the deeds of the LORD."

The fourth antithesis (v. 9c) continues this allusion to the Ps 118:18: "The LORD has *punished* me severely, but he did not give me over to death" (emphasis added). Like the psalmist, Paul views his hardships on behalf of the gospel as divine discipline. Though others may have viewed this discipline as just punishment for one they perceive to be a deceiver, Paul again exhibits the faith of the psalmist (see 4:13) and understands that God's discipline does not lead to death for the righteous.

In the fifth antithesis (v. 10a) Paul describes himself "as grieving." Since he has already said that he determined not to come to Corinth again "in grief" (2:1), and since he said that he wrote his harsh letter to the Corinthians "with many tears" (2:4), it is evident that the apostle experienced moments of genuine grief because of his apostolic ministry. Nonetheless, "joy" characterizes Paul's ministry since it is "the fruit" of the Spirit who energizes his life (Gal 5:22). Consequently it is not surprising that he speaks so extensively of rejoicing in Philippians (1:18; 2:17, 18, 28; 3:1; 4:4, 10), even though he finds himself in prison. Paul experiences this joy anew when he hears of Titus's report (7:7, 9, 13, 16), and he tells the Corinthians that when he is weak and they are strong, he rejoices (13:9). He appropriately concludes this letter with an exhortation to rejoice (13:11).

In his sixth antithesis (v. 10b) Paul seems to be drawing upon a theme that he will develop in his discussion of the collection where he writes, "For you know the grace of our Lord, Jesus Christ: that for your sake he became poor, though he was rich, so that by his poverty you might be enriched" (8:9). With this understanding of the one for whom he is an ambassador, Paul describes himself as "poor but enriching many." Although the poverty to which he alludes is undoubtedly real, the riches he brings are more than material, though one should not forget the gracious gift he is presently preparing for the church at Jerusalem. Paul will also describe how the Macedonian churches brought forth an abundance of generosity despite the depths of their poverty (8:1–2).

Paul's final antitheses (v. 10c) is the most paradoxical and is clearly intended to sum up all that he has said. He is the destitute apostle who must support himself by his own labors (see the vivid description of 1 Cor 4:11–13). Possessing nothing, he somehow possesses everything. What Paul writes here is best understood in light of the metaphor of the "earthen vessel" (4:7) that holds an incalculable treasure: the gospel and the ministry of a new covenant. Consequently, although he numbers himself among the destitute of the world, Paul fully comprehends the treasure he possesses as God's minister and Christ's ambassador.

The portrait that Paul presents in this hardship list can be summarized in this way: As God's minister, Paul endures a variety of afflictions, some imposed by others, others self-imposed (vv. 4b–5). He can endure these afflictions because he is a man of integrity, an integrity made possible by the Spirit, the power of God (vv. 6–7a). And so he conducts himself in righteousness in all the changing circumstances of life (vv. 7b–8a). There is a paradoxical dimension to his life, then, that only those who understand the workings of the Spirit can perceive (vv. 8b–10). This list of hardships undergirds Paul's self-commendation to the Corinthians (vv. 3–4a) and his appeal not to receive the grace of God in vain (vv. 1–2). Viewed as a whole, 5:11–6:11 provides the Corinthians with something to boast in to those who boast in appearance (5:12), reminding the Corinthians that the ministry of reconciliation requires them to be reconciled with their apostle.

4. Paul's Appeal for Reconciliation (6:11–7:4)

This is the fourth and final section in Paul's exposition and defense of his apostolic ministry. Having explained that he is "the minister of a new covenant" (2:14–4:6), whose apostolic sufferings paradoxically manifest and anticipate resurrection life (4:7–5:10), and having declared that God has given him "the ministry of reconciliation" and made him "Christ's ambassador" through whom

B. The Integrity of Paul's Apostolic Ministry

God now appeals to humanity (5:11–6:10), Paul explicitly appeals to the Corinthians to be reconciled to him. Although this fourth and final section does not develop Paul's exposition of his ministry in a new direction, it is the outworking of what he has said thus far. It shows that in addition to defending his ministry, the purpose of Paul's exposition in 2:14–7:4 is to call the community to reconciliation with its apostle.

6:11 We have spoken candidly to you,[a] O Corinthians. Our heart is opened[b] to you. 12 You are not restricted by us; you are restricted by your own affections.[c] 13 I speak as to my own[d] children, in exchange[e] open your hearts[f] to us.

14 Do not be yoked[g] with unbelievers. For what partnership can there be[h] between righteousness and lawlessness, or what sharing can there be between light and darkness? 15 What accord can there be between Christ and Beliar,[i] or what common portion can there be between believer and unbeliever? 16 What agreement can there be between the temple of God and idols? For we are the temple of the Living God.
As God said:
"I will dwell among them and walk among them,[j]
  and I will be their God, and they will be my people.
17 Wherefore, go forth from their midst,
  and set yourselves apart,
  says the Lord,
and what is unclean do not touch,
  and I will gather you,
18 and I will be your father,
  and you will be my sons and daughters,
  says the Lord Almighty."

7:1 Therefore, beloved, since we have these promises, let us cleanse ourselves from every defilement of flesh and spirit. Let us bring holiness to completion by fear[k] of God.

2 Make room for us in your hearts![l] We have injured no one. We have corrupted no one. We have taken advantage of no one. 3 I am not speaking to condemn you, for I have already said that you are in our hearts that we might die together and live together. 4 I have spoken frankly[m] to you, I have great confidence in you. I am filled with encouragement. In all our affliction, I am overflowing with joy.

a. Literally, "our mouth is open to you."
b. Literally, "our heart is enlarged," or "our heart is widened." The sense is that Paul's heart is completely open to the Corinthians.

c. "Affections" translates *splanchnon*, which refers to the innermost organs of a person, the seat of the emotional and affective life.

d. The words "my own" are supplied lest it appear that Paul views the Corinthians as children. What he means is that they are *his* children because he is the founding "father" of the community.

e. "In exchange" translates *de autēn antimisthian*, literally, "the same response," "the same recompense."

f. The words "your hearts" are supplied to complete the meaning of the verb.

g. The meaning of *heterozygeō* is "to be yoked unevenly." That is, to yoke different kinds of animals together, thus, "to be mismated."

h. This is the first of five interrogative phases, none of which has a verb. The verb "can there be" has been supplied in all five instances.

i. Some manuscripts read "Belial," which is related to the Hebrew word *beliyyal* used to denote wrongdoers. However, the word is not personified in the Old Testament to represent Satan.

j. The phrase "among them," which occurs only once in the Greek text, needs to be supplied here.

k. The Greek could be rendered as a dative of place, "in the fear of the Lord," or a dative of means, "by fear of the Lord." P^{46}, an important witness, reads "love of God" in place of "fear of God."

l. The phrase "in your hearts" has been supplied to complete the meaning of the verb.

m. "Frankly" translates *parrēsia*, which could also be rendered "boldly." But in light of 3:12, "frankly" or "openly" is the better translation. Paul has hid nothing from the Corinthians.

In terms of structure, the material of this section can be divided into three units that fall into yet another ring pattern. In the first unit (6:11–13) Paul makes an initial appeal to the Corinthians to open their hearts to him, just as he has opened his heart to them. In the second (6:14–7:1) he exhorts the community not to defile itself by "yoking" itself with unbelievers, since the community is "the temple of the Living God." This second unit is structured as follows:

6:14a	An initial exhortation not to be yoked with unbelievers
6:14b–16a	Five rhetorical questions showing that believer and unbeliever have nothing in common
6:16b	*For* the Corinthians are the temple of the Living God
6:16c–18	Scriptural proof that the Corinthians are God's temple
7:1	*Therefore*, possessing these promises, the Corinthians should avoid every defilement

In the third unit (7:2–4), Paul resumes the appeal he made in verses 11–13 for the Corinthians to open their hearts to him and adds that he has injured no one and has full confidence in the community. The entire section can be outlined as follows:

B. The Integrity of Paul's Apostolic Ministry

6:11–13	Appeal for reconciliation
6:14–7:1	Moral exhortation not to be yoked with unbelievers
7:2–4	Resumption of the appeal for reconciliation

The central portion of this section (6:14–7:1) has been the focus of an intense controversy for more than a century, with commentators questioning the Pauline authenticity of these verses and, more importantly, their relationship to the material that precedes and follows.[60] Commentators who question the Pauline authenticity of the passage have pointed to the numerous words in the passage that occur nowhere else in Paul's writings[61] as well as to the apparent "non-Pauline" or—in the view of a few— "anti-Pauline" theology that the passage exhibits, especially its dualism and call for believers to separate themselves from unbelievers. Consequently many view the passage as an interpolation introduced by Paul or a later editor. In support of this, they argue that this material "interrupts" the flow of Paul's thought between 6:11–13 and 7:2–4. Although more recent scholarship seems less inclined to view the passage as a non-Pauline fragment introduced by a later editor, and even though many commentators are more disposed to defend the Pauline authenticity of the passage, most still find it difficult to explain how these verses function within their present literary setting. For example, Furnish (383), who argues that the passage is non-Pauline in composition and that Paul incorporated it into the letter, writes, "The origin of 6:14–7:1, its place in the context, and therefore its meaning remain unclear."

In the view of this commentary, 6:14–7:1 is not an interpolation, since Paul's remark in 7:2 clearly indicates that he is resuming the appeal of 6:11–13, "for *I have already said* that you are in our hearts that we might die together and live together" (emphasis added). Moreover, there is a close connection between the

---

60. For a brief and helpful overview of the problem and the solutions that have been proposed, see Larry Kreitzer, *2 Corinthians* (NTG; Sheffield: Sheffield Academic Press, 1996), 30–35. For a classic discussion on the relationship of this text to the literature of Qumran, see Joseph A. Fitzmyer, "Qumran and the Interpolated Paragraph in 2 Cor 6:14–7:1," in *Essays on the Semitic Background of the New Testament* (Sources for Biblical Study 5; Missoula, Mont.: Scholars Press, 1974), 205–17. For a stimulating essay that explores the relationship of this passage to the whole of 2 Corinthians, see Nils Alstrup Dahl, "A Fragment and Its Context: 2 Cor. 6:14–7:1," in *Studies in Paul: Theology for the Early Christian Mission* (Minneapolis: Augsburg, 1977), 62–69. For a careful argument for the Pauline integrity of this text, see Lambrecht, "The Fragment 2 Corinthians 6,14–7,1," in *Studies on Second Corinthians*, 531–49. For a thorough history of scholarship on the text, see Bieringer "2 Korinther 6,14–7,1 im Kontext des 2. Korintherbriefes: Forschungsüberblick und Versuch eines eigenen Zugangs," in *Studies on 2 Corinthians*, 551–70.

61. Words that occur here, but nowhere else in the New Testament, are *heterozygeō* ("to be unevenly yoked"), *metochē* ("sharing"), *symphōnēsis* ("agreement"), *synkatathesis* ("agreement"), *eidōlon* ("idol"), *emperipateō* ("to walk about"), *eisdexomai* ("to gather"), *molysmos* ("defilement").

imperative of 6:13, "open your hearts to us," and the imperative that immediately follows in 6:14, "Do not be yoked with unbelievers." For the Corinthians to open their hearts to Paul, they must separate themselves from unbelievers. If they do not—and apparently some have not—their hearts will remain closed to Paul. In 6:14–7:1, then, Paul clearly employs moral exhortation to show the Corinthians what they must do to open their hearts to him, as he has opened his heart to them: they must not align themselves with unbelievers, since such people are not aligned with the gospel he preaches (see 2:15–16; 4:4).

If 6:14–7:1 is not an interpolation but an integral part of 6:11–7:4, what is its function? As already suggested, this section is the "outworking" of Paul's discussion of his apostolic ministry (2:14–7:4), inasmuch as it explicitly calls the Corinthians to be reconciled with their apostle, who is God's minister (6:4). Paul hinted at the need for such reconciliation in 3:1 when he asked, "Are we beginning to commend ourselves again? Or do we need—as some do—letters of recommendation to you, or from you?" Likewise, his remarks in 2:17; 4:1–6; 5:11–13; and most recently in 6:3–10 suggest that some at Corinth have questioned the manner in which he exercises his ministry. Consequently Paul has already made a general appeal to the Corinthians to "be reconciled to God" (5:20) and a more specific appeal for them "not to receive the grace of God in vain" (6:1). In this section, his appeal becomes explicit. The Corinthians must be reconciled *with him* (6:11–13; 7:2–4) by separating themselves from unbelievers, since those in Christ are "the temple of the Living God" (6:14–7:1).

The introduction of a specific moral exhortation in 6:14–7:1, one of the few such exhortations in 2 Corinthians, shows that the "crisis" at Corinth involves more than hurt feelings over a change in Paul's travel plans and the harsh letter that he sent to the community. As Paul indicates in 12:21, there is a moral crisis at Corinth (similar to that described in 1 Corinthians) because many of those who sinned previously "have not repented of the vileness, immorality, and licentiousness with which they acted." Thus Paul's call for reconciliation requires a moral conversion on the part of the Corinthians, and what he writes here anticipates what he will deal with in chapters 10–13. To summarize, the material of this section is the climax of Paul's exposition of his apostolic ministry, inasmuch as it calls the Corinthians to be reconciled with Christ's ambassador. In addition to functioning as the climax of what has preceded, it foreshadows the serious community problems that Paul will discuss in the final chapters of this letter.

[**6:11–13**] With these verses Paul begins his appeal for the Corinthians to be reconciled to him, even though he never explicitly uses the word "reconcile" in this section. This appeal comes immediately after a section in which Paul has exhorted the Corinthians "not to receive the grace of God in vain" (6:1) and provided them with an extended list of his hardships on behalf of the gospel (6:4–10), and therefore on their behalf as well. Consequently the Corinthians

B. The Integrity of Paul's Apostolic Ministry

should hear this appeal with the echo of Paul's hardships still ringing in their ears. From a rhetorical point of view, they should be well disposed to his appeal.

This appeal consists of three parts. In the first, Paul presents himself as fully and completely disposed to the Corinthians: he has spoken frankly to them, his heart is open to them (v. 11). In the second, he identifies the problem that the Corinthians must overcome: whereas he has opened his heart to them, their affections for him are cramped and constricting (v. 12), leading Chrysostom to note that whereas they need only to receive him, Paul is ready to receive "a whole city, and so great a population" (*Homily* 13). Finally, addressing the community as his "children," since he is the founder and so the "father" of their community, he explicitly asks them to open their hearts to him (v. 13). Paul's initial appeal, then, is a call for "reciprocity," for a "fair exchange" of affection. As he has opened his heart to them, so they should do the same.

This initial appeal is significant in several ways. First, it is characterized by a personal tone which immediately indicates that even though Paul reprimands the Corinthians, he is not condemning them (see 7:3). There is need for the community to be reconciled with its apostle, but Paul is not at enmity with the Corinthians. In this regard—though the point should not be pressed too far—his relationship to the community mirrors God's relationship to humanity; for just as it is humanity that needs to be reconciled to God, not God to humanity, so it is the community that needs to be reconciled to Paul, not Paul to the community. Accordingly he reprimands but does not condemn those whom he calls to reconciliation.

The personal tone of Paul's appeal is heightened by the direct address that he makes to the community, "O Corinthians." Although he addresses the Galatians (Gal 3:1) and Philippians (Phil 4:15) in a similar fashion, such personal appeals are rare in Paul's letters, suggesting his profound concern for those whom he now calls to reconciliation. Paul is openhearted to the Corinthians because they are his "children." As a parent reprimands but still loves his children, so he reprimands but still loves his children (for other examples of Paul calling his converts his "children," see 1 Cor 4:14; Gal 4:19; and 1 Thess 2:7, where the imagery is feminine; and 1 Thess 2:11, where the imagery is masculine).

The second way in which this appeal is significant is Paul's reference to his "heart," which echoes what he said when he called the community his letter of recommendation "written in our hearts, known and read by all" (3:2) and when he identified the community as "a letter from Christ," written by the Spirit of the Living God "on tablets (which are) human hearts" (3:3). In telling the community that his heart is open to it, then, and in summoning the Corinthians to open their hearts to him, Paul echoes themes of his new covenant ministry that will also appear in the scriptural quotations that he will soon employ. Paul's heart cannot but be open to the community, since the community is his letter of recommendation written on his heart. Conversely, if the Corinthians are a letter of Christ written by the Spirit on tablets of human hearts, their hearts should be open to him.

[6:14a] With this imperative, Paul employs an image that will control the following exhortation: the Corinthians are not to "be yoked" (*heterozygountes*) with unbelievers. The image is indebted to Deut 22:10, which prohibited the Israelites from plowing with two different kinds of animals, and to Lev 19:19, which forbade the crossbreeding of different kinds of animals ("You shall not let your animals breed with a different [*heterozygō*] kind"). In both instances the law forbids bringing together different kinds of animals for a common purpose, thereby maintaining the "boundaries" between animals that the law views as incompatible with each other. Paul's image functions in a similar way: the Corinthians are to maintain appropriate boundaries between themselves and unbelievers.[62]

As Paul clearly indicates in 1 Cor 5:9–12, the maintenance of such boundaries does not mean that the Corinthians may not associate with unbelievers. Rather, he is saying that although they may associate with unbelievers in the ordinary affairs of life, they must maintain boundaries between themselves and unbelievers in those things that lead to idolatry, a point that he will reinforce in what follows. Paul makes a similar (though more nuanced) point in 1 Cor 8:1–11:1, especially 10:14–22, where he provides the Corinthians with an extensive discussion about the danger of participating in cultic meals associated with the worship of idols. What he writes here and in 12:21 suggests that those problems have not yet been resolved.

But who are the "unbelievers" to whom Paul refers? Though some suggest that they are Paul's opponents, especially since Paul identifies the super-apostles as servants of Satan in 11:14–15, in Paul's letters "unbelievers" (*apistoi*) normally designates those who are not Christians, usually Gentiles (1 Cor 6:6; 7:13, 15; 10:27; 14:22, 23, 24; 2 Cor 4:4). The exhortation that follows, with its emphasis on the Corinthians as "the temple of the Living God," also points in this direction. The meaning of Paul's exhortation, then, can be summarized in this way: the Corinthians are not to be united in religious matters with those who are not Christians, for such behavior inevitably leads to idolatry.

[14b–16a] To clarify what he means by the imperative of v. 14a, Paul asks five rhetorical questions. In this series of questions, the first and second questions, as well as the third and fourth, are related to each other by the conjunction "or" (*hē*), whereas the fifth and most important question stands somewhat apart from the first four. The material can be outlined as follows:

---

62. Since Paul clearly affirms the validity of existing marriages between believers and nonbelievers in 1 Cor 7:12–16, it seems unlikely that he is forbidding believers from marrying unbelievers when he instructs the Corinthians not to be "yoked" with unbelievers (though this interpretation cannot be excluded). Rather, he appears to be urging the Corinthian believers to maintain appropriate boundaries between themselves and unbelievers by avoiding all immorality.

B. The Integrity of Paul's Apostolic Ministry

v. 14	what partnership	righteousness	and	lawlessness
or	what sharing	light	and	darkness
v. 15	what accord	Christ	and	Beliar
or	what portion	believer	and	unbeliever
v. 16	what agreement	temple of God	and	idols

The structure shows that there are two opposing camps that have nothing in common because each belongs to a different sphere or realm of influence. Accordingly, if the two are "yoked together," they will be "mismated" and inevitably be at odds with each other. Because the Corinthians are the fruit of Paul's new covenant ministry, they belong to the sphere of "righteousness," "light," "Christ," "believer," and "the temple of God." It should be obvious to them, therefore, what Paul means when he exhorts them not to be yoked with unbelievers. The series of words that Paul employs to designate a common sphere of interest ("partnership," "sharing," "accord," "portion," and "agreement") are almost interchangeable. In every instance these verbs presuppose participation in a common reality in which like-minded partners share. There cannot be such sharing with "lawlessness," "darkness," "Beliar," "unbeliever," and "idols."

"Righteousness" (*dikaiosynē*) has no partnership with "lawlessness" since the former presupposes a moral life in accord with God's will, made possible by the power of the Spirit, whereas the latter is a life at odds with God's law (*anomia*, "lawlessness"). The righteous belong to the realm of "light," whereas the lawless belong to the realm of "darkness." Such "light" has no sharing in "darkness" since the two are polar opposites. So Paul reminds the Thessalonians that they are "children of light and children of the day," not "of the night or of darkness" (1 Thess 5:5, see Eph 5:8). There is no accord between "Christ" and "Beliar" because each has his own sphere of influence.[63] Whereas the former heads the realm of "righteousness and light," the latter rules the realm of "lawlessness and darkness." Accordingly, "believer" and "unbeliever" belong either to "Christ" or to "Beliar," but there is no "common portion" or "inheritance" between "believer" and "unbeliever."

In his fifth and final rhetorical question, Paul establishes the contrast that will function as a thematic statement for the scriptural quotation that he will soon

---

63. "Beliar" is the Greek equivalent of "Belial." "Belial" does not occur as a proper name in the Old Testament, though it is often used in compounds to denote evil people, e.g., " a man of wickedness" (*beliyyal*). "Belial" does occur in intertestamental writings such as *Jubilees*, *Testament of the Twelve Patriarchs*, *Sibylline Oracles*, *Martyrdom of Isaiah*, and *Ascension of Isaiah*, where it is personified. Most significantly for this text, "Belial" frequently occurs in the writings of Qumran, where it designates the leader of the forces of darkness. For a full discussion, see "Belial," by Theodore J. Lewis in *The Anchor Bible Dictionary* (ed. David Noel Freedman; New York: Doubleday, 1992), 1:654–56.

introduce. There can be no agreement between "the temple of God" and "idols," since false gods cannot reside in the house of the Living God.

[16b] With this brief statement ("For [*gar*] we are the temple of the Living God") Paul draws an important conclusion that affects him as well as the Corinthians. As the sanctified community of the new covenant empowered by the Spirit prophesied by Jeremiah and Ezekiel, the Corinthians are the dwelling place of God; they are "the temple of the Living God." Therefore, the church, which is composed of many members, is the temple of "the Living God," as Paul reminds the Corinthians when he asks, "Or do you not know that your [plural] body is a temple of the Holy Spirit within you?" (1 Cor 6:19). Paul's reference to "the Living God" echoes his statement in 3:3 that the Corinthian community is "a letter from Christ administered by us, not written with ink but by the Spirit of the Living God," indicating in yet another way that the new covenant community is the "temple of the Living God" precisely because the Spirit of God dwells in it.

Paul's line of thought, then, can be summarized in this way: As the minister of a new covenant, he has been instrumental in bringing the Spirit of "the Living God" to Corinth. Because that Spirit dwells within the entire community of the church, the Corinthian community is "the temple of the Living God."

[16c–18] Having reminded the Corinthians that "we are the temple of the Living God," Paul introduces an extended quotation from Scripture to substantiate what he has said. Although the quotation consists of several texts from various Old Testament writings, Paul introduces it as if it were a single quotation, without identifying the writings in which it is found.[64] Rather, using an introductory formula that is not otherwise found in his letters, he writes, "As God said." The formula is important for two reasons. First, it discloses that Paul views the whole of Scripture as God's word. Consequently it is not necessary for him to identify the particular writing or writings from which he quotes, although he does do so in other instances. Second, by introducing the quotation in this manner, he reinforces what he wants to say by appealing to the authority of God. It was God who promised to dwell among his people, and God has now fulfilled that promise in the new covenant community that Paul has established at Corinth.

In addition to this strong introductory formula, Paul employs two other formulas, one in the middle of the quotation ("says the Lord") and another at the end ("says the Lord Almighty"), thereby underscoring the authority of this citation at its beginning, middle, and end. The material can be outlined in this way:

---

64. Paul may have "inherited" this quotation from another. For the purposes of this commentary, however, which focuses on the final form of the text, "Paul" is identified as its author. For even if he inherited the text, he surely agreed with the main lines of its theology since he employed it.

B. The Integrity of Paul's Apostolic Ministry

v. 16c	*"As God said."*
v. 16d	God's promise to dwell among the people and be their God. In turn the people will be God's people (Lev 26:11–12; Ezek 37:27).
v. 17a	A divine imperative to depart from an unclean people (Isa 52:11b).
v. 17b	*"says the Lord."*
v. 17c	A divine imperative not to touch anything unclean, coupled with a promise that God will gather the people (Isa 52:11a; Ezek 20:34).
v. 18a	A promise that God will be their father, and they will be God's sons and daughters (2 Sam 7:14; Isa 43:6).
v. 18b	*"says the Lord Almighty."*

The line of thought within the quotation can be summarized in this way: God promises to dwell among the people and be their God. Therefore, the people must depart from an unclean people without touching anything unclean. Then God will gather them and be their father, and they will be God's sons and daughters. Although there is no reference to "the temple of the Living God" in this quotation, the application of the text to the Corinthians is clear. God's promise to dwell among the people has found its fulfillment in their new covenant community. Consequently they must separate themselves from the midst of unbelievers by avoiding whatever is unclean, that is, by avoiding immorality. For God will gather them, and they will be God's sons and daughters.

The Corinthians, of course, would have heard this quotation as if it were a single citation from Scripture. For them, as for Paul, it was more important to understand that these imperatives and promises were the very words of God than to know from where they came. A knowledge of the quotation's historical background, however, can be helpful to contemporary readers for comprehending the meaning of the text and Paul's use of Scripture.

The first part of the quotation ("I will dwell among them and walk among them, and I will be their God, and they will be my people") comes from Lev 26:11–12, and perhaps from Ezek 37:27 as well. The text of Leviticus is the conclusion of a series of blessings that God will confer upon the people if they observe God's commandments. The blessing promised in Lev 26:11–12—that God will dwell among the people—is the greatest of these. Here, as in all of the quotations that follow, Paul is primarily dependent upon the Greek version of the Old Testament, the Septuagint. A translation of the Septuagint reads:

And *I will set my covenant among you,*
and my soul shall not abhor you;

> And *I will walk among you, and be your God,*
> and *you shall be my people.*
> (trans. Brenton, modified)

Ezekiel 37:27 may also have influenced the quotation, since the final part of the Corinthian text is closer to the text of Ezekiel than it is to the text of Leviticus. Moreover, the text of Ezekiel is especially interesting, since it occurs in the context of God's promise to establish "a covenant of peace" (Ezek 37:26) with the people. A translation of the Septuagint of Ezek 37:26–27 reads:

> And I will make with them a covenant of peace; it shall be an everlasting covenant with them; and I will establish my sanctuary (*ta hagia mou*) in the midst of them forever. And my tabernacle (*hē kataskēnōsis mou*) shall be among them; and *I will be to them a God, and they shall be my people.* (Brenton, emphasis added)

As in the text of Leviticus, God promises to dwell in the midst of the people and be their God. But in addition to this, the promise comes in the context of a covenant promise. If Paul was the one who compiled the quotation, and if the context of the quotation from Ezekiel was important to him, then Paul may have been attracted to this text because it coheres with his new covenant theology.

In the second part of the quotation ("Wherefore, go forth from their midst, and set yourselves apart, says the Lord, and what is unclean do not touch, and I will gather you.") Paul draws upon Isa 52:11 and Ezek 20:34, again from the Septuagint. The historical setting of the Isaiah quotation is the Babylonian exile and God's command for the people to leave Babylon, avoiding contact with anything unclean. Those carrying the sacred vessels are to touch nothing unclean as they return to their homeland. A translation of the Septuagint reads:

> Depart, depart. Go out from there, and touch not the unclean thing;
> Go out from the midst of her;
> separate yourselves, you that bear the vessels of the Lord.
> (Isa 52:11, trans. Brenton modified)

Although the original quotation exhorts the people and those bearing the sacred vessels to avoid impurity, since they were leaving an unclean people and returning to the sacred land, Paul's concern in appropriating this text is the ethical behavior of the Corinthians, who must not participate in the idolatrous and immoral practices of their non-Christian Gentile neighbors.

The final portion of the quotation ("I will gather you") is from Ezek 20:34. Once more the historical context is the exile: "I will bring you out from the peoples, and gather you (*kai eisdexomai hymas*) out of the lands where you were dispersed" (trans. Brenton, modified). As with the quotation from Isaiah, the emphasis of this text is on the restoration of the people: God will gather the people from exile and return them to their sacred land, where God will dwell in

B. The Integrity of Paul's Apostolic Ministry

their midst. For Paul this restoration is already occurring through his new covenant ministry, whereby God is gathering Gentile converts, such as the Corinthians, into the sanctified community of the church.

The third part of the quotation ("and I will be your father, and you will be my sons and daughters, says the Lord Almighty") is a mixed quotation from 2 Sam 7:14 (= 2 Kgdms 2:14 in LXX) and Isa 43:6. The text from 2 Samuel is God's promise to David that God will be a father to David, and David will be his son ("I will be a father to him, and he shall be a son to me"). With these words, God promises that David's dynasty will endure forever. But since Paul is more interested in God's promise to the people of a new covenant, he alters this promise to David with a quotation from Isa 43:6 ("bring my sons [*tous huious mou*] from far away and my daughters [*tas thygateras mou*] from the end of the earth"). Consequently the promise to David now includes all of God's sons and daughters, who for Paul are the people of his new covenant ministry.

To summarize, Paul or the tradition he received brought together a series of quotations from Leviticus, Isaiah, Ezekiel, and 2 Samuel (= 2 Kingdoms) to produce a single quotation that contains exhortation and promise: an exhortation to depart from an unclean people and a promise that God will dwell in the midst of this restored people. Even if Paul is not the compiler of this quotation, he undoubtedly saw its fulfillment in the new covenant ministry he exercised, whereby the sanctified Gentile communities that he established, such as the church at Corinth, have become "the temple of the Living God."

[7:1] Paul now draws out the practical implication of this extended quotation, moving from the indicative (the possession of these promises) to the imperative (the need to cleanse oneself from defilement) to the goal of the Christian life (bringing holiness to completion). The promises to which Paul refers, of course, are contained in the scriptural text that he has just quoted: God will gather the people and dwell among them as their God, and they will be God's sons and daughters. These promises summarize the restoration theology of the exilic period and substantiate Paul's earlier statement, "we are the temple of the Living God." As such, they cohere with what Paul has already said in chapter 3 about a new covenant empowered by the Spirit of God, which Jeremiah and Ezekiel foretold.[65]

The designation of the Corinthians as "beloved" (*agapētoi*) reinforces the relationship between Paul and the community. For even though he has accused

---

65. This is the only place where such restoration promises appear so explicitly in Paul's writings. Although it is true that Paul normally employs "promise" in the singular in Romans and Galatians, and usually in reference to the promise made to Abraham, there are instances when he uses the plural (Rom 9:4; 15:8; 2 Cor 1:20; Gal 3:16, 21) and when he refers to promises that are more embracing than the promise made to Abraham (Rom 9:4; 2 Cor 1:20). Thus, even though the present instance is somewhat unique, it is not necessarily at odds with Paul's theology, especially his theology of restoration, as defended in the recent commentaries of Scott J. Hafemann and James M. Scott.

the Corinthians of being constricted in their affections toward him (6:12), he still addresses them in a way that highlights his affection for them. Paul employs the same designation for the Corinthians at the end of this letter (after he has spoken rather harshly to them), as he assures them that everything he does is for their edification (12:19). The appearance of the word here, then, is significant for understanding how Paul views the community, even though he finds himself at odds with it.

People who possess such promises (that they are "the temple of the Living God") have the strongest motivation to cleanse themselves "from every defilement of flesh and spirit," as God commands in the scriptural citation that Paul has just quoted. Whereas the several texts that comprise that quotation originally had ritual impurity in view, the quotation as it now stands has ethical behavior in view. Accordingly Paul employs an inclusive expression to explain what he means: the Corinthians must cleanse themselves from every defilement of "flesh and spirit." In writing this, Paul is not supposing a dualistic view of the human person (body and soul) so much as an inclusive understanding of human life. He does not mean that there are some sins that belong to the realm of the "flesh" and others which belong to the realm of the "spirit." Rather, the expression emphasizes that the Corinthians must avoid any moral defilement whatsoever, whether blatant, like cultic prostitution, or less obvious, like pride and foolish boasting.

By avoiding every defilement, the Corinthians will achieve the goal of the Christian life: "holiness." Although the word *hagiosynē* occurs rarely in the New Testament (Rom 1:4; 1 Thess 3:13), its cognates occur rather frequently and cohere with Paul's view of the community as "the temple of the Living God." Thus Paul instructs the Thessalonians that God's will for them is their "holiness" (*hagiasmos*; 1 Thess 4:3), and he has already told the Corinthians that Christ is their "holiness" (1 Cor 1:30). Moreover, he consistently identifies those to whom he writes as "holy" or "sanctified" (*hagioi*), because they have been called, consecrated, and set apart for service to God. In summoning the Corinthians to "bring holiness to completion by fear of God" (7:1), then, Paul exhorts the community to fulfill its calling by living a life of moral holiness that accords with the gift of holiness that God has bestowed upon it. The Corinthians will accomplish this if they live with the same reverential awe ("the fear of God") that guides Paul's moral conduct (5:11). Bringing such holiness to completion is an appropriate task for those who are "the temple of the Living God."

[7:2–4] With these verses, Paul makes an appeal that echoes that of 6:11–13, once more appealing to the Corinthians to let him into their hearts. In addition to making this appeal, he defends himself with three specific statements that reveal something of the situation at Corinth: Paul has injured no one, corrupted no one, taken advantage of no one. But lest the Corinthians misunderstand his rebuke, he assures them that he is not condemning them. To support this, he

B. The Integrity of Paul's Apostolic Ministry

reminds them of his readiness to die and live with them, as well as his frankness, confidence, encouragement, and joy in regard to them. The material brings to a close Paul's defense and exposition of his apostolic ministry, begun at 2:14, and serves as a transition to the next section (7:5–16), in which he will describe the joy he experienced at finding Titus at Macedonia and learning of the community's concern for him.

In summoning the Corinthians to open their hearts to him, Paul makes three statements in his defense. First, he "injured" (*ēdikēsamen*) no one (v. 2a). The verb he employs here is rather general (Thrall, 1:481): Paul has not treated anyone "unjustly." The same verb appears twice in 7:12 in reference to "the offender" and the "offended" party. The offender mentioned in 7:12 is most likely the same person to whom Paul referred in 2:5–11, and although the identity of the offended party is not so clear, the person offended may well have been Paul. If he was the offended party, then he has followed his own injunction to suffer wrong rather than to retaliate (1 Cor 6:7).

Second, Paul insists that he has not "corrupted" (*ephtheiramen*) anyone (v. 2b). Here the verb suggests that others may have accused him of corrupting people by the gospel he preaches. Paul uses the word in 1 Cor 3:17, in speaking of the one who "destroys" the temple of God (the Christian community), presumably by false teaching, and in 1 Cor 15:33, where he warns the Corinthians that bad company "ruins" good morals. Finally, in 11:3 Paul expresses his concern that the Corinthians will be "corrupted" from their sincere devotion to Christ, presumably by the teaching of the super-apostles. The verb that Paul employs here, then, may be echoing a charge made against him.

Third, Paul says that he has not "taken advantage" (*epleonektēsamen*) of anyone (v. 2c), employing a verb that he uses twice in 12:17–18, when he asks the Corinthians if he or any of those whom he sent to Corinth "defrauded" (*epleonektēsa*) them. There and here, Paul seems to be defending himself from charges that even though he refused to accept financial support from the community, he and his coworkers took advantage of the community by means of the collection designated for the church of Jerusalem.

Realizing that his comments are liable to be misunderstood, Paul assures the Corinthians that he is not speaking to condemn them (v. 3). To the contrary, they are in his heart "that we might die together and live together." This expression, which is striking in its word order ("to die," then "to live"), enjoys several parallels in secular literature,[66] which leads many commentators (Chrysostom included) to argue that Paul is referring to his deep and abiding friendship for the Corinthians. But even if this is true, it is difficult to avoid the impression that Paul is alluding to death and resurrection in the light of Christ, given his

---

66. Furnish (*II Corinthians*, 367) and Martin (*2 Corinthians*, 219) provide a number of such parallels.

extensive treatment of this topic in 4:7–5:10.[67] Thus Paul may be saying something such as the following: He and the Corinthians are bound by a bond of friendship that is ultimately rooted in the death of Jesus, which leads to life. Because of this Paul is ready if necessary to die with and for the Corinthians as a true friend, because he already lives together with them in the life of Christ, and he will continue to live with them at the resurrection of the dead.

In verse 4 Paul concludes with four statements that complete his appeal in such a way that there can be no doubt about *his* affections for the community. First, he has spoken "frankly" or "openly" (*parrēsia*), a claim that echoes what he said earlier when comparing his ministry with the ministry of Moses (3:12). Thus his gospel conceals nothing from the community. Second, despite the present rift between Paul and the Corinthians, he has great "confidence" (*kauchēsis*) in them, for they will be his boast on the day of the Lord (1:14). Third, he is filled with "encouragement" (*paraklēsis*), the very "comfort" of which he spoke so eloquently at the beginning of this letter (1:3, 4, 5, 6, 7) and which he will experience upon hearing Titus's report (7:6–7). Finally, Paul expresses his "joy" in "our affliction." If "our" includes the community, then Paul is saying that despite their common troubles his joy abounds because not even affliction can separate a father from his beloved children.

By the end of this section Paul's line of thought should be clear. Because he is the minister of a new covenant through whom God summons people to reconciliation, Paul appeals to the Corinthians to be reconciled to him. To do this, they must not join with unbelievers in immorality, for they are the temple of the Living God. For his part, Paul has done nothing to harm the Corinthians. On the contrary, he holds them in the highest esteem.

C. Paul's Narration of Recent Events Resumed 2 Corinthians 7:5–16

Having defended his integrity and the nature of his new covenant ministry in 2:14–7:4, Paul now returns to his narration of the recent events that have transpired between him and the community. Thus far in that narration he has defended his reliability (1:15–22), explained why he did not visit Corinth as he had promised but sent a harsh letter instead (1:23–2:4), exhorted the commu-

---

67. Lambrecht, "To Die Together and to Live Together: A Study of 2 Corinthians 7,3," in *Studies on 2 Corinthians*, 571–87, has made the most extensive case for this, but his arguments have not gained broad support.

C. Paul's Narration of Recent Events Resumed

nity to forgive the offender (2:5–11), and described his anxiety at not finding Titus at Troas, leading to his decision to go to Macedonia to search for him (2:12–13). In this section (7:5–16) Paul finally recounts how he found Titus at Macedonia and learned of the community's repentance. Although the Corinthians were surely interested in Paul's version of the events recounted in 1:15–2:13, they would have been most concerned about his reaction to Titus's report of their repentance. This section shows that Paul's response did not disappoint them. For in addition to expressing his profound joy at Titus's report, Paul absolves the community of all guilt in the affair now that it has repented (7:11), and he expresses his supreme confidence in the Corinthians (7:16).

Because Paul's discussion of his apostolic ministry in 2:14–7:4 separates these two parts of the narration (1:15–2:13 and 7:5–16), many commentators argue that 2:14–7:4 represents a fragment from another letter that a later editor interpolated between 2:13 and 7:5. Although this is possible, the majority of commentators maintain that it was Paul who did the interpolating, thereby establishing yet another ring pattern. If this is so, as this commentary maintains, then Paul set aside his narration of the events that led to the crisis at a particularly crucial moment—his distress at not finding Titus at Troas—thereby delaying the account of his reaction to Titus's report, the very thing about which the Corinthians most wanted to hear. Holding his response in abeyance, Paul presents and defends the nature of his new covenant ministry. Only when this defense is complete does he return to the narration and recount his meeting with Titus and his reaction to the community's response. By doing this, Paul implicitly draws a comparison between the exposition of his apostolic ministry and his narration of the events surrounding the conflict between him and community. That comparison shows that just as God always comforts Paul in the afflictions of his apostolic ministry, so God has comforted Paul in the present crisis by Titus's arrival and the community's repentance. Paul's exposition of his apostolic ministry and the resolution of the present crisis, therefore, demonstrate how "the Father of mercies and God of all consolation" (1:3) is active in this particular crisis, as well as the whole of Paul's ministry.

7:5 For, even when we came to Macedonia, our flesh[a] had no relief, but we were afflicted in every way: external struggles, internal fears. 6 But the God who comforts the downcast comforted us by the coming of Titus, 7 and not only by his coming but also by the comfort by which he was comforted by you, as he reported to us your longing, your grieving, your zeal on my behalf so that I rejoiced even more.

8 Because even if I saddened you by that[b] letter I do not regret it. And if I regretted it—for I see[c] that letter saddened you if only for a time—9 now I rejoice, not because you were saddened but because you were saddened to repentance. For you were saddened in a way God intends[d] that

you might not suffer loss in any way because of us. 10 For sorrow in a way that God intends effects repentance with no regret[e] that leads to salvation, but worldly sorrow effects death. 11 See what earnestness this very sorrow as God intends has effected for you; not only that but[f] a defense, indignation, fear, longing, zeal, punishment. In every way you have commended yourselves as innocent in the matter. 12 Therefore, even if I wrote to you, it was not for the sake of the offender, nor for the sake of the one offended, but for the sake of revealing to you, before God, your zeal for us. 13 This is why we are comforted.

In addition[g] to our comfort, we rejoice all the more over the joy of Titus, because his spirit was refreshed by all of you. 14 Because if I boasted to him about you in any way, I have not been put to shame; but as we spoke truthfully to you in everything, so even our boasting to Titus was true. 15 And his affection for you is all the greater as he recalls the obedience of all of you, how you received him with fear and trembling. 16 I rejoice, because in every way I have confidence in you.

a. The word "flesh" (*sarx*) does not have a moral connotation here. Rather, it refers to the person of Paul and could be rendered "we." A literal translation has been adopted here, however, since Paul employs "spirit" (*pneuma*) in 2:13, where he writes "my spirit was ill at ease because I did not find Titus." There, as here, Paul is referring to his whole person. Thus "my spirit" could be rendered "I."

b. The Greek reads "the letter," but the context clearly indicates that Paul is referring to the harsh letter that he has already discussed in 2:2–4, 9.

c. The Greek as well as the English translation of v. 8 is somewhat contorted because, immediately after saying that he did not regret sending the letter, Paul admits that he did regret sending it since it caused pain to the Corinthians. Scribal attempts to clarify Paul's meaning are apparent in the variants of the manuscript tradition. The reading *blepō gar* ("for I see"), attested by ℵ, C, D,[1] F, G, is adopted here. This reading views the phrase "for I see that letter saddened you if only for a time" as a side comment that explains why Paul regretted sending the letter. Accordingly, it is set off by dashes.

d. The phrase "in a way God intends" translates *kata theon* ("according to God").

e. The words "with no regret" (*ametamelēton*) could also modify "salvation." But the sense of the text requires that they modify "repentance" (*metanoian*).

f. The phrase "not only that but" translates *alla*, which occurs before each of the six words that follow, even though it is not apparent in this translation. The sense is that in addition to their "earnestness" for Paul, their sorrow led to these other reactions as well.

g. The words "in addition" translate the Greek *epi*. A more literal translation would be "over" or "above" our comfort.

This section consists of three units. In the first (vv. 5–7) Paul explains how God comforted him in the midst of his many afflictions by Titus's arrival and his report of the community's repentance. In the second (vv. 8–13a) Paul discusses the harsh letter he sent to the Corinthians. Although he experienced some

C. Paul's Narration of Recent Events Resumed

regret in sending that letter because it grieved the Corinthians, now he rejoices because it led to their repentance (vv. 8–9). Paul then distinguishes between two kinds of grief, one according to the world, the other as God intends (vv. 10–11). He explains that he wrote to manifest their zeal for him (vv. 12–13a). In the third unit (vv. 13b–16), the discussion returns to Titus, thereby establishing a ring pattern. Titus has also experienced joy because of the community's response, since Paul's boasting on behalf of the community has proven true (vv. 13b–15). Consequently Paul is supremely confident in the community (v. 16). The words "comfort," "joy," and "sorrow" occur throughout the material, and Paul's final comment in verse 16 regarding his complete confidence in the community prepares for his discussion of the collection in chapters 8–9.

Although the material of this section seems to be a rather straightforward report of Paul's joy at meeting Titus and yet another explanation as to why Paul wrote the harsh letter (see 2:2–4, 9 for earlier explanations), Paul's point of view in this section is remarkable for its theological insight. The first unit (vv. 5–7) explains how *God* comforted Paul, and the central point of the second unit (vv. 8–13a) is the kind of sorrow that is in accordance with *God's* will because it leads to repentance and salvation. Although there is no explicit mention of God in the third unit (13b–16), it is apparent from the context that the joy Paul and Titus experienced ultimately derives from God. The material continues a theme, therefore, that has appeared throughout this letter: the active presence of the God and Father of Jesus Christ in Paul's ministry and in the life of the Corinthian community.

[7:5–6] These verses resume the narrative that Paul had set aside after 2:12–13: "When I came to Troas to preach the gospel of Christ and a door was opened for me by the Lord, my spirit was ill at ease because I did not find Titus, my brother. But saying farewell to them, I went on to Macedonia." Having explained the nature of his apostolic ministry in 2:14–7:4, Paul now recounts his meeting with Titus at Macedonia. From a theological point of view, the most important statement of the unit is verse 6, "But the God who comforts the downcast comforted us by the coming of Titus." This description of God as the one who comforts the downcast (*ho parakalōn tous tapeinous*) recalls Paul's initial description of God in the letter's benediction, "the Father of mercies and God of all consolation, who consoles us in our every affliction so that we can console those in every affliction through the consolation by which we ourselves are consoled by God" (1:3b–4). It also echoes a description of God found in the Septuagint of Isa 49:13, "For the Lord has had mercy on his people, and has comforted (*parekalesen*) the lowly ones of his people (*tous tapeinous tou laou autou*)" (trans. Brenton). Accordingly the focus of this unit is thoroughly theological in nature. For although Titus's arrival has comforted Paul, Paul understands that God is the ultimate source of his comfort and joy.

Having already presented two lists of his apostolic hardships (4:7–12; 6:4–10), Paul now portrays himself as "the afflicted apostle" (v. 5). Thus when he finally arrived in Macedonia in search of Titus, he found himself "afflicted in every way." On the one hand, there were "external struggles," on the other, "internal fears." Although there is no certainty about the precise nature of these fears and struggles, one suspects that the "external struggles" refer to the opposition of nonbelievers, and even certain believers, to the gospel Paul preached, whereas the "internal fears" denote his anxiety at not finding Titus at Troas and his concerns, perhaps even second thoughts, about his harsh letter to the Corinthians and the negative reaction it might provoke. These struggles and fears are the kinds of afflictions Paul has already described in his hardship lists.

In an instant, however, at the "coming" (*parousia*) of Titus, God wipes away Paul's afflictions (v. 6). The identification of God as the one who comforts Paul should not be passed over too quickly, for "God" enjoys a prominent role in this letter. For example, God is "the God of all consolation" (1:3), "the God who raises the dead" (1:9), the "faithful God" (1:18), the God who "strengthens," "anoints," "seals," and "gives" believers the first installment of the Spirit (1:21–22), the God who leads Paul in "triumphal procession" (2:14), the "living God" (3:3), the God who "reconciles" humanity to himself (5:18). In saying that it was *God* who comforted him, then, Paul acknowledges the active presence of God in his ministry and explains how he is able to endure his apostolic sufferings: the God in whom he believes is the God who comforts the downcast. The downcast (*tapeinous*) with whom Paul associates himself are those of lowly status, the very people whom the mighty God raises up (see Luke 1:52; Jas 1:9), the people with whom believers should associate (see Rom 12:16).

Paul's rendezvous with Titus in the Roman province of Macedonia (northern Greece) suggests that Paul is writing from there, perhaps from Philippi (so Furnish, 393–94), although there is no certainty on this point.

[7] Having spoken of how God comforted him by Titus's arrival, Paul now points to Titus's report about the community's response as yet another way in which God comforted him. Thus it was not only by the arrival of Titus that God comforted Paul but by the news that Titus brought about the community's "longing," "grieving," and "zeal" on Paul's behalf. These three reactions suggest an ascending order of response on the part of the community. First, having received the harsh letter, the community, which has been at odds with Paul, now desires to see him, fearful that he might not return to Corinth. Next, fearful that he might not return, the community is already lamenting its role in the affair. Finally, mourning what it has done, it is now zealous in its efforts to rectify the situation, perhaps by punishing the offending party (see 2:5–11).

The threefold reaction of the community results in even greater joy for Paul, and it shows the community how God makes use of its own response to comfort the apostle in his affliction and so to increase his joy. What Paul writes here should also be read in light of his statement in 7:4, "I am filled with encouragement. In all our affliction, I am overflowing with joy." It now becomes apparent why Paul

C. Paul's Narration of Recent Events Resumed

can make such a boast: although affliction brings hardship to the apostolic minister, it cannot take away the joy that comes from the Spirit of the Living God.

[8–9] Having recounted his meeting with Titus and the favorable report that Titus brought about the community, in verses 8–13a Paul reflects upon the harsh letter that he sent to the Corinthians in terms of his initial ambivalence about the letter (vv. 8–9), the kind of grief it produced (vv. 10–11), and his purpose in writing it (vv. 12–13a).

Verse 8 begins with a rather clear statement, which Paul quickly qualifies, suggesting that he had second thoughts about his action. He begins by asserting that he did not regret sending the letter, even though it caused them sorrow. (While "the letter" is not identified, it is undoubtedly the harsh letter about which he has already written in 2:2–4, 9.) However, he quickly qualifies what he writes, "And if I regretted it," concluding, "now I rejoice." Between these two statements, Paul inserts a comment to explain his misgivings: he realizes that the letter saddened them temporarily. The tension caused by these two statements suggests that Paul may have had second thoughts about the harsh letter resulting in the "internal fears" he mentions in verse 5. More importantly, however, the tension and ambivalence are further indications of his love and concern for the community—for he realizes the sorrow that the letter produced among them.

But now, having heard Titus's report, Paul can only rejoice. Continuing to play on the verb "to sadden" (*lypeō*) and the noun "sadness" or "grief" (*lypē*), which occur eight times in verses 8–11, he dispels any notion that he found joy in their sadness. Rather, he rejoices in the "repentance" (*metanoia*) that their grief produced, since they were saddened in the way that "God intended" (*kata theon*). Exactly what Paul means by this phrase will be discussed in the commentary on verses 10–11.

Because their grief led to repentance, Paul can now say that the community did not suffer any loss because of him. By this he means that the harshness of his letter did not ultimately harm them, even if it temporarily saddened them, since it ultimately led to their repentance. But if Paul had not written to them, or if his letter had not resulted in a grief that had led to repentance, then they would surely have suffered an irreparable loss.

[10–11] Having said that the letter saddened the Corinthians "in a way that God intends," Paul now draws a distinction between "sorrow as God intends" (*hē kata theon lypē*) and "worldly sorrow" (*hē tou kosmou lypē*), stating that, whereas the latter leads to "death," the former effects a repentance that one does not regret, leading to "salvation." Worldly sorrow, then, is mere regret. Offenders regret what they have done because they have been caught or shamed. Such sorrow is merely pragmatic and does not result in a change in one's life. Accordingly it leads to eschatological death, which is separation from God. Sorrow as God intends, however, effects repentance because offenders now understand the nature of the offense. Consequently they repent, and without regret, since they comprehend the evil they have done. Such repentance leads to eschatological salvation, which is union with God. The sorrow of the Corinthians is as God intends, because they now understand that they have offended Paul. Recognizing that they have offended God's apostle, they have repented without regret.

Confident of their repentance, Paul now lists a series of reactions that characterize their changed attitude toward him: earnestness, a defense, indignation, fear, longing, zeal, punishment. Their "earnestness" (*spoudē*) is their newfound zeal for him, now that they have understood the gravity of the situation. Their "defense" (*apologia*) is probably not so much a defense of their behavior as an attempt to clarify certain facts of the matter of which Paul may not have been aware. Their "indignation" (*aganaktēsis*) would be directed either at themselves for having offended Paul or at the offender whom Paul will mention in verse 12. Their "fear" (*phobos*) may be their reverential fear of Paul. Their "longing" (*epipothēsin*), also mentioned in verse 7, is their desire to see him again. Their "zeal" (*zēlos*), also mentioned in verse 7, is manifested in the "punishment" (*ekdikēsin*) they have already inflicted on the offending party, perhaps to a point of excess (see 2:5–11). Consequently, their repentance has manifested itself in action, and Paul can now say that they have proven themselves "innocent in the matter." This does not mean that the whole affair was simply a misunderstanding. Rather, they are "innocent" because they have repented. To that extent, they are no longer tainted by the "affair." The reference to the "affair" (*pragma*) is significant, because, although Paul can pronounce them innocent of *this* particular affair, there are other issues that remain unresolved (see 12:20–13:4).

[12–13a] Paul now draws a conclusion from what he has been saying about the harsh letter. He did not write because of the offender or because of the offended party but to manifest to the Corinthians their "zeal" (*spoudē*) for him. The language Paul employs here is rather striking, since one might have expected him to say that he wrote in order to manifest to the Corinthians "his" zeal for "them," and indeed there are variant readings of lesser importance that support this reading. Moreover, in 2:4 Paul did say that he wrote so that the Corinthians might become aware of his love for them. Here, however, Paul's focus is not so much on himself as on the community. The purpose of the letter was not only to manifest *his* love for the community (so 2:4) but to make the Corinthians aware of their zeal for him, the very thing that has happened. The community's response to the letter has shown its obedience, just as Paul had hoped it would (see 2:9).

It is now clear why Paul concludes this unit by writing, "This is why we are comforted" (v. 13). The harsh letter about which Paul had second thoughts resulted in the community's repentance. And in a way that the community did not anticipate, the letter also resulted in God's work of comforting the afflicted apostle.

C. Paul's Narration of Recent Events Resumed

The precise identity of "the offender" and "the offended" is a matter of conjecture. Although earlier commentators understood the "offender" to be the incestuous man mentioned in 1 Cor 5:1–2, contemporary commentators argue that "the offender" is an individual who offended Paul or one of his delegates at the time of Paul's painful visit to Corinth. If this is the case, then Paul would be the offended party.

[13b–15] Having clarified why he wrote the harsh letter, Paul once more turns his attention to Titus. But whereas earlier he spoke of the comfort that God granted him through Titus, now he speaks of Titus's joy because of the reception that the Corinthians accorded him. By focusing on Titus in this third and final unit (vv. 13b–16), Paul anticipates what he will say about Titus's eagerness to return to Corinth and complete the work of the collection (see 8:16–17).

Paul finds two reasons to rejoice in Titus's joy. First, and most importantly, Titus's "spirit was refreshed by all of you" (note the contrast with 2:13, where Paul writes that his own spirit was "ill at ease" because he did not find Titus at Troas). Second, Paul's "boasting" to Titus about the Corinthians has not been in vain. These statements suggest that Titus may have been ill at ease about going to Corinth; and well he might have been, given the recent painful visit that Paul had experienced there. However, despite that painful visit, Paul assures the Corinthians that his own confidence in them did not waver. To the contrary, at the moment when the crisis was most severe, he could still find reason to boast in them.

Paul's boast in the community has been a constant motif in this letter. In the letter's thematic statement, for example, he reminds the Corinthians that they will be his cause for boasting on the day of the Lord (1:14), and at the end of his discussion of his apostolic ministry he speaks of his great "confidence" (*kauchēsis*) in them (7:4). Moreover, throughout the first part of the letter, Paul has been trying to provide the Corinthians with an opportunity to boast in him (5:12). What Paul writes here, then, provides the Corinthians with proof of his enduring love for them. Although it is impossible to recover the content of Paul's boast to Titus, Paul's statement in 1:24—that he does not seek to exercise authority over their faith, since they stand firm in faith—suggests that, even in the midst of the crisis, Paul was confident of the work that God's Spirit had accomplished through him.

Recalling his mission to Corinth, Titus is filled with affection for the Corinthians as he recalls their "obedience" and how they received him "with fear and trembling." This obedience, of course, was the goal of the harsh letter according to 2:9—obedience to Paul, the apostolic founder of the community (3:2), the minister of a new covenant (3:6), Christ's ambassador (5:20), and God's minister (6:4). That the Corinthians received Titus with "fear and trembling" (the same phrase occurs in Eph 6:5 and Phil 2:12 in the context of obedience) suggests that they had now understood the gravity of the situation and the significance of the one who had been offended.

Was Titus the bearer of the harsh letter? Had he visited Corinth previously (so Thrall, 1:498–99), or was this his initial visit (so Furnish, 397)? The fact that Paul boasted to Titus about the community could indicate that this was Titus's first visit, and the "fear and trembling" with which the Corinthians received him might indicate that the harsh letter arrived before Titus. Paul's comment in 8:6, however, that he appealed to Titus to complete the work of the collection he (Titus) had begun, suggests a visit prior to this most recent visit.

[16] Paul's final words, "I rejoice, because in every way I have confidence in you," echo the statement that closes his exposition of his apostolic ministry, "I have spoken frankly to you, I have great confidence in you. I am filled with encouragement. In all our affliction, I am overflowing with joy" (7:4). The net effect of these statements, which enclose this unit, is to assure the Corinthians that despite the recent crisis Paul has not lost confidence in them. On the contrary, his confidence is so firmly established that in chapters 8–9 he will call upon them to complete the collection for Jerusalem they began a year ago (8:10).

Looking back, it is now apparent that the material of this section has had a twofold result. First, it has brought Paul's narrative of his altered travel plans, the painful visit, and the harsh letter to a successful conclusion by showing how God has once more triumphed in the ministry of the afflicted apostle. Second, it has assured the Corinthians of Paul's abiding confidence in them, allowing him to raise the delicate question of the collection for Jerusalem, to which he now turns in chapters 8–9.

Part 2

An Appeal to Complete the Collection 2 Corinthians 8:1–9:15

In the first part of this letter (1:12–7:16) Paul defended his apostolic integrity by narrating his version of the recent events that transpired between him and the Corinthian community (1:12–2:13 and 7:5–16) and by presenting the community with an exposition of his apostolic ministry, at the end of which he called the Corinthians to reconciliation (2:14–7:4). The favorable report of Titus in 7:5–16 indicated that the harsh letter, which Paul sent to the community, resulted in repentance and a renewed fervor for the apostle on the part of the Corinthians. In light of Titus's report, Paul expressed his profound confidence in the community (7:16). With the crisis occasioned by the painful visit apparently settled, and with this expression of confidence, Paul now embarks upon the second major part of this letter: an appeal to the Corinthians to resume the collection for Jerusalem that they began "last year" (8:10; 9:2). Thus the material of these chapters is closely related to what precedes. Titus, who appears in both chapter 7 and chapter 8, serves as a kind of bridge from one chapter to the other (7:6, 13; 8:6, 16, 23).[1]

---

1. Whereas there is a clear relationship between chapters 8–9 and the material that precedes them, the relationship of these chapters to Paul's critique of the intruding apostles in chapters 10–13 presents a formidable challenge for interpreters. For immediately after appealing to the generosity of the Corinthians, Paul embarks upon an unrelenting polemic against a group of intruding apostles whom he sarcastically identifies as super-apostles, and in the process he chastises the Corinthians. Thus it is not surprising that many maintain that chaps. 10–13 represent a separate letter written either before or after the material in these chapters. But if Paul was dealing with two distinct problems at Corinth (the crisis over the painful visit and the crisis of the intruding apostles), then the literary relationship between chapters 8–9 and chapters 10–13 may not be as awkward as many suppose. For having settled the dispute occasioned by the painful visit and having encouraged the Corinthians to

There is little agreement about the literary structure of chapters 8–9, in part, because some commentators argue that one or both of these chapters once functioned as separate administrative letters for organizing the collection. But even if one or both of these chapters were separate letters that a later editor interpolated into what is now called 2 Corinthians, they now function as a literary unit within the present form of the letter—the only form to which the manuscript tradition testifies. Most commentators recognize the following units within the canonical form of the letter: 8:1-5 (or 1-6); 8:6-15 (or 7-15); 8:16-24; 9:1-5; and 9:6-15.[2] This commentary structures the material in the following way:

8:1-6 Paul explains how the grace of God was manifested in the earnestness and generosity of the Macedonians for the collection, resulting in Paul's appeal to Titus to resume the work of the collection.
8:7-15 Paul appeals to the Corinthians to resume the collection that they began last year, so that there will be an equality among the churches.
8:16-24 Paul commends to the Corinthians a delegation consisting of Titus and two unnamed brothers.
9:1-5 Paul explains that he sent the delegation to ensure that the collection would be ready, lest he and the Corinthians lose face before the Macedonians.
9:6-9 Paul summons the Corinthians to liberal giving.
9:10-15 Paul explains how God will enrich the Corinthians to give liberally. As a result, God will be praised, and there will be a profound unity between Gentile and Jewish Christians.

As this structure indicates, chapters 8 and 9 are closely related, and there is no need to view chapter 9 as repeating what has already been said in chapter 8. For although chapter 8 appeals to the Corinthians to resume the collection and commends the delegation headed by Titus, chapter 9 explains the purpose for the delegation and assures the Corinthians that God will provide them with what they need to participate in the collection.

---

resume the collection, Paul can now turn to the problem of the intruding apostles, which he hopes to settle on the basis of the goodwill he has established with the Corinthians. Thus the canonical shape of the letter places Paul's appeal to resume the collection between two distinct conflicts, one that has already been resolved (1:12–7:16) and another that still needs to be resolved (chaps. 10–13).

2. For a rhetorical study of the structure of these chapters, see Hans Dieter Betz, *2 Corinthians 8 and 9: A Commentary on Two Administrative Letters of the Apostle Paul* (Hermeneia; Philadelphia: Fortress, 1985); and Kiernan J. O'Mahony, *Pauline Persuasion: A Sounding in 2 Corinthians 8–9* (JSNTSup 199; Sheffield: Sheffield Academic Press, 2000). The structure adopted in this commentary follows that proposed by Lambrecht in his commentary and is somewhat similar to that proposed by O'Mahony.

An Appeal to Complete the Collection

Those who read through these chapters will immediately be struck by the frequent use of *charis* ("grace")[3] and the variety of words that Paul employs to describe the collection, without ever mentioning money:

"ministry" (*diakonia*) 8:4; 9:1, 13
"partnership" (*koinōnia*) 8:4; 9:13
"gracious gift" (*charis*) 8:6, 7, 19
"generous gift" (*hadrotēs*) 8:20
"in this matter" (*en tō merei toutō*) 9:3
"in this undertaking" (*en tē hypostasei tautē*) 9:4
"bountiful gift" (*eulogia*) 9:5
"service" (*leitourgia*) 9:12

In addition to this vocabulary, Paul makes frequent use of words such as "abound" (8:2, 7; 9:8, 12), "abundance" (8:2, 14), "need" (8:14; 9:12), and "generosity" (8:2; 9:11, 13) to emphasize the gracious aspect of the collection, since the collection is more than an appeal for money; it is an invitation to participate in God's abundant grace. Thus it is God, the source of all grace, who plays the central role in these chapters, enabling believers to be gracious and generous by supplying them with the means to be so. Put simply, believers can be generous because God is the source and origin of all generosity.

Although chapters 8–9 represent Paul's most sustained discussion about the Jerusalem collection, Paul makes reference to the collection in Galatians, 1 Corinthians, and Romans. In Gal 2:10, at the end of his account of the conference at Jerusalem—at which James, Cephas, and John acknowledged that the grace of God was at work in his mission among the Gentiles—Paul writes, "They asked only one thing, that we remember the poor, which was actually what I was eager to do." Next, in 1 Cor 16:1–4, Paul provides the Corinthians with instructions for preparing the collection.[4]

> Now concerning the collection (*tēs logeias*) for the saints: you should follow the directions I gave to the churches of Galatia. On the first day of every week, each of you is to put aside and save whatever extra you earn, so that collections (*logeiai*) need not be taken when I come. And when I arrive, I will send any whom

---

3. *Charis* occurs in 8:1, 4, 6, 7, 9, 16, 19; 9:8, 14, 15. But it is not always translated as "grace," since it carries a variety of meanings that range from the "grace of God" to "the gracious gift" of the collection.

4. This is another example of "the economics of abundance" that characterizes Paul's thought about God's economy of salvation, a salvific economy that continually overflows in abundance and is never found wanting. The theme is insightfully developed, as noted earlier, by Young and Ford, *Meaning and Truth in 2 Corinthians*, 166–85.

you approve with letters to take your gift (*tēn charin hymōn*) to Jerusalem. If it seems advisable that I should go also, they will accompany me.

Finally, in Rom 15:25–28 Paul tells the Romans that he will go to Jerusalem with the collection before visiting them.

> At present, however, I am going to Jerusalem in a ministry to the saints (*diakonōn tois hagios*); for Macedonia and Achaia have been pleased to share their resources (*koinōnian tina poiēsasthai*) with the poor among the saints (*eis tous ptōchous tōn hagiōn*) at Jerusalem. They were pleased to do this, and indeed they owe it to them; for if the Gentiles have come to share in their spiritual blessings, they ought also to be of service to them in material things. So, when I have completed this, and have delivered to them what has been collected (*sphragisamenos autois ton karpon touton*), I will set out by way of Spain to you.

On the basis of these texts and what Paul says in 2 Cor 8–9, the historical background to the Jerusalem collection may be summarized as follows, provided that one acknowledges the fragile and tentative nature of any reconstruction.[5] First, the collection seems to have originated at the Jerusalem conference (approximately 49 C.E.) with the formal request of James, Cephas, and John that Paul "remember the poor." Paul's remark about his eagerness to do this, however, might suggest that he had already begun the work of the collection. Though there is no appeal for the collection in Paul's letter to the Galatians, his remarks in 1 Cor 16 indicate that he had already instructed the Galatians (orally or in another letter) how to prepare the collection. In 1 Cor 16 Paul gives the Corinthians the same instructions he gave the Galatians, indicating that he will write letters of recommendation for those whom the Corinthians designate to take the collection to Jerusalem. As for Paul, he is not yet sure if it is advisable for him to go to Jerusalem with the delegates of the church, though he is willing to do so. The crisis surrounding Paul's painful visit to Corinth (after the writing of 1 Corinthians), however, impeded the progress of the collection. Consequently in 2 Corinthians Paul must exhort the Corinthians to complete what they began "last year" (2 Cor 8:10), and he sends a team of envoys to ensure that the collection will be ready when he arrives on his third and final visit (2 Cor 8:16–9:5). By the time that Paul writes to the Romans (from Corinth in the mid 50s), both Macedonia and Achaia have contributed to

---

5. For the historical background and theological meaning of the collection, see Dieter Georgi, *Remembering the Poor: The History of Paul's Collection for Jerusalem* (Nashville: Abingdon Press, 1992); Keith F. Nickle, *The Collection: A Study in Paul's Strategy* (SBT 48; Naperville, Ill.: Alec R. Allenson, 1966), and A. J. M. Wedderburn, "Paul's Collection: Chronology and History," *NTS* 48 (2002): 95–110. For a helpful description of the role of Paul's delegates, see Margaret M. Mitchell, "New Testament Envoys in the Context of Greco-Roman Diplomatic and Epistolary Conventions: The Example of Timothy and Titus," *JBL* 111 (1992): 641–62.

the collection (there is no mention of Galatia), and Paul is about to go to Jerusalem with the collection, somewhat apprehensive about the reception he will receive in Jerusalem (Rom 15:30–32).

Although Paul undoubtedly brought the collection to Jerusalem, there is no mention of the collection in Philippians, or in Ephesians, Colossians, and the Pastorals, letters whose Pauline authorship is disputed. Likewise there is only a passing and somewhat uncertain reference to the collection in the Acts of the Apostles, when the Lukan Paul defends himself before the Roman governor Felix: "Now after some years I came to bring alms (*eleēmosynas*) to my nation and to offer sacrifices" (Acts 24:17). This suggests that although the collection was immensely important to Paul, it may not have had the impact upon the Jerusalem church for which he so fervently hoped (see 2 Cor 9:13–14). For in addition to "remembering the poor," Paul seems to have attached a significance to the collection that the church at Jerusalem did not; namely, the monetary gift of the Gentiles would demonstrate their solidarity with the Jewish-Christian mother church of Jerusalem and, conversely, the solidarity of that church with them. Paul may have even hoped that the collection would "provoke" Israel to believe in the Messiah as it witnessed the Gentiles coming to Jerusalem with offerings (see Isa 2:2–4).[6] In the end, the collection probably did little more than temporarily relieve the needs of the poor at Jerusalem, but what Paul writes in these chapters about the collection stands as an enduring theology of God's abundant and overflowing grace.

---

6. See the article by S. McKnight, "Collection for the Saints," in *DPL* and the classic study of Johannes Munck, "Paul and Jerusalem," in *Paul and the Salvation of Mankind* (London: SCM Press, 1959), 282–308.

A. The Grace Given to the Churches of Macedonia
2 Corinthians 8:1–6

8:1 We want you to know, brothers and sisters,[a] the grace of God[b] given to the churches of Macedonia: **2** that in a severe ordeal of affliction the abundance of their joy and their extreme poverty abounded in an extraordinary generosity;[c] **3** that according to their ability—I testify—and beyond their ability, of their own accord, **4** they implored[d] us most insistently for the favor of sharing in this ministry[e] to the holy ones. **5** This they did,[f] and not as we hoped, but they first gave themselves to the Lord[g] and to us in accordance with God's will.[h] **6** As a result we appealed to Titus that as he began so he should complete this generous gift[i] among you.

a. Although Paul employs *adelphoi* ("brothers"), he undoubtedly has all the members of the community in view, women as well as men.

b. *Charis* ("grace") occurs ten times in chapters 8–9 (8:1, 4, 6, 7, 9, 16, 19; 9:8, 14, 15) with a variety of nuances that prevent it from being translated by the same word in every instance. Here, the "grace of God" refers to God's "beneficent disposition" (BDAG) toward the Macedonians.

c. "Generosity" translates *haplotēs*, which normally means "simplicity," "sincerity," "uprightness," "frankness" (BDAG). BDAG says that the meaning "sincere concern" or "simple goodness" is sufficient here, but most translators and commentators render the word "generosity" or "liberality" in light of the wider context. Thrall (2:523–24), however, does not.

d. The participle *deomenoi* has been rendered as a verb.

e. The phrase "the favor of sharing in this ministry" renders a Greek phrase that translated literally is "the grace and the participation of the ministry." Here *charis* is rendered as "favor" rather than "grace," since it concerns Paul's "beneficent disposition" toward the Macedonians. Because *charis* and *koinonia* are so closely related, they are taken as a hendiadys, the latter being subordinated to the former, thus the translation "the favor of sharing in this ministry."

f. This translation begins a new sentence at v. 5. In order to do this, the translation supplies the words "This they did."

g. The "Lord" most likely refers to Christ. However, P[46] reads "God" (*theō*), probably in an attempt to clarify the meaning of "Lord."

h. Literally, "through God's will" (*dia thelēmatos tou theou*).

i. "This generous gift" translates *tēn charin tautēn*, since here *charis* refers to the collection.

A. The Grace Given to the Churches of Macedonia

Aware that his relationship to the Corinthian community is still somewhat fragile, despite Titus's encouraging report (7:7) and his own extravagant expression of confidence in the community (7:16), Paul broaches his appeal to resume the collection for Jerusalem somewhat indirectly, by telling the Corinthians of the extraordinary generosity the Macedonians have already demonstrated in their giving. Although Paul will eventually warn the Corinthians of the shame that will come upon him and them if the collection is not prepared when he arrives (9:4), his purpose in this unit is to disclose how the grace of God empowered the extraordinary generosity of the Macedonians, implying that the same grace will be available to them if they resume the collection. In this way, Paul hopes to rouse the Corinthians to complete the work of the collection they began "last year" (8:10).

The Greek text of this unit consists of a single sentence that begins in verse 1 with a disclosure formula ("we want you to know") and concludes in verse 6 with Paul's decision to send Titus to Corinth once more ("so that we appealed to Titus").[7] Verses 2 and 3 introduce subordinate clauses, each beginning with *hoti* ("that"), in which Paul explains how the grace of God manifested itself among the Macedonians. This unit consists of three subunits. In the first (v. 1) Paul employs a disclosure formula to announce his theme, "the grace of God." In the second (vv. 2–4) he explains how the grace of God manifested itself among the Macedonians. In the third (vv. 5–6) he relates how the extraordinary response of the Macedonians to the collection for the holy ones at Jerusalem encouraged him to ask Titus to resume the collection among the Corinthians.

[8:1] Paul begins his appeal by revealing or disclosing the "grace of God" (*charis tou theou*) bestowed upon the churches of Macedonia. In 1 Cor 12:3; 15:1 and Gal 1:11 he employs a similar formula, but in the first person singular ("I want you to know") to introduce new or important topics. Rather than speak directly of the collection, however, he draws the attention of the Corinthians to "the grace of God" at work in the generosity of the Macedonians. For even if the Corinthians already knew that the Macedonians had given to the collection, Paul finds it necessary to explain *how* the grace of God was at work in their generosity. In this way he establishes the leitmotif for the discussion that follows.

The "grace" of God is the gracious, salvific favor of God manifested in the saving death and resurrection of Christ. This is the divine favor to which Paul refers at the beginning of this letter, when he wishes the Corinthians "grace and

---

7. The limits of the text for this unit present a problem, as can be seen by comparing the paragraphing of Nestle-Aland's *Novum Testamentum Graece* with that of the *Greek New Testament* of the United Bible Societies. Whereas the former identifies vv. 1–6 as a literary unit, the latter extends the unit to include v. 7 (as do Barnett, Hafemann, and O'Mahony). This commentary follows the paragraphing of Nestle-Aland, viewing v. 7 as the beginning of an appeal based on the grace of God manifested in the Macedonians (vv. 1–6). However, v. 7 is somewhat transitional in nature, and it is understandable that it is taken with what precedes as well as with what follows.

peace" from God the Father and the Lord Christ (1:2). It is the same favor with which he concludes the letter, when he speaks of the "grace of our Lord Jesus Christ" (13:13). Here Paul writes that this divine favor manifested itself through the extraordinary generosity of the Macedonians.

The churches of Macedonia are those found in the Roman province of Macedonia, the northern part of Greece: Philippi, Thessalonica, and Beroea. Since Paul may have written 2 Corinthians from one of these congregations, perhaps Philippi, he would have had firsthand knowledge of how the collection had progressed in these congregations. From that vantage point, he understood the extraordinary generosity of the Macedonians as something God-given. And so he speaks of the grace of God "given" (*dedomenēn*) to the churches of Macedonia, thereby reinforcing the leitmotif of grace that will occur throughout chapters 8–9. It is this working of God's grace that Paul wishes to reveal or disclose to the Corinthians, whom he calls "brothers and sisters" (*adelphoi*) for the first time since 1:8, thereby affirming the initial reconciliation that has occurred between him and the community. Paul is not writing simply about the collection; he is writing about the grace of God.

[2–4] Making use of two subordinate clauses, each beginning with *hoti* ("that"), Paul explains how the grace of God was given to the churches in Macedonia. In the first clause (v. 2), he employs two paradoxes to make his point: an abundance of joy overflowed in the midst of the most extreme affliction, and an extraordinary generosity overflowed from an extreme poverty. These paradoxes suggest the presence of God's favor, since affliction does not ordinarily result in joy and poverty does not produce riches, unless some other power is at work. This, of course, is precisely the point Paul wishes to make. There is joy amid affliction only if one suffers for the sake of the gospel, and if joy is the fruit of the Spirit (Gal 5:22). Likewise, only the God who manifests power in weakness (13:4) can bring forth riches from poverty, a point Paul will substantiate by the example of Christ, who became poor to enrich others (8:9). Since Paul has already experienced these paradoxes as the grace of God in his own life (see esp. 6:9–10), he immediately recognizes the workings of God's grace in the affliction and poverty of the Macedonians.

Exactly how poor the Macedonians were is disputed (see Thrall, 2:522–23). There is little doubt, however, that the churches of Macedonia suffered persecution of some sort (Phil 1:29–30; 1 Thess 1:6; 2:14; 3:3–4). If this affliction led to social ostracism, then there may even be a relationship between the affliction the Macedonians endured and the poverty of which Paul speaks. Whatever the actual historical circumstances, Paul views the joy they manifested and the generosity they displayed as God-given grace.

In the second clause (vv. 3–4) Paul turns his attention to the generosity with which the Macedonians understood the collection and the urgency with which they petitioned him to be allowed to participate in it. Again the language is

A. The Grace Given to the Churches of Macedonia

somewhat paradoxical, thereby pointing to the presence of God's grace. For they gave, on the one hand, "according to their ability" but, on the other, "beyond their ability," suggesting that God's grace enabled them to do more than their own ability could. In all of this they acted freely, "of their own accord" (*authairetoi*; v. 3), the same word employed to describe Titus's willingness to return to Corinth (8:17).

Paul illustrates the freedom of their giving by recalling how the Macedonians petitioned him for "the favor of sharing in this ministry" (*tēn charin kai tēn koinōnian tēs diakonias*; v. 4), thereby suggesting to the Corinthians how the grace of God will work in them if they resume their participation in the collection. Paul's language here is dense but significant. *Charis* now takes on another meaning: Paul's own favor or goodwill toward the Macedonians. But given the importance of Paul's leitmotif, "the grace of God," one suspects that the two uses of *charis* are related, for the Macedonians seem to have understood that their "participation" (*koinōnia*) in this "ministry" (*diakonia*) will itself be a divine gift. In asking the apostle for the "favor" of sharing in this ministry, therefore, they seek to participate in the divine favor that this ministry will bestow upon the holy ones of Jerusalem (see 9:12–14).

Since Paul's new covenant ministry has played such an important role in this letter thus far, the use of *diakonia* here is related to Paul's ministry, albeit in connection with the collection (Barnett, 397). Thus the Macedonians seek to be participants in Paul's ministry to the holy ones of Jerusalem by contributing to the collection he is taking up for them.

[5–6] Paul is astonished because the self-giving of the Macedonians exceeded his every expectation. Even before they undertook the collection, they "first" gave themselves "to the Lord [Christ] and to us [Paul]." The expression is somewhat awkward because it suggests that the Macedonians gave themselves first to the Lord and then to Paul. It is also somewhat bold because of the way in which Paul associates himself with the Lord. Its meaning, however, coheres with Paul's understanding of the apostleship that he has received "through the will of God" (1:1). Thus he means that even before the Macedonians undertook the collection, they had given themselves (in a single act) to Christ *and* his apostle, and this in accordance with God's will. This, of course, is precisely what the Corinthians must also do if their participation in the collection is to be successful.

The result of such generosity and self-giving is that Paul was encouraged to do something he seemed hesitant of doing, until he witnessed the grace of God bestowed upon the churches of Macedonia: he appealed to Titus to complete "this generous gift" (*tēn charin tautēn*; v. 6). Here *charis* refers to the collection. By describing the collection as *charis*, Paul implies that it is related to the divine favor with which he introduced this unit. Just as God freely bestows "favor" (*charis*) upon humanity through Jesus Christ, so the collection is an expression of the "favor" of its contributors, who have been empowered by "the grace of God."

The introduction of Titus at this point recalls his prominent role in 7:5–16, where Paul speaks of Titus's deep affection for the Corinthians because of the "fear and trembling" with which they received him (7:13–15), and it prepares for the recommendation of Titus and the brothers that Paul will make in 8:16–9:5. But it also raises the question of when Titus began the work of the collection among the Macedonians. It is possible that Titus initiated the work of the collection—if not directly—then indirectly, by the reconciliation he effected in his most recent visit to Corinth (Allo, 215). But some commentators suggest that Titus may have begun the work of the collection on a visit previous to that one (Barnett, 401). As is so often the case in 2 Corinthians, the evidence is insufficient to settle the matter. Paul's remark that the Corinthians began the collection "last year" (v. 11), however, could indicate that Titus had been in Corinth to arrange for the collection, previous to his most recent visit.

From a rhetorical point of view, this unit provides Paul with a shrewd way to broach the question of resuming the collection, and the example of the Macedonians provides the Corinthians with the necessary motivation to do so. But the theological point of view is the most important, inasmuch as it clarifies the meaning and significance of the collection. Participation in the collection is participation in God's grace, for it is the grace of God that allows believers to be gracious to others, a point that Paul will make most clearly in 9:6–15.

B. An Appeal to Complete the Collection
2 Corinthians 8:7–15

8:7 But just as you abound in all things, in faith, and speech, and knowledge, and all earnestness, and in the love we bring to you,[a] may you abound in this gracious gift.[b] 8 I am not commanding you,[c] but through the earnestness of others I am testing the genuineness of your love. 9 For you know the grace[d] of our Lord, Jesus Christ: that for your[e] sake he became poor, though he was rich, so that by his[f] poverty you might be enriched. 10 In this matter[g] I give my opinion, for it is advantageous for you who not only began the work[h] but even desired[i] it last year[j] 11 now to finish the work so that as there was a willing desire,[k] so there will be a completion in proportion to what you have. 12 For if the willingness lies at hand, it is acceptable in proportion to what one has, not in proportion[l] to what one does not have. 13 For it is not that the relief of others should result[m] in hardship for you but in equality. 14 At the present time, your

B. An Appeal to Complete the Collection

abundance should overflow[n] to their need, so that their abundance might be applied to your need; thus there will be an equality. 15 As it is written, "the one who had much did not have too much, and the one who had little did not have too little."

a. The expression "the love we bring to you" translates the awkward expression *tē ex hēmōn en hymin* ("the love from us to you"). One might have expected Paul to speak of "your love for us," a reading found in several witnesses (ℵ, C, D, F, G). The more difficult reading, however, has the support of P[46] and B and is to be preferred. Although the phrase could refer to Paul's own love for the community, here it is construed as the gift of love that Paul has brought to the community.

b. "Gift" translates *charis* ("grace").

c. Literally, "I am not speaking by way of command."

d. As in v. 1, *charis* has been translated as "grace" because it refers to Christ's "beneficient disposition" toward the Corinthians that Christ manifested in making himself poor for their sake.

e. One might expect "our sake," and this is found in a few manuscripts (C, K), but "your" is the better reading, emphasizing Christ's love for the Corinthians.

f. Literally, by the poverty of "that one" (*ekeinou*).

g. Literally, "in this." Here Paul is referring to the collection.

h. "The work" translates the articular infinitive *to poiēsai*.

i. "Desired" translates the articular infinitive *to thelein*.

j. The time span indicated by "last year" (*apo perysi*) could refer to only a few months if Paul was writing at the beginning of the year or to several months if he was writing at the end of the year. The problem is complicated because it is difficult to know if Paul was employing the Roman calendar year, which began in January, or the Jewish or Macedonian calendar year, both of which began in the fall. For a full discussion see Allo, 218–19, and Furnish, 405–6.

k. Literally, "the willingness to desire" (*hē prothymia tou thelein*).

l. The words "in proportion" are supplied to complete the meaning of the Greek text.

m. The verb has been supplied to render the meaning of the Greek more clearly.

n. The words "should overflow" have been supplied to complete the meaning of the Greek text.

Having disclosed how God's grace produced an overflowing generosity among the churches of Macedonia, Paul makes his appeal to the Corinthians to resume the collection they so eagerly took up "last year." The appeal, like much of chapters 8–9, is couched in careful and sometimes contorted language to avoid any impression that Paul is ordering or commanding the Corinthians. Instead of commanding or ordering, he appeals to the example of Jesus, gives his "opinion" about what will be beneficial to the community, assures the Corinthians that he is not trying to impoverish them, describes the goal of the collection in terms of attaining a certain equality, and appeals to Scripture to support his argument.

The material can be divided into three subunits. In the first (vv. 7–9) Paul makes his appeal, suggesting that there is no need for him to command those who understand the grace of their Lord Jesus Christ. In the second (vv. 10–12) he gives his opinion that it is expedient for the Corinthians to complete what they began last year. In the third (vv. 13–15) he presents the attainment of a certain "equality" among the churches as the goal of the collection.

[8:7–9] Turning his attention from the Macedonians to the Corinthians, Paul makes his first explicit appeal to the Corinthians to "excel" or "abound" (*perisseuete*) in the work of the collection, which he again calls "this gracious gift" (*en tautē tē chariti*), as he did in verse 6. The exhortation to "abound" recalls what Paul has already written about the Macedonians, whose poverty "abounded in an extraordinary generosity" (v. 2). But rather than directly compare the Corinthians to the Macedonians, Paul reminds the Corinthians of the many gifts that already "abound" in their lives (faith, speech, knowledge, earnestness, and love) and exhorts them that as they "abound" in these gifts, so they should abound in the "gracious gift" of the collection. In this way Paul makes his initial appeal on the basis of the gifts that the Corinthians have already received and indicates that these gifts should result in a gracious gift on their part.

The faith, speech, knowledge, earnestness, and love of which Paul speaks should not be confused with the personal virtues of the Corinthians, as if Paul were making his appeal on the basis of their virtuous lives. Rather, the items in this list are more properly understood as gifts of the Spirit, as can be seen from a similar statement in 1 Cor 1:5, "for in every way you have been enriched in him, in speech and knowledge of every kind." The gifts of "speech," "knowledge," and "faith" also appear in Paul's discussion of the gifts of the Spirit (see 1 Cor 12:9; 13:2, 13 for "faith"; 1 Cor 12:8; 13:2, 8; 14:6 for "knowledge"; and 1 Cor 12:8; 14:9 for "speech"). "Earnestness" (*spoudē*), which has the sense of "zeal" or "willingness," does not appear among the gifts of the Spirit, but in verse 16 Paul gives thanks for the "earnestness" that God has placed in the heart of Titus, suggesting that the earnestness of the Corinthians is also God-given. The manner in which Paul refers to love ("the love we bring to you") could refer to Paul's personal love for the community. The context, however, suggests that it is the gift of love, the fruit of the Spirit (Gal 5:22), that Paul's ministry has brought to Corinth. Recalling these many gifts that already abound in the community, Paul appeals to the community to abound "in this gracious gift."

Although it should be apparent that he is exhorting rather than commanding the Corinthians, Paul immediately qualifies what he has said. He is not commanding the community but "testing" (*dokimazōn*) the genuineness of its love "through the earnestness of others" (v. 8). The earnestness of others is the zeal or willingness the Macedonians have already manifested for the collection because the grace of God was at work in them. Paul's "testing" of the Corinthi-

B. An Appeal to Complete the Collection

ans, then, implies a comparison between them and the Macedonians. Will they manifest the same willingness or earnestness for this gracious gift as the Macedonians? This "testing" becomes the second great test of this letter for the Corinthians, the first being the harsh letter that Paul sent them to determine if they are obedient in all things (2:9). The Corinthians passed that test, according to Titus's report (7:5–16), so Paul can be hopeful that they will pass this test of the collection as well. The third test will come with his final visit to Corinth, when he expects those who have sinned to repent (13:1–2).

Having clarified the nature of his appeal, Paul provides the Corinthians with the strongest possible reason for contributing generously to the collection, namely, they are aware of "the grace" (*tēn charin*) of the Lord Jesus Christ, who, though he was rich, became poor for their sake, in order to enrich them (v. 9). With this verse, one instinctively thinks of Phil 2:5–11, the hymnlike passage in which Paul describes the self-emptying of Christ, whom God exalted by giving the name above every other name. Unlike that christological passage, however, 2 Cor 8:9 has a soteriological dimension: Christ became poor *in order to* enrich those who were poor. Thus Paul establishes another "divine interchange," similar to those found in 2 Cor 5:21 (Christ becomes sin, and humanity becomes the righteousness of God) and Gal 3:13 (Christ takes on the curse of the law to free those under the law from the curse).

In saying that Christ became poor, Paul implies a prior condition of "being rich" that most exegetes interpret in light of the incarnation: the preexistent Son of God who took on the poverty of humankind. Thus the best commentary on this verse is Phil 2:5–11 (Allo, 217).[8] This said, it is important to remember that Paul's primary purpose in this passage is exhortation rather than an exposition of Christ's preexistence.[9]

Since the Corinthians have experienced the gracious favor of the Lord Jesus Christ, who became poor "for them," there is no need for Paul to "command" them. Just as he reminded the Corinthians of "the grace of God" given to the Macedonians, so he reminds them of "the grace of our Lord Jesus Christ" that has touched them. In both instances, it is the same "grace," that divine favor and beneficence God graciously bestows upon humankind for the sake of saving and redeeming it.

---

8. Some have argued that Paul does not have preexistence in view, either in this passage or in the passage from Philippians 2:5–11. See James D. G. Dunn, *Christology in the Making: A New Testament Inquiry into the Origins of the Doctrine of the Incarnation* (Philadelphia: Westminster Press, 1980), 98–128. Although Paul's writings do not yet exhibit the explicit teaching on the incarnation and the preexistence of Christ that is found in the Fourth Gospel, it would seem that his thinking has begun to move in the direction of Christ's preexistence and incarnation, even if not explicitly stated.

9. Because this text is used as part of Paul's exhortation rather than a theological exposition of the preexistence of Christ, one should not read more into the text than is there. Taken literally, it might suggest a radical kenosis whereby Christ set aside his divinity.

[10–12] Paul's exhortation now turns to "advice." It will be more advantageous for the Corinthians to complete what they have begun. What Paul writes here indicates that the Corinthians began the collection "last year," a detail that he repeats in 9:1–5, when he explains how he has already boasted to the Macedonians, "Achaia has been ready since last year" (9:2). Though the boast has spurred on the Macedonians, it has also overstated the situation at Corinth.

Although it is difficult to determine exactly how much time had elapsed since "last year," one suspects that Paul is speaking of several months, since the work of the collection appears to have been suspended by the events of the painful visit and the harsh letter. Indeed it seems—although it is difficult to prove—that there is a relation between Paul's painful visit to Corinth and the collection (see Thrall's reconstruction, 1:68–69). And so it is only now, when the Corinthians have been reconciled to him, that Paul can broach the topic once more. The careful and contorted manner in which he approaches the subject, however, indicates that he does so with hesitancy.

Instead of petitioning the community to give beyond its means, as the Macedonian churches have done, Paul asks the Corinthians to give in proportion to their means. This could suggest that the Corinthians were excusing themselves from completing the collection because they could not or did not gather a large enough sum (Furnish, 419). Whatever the case, Paul insists that what makes the gift acceptable is not the amount but one's "willingness," "readiness," or "zeal" (*prothymia*). The rule that Paul establishes here (give willingly in accordance with your means) coheres with his advice in 1 Cor 16:2 ("On the first day of every week, each of you is to put aside and save whatever extra you earn"). One suspects that the Corinthians have not heeded this advice and now find themselves in an embarrassing situation.

Paul's instructions about the collection in 1 Cor 16:1–4 indicate that he was responding to a query from the Corinthian church about the collection, perhaps a request to participate in it or questions about how it will be conducted. Thus the initial enthusiasm of the Corinthians for the collection of which Paul speaks here is corroborated in part by 1 Cor 16:1–4. Despite that initial enthusiasm, the work of the collection has remained unfinished, belying Paul's boast, "Achaia has been ready since last year" (9:2).

[13–15] In Paul's view, the collection should result in a certain "equality" (*isotētos*) among the churches (v. 13). Thus it is not the purpose of the collection to relieve one church by impoverishing another but to arrive at a certain "balance" among the churches of God (see BDAG, which explains the concept of *isotētos* as a "state of matters being held in proper balance"). At the present time, in Paul's view, this balance has been disrupted because, although there is an "abundance" at Corinth, there is "need" in the church of Jerusalem. Accord-

B. An Appeal to Complete the Collection

ingly Paul proposes that the "abundance" of the Corinthians and other Gentile congregations make up for the "need" of the Jerusalem congregation, thereby reestablishing the balance or "equality" among the churches. Realizing that this "balance" may have to be readjusted, Paul also speaks of an "abundance" of the Jerusalem church supplying the "need" of the church at Corinth.

> at the present time
>   your abundance   applied to their need
> so that
>   their abundance   applied to your need
> thus there will be equality

Although it is clear what Paul means when he says that the Corinthians should supply the need of the Jerusalem church "at the present time," it is not so apparent what he intends when he writes that the abundance of the Jerusalem church will be applied to the need of the Corinthian church. Since Paul is speaking about the collection, it would seem that he envisions a time when the church of Jerusalem may need to contribute to the material need of the Corinthian church in order to redress the balance (see Thrall, 2:541–42). But in Rom 15:27 Paul writes, "for if the Gentiles have come to share in their [the holy ones of Jerusalem] spiritual blessings, they ought also to be of service to them in material things." Beginning with Chrysostom, this has suggested to some commentators (Allo, 220; Betz, 68–69) that Paul is referring to the spiritual wealth of the Jerusalem church. Thus the "balance" or "equality" is established by the Gentiles' meeting the economic need of the church at Jerusalem, whereas that church meets the spiritual need of the Gentile churches. Both interpretations are attractive, and it is difficult to decide between them, but the context of the discussion and the fact that Paul does not define the abundance of the Jerusalem church in terms of its spiritual wealth suggest that he may have an economic equality in view.

Paul concludes his appeal with a quotation from Exod 16:18, which occurs in the account of how God provided Israel with manna in the wilderness (Exod 16:1–36). Each day the Israelites gathered the manna, some gathering more, some less. Those who gathered more, however, did not have anything left over, and those who gathered less had no shortage of manna to eat. Paul draws upon this episode to remind the Corinthians that God provided for and established an "equality" among the Israelites of old. Consequently those who hoarded the manna did not have more than those who gathered only a little of it. Rather, all enjoyed the same abundance. Applied to the Corinthians, this means that hoarding their abundance will not assure that they will have more for themselves; for if they do not establish a balance among the churches, then God will.

C. A Recommendation for Titus and the Two Brothers
2 Corinthians 8:16-24

8:16 Thanks be to God, who has placed[a] the same earnestness on your behalf in the heart of Titus, **17** because he accepted our[b] appeal, and being the more earnest he is going[c] to you of his own accord. **18** With him we are sending[d] the brother who is renowned as regards the gospel[e] throughout all the churches, **19** not only that, but he has even been chosen by the churches as our traveling companion with this gracious gift[f] that is being administered by us for the glory of the Lord and as an expression of[g] our goodwill. **20** We are taking care,[h] lest someone blame us regarding this generous gift we are administering. **21** For we have in view what is honorable not only before the Lord[i] but even before humans. **22** And we are sending[j] with them our brother whom we have tested frequently in many ways since he is earnest and now more earnest because of his great confidence in you. **23** If there is a question about[k] Titus, he is my partner and coworker for you, or if there is a question about[k] our brothers, they are envoys[l] of the churches, Christ's glory.[m] **24** Therefore, give proof[n] of your love and our boast on your behalf to them before the churches.

a. Several manuscripts (ℵ, B, C) read the present participle (*didonti*). This translation follows P^{46}, D, F, G, L, which read the aorist participle.

b. The Greek reads "the appeal."

c. The verb *exēlthen* ("he went") is construed as an epistolary aorist ("he is going") because at the time that Paul writes, Titus has not yet left. But by the time the Corinthians receive the letter, Titus will have arrived at Corinth.

d. This verb, *synepempsamen* ("we have sent"), is also construed as an epistolary aorist ("we are sending") for the reason noted above.

e. The Greek is somewhat vague. Translated literally, it reads "renown in the gospel." This may refer to the work of evangelizing carried out by this unnamed brother.

f. *Charis* is translated "gracious gift" because it refers to the collection.

g. The phrase "an expression of" has been supplied to bring out the meaning of the Greek.

h. These words translate the participle *stellomenoi* ("avoiding," "shunning"). Thrall (2:551), however, argues that the sense of the verb is "to prepare for."

i. The "Lord" refers to Christ. As in the variant of v. 5, however, P^{46} reads "God."

j. The verb *synepemsamen* ("we have sent") is again taken as an epistolary aorist ("we are sending") for the reason noted above.

C. A Recommendation for Titus and the Two Brothers 195

k. This translation renders the elliptical phrase *eite hyper* (literally, "whether, on behalf of").

l. The Greek word underlying "envoys" is *apostoloi* (literally, "apostles"). Here the word refers to someone designated by the churches rather than to an apostle commissioned by the risen Lord, the kind of apostleship that Paul claims for himself.

m. The phrase "Christ's glory" stands at the end of the verse, somewhat detached from what precedes it. It refers to the brothers rather than to the churches. In addition to being the envoys of the churches, they manifest the glory of Christ by their work.

n. The participle *endeiknymenoi* ("giving proof") is rendered as an imperative.

Having appealed to the Corinthians to resume the collection, Paul commends Titus and two unnamed brothers, all of whom will serve as envoys to the Corinthians to prepare the collection before Paul arrives (see 9:1–5). Thus this section functions as a kind of "letter of recommendation" for Titus and his companions, a rather ironical twist, since Paul has disclaimed any personal need for letters of recommendation (see 3:1–3). Although Paul may not have needed or cared for such letters, his envoys did, since they were about to embark upon a delicate task: the completion of the collection in a community that appears to have questioned Paul's integrity in financial matters (12:16–18). Accordingly Paul commends a carefully balanced team of associates (Betz, 78), consisting of Titus, Paul's trusted coworker, an envoy chosen by the churches, and still another chosen by Paul. Titus, last mentioned in verse 6, will head the delegation.

The unit consists of five subunits. In the first (vv. 16–17) Paul expresses his gratitude for the earnestness that God has placed in Titus's heart for this sensitive mission. In the second (vv. 18–19) he says that in addition to Titus, he is sending a renowned brother who has been chosen by the churches. In the third subunit (vv. 20–21) Paul explains the care he is taking to avoid any suspicion of impropriety. In the fourth (v. 22) Paul mentions yet another brother whom he is sending to the Corinthians. Finally (vv. 23–24) Paul formally commends the three envoys to the Corinthians. Structured in this way, the material exhibits a certain chiastic structure: (a) Titus; (b) an unnamed brother; (c) Paul's intentions; (b') an unnamed brother; (a') Titus and the brothers. If the chiasm is intentional, the focus would be upon the sincerity of Paul's intentions (c), but since Paul's primary purpose seems to be the recommendation of these envoys, it would be imprudent to place too much emphasis on this chiasm.

[8:16–17] Paul begins this unit with an exclamation of "thanks" (*charis*) to God for granting Titus the "same earnestness" for the Corinthians, inasmuch as Titus willingly embraced Paul's appeal, first mentioned in verse 6, to return to Corinth and resume the work of the collection. Thus, just as Paul began his appeal by disclosing how "the grace of God" manifested itself in the extraordinary generosity of the Macedonians (8:1), so he begins his formal recommendation of Titus and the two brothers by showing that it is God who wills and enables the work of this great collection. For if God had not filled Titus's heart with earnestness and zeal for the Corinthians, Titus would not have returned to Corinth of his own accord, as he is presently doing.

"Earnestness" or "zeal" (*spoudē*) has played an important role in this and the preceding chapter. Paul has spoken of the "earnestness" of the Corinthians (7:11, 12; 8:7), as well as the "earnestness" of the Macedonians (8:8), raising the question of what he intends when he writes "the *same* earnestness." Although some commentators (Betz, 70) believe that Paul is making a comparison with the "earnestness" of the Corinthians or Macedonians, others (Plummer, 237; Barrett, 227; Barnett, 418) argue that the comparison is with Paul's own "earnestness" for the community. Whatever the answer, the "earnestness" of which Paul speaks here is God-given, for the eagerness and willingness to complete the work of the collection, and the willingness to give generously, come from God.

The portrayal of Titus's willingness to go to Corinth "of his own accord" (*authairetos*) employs the same word found in 8:3 (the only other use of the word in the New Testament) to describe the willingness of the Macedonians to contribute to the collection. Therefore, just as the grace of God was at work in the Macedonian churches when they gave generously "of their accord," so God granted Titus the eagerness to return "of his own accord" to Corinth. Although Paul is not formally developing a theology of grace in this chapter, one cannot but notice that here and throughout the chapter God is the one who inspires and enables the good that humans do.

The thanksgiving formula that Paul employs calls to mind a similar formula in 2:14, "thanks be to God who, in Christ, is always leading us in a triumphant procession." Here as there, Paul is deeply aware that it is God who oversees every aspect of his ministry. Accordingly the fact that his request and Titus's eagerness coincide is for Paul a manifestation of divine grace. Returning to Corinth, Titus undoubtedly carries this letter, in which Paul recommends him as well as two other envoys to the Corinthians (Furnish, 433).

[18–19] Having announced that Titus is returning to Corinth, Paul informs the Corinthians that, in addition to Titus, he is sending a "brother," whom he identifies in two ways. First, this brother is renowned throughout all the churches because of his work for the gospel. Second, the churches have elected him as Paul's traveling companion to Jerusalem. Although the designation "brother" (*adelphos*) could be applied to any believer, since those "in Christ" form a new family, here it appears to take on a technical meaning, referring to someone entrusted with a special task.

Employing a literary plural ("we are sending"), Paul emphasizes that *he* is the one who is sending this brother to the Corinthians, clearly indicating that this brother has his full approval. Paul, however, wants to show that this brother has a certain independent standing, inasmuch as he has been appointed by "the

C. A Recommendation for Titus and the Two Brothers

churches" as Paul's traveling companion to bring "this gracious gift" to Jerusalem. The "churches" to which Paul refers are probably Pauline congregations of Asia Minor and Macedonia that have already contributed to the collection. Their decision to designate someone to accompany Paul with the collection makes eminent sense for a number of reasons. First, since the gift is theirs, it is appropriate that one of their own accompany Paul. Second, since the gift is generous (see v. 20), a traveling companion will forestall any suspicion of financial impropriety, as well as help to protect Paul and the collection from brigands.

The question of this envoy's identity (as well as that of the brother mentioned in v. 22) has given rise to endless speculation: Luke, Barnabas, Silas, Aristarchus, Sopater, Secundus, Mark, Tychicus, Trophimus (see Allo, 224–26; Hughes, 312–16; Thrall, 2:561–62, for surveys). Most commentators, however, recognize that the question cannot be solved, nor would the answer substantially alter the exegesis of this text, though it would provide some insight into the history of the Pauline mission. Exegetically the most important point is the brother's reputation due to his work on behalf of the gospel. This has led the churches to designate him as Paul's traveling companion, thereby assuring the integrity of the entire project, whose goal is "the glory of the Lord" and an expression of Paul's "goodwill." The last phrase is best understood as Paul's eagerness to show how his mission among the Gentiles is related to the mother church of Jerusalem.

Although some (Leitzmann, 137) have argued that the name of this brother, as well as the brother mentioned in verse 22, were excised from the text at a later date because these brothers had fallen out of favor, others (Plummer, 238; Barrett, 228) maintain that Paul did not identify them, since they would be introduced by Titus when he arrived or when the letter was read. By not identifying the brothers, Paul may be indicating that Titus is the head of the delegation, thereby preventing the brothers from acting independently of him (Betz, 80).

[20–21] Aware that the collection has been a source of friction between him and the community, Paul pauses for a moment to defend his integrity before introducing the third member of the delegation. Since Paul is the one who is administering the collection, which he now describes as a "generous gift" (*hadrotēs*, the only occurrence of the word in the New Testament), he has taken every precaution lest someone "blame" (*mōmēsētai*; v. 20) him in its administration. Paul's desire to avoid any kind of "blame" recalls what he said in 6:3 about his apostolic conduct: "We give no occasion for offense whatsoever, lest the ministry *be faulted*." As in that text, here Paul's primary concern is the integrity of the ministry, which is intimately related to his apostolic persona. To blame him is to find fault with the ministry; to blame the ministry is to find fault with Paul.

Accordingly he always seeks to do what is "honorable" (*kala*; v. 21), not only before the Lord but before human beings. The manner in which Paul expresses himself here is puzzling, since one might have expected him to say that he seeks to do what is honorable, not only before human beings but before the Lord (see Gal 1:10, where he insists that he seeks to please God rather than humans). Here, however, Paul may be influenced by the Septuagint text of Proverbs 3:4 ("in the sight of the Lord, and of men," *enōpion kyriou kai anthrōpōn*; trans. Brenton). Thus, he acts honorably before the Lord (Christ), and the Lord is always aware of this. But unlike the Lord, human beings do not always comprehend Paul's honorable intentions. It is all the more important, therefore, that he seek to act honorably before them so that they understand his intentions, especially in this matter.

[22] Having clarified his motives in regard to the collection, Paul now introduces the third and final member of the delegation. As was the case in verses 18–19, Paul does not identify the brother. He again insists that *he* is sending the brothers ("we are sending"), clearly indicating that the delegation comes with Paul's authority. As in his description of Titus, Paul emphasizes the "earnestness" of the brother to undertake this work. But there is a striking difference between this brother and the one mentioned in verses 18–19. Whereas Paul described that brother as designated by the churches to be his traveling companion, he identifies this envoy as "our brother," someone whom he has frequently "tested," perhaps by entrusting him with other missionary tasks. Thus the brother seems to have a close relationship to Paul. The statement that this brother is all the more earnest because of his confidence in the community suggests that he has been with Paul during the difficult period of Paul's conflict with the Corinthians.

The delegation that Paul sends to Corinth is carefully balanced to the extent that one of the envoys has been chosen by "the churches" and the other is a proven associate of Paul (though in v. 23 Paul will describe both brothers as envoys of the churches). Since Paul mentions only Titus by name, however, it is apparent that he has placed Titus in charge of this delicate mission.

[23–24] With these verses, Paul gives his formal recommendation of Titus and the two brothers: the Corinthians are to give proof of their love, and of Paul's boast on their behalf, by receiving this delegation. Realizing that there might be some question about the members of the delegation, Paul draws a careful distinction between Titus and the two brothers. Titus enjoys the designation of "partner" (*koinōnos*) and "coworker" (*synergos*), whereas the brothers are "envoys of the churches" (*apostoloi ekklēsiōn*) and "Christ's glory" (*doxa Christou*). The differences in these designations appear to give a certain primacy of place to Titus without denigrating the two unnamed brothers. Titus will hold the first place because as Paul's "partner" and "coworker" he speaks for, and with the full authority of, Paul. As for the two brothers, they will represent the churches of the Pauline mission, who stand in solidarity with their apostle as regards the collection. Thus Paul calls them "envoys" or "apostles" of the churches, inasmuch as they have been "sent" or "appointed" by the churches.[10] The brief phrase that Paul adds in his description of these two envoys, "Christ's glory," is somewhat enigmatic, but it is best understood as an expression of praise for the service that these men are rendering to the churches. By what they are doing, they render glory to Christ and manifest that glory to others.

Paul's exhortation that the Corinthians give proof of their love is clear enough. By receiving the delegation, the community will manifest its love for Paul. His remark that they should give proof of his boast on their behalf, however, can be understood only in light of 9:1–5. Paul has already boasted to the Macedonians that Achaia has been ready since last year (9:2). That boast, it now seems, was premature, and Paul must encourage the Corinthians to live up to it.

D. Paul's Purpose in Sending the Delegation
2 Corinthians 9:1–5

9:1 Concerning[a] the ministry for the holy ones, it is superfluous for me to continue writing[b] to you, 2 for I know your willingness of which I boast about you to the Macedonians, "Achaia has been ready since last year," and your zeal has roused most of them. 3 But[c] I am sending[d] the brothers, lest our boasting about you prove empty in this matter, so that you might be ready as I said, 4 lest the Macedonians should come with me and find you unprepared, and we be put to shame (not to mention you[e]) in this undertaking.[f] 5 Therefore, I considered it necessary to encourage the brothers that they should go to you and make advance arrangements for your bountiful gift[g] previously promised.[h] Thus it will be ready as a bountiful gift and not as something given grudgingly.[i]

a. This verse begins *peri men gar*, which is rendered "Concerning." The *gar* ("for"), which is not expressed in the translation, relates this unit to the previous unit (8:16–24). Thus this unit will explain *why* Paul is sending the delegation to Corinth. The *men*, which is not expressed in this translation, coordinates v. 1 with v. 3, which begins *epempsa de* ("But I am sending"). Thus Paul says, "on the one hand" (*men*) it is superfluous for me to continue writing about the collection, "but on the other hand" (*de*) I am sending the brothers to ensure that it is prepared.

10. There is, of course, a certain tension here, since Paul did not identify the second brother as a delegate of the churches when he introduced him in v. 22. However, it is now apparent that in addition to being a close associate of Paul, he functions as an envoy of the churches.

b. The Greek phrase *to graphein* is anaphoric; that is, it refers back to what Paul has been saying in chapter 8. Therefore, it is translated "to continue writing." See Furnish, 426; Lambrecht, 149.

c. "But" represents the *de* mentioned above that coordinates this verse with v. 1.

d. The verb *epempsa* ("I have sent") is taken as an epistolary aorist ("I am sending") because the brothers will have arrived at Corinth by the time that Paul's letter arrives.

e. This translates *hina mē legō hymeis* ("lest I say you").

f. The Greek, *en tē hypostasei tautē*, is often rendered "by this confidence," but many modern commentators (Furnish, 427; Lambrecht, 146, Thrall, 2:568) as well as BDAG construe it "in this undertaking or project," referring to the collection. It should be noted, however, that some manuscripts (ℵ², D¹) add "of boasting" after this phrase, suggesting that they understood the sense of the phrase to be "by this confident boasting."

g. "Bountiful gift" translates *eulogia* ("blessing"), since a blessing is a generous gift. Here the gift again refers to the collection. In 1 Cor 16:1 Paul uses a cognate word, *logeia*, to designate the collection.

h. The Greek employs an artful alliteration that this translation does not convey: *proelthōsin* ("go on ahead") *prokatartisōsin* ("prepare ahead of time") *proepēngelmenēn* ("promised ahead of time").

i. "Something given grudgingly" translates *pleonexia* ("greed" or "covetousness"). Since *pleonexia* is being contrasted with *eulogia*, it seems to refer to an attitude of the Corinthians that would result in stingy rather than liberal giving because of greediness on their part, thus the translation "given grudgingly." See the discussion in Thrall, 2:572–73.

The relationship of chapter 9 to chapter 8 has always presented a problem for interpreters, since it appears to many that chapter 9 is taking up the topic of the collection for the first time, as if it had not been discussed in chapter 8. Thus some argue that this chapter represents a separate, administrative letter about the collection that a later editor interpolated at this point. Hans Dieter Betz has argued most forcefully for this position, but other commentators (Allo, Furnish, Lambrecht, Martin) support the unity of chapters 8–9. This commentary follows their line of argumentation.[11]

The opening words of this unit *peri men gar* (literally, "for, concerning") relate what follows to what has preceded: Paul's commendation of Titus and the two unnamed envoys (8:16–24). The *gar* indicates that Paul is now explaining *why* he is sending the delegation, and the *men*, which carries the meaning "on the one hand," is coordinated with the *de*, which stands at the beginning of verse 3 and carries the meaning "on the other hand." Thus the sense of these opening verses may be paraphrased as follows: "*On the one hand*, it is super-

---

11. Two studies are especially helpful in establishing the unity of chapters 8 and 9. Jan Lambrecht, "Paul's Boasting about the Corinthians: A Study of 2 Cor. 8:24–9:5," *NovT* 40 (1998): 352–68; and Stanley K. Stowers, "*Peri Men Gar* and the Integrity of 2 Cor. 8 and 9," *NovT* 32 (1990): 340–48. Whereas Stowers establishes that *peri men gar* does not begin a new topic, as Betz argues, Lambrecht establishes the thematic unity of the two chapters.

D. Paul's Purpose in Sending the Delegation

fluous for me to go on writing to you about the collection as I have been doing, for I am fully aware of your eagerness about the collection, about which I boast to the Macedonians, *but on the other hand*, I am continuing to write because I am sending this delegation to ensure that everything is ready, lest my boasting prove to be false." In verses 1–5, then, Paul is not so much taking up the topic of the collection anew as he is providing the Corinthians with his reasons for sending the delegation.

The *men . . . de* construction noted above and the use of *oun* ("therefore") in verse 5 indicate that the material of this unit consists of three subunits. In the first, governed by *men* (vv. 1–2), Paul explains why it is superfluous for him to go on writing about the collection: he knows the willingness of the Corinthians. In the second, governed by *de* (vv. 3–4), he explains why he is sending the delegation: to avoid losing face before the Macedonians if the collection is not ready. In the third, governed by *oun* (v. 5), he explains why he has found it necessary to encourage the delegation to go ahead of him: to prepare the collection so that it will truly be a "blessing" (*eulogia*) rather than something forced upon them, thereby manifesting their "greed" (*pleonexia*).

[9:1–2] At the conclusion of chapter 8, in his commendation of the delegation that he is sending to Corinth, Paul exhorted the Corinthians to give proof not only of their love but of his boasting on their behalf (8:24). As he begins chapter 9, Paul clarifies what he means by this boasting.

Expressing his confidence in the "willingness" (*prothymia*; see 8:11–12, where the same word occurs twice) of the Corinthians to participate in the collection, Paul acknowledges that there is no need for him to go on writing about "the ministry to the holy ones" (see 8:4, where Paul also employs "ministry" to describe the collection). Indeed he has already boasted to the Macedonians that Achaia has been ready since last year, and the "zeal" of the Corinthians has roused most of the Macedonians (see 8:1–5). Thus, playing on the rivalry between the provinces of Achaia and Macedonia, Paul uses the zeal of the Achaians to stir up the generosity of the Macedonians. In 8:1–5, of course, Paul employed the example of the Macedonians—some of whom may accompany Paul when he visits Corinth (9:4)—to rouse the Corinthians to complete the collection. Thus, whereas Paul speaks favorably of the "willingness" of the Corinthians here, in 8:11–12 he must remind them of their former willingness and encourage them to complete what they so eagerly began.

"Achaia" refers to the Roman province, established in 146 B.C.E., in the southern part of Greece, of which Corinth was the capital. Although most of the believers to whom Paul wrote in this letter lived in Corinth, the greeting of this letter ("to the church of God in Corinth, with all the sanctified throughout Achaia"; 1:1) suggests that Paul was also addressing believers who lived beyond the city in the province of Achaia. Other uses of "Achaia" occur in 1 Corinthians 16:15, where Paul writes that the members of the household of

Stephanas were "the first converts in Achaia," and in 2 Cor 11:10, where he insists that his boast of not accepting support from the Corinthians "will not be silenced in the regions of Achaia." If Paul was trying to establish a sense of competition between these two provinces, it would have been natural for him to employ "Achaia" here rather than "Corinth," since he speaks of his boast to the believers in Macedonia. Furthermore, whereas most believers probably lived in Corinth, there were others outside of the city (for example, the congregation at Cenchreae; see Rom 16:1), to whom Paul must have appealed for funds, and their portion of the collection may have been ready, whereas that of the Corinthians was not. Paul's statement in Rom 15:26, "for Macedonia and Achaia have been pleased to share their resources with the poor among the saints at Jerusalem," however, indicates that Achaia (and so the Corinthians) eventually contributed to the collection. The order in which Paul lists the provinces, however, may indicate that the contribution of Macedonia was greater.

[3–4] Although it is superfluous for Paul to continue writing about the collection, he explains why he finds it necessary to do so. He is confident of their "willingness," but he is apprehensive that preparations for the collections may not be complete when he arrives at Corinth, especially if he comes with representatives from the Macedonian congregations. Accordingly, lest he and the Corinthians lose face (a frightful prospect in an honor and shame culture, where the inability or the failure to fulfill one's word meant the loss of status and dignity in the esteem of others), he is sending the "brothers" to handle the administrative details of the collection. The "brothers" refers to the entire delegation that Paul recommended in 8:16–24, even though he made a distinction between Titus and the two brothers in 8:23 (but see 2:13, where Paul calls Titus "my brother").

If the collection is not ready, Paul will be shamed because he has publicly boasted that Achaia has been ready since last year, and the Corinthians will lose face because they have not been able to complete what they began last year. Consequently, although it may be superfluous from the point of view of the Corinthians for Paul to continue writing about the collection, from Paul's point of view there is every reason to write: his third and final visit to Corinth is at hand, and he is apprehensive that the collection may not be ready.[12]

In boasting to the Macedonians, did Paul exaggerate or miscalculate? Although it is possible that his enthusiasm for the collection led him to overstate the readiness of Achaia, one suspects that the conflict between him and the Corinthian community severely impeded the progress of the collection. When

---

12. Whereas Paul speaks somewhat vaguely about the Macedonians who might accompany him on his third visit, Acts 20:4 provides a list of those who accompanied Paul as he journeyed through Achaia and Macedonia, the first three of whom were from Macedonia: Sopater of Beroea, Aristarchus and Secundus of Thessalonica, Gaius of Derbe, Timothy, and the Asians Tychicus and Trophimus.

D. Paul's Purpose in Sending the Delegation

Paul first boasted that Achaia had been ready since last year, therefore, it is likely that he had good reason for such confidence. But in the time that elapsed since that boast, the situation at Corinth had deteriorated, and Paul is now threatened with the prospect of losing face before the Macedonians.

In this chapter, Paul has already referred to the collection as "the ministry for the holy ones" (v. 1). Here he refers to it in two other ways, "in this matter" (*en tō merei toutō*) and "in this undertaking" (*en tē hypostasei tautē*), but in no instance does he employ an explicit monetary term to designate the collection. In the next verse he will introduce yet another term, "bountiful gift" (*eulogia*, literally "blessing").

[5] Paul introduces his conclusion with the adverb "therefore." Lest he and the Corinthians lose face, he has appealed to the brothers to go to Corinth ahead of him to prepare "the bountiful gift" (*eulogia*) that the Corinthians have previously promised. For if the gift is not prepared, the Corinthians will find themselves in a situation whereby they will be forced to contribute to the collection in order not to lose face before the Macedonians. In that instance, their gift will no longer be given as an expression of the "blessing" (*eulogia*) it should be but of their "greed" (*pleonexia*) since it will have been given under duress. The introduction of *eulogia* to designate the collection adds to the repertoire of words that Paul has been employing since chapter 8 to describe the collection. Like *charis*, it focuses on the generous and gracious aspect of the gift that has its origin in God's *charis* and *eulogia* toward humankind. The contrast between *pleonexia* and *eulogia*, therefore, is especially apropos. For whereas "greed" is characteristic of human beings who refuse to trust in God's help, "blessing" points to the gracious aspect of the God who freely bestows his abundance upon others.

Paul's "appeal" to the brothers echoes his earlier appeal to Titus to complete the work of the collection that he began earlier by returning to Corinth (8:16), but it also stands in some tension with Paul's statement about the willingness of Titus (8:17) and the brother mentioned in 8:22 to carry out the mission. The tension, however, is more apparent than real for, whereas Paul does and must initiate the appeal, he seems to have found an eager response among the members of the delegation that he is sending to Corinth.

Overall, this unit is closely related to 8:16–24, and it is not surprising that some commentators (Furnish, Hafemann) view 8:16–9:5 as a single unit or as part of the same unit. Apart from 8:16–24 Paul's reference to "the brothers" in 9:3 would make little sense, and without 9:1–5 one would not understand what he means in 8:24 about his boasting on behalf of the Corinthians. In the first unit (8:16–24) Paul describes the composition of the delegation and formally commends it to the Corinthians; in the second (9:1–5) he explains why he is sending the delegation and what it will do. Having done this, Paul returns to the topic of generous giving.

E. The Relationship between Sowing and Reaping
2 Corinthians 9:6–9

9:6 This is what I mean:[a] the one who sows sparingly, sparingly reaps, whereas the one who sows bountifully,[b] bountifully reaps. **7** Each should give[c] as he has determined in his heart, not reluctantly or as if under pressure,[d] for God loves a cheerful giver. **8** God can make every blessing[e] abound among you, so that in every way, always having enough of everything,[f] you may abound in every good work. **9** As it is written,

"he scattered,[g] he gave to the poor,
his righteousness[h] endures forever."

a. This phrase translates *touto* ("this").

b. "Bountifully" translates *ep' eulogiais* (literally, "to blessings"). Since "blessing" refers to something generously given or bestowed upon another, the phrase is here translated "bountifully."

c. The words "should give" have been supplied.

d. A literal rendering of the Greek would be "not out of sorrow or out of necessity."

e. Here *charis* is translated as "blessing," because it refers to the favor (spiritual and material) that God bestows.

f. The Greek contains an alliteration that the English translation does not reproduce, *panti pantote pasan*.

g. "He scattered," that is, he dispersed his goods in almsgiving. The generous man shows his generosity by "scattering" or "dispersing" his goods to the poor.

h. Here "righteousness" could refer to almsgiving or to moral conduct.

Having explained that he is sending a delegation to ensure that the collection will be ready when he arrives, Paul now exhorts the Corinthians to give generously, assuring them that God will support their generosity. The limits of this unit are difficult to determine. Although some commentators view verses 6–15 as the unit, others regard verses 6–9 and vv. 10–15, or 6–10 and 11–15, as discrete units. There is a strong case for construing verses 6–10 as a unit, since the theme of "sowing" encompasses these verses (Furnish, 446). But one could argue, as does this commentary, that verses 6–9 focus on the one who gives and verses 10–15 speak of God and God's purpose for the collection (so Lambrecht, 150–51).

If one accepts verses 6–9 as the unit, the material can be structured in the following way. In verses 6–7 Paul introduces a maxim (v. 6) that he applies to

E. The Relationship between Sowing and Reaping

the collection (v. 7). In verses 8–9, he reinforces his exhortation by explaining what God can do (v. 8), supporting this by a quotation from Scripture (v. 9). Thus, whereas in 8:7–15 Paul exhorted the Corinthians to give according to their means in order to establish a certain equality, here he provides them with reasons for liberal giving.

[9:6–7] Having completed his commendation of the delegation, Paul returns to the topic of liberal giving with a carefully crafted maxim that serves as the leitmotif for the whole unit:

> the one who sows *sparingly*, *sparingly* reaps.
> the one who sows *bountifully*, *bountifully* reaps.

Similar maxims abound in Hellenistic literature (Betz, 102–5, provides examples from Aristotle and Cicero), and Paul may have been aware of such sayings. It is possible that he is also indebted to the Septuagint form of Proverbs 11:24, which employs the agriculture image of sowing.

> There are *some* who sow (*speirontes*) their own and make it more:
> and there are *some* who gather (*synagontes*), yet have less.
> (trans. Brenton)

Whatever the original source of the Pauline maxim, its meaning is clear. There is a direct proportion between sowing and reaping: those who plant little will harvest little, whereas those who plant generously will harvest generously. The phrase that has been translated "generously" (*ep' eulogiais*) employs the same word that Paul used in verse 6 in reference to the collection that he describes as a "bountiful gift" (*eulogia*). By employing that word in this maxim, Paul draws a literary connection between the maxim and the collection, suggesting that those who give "generously" (*ep' eulogiais*) to this "bountiful gift" (*eulogia*) will harvest generously.

But giving generously is not sufficient if one gives under compulsion. Accordingly Paul instructs the Corinthians to give as their heart dictates, not "reluctantly" (*ek lypēs*, "from sorrow") or "under pressure" (*ex anankēs*, "from necessity"). Deuteronomy 15:10 contains a similar injunction: "Give liberally and be ungrudging when you do so, for on this account the LORD your God will bless you in all your work and in all that you undertake." Next Paul grounds what he says in a quotation from the Septuagint form of Proverbs 22:8 "God blesses a cheerful and liberal man" (trans. Brenton). But whereas Proverbs speaks of God "blessing," Paul writes, God "loves" a cheerful giver. Although some commentators maintain that here "loves" means little more than "approves" or "values" (Furnish, 441), others argue that Paul intends the full force of the verb "love" (Thrall, 2:577); otherwise he would not have altered the wording of Proverbs from "blesses" to "loves."

[8–9] In order to substantiate his exhortation to give liberally, Paul instructs the Corinthians that God is always able to make every "blessing" (*charis*) abound in them so that, always having what is "sufficient" (*autarkeian*), they will abound in every good work. In effect, Paul affirms that God is the source of all human generosity, because it is God who supplies the "blessing" to make one "sufficient" in order to perform every "good work." The sufficiency of which Paul speaks here is not inner self-sufficiency, a favorite virtue among Cynic and Stoic philosophers. Rather, Paul views *autarkeia* as a sufficiency of material wealth, supplied by God, which believers can disperse to those in need. Thus God provides believers with the sufficiency necessary to do "every good work" (*pan ergon agathon*). Here, "every good work" is best understood as the work of generosity to which Paul exhorts the Corinthians.

To conclude his argument, Paul quotes the Septuagint form of Psalm 111:9 (=MT 112:9), "He scattered, he gave to the poor, his righteousness endures forever" (2 Cor 9:9). Although some commentators (Barnett, 440; Betz, 111) argue that the subject of the psalm is God and so "righteousness" refers to God's righteousness, which endures forever, the context suggests that the subject of the psalm is the human person (Lambrecht, 147), since Paul has been exhorting the Corinthians to liberal giving throughout this unit. Understood in this way, Paul is saying that it is God who supplies the believer with the sufficiency to do every good work. As Scripture testifies, when the righteous give to the poor, their righteousness endures forever. The meaning of this "righteousness," however, is disputed. Whereas some view it as the act of almsgiving, others interpret it as the moral conduct of the righteous person that leads to such almsgiving. In the first instance, the results of one's generosity endure forever in the good produced for those in need. In the second, it is one's moral righteousness that endures forever. It is difficult to choose between these alternatives, but since Paul normally understands righteousness in terms of God's gift or human conduct before God, this commentary adopts the second interpretation.

F. The Theological Significance of the Collection
2 Corinthians 9:10–15

9:10 The one who supplies seed for sowing and bread for eating will provide and multiply your seed and increase the harvest of your righteousness. 11 In every way, you are being enriched[a] for all generosity,[b] which produces thanksgiving to God through us, 12 because the ministry of this service[c] is not only supplying the needs of the holy ones, but it

F. The Theological Significance of the Collection 207

even abounds in many acts of thanksgiving to God. 13 Through the proof of this ministry you[d] are glorifying God by your obedient confession of the gospel of Christ[e] and by the generosity[f] of your partnership toward them and all. 14 And they long for you by their prayer on your behalf because of the immeasurable grace of God bestowed[g] upon you. 15 Thanks[h] be to God for his indescribable gift.

a. "You are being enriched" renders the participle *ploutizomenoi* as a finite verb.

b. As in 8:2, *haplotēs* is construed as "generosity," though its basic meaning is "sincerity," "frankness," "uprightness."

c. Here Paul employs *leitourgia* ("service") in conjunction with *diakonia* ("ministry") to designate the collection. This somewhat formal expression could also be translated "in the administration of this service."

d. The subject of the participle *doxazontes*, which has been rendered as a finite verb, is not expressed. Here the subject is taken as the Corinthians, "you." Most commentators, however, supply "they" as the subject; that is, the believers in Jerusalem.

e. The Greek could also be rendered "by your obedience, which is your confession of the gospel of Christ."

f. Since *haplotēs* usually means "sincerity," the phrase could be rendered "by the sincerity of your partnership."

g. The word "bestowed" has been supplied.

h. "Thanks" translates *charis* which, in this instance, simply refers to gratitude.

This unit is related to the preceding unit in two ways. First, it begins with, and it develops, the agricultural image of "sowing" that Paul employed in verses 6–9. Second, it resumes the theme announced in verse 8: that God is able to make every grace abound in the Corinthians. But whereas in verses 6–9 Paul exhorted the Corinthians to liberal giving, in these verses he turns his attention to the God who is the source of their liberal giving. The material can be divided into three subunits. In the first (vv. 10–11) Paul explains how God will supply the Corinthians with all they need to be liberal givers. In the second (vv. 12–14) he reveals that in addition to supplying the needs of the holy ones, the collection will result in many acts of thanksgiving. On the one hand, then, the Corinthians themselves will praise God. On the other, those in Jerusalem will desire to see them because of the gracious favor God has bestowed upon them. In the final subunit (v. 15), Paul expresses his thanks to God for the gift of salvation. Taken as a whole, verses 10–15 present an exalted vision of the collection. In addition to responding to the needs of the holy ones, the gracious gift of the Corinthians will result in a profound union between them and those in Jerusalem.

[9:10–11] These verses are theocentric in their presentation, for having told the Corinthians that as they sow so they will reap, Paul assures them that the God who supplies seed for sowing and bread for eating will provide and even increase their seed, so that they will enjoy an abundant harvest of righteousness. Indeed

God is already enriching them with a generosity that will result in thanksgiving to God. In this way Paul returns to the theme introduced in verse 8: it is God who is the source of all human generosity.

Paul's description of God as the one "who supplies seed for sowing and bread for eating" finds an echo in the prophet Isaiah, whereas the promise that God will increase "the harvest of your righteousness" alludes to the prophet Hosea.

> For as the rain and the snow come down from heaven,
>   and do not return there until they have watered the earth,
> making it bring forth and sprout,
>   *giving seed to the sower and bread to the eater*,
> so shall my word be that goes out from my mouth;
>   it shall not return to me empty,
> but it shall accomplish that which I purpose,
>   and succeed in the thing for which I sent it.
>   (Isa 55:10–11)

> Sow to yourselves for righteousness. . . . seek the Lord till the fruits of righteousness (*genēmata dikaiosynēs*) come upon you. (LXX Hos 10:12; trans. Brenton)

The "seed" with which God will provide the Corinthians is the material means necessary to give liberally. The precise meaning of "the harvest of your righteousness," however, is more difficult to determine. It could refer to the blessings that will accrue to the Corinthians because of their righteousness (which they manifest in their generous giving). Or it could mean that righteousness itself will be their harvest. In either case, the main line of Paul's thought is clear. Not only will God provide the Corinthians with the means to contribute to the collection; God will increase the harvest for which they sow, a harvest of righteousness or perhaps the blessings that accrue from righteousness.

For Paul the work of the collection is the work of God. Consequently he began his exhortation by telling the Corinthians of "the grace of God" that was given to the churches of Macedonia and resulted in an extraordinary generosity on their part. Now he tells the Corinthians that the same grace is enriching them so that they can be generous as well. As a result, through the ministry of the collection that Paul is administering, thanksgiving will be given to God. From start to finish, then, the collection is God's work. It begins with God's grace, and it ends in thanksgiving to God.

[12–14] In chapter 8 Paul described the purpose of the collection in terms of attaining a certain "equality" among the churches. He exhorted the Corinthians to contribute from their abundance in order to offset the present need (*hysterēma*) of the Jerusalem congregation (8:13–14). In these verses Paul provides another reason for the collection, one that is thoroughly theological: the collection will overflow in an abundance of thanksgiving to God (v. 12), presum-

F. The Theological Significance of the Collection

ably from the recipients of the collection as well as from those who learn of it. In verses 13–14 Paul explains how and why this will happen. The collection is a "test" or "proof" (*dokimē*) of the character of the Corinthians inasmuch as it discloses whether or not they understand the full implications of the gospel they confess, namely, that the gospel of Christ unites Gentile and Jew. By responding generously to the collection, therefore, the Corinthians will give proof of their obedience to the gospel and so their partnership (*koinōnia*) with "the holy ones" at Jerusalem and indeed with all believers (v. 13). For their part, Jewish Christians in Jerusalem will show their appreciation by their prayerful longing for them because of the grace of God manifested in them.

Paul's understanding of the collection in these verses approaches an eschatological vision that anticipates a profound unity between the congregations of his mission and the church of Jerusalem. In his view the ministry of the collection will allow the Jewish mother church to see in the generous contributions of the Gentile churches the work of God's grace in the churches of the Pauline mission. Paul's apprehensive remarks in Rom 15:30–31—that he might be rescued from the unbelievers in Judea and that his ministry to Jerusalem will be acceptable—suggest that the apostle was not so confident about the reception the collection would receive in Jerusalem. Despite these misgivings, in this passage he has set aside such apprehensions (or has not yet had to deal with them) in order to provide the Corinthians with a profoundly theological understanding of the collection and its importance for the life of the church. Not only will it relieve the needs of the "holy ones" in Jerusalem; it will unite the Gentile and Jewish wings of the fledgling church in praise, prayer, and thanksgiving.

The language that Paul employs for the collection at the beginning of this unit is formal to the point of being cultic. Whereas he described the collection as the "ministry to the holy ones" in 8:4 and 9:1, he now speaks of "the ministry of this service" (*hē diakonia tēs leitourgias*). In the ancient world, *leitourgia* referred to "service of a formal or public type" or "service of a personal nature" (BDAG), such as that provided by this collection. Thus Paul uses the verbal form of the noun in Rom 15:27, where he writes: "They [the Gentile Christians] were pleased to do this, and indeed they owe it to them [the Jewish Christians]; for if the Gentiles have come to share in their spiritual blessings, they ought also to be of service (*leitourgēsai*) to them in material things." Likewise in Phil 2:30 he acknowledges the "service" that Epaphroditus rendered to him, presumably in bringing him a gift of money from the Philippians (see Phil 4:10–13). But in that same letter Paul also employs *leitourgia* in a cultic sense, "the sacrifice and offering of your faith" (*tē thysia kai leitourgia tēs pisteōs*; Phil 2:17). Inasmuch as he expects the collection to evoke thanksgiving in many people, this phrase may indicate that he views his ministry in regard to the collection as more than a personal service to the church of Jerusalem. It is a public service with cultic overtones (see Thrall, 2:587).

In verse 13 Paul employs *diakonia* ("ministry") to designate the collection and writes that through this ministry the Corinthians will "praise" (*doxazontes*) God by the obedience of their faith in the gospel and their generous partnership with those in Jerusalem. As the notes indicate, the subject of the participle *doxazontes* must be supplied. If the subject is the Corinthians ("you"), as suggested by the translation of this commentary (also by the NAB, NRSV, and Lambrecht, 148), then the sense of the text is as follows: the Corinthians will praise God because their participation in the collection will demonstrate the obedience of their faith and their partnership with the Jerusalem church. If the subject is the Jerusalem Christians ("they"), however, as most commentators argue, then the sense is as follows: the Jerusalem Christians will praise God for the obedient faith of the Corinthians and for their partnership, both of which have been manifested through the gift of the collection. Although the second of these translations offers a richer interpretation of the text, the introduction of "they" as the subject of the participle comes somewhat abruptly. But since there is no overriding argument for either interpretation, it is prudent to keep both in view.

The mention of "the immeasurable grace of God" (v. 14) recalls the manner in which Paul began his discussion of the collection: "We want you to know, brothers and sisters, *the grace of God* given to the churches of Macedonia" (8:1). Having told the Corinthians how "the grace of God" was at work in the extraordinary generosity of the Macedonians, Paul anticipates the longing of the Jerusalem Christians for the Corinthians when they recognize how "the immeasurable grace of God" is at work in the Corinthians. Thus two references to God's grace enclose Paul's discussion of the collection: "the grace of God" given to the Macedonians (8:1) and "the immeasurable grace of God" that will be manifested in the Corinthians when they have completed the work of the collection (9:14).

[15] Paul concludes his discussion by giving "thanks" (*charis*) to God for "his indescribable gift" (*anekdiēgētō autou dōrea*). Although it is possible to understand the gift in light of the collection, it is more likely that Paul has God's gift of salvation in view, as in other instances where he employs *dōrea*. See Rom 5:15 ("the free gift"), Rom 5:17 ("the free gift of righteousness"), as well as Eph 3:7 ("the gift of God's grace"), and Eph 4:7 ("the measure of Christ's gift"). With this concluding thanksgiving, therefore, Paul again emphasizes the relationship of the collection to God's overall work of redemption. To the extent that the generosity of the Macedonians and the Corinthians is an expression of God's grace, it reflects the work of God's salvation—the indescribable gift—in their lives.

The line of thought in chapters 8–9 can now be summarized. Paul begins by telling the Corinthians how the grace of God manifested itself in the generosity of the Macedonians, exhorting the Corinthians to resume what they began a year ago so that there will be a certain equality among the churches (8:1–15),

F. The Theological Significance of the Collection

and it concludes with Paul exhorting the Corinthians to liberal giving so that others will recognize and praise the same grace in them (9:6–15). Between these two exhortations, Paul recommends the delegation headed by Titus, which will make preparations for this gracious gift (8:16–9:5). Although these chapters are an appeal for money, they also provide a theology of grace, namely, the graciousness of the God revealed in Jesus Christ, which allows and empowers people to be generous to each other.

Part 3

Defense and Warnings in Preparation for Paul's Third Visit
2 Corinthians 10:1–13:10

In the first part of this letter (1:12–7:16), Paul provided the Corinthians with his account of the recent events that had transpired between him and the community. In doing so, he defended his reliability and explained why he had sent a harsh letter rather than visit them in painful circumstances again (1:12–2:13). Before concluding his narration, however, Paul embarked upon a rich theological exposition of his new covenant ministry (2:14–7:4), a ministry in which apostolic suffering and reconciliation play central roles. Paul then ended his narration with his account of Titus's good news that the community had repented of its part in the painful visit (7:5–16). Thus it would appear from 1:12–7:16 that at least one aspect of the conflict between Paul and the Corinthian community had been successfully resolved, although Paul's call for reconciliation in 6:11–7:4 suggests that not all of the difficulties between him and the community had been settled.

Since the problem surrounding the painful visit had been concluded, however, Paul felt confident enough to encourage the community to complete the work of the collection that it had begun "last year" (8:10). Consequently, in the second part of his letter (8:1–9:15) he appealed to the Corinthians to finish the work of the collection, recommending the delegation, headed by Titus, that would make advance preparations for the collection (8:16–24).

In this third part of this letter (10:1–13:10) Paul prepares for his final visit to Corinth with a staunch defense of his apostolic integrity, a relentless attack upon a group of intruding apostles who have turned some of the Corinthians against him, and a number of warnings to those who had previously sinned and not yet repented (see 12:20–21; 13:1–2).

Although commentators agree that 10:1–13:10 forms a distinct unit within 2 Corinthians, many, beginning with Johann Salomo Semler (1776), have argued that chapters 10–13 represent the whole or part of an independent letter. Thus whereas some (Hausrath, Kennedy, Plummer, Héring) maintain that chapters 10–13 are the whole or part of the harsh letter Paul sent to the Corinthians and so were written before chapters 1–9, others (Barrett, Martin, Thrall, Furnish) argue that these chapters are Paul's response to a deteriorating situation at Corinth and were written some time after chapters 1–9. In both instances, those who view chapters 10–13 as the whole or a part of a separate letter point to the harsh tone of these chapters, and they ask why Paul would write in this manner if he had such perfect confidence in the community (7:16). They also question his strategy of reprimanding the community in chapters 10–13 after so delicately appealing to the Corinthians to resume the work of the collection.

This and several other recent commentaries (Barnett, Garland, Hafemann, Lambrecht, McCant, Scott) argue that these chapters are an integral part of 2 Corinthians, and there is no need to resort to partition theories to explain them. For even though the tone of these chapters is more strident than what precedes, Paul's reprimand is not unexpected, since he has given several indications that other preachers have come to Corinth. For example, see his remark about those who trade on the word of God (2:17), his defensive claim that he does not need letters of recommendation (3:1), and his comment about those who boast in "appearance and not in the heart" (5:12). Moreover, even though Titus reported that the community repented of its role in the painful visit (7:5–16), Paul's call for reconciliation in 6:11–7:4 indicated that something was still amiss at Corinth, a point that finds confirmation in his warnings to those who have sinned and not yet repented (12:20–21; 13:1–2). Consequently, although one issue had been settled (the incident of the painful visit and the harsh letter), other problems remained (unrepentant sinners and the presence of the intruding apostles). Having settled the first issue, Paul turns to these problems.

Chapters 10–13, then, are best viewed in light of Paul's third and final visit to Corinth. Having prepared the way for the visit of Titus's delegation (chaps. 8–9), Paul now prepares the way for his own visit. If this third and final visit is to be successful, the Corinthians must disassociate themselves from the intruding apostles who have called into question his ministry, and those who have not repented of their immorality must do so.

The overall structure of these chapters can be viewed in this way: In 10:1–18 Paul defends his integrity, as well as the integrity of his missionary activity, by arguing that whether present or absent he is bold (10:1–11) and that he has not gone beyond the missionary limits the Lord assigned to him (10:12–18). In 11:1–12:13 Paul is "forced" (12:11) into a display of foolish boasting in order

Defense and Warnings in Preparation for Paul's Third Visit 215

to deal with the intruding apostles to whom he had already alluded in 10:1–18. Finally, in 12:14–13:10 Paul warns the community to test itself and put itself in order for his impending visit, since he will act with boldness when he arrives, as he already warned them in 10:1–18. The great central section, in which Paul engages in foolish boasting (11:1–12:13), then, is bracketed by two smaller sections (10:1–18 and 12:14–13:10), in which Paul asserts that if he must, he can and will act boldly when he comes to Corinth.

A. Paul's Integrity and Missionary Assignment
2 Corinthians 10:1–18

Chapter 10, the first of the three major sections that make up the third part of 2 Corinthians, can be divided into two units. In the first (10:1–11) Paul defends his personal integrity against charges that his letters are "severe and strong" but, when he is present to the community, he is weak and his speech is despicable (10:10). Already anticipating his impending visit to the Corinthians, Paul argues that the boldness he displays in his letters is the same boldness that he will show when he comes to Corinth. In the second unit (10:12–18) Paul deals more directly with the intruding apostles, although he does not yet identify them as "super-apostles," as he will in 11:5 and 12:11. Arguing that he has not gone beyond the missionary limits assigned to him, Paul implicitly accuses the intruding apostles of encroaching upon his assigned missionary task. The theme of "boasting," with which this unit concludes, prepares for Paul's foolish boasting in 11:1–12:13.

Although the two units of 10:1–18 are somewhat distinct, both anticipate what follows. Thus Paul's defense of his integrity in verses 1–11 prepares for the discussion in 12:14–13:10 of his third visit, as can be seen from references to his "absence" and "presence" (10:1–2, 11; 13:1–2, 10) and to "tearing down" and "building up" (10:4–5, 8; 12:19; 13:10), which occur in both sections. In a similar fashion Paul's defense of his "assignment" in verses 12–18, which concludes with an exhortation that the one who boasts should boast in the Lord, provides the context for interpreting his comparison with the super-apostles and his foolish boasting in 11:1–12:13.

1. Bold Whether Absent or Present (10:1–11)

10:1 I, Paul, appeal to you through the meekness and clemency of Christ, who[a] am humble when present among you but bold toward you when absent. 2 I ask[b] that when I am present I may not have to act boldly with the confidence that I am counting on to act boldly toward some who consider us as walking according to the flesh.[c]

3 For while we walk in the flesh, we do not wage war according to the flesh.[d] 4 For the weapons of our warfare do not belong to the realm of the flesh[e] but are powerful in the service of God[f] for the destruction of fortresses.

We tear down sophistries[g] 5 and every proud obstacle[h] arising in opposition to the knowledge of God,[i] and we take captive every thought for

A. Paul's Integrity and Missionary Assignment

obedience to Christ. 6 And when your obedience is complete,[j] we are ready to punish every disobedience.

7 Look at what is before your eyes![k] If someone is convinced in his own mind that he belongs to Christ,[l] let him consider again, for himself, that just as he belongs to Christ, so do we. 8 For even if I should boast a bit much about our authority that the Lord gave to me for building up, and not for your destruction, I will not be put to shame.[m]

9 Lest I appear as frightening you[n] through letters—10 because someone says,[o] "the letters are severe and powerful, but his physical presence is weak and his speech contemptible"—11 let this one consider this, that what we are in word through our letters when absent, we are in action when present.

a. A smoother translation would be achieved by supplying "I" before "who." This translation, however, tries to reflect the ambiguity of the Greek in which "who" (*hos*) appears at first to refer to Christ. Although it is clear by the end of the verse that Paul is referring to himself, the initial ambiguity suggests a close relationship between the behavior of Paul and Christ.

b. The Greek verb for "ask" (*deomai*) is even milder in tone than the initial verb in which Paul "appeals" (*parakaleō*) to the Corinthians.

c. This is a rather literal translation of the Greek. "To walk according to the flesh" is a Pauline idiom for behaving in a purely worldly manner that does not take into account the power of God's Spirit. The REB translates the phrase: "who assume my behavior to be dictated by human weakness."

d. The translation of this verse is also rather literal. To walk *in* the flesh is to be constrained by the circumstances of human existence. There are no moral overtones attached to the expression here. To wage war "according to the flesh" means to fight in a purely human manner. The REB translates the verse: "Weak and human we may be, but that does not dictate the way we fight our battles."

e. "The realm of the flesh" translates *sarkika*. Paul's weapons are not "fleshly" or "carnal."

f. The Greek phrase *tō theō* is taken as a dative of advantage. It could be construed as a dative of means, "empowered by God," or a dative of presence, "in the presence of God."

g. Literally, "thoughts" or "reasonings." But since Paul seems to be referring to a kind of reasoning that he views as false, many translations and commentators use "sophistries."

h. According to BDAG, *hypsōma* refers to "that which postures arrogantly," thus "arrogance."

i. "The knowledge of God" can be taken as an objective genitive (knowledge about God) or a subjective genitive (God's own knowledge that God reveals to humans in the gospel). This commentary construes it as the latter: God's knowledge revealed through the gospel.

j. The phrase "when your obedience is complete" occurs at the end of the verse in the Greek text. It has been transposed to the beginning for the sake of clarity.

k. The phrase could be taken as a statement ("You only see what is before your eyes"), as a question ("Do you see what is before your eyes?"), or as an imperative, as in this translation. In the first instance, Paul would be rebuking the Corinthians, in the second he would be expressing his puzzlement, and in the third he would be issuing a command. This translation, as well as most commentaries, construes *blepete* ("look") as an imperative, since Paul tends to use *blepete* as an imperative (Thrall, 2:619). See 1 Cor 1:26; 8:9; 10:18; 16:10; Gal 5:15; Phil 3:2. Also see Col 2:8; Eph 5:15.

l. Some manuscripts (D*, F, G) read "servant of Christ." The phrase, however, is probably an attempt to clarify what Paul means when he writes that he "belongs to Christ." The exegesis deals with this question.

m. This may be a "divine passive" (Lambrecht, 157). The sense is that God will not shame or disappoint Paul, because Paul has received his authority from the one who is dependable.

n. The abrupt manner in which this verse begins, "lest I appear as frightening you" (*hina mē doxō hōs an ekphobein hymas*) presents a problem for translators and commentators. Some (Barrett, 259; Thrall, 2:627) view these words as elliptical and supply a brief introduction such as "*I forebear to do this* [exercise my authority] lest I appear as trying to frighten you." Others (Lambrecht, 157) take *hina* as an imperative particle, as does the NAB, "*May I not seem* as one frightening you through letters." This commentary (along with Garland, 445, and Martin, 310) connects v. 9 with v. 11, viewing v. 10 as a parenthetical remark. Paul would be saying, lest he appear as frightening them by his letters (since someone is saying that his letters are strong but his appearance weak), that person should understand that what Paul is in word, he is in action.

o. Some manuscripts (B, Latin, and Syriac) read the plural, "they say" (*phasin*), but the better manuscript tradition reads the singular. Here, and in v. 7 (*tis*) and v. 11 (*toioutos*), Paul seems to be referring to an individual.

Having appealed to the Corinthians to resume the collection they began last year for Jerusalem, Paul embarks upon the third part of this letter with yet another appeal so that he will not have to act boldly when he comes to Corinth. The ironic tone of the opening verses foreshadows the irony that will appear throughout chapters 10–13, and the contrast between "being absent" and "being present" presages Paul's third and final visit, which will be discussed in 12:14–13:10.

The material can be divided into several subunits. In the first (vv. 1–2) Paul appeals to the Corinthians so that he will not have to act boldly, when he comes to Corinth, with the boldness which he is confident he can muster, since some are accusing him of "walking according to the flesh." The precise content of Paul's appeal, however, is never explicitly stated. In the second (vv. 3–4a) he plays on the accusation that he walks "according to the flesh" to argue that although he walks "in the flesh," the weapons of his warfare do not belong "to the realm of the flesh." In the third subunit (vv. 4b–6), which is closely tied to the second, Paul develops the warfare metaphor further, comparing himself to a soldier who tears down fortresses, takes prisoners, and then punishes the

A. Paul's Integrity and Missionary Assignment

rebellious. In the fourth (vv. 7–8) Paul affirms his relation to Christ and the authority that Christ has given him. In the final subunit (vv. 9–11) Paul returns to the theme of the first subunit and asserts that when he is present, his actions will correspond to the letters that he has written while absent. Thus verses 1–2, which speak of Paul's "presence" and "absence," and verses 9–11, which contrast Paul's "letters" with his "physical presence," enclose Paul's description of his powerful weapons and apostolic authority (vv. 3–8), indicating that Paul acts with boldness whether absent or present. The material can be outlined as follows:

>vv. 1–2 Bold whether present or absent
>vv. 3–4a The power of Paul's weapons
>vv. 4b–6 Tearing down, taking prisoners, and punishing
>vv. 7–8 Paul's authority and relation to Christ
>vv. 9–11 The same whether present or absent

[10:1–2] The manner in which these verses begin clearly indicates that Paul is embarking upon a new topic. First he "appeals" (*parakaleō*) to the Corinthians as if he were about to introduce an extended moral exhortation (cf. Rom 12:1; Eph 4:1; 1 Thess 4:1). Then he makes an emphatic self-reference ("I, Paul") that has the effect of emphasizing his apostolic authority.[1] But instead of the expected moral exhortation, Paul launches into a vigorous defense of his apostolic integrity against those who accuse him of being bold in his letters when he is absent from the community but humble, in the sense of "timid" or "base," when he is present to the community.[2]

In these opening verses Paul accomplishes two things. First, by mentioning the boldness with which he will act when he comes to Corinth, he implicitly announces his third and final visit. Second, by making his appeal through the "meekness and clemency of Christ" and then speaking ironically of his "humble"

---

1. Brian K. Peterson, *Eloquence and the Proclamation of the Gospel in Corinth* (SBLDS 163; Atlanta: Scholars Press, 1998), 76. Peterson provides an interesting rhetorical study of chaps. 10–13, arguing that 10:1–6 is the *exordium*, 10:7–11 the *propositio*, 10:12–18 the *narratio*, 11:1–12:18 the *probatio*, and 12:19–13:10 the *peroratio*. His work adds to a growing body of literature on the rhetoric of 2 Corinthians. Such studies are helpful for highlighting Paul's rhetorical strategy, but one must remember that ancient rhetorical handbooks were primarily concerned with public discourse, whereas Paul was writing a letter, albeit a letter that would be read aloud. Moreover, one should not assume that a rhetorical analysis of a portion of 2 Corinthians, for example chaps. 8–9 or chaps. 10–13, can prove that these chapters were once independent units.

2. Jan Lambrecht ("Paul's Appeal and the Obedience of Christ: The Line of Thought in 2 Corinthians 10,1–6," *Bib* 77 [1996]: 398–416) suggests that Paul begins an exhortation in 10:1a that is not resumed until 12:19–13:11, with 10:1b–13:10 (or perhaps 10:1b–12:18) functioning as a lengthy excursus somewhat analogous to the excursus of 2:14–7:4. This is an interesting suggestion, but the excursus that Lambrecht proposes is not as immediately apparent as is that of 2:14–7:4.

presence among them, he suggests that the Corinthians have mistaken the "meekness" (*prautēs*) and "clemency" (*epieikeia*) that he has exhibited for servile and cowardly behavior. Thus some accuse Paul of being "humble" (*tapeinos*) in the sense of "base" or "of no account" when in fact his humble bearing in their presence is a manifestation of Christ's meekness and clemency. Consequently to reject Paul as lowly and of no account is to reject the one whose life manifests the very meekness and clemency of Christ. Put another way, in misinterpreting Paul's humble bearing toward them, the Corinthians have misunderstood the gospel he has proclaimed to them.

The emphatic manner in which Paul identifies himself in these opening verses finds its closest parallel in Gal 5:2, "Listen! I, Paul, am telling you that if you let yourselves be circumcised, Christ will be of no benefit to you." In Galatians, this emphatic self-identification comes at a crucial point in the letter, the moment when Paul finally warns the Galatians of the dire consequences they will face if they allow themselves to be circumcised.[3] This emphatic manner in which Paul identifies himself in 10:1,[4] after having employed a literary plural ("we") throughout most of the first nine chapters of this letter,[5] suggests that Paul has come to a critical juncture in this letter when he must finally deal with the intruding apostles who have called into question the style and perhaps the content of his apostolic ministry. A similar expression, though not quite as emphatic, occurs in 12:13 (the conclusion to Paul's foolish boasting), where the apostle writes, "For in what respect were you worse off than the other churches except that I myself (*autos egō*) did not burden you financially? Forgive this injustice!"

Although he refers to himself in this emphatic way, Paul makes his appeal "through the meekness and clemency of Christ." Lambrecht (137) notes that similar appeals occur in Rom 12:1 ("Now I appeal to you . . . by the mercies of God"), Rom 15:30 ("I appeal to you . . . by our Lord Jesus Christ and by the love of the Spirit"), and 1 Cor 1:10 ("I appeal to you . . . by the name of our

---

3. Prior to this point in Galatians, Paul has not explicitly taken up the question of circumcision, even though it is the central issue of the letter. One could argue that something similar occurs in 2 Corinthians. Paul has not yet taken up the main issue, the intruding apostles, though he has hinted at the issue in earlier parts of the letter; see 2:17; 3:1; 5:12.

4. For other instances where Paul refers to himself by name, apart from the letter greeting, in order to provide emphasis, see 1 Cor 1:13; 3:5, 22; 16:21; 1 Thess 2:18; Phlm 9, 19; and in the deuteropaulines 2 Thess 3:17; Eph 3:1; Col 1:23. For other instances where Paul employs "I, myself" (*autos egō*), see Rom 7:25; 9:3; 15:14.

5. The use of this emphatic form of address, as well as the more frequent use of the first person singular in chaps. 10–13, is often presented as an argument against the literary integrity of 2 Corinthians. However, it should be noted that Paul does not abandon the literary plural in these chapters. For example, although he employs the first person singular in vv. 1–2, he uses the literary plural in vv. 4–6. Likewise, although the first person singular appears in vv. 8 and 9, the literary plural occurs in vv. 7 and 11, as well as in vv. 12–17.

A. Paul's Integrity and Missionary Assignment

Lord Jesus Christ"). In highlighting the meekness and clemency of Christ, Paul is implicitly applying these qualities to himself as well.

"Meekness" (*prautēs*) according to BDAG is "the quality of not being overly impressed by a sense of one's self-importance." Thus it often has the meaning of "gentleness," "humility," "courtesy," or "consideration," as well as "meekness." In Gal 5:23 Paul lists *prautēs* among "the fruit" of the Spirit, and it occurs in Eph 4:2 and Col 3:12 as one of the virtues or qualities that should characterize the Christian life. Although this noun never appears in the Gospels, the adjective *praus* does, once in the Beatitudes (Matt 5:5, "Blessed are the meek") and twice in reference to Jesus (Matt 11:29, "for I am meek [NRSV "gentle"] and humble in heart"; Matt 21:5 "Look, your king is coming to you, meek [NRSV "humble,"] and mounted on a donkey," a citation from Zech 9:9). This concept of meekness had a rich and varied background in Hellenistic culture, but in the Septuagint it tended to take on the religious quality of "radical submission to God and modesty in dealing with other people."[6] One suspects that Paul has a similar understanding of meekness, since he views it in light of Christ.

"Clemency" (*epieikeia*) according to BDAG is "the quality of making allowances despite facts that might suggest reasons for a different reaction." Thus it is translated as "gentleness," "graciousness," "courtesy," "indulgence," "tolerance," as well as "clemency." Wisdom 12:18 describes God as governing "with great forbearance," and in 2 Macc 10:4 Maccabeus and his followers pray that God will discipline them "with forbearance" should they sin. In Phil 4:5 Paul exhorts his converts to let their *epieikeia* be known to everyone, whereas in the Pastorals, *epieikeia* is listed as one of the qualities required of a bishop (1Tim 3:3). James 3:17 employs *epieikeia* to describe "the wisdom from above," and in Acts 24:4 the orator, Tertullus, asks the Roman governor Felix to hear him briefly with his customary *epieikeia*.

In *1 Clem.* 30:8 and *Diogn.* 7:4 the two words occur together, as they do here. *First Clement* names "meekness and clemency" among the qualities that identify a person as blessed by God, whereas the *Epistle to Diognetus* says that God sent his Christ in "meekness and clemency" as a king might send his son. Although the two words are similar in meaning and might be viewed as an hendiadys (so Barrett, 247), the concept of *epieikeia* carries a greater sense of "indulgence" or "clemency," whereas *prautēs*, especially in the biblical period, begins to focus on submission to God. In making his appeal "through the meekness and clemency of Christ," then, Paul probably has in view the submissive

---

6. Ceslas Spicq, *Theological Lexicon of the New Testament* (Peabody, Mass.: Hendrickson, 1994), vol. 3, s.v. *praupathei*. Spicq's article covers the Hellenistic as well as the biblical background of the word. He notes that in the classical period it denoted a "calm and soothing disposition," whereas among the orators it becomes "leniency and indulgence." Eventually it became "a constant epithet for the emperor, kings, and high officials." Plato sees it as a "quality of a good person," and Aristotle makes it a virtue.

and gracious dimension of Jesus' earthly life as well as the graciousness that the preexistent one manifested in assuming the human condition (see 2 Cor 8:9; Phil 2:5–11), although some commentators (Furnish, 460; Thrall, 2:600) prefer to view the phrase only in light of the weakness and lowly condition that the preexistent Christ assumed. It is interesting to note that whereas many modern commentators portray Paul as cantankerous and irascible, Paul presents himself as someone who has modeled himself on the "meekness and clemency of Christ."[7]

Having made his appeal "through the meekness and clemency of Christ," Paul describes himself in yet another way, "[I] who am humble (*tapeinos*) when present among you but bold toward you when absent." The phrase is ironic and can be taken in different ways, depending upon one's point of view. For example, from the point of view of the Corinthians, who misunderstand the nature of Paul's apostolic ministry, Paul is *tapeinos* in the sense of being "lowly" and "of no account," for he works as a common tradesman rather than accept their financial support. Thus in 11:7 he writes, "Did I commit a sin by abasing myself (*emauton tapeinōn*) so that you might be exalted because I proclaimed God's good news to you free of charge?" Moreover, if Paul acted with "meekness and clemency" toward the Corinthians on the occasion of the painful visit, some may have mistaken his behavior as an inability to act boldly and decisively as they expected he should.[8] But from the perspective of Paul, who understands his behavior in light of Christ, his *tapeinos* is a manifestation of "the meekness and clemency of Christ" (see Matt 11:29, where Jesus describes himself as "meek" [*praus*] and "humble" [*tapeinos*]). Therefore, just as Christ was not overbearing in the exercise of his authority, neither is Paul (see Paul's statement in 1:24 that he does not rule over their faith). The conflict at Corinth, then, is rooted in conflicting perceptions of how Paul exercises his ministry.

Aware of this problem, Paul begins his appeal anew in verse 2, implicitly asking the Corinthians to alter their perceptions of his apostolic service, lest it become necessary for him to act with the boldness that he is capable of exercising "toward some" (*epi tinas*) who judge that he walks "according to the flesh." Although the people to whom he refers are not specified, Paul probably has in mind the intruding apostles (who will loom ever larger as these chapters progress) and their Corinthian sympathizers. "Walking according to the flesh" normally has a negative moral connotation in Paul's letters, but here the phrase represents a charge leveled against the nature of Paul's ministry rather than an accusation of sinfulness (namely, that Paul lacks the power of the Spirit to act boldly), a point he will address in the following verses.

---

7. The point is made in the commentary of David Garland (434), who suggests that it may be necessary for modern commentators to reevaluate their portrait of Paul.

8. Paul's apparent inability to resolve the crisis of the painful visit in a decisive or powerful manner may have been one of the accusations made against him by his detractors.

A. Paul's Integrity and Missionary Assignment

To summarize, these opening verses set out the parameters of the problem and the theological grounds for settling it. The Corinthians have misunderstood Paul's humble presence among them as a sign of weakness and servileness. They have not understood that his humble bearing in their midst is nothing less than "the meekness and clemency of Christ," the very essence of the gospel he preaches.

[3–4a] Having implicitly warned those who misunderstand the nature of his "humble" (*tapeinos*) presence when among them, Paul now affirms that although he walks "in the flesh," the weapons of his warfare do not belong to the realm of the flesh. For although his critics may view him as weak, servile, and bereft of the boldness that comes from the Spirit, he possesses "weapons" that are powerful to destroy fortresses. This military metaphor, which will continue through verse 6, is reminiscent of the other military metaphors that Paul employed in 2:14. But whereas in 2:14 Paul portrayed himself as a prisoner in God's triumphal procession, here he presents himself as a soldier who assaults and tears down powerful fortresses that stand in opposition to the gospel.

In asserting that his weapons do not belong to the realm of the flesh, Paul implies that they belong to the realm of the Spirit. Thus they can be equated with the "weapons of righteousness" that he mentions in 6:7 and the "armor of light" that he notes in Rom 13:12. The context, however, suggests that his weapons are the gospel he preaches, since the military installations or "fortresses" that he destroys are the false reasonings or sophistries of those who oppose his gospel. In effect Paul views himself as a soldier, armed with the Spirit-empowered weapons of the gospel, who assaults the powerful fortress of those who oppose his ministry by their false and misleading reasoning.

Although this threatening military metaphor stands in contrast to Paul's gentle appeal "through the meekness and clemency of Christ," it does not contradict it, as if Paul were threatening to replace meekness and clemency with an exercise of power and force as the world understands these realities. The powerful weapons that Paul will employ to tear down the fortresses opposed to the gospel are the persuasive words of the gospel. Indeed Paul has been employing these weapons all along, but the Corinthians have not understood that in meekness and boldness, in clemency and in battle, Paul is always the same.

[4b–6] These verses expand upon Paul's military metaphor with three participles that highlight three aspects of his warfare: (1) Paul "tears down" (*kathairountes*) sophistries; (2) he "captures" (*aichmalōtizontes*) every proud obstacle; and (3) he "stands ready to punish" (*en hetoimō echontes ekdikēsai*) every disobedience. The three phases of warfare that Paul describes here are similar to the stages of battle that the Romans employed against the Greeks, as portrayed in 1 Macc 8:9–10, when the Romans tore down the strongholds of the Greeks, took their wives and children captive, and then enslaved them.

The Greeks planned to come and destroy them [the Romans], but this became known to them, and they sent a general against the Greeks and attacked them. Most of them were wounded and fell, and the Romans took captive (*ēchmalōtisan*) their wives and children; they plundered them, conquered the land, tore down their strongholds (*katheilon ta ochyrōmata autōn*), and enslaved them to this day.

Understood metaphorically, the stages of Paul's warfare can be described in this way: First, he will tear down the strongholds of his opponents, which he identifies as their "sophistries" (*logismous*) and "arrogance" (*hypsōma*), fortresses in which they seek to protect themselves from attack and which they raise up in opposition to "the knowledge of God." This knowledge, which Paul has already mentioned several times in 2 Corinthians (2:14; 4:6; 6:6), is the gospel, inasmuch as its proclamation makes known God's plan for salvation. In the second stage of his warfare, Paul will rescue those who have been seduced by the sophistries and arrogance of his opponents and "take captive every thought (*noēma*) for obedience to Christ." The use of *noēma* recalls Paul's earlier comment in 4:4 that the "god of this age has blinded the minds (*noēmata*) of the unbelieving lest they see the light of the gospel of the glory of Christ," and it anticipates his remark in 11:3 that he fears that as the serpent deceived Eve, the "thoughts" or "minds" of the Corinthians will be led astray by the intruding apostles. In the third stage of his warfare, after he has torn down the fortresses of his opponents by exposing their false arguments and rescued those whose minds have been captivated by them, he will punish the disobedient. Paul does not explicitly identify whom he has in mind, but since he will punish the disobedient when the obedience of the community is complete, he may have the intruding apostles in view. But the threat is open-ended enough to include those Corinthian sympathizers who do not repent.

From one point of view, Paul portrays himself like the wise person of the Wisdom literature:

> One wise person went up against a city of warriors and brought down the stronghold (*katheile to ochyrōma*) in which they trusted. (Prov 21:22)

> There was a little city with few people in it. A great king came against it and besieged it, building great siege works against it. Now there was found in it a poor wise man, and he by his wisdom delivered the city. Yet no one remembered that poor man. (Eccl 9:14–15)

In addition to these texts, Abraham Malherbe has drawn attention to a number of Greco-Roman parallels and argued that Paul "describes his own weapons in terms approximating the self-description of the rigorist Cynics and describes his opponents' fortifications in terms strongly reminiscent of the Stoic sage."[9]

---

9. "Antisthenes and Odysseus, and Paul at War," in *Paul and the Popular Philosophers* (Minneapolis: Fortress, 1989), 112.

A. Paul's Integrity and Missionary Assignment

But Paul is more than a wise man or philosopher who conquers the sophistries of his opponents by clever and wise arguments. He is the herald of the gospel who has been fully fitted for battle with the armor of God (see Eph 6:11–17). When he finally comes to Corinth, his physical presence may not be any more forceful than it was when he first came (see 1 Cor 2:1–5), but armed with the weapons of God's warfare, he will act boldly.

[7–8] Having described the boldness with which he will act when he comes to Corinth—and still hoping that he will not have to display such boldness—Paul calls upon the Corinthians to see what is before their very eyes: the new covenant community that has been established in their midst. Thus, just as he argued that he does not need letters of recommendation to or from the community, since the community is his letter of recommendation (3:1–3), so he now defends his relationship to Christ by pointing to the work that has been done at Corinth. If the Corinthians look at the work of building up the church that he has accomplished in their midst, they will recognize that just as others claim that they belong to Christ, so does Paul.

The expression that Paul employs at this point ("just as he belongs to Christ, so do we," *kathōs autos Christou, houtōs hēmeis*) is somewhat vague, and most commentators take it in one of the following ways: (1) belonging to the "Christ party" mentioned in 1 Cor 1:12; (2) being a Christian; (3) having a special relationship to the earthly Jesus; (4) having a Gnostic-mythical relationship to the risen Christ; (5) having the status of Christ's apostle. However, since Paul has been defending his apostolic ministry throughout this letter, it is best to take the expression "belonging to Christ" as a kind of shorthand for his status as an apostle, since he will soon argue that he is in no manner inferior to the super-apostles (11:5), who apparently identify themselves as "ministers of Christ" (11:23). Moreover, the use of the singular here ("if someone"), as well as in verses 10 and 11 ("someone says" . . . "let this one consider"), could indicate a particular individual, such as the ring leader of the opposition (Lambrecht, 156), though many commentators interpret the singular as embracing the whole of the opposition (Barnett, 469; Martin, 307). In either case, Paul affirms his credentials as Christ's apostle on the basis of the work that he has already done at Corinth, a theme that he will develop further in verses 14–16.

Having asserted that he also belongs to Christ, Paul grounds his claim in the authority that "the Lord" (Christ) gave him for building up and "not for your destruction" (*ouk eis kathairesin hymōn*), arguing that even if he should boast too much in this authority, he will not be put to shame (v. 8). Paul's line of reasoning works in this way: First, it was Christ who gave him the authority to "build up" the church at Corinth (for other uses of this verb, see 1 Cor 8:1; 10:23; 14:4, as well as 2 Cor 12:19). Second, because Christ gave him this authority, Paul can boast of it to the Corinthians. Third, even if he should boast a bit much in his Christ-given authority, Paul knows that God will not shame or disappoint him, since Paul does not boast in his own authority but the authority that the Lord has given him. Thus Paul anticipates what he will say in the next unit about boasting in the Lord (v.17) and his refusal to boast beyond the limits appointed to him (v. 13) or in the work of others (v. 16).

In affirming that the Lord gave him authority to "build up" the community, Paul adds that this authority does not include destroying the community, a point that he will repeat in 13:10. For even though Paul has been equipped with powerful weapons to destroy the proud fortresses of those who oppose the gospel (v. 4), Christ did not give him this authority for the purpose of destroying the church of God, although Paul will punish those who try to destroy the church. Indeed, he views the intruding apostles as false apostles precisely because they are destroying the church of God by leading the Corinthians astray (11:3–4). Because they are doing this, they are false apostles (11:13), without authority from Christ (Barrett, 258), and they will be destroyed for destroying the temple of God (see 1 Cor 3:17).

[9–11] Having asserted that he fights with powerful weapons that are capable of tearing down the fortresses of those who oppose his gospel (vv. 3–6) and that he "belongs to Christ," who has given him authority for building up the church, Paul returns to the accusation that he introduced in the opening verses: although he is bold when absent from the community, he is humble in the sense of being "timid" or "base" when he is present to the community. In these final verses, however, the accusation becomes more specific and establishes a contrast between Paul's letters, which are "severe and powerful," and his physical presence and speech, which are "weak" and "contemptible." As in the opening verses, Paul insists upon the consistency of his behavior, whether he is present or absent. The relationship between verses 1–2 and verses 9–11 can be summarized as follows:

Absent	*Present*
bold	humble
severe and powerful letters	weak presence and contemptible speech

As the notes indicate, the beginning of verse 9 presents a difficult problem of translation, since the opening words of this verse, "lest I appear as frightening you" (*hina mē doxō hōs an ekphobein hymas*), seem to be elliptical, unless they are taken as having the force of an imperative. The difficulty, however, can be resolved in another way by viewing verse 10 as a parenthetical remark in which Paul alludes to an accusation leveled against him that though he can write in a severe and powerful manner, his physical presence and speech do not match the powerful oratory of his letters. Although the accusation refers to "letters," the immediate reference may be to the harsh letter that Paul mentions in 2:3–4, 9; 7:8–13. Moreover, although Paul acknowledges that when he first came to

A. Paul's Integrity and Missionary Assignment

the Corinthians it was in "in weakness and in fear and in much trembling" and that his speech and proclamation "were not with plausible words of wisdom" (1 Cor 2:3–4), here the accusation probably has in view Paul's second visit to Corinth, the painful visit mentioned in 2 Cor 2:1. If so, someone has drawn a comparison between Paul's apparent "timidity" on the occasion of that visit and the harshness of the letter he wrote after that visit, in order to discredit Paul by showing the discrepancy between how he writes and how he behaves. Aware of this accusation and that another harsh letter will only compound the problem, Paul assures the Corinthians that there is a correspondence between the Paul who writes to them and the Paul who will soon be present to them.

Paul's line of thought in verses 8–11 develops in this way: He begins by assuring the Corinthians that he is not writing to frighten them (v. 9). Next, aware of the accusation that has been leveled against him, he quotes it back to the Corinthians (v. 10). Finally, he asks the one who makes such an accusation to understand that what he (Paul) writes when absent will be matched by his deeds when he comes to Corinth. As in verse 7 Paul employs the singular in verse 10 ("some one says") and verse 11 ("this one"), suggesting that he may have a particular individual in view, though he will use the plural in verse 12 when he criticizes those who classify or compare themselves with themselves.

In 11:6 Paul will acknowledge that he is not a professional or trained speaker, and in 11:30 and 12:5, 9 he will boast in his weakness,[10] suggesting that there is a certain aspect of the accusation that is true. Paul makes no claim to be a professional orator; indeed when he first came to Corinth he explicitly avoided "words of wisdom" (1 Cor 2:3) so that the faith of the Corinthians would not rest on human wisdom but "on the power of God" (1 Cor 2.5). Likewise he can rejoice in his weakness, because when he is weak, then the Corinthians are "strong" (13:9). The Corinthians, however, should not confuse appearance with reality, for there is a paradoxical sense in which, when Paul is weak, then he is strong (12:10).

When he writes that "what we are in word through our letters when absent, we are when present in action," Paul does not mean that he will suddenly appear as a highly skilled speaker and manifest a powerful physical presence to the Corinthians. Rather, he will come armed with the powerful spiritual weapons of the gospel that he preaches. In this sense, what he does will correspond to what he writes, since the boldness and courage that he will demonstrate will not come from himself but from the gospel that he preaches.

This first unit can be summarized as follows: Whether present or absent, Paul acts with boldness, because he is armed with powerful weapons of the gospel, and he has received his authority from Christ. Although his detractors misin-

---

10. For other uses of the noun "weakness" (*astheneia*), see 12:10; 13:4. For Paul's use of the verb "to be weak" (*astheneō*), see 11:21, 29; 12:10; 13:3, 4, 9.

terpret his humble bearing for weakness, his apparent weakness is the meekness and clemency of Christ.

2. Paul's Assignment (10:12–18)

10:12 For we are not bold enough to classify or compare[a] ourselves with some who commend themselves; but in evaluating themselves with themselves and comparing themselves with themselves, they do not understand.[b]

13 We do not boast beyond limits but according to the assigned measure[c] that God has apportioned us for a measure to come all the way to you. 14 For we are not going beyond our limits—as if we did not come to you— for we were the first to come[d] to you with the gospel of Christ. 15 We are not boasting beyond limits in the work of others but hoping that as your faith increases we might be praised among you[e] to a greater degree, in accordance with our assignment,[f] 16 so that lands[g] beyond you might be evangelized, without our[h] boasting in work already done in the assignment[f] of another.

17 Let the one who boasts, boast in the Lord. 18 For, it is not the one who commends himself who is approved but the one whom the Lord commends.

a. The Greek has a play on words that is not apparent in this translation (*enkrinai ē synkrinai*). Plummer (286) suggests the phrase "to pair or compare" as a way of reproducing this wordplay.

b. Some Greek manuscripts (D*, F, G) do not have the final two words of verse 12 (*ou syniasin*) and the first two words of v. 13 (*hēmeis de*). If this reading is correct, then v. 12 should be translated: "For we are not bold enough to classify or compare ourselves with those who commend themselves, *but we measure ourselves and compare ourselves with ourselves.* . . ." Although this is the shorter reading and makes better sense of the *ou . . . alla* ("not" . . . "but") construction in this verse, most modern commentators (Windisch, Bultmann, and Héring being notable exceptions) and translations adopt the longer reading for the following reasons. First, the shorter reading "is doubtless the result of an accident in transcription, when the eye of a copyist passed from *ou* to *ouk* and omitted the intervening words" (Metzger, *A Textual Commentary on the New Testament*, 583). Second, the shorter reading, which has Paul comparing himself with himself, contradicts what Paul says in v. 18 about the approved person being the one whom the Lord commends.

c. "The assigned measure" translates *to metron tou kanonos*, literally "the measure of the rule." The phrase, which is discussed in the exegesis, is notoriously difficult to interpret. In this translation *to metron* is construed as what has been measured out and, following BDAG, *kanōn* is interpreted as a "set of directions or formulations for an activity," thus an "assignment." Understood in this way, God has measured out a certain apostolic assignment for Paul that includes bringing the gospel to Corinth.

A. Paul's Integrity and Missionary Assignment

d. Since the verb *phthanō* has the sense of "preceding" and the context requires that Paul arrived in Corinth before the intruding apostles, the verb is translated "first to come."

e. Although "among you" could be taken with the phrase "as your faith increases," its position in the Greek text suggests that it should be taken, as it is here, with "be praised." Since there is no expressed subject for "be praised" (*megalynthēnai*), one must be supplied. In this translation, Paul asks that he ("we") be praised among the Corinthians, so that the gospel might be preached to others. One could supply another subject, however, as does the NRSV, "our sphere of action."

f. The word "assignment" translates the Greek *kanōn*, whose basic meaning is "rule" or "standard."

g. The meaning of *hyperekeina* is "beyond." The noun "lands" is supplied in order to clarify what Paul intends.

h. The words "without our" have been supplied to clarify the meaning of the Greek.

These verses are related to the preceding unit in several ways. First, in verse 2 Paul tells the Corinthians that he is ready to act "boldly" toward those who criticize him as walking according to the flesh, and in verse 12 he says—with evident irony—that he is not "bold enough" to classify or compare himself with his detractors who indulge in such self-commendation. Second, having said in verse 7 that the one who considers himself as belonging to Christ ought to examine himself again, in verse 12 Paul ridicules the manner in which his detractors compare themselves with themselves rather than examine themselves. Third, having spoken in verse 8 of the authority that the Lord gave him for building up the church, in verses 13–14 Paul discloses the "standard" or "norm" that God apportioned to him so that he could come to Corinth. Finally, having said in verse 8 that even if he should "boast" he will not be put to shame, in verses 15–18 Paul explains that he does not "boast" beyond the measure that God assigned to him or in the work apportioned to others, for the one commended by the Lord boasts in the Lord.

If Paul's purpose in the first unit was to show the Corinthians that he is the same, whether absent or present, in this unit his goal is to explain the "norm" or "standard" (*kanōn*) that guides his apostolic activity. Because he acts in accordance with this *kanōn*, he is boasting in the Lord when he boasts in the work that he has done at Corinth. In contrast to him, the intruding apostles have no "standard" or "norm" for their boasting except themselves, consequently they boast in themselves rather than in the Lord.

The material can be divided into three subunits. In the first (v. 12) Paul derisively says that he is not bold enough to compare himself with those who *commend* themselves by comparing themselves with each other. In the second subunit (vv. 13–16), however, Paul implicitly compares himself with the intruding apostles by showing that his missionary activity is determined by the measure that God assigned to him, whereas the intruding apostles have no norm or standard of measurement beyond themselves. In this subunit the phrase "we do not boast beyond our limits" occurs twice, at the beginning of verse 13 and at the beginning of verse 15, setting off verses 13–14 from verses 15–16. In the third subunit (vv. 17–18) Paul returns to the theme of commendation introduced in verse 12, arguing that only those whom the Lord commends are approved. Thus he encloses his discussion of the "rule" or "standard" that guides his missionary activity with two references to commendation.

v. 12 Paul's refusal to engage in self-commendation
    vv. 13–16 The *kanōn* of Paul's activity
    vv. 17–18 Boasting in the Lord as the criterion for commendation

[10:12] Having defended himself from the charge that he speaks boldly through his letters but acts in a timid and servile way when he is present to the Corinthians, Paul now criticizes those who commend themselves by comparing themselves with each other. This unit, as did the previous unit, begins with an ironic and derisive comment, namely, although he has already told the Corinthians that he will act "boldly" toward those who esteem him as powerless to act boldly (vv. 1–2), he admits that he is not "bold enough" to classify or compare himself with those who commend themselves (*heautous synistanontōn*). What Paul really means, of course, is that he will not engage in their kind of self-commendation, because, as he will explain, self-commendation is boasting in oneself rather than in the Lord.

Paul will eventually engage in "foolish boasting" (11:1–12:13) and even affirm his boldness to do so (11:21). But he will do this *after* he has disclosed the *kanōn* of his apostolic work that allows him to boast in the work that he has done at Corinth. The boasting in which he will engage (11:1–12:13) will indeed be foolish and dangerous, since it will serve no real purpose apart from a comparison with the super-apostles, but it will not be entirely illegitimate, since Paul will boast within the limits of the "standard" or "assignment" (*kanōn*) that God has established for his apostolic activity.

The theme of "commendation" has played and will continue to play an important role in 2 Corinthians. Thus in 3:1 Paul asks, "Are we beginning to commend ourselves again?" In 4:2 he affirms that he commends himself "before God, to everyone's conscience." In 5:12, he writes, "We are not commending ourselves to you again but giving you an opportunity for boasting on behalf of us, so that you might have something to say to those who boast in appearance and not in the heart." In 6:4 he commends himself as God's minister through the hardships he has endured for the gospel. Finally, in 12:11, after he has concluded his foolish boasting, Paul will acknowledge, "I have become a fool. You drove me to it. For I should have been commended by you. For in no way am I inferior to the super-apostles, even though I am nothing."

A. Paul's Integrity and Missionary Assignment

On first reading, these texts are puzzling and contradictory. On the one hand, Paul apparently denies a charge that he commends himself (3:1), but on the other he does commend himself (4:2; 6:4) and expects the Corinthians to do the same (5:12; 12:11). But Paul relieves this tension when he explains that "it is not the one who commends himself who is approved but the one whom the Lord commends" (10:18). In verses 13–16 he will show that he is approved by the Lord because he acts according to the measure of the "rule" or "standard" that God apportioned to him. Consequently Paul has every right to expect the Corinthians to commend him, and he can even commend himself to them, provided that he works within the limits of this "rule," "standard," or "assignment" that God has established for him.

In contrast to Paul, the intruding apostles have no *kanōn* to measure themselves against apart from themselves. Consequently they engage in self-commendation and foolish boasting by comparing themselves with themselves. What the intruding apostles "do not understand" (v. 12), then, is the need for an external God-given standard to which they can compare themselves. Only then will their boasting be in the Lord rather than in themselves. For this reason Paul confesses that he is "not bold enough" to compare himself with them. For if he did, he would be engaging in the same foolish boasting.

[13–16] With these verses Paul embarks upon a process of legitimizing his apostolic activity among the Corinthians by appealing to an external criterion, given by God, that bestows a unique status upon him in relation to the Corinthians: he is their father in Christ because he was the first to bring the gospel to them. In contrast to Paul, the intruding apostles, who have come to Corinth after Paul founded the church, do not possess a standard or criterion that allows them to boast in the Corinthians. In addition to providing the central argument for this unit, the point that Paul makes in these verses will allow him to engage in the foolish and dangerous boasting upon which he will soon embark (11:1–12:13). For although boasting is always dangerous, it is not excluded if one boasts within the measure, determined by the norm, that God apportions.

Paul begins with a phrase that will be repeated in a slightly different way at the beginning of verse 15, "We do not boast beyond limits," implying that the intruding apostles, who commend themselves by comparing themselves with themselves, do. Although Paul does not repeat the verb "to boast" in the second part of verse 15, it is implied: Paul does not boast beyond limits, but he can boast according to "the assigned measure" that God has apportioned for him. Thus, as Paul has already suggested in verse 8 and as he will explain in verse 18, boasting is not excluded, provided that one boasts within the measure that God allows; for such boasting is boasting in the Lord. The crucial question, however, is, What does Paul mean when he refers to *to metron tou kanonos* as the norm or standard of his apostolic activity, and so of his boasting?

The word *metron* can designate either "an instrument for measuring" or "the result of measuring" (BDAG), whereas *kanōn* normally designates "a means to determine the quality of something." Thus *kanōn* is commonly translated "rule" or "standard." If *metron* designates the instrument of measure, *metron* and *kanōn* are referring to the same thing in this expression, giving the sense "the measure that is the rule." But if *metron* refers to what has been measured out, then it is the *kanōn* that determines the *metron*, and the phrase would be rendered "the measure [which is measured out and] determined by the standard." Overall, this seems to be the better way of understanding the phrase, since Paul immediately adds, "that God has apportioned us for a measure" (*hou emerisen hēmin ho theos metrou*). If this is correct, then Paul is saying that God has established a "standard" (*kanōn*) for Paul's apostolic activity by which God determines a specific "measure" or "portion" for Paul. Thus Paul does not boast "beyond the limits" (*eis ta ametra*) that God has established for him but within the measure, determined by the standard, that God has apportioned for him.

But what is this "measure" that has been determined by the "standard"? Arguing on the basis of Gal 2:9, some commentators (Scott, 198–99)[11] construe "the measure determined by the standard" in terms of the geographical sphere that the "pillar apostles" allotted to Paul and Barnabas on the occasion of the apostolic conference: "and when James and Cephas and John, who were acknowledged pillars, recognized the grace that had been given to me, they gave to Barnabas and me the right hand of fellowship, agreeing that we should go to the Gentiles and they to the circumcised." Thus the NRSV translates this phrase "the *field* that God has assigned to us," and the REB, "our *sphere* is determined by the limit God has laid down." This interpretation is attractive, since Paul is defending Corinth as his missionary sphere of activity against the intruding apostles. But even though the text of Galatians says that the "pillar apostles" agreed that Paul and Barnabas should go to the Gentiles, it does not explicitly assign a geographic sphere to them. Indeed it would have been impractical to do so, since Gentiles and Jews often inhabited the same towns in the Hellenistic world. Moreover, even though Paul is defending his "territorial rights" at Corinth, he does not appeal here to the agreement with the "pillar apostles."

Other commentators maintain that there is little, if any, linguistic evidence that *kanōn* carries the geographical sense of "field" or "sphere."[12] They argue

---

11. See James M. Scott, *Paul and the Nations: The Old Testament and Jewish Background of Paul's Mission to the Nations with Special Reference to the Destination of Galatians* (WUNT 84; Tübingen: J. C. B. Mohr, 1995), 159–62, for a fuller exposition of this position.

12. However, BDAG, s.v. *kanōn*, points to an inscription found in *New Documents Illustrating Early Christianity* that may give some support to the notion of sphere: "I have promulgated in the individual cities and villages a *schedule* of what I judge desirable to be supplied" (*kata polin kai kōmēn etaxa kanona tōn hypēresiōn* [trans. Horsley]). BDAG then provides a second meaning for *kanōn*: a "set of directions or formulation for an activity," thus "assignment" or "formulation," suggesting that the missionary "assignment" given to Paul "included directions about geographical area."

A. Paul's Integrity and Missionary Assignment

for the common meaning of the word as "norm" or "standard" and interpret the phrase in light of the concluding words in verse 13, "to come all the way to you." Understood in this way, the "standard" (*kanōn*) that determines the "measure" (*metron*) that God has apportioned Paul for a measure (*hou emerisen hēmin ho theos metrou*) is disclosed in the indisputable fact that Paul was the first to come to Corinth. Beyer writes, "Paul does not appeal to an exclusive right to come to Corinth as a missionary, but to the historical fact that it was granted to him to do this."[13] In a similar vein Hafemann notes, "Paul's arrival in Corinth and the ensuing birth of the church are thus the *divinely* appointed indication and objective evidence that Paul's claim to authority in Corinth is valid."[14]

It is difficult to choose between these alternatives. The context suggests that "place" or "sphere" plays a role in what Paul is saying, but *kanōn* usually means "standard" or "norm," and in this case it seems to be defined by the phrase "to come all the way to you." Moreover, in Gal 6:15–16, the only other instance when Paul employs the word, apart from the variant reading of Phil 3:16, *kanōn* clearly means "standard," "norm," or "rule": "For neither circumcision nor uncircumcision is anything: but a new creation is everything! As for those who will follow this *rule*—peace be upon them, and mercy, and upon the Israel of God."

The translation adopted in this commentary, "the assigned measure," is indebted to the second meaning of *kanōn* ("assignment") provided by BDAG. On the one hand, "assignment" presupposes instructions given by another and so does justice to the sense of *kanōn* as a "norm" or "standard." On the other hand, an assignment could, but it does not need to, include instructions to work in a particular geographical sphere.

Having explained in verse 13 that he does not boast beyond limits because he works within the "assigned measure" that God has apportioned for him, in verse 14 Paul substantiates what he says by reminding the Corinthians that he was the first to come to them. Echoing the final words of verse 13 ("to come all the way to you"), he writes that it is not "as if we did not come to you." That is, if Paul had not come to Corinth first, so that others had preached the gospel there before he arrived, then he would be going beyond his limits. But what the Corinthians know, and what Paul's detractors cannot deny, is that he was the first to preach the gospel at Corinth (see 1 Cor 4:15). The external "norm" or "standard" that guides his apostolic service and allows him to boast in the Lord, then, is the indisputable fact that he is the father-founder of the Corinthian church, the first to preach the gospel at Corinth. When Paul writes that he does not boast beyond limits, therefore, he means that he does not boast in the work that others have done, as he will explain in verses 15–16.

Having said in verses 13–14 why he is not boasting beyond his limits (when he boasts about his work among the Corinthians), in verse 15 Paul repeats and

---

13. H. W. Beyer, *TDNT*, vol. 3, s.v. *kanōn*.
14. Scott Hafemann, *NTS* 36 (1990): 79.

expands upon the opening words of verse 13, "We are not boasting beyond our limits *in the work of others*." The addition of "in the work of others" suggests that the intruding apostles are boasting to the Corinthians as if they, and not Paul, were the first to bring the gospel to Corinth. Unlike the intruding apostles, when Paul boasts to the Corinthians, he is boasting in his own work: the task assigned to him by God and disclosed by the incontrovertible fact that he was the first to come to Corinth with the gospel.

Rather than boasting in another's work, Paul hopes that as the faith of the Corinthians increases, he will be praised among them to a greater degree in accordance with his "assignment" (*kata ton kanona hēmōn*). Thus he will be able to bring the gospel to lands beyond Corinth without boasting in another person's "assignment" (*en allotriō kanoni*). The references that Paul makes here, first to his own "assignment" and then to the "assignment" of another, clearly indicate that he does not deny that others have received an "assigned measure" from God. Aware that there are places where others have preached the gospel before him, Paul writes in Rom 15:20, "Thus I make it my ambition to proclaim the good news, not where Christ has already been named, so that I do not build on someone else's foundation, but as it is written, 'Those who have never been told of him shall see, and those who have never heard of him shall understand.'"

At the present moment Paul is poised to preach the gospel in lands beyond Achaia, as he notes in Rom 15:23–24a, "But now, with no further place for me in these regions [he is writing from Corinth], I desire, as I have for many years, to come to you when I go to Spain." Before embarking upon uncharted territories, however, Paul must solidify his position at Corinth. This is why he expresses his hope that as their faith increases, he (and his work) may be "magnified" or "praised" among the Corinthians to a greater degree. Paul, of course, has already affirmed that the Corinthians stand firm in faith (1:24), and he has said that the Corinthians abound "in faith, and speech, and knowledge" (8:7). But in the final chapter of this letter, he will challenge them to examine and test themselves to see if they are "in the faith" (*en tē pistei*; 13:5). Thus, whereas Paul affirms the faith of the Corinthians, he also challenges it, and he asks them to test themselves as they have tested him. In 10:15, however, Paul does not so much challenge their faith as express a wish that their faith will continue to grow as a result of, and as a sign of, the work that he has done among them. In that way, he will be praised or magnified among them because the assigned work that he has accomplished will be evident for all to see.

The work that he has done among the Corinthians will allow him to bring the gospel to lands beyond Achaia; for having planted the gospel firmly in one place, it will be necessary for him to move to another, where the gospel has not yet been preached. There is a sense, then, in which Paul must settle the troubles in Corinth before moving to new missionary territories, since the Corinthians

A. Paul's Integrity and Missionary Assignment

are his letter of recommendation (3:2). Failure at Corinth would have seriously called into question his apostolic credentials elsewhere.

Paul's line of argument in these difficult verses may be summarized in this way: The fact that he was the first to preach the gospel at Corinth is the *kanōn* that determines and discloses the "measure" (*metron*) of apostolic authority that God has apportioned to him. As long as Paul works within the limits established by this *kanōn*, he is not boasting beyond the limits God established for him. Indeed, it is legitimate for Paul to boast in the work he has done at Corinth. Since God has established a *kanōn* for others, Paul does not boast in their work. Rather, he hopes that as the faith of the Corinthian community continues to grow, it will recommend him as an apostolic minister to those to whom the gospel has not yet been preached. Paul's letter of recommendation is and remains the Corinthians.

[17–18] Having presented the *kanōn* that legitimizes him as an apostle to the Corinthians (vv. 13–16), Paul returns to the theme of "commendation" that he introduced in verse 12, thereby completing the ring pattern of this unit (vv. 12–18). But whereas verse 12 focuses on those who commend themselves by comparing themselves with each other, these verses establish the authentic grounds for commendation: it is not those who commend themselves who are approved but those whom the Lord commends.

Paul begins the final phase of his argument with an allusion to the text of Jer 9:23–24 (LXX 9:22–23), which reads:

> Thus says the LORD: Do not let the wise boast in their wisdom, do not let the mighty boast in their might, do not let the wealthy boast in their wealth; but let those who boast boast in this (*all' ē en toutō kauchasthō ho kauchōmenos*), that they understand and know me, that I am the LORD; I act with steadfast love, justice, and righteousness in the earth, for in these things I delight, says the LORD.

Whereas the text of Jeremiah exhorts those who boast to boast "in this" and then explains the content of the demonstrative pronoun as knowledge and understanding of the Lord, who acts with steadfast love, justice, and righteousness, Paul abbreviates the text from Jeremiah and exhorts those who boast to boast "in the Lord"; which in this instance most likely refers to Christ.

The Corinthians would have been familiar with this text, since Paul had already employed it in 1 Cor 1:31, after explaining how God chose "what is low and despised in the world ... so that no one might boast in the presence of God" (1 Cor 1:28–29). "He [God] is the source of your life in Christ Jesus, who became for us wisdom from God, and righteousness and sanctification and redemption, in order that, as it is written, 'Let the one who boasts, boast in the Lord'" (1 Cor 1:30–31).

In 2 Cor 10 the context is different. Paul has affirmed that even if he should boast a bit too much about the authority that God gave him for building up the church, he will not be put to shame, for he "belongs to Christ" (vv. 7–8). And in this unit, he has insisted that he does not boast beyond the limits that God assigned to him (v. 13), nor does he go beyond his limits by boasting in the work that others have done (v. 15). The exhortation that those who boast should boast in the Lord, therefore, stands at an important juncture in his argument. For having asserted that he does not boast beyond the limits assigned to him, and having expressed his confidence that even if he boasts he will not be put to shame, Paul now explains the grounds for authentic boasting: boasting is allowed if one boasts in what the Lord has done. In Paul's case God has given him a missionary "assignment" (*kanōn*) that is revealed in the indisputable fact that he was the first to preach the gospel to the Corinthians. Consequently, when Paul boasts in his work at Corinth, he is boasting in the Lord, because this is the work that God assigned and accomplished in him (see 1 Cor 3:6: "I planted, Apollos watered, but God gave the growth"). In light of the full quotation from Jeremiah, noted above, it now becomes clear what Paul means when he writes in verse 12 that those who commend themselves "do not understand." They do not "know" and "understand" the Lord (see Jer 9:24), who has acted in their midst with steadfast love, justice, and righteousness.

With the assistance of this allusion from Jeremiah, Paul now concludes his argument. The reason for boasting in the Lord is that only the one whom the Lord commends is approved (*dokimos*). In commending themselves by comparing themselves with each other, the intruding apostles may demonstrate to themselves and to the Corinthians that they are "approved" (*dokimos*) for apostolic service; but they are not approved by the Lord, since they do not boast in the Lord. In the process of their self-commendation, however, they have undoubtedly inferred or told the Corinthians that, unlike them, Paul is "unfit" (*adokimos*) for apostolic ministry. Thus, in 13:5–6 Paul challenges the Corinthians, "Put yourselves to the test to see if you are in the faith. Examine yourselves (*heautous dokimazete*). Or do you not realize that Jesus Christ is in you? Unless, perhaps, you have failed to meet the test (*adokimoi este*). I trust that you know that we are not failing to meet the test (*ouk esmen adokimoi*)." In addition to this text, see 1 Cor 3:13, where Paul tells the Corinthians that fire will "test" (*dokimasei*) the work of apostolic ministers, and 1 Thess 2:4, where he writes, "but just as we have been approved (*dedokimasmetha*) by God to be entrusted with the message of the gospel, even so we speak, not to please mortals, but to please God who tests (*dokimazonti*) our hearts."

The line of thought in 10:1–18 can be summarized in this way: Paul appeals to the Corinthians with the very meekness and clemency of Christ, so that he will not have to act boldly when he comes to Corinth. Although some accuse him of being servile and lacking the boldness that comes from the Spirit, he possesses the powerful weapons of the gospel that allow him to destroy false arguments, take minds captive for Christ, and punish the disobedient. The Corinthians only need to look at what Paul has accomplished in their midst to realize that he is Christ's minister. In writing these things, Paul is not trying to frighten them by his letters, as if he were incapable of acting boldly in their midst; for the absent apostle portrayed through the letters is the same apostle who will be present in their midst. Paul, however, is not bold enough to commend himself, as do the intruding apostles, who do not understand the power of God. Rather, if he boasts it will always be within the limits established by the measure that God has assigned to him, an assignment authenticated by the indisputable fact that he was the first to preach the gospel to the Corinthians. If he boasts, therefore, it is in the Lord; for only the one whom the Lord approves is commended. Paul can claim such approval because he has been granted an assignment from the Lord, who guides his apostolic activity.

B. Boasting Foolishly
2 Corinthians 11:1–12:13

Having defended his apostolic integrity in 10:1–18, Paul embarks upon a foolish and dangerous project of "boasting" in 11:1–12:13. The project is dangerous because boasting runs in the face of what Paul has just written, "Let the one who boasts, boast in the Lord" (10:17). Aware of this, and deeply distressed that he must engage in such boasting, Paul makes several references to himself as a "fool" and to the "foolishness" of what he is doing (11:1, 16, 17, 21), concluding that his boasting has made him "a fool" (12:11).

The Corinthians, however, have left Paul with little room to maneuver. Since they have not defended him against the intruding apostles, he has been forced to defend himself by this foolish and dangerous boasting, lest his ministry at Corinth be brought to naught (12:11).

Although nearly all commentators view 11:1 as the beginning of this section, there is little agreement about its ending, some concluding the section at 12:10 (Allo, Martin), others at 12:13 (Barnett, Furnish, Garland), and still others at 12:18 (Barrett, Bultmann, Plummer, Thrall). Despite this lack of agreement, there are several good reasons for viewing 12:11–13 as the conclusion or epilogue of this section. First, Paul's statement in 12:11 that he has "become a fool" echoes his appeal to the Corinthians in 11:1 to bear with "a little foolishness" from him, thereby forming a bracket around 11:1–12:13. Second, Paul's frequent references to "foolishness" and to being a "fool" (11:1, 16, 17, 19, 21; 12:6, 11) are confined to 11:1–12:13. Third, the opening words of 12:14

("Behold, I am ready to come to you this third time") appear to mark the beginning of the third and final section of 10:1–13:10, which will deal with Paul's impending visit to Corinth.[15]

This section, which is often called "the fool's speech," begins with an extended introduction (11:1–21a) in which Paul calls upon the Corinthians to "bear" with him in this exercise of foolish boasting, insisting that he is not inferior to the intruding apostles, even though he has not accepted the financial patronage of the Corinthian community as they have. After this extended introduction, Paul reluctantly takes up his project of foolish boasting (11:21b–12:10), boasting in his Jewish lineage and ministry, his apostolic sufferings, his visions and revelations, and his weaknesses. The speech then concludes with an epilogue (12:11–13) in which he admits that he has become a "fool" by boasting in this way, accusing the Corinthians of forcing him into such boasting. The speech may be outlined as follows:

11:1–21a   Introduction
   vv. 1–4   An initial appeal to bear with Paul
   vv. 5–15   Paul not inferior to the super-apostles
   vv. 16–21a   A renewed appeal to bear with Paul
12:21b–12:10   Paul's Boasting
   vv. 21b–29   Daring to boast as a fool
   vv. 30–33   Boasting in weakness
   vv. 12:1–10   Boasting in visions and revelations
12:11–13   Peroration

The precise nature of the speech is a matter of dispute. Although acknowledging that the speech makes extensive use of irony, many commentators argue that Paul intends his boasting to be taken seriously, even if it is foolish and dangerous. But other commentators maintain that that speech is a parody of the boasting in which Paul's opponents engage and should not be taken seriously. Thus Paul derides the boasting of his opponents by recounting his sufferings, his embarrassing escape from Damascus, and a journey to paradise that reveals nothing apart from his weakness (see the exposition of McCant, 114–57). Although there may be an element of parody in this section, it seems unlikely that Paul is *merely* parodying the boasting of his opponents, since what he narrates is true (12:6), though he would prefer not to boast about it. The sufferings Paul has endured for the gospel and his vision of paradise confirm his relationship to Christ, but Paul would prefer not to boast of them, since such boasting

---

15. It is true that Paul discusses the subject of financial support in 12:14–18, as he did in 11:7–15, causing many commentators to attach 12:13–18 to the material that precedes it rather than to the material that follows it. This second discussion of financial support, however, is subservient to the matter of Paul's third and final visit, which is explicitly mentioned in 13:1 as well as in 12:14.

B. Boasting Foolishly

does not build up the church. But if forced to defend his apostleship for the sake of the church, as he must here, he will boast, even if it is foolish.

1. An Initial Appeal to Bear with Paul (11:1–4)

1 Would that you would bear with me[a] a little foolishness. But bear[b] with me. 2 For I am jealous of you with a jealousy like God's,[c] for I betrothed you to one man to present you as a chaste virgin to Christ. 3 But I am afraid that as the serpent deceived Eve by its cunning, your minds may be corrupted from sincerity and purity[d] of devotion toward Christ.[e] 4 For if someone[f] comes preaching another Jesus whom we did not preach, or you receive another spirit different from what you received, or a gospel different from what you received, you gladly[g] bear it.

a. The pronoun "me" (*mou*) can be taken with the verb that immediately precedes it ("bear with me") or with the noun that follows ("bear with a little of my foolishness"). Commentators are not in agreement on this point. This translation construes the pronoun with the verb, since it is taken with the verb at the end of the verse ("Indeed, bear with me").

b. The verb *anechesthe* ("to bear") can be construed as an indicative ("Indeed, you are bearing with me") or, as in this translation, an imperative. Most commentators (Bultmann being an exception) take it as an imperative, since the context seems to require an imperative: Paul wants the Corinthians to do something they are not yet doing.

c. The genitive is a genitive of quality (so Bultmann, 220). Paul's "jealousy" for the Corinthians is like God's covenant jealousy for the people whom God has espoused as God's bride.

d. The words *kai tēs hagnotētos* ("and the purity") are not found in some important manuscripts ($\aleph^2$, D^2). It is possible that they were added in order to make the marriage imagery of this passage more explicit. But since they occur in P^{46}, B, and the original text of $\aleph$, they are included here.

e. The word "devotion" is supplied to clarify the text, which, if translated literally, would read, "from the sincerity and purity that are in (or toward) Christ."

f. "Someone" (*ho erchomenos*) could be taken generically, "anyone," or it could refer to an individual, as seems to be the case in 10:7, 10, 11.

g. "Gladly" translates *kalōs* ("well"). The word is being used in an ironic sense.

These verses are the first of three subunits (1–4, 5–11, 15–21a) that comprise Paul's extended introduction to his foolish boasting. Since he has just said that the one who boasts should boast in the Lord (10:17), it is not surprising that he characterizes the boasting in which he will engage as "a little foolishness" and prefaces it with an extended introduction. Paul understands that what he is about to do is foolish. Therefore, he ironically asks for the indulgence of the Corinthians, fully aware that they are all too ready to delight in such boasting. But he also realizes that he must engage in this foolish boasting, since the integrity of Christ's bride, the church at Corinth, is at stake.

This unit has two parts. In the first (vv. 1–2) Paul asks the community to "bear" with him (v. 1), "for" (*gar*) he has a Godlike jealousy for the community that he must present as "a chaste virgin" to Christ (v. 2). In the second (vv. 3–4), Paul begins with an adversative statement that discloses his anxiety: "But" (*de*) he is fearful that the Corinthians are in danger of being corrupted (v. 3). He then provides the grounds for his anxiety, "for" (*gar*) if someone preaches another Jesus, the Corinthians willingly "bear" it. Paul's final remark, that the Corinthians willingly "bear" the preaching of another Jesus, forms a literary bracket with his request in verse 1 that the Corinthians "bear" with him in a little bit of foolishness. The material can be outlined in this way:

vv. 1–2   A request to *bear* with Paul, "for" (*gar*) he has a Godlike jealousy for the Corinthians.
vv. 3–4   "But" (*de*) the Corinthians are in danger of being corrupted by intruders, "for" (*gar*) if someone preaches another Jesus they willingly *bear* it.

[11:1–2] Paul begins by expressing his desire that the Corinthians "bear with" him as he indulges in a bit of foolishness. This wish that the community "bear with" him serves as a leitmotif for this entire unit (vv. 1–21a), in which Paul prepares for his foolish and dangerous boasting. (See vv. 4, 19, and 20, the only other places where the verb "to bear with" [*anechō*] occurs in 2 Corinthians.) Paul's initial statement, however, is ironic and somewhat reprimanding, as is his statement in verse 19, "For being wise you gladly bear with fools." A somewhat similar reprimand occurs in 1 Cor 4:8, "Already you have all you want! Already you have become rich! Quite apart from us you have become kings! Indeed, I wish that (*ophelon*) you had become kings, so that we might be kings with you!"

The Corinthians are already "bearing with" the intruding apostles, who have preached "another Jesus" (v. 4) and in the process "enslaved" them (v. 20). Accordingly Paul asks the Corinthians to extend the same indulgence to him that they have so willingly granted the intruders. Unlike the intruders, however, Paul understands the foolishness of such boasting. Consequently, as he embarks upon this foolish and dangerous project, he asks the Corinthians to bear with him in "a little foolishness." This "little foolishness" is the boasting he will take up in verse 21b.

Paul's boasting will be an exercise in foolishness, because, even though it will be true, it will not build up the community. Indeed it is inherently dangerous, since it shifts the focus of attention from Christ to the human person. But since it has become necessary in the present circumstances, Paul will engage in such boasting, provided that the Corinthians understand that it is utter foolishness.

B. Boasting Foolishly

Like the verb "to bear" (*anechō*), the noun "foolishness" (*aphrosynē*) is a leitmotif of this section. In verse 17, for example, Paul insists that he is not speaking "according to the Lord" (*kata kyrion*) but "foolishly" (*hōs en aphrosyē*), and in verse 21, immediately before embarking upon his boasting, he writes, "I am speaking foolishly." In addition to this noun, Paul employs the adjective "foolish" (*aphrōn*, see 11:16, 19; 12:6, 11). On the one hand, he insists that he is not a fool (11:16), and even if he continues to boast, he will not be a fool (12:6). But on the other hand, he will eventually acknowledge that he has become a fool (12:11) because he has been "forced" into this unprofitable exercise of boasting.

Paul's initial appeal for the Corinthians to bear with a little foolishness from him establishes the proper framework for understanding what follows. His boasting will be true. Indeed, even the boasting of the intruding apostles may be true. But the kind of boasting in which Paul will engage, and in which the intruders have already been engaged, is "foolishness" and makes those who participate in it foolish. With this understanding, and only with this understanding, will Paul dare to engage the intruders in this foolish and dangerous contest of boasting.

Having asked the Corinthians to bear with him in a little bit of foolishness, in verse 2 Paul provides a reason for this request: by establishing the church at Corinth, he betrothed the community to Christ. Thus he views himself as if he were the father of a young virgin who has been promised in marriage. Just as a father bears the responsibility for presenting his daughter as an undefiled virgin to her intended husband, so he bears the responsibility of presenting the church at Corinth "as a chaste virgin to Christ."

The metaphor that Paul employs here presupposes the Jewish practice of an extended period of betrothal during which the father watched over his daughter to assure that her virginity would not be compromised. This responsibility is reflected in Deut 22:13–21, a legal text that deals with the case of a husband who charges that the woman whom he married was not a virgin. In such a case, "The father of the young woman and her mother shall then submit the evidence of the young woman's virginity to the elders of the city at the gate" (22:15), with the father presenting the case to the elders (vv. 16–17). The author of Sirach must have been aware of this responsibility; for he writes: "A daughter is a secret anxiety to her father, and worry over her robs him of sleep; when she is young, for fear that she may not marry, or if married, for fear that she may be disliked; *while a virgin, for fear she may be seduced and become pregnant in her father's house*" (Sir 42:9–10).

The imagery that Paul employs here presupposes three stages in the life of the Corinthian community. The first was the betrothal of the community to Christ when Paul established the church at Corinth. The second is the period of betrothal or engagement in which the church now finds itself as it awaits the parousia. The third will occur at the parousia when Paul will finally "present" the church "as a chaste virgin to Christ."

This imagery of the church as the bride of Christ is deeply rooted in Israel's Scriptures, which frequently employ marriage as a metaphor to explain the covenant relationship between YHWH and the people of Israel or, sometimes, the city of Jerusalem. In its use of this metaphor, however, the Old Testament often points to the unfaithfulness of Israel or Jerusalem to the covenant, which then results in God dismissing and divorcing his people for their adultery, though the hope of restoration is always close at hand (see Hos 1–3; Ezek 16; Isa 50:1). The New Testament continues this imagery by applying it to the church and to Christ. For example, the book of Revelation speaks of "the holy city, the new Jerusalem, coming down out of heaven" (Rev. 21:2) as "the bride, the wife of the Lamb" (Rev 21:9). In Ephesians Paul or another writing in his name exhorts husbands to love their wives as "Christ loved the church and gave himself up for her, in order to make her holy by cleansing her with the washing of water by the word, so as to present (*hina parastēsē*) the church to himself in splendor, without a spot or wrinkle or anything of the kind—yes, so that she may be holy and without blemish" (Eph 5:25–27).[16] But whereas in 2 Corinthians it is Paul who will present the church to Christ, in Ephesians it is Christ who presents the church to himself.[17] Moreover, whereas Ephesians has the whole church in view, 2 Corinthians is primarily concerned with the church as a local community.

To summarize, Paul asks the Corinthians to bear with him because he has a unique relationship to their community that the intruding apostles cannot claim. By founding the church, he betrothed it to Christ and now guards it with a "jealousy" akin to God's "jealousy" for his covenant people, so that he may present the church "as a chaste virgin to Christ." Because Paul must protect his "virgin" for Christ, he will engage in foolish and dangerous boasting.

[3–4] Having explained his parental responsibility to the Corinthians, Paul now expresses his fear that as the serpent deceived Eve by its cunning, so their minds will be corrupted from a proper devotion or commitment to Christ. To support what he says, he accuses the Corinthians of being all too ready "to bear with" those who preach "another Jesus," thereby drawing a comparison between the serpent who deceived Eve and those who preach "another Jesus." For just as the serpent deceived Eve by its cunning, so the intruding apostles are deceiving the Corinthians by their preaching.

---

16. The text of Ephesians, of course, is primarily an analogy of the relationship between Christ and the church. Accordingly, it should not be interpreted as the foundation for a theological anthropology that subordinates woman to man.

17. Colossians also uses the language of "presenting," though it does not make use of the marriage metaphor as does Ephesians. Colossians 1:22 says that Christ will "present" believers "blameless and reproachable" to God, whereas in Col 1:28 the author writes, "so that we may present everyone mature in Christ."

B. Boasting Foolishly

The verb "deceived" (*exēpatēsen*) clearly relates this text to the words of Eve in Gen 3:13, "The serpent tricked me (*ho ophis ēpatēse me*), and I ate," a text to which 1 Tim 2:14 also alludes, "Adam was not deceived, but the woman was deceived (*exapatētheisa*) and became a transgressor."[18] Other traditions about the deception of Eve are found in *The Apocalypse of Abraham* (chap. 23) and *The Life of Adam and Eve* (chaps. 9–11), the latter relating how Satan transformed himself "into the brightness of angels" and seduced Eve a second time. Although Paul does not explicitly identify the serpent with Satan, his characterization of the intruding apostles in 11:15 as "ministers" of Satan suggests that he views the serpent as Satan, whom he has already identified as a constant danger to the church (2:11).

When Paul describes the serpent as deceiving Eve by its "cunning," he undoubtedly has in mind the behavior of the intruding apostles, who in his view have been "cunning" in their preaching to the Corinthians. The word "cunning" (*panourgia*) is significant because Paul will allude to an accusation against him that, although he did not accept support from the community, he was "cunning" and took advantage of the Corinthians (12:16). It is not surprising then that earlier in this letter Paul insisted that he does not act "cunningly" (4:2). Somewhat analogously, having written of himself, "We have injured no one. We have corrupted (*ephtheiramen*) no one. We have taken advantage of no one" (7:2), he now expresses his fear that the Corinthians are being "corrupted" (*phtharē*) by the intruding apostles (v. 3).

By their cunning the intruders are corrupting the Corinthians from the "sincerity" and "purity" that should characterize their commitment to their betrothed. "Sincerity" (*haplotētos*) recalls Paul's description of his own conduct toward the community (1:12), and "purity" (*hagnotētos*) emphasizes the complete and total devotion that should be the hallmark of the community as the chaste bride of Christ. Like Israel of old, the community is in danger of abandoning its betrothed in order to pursue "another Jesus" (v. 4).

What Paul means by "another Jesus" is problematic, since he never explicitly explains how the teaching of the intruders differs from the gospel he preaches. Consequently, one must be careful not to read too much into this statement by suggesting, for example, that the intruders espoused a "heretical" Christology. It is more likely that the real conflict between Paul and the intruders concerned issues of ministerial style and jurisdiction, which in Paul's perspective cannot be separated from the gospel, since they reflect one's view of Christ. As Paul will show in his foolish boasting, there is an intimate connection between the way in which one exercises apostolic ministry and the gospel message that one preaches. For example, because suffering, hardship, and

---

18. It should be noted that whereas the comparison in 1 Tim 2:14 reflects negatively on Eve, the comparison in 2 Corinthians does not.

weakness are such integral parts of his ministry, the gospel that he preaches necessarily focuses on the paradox of the cross and the crucified Christ who manifests God's power through weakness. Conversely, because Paul's gospel focuses on the cross and the crucified Christ, he understands suffering, hardship, and weakness as integral parts of his apostolic ministry. If, in contrast, the intruding apostles focused attention on their powerful deeds, eloquent speech, and ecstatic experiences, it is unlikely that the cross of the crucified Christ played as central a role in their preaching. Conversely, if their preaching was concerned first and foremost with the power of the pneumatic Lord, they would have been more inclined to boast of the outward manifestations of that power in their own ministry. Understood in this way, Paul is quite correct when he accuses the intruders of preaching "another Jesus."

Although an outsider might view these approaches to ministry merely as different ways of preaching the same gospel, it is clear that Paul did not, since there can be no other gospel (Gal 1:7). Just as there is an inseparable relation between the minister of the gospel and the gospel that is preached, so there is an intimate relation between the "Jesus" that is preached and the "Spirit" and the "gospel" that is received. In accepting the preaching of the intruders, the Corinthians have experienced a different Spirit, but in Paul's view it is not the authentic Spirit of Jesus. Likewise they have received another gospel, but since there is only one gospel, it is not the gospel that he preached.

To summarize, Paul must engage in foolish and dangerous boasting because the church that he hopes to present to Christ as a chaste virgin is being deceived by the cunning preaching of intruders who preach "another Jesus," as is evident from the way in which they exercise their ministry.

2. Not Inferior to the Super-Apostles (11:5–15)

11:5 In[a] no way do I think of myself as being inferior to the super-apostles. 6 And, even if I am not a professional speaker,[b] I am not[c] as regards knowledge, rather, in every way we have made this clear[d] to you in all things.[e]

7 Did I commit a sin by abasing[f] myself so that you might be exalted because I proclaimed God's good news[g] to you free of charge?[h] 8 I plundered[i] other churches accepting wages to minister to you.[j] 9 And when I was present among you and in need, I did not burden anyone, for the brothers who came from Macedonia provided for my needs. So I kept and will keep myself from being a burden to you in any way. 10 By the truth of Christ that is in me,[k] this boast of mine[l] will not be silenced in the regions of Achaia. 11 Why? Because I do not love you? God knows I love you.[m]

12 I will continue to do what I am doing in order that I may remove the occasion of those seeking an occasion in order that in their boasting they

B. Boasting Foolishly

might be found to be even as we are.[n] 13 For such people are false apostles, deceitful workers, disguising themselves as apostles of Christ. 14 This is not to be wondered at,[o] for Satan himself disguises himself as an angel of light. 15 Therefore, it is not a marvel if his ministers disguise themselves as ministers of righteousness.[p] Their destiny[q] will correspond to their deeds.

a. *Gar* ("for"), which stands toward the beginning of this sentence in the Greek text and which often has a causal force, has been left untranslated, since it appears to function merely as a connective (Furnish, 489). Note that the text of Vaticanus (B) reads *de* rather than *gar*, suggesting that it does not view this verse as providing a reason for what Paul has written in the preceding verses.

b. According to BDAG *idiōtēs* designates "a person who is relatively unskilled or inexperienced in some activity or field of knowledge." The translation "not a professional" tries to reflect this without giving the impression that Paul was an inept speaker.

c. "I am" is supplied since the Greek, which reads *all' ou* ("but not"), lacks a verb.

d. "We have made this clear" renders the participle *phanerōsantes*. "This" has been supplied to clarify that Paul is referring to his "knowledge."

e. *pasin* ("in all things") could be taken as masculine, in which case the translation would be "we have made this clear to you *before all*."

f. The participle *tapeinōn* is rendered "abasing," since Paul is referring to his practice of supporting himself by manual labor, which in the eyes of the Corinthians was an act of abasement. Paul, however, did not necessarily view the matter in the same way and probably thought of his manual labor as an act of humble service.

g. The phrase *to tou theou euangelion* is taken as a subjective genitive: God's own gospel; God's good news about what God did in Christ.

h. The adverb *dōrean* is translated "free of charge," because Paul has refused to accept financial support from the Corinthians for his preaching.

i. The verb *esylēsa* is translated "plundered" to highlight the military metaphor that Paul develops here. The metaphor is reinforced by the use of *opsōnion* ("wages"), which often refers to the wages paid to a soldier.

j. Literally, "for your service."

k. "By the truth of Christ that is in me" functions as an oath formula. Christ's own truth assures the truth of what Paul is saying.

l. Literally, "in me."

m. The words "I love you" have been supplied in order to complete Paul's thought.

n. This verse is complicated because it contains two purpose clauses ("in order that"). In this translation the second purpose clause depends on the first. Paul acts as he does *in order to* remove any occasion from his opponents *in order that* they may not boast that they are like him. But if the second purpose clause is taken with the main verb ("I will continue to do what I am doing"), then Paul means that he will continue to do what he is doing *in order that* his opponents may be like him. This second interpretation is unlikely.

o. Literally, "this is no wonder."

p. The Greek (*diakonoi dikaiosynēs*) could be rendered "righteous ministers," but in light of chapter 3 it is more likely that the opponents claim to be ministers of righteousness who dispense God's righteousness.

q. "Destiny" translates *telos* ("end").

Having accused the Corinthians of gladly "bearing with" someone who preaches "another Jesus," Paul turns his attention to the intruding apostles, whom he identifies for the first time as "super-apostles." In chapter 10 Paul accused the super-apostles (although he had not yet identified them as such) of comparing themselves with themselves and of intruding upon his "assignment," the church at Corinth (10:12–18). As he prepares to engage in what he knows is foolish and dangerous boasting, he shows that there is another decisive difference between him and the intruding apostles, a difference that he will not surrender in order to show that he is not inferior to the super-apostles: whereas they accept the patronage and financial support of the Corinthian community, he does not. Nor will he. Thus, even if he engages in foolish and dangerous boasting, there are two reasons why there can be no real comparison between him and the super-apostles: First, the Corinthian church is his missionary assignment, because he is the church's apostolic founder (10:12–18). Second, Paul preaches the gospel to the Corinthians free of charge (11:5–15).

The material can be divided into three subunits. In the first (vv. 5–6) Paul affirms that he is not inferior to the super-apostles. In the second (vv. 7–11) he defends his practice of refusing the financial support of the Corinthian church. In the third (vv. 12–15) he returns to the problem of the intruders and explains why he will not alter his missionary practice at Corinth. The material can be outlined in this way:

vv. 5–6   Paul not inferior to the super-apostles
vv. 7–11   Preaching the gospel free of charge
vv. 12–15   The difference between Paul and the intruders

[11:5–6] Claiming that he is not inferior to the super-apostles, Paul makes a qualifying statement. Although he is not a "professional speaker," he possesses "knowledge," which he has shown the Corinthians in many and different ways.

The designation "super-apostles" occurs twice in the New Testament, here and at the end of Paul's foolish boasting (12:11), suggesting that Paul himself may have coined the expression. The term is a compound of the adverb *hyperlian* ("exceedingly," "beyond measure") and the noun *apostolos* ("apostle"), indicating an apostle of superlative degree or of the highest rank, thus a "superlative" or "super" apostle.

This commentary argues that Paul applies this designation to the intruding apostles who have come to Corinth and preached "another Jesus." Beginning with John Chrysostom (*Homily* 23:2), however, a number of commentators

B. Boasting Foolishly

(Heinrici, 354; Barrett, 28–32; Martin, 342) have argued that Paul is referring in a mildly ironic way to the apostles of Jerusalem (James, Peter, and John), whom he also calls "pillars" (of the church) in Gal 2:9. Thus he would be making a distinction between the "super-apostles" who reside in Jerusalem, on the one hand, and the intruding apostles who have come to Corinth, either with the explicit support of or claiming the support of these "super-apostles." Those who espouse this interpretation note that the super-apostles cannot be the intruders, whom Paul castigates as "false apostles" and "deceitful workers" in verse 13, and as "ministers" of Satan in verse 15, since Paul claims the same rank as the super-apostles. Rather, the intruders must be a second group that has come to Corinth with "letters of recommendation," from the super-apostles, that is, the Jerusalem apostles.

Paul's statement that he is not inferior to the super-apostles, however, can be construed in another way. Rather than merely claiming a status comparable to the super-apostles, Paul is asserting his overall superiority to them. On this reading, he applies the term "super-apostles" to the intruding apostles in a manner that is harsh as well as ironic. The intruders have come to Corinth and boasted of their extraordinary talent and work on behalf of the gospel, forcing Paul into a contest of foolish boasting. He then dubs them "super" or "superlative" apostles, not because he believes that they are extraordinary apostles but because this is how they present themselves or perhaps how the Corinthians view them. In Paul's view, however, they are "false apostles" (11:13).

This interpretation, which equates the super-apostles with the intruding apostles, makes the best sense for three reasons. First, if the super-apostles are not the intruders, then their appearance in verse 5 is unexpected, since Paul is clearly referring to the intruders in verse 4 and surely has them in view in 11:6–12:10. Second, Paul's concession that he is not a "professional speaker" seems to imply that the super-apostles are more skilled in speech than he is, but this hardly fits the description of the Jerusalem apostles, James, Peter, and John (see Acts 4:13). Finally, Paul's reference to the super-apostles in the peroration of this speech (12:11–13) is a retrospective comment on everything that he has said in chapter 11 about the intruding apostles. In light of this comment, there should be little doubt that the super-apostles and the intruding apostles are one and the same.[19]

In conceding that he is not "a professional speaker," Paul appears to be echoing a criticism of his oratorical skill that he quoted in 10:10, "the letters are severe and powerful, but his physical presence is weak and his speech is contemptible (*ho logos exouthenēmenos*)." Similarly, in 1 Cor 2:1 Paul reminded

---

19. Allo, 280; Barnett, 522–23; Bultmann, 208; Furnish, 502–5; Garland, 469; Lambrecht, 175; Thrall, 2:671–76; and Windisch, 330, argue that the super-apostles and the intruders are one and the same.

the community, "When I came to you, brothers and sisters, I did not come proclaiming the mystery of God to you in lofty words (*ou kath' hyperochēn logou*) or wisdom." The acknowledgment that he did not preach the gospel to the Corinthians "in lofty words" and the concession that he is not a "a professional speaker," however, do not necessarily mean that Paul was an inept orator. Indeed, the rhetorical artistry of his letters argues against such a conclusion, leading Barrett (279) to speculate that Paul may have suffered from "an impediment in his speech."

Paul's description of himself in verse 6 as *idiōtēs tō logō*, however, suggests another possibility. In conceding that he is an *idiōtēs*, Paul acknowledges that he is an "amateur" or "layperson" in the field of oratory, not a professional who makes his livelihood from the profession that he exercises. Unlike such professional speakers, Paul supports himself by working with his hands so that he can preach the gospel free of charge. To that extent he is an "amateur" (*idiōtēs*) when it comes to public oratory, but he is not necessarily inept. In contrast to him, the super-apostles have accepted financial support from the community (this is the implicit point of v. 12), and on the basis of this they may have presented themselves as truly "skilled" as regards speaking, whereas in their eyes Paul was only an "amateur" and his speech was "despicable."[20]

If Paul is willing to concede that he is only an "amateur" in regard to speaking, he refuses to concede the same as regards knowledge. He has already referred to "knowledge" several times in relation to his ministry and the gospel that he preaches. For example, God leads him as his captive in a triumphal procession, and Paul manifests "the fragrance of the knowledge of him in every place" (2:14). The light of God has shown in Paul's heart "to bring to light the knowledge of the glory of God on the face of [Jesus] Christ" (4:6). Furthermore, in 6:6 Paul lists "knowledge" along with "sincerity," "patience," and "kindness" as qualities that characterize his ministry. Finally, in 10:5, Paul presents himself as a powerful soldier who destroys every "proud obstacle arising in opposition to the knowledge of God." This knowledge, which Paul will not concede to the super-apostles, is nothing less than the knowledge that is the gospel: the glory of God shining on the face of Christ. Thus, although Paul may not be a "professional orator," as his opponents apparently present themselves, he is fully equipped with the knowledge that is the gospel, something he has repeatedly demonstrated to the Corinthians by his ministry among them.

[7–11] Having asserted that he is not inferior to the super-apostles, Paul appears to take up a new and unrelated topic: his refusal to accept the financial

---

20. Brian Peterson (*Eloquence and the Proclamation of the Gospel*, 109) writes, "Paul refused to accept the kind of salary from the Corinthians that any decent teacher would expect; this made it look to his opponents in Corinth as though Paul did not deserve to be paid, and thus Paul seems to be an *idiōtēs* in contrast to these newcomers, who did accept (if not demand) payment."

B. Boasting Foolishly

support of the Corinthian community that would have allowed him to exercise his ministry without working at a trade. The topic, however, is related to the problem posed by the intruding apostles, as will become evident in verses 12–15, where Paul returns to the intruders once more. For whereas he has not accepted the financial patronage of the Corinthians, the super-apostles apparently have, thereby distinguishing their ministry from his.

Paul begins with a rhetorical question, asking if he committed a "sin" by preaching the gospel without cost to the Corinthians (v. 7). Then, employing a strong dose of irony, he acknowledges that he accepted support from other churches in order to minister to the Corinthians without being a burden to them (vv. 8–9). Finally, he concludes that he will not allow this "boast" of his to be silenced, and he affirms his deep love for the community (vv. 10–11).

Although *hamartia* ("sin") occurs frequently in Paul's writings to describe sin as a destructive or evil power (see Rom 5:11–21), the rhetorical question that opens this unit (v. 7) is the only instance, apart from Rom 4:8, in which Paul uses *hamartia* in reference to an individual sin. Although it is possible that the question reflects an accusation that Paul has sinned against the commandment of the Lord that he quotes in 1 Cor 9:14 ("those who proclaim the gospel should get their living by the gospel") by refusing the support of the Corinthians, there is an unmistakable tone of irony in Paul's remark that is meant to put the Corinthians on notice. Far from sinning, he abased himself in order to exalt them.

The Corinthians undoubtedly interpreted Paul's refusal of their support as an indication that he did not love them, or that he loved them less, because he accepted the support of other communities. In verse 11, therefore, Paul must affirm his love for the Corinthians, and in 12:13 he will ask in what way they were any worse off "than the other churches except that I myself did not burden you financially," and conclude with a strong dose of irony, "Forgive me this injustice!" Aware that the Corinthians have questioned his love for them, Paul casts his refusal of their support in terms of abasement and exaltation: He "abased" himself by preaching the gospel without cost, so that he might "exalt them." In saying that he "abased" (*tapeinōn*) himself, Paul has in mind his custom of working with his own hands as a tentmaker in order to support himself.[21] In addition to this, Paul may also be viewing his abasement in light of Christ, who "humbled himself (*etapeinōsen heauton*) and became obedient to the point of death" (Phil 2:8). Whereas God exalted Christ for his humble service, however, it is the Corinthians who are exalted by Paul's abasement.

21. Ronald F. Hock, *The Social Context of Paul's Ministry: Tentmaking and Apostleship* (Philadelphia: Fortress, 1980), 60, notes, "To those of wealth and power, the appearance (*schēma*) of the artisan was that befitting a slave (*douloprepes*). . . . To Corinthians who, relative to Paul, appeared to be rich, wise, powerful, and respected (cf. 4:8, 10), their lowly apostle had seemed to have enslaved himself with his plying a trade."

In verses 8–9 Paul makes use of military imagery once more, much as he did in 10:3–6. Employing the verb "to plunder" (*sylaō*) and the noun "wages" (*opsōnion*), he portrays himself as a soldier "plundering" other churches and then accepting "wages" from them so as not to burden the Corinthians with his financial support. Moreover, he acknowledges that the Macedonians provided for his needs while he was at Corinth. Again Paul writes ironically, and with good reason. His willingness to accept support from other churches, but not from the Corinthians, has become the point of contention between him and the Corinthians who, one suspects, have only recently learned of what, to them, was a double standard.

If, as Peter Marshall proposes, there was a group, or there were groups, of wealthy people among the Corinthians who offered Paul a gift of financial support that he refused, but that the intruding apostles eventually accepted, then it becomes easier to understand the difference in reasoning between Paul and the Corinthians.[22] By offering Paul their patronage, some wealthy Corinthians made him an offer of "friendship." By refusing their patronage Paul offended them, raising doubts about his love for them and the community. The arrival of the intruding super-apostles, who apparently accepted this offer, would only have complicated matters between Paul and the Corinthians. For the intruders could now call into question Paul's apostleship and compare him unfavorably with themselves. As for Paul, he probably refused this offer, not because he loved the Corinthians less than his other converts, but because he understood all too well that such "friendship" would have made him the client of certain wealthy Corinthians. Since Paul was the apostolic father of the community, whose duty it was to provide for his children (12:14), he could not countenance any arrangement in which someone else would become his patron.

Why then did Paul accept support from other churches? The "other churches" to which he refers were probably the congregation (or congregations) at Philippi, of whom he writes:

> You Philippians indeed know that in the early days of the gospel, when I left Macedonia, no church shared (*ekoinōsēsen*) with me in the matter of giving and receiving, except you alone. For even when I was in Thessalonica, you sent me help for my needs more than once. Not that I seek the gift, but I seek the profit that accumulates to your account. (Phil 4:15–17)

The verb that Paul employs here (*ekoinōsēsen*, "shared") is significant, since in Phil 1:5 he speaks of the "sharing" or the "partnership" (*koinōnia*) of the Philippians in the gospel. It would seem, therefore, that Paul enjoyed a special mis-

---

22. Marshall has a detailed presentation of this scenario in *Enmity in Corinth: Social Conventions in Paul's Relations with the Corinthians* (WUNT 2/23; Tübingen: J. C. B. Mohr (Paul Siebeck), 1987), esp. 165–258, the main lines of which are summarized here.

B. Boasting Foolishly

sionary relationship with the Philippians that he had not yet extended to the Corinthians, whereby the Philippians supported him in some of his missionary endeavors. Understood in this way, the support that they extended to Paul was different from that which the Corinthians, or certain members of the Corinthian community, were offering. For whereas the Philippians supported the apostle as he evangelized in new missionary territories, the Corinthians were proposing to support him as he preached the gospel in their own church, an offer that Paul was unwilling to accept, since it had the potential for hampering his freedom to preach the gospel to them.

In verses 10–11, Paul concludes this subunit with an oathlike formula that his "boast" will not be silenced in the regions of Achaia and with an assurance of his love for the community. The introduction of the word "boast" is the first appearance of this word group, which will play an increasingly important role in the rest of the speech. Moreover, it provides Paul with a transition to the next subunit, in which he will explain why he will not change this practice, namely, so that the super-apostles will not be able to boast that they exercise their ministry in the same way that he does. Paul understands that his practice of not accepting support is known throughout the Roman region or province of Achaia, of which Corinth was the capital. Whereas many questioned this practice, Paul presents it as his "boast," since his refusal of their support distinguishes his ministry from that of the intruding apostles. Because the Corinthians have interpreted his practice as a refusal of their friendship and love, Paul must now affirm his love for them, as he did in 2:4, when he explained his purpose in sending them the harsh letter, and as he will do in 12:15, when he returns for the last time to this issue of support.

The question of financial support plays an important role in the Corinthian correspondence. In 1 Corinthians Paul dedicates much of chapter 9 to the topic. On the one hand, he argues that he has the same right as other apostles to be supported by the gospel that he preaches, as the Lord commands (1 Cor 9:1–12a), but on the other, he insists that he has not made use of this right, nor does he intend to (1 Cor 9:12b–18), lest he put "an obstacle in the way of the gospel of Christ" (1 Cor 9:12b) and be deprived of his "ground for boasting" (1 Cor 9:15), that he preaches the gospel "free of charge" (1 Cor 9:18). By the time that Paul writes 2 Corinthians, however, the situation seems to have worsened, because the intruding apostles have arrived and accepted support for their preaching. Furthermore, there are rumors that even though Paul did not burden the community by accepting its support, he took advantage of it (12:16). Therefore, in the final chapters of 2 Corinthians Paul takes up the question of financial support twice, first in this passage, and then in 12:11–18. But here the emphasis is on Paul's motives and integrity, and he must defend his apparent double standard of accepting support from some congregations but not from the Corinthians. Although Paul's practice of working in order to support himself is well documented (1 Thess 2:5–12; 2 Thess 3:7–9; Acts 20:33–35), Rom 16:23 indicates that he did accept hospitality at Corinth from Gaius, and Paul's statement in 1 Cor 16:6 ("that you may send me on my way, wherever I go") suggests that he anticipated receiving some support from the Corinthians when he left Corinth for his next destination. Thus, though Paul declined to become the "client" of certain factions at Corinth, he may have been willing to extend a certain partnership in the gospel to the Corinthians, as he did with the Philippians, after leaving Corinth.[23]

[12–15] With these verses, Paul returns to the super-apostles, whom he introduced in verses 5–6, in order to explain why he will not alter his practice of refusing the community's financial support: he will not give the super-apostles an occasion to boast that they are apostles in the way that he is (v. 12). After this opening verse, Paul makes a harsh attack upon the super-apostles, to the point of identifying them as Satan's ministers (vv. 13–15a). Finally, Paul proclaims that their deeds will receive an appropriate judgment (v. 15b). His language is extreme, leading the reader to ask if the acceptance of financial support merits such opprobrium. From Paul's point of view, however, it is not merely a question of financial support; the super-apostles have intruded themselves into his missionary assignment (10:12–18) and preached "another Jesus" (11:4).

In verse 10, Paul told the Corinthians that he would not allow his "boast," that he preaches the gospel without cost, to be silenced. Now in verse 12 he explains why. By refusing to be the "client" of the Corinthians, Paul has and will continue to cut off any "occasion" (*aphormēn*; v. 12) for those who seek an "occasion" to boast that their ministry is comparable to his. Thus it appears that the intruding apostles, whom Paul has ironically called "super-apostles," have become "clients" of the Corinthians, or at least certain factions of the Corinthians, by accepting their financial support. From Paul's vantage point, they are trying to persuade the Corinthians that their ministry is equal to his own. In Paul's estimation, however, this cannot be, since he was the first to come to Corinth with the gospel, thereby confirming the "assigned measure" that God apportioned to him (10:13–14). Consequently, even though Paul knows that "those who proclaim the gospel should get their living by the gospel" (1 Cor 9:14), he seems to deny this right to the intruding apostles. Why? First, they have gone beyond the limits assigned to them (10:13–16). Second, going beyond these limits and accepting the support of the Corinthians, they have caused dissension within the church by calling into question his missionary practice. Thus the apparently simple matter of whether or not to accept financial support becomes, in this instance, a determining factor for assessing apostolic credentials.

---

23. On the question of financial support and Paul's consistency or lack of in this matter, see the excursus in Thrall, 2:699–708.

B. Boasting Foolishly

In light of this understanding of his apostolic responsibility Paul pours out a series of invectives on the super-apostles in verses 13–15a. They identify themselves as "apostles of Christ" and "ministers of righteousness," and the Corinthians have accepted them as such. But Paul exposes them as "false apostles," "deceitful workers," and "ministers" of Satan.

Appearance	*Reality*
apostles of Christ	false apostles and deceitful workers
ministers of righteousness	ministers of Satan

Paul's process of reasoning in these verses is based on an enthymeme or implied syllogism that can be formulated in this way:

- *Major Premise*: Satan *disguises* himself as an angel of light.
- *Minor Premise*: The super-apostles are ministers of Satan and can also *disguise* themselves.
- *Conclusion*: Therefore, they *disguise* themselves as apostles of Christ and ministers of righteousness, proving that, in fact, they are false apostles and deceitful workers.

The threefold use of the verb *metaschēmatizō* (vv. 13, 14, 15), which has been translated as "disguise," is significant for Paul's argument, because it allows him to explain how the super-apostles have been able to deceive the Corinthians: Satan is working through them.

Apart from this passage, the only other occurrences of *metaschēmatizō* in the New Testament are in 1 Cor 4:6 (whose precise meaning is difficult to determine) and Phil 3:21. In the Philippian passage, Paul writes, "He [the Lord Jesus Christ] will transform (*metaschēmatisei*) the body of our humiliation that it may be conformed (*symmorphon*) to the body of his glory, by the power that also enables him to make all things subject to himself." In this passage Paul clearly employs the verb in a positive manner and uses a second verb *symmorphon* ("conformed") to clarify what he means. By the power of his resurrection, the risen Christ will "transform" the present earthly body of believers so that they will be "conformed" to his glorious resurrection body. Consequently, to belong to Christ is to belong to a Lord who has the power to change and transform one's earthly bodily existence into a glorious resurrection existence. Paul belongs to this Lord.

In 2 Corinthians, however, Paul employs the verb in its middle form in a negative manner. Satan and his ministers can transform or disguise their outward appearance. Thus, according to *The Life of Adam and Eve* (9:1) Satan becomes angry and transforms himself "into the brightness of angels" in order to seduce Eve a second time, and in the *Testament of Reuben* (5:6) angels transform themselves into human males in order to have sexual relations with women. Aware that Satan and his ministers have such powers, Paul explains how the intruding apostles have been able to deceive the Corinthians. They have come to Corinth appearing to be "apostles of Christ" and "ministers of righteousness," but in fact their appearance is merely a disguise; for unlike Christ, who has the power to change and conform believers to himself, Satan and his ministers cannot truly change or conform themselves to be Christ's apostles and ministers of righteousness. Their appearance is merely a disguise, a masquerade, a sham.

The language that Paul employs here raises an important question. How did he understand his own invectives? Did he really believe that the intruding apostles were knowing and willing ministers of Satan who deliberately set out to thwart the gospel? Or did he view the intruding apostles as the unwitting tools of Satan who thought that they were doing Christ's work but were in fact being used by Satan? Since in verse 23 Paul seems to acknowledge that the intruders are "ministers of Christ," Bultmann's comment on Paul's language at this point is apropos: "This certainly need not describe their subjective intent, as though these persons really did not desire to work for Christ at all; it is merely stated that they actually do not do so" (208). Paul would probably have acknowledged the intruders as apostles of Christ if they worked within the limits that God had assigned to them, but not when they intruded upon his "assignment."

Paul's description of the intruders as apostles who present themselves as "ministers of righteousness" recalls the description of his new covenant ministry as "the ministry of righteousness" (3:9). Thus, since Paul can call his own ministry "the ministry of righteousness," it is not necessary to identify the intruders as "Judaizers," or as advocating a righteousness based on the law (as does Barnett, 527); for there is no polemic against circumcision or doing the works of the law in 2 Corinthians, as there is in Galatians. This said, one must acknowledge that there is little in 2 Corinthians about the actual "teaching" of the intruders, suggesting that the conflict may have been more concerned with their ministerial style and intrusion into Paul's missionary field than with their teaching, though the latter is related to the former.

Having already reminded the Corinthians that everyone will have to stand before the judgment seat of Christ (5:10), in verse 15b Paul assures them that the intruders will have to give an account for their own works (for related texts, see Rom 2:6; 6:23; Gal 6:7; 1 Thess 2:16; 2 Tim 4:14). But whereas in 1 Cor 3:15 Paul provides some hope for apostolic ministers whose work proves to be defective, here he does not.

3. A Renewed Appeal to Bear with Paul (11:16–21a)

11:16 I repeat, let no one suppose that I am a fool,[a] but if you do,[b] receive me as a fool so that I may boast a bit.[c] 17 What I am saying, I am not saying according to the Lord but foolishly in this project of boasting.[d] 18 Since

B. Boasting Foolishly

many boast according to the flesh,[e] I will also boast. 19 For being wise you gladly bear with fools. 20 For you bear it if someone dominates[f] you, if someone exploits[g] you, if someone takes advantage[h] of you, if someone acts haughtily, if someone strikes your face.[i] 21 To my shame[j] I admit that[k] we have been weak.

a. The Greek reads "foolish," but it is probably best to take the adjective *aphrona* as a noun.

b. The Greek *ei de mē ge* is usually rendered "otherwise." The translation "but if you do" emphasizes that some of the Corinthians probably consider Paul a fool.

c. This translates *mikron ti* ("a little something").

d. "This project of boasting" (*en tautē tē hypostasei tēs kauchēseōs*) could also be rendered "in this confidence of [or that comes from] boasting." However, here, as in 9:14, *hypostasis* is taken as referring to a "plan" or "project," as suggested by BDAG.

e. "According to the flesh" (*kata sarka*) refers to a norm of conduct that accords with what is merely human and mortal. It could also be rendered "acting in a worldly manner." Several important witnesses (ℵ,² B, D¹) read *kata tēn sarka*, whereas others (P⁴⁶, ℵ,* D*) read *kata sarka*. Although the reading of the latter witnesses is adopted here, the English translation requires the article "the."

f. Literally, "enslaves you" (*katadouloi*).

g. Literally, "eats up," "consumes," "devours" (*katesthiei*).

h. Literally, "takes" or "receives" (*lambanei*) but here clearly in a negative sense.

i. This is a literal translation of *eis prosōpon hymas derei* that is probably intended to be taken metaphorically.

j. The Greek *kata atimian legō* does not possess the possessive pronoun ("my"), and it is possible that Paul may have in view the shame of the Corinthians for acting as they have. However, since he is speaking ironically, "my shame" makes good sense.

k. The phrase *hōs oti* also occurs in 5:19 where it functions as an elliptical expression to introduce a quotation ("as it is said"). Here it appears to be the equivalent of *hoti* ("that"). Paul is admitting, somewhat ironically, "that" he is too weak to dominate the Corinthians as the intruding apostles have.

These verses complete Paul's extended introduction (11:1–21a) to his foolish boasting that will begin at 11:21b and continue through 12:10. As the third subunit of this introduction, the other units being 11:1–4 and 11:5–15, these verses (verses 11:16–21a) complete the ring pattern that Paul began when he asked the Corinthians to bear with him as he engages in some foolishness (vv. 1–4). Paul now takes up that appeal anew in the opening words of this unit ("I repeat"), which clearly refer back to verses 1–4. In addition to these introductory words, the double appearance of the verb "to bear" (*anechō*) in verses 19 and 20 also relates these verses to verses 1–4. In this way, Paul encloses this discussion of his missionary practice of refusing financial support from the Corinthians (vv. 5–15) with two units (vv. 1–4 and vv. 16–21a) in which he implores the Corinthians to bear with him in the project of foolish boasting upon which he is about to embark. A consequence of this ring pattern is that Paul encloses his "boast" of not accepting financial support from the Corinthians between two subunits that disclose his awareness of the foolishness of boasting.

The material begins with Paul's reprise of verses 1–4 in which he asks the Corinthians not to view him as a fool (v. 16a) and then qualifies this by saying that if they insist upon viewing him as such, they should receive him as a fool, so that he can boast as a fool (v. 16b). Next, Paul makes a parenthetical comment that indicates he understands the foolishness of what he is doing (v. 17). In verses 18–20, he explains why he will boast nonetheless. Finally, in verse 21a, he concludes with an ironic statement of his "weakness" that presages the theme of boasting in weakness. The material can be outlined in this fashion:

v. 16   Introduction: a renewed appeal to the Corinthians
v. 17   A caution: Paul's boasting will not be according to the Lord
vv.18–20   Why Paul will boast nonetheless
v. 21a   Conclusion: Paul's weakness

[11:16] At the beginning of this unit, Paul implored the Corinthians to bear with him as he engaged in some foolishness, but he did not mention the word "boasting," nor did he present himself as a "fool" (11:1). Now, as he draws ever closer to the foolish boasting he would prefer to avoid, he goes a step further and asks the Corinthians to receive him as "a fool" (Allo, 289). Paul, of course, does not view himself as a fool, although he will eventually admit that he has become a fool by engaging in such boasting (12:11). Moreover, he would prefer that the Corinthians not take him for a fool. But as in verses 1–4, he is searching for a way to boast without becoming identified with the intruding apostles. In this verse he finally reveals how he will approach his task: he will ask the Corinthians to accept him as a fool so that he can boast as a fool. Consequently, as the Corinthians listen to Paul's boasting in 11:21b–12:10, they will be hearing someone who, unlike the intruding apostles, wants his boasting to be taken for what it is, foolishness.

[17] Having asked the Corinthians to receive him as a fool so that he can boast, Paul immediately qualifies what he has said, lest there be any misunderstanding. In asking them to receive him as a fool in order that he may be able to boast, he insists that he is not speaking *kata kyrion,* that is, he is not speaking in accordance with, or in conformity with, a norm established by the Lord. For this reason, he will not be "boasting in the Lord" (10:17), except when he boasts in his weaknesses (11:30; 12:9). Rather he will be boasting foolishly because he will be boasting in those things that appear to commend him on the basis of what he has done. Thus Paul describes his boasting as "this project of boasting" (*en tautē tē hypostasei tēs kaukēseōs*), an expression that characterizes what he is about to do as a "plan," an "endeavor," or an "undertaking" (see

B. Boasting Foolishly

BDAG; s.v. *hypostasis*) that focuses on externals. "In other words," as Danker (176) puts it in his commentary, "if Paul were to keep the Lord strictly in mind, he would never brag as he is about to do in vv. 22–33."

[18–20] However, circumstances beyond Paul's control have forced him into a situation he would have preferred to avoid. First, many are already boasting *kata sarka* (v. 18). Second, the Corinthians are already "bearing with" such fools (vv. 19–20). Consequently Paul will boast.

In writing that there are many who are already boasting *kata sarka*, Paul clearly has the intruding super-apostles in mind, as he apparently did in 5:12. By saying that they boast *kata sarka*, he means that the standard or norm of their boasting is merely human and mortal; it is what the world sees at the level of appearance. Such boasting is clearly opposed to what is *kata kyrion*, and Paul now takes the dangerous step of implying that his own boasting will be *kata sarka*, though he never explicitly says that he will boast *kata sarka*. But even if his own boasting is *kata sarka*, it is distinguished from that of the intruders in a significant manner, namely, whereas he acknowledges that his boasting will not be *kata kyrion*, they do not understand that their boasting is *kata sarka*.

Speaking with yet greater irony and not a little sarcasm, Paul portrays the Corinthians as willingly bearing with fools because they are "wise," much as he did in 1 Cor 4:10, where he wrote:

> *We* are fools for the sake of Christ, but *you* are wise in Christ.
> *We* are weak, but *you* are strong.
> *You* are held in honor, but *we* in disrepute. (emphasis added)

Although this may have been the appearance of the matter to the Corinthians, the reality in Christ is quite different, as it is here. The Corinthians do not "bear with" fools because they are wise but because they have become as foolish as those who boast *kata sarka*. For this reason, they put up with a series of insults to which those who are wise in Christ would never submit.

The list of insults that the Corinthians endure contains five items, each beginning with the words "if someone" (*ei tis*), each item building upon the one that precedes it. First, the Corinthians have allowed themselves to become "dominated" or "enslaved" (*katadouloi*) by the intruders who, in contrast to Paul (see 1:24), have apparently exercised their authority over the faith of the Corinthians. The only other occurrence of this word is in Gal 2:4 in reference to the false brothers who "slipped in to spy on the freedom we have in Christ Jesus, so that they might *enslave* us." One might be tempted to identify the intruders of 2 Corinthians with the false brothers of Galatians, but there is no indication that circumcision or the works of the law were an issue at Corinth as they were at Galatia.

Second, having allowed the intruders to exercise authority over them, the Corinthians are now being "exploited" (*katesthiei*) by the very people whom they are supporting (see Gal 5:15 for the only other occurrence of this verb in Paul's writings). Thus, whereas Paul works with his own hands so that he will not be a burden to the Corinthians (11:8–9), the intruders exploit the Corinthians by depending upon them for support and "devouring" their goods.

Third, the intruders have "taken advantage" (*lambanei*) of the Corinthians. The verb that Paul employs here is the least descriptive of the five verbs that he uses, but it serves the purpose of reinforcing what he has just said, namely, by "exploiting" the Corinthians the intruders have taken advantage of them. Although Paul is accused of such behavior, he forcefully denies that he, Titus, or "the brother" has ever taken advantage of the Corinthians (12:16–18).

Fourth, having enslaved, exploited, and taken advantage of the Corinthians, the intruders are now in a position to "act haughtily" (*epairetai*). Here Paul employs the same verb as in 10:4b–5, where he wrote, "we tear down sophistries and every proud obstacle arising (*epairomenon*) in opposition to the knowledge of God." Whereas Paul has "abased" himself in order to "exalt" the Corinthians (11:7), the intruders have "enslaved" the Corinthians in order to act "haughtily" or exalt themselves.

The end result is that the intruders have abused the Corinthians. Paul's fifth and final item, therefore, is that the super-apostles have "struck" (*derei*) the Corinthians. Whether this last item is to be taken metaphorically or literally, it is apparent that in Paul's view the behavior of the intruders has been abusive. In contrast to them, he has acted as the father of the community who has spent himself and will willingly be spent for his children, since parents should provide for their children, not children for their parents (12:14–15).

The Intruders' Behavior	*Paul's Behavior*
domineering	does not exercise authority over their faith
exploitative	not a burden to them
take advantage of	not crafty or cunning
haughty	abases himself to exalt them
abusive	acts as their father

[21a] Paul concludes this subunit with an ironic and satirical statement that probably responds to a charge made against him: he was and is too weak for such behavior, for he did not exercise his authority over the Corinthians (1:24) in the manner that some expected him to, especially at the occasion of the painful visit. The statement, however, is ironical because Paul understands the paradox of the gospel: when he is weak, the power of Christ comes upon him (12:9), so that when he is weak, then he is strong (12:10). The mention of weakness here is the first occurrence in 2 Corinthians of either the noun or the verb. From this point forward, however, the noun (11:30; 12:5, 9 [twice], 10; 13:4) and the verb (11:21; 29 [twice]; 12:10; 13:3, 4, 9) will play a prominent role in the "fool's

B. Boasting Foolishly

speech." Indeed the key to Paul's boasting will be found in his willingness to boast in his weaknesses (11:30; 12:9), and it will be this characteristic more than any other that will distinguish his boasting from that of the intruders.

The line of thought in Paul's extended introduction (11:1–21a) can now be summarized in this way: Paul wants the Corinthians to "bear with" him in a little foolishness because he is the "father of the bride," who must present the community to Christ as a chaste virgin on the day of the parousia. At the present time, however, Paul is fearful that his virgin is being seduced, for the Corinthians are willingly "bearing with" suitors who preach "another Jesus." Paul is not inferior to these "super-apostles." Indeed what distinguishes him from them is that he has not burdened the community financially in order to preach the gospel to the Corinthians free of charge. In contrast to him, the intruders work on a different basis, accepting and perhaps insisting upon support from a community that has not been assigned to them. In this regard they show themselves to be false apostles and Satan's ministers. Like the serpent who deceived Eve, they are deceiving the community. For this reason it is all the more urgent that the Corinthians "bear with" Paul, even if it means receiving him as a fool. After all, they "bear with" fools already, allowing themselves to become enslaved to them. If so, why not listen to a little foolish boasting from Paul?

Before proceeding to Paul's boasting, it will be helpful to summarize what can be said about the intruders on the basis of 11:1–21a. First, as Paul has already suggested in 10:12–18, they have intruded upon his mission field. Second, they preach "another Jesus." But since Paul never explains the content of this statement, it is best not to read too much into it. Third, they have accepted the patronage of the Corinthians and, to that extent, they may have presented themselves as professional orators of the gospel. Fourth, they have boasted in their achievements to the Corinthians. Fifth, they have imposed their authority over the community.

4. Daring to Boast as a Fool (11:21b–29)

11:21b In whatever respect anyone is bold—I am speaking foolishly—I too am bold.

22 Are they Hebrews? So am I!
Are they Israelites? So am I!
Are they Abraham's seed? So am I!
23 Are they ministers of Christ?
   —I am speaking as if I were out of my mind—
   I am even more so,[a]
with[b] far more labors,
with far more imprisonments,

with more severe beatings,[c]
with more frequent brushes with death.
24 Five times at the hands of Jews,[d] I received forty lashes minus one.
25 Three times I was beaten with sticks.
Once I suffered a stoning,
three times I suffered shipwreck,
a day and night I spent on the sea,[e]
26 frequently in my journeys,[f]
in danger from rivers,
in danger from robbers,
in danger from my fellow countrymen,
in danger from Gentiles,
in danger in cities,
in danger in desolate places,[g]
in danger at sea,
in danger from false brethren,
27 by[h] labor and toil,
often in sleepless nights,
in hunger and thirst,
often without food,
in the cold and poorly clothed.
28 Apart from these external things,[i] there is the daily pressure[j] on me, that anxiety for all of the churches.
29 Who is weak, and I am not weak?
Who is scandalized, and I am not indignant?[k]

a. "I am even more so" translates *hyper egō*. In this translation *hyper* is taken as an adverb, "even more." This use of *hyper* echoes the manner in which Paul has designated the "super-apostles" (*hyperlian apostoloi*).

b. The word "with," here and in the following phrases, translates *en,* which can indicate the means by which something is done, the circumstances in which it is done, or the reason it is done (BDAG). Paul probably intends the first: by means of such hardships he shows that he is a far greater minister of Christ.

c. Several manuscripts place "beatings" before "imprisonments," perhaps because this seems to be the more logical sequence. The present reading, however, has the support of P^{46}, $\aleph^1$, B, D*.

d. Literally, "by Jews."

e. Literally, "on the deep."

f. Paul's reference to his journeys is the heading for the list of eight dangers that follows. They are the kinds of dangers that he has faced on his journeys.

g. In the Greek text "cities" and "desolate places" are in the singular, but since Paul seems to have several occasions in mind, and since it is awkward to translate these words using the singular, the plural is used here.

B. Boasting Foolishly

h. Some manuscripts read *en* ("in") before "labor and toil, " probably because *en* occurs with each of the four items that follow. The best manuscript tradition (P^{46}, $\aleph^2$, B, D), however, does not read *en*, which suggests that "toil and hardship" functions as a heading for what follows. "By" has been introduced here for the sake of English usage.

i. The phrase *chōris tōn parektos* could also be rendered "apart from what is left unsaid," but the present translation seems to fit the context better. Having listed his external trials, Paul mentions his internal trials occasioned by his concern for the churches.

j. A few manuscripts of lesser importance have the interesting reading *episystasis* ("uprising" or "disturbance"). If this reading were correct, Paul would be referring to the "disturbances" caused in churches such as those in Corinth. Although not the original reading, this variant describes the kinds of concerns that Paul had.

k. Literally, "I am burning" (with indignation).

By imploring the Corinthians to bear with him in a little foolishness and, if they must, to receive him as a fool so that he can boast as a fool (11:1–21a), Paul has established the framework necessary for understanding what he is about to do. He will boast as a fool, and what he says will not be "according to the Lord." Thus in verse 21b, no longer able to delay the inevitable, he begins his boasting, which continues until 12:10 and moves through different stages. This unit (vv. 21a–29) represents the first stage of Paul's boasting, in which he chronicles what he has courageously endured for the sake of the gospel. In the second stage (vv. 30–33) Paul's boasting takes a different turn as he highlights his weaknesses. Finally, in the third stage (vv. 12:1–10) he moves to "visions and revelations." He then returns to the only thing in which he will ultimately boast, his weaknesses (vv. 1–10).

As the arrangement of the translation indicates, this is a highly rhetorical section in which Paul's rhetoric determines the outline of the material. After a brief introduction in which he announces his courage on behalf of the gospel (v. 21b), Paul establishes his pedigree in terms of his Jewish ancestry and apostolic ministry (vv. 22–23a). However, since it is his calling as a "minister of Christ" that is most important to him, in verse 23b he highlights his more frequent (1) labors, (2) imprisonments, (3) beatings, and (4) brushes with death on behalf of the gospel as compared with those of the super-apostles. He then chronicles his close encounters with death by listing five items, each of which has a numerical value or time period attached to it (vv. 24–25). Next (v. 26), Paul lists eight dangers that he has faced on his frequent journeys when preaching the gospel. This is followed by a list of four items endured during his labors and hardships for the gospel (v. 27) and a reference to his concern and anxiety for the churches (v. 28). The list concludes with two rhetorical questions (v. 29). The material may be outlined as follows:

v. 21b	Introduction
vv. 22–23a	Paul's Jewish and apostolic pedigree
v. 23b	Four indications of Paul's apostolic pedigree: his labors, imprisonments, beatings, and brushes with death
vv. 24–25	Five brushes with death
v. 26	Eight dangers while traveling
v. 27	Four hardships resulting from labor and toil
v. 28	Anxiety for the churches
v. 29	Conclusion

Although some view the material as a parody of the boasting done by the super-apostles, Paul's tone in this passage is far too serious and somber to reduce what he writes to parody. As the introductory passage of this section indicates, he intends to establish that as a minister of Christ he has been as courageous as—indeed, more courageous than—the intruders who boast of their exploits. Once he has established his own courage, Paul will turn to those things that show his weakness: his escape from Damascus and the thorn for the flesh.

[11:21b] Having postponed the inevitable for as long as he could, Paul must now engage in the very boasting he has tried to avoid. Therefore, drawing a comparison between himself and the super-apostles, he affirms that in whatever respect they are bold or courageous (*tolmaō*), so is he. The material that follows this introductory statement deals with Paul's Jewish pedigree, his sufferings on behalf of the gospel, and an ecstatic experience, all of which could suggest that the super-apostles had already boasted to the Corinthians of their Jewish pedigree, their apostolic labors, and their ecstatic experiences.[24] Paul's parenthetical remark, however, "I am speaking foolishly" (*en aphrosynē legō*) immediately alerts the audience that his "bravado" (the translation of the REB) will ultimately be an exercise in futility, as he already indicated when he wrote at the beginning of this section, "Would that you would bear with me a little foolishness" (*mikron ti aphrosynēs*; 11:1).

The theme of boldness plays an important role in 2 Corinthians, in part, because the super-apostles and some of the Corinthians have apparently accused Paul of lacking the courage or boldness that should characterize an apostle. In 10:2, therefore, Paul affirms his boldness and expresses his hope that he will not have "to act boldly" (10:2) when he comes to Corinth for his third and final visit. And in 10:12, he makes the ironical statement that he is not "bold

---

24. However, one must be careful not to read the text as though it were a mirror that reflects the position of Paul's opponents, what New Testament scholars call and criticize as "mirror reading." Although it is possible that the topics in which Paul boasts are an indication of those in which the super-apostles boasted, it is also possible that he has chosen to boast in topics other than those chosen by the super-apostles.

B. Boasting Foolishly

enough" to classify or compare himself with those who commend themselves. Paul would prefer to act with "the meekness and clemency of Christ" (10:1), and he would like to avoid a contest of foolish boasting (10:12), but he is bold enough to engage in such boasting if he must (11:21a), just as he is capable of acting boldly when necessary (10:2).

[22–23a] Paul is bold enough to engage in such foolish boasting because he enjoys the same Jewish pedigree as do the intruders. More importantly, just as they are—or claim to be—"ministers of Christ," so is he, but to a superlative degree. Employing four rhetorical questions to which he gives his own response, Paul establishes his Jewish pedigree in the first three and then boldly affirms the superlative nature of his ministry in the fourth. The first three questions, all of which deal with Paul's Jewish pedigree, receive the same answer ("So am I!"), but the fourth, which identifies him as a minister of Christ, points to the superlative nature of his ministry ("I am even more so"). However, because he is being forced to boast, Paul prefaces his response with a qualifying statement, "I am speaking as if I were out of my mind."

The three questions that deal with Paul's Jewish pedigree highlight the ethnic, religious, and privileged nature of what it means to be a Jew, and they appear to be arranged in an ascending order of importance, moving from racial purity, to religious identity, to Abrahamic descent. In calling himself a "Hebrew," he boasts of his racial purity, or perhaps his ability to speak Hebrew.[25] In identifying himself as an "Israelite," he boasts of his membership in God's chosen people. And in proclaiming that he is "Abraham's seed," he lays claim to the promises that God made to the great patriarch, promises that have found their fulfillment in Christ.

Paul makes similar claims about himself in Phil 3:4b–5, where he writes, "If anyone else has reason to be confident in the flesh, I have more: circumcised on the eighth day, a member of the people of Israel, of the tribe of Benjamin, *a Hebrew born of Hebrews*; as to the law a Pharisee" (emphasis added). The manner in which Paul identifies himself here, "a Hebrew born of Hebrews," suggests that he is pointing to his ethnic purity, though many commentators maintain that the focus is rather on his ability to speak Hebrew (see the use of

---

25. The meaning of "Hebrews" (*Hebraioi*) is disputed. Thrall (2:723–27) notes four possible meanings: (1) Jews by birth, as distinct from proselytes; (2) those who speak Hebrew or Aramaic, see Acts 6:1; (3) those with close family ties in Palestine; (4) a reference to the special character of the Jewish people. Thrall (730) acknowledges that "like his rivals, he may intend to indicate competence in Aramaic." But she then concludes, "He may simply be making the basic claim that he is fully a Jew by birth and ancestry, as he does in Phil 3.5." The meaning of "Hebrew" in the Philippians text is also disputed. Thus BDAG places the references to 2 Cor 11:22 and Phil 3:5 under two headings: "ethnic name for an Israelite," "Hebrew/Aramaic-speaking Israelites in contrast to a Gk.-speaking Israelite." See BDAG, s.v. *Hebraios*. This commentary has opted for the former meaning (ethnic name for an Israelite) because the other appellations ("Israelites," "Abraham's seed") concern Jewish descent.

the term in Acts 6:1). But if the point of the text in Philippians is Paul's ethnic heritage, then it would help to explain how he understands the term in 2 Corinthians; namely, he is a pure-blooded Hebrew and not the offspring of a mixed union (a Hebrew and a proselyte). The manner in which he begins this statement from Philippians ("If anyone else has reason to be confident in the flesh"), however, clearly indicates that even though Paul can boast in his ethnic purity (or his ability to speak Hebrew), it has lost its former importance for him, since "whatever gains I had, these I have come to regard as loss because of Christ" (Phil 3:7).

In Phil 3:5 Paul also identifies himself as "a member of the people of Israel" (*ek genous Israēl* rather than as an *Israēlitai*, as in 2 Corinthians), and in Rom 11:1 he makes a statement similar to the text of Phil 3:5. "I ask, then, has God rejected his people? By no means! I myself am an Israelite (*Israēlitēs*), a descendant of Abraham, a member of the tribe of Benjamin." It is Rom 9:4–5, however, that best clarifies what Paul means by "Israelite": "They are Israelites, and to them belong the adoption, the glory, the covenants, the giving of the law, the worship, and the promises; to them belong the patriarchs, and from them, according to the flesh, comes the Messiah, who is over all, God blessed forever. Amen." To be an Israelite is to belong to the people whom God has adopted as his own and to whom God revealed his glory, making covenants with them and granting them the Mosaic law, the temple worship, and the promises made to Abraham, Isaac, and Jacob, all of which lead to the Messiah. But as in the case of his Hebrew ancestry, Paul is aware that there is a new dimension to being a member of God's people, which he expresses in the phrase "the Israel of God" (Gal 6:16).

Although Paul's third way of identifying himself ("Abraham's seed") is logically prior to the first two, since Abraham is the progenitor of the people, it occurs last because of its importance: "Now the promises were made to Abraham and to his offspring/seed" (Gal 3:16). The promises that God made to Abraham play a major role in Rom 4 and 9, and in Gal 3. In Gal 3, Paul argues that those who are "in Christ" are Abraham's seed because Christ is Abraham's singular "seed" or "descendant," and in Rom 9:7 Paul writes that "not all of Abraham's children/seed are his true descendants." But here and in Rom 11:1, Paul is primarily intent upon identifying himself as "Abraham's seed." Because he is Abraham's seed, he can claim the same pedigree as the intruders. He is an ethnic Jew born of Hebrew parents; he is a member of God's chosen people; he is a descendant of the great patriarch to whom God made the promises, which are fulfilled in Christ.

It is clearly the fourth and final question, however, that is of paramount importance to Paul. Since the intruders claim to be "ministers of Christ," can Paul claim the same? Whereas Paul does not draw any distinction between himself and the intruders in respect to his Jewish pedigree, here he does. Not only

B. Boasting Foolishly

is he a minister of Christ; he insists that he is "even more so" (*hyper*) than they are, or claim to be. The use of *hyper* as an adverb results in an interesting play on words, since Paul has already identified the intruders as *hyperlian apostoloi* ("super-apostles"). Having given them that ironic title, he now claims to be Christ's minister in a superlative manner, which he will verify by the list of apostolic hardships that follows.

Apart from Col 1:7, which applies this title to Epaphras, and 1 Tim 4:6, which applies it to Timothy, 2 Cor 11:23 is the only occurrence of *diakonoi Christou* in the Pauline writings. Its appearance, however, is not surprising, since Paul has already identified himself and Apollos as *diakonoi* through whom the Corinthians have come to believe (1 Cor 3:5). More importantly, in 2 Cor 3:6 Paul called himself the "minister of a new covenant" and in 6:4 a "minister of God." Thus he probably identified himself and his coworkers as *diakonoi* in a variety of ways.

If the intruding apostles viewed themselves as *diakonoi*, it is likely that they called themselves "ministers of Christ." But did Paul view them as such? On the one hand, he appears to concede the title to them, much as he acknowledges that they are Hebrews, Israelites, and Abraham's seed. But on the other, it is clear that he has grave reservations about their ministry, since he calls them "false apostles" who disguise themselves as "apostles of Christ." In his view, they are Satan's ministers, disguising themselves as "ministers of righteousness" (11:13–15). Despite these strong invectives, Paul may have been willing to acknowledge that the "super-apostles" were "ministers of Christ," but not at Corinth; for at Corinth they were intruding upon his missionary assignment to the detriment of the church. To that extent they have become Satan's ministers, even if they do not realize it. But even if they are what they claim to be, and even if Paul is willing to grant them this title, he is Christ's minister in a superlative manner as the following list of hardships will show.

[23b] Paul has already presented the Corinthians with three lists of his hardships, one in 1 Cor 4:9–13, and two in this letter thus far (4:8–12; 6:4–10). Beginning with this verse and continuing through verse 33, he now presents them with a fourth list of hardships, and in 12:10 he will present them with a fifth. This particular list, however, is the longest and most detailed, and it is distinguished from the others inasmuch as it points to specific moments of hardship, whereas the other lists are more general in nature. Thus in 2 Cor 11:23b–33, as in Gal 1:11–2:14, Paul provides his audience with an extensive autobiographical section. Unlike the text of Galatians, however, the material of this section is not arranged in chronological order. Consequently, although it provides important information about Paul's apostolic sufferings, it is difficult to identify when or where these events took place. But since the primary purpose of the material is to substantiate Paul's claim that he is a minister of Christ in a superlative manner, it fulfills its intended purpose.

This half verse (v. 23b) serves as a general heading for all that will follow. Paul has a greater claim to be a "minister of Christ" because of his more numerous (1) labors, (2) imprisonments, (3) beatings, and (4) more frequent brushes with death. His "labors" (*en kopois*) could refer to his practice of working with his own hands in order to support himself (so Furnish, 515), since this is how he appears to employ the word in 6:5, 11:27, and 1 Thess 2:9 (also see 2 Thess 3:8). But it could also refer to his apostolic labors on behalf of the gospel (so Thrall, 2:735; Martin, 376), as it does in 10:15; 1 Cor 3:8; 15:58; and 1 Thess 3:5. Since Paul is defending his claim to be a minister of Christ, the latter seems the more likely, though the former cannot be excluded.

First Clement 5:6 attests to Paul's frequent imprisonments (*en phylakais*) for the gospel when it notes that he was imprisoned seven times. Although it is difficult to determine how the author of *1 Clement* arrived at this number, it is not hard to understand why this author would have made such a statement, since several of the Pauline letters (Ephesians, Colossians, Philippians, 2 Timothy, Philemon) were purportedly written from prison, see Eph 3:1; 4:1; Phil 1:13; Col 4:10; 2 Tim 1:8, and Phlm 1, 9. Furthermore, the Acts of the Apostles recounts that Paul was imprisoned at Philippi (16:23–24), Jerusalem (21:31–23:30), Caesarea (23:31–26:32), and Rome (28:16). Three of the imprisonments that Acts narrates (Jerusalem, Caesarea, and Rome), however, would have occurred after Paul had written 2 Corinthians. Moreover, even if Paul was the author of Ephesians, Colossians, and 2 Timothy, these imprisonments would also have occurred after the writing of 2 Corinthians. The most likely candidates for the imprisonments mentioned here, therefore, are those at Philippi (mentioned in Acts 16) and those noted in Philippians and Philemon, though it is possible that these letters were written after 2 Corinthians. In addition to these imprisonments, Paul's remark in 1 Cor 15:32 about fighting "with wild animals" and his statement in 2 Cor 1:8 about the "affliction which occurred in Asia" may point to an imprisonment in Asia, most likely at Ephesus.

Since "beatings" (*en plēgais*) often accompanied imprisonment (see Acts 16:23, 37), Paul includes them among the hardships that he has endured for the gospel, as he did in 6:5. In 6:5, however, "beatings" comes before "imprisonments," reflecting the order in which the two hardships probably occurred and leading some manuscripts to rearrange the order of these items in this verse. Paul, however, is not so much interested in the order of the events as the rhetorical affect his recounting of them will have on his audience. Consequently, having begun with his labors for the gospel, he turns to the harsh consequences of those labors, namely, imprisonments and beatings. The climax of the hardships that he mentions here, however, are his frequent encounters with death (*en thanatois*), a theme that he has already developed in 1:9–10 and 4:11 and that can also be found in Rom 8:36 and 1 Cor 15:32. Apostolic ministry for Paul is a process of "continually being handed over to death on account of Jesus"

B. Boasting Foolishly 267

(2 Cor 4:11). To explain what he means, Paul will list five hardships, three of which he endured multiple times, and any one of which could have led to his death (vv. 24–25).

[24–25] The five kinds of hardships Paul lists in these verses provide specific examples of sufferings he has endured for the gospel, and in each instance he refers to the number of times or time period that he endured them ("five times," "three times," "once," "three times," "a day and night"). Although some commentators suggest that this enumeration may be Paul's way of parodying the list of deeds or exploits that Roman emperors and other distinguished figures produced to proclaim their accomplishments, the sober manner in which he recounts this list indicates that he is referring to specific occasions when he actually came close to losing his life because of the scourgings, beatings, a stoning, and shipwrecks that he suffered for the sake of the gospel.

That Paul was scourged five times by the synagogue authorities indicates that he was punished by them for preaching a gospel that did not require Gentiles to do the works of the Mosaic law in order to be justified. These scourgings also suggest that Paul continued to preach to his Jewish compatriots, at least from time to time, despite the harsh reception he received from them. As Luke indicates in the Acts of the Apostles, Paul frequented synagogues because they provided a ready-made assembly of Jews, proselytes, and God-fearers whom he could evangelize. His preaching about Jesus and the law, whether to Jews or to Gentiles, led the synagogue authorities to discipline him with the punishment prescribed in Deut 25:3: "Forty lashes may be given but not more; if more lashes than these are given, your neighbor will be degraded in your sight." To ensure that the law would not be violated, however, only thirty-nine lashes were administered. That Paul was scourged fives times is an indication of his perseverance in preaching as well as of his physical stamina. It also indicates that at this early stage the synagogue authorities were content to punish rather than expel him for his messianic preaching.

When Paul writes that he was beaten with sticks three times (*tris errabdisthēn*), he is referring to the Roman punishment of scourging. In Acts 16:22, Luke recounts how the magistrates at Philippi had Paul and Silas "stripped of their clothing and ordered them to be beaten with rods" (*rabdizein*). Then, after they were flogged, they were thrown into prison. The next day, when the magistrates released them, Paul protested, "They have beaten us in public, uncondemned, men who are Roman citizens" (Acts 16:17). Paul's protest was justified, as was the fear that it inspired in the magistrates (Acts 16:38), since the *Lex Porcia* and the *Lex Julia* protected Roman citizens from such scourging (see the extended discussion of Thrall, 2:939–42). Magistrates, however, could be arbitrary in their administration of justice, especially in the case of a religious missionary such as Paul, whose preaching they undoubtedly viewed as a disruption of the public order.

It is not surprising that Paul mentions only one stoning (*hapax elithasthēn*) since this was a form of capital punishment (see Deut 17:5–7; 22:22–24), and Paul was fortunate to escape with his life. But since the Romans probably did not allow the Jews to exercise the right of capital punishment, as the Fourth Gospel notes (John 18:31), the stoning that he endured may have been the result of mob violence or vigilante justice as in the case of Stephen (Acts 7:54–60). Luke narrates just such an incident of mob violence against Paul at Lystra (Acts 14:19–20), and this may be the incident to which Paul is referring.

The three shipwrecks (*tris enauagēsa*) that Paul notes, one of which resulted in him spending a night and a day on the sea, would almost have been inevitable for someone who made as many sea journeys as Paul did to visit his congregations in Asia Minor, Macedonia, and Achaia. The only shipwreck that Luke describes (Acts 27), however, occurred a considerable time after Paul wrote 2 Corinthians. Thus, although Luke narrates a few of the sufferings that Paul chronicles here, neither Acts nor Paul's letters relate all of the hardships that Paul lists here, an indication of how much of the apostle's life and ministry remains unknown.

[26] Having specified five ways in which he came close to death on numerous occasions, Paul catalogues a series of dangers that he experienced during his frequent journeys on behalf of the gospel. Although he introduces each of the eight items in this list with the same phrase, "in danger from," the items can be arranged in four groups. In the first, "in danger from rivers, in danger from robbers," Paul points to the perils that he has encountered as he walked through the Roman provinces of Asia, Galatia, Macedonia, and Achaia. On such journeys it would have been necessary for him to ford rivers and streams and, like most travelers, he would have been at the mercy of roving brigands. In the second, "in danger from my fellow countrymen, in danger from Gentiles," Paul employs an inclusive expression to indicate that Jews and Gentiles persecuted him because of the gospel he preached, a fact to which the Acts of the Apostles testifies throughout its narrative, though Acts tends to give greater emphasis to Jewish opposition. In the third, "in danger in cities, in danger in desolate places, in danger at sea," Paul employs yet another inclusive expression to show that no matter where he traveled, he was in constant danger. Thus, whether he was in the city or outside of it, on land or on sea, he was in danger because of the gospel he preached. It is the fourth and last item of the list, however, that is the most important, "in danger from false brethren." Although the only other occurrence of "false brethren" is Gal 2:4, in Paul's account of the Jerusalem conference, he probably has in view Jewish Christian missionaries such as those who came to Galatia and those whom he is now encountering at Corinth; that is, the intruders whom he has labeled "false apostles." Paul is in danger from them because if they have their way, they will destroy his work and leave him without the very community he founded. Although this extended list of hardships is

B. Boasting Foolishly

more general than the preceding list, the repeated use of the phrase "in danger from" is a powerful reminder that Paul continually risked his life for the sake of the gospel and, therefore, for the sake of the Corinthians.

[27] Having catalogued the multiple ways in which he has been in danger on account of preaching the gospel, Paul turns to the hardships that he has imposed upon himself because of his "labor and toil" (*kopō kai mochthō*). The same phrase occurs in 1 Thess 2:9 and 2 Thess 3:8; in both instances it clearly refers to Paul's efforts to support himself by working with his own hands, as can be seen from the text of 1 Thessalonians: "You remember our labor and toil, brothers and sisters; we worked night and day, so that we might not burden any of you while we proclaimed to you the gospel of God." Thus, whereas Paul employed *kopos* ("labor") in 11:23 to describe his apostolic work, here he appears to have his manual labor in view, just as he does in the hardship list of 6:4–10, where, as in this list, "sleepless nights" (*agrypniais*) and being "without food" (*nēsteiais*) are mentioned along with Paul's "labor" (*kopos*; 6:5). The phrase "labor and toil," then, functions as a heading for the hardships that follow, hardships that Paul has imposed upon himself because he insisted upon supporting himself for the sake of the gospel.

The hardships in this list fall into four groups, each group introduced by the particle *en* ("with"). In the first and third group, Paul lists a single hardship modified by *pollakis* ("often"). In the second and fourth he lists two hardships joined by the conjunction *kai* ("and"). The list can be arranged in this way:

> labor and toil
> *often* in sleepless nights,
>   in hunger *and* thirst,
> *often* without food,
>   in the cold *and* poorly clothed

The structure of Paul's language indicates that the hardships he catalogues here are the result of his decision to "labor and toil" in order to support himself so that he could offer the gospel to others free of charge. As a result of that decision, it often became necessary for him to forgo sleep and meals in order to work or to preach the gospel. Paul may also be saying that although he labored and toiled with his own hands, his work did not always provide him with a sufficient income for food, clothing, and shelter. Whatever the exact meaning, he indicates that his decision to support himself, rather than to be supported, resulted in self-imposed hardships that the super-apostles have not had to endure because they accept, and perhaps even demand, support from the Corinthians.

[28] Paul now draws the first stage of his boasting to a conclusion. Having mentioned those hardships that can be seen, he turns to the kind of hardship that cannot be externally verified: the daily pressure he experiences in his anxiety and concern for the churches. The disputed phrase that begins this verse, *chōris tōn parektos*, can be taken in two ways: "apart from what is left unmentioned," or "apart from what is external." In the first instance, Paul would be saying that he is cutting short the list of his hardships (since what he has said is sufficient) in order to go on to other kinds of hardships that he endures. In the second, he would be establishing a contrast between the visible and external hardships that he has just listed and his daily anxiety for the churches that cannot be seen. The majority of commentators argue for the first interpretation on philological grounds but the second certainly makes good sense within this context. In either case, Paul's main point remains the same: his daily anxiety and concern for the churches is a hardship that most do not know of, even though it afflicts him every day. Unlike the super-apostles, he is presently experiencing such anxiety for the church of Corinth, just as he experienced care and concern for the congregations at Thessalonica and Galatia (1 Thess 3:1–5; Gal 4:19–20; see Garland, 501–2). Although the intruding apostles may have boasted in their labors and hardships on behalf of the gospel, one suspects that they did not boast of their daily concern for the churches as does Paul.

[29] Paul's concern for the churches leads him to conclude the first stage of his boasting with two rhetorical questions. In the first, he asks who is weak, and then proclaims that he is weak. In the second, he asks who is scandalized, and then proclaims his indignation. The reference to the "weak" recalls Paul's extended discussion in 1 Cor 8:1–11:1 about idolatry and the appropriateness of eating food sacrificed to idols, practices that scandalized those whose consciences were "weak" or delicate (1 Cor 8:7). Although Paul could number himself among those whose conscience is "strong," he proclaimed his willingness, if necessary, never to eat meat again "so that I may not cause one of them [the weak] to fall (*skandalizō*)" (1 Cor 8:13). Then, in 1 Cor 9:22 he associates himself with the weak when he writes, "To the weak I became weak, so that I might win the weak. I have become all things to all people, that I might by all means save some." Even if Paul no longer has this incident in mind, what he says here clarifies these rhetorical questions. First, because of his daily anxiety for the churches, he associates himself with the weak members of the community lest "those weak believers for whom Christ died are destroyed" (1 Cor 8:11). Second, because he associates himself with the weak, he burns with indignation when others scandalize them. Could it be that the faction that aligned itself with the intruding apostles against Paul was the same group of people whose behavior had previously scandalized the weaker members of the community?

The first stage of Paul's boasting can be summarized in this way: Like the super-apostles, he can boast in his Jewish pedigree. Moreover, even if they are "ministers of Christ," he is a superior minister because of the hardships that he has endured for the sake of the gospel: hardships that have brought him close to death on numerous occasions; hardships that constantly endanger him, hard-

B. Boasting Foolishly

ships that he has imposed upon himself; hardships that result from his personal concern for his congregations and lead him to associate with the weak and burn with indignation when others, such as the super-apostles, scandalize them.

5. Boasting in Weakness (11:30-33)

11:30 If I must boast, I will boast about the things that show[a] my weaknesses. 31 The God[b] and Father of the Lord Jesus[c] knows—the one[d] who is blessed forever—that I am not lying. 32 In Damascus the ethnarch of the king, Aretas, was guarding the city of Damascus[e] to arrest me, 33 and I was lowered in a basket through a window in the wall and escaped his clutches.[f]

a. The word "show" is supplied in order to complete the sense of the Greek.
b. D* reads "the God of Israel," thereby avoiding the translation difficulty discussed in the next note.
c. The Greek could be translated "God, the Father of the Lord Jesus" (so Furnish, 521), but the absence of an article before "Father" favors the translation, "The God and Father of the Lord Jesus" (so Thrall, 2:762). The resulting translation is somewhat striking, since it speaks of *ho theos* as the "God," as well as the "Father," of Jesus. This may be the reason that D* reads "the God of Israel," as noted above. See 1:3, where the same phrase occurs.
d. The "one" refers to the God and Father of Jesus.
e. Some manuscripts (א, D²) read *thelōn* at this point, "wishing to arrest me."
f. Literally, "hands."

The function of these verses has always been somewhat puzzling to commentators, occurring as they do after the extensive list of hardships recorded in 11:21b-29 and immediately before the account of Paul's visions and revelations in 12:1-10. It is not surprising, then, that Windisch (364) suggests that they are an interpolation from Paul's secretary and that Bultmann (218) can find no reason whatsoever for narrating the event at this point, asking if it is an interpolation, as Windisch proposes. Hughes (422) and Martin (384), however, maintain that the episode establishes a striking contrast with the account of Paul's visions and revelations: a descent from the city wall followed by an ascent to the third heaven. Furnish (542) and McCant (141) adopt a suggestion of E. A. Judge[26] and view the episode as a parody of the Roman practice of awarding the "mural crown" to the first soldier up the wall.

The real function of the unit, however, may be to mark a turning point in Paul's boasting. To this point (v. 29) he has boasted in his Jewish heritage and

---

26. "The Conflict of Educational Aims in NT Thought," *Journal of Christian Education* 9 (1966): 32-45.

the hardships that show the superlative degree to which he is a minister of Christ. In effect, he has boasted in the kinds of things in which the super-apostles may also have boasted. Having boasted in his hardships and heritage, he now turns to an episode that highlights his weakness, an ignominious escape from Damascus that paradoxically shows the power of God to save him despite his weakness. Paul's opening statement clearly introduces this theme of "weakness" (*asthenia*), which will be the leitmotif of the remaining units in this section (see 12:5, 9, 10; 13:4). Moreover, the manner in which he begins this statement ("if I must boast") will find an echo in 12:1 (*kauchastha dei*). For these reasons, it would appear that the function of the unit is to signal a turning point in Paul's boasting.

The material begins with an introduction that establishes the tone for the rest of the speech (v. 30). Paul then employs an oath formula to undergird what he has said (v. 31) before he proceeds to narrate his escape from Damascus (vv. 32–33).

[11:30] This verse marks a turning point in Paul's boasting. On the one hand, it has a retrospective function, inasmuch as the verb "to boast" echoes Paul's initial intention to engage in foolish boasting (11:16, 18). On the other, it introduces the theme of boasting in weakness that Paul has not yet developed but that will play an important role in the rest of the narrative (see 12: 5, 9, 10). The retrospective function of this verse, however, appears to be limited to the theme of boasting, and it does not necessarily characterize the nature of the hardships that Paul has catalogued thus far as weakness (as proposed by Lambrecht, 192–93). Viewed in this way, the hardships that Paul has listed are indications of his endurance rather than of his weaknesses. But from this point on he will boast in those things that show his weakness: his escape from Damascus and the thorn for the flesh that was given to him after his ascent to paradise. This will lead to Paul's climactic statement that he will gladly boast all the more, so that the power of Christ can rest upon him (12:9). In effect, having boasted like his opponents, Paul will now boast in a way they cannot even conceive of boasting.

[31] With this verse, Paul introduces an oath formula similar to those found in Rom 9:1 and Gal 1:20. The precise function of this oath, however, is not clear. Is it retrospective, guaranteeing the truth of what he has boasted of thus far (Martin, 384)? Or is it prospective, guaranteeing the truth of what he will now narrate (Hughes, 419)? Or does it simply undergird what Paul has said in verse 30 about boasting in weakness (Furnish, 540; Thrall, 2:762–63)? Whatever the intended meaning, Paul establishes a clear contrast between his veracity and the deceitfulness of the super-apostles, whom he has already characterized as "deceivers" and "false apostles" (11:13), and it coheres with his insistence elsewhere that he is speaking to the Corinthians in the presence of God (2:17; 12:19).

B. Boasting Foolishly

[32–33] The episode that Paul narrates in these verses differs from the hardships that he has chronicled thus far; for whereas his hardships point to his endurance, his escape from Damascus highlights his weakness. However, it is precisely for this reason that Paul now narrates this event; for, when he was helpless, then God delivered him (Lambrecht, 193).

The king to whom Paul refers is Aretas IV, who ruled over the Nabatean kingdom (a region east and southwest of the Dead Sea) approximately 9 B.C.E.–40–41 C.E. Whether or not Aretas ever exercised political control over the city of Damascus is disputed, since "the city had been in the possession of Rome from the time of Pompey in 66 B.C.E." (Thrall, 2:766), though there may have been a brief period under the emperor Gaius (37 C.E.) when it was under Nabatean control. The ethnarch to whom Paul refers is unknown, as is the precise meaning of this title. BDAG defines *ethnarchēs* as the "head of an ethnic community/minority." Since there was a Jewish ethnarch who was responsible for the Jewish population in Alexandria (Thrall, 2:767–68), Paul may be referring to an Arab ethnarch who was similarly responsible for the Nabatean population in Damascus, whether or not Aretas actually ruled over the city.

According to Gal 1:17 Paul went "into Arabia," that is, the region of the Nabateans, immediately after his call/conversion. If he began to preach the gospel at this time, as most commentators believe, his preaching may have disturbed segments of the Nabatean population, thereby incurring the wrath of Aretas. Accordingly, when Paul returned to Damascus, Aretas would have ordered the ethnarch of that city to apprehend him. Paul's ignoble flight through a window, down a wall, in a basket, would have forever reminded him of his own weakness. But his miraculous escape would also have taught him, perhaps for the first time, how the Lord manifests power in and through weakness.

Luke recounts a similar episode in Acts 9:23–25. In his account it is not Aretas and his ethnarch who pursue Paul but the Jews. Margaret Thrall (2:771), however, suggests that if there were Jewish complaints to the ethnarch about Paul, then "there might be some truth in Luke's indication of Jewish involvement in the threat to Paul," since the ethnarch would have taken notice of such complaints, whatever his feelings about the Jews, in order to preserve civil order. "After some time had passed, the Jews plotted to kill him, but their plot became known to Saul. They were watching the gates day and night so that they might kill him; but his disciples took him by night and let him down through an opening in the wall, lowering him in a basket." Since there is no literary evidence that Luke knew 2 Corinthians, the presence of this episode in Acts suggests that Paul's escape from Damascus was rather well known. If so, it is possible that some employed this narrative to his disadvantage. Paul, however, has found a way to boast in it.

6. Boasting in Visions and Revelations (12:1–10)

12:1 I must boast.[a] It is not profitable.[b] But I will move on to visions and revelations of the Lord.[c] 2 I know a man in Christ who fourteen years ago—whether in the body I do not know, whether outside of the body I do not know, God knows—this one was snatched up to the third heaven. 3 And I know such a man—whether in the body, whether apart from[d] the body, I do not know, God knows—4 that he was snatched up into paradise, and he heard unutterable utterances[e] that a mortal is not permitted to utter. 5 About this one, I will boast, but about myself I will not boast, except in weaknesses.[f]

6 By all means,[g] even if I should choose to boast, I will not be a fool, for I am speaking the truth. But I am refraining, lest someone consider me to be more than what he sees or hears from me.

7 Because of my surpassing revelations,[h] for this reason,[i] lest I be puffed up with pride, I was given a thorn for the flesh, an angel of Satan, to torment me lest I become puffed up with pride.[j] 8 Three times I begged the Lord about this[k] that it might leave me. 9 And he said to me, "My grace is sufficient for you; for power[l] is made perfect in weakness."

Therefore, I will gladly boast all the more in my[m] weaknesses so that the power of Christ might dwell in me. 10 Wherefore, for the sake of Christ I delight in weaknesses, in mistreatment and[n] distress, in persecutions and[o] anguish; for when I am weak, then I am powerful.

a. Some manuscripts (א², H) read "*If* I must boast" (*ei kauchasthai dei*), thereby bringing this verse in line with the opening words of 11:30. Others (א, D*) read *de* instead of *dei*, "It is not profitable to boast." The more difficult reading (*kauchasthai dei*), supported by P⁴⁶, B, D, is adopted here.

b. "It is not profitable" translates the participle *ou sympheron*. Some manuscripts improve this reading by substituting the verb *ou sympherei* ("it is not profitable") for the participle, while others read *ou sympherei moi* ("it is not profitable for me"). The more difficult reading of P⁴⁶, א, B is followed here.

c. The genitive can be taken as a genitive of origin ("visions and revelations from the Lord") or as an objective genitive ("visions and revelations about the Lord"). It could also include both notions: visions and revelations from the Lord in which the Lord is also the object of the visions and revelations.

d. Some manuscripts read *ektos* ("outside") in order to bring this verse in line with v. 2 where *ektos* ("outside") is also used. P⁴⁶, B, and D* read *chōris* ("apart from").

e. The Greek *arrēta rhēmata* could refer to heavenly words that cannot be expressed in human words or to heavenly words that one has heard but has been forbidden to divulge. The translation "unutterable utterances" is suggested by Plummer (345).

f. Several manuscripts read "my weaknesses" (as does v. 9). Although this provides a smoother reading, "my" is not found in several important manuscripts (P⁴⁶, B, D*).

g. The particle *gar* ("for") is taken as a clarifying marker, thus the translation "By all

B. Boasting Foolishly

means." The verb *thelēsō* ("choose," "wish") is taken as subjunctive rather than as future indicative.

h. Many translations (NAB, NRSV) and commentators (Allo, Furnish, Martin) read the phrase "because of my surpassing revelations" as the final words of v. 6, "But I am refraining, lest someone consider me to be more than what he sees or hears from me, *because of my surpassing revelations*." Paul, however, appears to begin a new thought with these words. Therefore they are taken as the beginning of a new sentence, even though the sentence is somewhat awkward.

i. Some manuscripts omit "for this reason" (*dio*) making it easier to read the phrase "because of my surpassing revelations" as the beginning of a new sentence rather than as the conclusion of verse 6. However *dio*, which has the support of P^{46} and D, should be retained as the more difficult reading.

j. Some manuscripts omit "lest I become puffed up with pride" as redundant. There is strong textual evidence (P^{46}, $\aleph^2$, B), however, for these words, even though they also occur earlier in the same verse.

k. The word translated "this" (*toutou*) could also be taken as masculine ("him"). The decision to treat it as masculine or neuter depends on one's interpretation of Paul's thorn for the flesh, whether it refers to a person or to a physical affliction.

l. Although some manuscripts read "my power," which is a richer theological reading because it explicitly identifies the power as belonging to Christ, the best manuscript tradition (P^{46vid}, $\aleph^*$, B, D^*) does not have the possessive pronoun "my." Paul's reference to "the power of Christ" in v. 9b, however, indicates that he is indeed referring to Christ's power.

m. A few manuscripts omit "my."

n. P^{46} and $\aleph^*$ read "and" rather than "in." This reading, which is adopted here, suggests that there are two couplets ("in mistreatment *and* distress, in persecution *and* anguish") with "weakness" serving as the heading for both.

o. Some manuscripts read "in" rather than "and" so that each of the five items has "in" (*en*) before it.

Having boasted in an incident that shows his weakness in the face of hostile human forces—his ignominious escape from Damascus—Paul goes on to boast in "visions and revelations." On first reading, he seems to contradict what he has just said about his intention to boast only in those things that show his weakness (11:30). As the passage unfolds, however, it becomes apparent that he does not employ this account of his ecstatic experience to boast in himself but to boast in his weaknesses (12:6, 9).

The episode presents a host of exegetical problems, not the least of which concerns the rhetorical goal of the material. Is Paul being satirical and merely offering a parody of his opponents' boasting by recounting a revelation that reveals nothing? Or is he narrating an ecstatic experience that was profoundly important for him but which he would have preferred not to disclose in light of his comment in 5:13 ("For, if we are beside ourselves, it is for God; and if we are sober-minded, it is for you")? Although some commentators argue that Paul engages in satire and parody at this point (see McCant, 141–50, who is indebted to Hans Dieter Betz), the way in which Paul narrates this episode, as well as the manner in which he portrays himself as a man in Christ, suggests that parody is not the appropriate genre for interpreting this episode (so Garland, 511). Rather, Paul has been forced into boasting about something he would have preferred not to divulge. But now that he must disclose it, he will use it to show how his ecstatic experience taught him to boast in his weaknesses.

The theme of boasting in weakness comes to its climax in this unit with the verb "to boast" (*kauchaomai*) occurring five times (vv. 1, 5 [twice], 6, 9) and the noun "weakness" (*astheneia*) four times (vv. 5, 9 [twice], 10). Thus, Paul begins by saying that he must boast even though it is not profitable (12:1). Midway through the narrative he then turns from boasting in the man in Christ who was snatched into paradise to boasting in his weaknesses (12:5). Finally, he concludes with his willingness to boast and rejoice in his weaknesses (12:9b–10). The material can be outlined as follows:

v.1   Boasting is necessary but not profitable
vv. 2–4   Paul's heavenly ascent
    v. 2   The first account
    vv. 3–4   The second account
vv. 5–6   Refraining from boasting except in weaknesses
    v. 5a   Willing to boast in "this man"
    vv. 5b–6   Refraining from boasting except in weaknesses
        v. 5b   thematic statement: boasting in weaknesses
        v. 6a   boasting and Paul's truthfulness
        v. 6b   refraining from boasting
vv. 7–9a   The result of Paul's heavenly ascent
    v. 7   the thorn for the flesh
    v. 8   Paul's petition to the Lord
    v. 9a   the Lord's response
vv. 9b–10 Paul's resolve
    v. 9b   to boast in weaknesses
    v.10   to delight in weaknesses

[12:1] This verse functions as a heading for the entire unit, stating that it has become necessary for Paul to boast, even though he recognizes that it will not be "profitable" (*sympheron*). Nonetheless he will move on to "visions and revelations." This suggests that Paul found it necessary to boast in his ecstatic experiences because the intruding apostles had already boasted of their ecstatic experiences, though Paul never explicitly refers to their ecstatic experiences.

Paul is keenly aware, as he has already told the Corinthians, that though all things are lawful for the believer, not everything is "beneficial" (*sympherei*; 1 Cor 6:12; 10:23), and that the gifts of the Spirit have been distributed for "the

B. Boasting Foolishly

common good" (*to sympheron*; 1 Cor 12:7). In this verse, he says something similar about his own ecstatic experiences, namely, though they were of great personal value to him, they are of less value for the common good or building up of the church. Consequently he is reluctant to recount them, since boasting in them will not be profitable to him or to the community. But if it is not profitable to boast, then why boast? Perhaps because others have engaged in such "foolish boasting," and Paul must show that he is not inferior to these super-apostles. As the narrative develops, however, it becomes clear that Paul is also using this boasting to develop the theme of boasting in weakness.

When Paul writes that he will go on to "visions and revelations," one immediately expects him to recount several episodes. But as in Rom 3:1, where he asks "What advantage has the Jew?" and answers "Much, in every way," but then only recounts *one* advantage, Paul only narrates one ecstatic experience. Thus, the phrase "visions and revelations" may be intended for literary effect, though Paul does refer to "revelations" in verse 7. Or if it was Paul's intention to narrate several examples, it soon became apparent to him that one extraordinary experience was sufficient to make his point.

The expression "visions and revelations" is an example of hendiadys (Lambrecht, 200) whereby Paul uses two concepts to express one; in this case, the ecstatic experience that transported him to paradise. "Visions" places the emphasis on what one sees, as in Luke 1:22 (the angelic vision to Zechariah), Luke 24:23 (the vision to the women at the tomb), and Acts 26:19 (Paul's vision of Christ); whereas "revelations" often concern the final, that is, the eschatological character of what has or will be revealed (Rom 8:19; 1 Cor 1:7). In Gal 1:12, however, Paul writes that he received the gospel "through a revelation (*di' apokalypseōs*) of Jesus Christ," that is, the Damascus road experience in which God revealed his Son to him, an experience that may have had a visionary dimension. In referring to "visions and revelations," therefore, Paul seems to have in view an ecstatic experience that was both visual and auditory whereby he was privileged to hear and see eschatological realities. The "Lord" to whom he refers in this expression ("visions and revelations of the Lord") is Christ, to whom Paul will appeal in verses 8–9 to remove the "thorn for the flesh." Although this expression of verse 1 can be understood as referring to visions and revelations that the Lord granted Paul, or to visions and revelations about the Lord, it is probably best to take it in a broader sense. Namely, not only did Christ grant Paul "visions and revelations," Christ was also the content of these revelations. Thus Paul would have seen a vision of Christ while in the third heaven, paradise.

[2–4] Paul goes on to narrate what happened to "a man in Christ" fourteen years earlier. The man in question is undoubtedly Paul, and this oblique manner of referring to himself could be Paul's way of deflecting attention from himself. But since it is apparent that Paul is talking about himself, the use of the third person could also reflect the very nature of the vision, whereby Paul experienced a certain distance from himself during this ecstatic experience.[27]

The expression, "a man in Christ," is Paul's way of referring to a believer, "a Christian." Thus, he is saying, "I know a believer," or "I know a Christian." The expression may also have a further purpose. Paul has already exhorted the Corinthians, "Let the one who boasts, boast *in the Lord*" (10:17), and in verse 5 he will write, "About this one [the man in Christ] I will boast, but about myself I will not boast except in my weaknesses." By obliquely referring to himself as "a man in Christ," then, Paul is boasting in the Lord who is the source of his ecstatic experience.

Some commentators argue that Paul is referring to two experiences,[28] one in which he was transported to the third heaven (v. 2) and another in which he was transported to paradise and heard "unutterable utterances" (v. 4). Most modern commentators, however, view these verses as an example of synthetic parallelism, a device whereby an author repeats, in a slightly different way, what he has just said in order to clarify or add a new perspective. The technique occurs frequently in the Psalms, and it is found here as the following comparison shows:

Verse 2	*Verse 3–4*
I know a man in Christ	And I know such a man
fourteen years ago	
whether in the body	whether in the body
whether outside of the body	whether apart from the body
I do not know, God knows	I do not know, God knows
this one	that he
was snatched up to the third heaven.	was snatched up into paradise
	and heard unutterable utterances
	that a mortal is not permitted to utter.

As this comparison shows, there are three important differences between verse 3 and verse 4. First, whereas in verse 3 Paul dates the ecstatic experience, in verse 4 he does not, an indication that he is referring to the same event (or, if

---

27. See the article by Margaret Thrall, "Paul's Journey to Paradise: Some Exegetical Issues in 2 Cor 12, 2-4," in *The Corinthian Correspondence* (ed. R. Bieringer; BETL 125; Leuven: Leuven University Press, 1996), 325–46. She writes, "The style may derive originally from the phenomenon of the retreat and displacement of the ego in ecstatic experience, and its use may indicate that the writer had himself actually experienced this condition" (352).

28. Plummer notes, "On the whole patristic writers seem to be mostly in favor of either two raptures, or one rapture in two stages, the first to the third heaven and then to paradise." Plummer favors two experiences, arguing "the *kai* at the beginning of *v.* 3 is rather strongly in favor of the view that we have two revelations without counting the Divine utterance in *v.* 9; for the *kai* is almost awkwardly superfluous if what follows simply repeats *v.* 3" (344).

B. Boasting Foolishly

there were two events, that they took place about the same time). Second, whereas in verse 3 he writes that the man in Christ was snatched up to the third heaven, in verse 4 he says this one was snatched up into paradise. Although Paul could be referring to two different places, it seems more likely that he is now identifying paradise with the third heaven. Finally, whereas in verse 3 Paul does not say what occurred in paradise, in verse 4 he discloses that he heard "unutterable utterances" that he was not permitted to reveal. Though the evidence may not be conclusive, the manner in which verse 4 develops verse 3 strongly suggests that Paul is referring to a single experience, even though he speaks of "visions and revelations."

In writing that this experience occurred "fourteen years ago," Paul reveals that it was not of recent vintage, suggesting that he is disclosing it to the Corinthians for the first time. In keeping with the opening verse of this unit, therefore, Paul did not consider it beneficial to speak of such revelations to his converts, no matter how edifying they were to him. If Paul wrote 2 Corinthians about 55–56 C.E., then this experience occurred around 42 C.E., well after the revelation on the road to Damascus and the temple vision recorded in Acts 22:17–21. Thus, Paul seems to be reporting one of several experiences that the Lord granted him, experiences that he did not normally disclose. One suspects that the apostle to the Gentiles was also a visionary.

Because of the transcendent nature of this experience, not even the one who participated in it knew whether he was in or out of his body when it occurred. In most instances, Jewish literature describes such experiences as bodily translations from this world to the other. For example, in the B Recension of the *Testament of Abraham* (8:1–3), the Lord instructs the angel Michael to bring Abraham "in the body," and in the J Recension of *2 Enoch* (1:1–10) two heavenly figures come for Enoch in order to bring him to heaven through a bodily ascension. Though the notion of a nonbodily ascent to heaven was not as familiar to Jewish thought, it was familiar to the Greeks, for example, the story of Er, in the tenth book of Plato's *Republic*, whose soul journeyed to the entrance of heaven and the underworld after his death.[29] Paul's purpose in this text, however, is not to leave the question open, so that what he says will be acceptable to all factions, but to highlight his ignorance and God's knowledge. The experience was of such a transcendent character that even now, fourteen years later, he does not know whether he was in or out of the body when it occurred. Only God, who guarantees the veracity of what Paul says, knows. Indeed, whether or not Paul was in the body is beside the point, since in or out of the body he was transported to the third heaven.

---

29. Thrall ("Paul's Journey to Paradise," 354) points to this example. She notes, however, that it is not an exact parallel, since Er never enters the realm of the gods and his journey occurs after his funeral. She discusses the issue of bodily and nonbodily journeys, 353–56.

In writing that he was "snatched up" to the third heaven, Paul uses that same verb that he employs in 1 Thess 4:17, where he describes how the living will be "caught up" (*harpagēsometha*) in the clouds at the Lord's parousia. The sudden and unexpected manner in which "the rapture" will occur at the parousia suggests that Paul's ecstatic experience came unexpectedly, snatching him up to the third heaven.

The mention of the "third heaven" indicates that Paul, like many of his contemporaries, thought of heaven as comprising multiple levels. But how many? Expressions such as "heaven and the heaven of heavens" (Deut 10:14) and "heaven and the highest heaven" (1 Kings 8:27; 2 Chr 2:6; 6:18) imply that there are at least two levels of heaven, a notion also found in *1 En.* 71:5. Certain intertestamental writings, however, reckon with even more levels. The *Testament of Levi* (chap. 3), for example, refers to three heavens: the first contains the spirits that will carry out God's judgment; the second holds the armies of God that are prepared for the day of judgment; and in the third the great glory of God dwells in the Holy of Holies. In the *Martyrdom and Ascension of Isaiah* (7–11), however, Isaiah journeys through seven heavens, and when he arrives at the seventh, he sees a wonderful light, innumerable angels, and all the righteous. Finally, the J Recension of *2 Enoch* speaks of ten heavens, identifying the tenth as the place where Enoch views the face of the Lord that is not to be talked about since it is so marvelous (chap. 22). Since Paul is intent upon showing the surpassing character of his own ecstatic experience, and since he appears to identify the third heaven with paradise,[30] he likely thinks of the third heaven as the highest heaven, the place where God dwells. Unlike the writers of the intertestamental books, however, he steadfastly refuses to describe the different levels of heaven or his journeys through them.[31]

In identifying the third heaven as "paradise" (*paradeisos*) Paul employs a Persian loan word that occurs in the Septuagint to describe the "garden" that God planted in Eden for Adam and Eve (Gen 2:8). The word occurs only twice in the New Testament apart from this text. In Luke 23:43 Jesus promises the repentant criminal, "today you will be with me in Paradise," and in the book of Revelation the risen Lord says to the church in Ephesus, "To everyone who conquers, I will give permission to eat from the tree of life that is in the paradise of God" (2:7), an allusion to the garden of Eden. There is no indication in the

---

30. The J recension of *2 En.* 8:1 identifies the third heaven as the location of paradise, but since it speaks of ten heavens, the third heaven is clearly not the highest heaven. However, paradise and the third heaven are identified in the Greek edition of *The Life of Adam and Eve* (=*Apocalypse of Moses*) 37:5, where the Archangel Michael takes Adam to paradise, the third heaven. For a further example, see 40:1–2 of the same writing.

31. For a fuller description of the Old Testament, intertestamental, and rabbinic background to "heaven," see the article of H. Traub on "heaven" (*ouranos*) in *TDNT*, vol. 5, and the article by J. Jeremias on "paradise" (*paradeisos*), also in *TDNT*, vol. 5.

B. Boasting Foolishly

passage of 2 Corinthians, however, that Paul thought of the third heaven as the eschatological garden of Eden, though this cannot be ruled out.

In the end Paul reveals little about "heaven" or his ecstatic experience, except that he heard "unutterable utterances." This expression, which is an oxymoron in both English and Greek (*arrēta rhēmata*), could indicate the inexpressible nature of the heavenly words that he heard, so that even if he wanted to communicate them, he could not. Or it could mean, as the command that follows intimates, that Paul was forbidden to communicate them. In either case, it now becomes apparent why it is not profitable for him to boast in this ecstatic experience: Although this experience may have assured him that he was Christ's apostle, it did not provide him with any "revelation" with which he could build up the church. To that extent it is unprofitable for him or any one else to boast in ecstatic experiences. If the super-apostles had already boasted in such experiences, Paul is surely making a pointed critique of them.

[5–6] With these verses Paul returns to the theme of boasting that began this unit and makes a distinction between himself and the man in Christ who was snatched up to the third heaven, a distinction that allows him to develop the theme of boasting in his weaknesses. The distinction that Paul makes is somewhat semantic, since he is the man in Christ who was taken into paradise. The detached manner in which he described that ecstatic experience, however, now allows him to make this distinction. Accordingly, he can boast in the man in Christ who was transported to the third heaven, because this ecstatic experience was not his own doing. The visions and revelations came from Christ, who presumably transported him to paradise. Boasting in this man is boasting in the Lord.

Aware that this ecstatic experience was graciously granted by Christ, Paul will not boast about himself except in relation to his weaknesses (v. 5b). This thematic statement echoes what he wrote in 11:30, "If I must boast, I will boast about the things that show my weakness," and it anticipates what he will write in verse 9a, "Therefore, I will gladly boast all the more in my weaknesses so that the power of Christ might dwell in me." The last item about which Paul will "boast" is the strangest of all: the thorn for the flesh that was given to him lest he become puffed up with pride on account of the surpassing revelations he received.

Before mentioning the "thorn for the flesh," Paul makes a qualifying statement that seems to stand in tension with what he has just said and what he will write in 12:11. For after stating that he will not boast except in his weaknesses, Paul affirms that even if he chooses to boast, he would not be a fool, since he would be speaking the truth. Then in 12:11, in a retrospective comment, he laments that he has become a fool, presumably by his boasting. Although these statements stand in tension with each other, each functions in a slightly different way. In verse 6, when he claims that if he boasts, he will not be a fool, because he will be telling the truth, Paul appears to have his rivals in view, thereby implying that their boasting is not truthful. In 12:11, however, he is looking back upon the entire "fool's speech" and lamenting that it has been a foolish exercise; for even though it is true, his boasting has not benefited the Corinthians. At best, it has allowed Paul to show them that he is not inferior to the super-apostles.

Since Paul wants the Corinthians to evaluate him on the basis of what they have seen and heard from him—rather than on the basis of what he boasts that he has done—he writes that he is refraining from such boasting (v. 6b). This statement is also a bit off-putting, since he has in fact engaged in boasting. But here Paul seems to have in mind any further boasting about his pedigree, hardships, and revelations. Having reluctantly boasted in these, he will not boast further, except in the thorn for the flesh. Unlike his rivals, he wants the Corinthians to evaluate him on the basis of what they can see (his ministry among them) and hear (the gospel he proclaims), rather than on the basis of what he boasts about himself.

Paul's line of thought can be summarized in this way: He is willing to boast in the man who was taken to paradise because this was not his own doing, but he does not want to boast in himself except in his weaknesses. Although he could boast further, since he would be telling the truth, he is refraining from this, so that the Corinthians can evaluate him on the basis of his preaching and work among them, rather than on the basis of his boasting.

[7–9a] Paul now discloses the outcome of his visions and revelations, the enigmatic thorn for the flesh (v. 7). Whatever the thorn was, it tormented Paul to the point that he asked the Lord three times to remove it (v. 8). The response he receives (v. 9a), however, is a paradoxical saying that becomes the basis for his boasting (vv. 9b–10). Thus one begins to suspect that Paul had an ulterior purpose in narrating his ascent to paradise. For in addition to enabling him to boast in the man who was taken into paradise, it now allows him to inform the Corinthians of the thorn for the flesh, from which he learned the paradox of boasting in his weaknesses.

Having reflected on this episode of the thorn, which seems to have occurred fourteen years earlier at the time of his ecstatic experience, Paul now understands God's purpose. The passive verb *edothē* ("given") suggests that the unexpressed subject of the action was God. If so, then it was God who gave Paul the *skolops tē sarki*, which is best rendered a "thorn *for* the flesh" (taking the dative as a dative of advantage rather than as a dative of place). God gave Paul the thorn as a kind of divine protection, lest the visionary become overly exalted in his self-estimation because of the abundant revelations he had received.

This text is the only occurrence in the New Testament of the Greek noun *skolops*, a noun that also occurs in the Septuagint (Num 33:55; Ezek 28:24; Hos 2:6; Sir 43:19), where it is best translated as "thorn." Originally the word meant anything pointed, such as a stake, but eventually it came to refer to something

B. Boasting Foolishly

that causes serious annoyance, such as a thorn or splinter (BDAG). In writing that he was given a thorn for the flesh, therefore, Paul is referring to something or someone that caused him serious and ongoing annoyance in his life, "flesh" being taken in the broad sense of physical life.[32]

Either assuming that the Corinthians know what he intends by the expression, or purposely using the expression so as not to divulge the precise nature of this particular weakness, Paul metaphorically identifies the thorn as a "messenger" or "angel" of Satan sent to "torment" (*kolaphizē*) him, a verb that is often used in the New Testament in reference to "striking" or "beating" someone, as in Matt 26:67 and Mark 14:65, where Jesus is mocked and struck after his trial before the Sanhedrin (also see 1 Cor 4:11 and 1 Pet 2:20). Here, however, it appears to have the more general sense of "torment." But who or what is this angel of Satan?

Overall, there have been three lines of interpretation.[33] The first and earliest has its origin in Tertullian, who suggested that Paul was afflicted by head pains, a reasonable assumption, since the verb *kolaphizō* can mean "to beat," or "to strike." Understood in this way, Satan "beat" or "struck" Paul with severe head pains. This line of interpretation (that the thorn refers to a physical illness) has led to other suggestions about the kind of ailment that afflicted Paul, one of the most popular conjectures being an eye ailment, given Paul's remarks in Gal 4:13–16 about the infirmity that brought him to Galatia and the willingness of the Galatians to give him their eyes if they could.

The second line of interpretation has its origin with Chrysostom (*Homily* 26: 2), who was aware of Tertullian's opinion but rejected it since he could not conceive of Paul's body being given over to Satan, since Satan himself had often submitted to Paul. Therefore, noting that in Hebrew "Satan" means "adversary," Chrysostom proposes that the messenger or Satan is Alexander the coppersmith (2 Tim 4:14), Hymenaeus and Philetus (2 Tim 2:17), and all the adversaries of the Word. Although contemporary scholars are less inclined to identify Paul's adversaries so specifically, many follow Chrysostom's lead by viewing Paul's opponents, either in general or those mentioned in chapters 10–13, as his "thorn for the flesh."

The third line of interpretation derives from the manner in which the Vulgate translates the Greek, *stimulus cari* ("sting of the flesh"), which suggests temptations of a sexual nature. This interpretation, which is based on a mistranslation of the Greek, was nearly the universal view in the West until the Reformation, when it was severely criticized by Luther and Calvin (Plummer, 350).

---

32. See Delling, *TDNT*, vol. 7, s.v. *skolops*.

33. The commentaries of Allo (313–23), Furnish (548–49), Plummer (349–51), and Thrall (2:809–18) provide detailed surveys of these lines of interpretation. Thrall (809) summarizes the various approaches under three headings: "(i) an internal psychological state, whether of temptation or of grief; (ii) external opposition; (iii) physical illness or disability."

Although there is no end to speculation about the meaning of the thorn and the angel of Satan, most commentators agree that it is impossible to know for certain what Paul intended. Indeed Paul may have purposely employed the metaphor to conceal as well as to reveal what he means. On the one hand, he reveals that God allowed Satan to torment him in order to protect him from being overcome by pride—something the Corinthians may not have realized. On the other hand, Paul does not reveal what this thorn was, be it the opposition he encountered or some chronic infirmity.

In verse 8, Paul discloses that he did not immediately understand God's purpose in allowing Satan's angel to torment him. Or if he understood it, he had not yet reconciled himself to God's purpose. Consequently, just as Jesus prayed to his Father to let the cup of suffering pass from him (Matt 26:36–46), so Paul prayed to the Lord (Christ) that the thorn, the angel of Satan, might leave him. The language here is rather remarkable, since it is the only example in the nondisputed Pauline correspondence of Paul praying to Christ (Windisch, 388). But since it is Christ who granted Paul "visions and revelations" (v. 1), the prayer is not inappropriate.

The risen Lord, however, refuses Paul's request (v. 9a). Instead he provides his apostle with a new and profound understanding of power and weakness that changed and transformed his life. The divine "favor" (*charis*) that Christ has already granted Paul in calling him is sufficient, for a reason that can be understood only in light of the paradox of the cross: "power is made perfect in weakness." This power is the "grace" or "favor" that Christ has already extended to Paul. But just as the power of the resurrection could not be brought to perfection apart from the suffering of the cross, so the divine favor or grace that Christ granted Paul cannot be perfected or brought to completion apart from the weakness and suffering that accompany apostolic ministry. The thorn for the flesh then is the necessary antidote to the superexaltation that accompanies visions and revelations, the constant reminder of Paul's weakness and dependency on Christ. Without this antidote, it is all too easy to boast in oneself and forget the paradox of the cross that underlies the gospel message.

[9b–10] These verses function as the climax of this unit. Recalling the theme of boasting in weakness introduced in 11:30 and repeated in 12:5, they disclose the paradoxical logic that underlines his understanding of boasting: when Paul is weak, then he is strong. Consequently, Paul will gladly boast in his weaknesses so that the power of Christ may dwell in him. And for the sake of Christ he now delights in his weaknesses. These verses, more than any other, explain Paul's aversion to the kind of boasting in which he has been compelled to engage—boasting that would elevate him in the eyes of others, rather than focus attention on his weakness. The paradox of the gospel that Paul proclaims reveals how power has been made most effective in and through the weakness of the cross.

B. Boasting Foolishly

Making use of a purpose clause, Paul begins by explaining why he gladly boasts in his weaknesses: so that the power of Christ might dwell in him (v. 9b). On the basis of this, he then draws the conclusion toward which he has been moving since 11:1: for the sake of Christ he delights in his weaknesses (v. 10).

In verse 9a the risen Lord answered Paul's request by revealing that "power is made perfect in weakness." Now, in verse 9b, Paul mentions "the power of Christ," clearly indicating that Christ was speaking of his own power. Accordingly, it is the very power of Christ, which Paul has already identified with Christ's grace (v. 9a), that comes to perfection in weakness. Since the risen Lord is no longer subject to weakness, his power is now perfected in and through the weakness of believers such as Paul. In light of this understanding of Christ's power and his own weakness Paul affirms his willingness to boast in his weaknesses. As the purpose clause indicates, when he boasts in his weaknesses, then Christ's power will dwell in him.

Although the compound verb that Paul employs here, *episkēnōsē* ("might dwell in me"; v. 9b), does not occur elsewhere in the New Testament, the simple form of the verb, *skēnoō* ("to settle," or "to take up residence") does. John 1:14 says that "the Word became flesh and *lived* among us," and Rev 21:3 reads, "See, the home of God is among mortals. He will *dwell* with them." In both instances God or God's Word takes up residence and dwells among mortals. In this text, Paul's statement is more personal; the divine "favor" (*charis*), which is the manifestation of Christ's power, takes up residence in Paul's weakness. Although the reality of which Paul writes here may be similar to the experience he relates in Gal 2:20, "it is no longer I who live, but it is Christ who lives in me," Paul now focuses on the experience of Christ that comes from this divine favor.

The theological point that Paul makes here—that Christ will take up residence in him when he is weak—is analogous to a statement that Paul will make about Christ in 13:4, "For indeed he was crucified by reason of weakness, but he lives by reason of the power of God." Thus, just as the power of God took up residence in the weakness of Christ, so the power of Christ now takes up residence in the weakness of Paul.

Recognizing that the power of Christ takes up residence in him, he boasts in his weaknesses. Paul even delights in his weaknesses, for when he is weak, then he is strong (v. 10). The relationship between verse 9b and verse 10 can be set out in this way:

Paul boasts in *weaknesses* in order that Christ's *power* might dwell in him
Paul delights in *weakness* for
when he is *weak* then he is *powerful*

As the structure of the verses shows, the paradox is one of weakness and strength. But whereas in verse 9b Paul refers to Christ's power, in verse 10 he refers to his own power. His power, of course, is not merely his own power but the power he receives from Christ as a divine favor. Accordingly, he participates in the *dynamis* ("power") of Christ because he is weak, and the *dynamis* of Christ resides in him when he is weak. In drawing out this paradox, Paul is *not* saying that weakness *is* power. Rather, weakness becomes the place or the occasion for Christ to manifest power, just as the weakness of the cross was the occasion for God to manifest power in Christ.

To explain what he means by weakness, Paul draws up a brief list of hardships in which his weakness is apparent, "in mistreatment and distress, in persecutions and anguish." At such moments he is weak because others have power and control over his destiny. Precisely at those moments, however, the power of Christ takes up residence in him.

Looking back on Paul's line of argument in this unit, one is struck by the manner in which he has moved from boasting in visions and revelations to boasting in his own weaknesses. Because of these extraordinary revelations, God protected Paul from succumbing to pride by giving him a thorn for the flesh. Although Paul did not immediately understand the reason for this, he soon learned that the power of Christ comes to perfection in weakness. Thus even Paul's visions and revelations have taught him to boast in his weaknesses.

7. Peroration (12:11–13)

12:11 I have become a fool.[a] You[b] drove me to it. For I should have been commended by you. For in nothing am I inferior to the super-apostles, even though I am nothing. 12 The signs of an[c] apostle were worked among you with unfailing[d] endurance, by signs and wonders and mighty deeds. 13 For in what respect were you worse off than the other churches except that I myself did not burden you financially?[e] Forgive me this injustice!

a. Many manuscripts include the participle "by boasting" (*kauchōmenos*), which is not found in the manuscript tradition represented by P⁴⁶ and ℵ. The participle was undoubtedly introduced to clarify that Paul has become a fool by his boasting.

b. The Greek pronoun *hymeis* ("you") makes this an emphatic statement, highlighting the responsibility of the Corinthians.

c. The Greek has the definite article "the" before "apostle."

d. Literally, "all." The sense is that these apostolic signs were worked as Paul endured hardships.

e. The word "financially" has been supplied for the sake of clarification.

Verses 11–13 serve as the peroration to this section, which began with Paul's appeal to the Corinthians to bear with him in a little foolishness (11:1). As such it highlights themes that Paul wishes to reinforce and serves as a transition to

B. Boasting Foolishly

the last section of chapters 10–13, in which he will focus on his third and final visit to Corinth (12:12–13:10).

Paul begins with a retrospective statement in which he acknowledges that he has become a fool by engaging in the very boasting he has sought to avoid. Excusing himself, he blames the Corinthians for forcing him to act foolishly. For since they did see fit to commend him when the intruding apostles came to Corinth, he had to commend himself, thereby becoming a fool. Alluding to the super-apostles one last time, he asserts, as he did in 11:5, that he is not at all inferior to them, since the signs of an apostle were worked in their midst through his ministry. Paul then concludes by caustically asking the Corinthians in what way—apart from not burdening them—his ministry has left them inferior to other churches. The remark about not burdening the Corinthians recalls his earlier discussion about his refusal to accept the community's support (11:7–15) and serves as a transition to the next unit, where that topic will be taken up again in conjunction with Paul's third and final visit to Corinth (12:14–18).

The material begins with a retrospective statement in which Paul blames the Corinthians for not commending him (v. 11a). He then explains why the Corinthians should have commended him (vv. 11b–12), concluding with a rhetorical question and mock apology (v. 13). The unit may be structured in this way:

v. 11a   Paul's foolishness and the Corinthians' responsibility
vv. 11b–12   Why the Corinthians should have commended Paul
   v. 11b   Paul not inferior to the super-apostles
   v. 12   the signs of an apostle worked in their midst
v. 13   Rhetorical question and mock apology

[12:11a] The manner in which Paul begins this unit, "I have become a fool," is clearly retrospective and indicates that there will be no more boasting. There is also a sense of regret in this remark. For although Paul has shown that he is not inferior to the super-apostles, he has done so at great personal cost. He has become a fool by engaging in the very boasting he sought to avoid.

Plummer (357) notes that the perfect tense of the verb ("I have become," *gegona*) is emphatic, giving the sense "that what was expected or predicted has come to pass." At the outset of this section Paul indicated that what he was about to do was an exercise in foolishness (11:1). And even though he insisted that he was not a fool (11:16; also see 12:6), he acknowledged that his boasting was foolishness (11:17). But now, even though everything he has said is true, he realizes that he has indeed become a fool because of his foolish boasting.

Somewhat unexpectedly, however, he blames the Corinthians for his predicament. For if they had commended him by boasting on his behalf, there would have been no need for him to commend himself by boasting on his own behalf. Paul's use of the verb "to commend" (*synistēmi*), which occurs throughout this letter (3:1; 4:2; 5:12; 6:4; 7:11; 10:12; 10:18), comes to a climax. The Corinthians, or certain factions within the community, have accused him of commending himself and lacking letters of recommendation (3:1). Paul, however, sees no need for such letters, since the community is his letter of recommendation (3:2). If he commends himself, it is before God and everyone's conscience (4:2). What he has tried to do is to provide the Corinthians with an opportunity for boasting on his behalf so that they will have something to say "to those who boast in appearance and not in the heart" (5:12). Paul has made a fool of himself because the Corinthians have failed in the task of commending him.

[11b–12] Having said that if the Corinthians had commended him it would not have been necessary for him to commend himself by foolish boasting, Paul now provides the Corinthians with two reasons why they should have commended him. First, he is not inferior to the super-apostles. Second, the signs of an apostle were performed in their midst through his ministry.

Paul's first reason (that he is not inferior to the super-apostles) is a clear and strong echo of what he wrote at the beginning of this section, "In no way do I think of myself as being inferior to the super-apostles" (11:5). This second reference to the super-apostles clearly indicates that all of Paul's boasting between these two remarks (11:5 and 12:12) has had the super-apostles in view and that the super-apostles are to be identified with the apostles whom Paul accused of commending themselves and intruding upon his missionary field (see 10:12–18). These super-apostles accepted, and perhaps even demanded as their apostolic right, the financial support of the Corinthian community (11:12–15). They may also have come to Corinth with letters of recommendation, causing the Corinthians to ask for Paul's letters of recommendation. If the Corinthians had commended Paul when the super-apostles and their partisans had criticized him, then there would have been no need for him to engage in boasting. But since they did not, it was necessary for Paul to show that he is not inferior to the super-apostles. He has done this by his boasting, but his boasting has made him a fool.

In reaffirming that he is not inferior to the super-apostles, Paul adds, "even if I am nothing," leading some commentators to ask if Paul is ironically responding to a charge levied against him by the super-apostles and their partisans (Martin, 427) or if he is employing a figure of speech current in philosophical circles (Furnish, 555). Although both suggestions are possible, one should also reckon with the possibility that the remark "is Paul's honest evaluation of his status before God" (Garland, 528), since he has already acknowledged that his qualification for ministry comes from God rather than from himself (3:5). Such a self-evaluation coheres with Paul's willingness to boast in his weaknesses so that the power of Christ might dwell in him (12:9). Thus even if Paul was employing a Socratic topos, he understands it in an entirely new way. And if he is responding to an accusation, he gladly accepts it; for even if he is nothing, the power of Christ is at work in him (12:9b–10).

B. Boasting Foolishly

Paul's second reason why the Corinthians should have commended him introduces an argument that he did not develop during the fool's speech but that the Corinthians would have known from his ministry and could not deny: "the signs" (*ta sēmeia*) that were worked in their midst when he was among them. According to BDAG *sēmeion* can refer to "a sign or distinguishing mark whereby something is known" or "to an event that is an indication or confirmation of intervention by transcendent powers," thus, a miracle. The passive voice of the verb that follows (*kateirgasthē*, "were worked"), however, as well as the reference to "signs," "wonders," and "mighty deeds," suggests that Paul has some sort of miraculous activity in view. That is, his ministry was attended by miraculous signs that God worked through him in the midst of the Corinthian community. Although it was not these signs that made Paul an apostle (since God had already called him to be an apostle), they confirmed his apostleship.

Paul specifies the signs that God worked through his ministry as "signs and wonders and mighty deeds." The use of this threefold expression highlights different aspects of the miraculous. Understood as "signs," miracles point to the transcendent power that effects them. Understood as "wonders," they astound people because they are the transcendent work of God. Understood as "mighty deeds," they indicate the surpassing power of God, who effects them. In most instances, the biblical writings tend to couple "signs" with "wonders" (Exod 7:3; Deut 4:34; 6:22; 7:19; Acts 2:43; 4:30; 5:12; 6:8; 7:36; 14:3; 15:12), whereas the threefold expression that Paul employs here occurs less frequently, for example, Acts 2:22, where it appears in reference to Jesus. In Rom 15:18–19 Paul employs the three words together but with "signs" and "wonders" as manifestations of divine power: "For I will not venture to speak of anything except what Christ has accomplished through me to win obedience from the Gentiles, by word and deed, by the power of signs and wonders (*en dynamei sēmeiōn kai teratōn*), by the power of the Spirit of God." As in this text, Paul does not attribute the power to himself but to another, in this case, Christ.

What Paul writes here and elsewhere (Gal 3:5; 1 Thess 1:5) clearly indicates that miraculous activity played an important role in his ministry. Indeed it is difficult to imagine Paul making such a statement about himself if God had not effected miraculous signs through him, since the Corinthians had firsthand knowledge of his ministry among them. Thus the Acts of the Apostles, which portrays Paul as a miracle worker, witnesses to an important dimension of his ministry, even if Acts does not recount any of the miracles that God worked through Paul at Corinth.

Lest the emphasis be put in the wrong place, Paul notes that the signs that God worked through him were done "with unfailing endurance." Such "endurance" (*hypomonē*) headed the hardship list of 6:4–10 by which Paul commended himself as God's minister "in great endurance" (6:4). Its presence here indicates that it was in the midst of Paul's apostolic hardships that God worked such miraculous signs. Thus it was not apart from hardships but in the midst of them that God worked signs through Paul.

[13] Paul brings his peroration to a close with a rhetorical question and a mock apology. Having reminded the Corinthians that the signs of an apostle were worked in their midst, he asks in what way they are worse off than other churches. Aware that his refusal to accept their support is a bone of contention between him and them, he acknowledges that there is only one difference. Whereas some churches have supported those who preached the gospel to them, and he has accepted support from some congregations, Paul identifies this as the one difference between the Corinthians and other churches. As in 11:9, however, he portrays such financial support as "burdening" the community, the very thing that he has refused to do to the Corinthians. Understood in this way, Paul's ministry has not left the Corinthians worse off than the other churches. On the contrary, because of his unselfish service they are better off financially. Therefore, echoing the rhetorical question of 11:7, in which he asked if he committed a sin by abasing himself (by supporting himself) in order to exalt them, he caustically asks them to forgive this "injustice," which, of course, is no injustice, just as his decision to support himself was not a sin. The issue, however, cannot be resolved with rhetorical questions and mock apologies, and Paul will deal with it again in the next unit as he discusses his third and final visit to Corinth.

Paul's line of thought in 11:1–12:13 can be summarized in this way. Fearful that the community he has betrothed to Christ is being led astray by the intruding apostles who have commended themselves to the Corinthians and accepted their support, Paul reluctantly embarks upon a project of foolish boasting to show the Corinthians that he is not inferior to these super-apostles. In doing so, he distinguishes himself from the intruding apostles in two ways. First, whereas they burden the community by accepting financial support, he does not. Second, whereas they take their boasting seriously, Paul knows that it is foolish to boast except in one's weaknesses.

C. Preparations for Paul's Third and Final Visit
2 Corinthians 12:14–13:10

The material of 12:14–13:10 is the third and final section of 10:1–13:10, which, in turn, is the third and final part of 2 Corinthians. In the first section (10:1–18), Paul warned the Corinthians of the boldness with which he is capable of acting when present, despite accusations that his bodily presence does not match the boldness of his letters (10:1–11), and he criticized those who had intruded upon

C. Preparations for Paul's Third and Final Visit

his missionary assignment (10:12–18). In the second section (11:1–12:13), Paul called the intruders "super-apostles" who are, in fact, false apostles. Insisting that he is not inferior to these super-apostles (11:5), he reluctantly engaged in a project of foolish boasting in order to show the Corinthians what they should have known: that he is not inferior to these super-apostles (12:11). With this boasting behind him, and having established his superiority to the super-apostles, in this section (12:14–13:10) Paul turns his attention to his third and final visit to Corinth, a visit to which he had already alluded in the first section (10:1–18), when he warned the Corinthians of the boldness he will exercise if necessary when he comes to Corinth (10:2, 11).

This final section (12:14–13:10) of Part 3 consists of two units (12:14–21 and 13:1–10), each of which begins with an announcement of Paul's impending visit (12:14; 13:1). In the first unit (12:14–21) Paul begins with the question of financial support, insisting that he will not burden the community financially by his visit and that neither he nor his associates have taken advantage of the Corinthians (vv. 14–18). He then expresses his fear that, because of the moral laxity of many, the Corinthians may not be prepared for his visit (vv. 19–21). In the second unit (13:1–10) Paul warns those who have not yet repented of their moral laxity that he will not spare them (vv. 1–4). He then calls upon the community to test and examine itself (vv. 5–9), so that he will not have to act severely when he comes (v. 10).

Since the first seven chapters of this letter deal with the events and questions surrounding Paul's second (painful) visit to Corinth, this section, which focuses on Paul's third and final visit, brings the letter to closure. The crisis of the second visit has been resolved (chaps. 1–7), and Paul has exhorted the Corinthians to resume the collection they began last year (chaps. 8–9). Therefore, he can now return to Corinth for his third and final visit, a visit that will bring about complete reconciliation with the church if the Corinthians heed his warnings about the intruding apostles, and if those who have sinned finally repent.

1. The Announcement of the Visit (12:14–21)

12:14 Behold, I am ready to come to you this third time,[a] and I will not be a burden; for I do not seek your possessions[b] but you. For it is not children who ought to store up treasure for their parents but parents for their children. 15 I[c] will gladly spend and be spent for the sake of your lives.[d] If I love you the more, am I to be loved the less?[e]

16 Agreed.[f] I did not burden you. But, being crafty, you say,[g] I took advantage of you. 17 I did not defraud you through any of those I sent to you, did I?[h] 18 I appealed to Titus and sent the brother with him. Titus did not defraud you, did he? Did we not walk in the same spirit?[i] Did we not walk in the same footsteps?

19 All this time[j] you have been thinking that we are defending ourselves to you.[k] We are speaking before God, in Christ. Everything, beloved, is for your edification. 20 For I am afraid lest somehow, when I come, I may not find you such as I wish, and you may not find me such as you wish.[l] I fear[m] lest somehow there be discord, jealousy, outbursts of anger, disputes, slanders, whisperings, conceit, disorders. 21 I fear[n] lest when I come, my God may humble me again[o] before you, and I shall have to grieve for many of those who sinned previously and have not repented of the vileness, sexual immorality, and licentiousness with which they acted.

a. Grammatically, "this third time" (*triton touto*) could modify "I am ready," in which case Paul would be saying that this is the third time that he is ready to come to Corinth. The clear statement in 13:1 that Paul is coming to Corinth *for a third time*, however, indicates that the phrase modifies the infinitive "to come" (*elthein*).

b. The phrase "your possessions" translates *ta hymōn* ("the things of you").

c. The use of the personal pronoun *egō* makes the "I" emphatic.

d. "Your lives" translates *tōn psychōn* ("your souls").

e. This phrase could be rendered as a declarative statement as well as a question, but most commentators take it as a question. There are a number of variant readings that, if adopted, would result in different translations. This translation follows the text of ℵ* and A, which read the finite verb *agapō* ("I love") rather than the participle *agapōn*.

f. Literally, "so be it" (*estō*).

g. The phrase "you say" is supplied because Paul seems to be referring to a real or hypothetical objection raised by the Corinthians or the super-apostles.

h. The contorted order of the Greek sentence has been rearranged for the sake of translation. This question and the next are introduced by Greek particles that indicate the question expects a negative answer.

i. The word "spirit" is not capitalized since it does not refer to the Holy Spirit.

j. Many manuscripts read "again" (*palin*). The reading *palai* ("all this time"), however, is well attested (ℵ*, A, B), even though this is the only occurrence of the word in Paul's writings.

k. The sentence could also be taken as a question (so Thrall, 2:858–59).

l. Literally, "and I will not be found by you such as you wish."

m. The verb "I fear" is supplied since the phrase depends on the main verb, "I am afraid," in v. 20.

n. As above, the verb "I fear" is supplied since this phrase is also dependent on the main verb in v. 20.

o. While the adverb *palin* ("again") could be taken with the participle *elthontos* ("when I come"), most commentators take it with the verb *tapeinōsē*.

The material of this unit is related to the preceding unit by the verb "to burden" (*katanarkaō*), which occurs at the end of that unit (12:13) and at the beginning of this unit (12:14). Paul has not been a financial burden to the Corinthians

C. Preparations for Paul's Third and Final Visit

in the past (12:13), and he will not be a burden to them during his third and final visit (12:14). He has already dealt with the question of financial support in the context of comparing himself with the super-apostles (11:5–11), and he now takes up that question once more, this time in the context of his third and final visit, in order to dispel any suspicion that his refusal to accept support from the Corinthians is a pretext for taking advantage of them.

The material of this unit is related to what follows by the verb *proamartanō* ("to sin previously," "to sin earlier") which occurs at the end of this unit (12:21) and at the beginning of the next (13:2). Thus at the end of this unit Paul expresses his fear that his third visit will find him grieving over those who sinned earlier and have not repented (12:21), and at the beginning of the next unit he warns such people that he will not spare them when he comes (13:2).

Paul begins by announcing that his third visit will not be a burden to the community (vv. 14–15). He then deals with suspicions that his practice of self-support is merely a ruse to take advantage of the community (vv. 16–18). He concludes by expressing his fears about the impending visit (vv. 19–21). The unit can be outlined as follows:

vv. 14–15 The visit announced
v. 14 Paul will not be a burden
v. 15 Paul's willingness to be spent
vv. 16–18 Questions about Paul's motives
v. 16 Paul has been devious
vv. 17–18 Paul's response
vv. 19–21 Paul's anxiety about the visit
v. 19 Paul has not been defending himself
vv. 20–21 The moral climate of the community

[12:14–15] Having dealt with the super-apostles who are intruding upon his missionary assignment, Paul turns his attention to preparations for his third and final visit to Corinth. His first visit was the occasion when he initially preached the gospel to the Corinthians (1 Cor 2:1–5; Acts 18:1–17), and the second was the painful visit to which he refers when he writes, "For I determined not to come to you in painful circumstances again" (2 Cor 2:1). Since Paul has encouraged the Corinthians to resume the collection for Jerusalem, which they began last year but which was disrupted by the crisis between him and the community (8:1–9:15), he undoubtedly hopes to receive the collection on this third visit. The third visit will also be an occasion for him to spend more time with the Corinthians, as he had promised in 1 Cor 16:6, before the events of the painful visit had transpired. But it will also be an opportunity to see if the community has heeded his admonitions about the intruding apostles and to determine if those who have sinned have repented. Thus the final visit will decide whether or not the community is fully reconciled to its apostle.[34]

Aware that the Corinthians have interpreted his decision not to accept their offering of financial assistance as a refusal of their friendship and as an indication that he does not love them (11:11), Paul returns to this issue, which he had already discussed in 11:5–15 and 12:13, and he insists that his visit will not burden them, that is, they will not have to support him. Although Paul presents his intentions in the best possible light (he will not burden them), he realizes that his insistence on supporting himself remains a point of contention between him and them. Consequently he provides the Corinthians with two reasons for this decision, each introduced by the conjunction *gar* ("for," "because"). First, he will not be a burden to them because he seeks them rather than what belongs to them. Second, he will not be a burden to them because parents ought to lay up treasures for their children rather than children for their parents.

The first of these supporting statements highlights the purity of Paul's intentions and implies that the intruding apostles have ulterior motives. For whereas he is primarily concerned with the welfare of the Corinthians, the intruders are concerned about what the Corinthians can do for them. The second statement is closely related to the first and develops Paul's argument further. He is concerned for the welfare of the Corinthians because, unlike the intruding apostles, he is the founding father of the community, and they are his beloved children. As he writes in 1 Corinthians, "I am not writing this to make you ashamed, but to admonish you *as my beloved children*. For though you might have ten thousand guardians in Christ, you do not have many fathers. Indeed, in Christ Jesus *I became your father* through the gospel" (1 Cor 4:14–15, emphasis added). Because he is the founder, and so the parent of the congregation, he refuses to view his relationship to the Corinthians in terms of the client-benefactor relationship that the Corinthians would have preferred to impose upon him, a relationship whereby he would become their client and they would be his benefactors. Although such a relationship may have been suitable to some peripatetic teachers and philosophers and perhaps to the super-apostles, it was unacceptable to Paul, since it had all the potential for compromising the gospel he preached.

---

34. The reference to a third visit in 12:14 and 13:1 is a strong argument against viewing chaps. 10–13 as all, or even as part, of the harsh letter written in tears to which Paul refers in 2:4 and 7:8, since Paul wrote that letter after his second (painful) visit as a substitute for a third visit (see 2:1–4). When Paul writes that he is about to make his third visit to Corinth, one must suppose that the harsh letter has already been sent and that the issues surrounding the painful visit have been settled.

Niels Hyldahl ("Die Frage nach der literarischen Einheit des Zweiten Korintherbriefes," *ZNW* 64 [1973]: 289–306) argues that Paul visited Corinth only once and that there was no second (painful visit), and he interprets 12:14 to mean that Paul is now preparing for a third time to come to Corinth, the other attempts being unsuccessful. Although the grammar might allow for such an interpretation of 12:14, what Paul writes in 13:1 clearly indicates that this will be his third visit.

C. Preparations for Paul's Third and Final Visit

Paul, of course, is not saying that children are exempt from aiding and supporting their parents in time of need, nor is he arguing against what he so vigorously supported in 1 Cor 9:1–14, the right of apostolic workers to receive support from the gospel they preach, a right he has chosen not to exercise (1 Cor 9:12). He employs this proverb-like saying to support his decision in this particular instance. For he wants to show the Corinthians that, far from rejecting their offer of friendship, his decision is an expression of parental affection for them. Because he is their parent and not their client, he will not burden them with the responsibility of supporting him, but like a good parent he will store up treasure for them. Since "treasure" can hardly refer to material goods in this instance, Paul is undoubtedly employing this proverb-like saying metaphorically. The gospel is the treasure that he stores up for them by his apostolic service to them.

In verse 15, Paul draws his argument to a conclusion. Since he is their parent who seeks their welfare, he will gladly spend and be spent for them. As in the case of the proverb about storing up treasure, the commercial language that Paul employs here is metaphorical. In addition to spending his own resources so that the community will not be burdened by him, he will pour out his very self and allow himself to be poured out in apostolic service to them, a point he eloquently makes in Phil 2:17, when, faced with the prospect of death, he writes, "But even if I am being poured out as a libation over the sacrifice and offering of your faith, I am glad and rejoice with all of you." Paul's argument contains an implicit syllogism that, when reconstructed, can be stated as follows:

- *Major premise*: It is the duty of parents to store up treasures for their children.
- *Minor premise*: Paul is the parent of the Corinthians, and they are his children.
- *Conclusion*: Therefore, rather than burden them by seeking their financial support, Paul will store up treasure for the Corinthians to the point of spending himself and being spent for their sake.

But logic rarely settles arguments. Therefore Paul concludes with a rhetorical question intended to rouse the pathos of the Corinthians and provide yet another answer to the question that he raised in 11:11 when, explaining his decision not to be supported by them, he asked, "Why? Because I do not love you?" Without offending or scolding the Corinthians, he now provides them with an opportunity to answer the question for themselves. Asking if he is to be loved the less for loving them the more, he implicitly invites them to respond. If they have been moved by the pathos of his question, then they will reply, "Of course not! The more you love us, the more we will love you!" Such a response is what Paul would most like to hear. Realist that he is, however, he understands that there may be lingering suspicions about the purity of his intentions.

[16–18] Paul now takes a new tack. Either in response to accusations made against him, or in an attempt to forestall such accusation, he raises an objection to what he has just said: the claim that his visit will not burden the community is merely a ruse for him to deceive them in some other way. If Paul is responding to real accusations, then the super-apostles or their partisans may have accused him of using or intending to use funds from the collection for his own purpose. Whatever lies behind the statement that Paul is "crafty" (*panourgos*), this is not the first time that he has dealt with this issue. In 4:2 he wrote, "we have renounced hidden deeds of which one is ashamed, *not acting cunningly*, not falsifying the word of God, but in full disclosure of the truth, commending ourselves before God, to everyone's conscience." Moreover, in 11:3 he implied that it is the super-apostles who have been crafty in dealing with the Corinthians, and he expressed his fear that just as the serpent deceived Eve "by its cunning," so the minds of the Corinthians are being corrupted, presumably by the cunning preaching of the super-apostles. Having been accused of cunning and trickery in dealing with the Corinthians, Paul replies that the real cunning comes from the intruding apostles.

Rather than respond directly to the accusation, Paul asks four rhetorical questions. The first two expect a negative answer and the last two a positive response. In each of the first two questions, Paul employs the verb *pleonekteō* ("to defraud," "to cheat," "to take advantage of"), which may suggest fiscal misconduct of some kind, such as might occur in the arrangement and management of the collection. It is the same verb that Paul used in 7:2 when he wrote, "We have injured no one. We have corrupted no one. We have *taken advantage* of no one." But whereas in 7:2 he used the verb in reference to himself, now he employs it in relation to those whom he has sent to represent him to the community, suggesting that if any of his delegates defrauded the Corinthians, then he has defrauded them. Paul can raise these questions because he is utterly confident of the response he will receive from the Corinthians, who know from their own experience that none of the delegates whom he sent has cheated or defrauded them. Indeed, after Titus returned from Corinth, he told Paul how obedient the community had been to him (Titus) and how the Corinthians received him with fear and trembling (7:15).

The argument Paul makes here is predicated on the intimate relation that exists between him and his delegates.[35] His delegates represent him not only in word but in deed. That is why, in the final two rhetorical questions, both of

---

35. For an informative study of the "delegates" or "envoys" in the ancient world, see Margaret M. Mitchell, "New Testament Envoys in the Context of Greco-Roman Diplomatic and Epistolary Conventions: The Example of Timothy and Titus," *JBL* (1992): 641–62. She concludes her article, "Hardly mere substitutes for the universally preferable Pauline presence, these envoys were consciously sent by Paul to play a complex and crucial intermediary role that he could not play even if present himself" (662).

C. Preparations for Paul's Third and Final Visit

which expect positive answers, Paul can ask if he and Titus did not walk in the same spirit and in the same steps. Thus Paul assumes that the Corinthians can evaluate his character by evaluating the character of his delegates. Once more his reasoning depends upon an implicit syllogism that, when made explicit, can be set forth in this way:

- *Major premise*: Paul's delegates represent him in word and deed.
- *Minor premise*: Paul's delegates did not defraud or take advantage of the Corinthians.
- *Conclusion*: Paul did not take advantage of the Corinthians.

What Paul writes here about Titus and the brother whom he sent with him to the Corinthians raises an important question about the number of visits Titus made to Corinth, a question that has important implications for the literary integrity of 2 Corinthians. Simply stated, the problem is this: Is the visit to which Paul refers in verse 18, when he speaks of sending Titus and the brother to Corinth, the same visit that is described in 8:16–9:5, where Paul recommends the delegation of Titus and the two brothers who were to prepare the collection for Jerusalem? If it is, then it would appear that chapters 10–13 were written after chapters 1–9, since Paul would be looking back at that visit as something that had already taken place, or at least was far advanced.

However, it is not so apparent from 12:18 that Paul is referring to the collection visit of 8:16–9:5, since he speaks of Titus and *two* unnamed brothers in 8:16–9:5 but of only one brother in 12:18. Furthermore, Paul's statement in 8:6, that he "appealed to Titus that as he began so he should complete this generous gift among you," suggests that Titus had already visited Corinth in order to arrange for the collection when the Corinthians first undertook the collection "last year" (8:10). Consequently Titus may have visited Corinth on at least three occasions: first, when he first undertook the work of the collection, 8:6; second, when he delivered the harsh letter to the Corinthians, 2:12–13 and 7:5–16; third, to complete the work of the collection, 8:16–9:5. If this reconstruction is accurate, then in 12:18 Paul is referring to Titus's first visit to Corinth, the one alluded to in 8:10, and Paul's statement in 12:18 is not an argument against the literary integrity of 2 Corinthians.

[19–21] In these verses, Paul expresses anxiety about his upcoming visit. He begins with a statement that clarifies what he has been trying to do in this letter: to build up and edify the community (v. 19). He then supports this statement by expressing his fear that when he comes he will find the community beset by strife and factions (v. 20), and he will again be humbled because he will have to grieve over those who have not repented (v. 21). Thus he will not find the community as he wishes, and the community will not find him as it wishes.

Given what Paul has just said in verses 16–18 and what he has been saying throughout this letter, the statement in verse 19 (that he has not been defending himself to the Corinthians) is somewhat surprising, since he has, in fact, defended himself in a variety of ways. For example, he found it necessary to explain the change in his travel plans and why he wrote the harsh letter. He explained his new covenant ministry and why he does not need letters of recommendations to the Corinthians. And he has just engaged in foolish boasting to show the Corinthians that he is not inferior to the super-apostles who have intruded upon his missionary assignment. On the basis of what Paul has written, one can readily understand why commentators view parts or the whole of 2 Corinthians as an apologia for his apostolic ministry (see 1 Cor 9:3, where Paul actually speaks of making such a "defense"). And indeed this is how Paul himself supposes that the Corinthians have interpreted his letter thus far, since he writes, "All this time you have been thinking that we are defending ourselves to you." Consequently, when he writes "We are speaking before God, in Christ" (*katenanti theou en Christō laloumen*), he is making an important statement about how *he* understands what he has been doing. Namely, he has been speaking with complete and total honesty to the Corinthians in God's presence as a Christian. He has not been on trial before the Corinthians. To the contrary, only God can judge him (see Paul's statement in 1 Cor 4:1–5, where he makes a similar point), and all must appear before the judgment seat of Christ (5:10). Therefore, Paul speaks before God, in Christ.

Paul uses the same language in 2:17, where he writes, "For we are not, as so many, trading on the word of God; rather we speak before God in Christ (*katenanti theou en Christō laloumen*) from sincerity, as from God." This language finds an echo in 4:2, where he avers that he has not falsified the word of God "but in full disclosure of the truth" commends himself "before God (*enōpion tou theou*), to everyone's conscience." Likewise in 5:11 he says, "Therefore, knowing the fear of the Lord, we persuade people, but we are known to God (*theō de pephanerōmetha*), and I hope to be known even to your consciences." In these texts, Paul insists that the integrity of his conduct is evident to everyone's conscience because he speaks and acts in God's presence. Therefore, although his letter is apologetic in tone, he does not view himself as a defendant before the tribunal of the Corinthians. Rather, in God's presence he speaks the truth for their edification.

In writing that he has spoken for their "edification" (*oikodomēs*; v. 19), Paul echoes what he wrote in 10:8 about the authority that the Lord gave him "for building up (*eis oikodomēn*), and not for destruction," a phrase that he will repeat in the closing of the letter, when he will again refer to "the authority that the Lord has given me for building up (*eis oikodomēn*) and not for tearing down" (13:10). Thus his purpose has been to speak as honestly as possible in God's presence in order to edify or build up the community. This is why Paul

C. Preparations for Paul's Third and Final Visit

found it so difficult to engage in boasting; he knew that boasting does not build up the community, unless it is boasting in one's weakness. Like Paul's statement in 5:12 ("We are not commending ourselves to you again but giving you an opportunity for boasting on behalf of us, so that you might have something to say to those who boast in appearance and not in the heart"), this verse is a key text for understanding Paul's purpose in writing to the Corinthians. He does not write to defend himself to them but to provide them with an opportunity to boast in him. In effect, it is the Corinthians who must defend Paul.

Having explained what he has been doing, in verses 20–21 Paul expresses concern about his impending visit. On the one hand, he is afraid that he will find a community torn by strife. On the other, he fears that God will humble him once more. In the first instance, he will not find the community as he would like; in the second, the community will not find him as it would like. Both statements need further explanation.

First, Paul is fearful that he will not find the community as he wishes. Instead of a community reconciled and at peace, he fears that he will find a community marked by "discord, jealousy, outbursts of anger, disputes, slanders, whisperings, conceits, disorders." This list of eight "vices" is similar to other lists found in Paul's letters, especially Rom 1:29–31; 13:13; and Gal 5:19–21. Most of the vices listed here can also be found in other Pauline letters, often in lists of vices.

> discord (*eris*) Rom 1:29; 13:13; 1 Cor 1:11; 3:3; Gal 5:20;
>   Phil 1:15; 1 Tim 6:4; Titus 3:9
> jealousy (*zēlos*) Rom 13:13; 1 Cor 3:3; Gal 5:20
> outbursts of anger (*thymoi*) Gal 5:20; Eph 4:31
> disputes (*eritheiai*) Rom 2:8; Gal 5:20; Phil 1:17; 2:3
> slanders (*kataliai*) Rom 1:30
> whisperings (*psithyrismoi*) Rom 1:29
> conceits (*physiōmoi*, noun) only here, but to be conceited
>   (*physioō*, verb) 1 Cor 4:6, 18, 19; 5:2; 8:1; 13:4
> disorders (*akatastasiai*) 1 Cor 14:33

From one point of view, this vice list is somewhat formulaic, since most of these terms appear elsewhere. Moreover, the first three items occur in the same order in Gal 5:19–21 (see Gal 5:20). Nonetheless, it is likely that Paul had the situation of the Corinthian community in mind, especially since the first of these vices, "discord" (or "rivalry"), figures so prominently in the difficulties that he originally faced at Corinth (1 Cor 1:11; 3:3), as does the reference to "conceits." The list gives the impression that the Corinthian community suffers from discord and disputes occasioned by jealousy, anger, and conceit, and that the whisperings and slanders of many are leading to further disorders. Although Paul does not identify the cause of this situation, one suspects that factions may have resulted at Corinth because some have sided with the intruding apostles against Paul, whereas others have remained loyal to him.

Second, Paul is fearful that the Corinthians will not find him as they wish. For, even though he has sent them a harsh letter, to this point in their relationship he has dealt with and appealed to them "through the meekness and clemency of Christ" (10:1). And even though they have treated him as if he were on trial, he has not reciprocated in kind. Since he can act boldly if necessary (10:2), this is precisely how he will act toward them, if he must, when he comes to Corinth. What he says here, then, recalls what he wrote in 1 Cor 4:21, "What would you prefer? Am I to come to you with a stick, or with love in a spirit of gentleness?"[36]

Paul understands that if it is necessary for him to act boldly and punish the community, it will be for him a moment not of personal victory but of humiliation. Thus in verse 21 he writes, "I fear lest when I come again, my God may humble me again before you." The precise meaning of this verse is difficult to determine for two reasons. First, the adverb "again" can be taken with the Greek participle *elthōn* ("when I come") or with the verb *tapeinōsē* ("may humble"). In the first instance, Paul would be saying that when he *comes again*, then God may humble him. In the second, he would be saying that God will *humble him again*, raising the question of when God humbled him earlier. Second, the identification of God as the subject of the action raises the questions why and how God will humble Paul. Since the answer to the first question is somewhat dependent upon the second, it is best to begin with the latter.

Chrysostom (*Homily* 28: 2) provides some guidance when he notes that if Paul's work had not been for the sake of God, then Paul would not have paid any attention or been anxious about the situation at Corinth. Paul's work, however, is not his own but belongs to God, who has made him his coworker (6:1). When Paul speaks of God humbling him before the Corinthians, therefore, he does so because he is doing God's work and not merely his own. Put another way, Paul is *not* saying that God will humble him to punish him. Rather, Paul is revealing his profound understanding of himself as God's coworker who endures everything for the sake of God. God humbles his coworkers by causing them to endure the insults and disobedience of others. Calvin (167) writes, "Their [the Corinthians'] progress in holiness would have been the honour and glory of Paul's apostleship, but being in the grip of so many faults, they had instead brought disgrace upon him."

---

36. Although Paul is not referring to the same visit in 1 Cor 4:21 to which he is referring here, 1 Cor 4:21 points to the need for ongoing reform at Corinth in regard to the problems of factions and divisions with which Paul deals in 1 Cor 1–4, and the ongoing problems of immorality and participation in sacral banquets with which he deals in 1 Cor 5–6 and 8–10, respectively. Paul may have hoped that his letter would be sufficient to bring about reform, but he is aware that he may still have to deal with these issues when he comes to Corinth.

C. Preparations for Paul's Third and Final Visit

If Paul thinks of God humbling him, as described above, then it is easier to understand what he means when he writes that he is fearful that God will humble him *again*. In writing "again," Paul is most likely referring to his second and painful visit. He made that visit as Christ's apostle and God's coworker, and the insults he endured then were for the sake of the gospel. When someone injured or insulted him (2:5–11; 7:12), therefore, and when the community did not come to his support, Paul was humbled in their midst by God for the sake of the gospel he preached.

In the final part of verse 21 Paul expresses his fear that he may have to grieve for those who sinned previously but still have not repented of their vileness, immorality, and licentiousness. The introduction of this second but shorter list of vices suggests that Paul is addressing two issues. On the one hand, there is the problem of general strife and disorder within the community. On the other, it appears that a serious situation of gross immorality still infects certain members of the community. If the immoral do not repent by the time he arrives, Paul's grieving for them will be part of the humiliation that he will have to endure as God's coworker, since such immoral behavior contradicts the very nature of the sanctified new covenant community that Paul has established at Corinth.

The three vices that Paul lists in verse 21 appear frequently in his writings, and all three occur in a slightly different order in the vice list of Gal 5:19–21 (see v. 19). The first, "vileness" (*akatharsia*), refers to "a state of moral corruption" (BDAG), especially in sexual matters. It also occurs in Rom 1:24; 6:19; Gal 5:19; Eph 4:19; 5:3; Col 3:5; and 1 Thess 2:3; 4:7. The last reference is especially interesting, since Paul reminds the Thessalonians that God did not call them to *akatharsia* but to holiness. The second, "immorality" (*porneia*), is a general word that covers a wide range of sexual misconduct, as well as idolatry, which is often associated with it. It stands at the beginning of the vice list of Gal 5:19–21. In 1 Cor 6:18 Paul exhorts his converts to flee all *porneia*, and in 1 Thess 4:3 he appeals to them to abstain from *porneia* because God's will for them is their sanctification. *Porneia* also occurs in 1 Cor 5:1; 6:13; 7:2; Eph 5:3; and Col 3:5. The third item, "licentiousness" (*aselgeia*), refers to a "lack of self-constraint which involves one in conduct that violates what is socially acceptable" (BDAG). Such conduct is often sexual in nature, as seems to be the case here. The term also occurs in Rom 13:13; Gal 5:19; and Eph 4:19.

Joined together, as they are here and in Gal 5:19, the words of this list suggest that there is still a serious problem of sexual immorality at Corinth, despite Paul's strong admonitions in 1 Cor 5–6. Paul had apparently warned the Corinthians about such immorality on the occasion of his second (painful) visit, and now he is fearful that the situation is still not resolved. When he writes that he is fearful that he will not find the Corinthians as he wishes, therefore, he is referring to their ongoing factions and to the sexual immorality in which some persist. When he says he is fearful that they will not find him as they wish, he is apprehensive that, as God's coworker, he will have to endure the humiliation that attends reprimanding the community and punishing sinners.

Paul's remarks in these verses about the moral state of the Corinthian community raise an important question. Why does he express such fears about the moral climate at Corinth when earlier he commended the Corinthians for their repentance, their earnestness, and their innocence (7:8–13), and then expressed his confidence in them (7:16)? The dissonance between Paul's description of the community here and the confidence that he expresses in chapter 7 upon receiving Titus's report about the community has led many commentators to argue for some kind of partition theory. Either chapters 10–13 belong to the harsh letter and so were written before chapter 7, or they represent a letter that Paul wrote after chapters 1–9, a response occasioned by a new crisis. In both cases, commentators point to this dissonance as an argument against the literary integrity of 2 Corinthians.

There is, however, a third possibility: Paul may be responding to two different situations. In chapters 1–7 he is primarily concerned with the affair concerning the painful visit. Because the Corinthians have repented of this incident, Paul pronounces them "innocent in the matter" (7:11) and expresses his confidence in them (7:16). But other issues have yet to be settled, namely, the problems caused by the intruding apostles and the lingering question of sexual immorality. This is why Paul calls the Corinthians to be reconciled to God (5:20) and not to receive the grace of God in vain (5:20; 6:1). It is also the reason he summons the Corinthians to open their hearts to him (6:11–13; 7:2–4) and to separate and cleanse themselves from every defilement (6:14–7:1). Indeed it is precisely the presence of these texts in chapters 1–7 that suggests, despite Titus's good report, that not everything is well at Corinth. If this scenario is correct, Paul's remarks in 12:20–21 and 13:1–4 are not an argument against the literary integrity of 2 Corinthians.

The line of thought in 12:14–21 can now be summarized in this way: Paul announces that his third visit to Corinth will not burden the community and defends himself against any suspicion that he or his delegates have taken advantage of the community. He has not been defending himself to the Corinthians but writing to them with complete honesty in the presence of God. He is fearful, however, that this third visit will not be satisfactory either to him or to them. Therefore, to avert further humiliation, he will call upon the Corinthians to test themselves in light of the faith they profess.

2. The Need to Prepare for Paul's Visit (13:1–10)

13:1 This is the third time that I am coming to you.[a] "Let every matter be established on the evidence of two or three witnesses."[b] 2 On my second

C. Preparations for Paul's Third and Final Visit

visit I forewarned, and now that I am absent I am forewarning,[c] those who previously sinned[d] and all the rest that when[e] I come again[f] I will not be lenient 3 since you seek proof of Christ speaking through[g] me, who is not weak toward you but powerful among you. 4 For indeed he was crucified by reason of[h] weakness, but he lives by reason of[i] the power of God, and indeed we are weak in[j] him, but we will live with him by reason of the power of God for you.

5 Put yourselves to the test to see if you are in the faith. Examine yourselves! Or do you not realize[k] that Jesus Christ[l] is among[m] you? Unless, perhaps, you are failing to meet the test.[n] 6 I trust that you know that we are not failing to meet the test. 7 We pray to God that you do nothing evil,[o] not that we might appear approved, but in order that you might do what is good, and we might appear as if we were failing to meet the test. 8 For we cannot do anything against the truth but only for the truth. 9 For we rejoice whenever we are weak, and you are strong. This is what we pray for, your restoration.[p]

10 This is why, though absent, I write these things, so that when present I may not have to act severely according to the authority that the Lord has given me for building up and not for tearing down.

a. Alexandrinus (A) reads "This is the third time that I am ready to come to you," thereby aligning this verse with 12:14. But the best manuscript tradition clearly indicates that Paul is now about to make his third visit to Corinth.

b. Quotation marks have been introduced to indicate that Paul is quoting from Deut 19:15. Translated more literally, the text reads "Let every matter be established *from the mouth* of two or three witnesses." By metonymy, "from the mouth" (*epi stomatos*) means from the "utterance," thus from the "evidence" of two or three witnesses.

c. The order of the Greek text has been restructured in order to present a clearer translation. Translated literally, the Greek reads, "I forewarned and I am forewarning, as when present the second time and now absent."

d. Those who had previously sinned would be those who sinned before Paul's second visit and whom he warned on the occasion of that visit.

e. Paul employs an eventual conditional clause. But since there is little doubt that he is coming to Corinth, *ean* ("if") is translated "when."

f. The adverb "again" (*palin*) is taken with the verb "come," but it could also be taken with the verb "be lenient," in which case Paul would be saying that when he comes he will not be lenient again.

g. Literally translated the Greek reads "in me" (*en emoi*), but the sense is that the Corinthians want proof that, when Paul speaks, Christ speaks through him.

h. The preposition *ek* can be rendered in several ways: "through weakness," "because of weakness," "out of weakness," "in weakness." The meaning of the phrase is discussed in the exegesis.

i. The same preposition (*ek*) occurs here as well. Most commentators render it as "by." The meaning of the phrase that it governs is discussed in the exegesis.

j. Some manuscripts (ℵ, A, F, G) read *syn* ("with"), thereby bringing this phrase in line with the next phrase, "we will live *with* him." Conversely, other manuscripts (P⁴⁶ vid, D*) change "we will live with him" to "we will live *in* him" to bring that phrase in line with this phrase, "we are weak in him." Paul, however, is distinguishing between being weak "in Christ" and living "with Christ."

k. The Greek reads "do you not know yourselves" (*epiginōskete heautous*), which suggests a thorough knowledge of oneself.

l. Several manuscripts (ℵ, A, F, G) read "Christ Jesus." The reading "Jesus Christ" is supported by B and D.

m. The Greek (*en hymin*) could also be rendered "in you." The decision to translate the phrase "among you" has been made because the context suggests that Paul is referring to the presence of Christ to the Corinthian community.

n. Here and elsewhere the phrase "failing to meet the test" translates the noun *adokimos*, which BDAG renders as "unqualified," "worthless," "base."

o. If *hymas* ("you") is taken as the object of the infinitive *poiēsai* ("to do") then the phrase should be rendered "that we may not have to do anything bad *to you*." Thus the NEB (1961) translated the phrase "that we may not have to hurt you." But the REB (1989) now translates the phrase "that you may not do any wrong."

p. BDAG suggests the translation "maturation," but the situation of the Corinthian community suggests the translation "restoration." Such a translation would be akin to the meaning of the verb *katartizō*, "to put in order," "restore."

Having expressed his apprehension about his impending visit to Corinth (12:14–21), Paul warns the Corinthians to prepare themselves for his third and final visit. Those who have not repented of their previous sins must do so (vv. 1–4), and all must test and examine themselves as they have tested and examined Paul (vv. 5–9), so that Paul will not have to use his authority in a severe and destructive manner (v. 10).

This unit is closely related to the previous one in two ways. First, Paul makes another reference to his impending visit (13:1, see 12:14). Second, having spoken of those who sinned previously and have still not repented (12:21), he warns the unrepentant for a second and final time, thereby ensuring that his action will be in accord with the prescription of Deut 19:15, which he quotes at the beginning of this unit (13:1).

The material of this unit also echoes a number of themes that Paul has already developed in chapters 10–12. For example, the statement about his weakness and the weakness of Christ (vv. 3b–4) completes the theme of weakness that played such a prominent role at the end of Paul's boasting (see 11:30; 12:7–10). Second, Paul's discussion about being approved (13:5–9) develops his statement in 10:17 that it is not the one who commends himself or herself who is approved but the one whom the Lord commends. Finally, Paul's reference to the authority that the Lord has given him for building up the community and not for destroying it echoes what he wrote in 10:8, as well as the threat

C. Preparations for Paul's Third and Final Visit

in 10:4 that he is like a powerful warrior who can destroy fortresses that have been raised up against God.

The unit consists of three parts. In the first Paul issues his final warning to the community (vv. 1–4). In the second he calls the community to test itself (vv. 5–9). In the third (v. 10) he explains why he has written this letter. The material can be outlined as follows:

vv. 1–4	A final warning to the unrepentant
vv. 1–3	The unrepentant will not be spared
v. 4	The weakness and power of Christ and Paul
vv. 5–9	The need for self-examination
v. 5	A call for self-examination
v. 6	Recognition that Paul has not failed the test
vv. 7–9	Paul's prayer for the community
v. 10	Paul's purpose in writing

[13:1–3] With these verses Paul issues a final warning to the Corinthians that on his third and final visit he will not spare those who have sinned. Since the Corinthians themselves have been asking him for evidence that Christ speaks through him, Paul will provide the proof they want by punishing those who have not repented when he comes to Corinth.

As he did at the beginning of the previous unit (12:14), Paul indicates that this will be his third visit to Corinth, the founding visit being his first and the painful visit being his second. The legal prescription of Deut 19:15 ("Let every matter be established on the evidence of two or three witnesses") gives an added note of seriousness to this announcement by suggesting that Paul intends to settle matters once and for all. This legal prescription, which also occurs in Matt 18:16 and John 8:17, was intended to protect a defendant from being convicted of a crime on the basis of the testimony of a single witness, lest a false witness come forward and maliciously accuse an innocent person. Accordingly, in order to convict a person of a crime, the legal prescription of Deuteronomy required the testimony of two or three witnesses whose testimony agreed (see Deut 19:15–21).

Although the basic meaning of the legal prescription from Deuteronomy is clear enough, Paul's purpose in quoting from it is not. Some commentators take the reference to the witnesses literally and maintain that Paul will hold court at Corinth and produce witnesses against those who have sinned before he punishes them (Allo, 337; Garland, 541). Others take the references to the witnesses figuratively and argue that they personify Paul's warnings (Bultmann, 241) or visits to Corinth (Barrett, 333; Plummer, 372), or both (Chrysostom, *Homily* 29:1). Though it is possible that Paul intended to produce witnesses against those who had sinned, there is no indication apart from this text that Paul actually intends to "hold court" in order to settle the situation at Corinth. However, the mention of the visits that Paul has already made ("on my second visit"), and the visit that he is about to make ("This is the third time that I am coming to you"), suggest that there is a relationship between these visits and the witnesses required by the legal prescription of Deuteronomy. Thus Barrett (333) notes, "The ordinals *third* and *second* in these two verses cannot fail to be connected with the cardinals *two* and *three* in the quotation." In effect, Paul is saying that he has already produced the necessary witnesses to convict the Corinthians if they do not repent, since on his second visit he warned those who had sinned, and all the rest, that he would not spare them when he came to Corinth again. Now, although he is absent, he is warning the Corinthians a second time, by this letter, that he will not spare them when he comes for his third visit. Understood in this way, the witnesses against the Corinthians are Paul's warnings and visits to the Corinthians.

The first witness   Paul's second visit and the warning he issued then
The second witness   Paul's third visit and the warning he issues now

The people who have sinned and not repented are those whom Paul identified in 12:21 as continuing to act with vileness, immorality, and licentiousness, whereas "all the rest" probably refers to the rest of the community, which is in danger of falling into "discord, jealousy, outbursts of anger, disputes, slanders, whisperings, conceit, disorders" (12:20). In 1:23 Paul wrote that it was to "spare" (*pheidomenos*) the Corinthians that he did not come to Corinth after the painful visit. He sent them the harsh letter instead. This time, however, since they have received the requisite warnings, which now stand as witnesses against them, Paul will not be "lenient" (*pheisomai*; 13:2).

Since it is the Corinthians who have asked for proof that Christ speaks through Paul, they will have no one to blame but themselves if Paul does not spare them when he comes. For even though the signs of an apostle were worked in their midst through his ministry (12:12), they have criticized him for failing to act according to their understanding of power and authority. Paul will indeed act with the power of Christ when he comes to Corinth, but the Corinthians have still not understood the paradoxical relationship between weakness and power that Paul has been developing throughout this letter.

Because of the paradoxical nature of Paul's apostolic ministry among them, the Corinthians have interpreted his hardships and sufferings as weakness. In their view, his weakness has not allowed them to experience the full power of Christ. Put another way, Christ has been weak toward them because Paul has been weak toward them. Aware of this criticism, Paul assures them that Christ has indeed been powerful among them. But since the power of Christ is paradoxically related to weakness, Paul must again explain the intimate relationship between these two realities of his apostolic life, which are rooted in the weakness and power of Christ.

C. Preparations for Paul's Third and Final Visit 307

[4] Having introduced the theme of weakness and power at the end of verse 3 in relationship to the Corinthians ("who is not weak toward you but powerful among you"), Paul now develops the same theme in relationship to Christ and then to himself. The material can be structured as follows:

> He was crucified by reason of *weakness*
> but
> he lives by reason of *the power of God*
> and indeed
> we are *weak* in him
> but
> we will live with him by reason of *the power of God* for you.

As the outline shows, the primary contrast is between "weakness" and "the power of God." Christ was crucified "by reason of" (*ex*) weakness, but he now lives "by reason of" (*ek*) the power of God. Employing a literary plural ("we"), Paul establishes a similar paradoxical relationship within his own life. He is weak in Christ but will live with Christ "by reason of" (*ek*) the power of God.

In writing that Christ was crucified "by reason of (*ek*) weakness," Paul could mean that (1) Christ was crucified because he was weak, or (2) Christ was crucified through the weakness of the human condition in which he shared. In the first instance, the emphasis would be upon Christ's own weakness, in the second upon the human condition in which Christ shared as a result of the incarnation. Although both interpretations contribute to an understanding of the text, each needs to be supplemented by the other. Christ was indeed crucified *because* of weakness, but this weakness was the human condition that he freely embraced in the act of emptying himself (Phil 2:7–9). In saying that Christ now lives by reason of the power of God, Paul has the power of the resurrection in view. There is a certain correspondence then between this text and that of Rom 1:3–4: "the gospel concerning his Son, who was descended from David, according to the flesh and was declared to be Son of God with power according to the spirit of holiness by resurrection from the dead." Descended from David according to the flesh, Christ was crucified by reason of weakness. He now lives, however, by reason of the resurrection of the dead.

Having established the fundamental paradox that undergirds his gospel, Paul applies the paradox to himself. In doing so he emphasizes his relationship to Christ as well as to the community. Because he is in Christ, Paul shares in the weakness of Christ. This is why he always bears "the dying of Jesus" in his body "so that the life of Jesus" might be manifested in his body (4:10). But though he is weak in Christ, he knows that he "will live with Christ by reason of the power of God *for you*." The final words of this phrase, "for you," indicate that

Paul is not thinking of life after death (Lambrecht, 221). Rather, he has in view that resurrection life that is an eschatological reality for those who are alive in Christ. It is precisely this life that enables him to make the power of Christ present to the community despite weakness.

The manner in which Paul develops the paradox of weakness and power in verses 3b–4 can now be summarized in this way: Christ is not weak in relationship to the Corinthians but powerfully present in their midst through Paul's ministry (v. 3b). Christ himself was crucified because of, and through, his human condition, but he now lives by the power of God (v. 4a). Therefore, because Paul lives in Christ, he shares in the weakness and power of Christ, which allows him to live *for the Corinthians* despite his weakness. Accordingly Paul's reflections on weakness and power move from the community, to Christ, to Paul, and then return to the community once more.

[5–6] Having warned the Corinthians that he will not spare them on his third and final visit if they have not repented, in these verses Paul embarks upon a different tack. Thus far, the community has put him to the test, asking for "proof" (*dokimēn*) that Christ speaks through him (13:3). Now he challenges the Corinthians to "examine themselves" (*heautous dokimazete*), expressing his hope that they will recognize that he has "not failed to meet the test" (*adokimoi*). Thus just as he called upon them to undertake a critical examination of themselves before participating in the Eucharist (1 Cor 11:28), so he summons them to a critical examination of themselves before he arrives at Corinth.

In calling upon the Corinthians to test themselves, Paul asks them to determine if they are "in the faith" (*en tē pistei*), a phrase that he also employs in 1:24, where he writes "Not that we exercise authority over your faith, rather we are coworkers for your joy, for you stand firm in the faith (*tē gar pistei hestēkate*)." In 1:24 the phrase refers to the realm of faith. To stand in the faith is to be "in the realm of faith," an apt description of what it means to be a Christian. In these verses, the expression means much the same thing. Its meaning is also determined by Paul's rhetorical question, "Or do you not realize that Jesus Christ is among you?" Thus the critical realization that Jesus Christ dwells among them, within their community, will be an indication that the Corinthians are in the faith.

If Paul has already expressed his confidence that the Corinthians are standing in the faith (1:24), why does he ask them to examine themselves to determine if they are in the faith? For some (Plummer, 376) the tension between Paul's statement of confidence in 1:24 and his exhortation to the Corinthians to examine themselves (13:5) is an indication that chapters 10–13 belong to another letter, perhaps the harsh letter. The tension between these statements, however, may be more apparent than real. For having expressed his confidence in 1:24 that the Corinthians are standing in the faith, Paul is now calling upon them to examine themselves so that they can determine this for themselves.

C. Preparations for Paul's Third and Final Visit

When he asks "Or do you not realize that Jesus Christ is among you?" he presumes that Jesus Christ dwells among them because of his apostolic work, and that all they need do is recognize this, unless they have failed the test. When they recognize that Jesus Christ dwells among them, then they will know that they are "in the faith" and that Paul has not failed the test, since he is the one who has brought them to this faith.

Paul's line of thought in these opening verses can be summarized in this way: Confident that the Corinthians are in the faith because Jesus Christ is in their midst, Paul calls upon them to examine themselves in order to determine this for themselves. Unless they have failed the test, they will discover that Jesus Christ is indeed in their midst, and when they realize this, then they will know that their apostle has not failed the test.

[7–9] Although Paul has warned the Corinthians that he will not spare them if they do not repent, these verses indicate that he is far more interested in their restoration than in his self-vindication, even if their restoration deprives him of the opportunity of acting in a bold and powerful manner. Therefore, playing on the words *dokimos* ("approved") and *adokimos* ("failing to meet the test"), he tells the Corinthians that he prays that they will do what is good or honorable, not for his own benefit but for their own. For when they do what is good, then they will indeed be "approved," and he will appear to have "failed the test," since there will be no need for him to exercise his authority. Paul, however, would rather appear to have "failed the test" than see them do what is evil, thereby forcing him to exercise his authority.

In verses 8–9a Paul substantiates what he has said with two arguments. First, since he acts on behalf of the truth, he cannot do anything against the truth. Since the truth is closely related to the gospel in 4:2–3 and 6:7, it is possible that Paul has the gospel in view here as well (so Bultmann, 248, but not Lambrecht, 222). But even if he does not, his meaning is clear. Paul is more concerned that the truth prevail than that he be approved at any cost (Barrett, 339). Therefore he prays for the good of the Corinthians, even if it means that it will make him appear as having failed the test. Second, he rejoices when the Corinthians are strong and he is weak. With this statement Paul returns to the theme of power and weakness (see 13:3b–4) and recalls a remark that he made in 4:12, "death is at work in us but life in you." Thus, just as his daily dying effects life for the Corinthians, so his weakness in Christ (12:4b) leads to the moral restoration of the Corinthians, who will be strong by doing good and avoiding evil (see Barrett, 240).

In the final words of v. 9, Paul returns to the theme of prayer with which he began these verses, thereby enclosing verses 7–9 by references to his prayer for the community. Paul prays that the Corinthians will avoid what is evil and do what is good (v. 7a), and he prays for their restoration (v. 9b). This restoration will occur if they avoid what is evil and do what is good, and if those who have sinned finally repent (11:21; 13:2). Then the Corinthians will be approved and strong at the expense of their apostle, who will still appear weak and as having failed the test, because he will not have had to exercise the authority the Lord has given him.

[10] This verse echoes a number of themes that Paul introduced in chapter 10, thereby bracketing this section (10:1–13:10) with references to Paul's absence and presence (10:1, 2, 11; 13:10) as well as remarks about the authority that the Lord has given him for building up and not for tearing down (10:4, 8; 13:10). Assuming that 2 Corinthians is a single letter rather than a collection of letters, this verse also provides a retrospective view of the entire letter: Paul has written so that he will not have to act severely toward the Corinthians, when he comes to Corinth, with the authority that the Lord has given him for building up and not for tearing down. Viewed from the perspective of this verse, then, Paul has written 2 Corinthians in order to prepare for his third visit. For even though the issue or issues that made Paul's second visit so painful have been successfully resolved (7:5–16), other matters have not yet been settled: the resumption of the collection, criticism of Paul's apostolic ministry, Paul's refusal to be supported by the community, divisions within the Corinthian church, and the continuing immoral behavior of some. If Paul's letter has been effective, the Corinthians will resolve these issues before he arrives.

The Letter Closing
2 Corinthians 13:11–13

Paul has now completed the three parts of 2 Corinthians that form the letter body: (1) his narration of the recent events that have transpired between him and the community (1:12–7:16), in which he presented the Corinthians with an extended exposition of apostolic ministry (2:14–7:4); (2) an appeal to complete the work of the collection (8:1–9:15); and (3) a vigorous defense of his ministry in preparation for his third visit to Corinth (10:1–13:10). He now concludes his correspondence with a greeting in which he appeals to the Corinthians one last time to mend their ways. The greeting is notable for its reference to the grace of Jesus Christ, the love of God, and the fellowship of the Holy Spirit (v. 13), a text that plays a prominent role in later Trinitarian theology.

> 13:11 Finally brothers and sisters,[a] rejoice,[b] mend your ways,[c] encourage each other,[d] be of one mind, be at peace, and the God of love and peace will be with you.[e]
>
> 12 Greet one another with a holy kiss. All the holy ones[f] greet you.

The Letter Closing

13 The grace of the Lord Jesus Christ, and the love of God, and the fellowship of the Holy[g] Spirit be[h] with all of you.[i]

a. Although the Greek employs *adelphoi* ("brothers"), Paul's final greeting has all the members of the community in view, women as well as men.
b. The Greek word *chairete* ("rejoice") is rendered as the first in a series of imperatives. Although some construe it as a greeting, "farewell," Omanson and Ellington (245) note that "there is no solid evidence that it was ever used at the conclusion of a letter to mean 'good-bye.'"
c. The Greek word *katartizesthe* is taken as a middle voice ("mend your ways") rather than as a passive ("be restored," "be made perfect"), since the Corinthians must be actively involved in the restoration of their community.
d. The Greek word *parakaleisthe* is taken as a middle voice ("encourage each other") rather than as a passive ("be encouraged," "heed our appeal"), since Paul is calling the community to unity.
e. The phrase "and the God of love and peace will be with you" could be construed as the apodosis of an implied conditional sentence ("if you rejoice, mend your ways, ... then the God of love and peace will be with you") or as a promise of God's presence.
f. *Hoi hagioi* is translated as "the holy ones" rather than as "the sanctified," as it is in 1:1, in order to draw a relationship between "the holy ones" and "the holy kiss."
g. "Holy" (*hagiou*) is absent from P[46].
h. Since the phrase is construed as blessing, the verb "be" is supplied. It would be possible to take the phrase as a declarative statement, in which case the verb "is" should be supplied. Such a translation, however, seems less likely.
i. Some manuscripts (ℵ,[2] D) conclude the letter with "amen." "Amen" is absent from P[46], ℵ*, A, B, F, G.

Having called upon the community to prepare itself for his impending visit (12:14–13:10), Paul concludes his letter with a series of staccato imperatives that function as a final exhortation (v. 11a), followed by a promise of God's presence (v. 11b). He then calls upon the Corinthians to greet each other with a holy kiss (v. 12a) and extends the greetings of all the holy ones to them (v. 12b). Finally he pronounces an elaborate tripartite blessing upon the community (v. 13).

The first two imperatives of verse 11, *chairete* ("rejoice") and *katartizesthe* ("mend your ways"), function as hook words that relate this material to the previous unit, where the same or related words, *chairomen* ("we rejoice") and *katartisin* ("restoration"), occur in verse 9. The material can be outlined as follows:

v. 11   Exhortation and promise
    v. 11a   Five imperatives
    v. 11b   Promise of God's presence
v. 12   Greetings
    v. 12a   Greet one another with a holy kiss
    v. 12b   Greetings from the holy ones

v. 13 Blessing
    v. 13a   The grace of the Lord Jesus Christ
    v. 13b   The love of God
    v. 13c   The fellowship of the Holy Spirit

[13:11] Having explained that he has written so that he will not have to act severely when he comes to Corinth (v. 10), Paul signals the conclusion of his letter with the simple adverb "finally" (*loipon*; see Phil 3:1; 4:8; 1 Thess 4:1; and 2 Thess 3:1, where the same word indicates the beginning of a new section). Moreover, for only the third time in this letter (see 1:8 and 8:1), he addresses the Corinthians as *adelphoi* ("brothers and sisters"), thereby showing that he still views them as members of the new family that God has established in Christ, despite the recent difficulties between him and the community. As in 1 Thess 5:16–22, Paul provides the Corinthians with a series of staccato imperatives that serve as his final exhortation. The Corinthians should rejoice, mend their ways, encourage each other, be of one mind, and be at peace. For the God of peace and love will be with them.

On first reading the first of these imperatives ("rejoice") appears somewhat incongruous, given the harsh manner in which Paul has written to the Corinthians. However, the theme of rejoicing has played an important role in this letter (2:3; 6:10; 7:7, 9, 13, 16), and Paul has just written that he rejoices when he is weak and the Corinthians are strong (13:9). The exhortation to rejoice, therefore, is neither frivolous nor out of place. Rather, it is an expression of Paul's profound confidence in the community. The Corinthians form a Spirit-filled community of the new covenant that God has reconciled to himself and to whom Paul is now extending an offer of reconciliation.

Such rejoicing should encourage the Corinthians to put things in order and "mend their ways" (*katartizesthe*), since Paul himself prays for their restoration (*katartisin*; v. 9). For some, mending their ways will mean repentance from the vileness, immorality, and licentiousness of which they have not yet repented (12:21). For all, it will entail avoiding discord, jealousy, slander, conceit, and the like (12:20). Accordingly, employing a verb that has played a major role throughout this letter, especially in the letter's benediction in which he spoke of the God who consoled or encouraged him (1:4, 6), Paul calls upon the Corinthians to "encourage each other" (*parakaleisthe*). If they do, then they will "be of one mind" (*to auto phroneite*). Paul makes similar appeals for unanimity of thought in Rom 12:16 and Phil 2:2; 4:2. The agreement he seeks, however, is always grounded in the Lord; thus he exhorts Euodia and Syntyche "to be of the same mind in the Lord" (Phil 4:2).

Finally, Paul calls upon the Corinthians to "be at peace" (*eirēneuete*: a similar injunction occurs in Rom 12:18 and 1 Thess 5:13). Since peace is the result of reconciliation, and since reconciliation has been a major motif of this letter, this fifth and final imperative is a fitting climax to this brief exhortation. This exhortation to be at peace leads to a promise: "and the God of love and peace will be with you." Paul has already told the Corinthians that "God is a God not of disorder but of peace" (1 Cor 14:33), and the epithet of God as "the God of peace" occurs with some frequency in Paul's letters (Rom 15:33; 16:20; Phil 4:9; 1 Thess 5:23; also see Heb 13:20). But this is the only description of God as "the God of love and peace," though the love of God plays an important role in Paul's writings (Rom 5:5, 8; 8:39), and Paul will explicitly mention the love of God in verse 13. This description of God, like Paul's earlier epithet of God as "the Father of mercies and God of all consolation" (1:3), is intended to remind the Corinthians of what God has done for them in Jesus Christ. In Christ, the God of peace has reconciled them to himself (5:19) and manifested his love for them through the love of Christ (5:14). Thus Paul is not so much establishing a condition—*if* the Corinthians are at peace with each other, *then* the God of love and peace will be with them—as he is reminding them that the God of love and peace will be with them, enabling them to be at peace with each other (Barrett, 343; Furnish, 586).

[12] Having given his final exhortation, Paul calls upon the Corinthians to greet each other with a "holy kiss," and he extends the greetings of all "the holy ones" to them. References to a "holy kiss" occur at the conclusion of other Pauline letters (Rom 16:16; 1 Cor 16:20; 1 Thess 5:26), as well as in 1 Pet 5:14. Although the kiss eventually became a liturgical action and remains such today, it is difficult to determine if it had a role in the worship of the Pauline churches. Since this letter would have been read to an assembly of believers at Corinth, however, it is likely that Paul intended the Corinthians to exchange a holy kiss immediately after hearing his letter, whether or not the letter was read in the context of a liturgical setting. In calling upon the Corinthians to exchange a holy kiss, Paul is reinforcing his exhortation to reconciliation, since the holy kiss was undoubtedly an expression of peace and reconciliation among those who exchanged it. The gesture is described as a "holy kiss" because those who exchanged it belonged to the assembly of "the holy ones," whom God had reconciled to himself through Christ.

Mindful that the Corinthians belong to a wider community of believers, Paul extends the greetings of all "the holy ones" to them. Exactly who "the holy ones" are depends in part on the location from which Paul writes. If he is writing from somewhere in Macedonia, such as Philippi, he might have the members of that community in view.[37] The general nature of this greeting, however,

---

37. Many manuscripts conclude with a subscription that identifies the location from which Paul writes. Some add, "I have written to the Corinthians from Philippi," and others, "I have written to the Corinthians from Philippi and Macedonia through Titus and Luke." These subscriptions, however, do not belong to Paul's original text.

could also suggest that Paul was extending greetings to the Corinthians from all his converts, those in Asia as well as those in Macedonia, thereby reminding the Corinthians of the extended family of believers to which they belong.

[13] Paul concludes his letter with a three-part blessing that highlights the grace of the Lord Jesus Christ, the love of God, and the fellowship of the Holy Spirit. This blessing is the most elaborate concluding blessing of the nondisputed Pauline letters, all of which employ the simpler form "the grace of the Lord Jesus Christ" (Rom 16:20; 1 Cor 16:23; Gal 6:18; Phil 4:23; 1 Thess 5:28; Phlm 25). Although there is general agreement that the first two members of the blessing are to be construed as subjective genitives (the grace that comes from the Lord Jesus Christ, and the love that comes from God), there is considerable debate about the third genitive. Taken as a subjective genitive, it would mean the fellowship that comes from the Holy Spirit whereby believers are united with the Holy Spirit. Taken as an objective genitive, it would mean the fellowship that the Holy Spirit creates among believers. Some commentators maintain that the presence of the subjective genitive in the first two instances argues for its use in the third (Bruce, 255), but others note "that elsewhere in the NT a genitive following *koinōnia* is usually objective" (Thrall, 2:917). But it may be that there is a surplus of meaning here, so that Paul has in view the fellowship whereby believers are united both with each other and the Holy Spirit.

Paul's tripartite formula focuses on the economy of salvation as effected by Christ, God, and the Spirit and as experienced by believers. Believers first experience the graciousness of Jesus Christ who died for all (5:11–12). On the basis of this gracious act, they come to know the love of God, who in Christ "was reconciling the world to himself" (5:19). Having been reconciled by God's love, believers are given "the first installment of the Spirit" (1:22) who establishes fellowship and communion among those who belong to the new covenant community. Paul's three-part blessing, therefore, prays for and reminds the Corinthians of the blessings of the economy of salvation. In and of itself, the blessing is not an explicit statement of the Trinity as developed by later theology, but there can be little doubt that this reflection on the divine economy of salvation is the proper starting point for such a theology.

Gloria Patri
et Filio
et Spiritui Sancto

INDEX OF ANCIENT SOURCES

OLD TESTAMENT

Genesis
1:3	104
1:26	102
2:7	280
2:8	280
3:13	243
8:21	73
28:15	109

Exodus
4:10	74
7:3	289
16:1–36	193
16:18	193
29:18	73
31:18	87
32:15	87
34:1	79
34:4	79
34:6	41
34:27–35	87, 90–91
34:28	79
34:29	79
34:30	87, 91, 91 n.22
34:33	91
34:34	12, 83–84, 95
34:35	91

Leviticus
1:9	73
1:13	73
1:17	73
6:28	108
11:33	108
19:19	162
26:11–12	165–66

Numbers
15:3	73
15:7	73
15:10	73
33:55	282

Deuteronomy
4:34	289
6:22	289
7:9	55
7:19	289
10:14	280
15:10	205
17:5–7	268
19:15–21	305
19:15	303, 305
22:10	162
22:13–21	241
22:15	241
22:22–24	268
25:3	267
30:6	81
31:6	109
31:8	109

1 Samuel
16:7	131

2 Samuel
7:14	165, 167

1 Kings
8:27	280

1 Chronicles
9:23	117
28:20	109

2 Chronicles
2:6	280
6:18	280

Job
37:15	104

Psalms
16:10	109
25:6	41
31:12	108
36:25	109
69:16	41
88:15	43
111:9	206
116:1–9	112 n.32
116:10	112, 112 n.32
116:10–19	112 n.32
118:17	155
118:18	155

Proverbs
1:7	130
3:4	198
11:24	205
21:22	224
22:8	205

Ecclesiastes
9:14–15	224

Isaiah
1:22	75
2:2–4	183
9:1	104
40:1	41
42	104 n.27
42:9	136–37
43:6	165, 167
43:18–19	137
48:6	137
49:1–6	104
49:1–13	150
49:1	104
49:6	104
49:8	150
49:13	41, 173
50:1	242
52:11	165–66
55:10–11	208
65:17	136

Jeremiah
4:4	81
9:23–24	235
9:24	236

Jeremiah (continued)

31:31	13
31:31–34	79–80
31:33	78
32:37–41	79 n.15, 80
32:40	79

Lamentations

4:2	108

Ezekiel

11:19	78, 80
16	242
18:31	78, 80
20:34	165–66
28:24	282
36:26–27	78, 80–81
37:1–14	81
37:26–27	165–66
37:27	165–66

Hosea

1–3	242
2:6	282
10:12	208

Zechariah

9:9	221

NEW TESTAMENT

Matthew

5:5	221
5:37	51
11:29	221–22
18:16	305
21:5	221
26:36–46	284
26:67	283
27:46	109

Mark

3:5	110
3:21	132
8:32	90
9:31	111
10:33–34	111
14:58	117, 120
14:65	283
15:34	109

Luke

1:22	277
1:52	174
1:68–79	40
13:7	87
22:20	79
23:43	280
24:23	277

John

1:14	285
7:18	143 n.52
7:26	90
8:17	305
8:46	143 n.52
12:31	102
14:30	102
16:11	102
16:29	90
18:31	268

Acts

2:43	289
4:13	90, 247
4:30	289
5:12	289
6:1	263 n.25, 264
6:8	289
7:36	289
7:54–60	268
9:23–25	273
13:43	130
13:50	152
14:3	289
14:19	152
14:19–20	268
14:27	63–64
15:12	289
15:21	83
16:1–3	38
16:17	267
16:22	267
16:22–23	152
16:23	266
16:23–24	266
16:37	266
16:38	267
17:5	152
17:14	38
17:15	38
18:1–17	293
18:1–18	16
18:4	130
18:5	39
18:12	152
18:27	77
19:22	39
19:23–41	43
19:29–30	152
20:4	202 n.12
21:21	155
21:31–23:30	266
22:17–21	279
23:31–26:32	266
24:4	221
24:17	183
26:19	277
26:28	131
27	268
28:16	266

Romans

1:1	103
1:3–4	307
1:4	168
1:9	58
1:10	38
1:13	43
1:17	144
1:18	144 n.53
1:18–3:20	139
1:23	102
1:24	301
1:29	299
1:29–31	299
1:30	299
2:4	152
2:6	254
2:8	299
2:12–16	126
2:15	48
2:17–24	81
2:29	81
3:1	277
3:3	87, 87 n.20
3:5	144
3:20	88
3:21	144
3:23	102, 144
3:25	143
3:31	87, 87 n.20
4	264
4:14	87 n.20
4:19	110
4:25	111, 141
5:1–2	40
5:1–11	137, 137 n.46
5:3	151
5:4	151
5:5	133, 313
5:6	133
5:8	133, 313
5:10	86
5:11–21	249
5:12–21	102, 134, 143
5:15	86, 141, 210
5:16	88
5:17	86, 141, 210
5:18	88
5:20	141

Index of Ancient Sources

6:3–4	134	15:8	167 n.65	3:17	169, 226		
6:5	134	15:13	41, 59	3:18	101		
6:6	87 n.20, 115	15:14	220 n.3	3:22	220 n.3		
6:11	134	15:20	234	4:1–5	298		
6:13	154	15:23–24	234	4:4	48		
6:18	96	15:25–28	181	4:6	253, 299		
6:19	301	15:26	202	4:8	240		
6:23	254	15:27	193, 209	4:9	73, 155		
7:2	87 n.20	15:30	220	4:9–13	265		
7:6	87 n.20	15:30–31	209	4:10	257		
7:7–12	88	15:30–32	183	4:11	283		
7:22	115	15:33	313	4:11–13	156		
7:23–24	115	16:1	77, 202	4:13	155		
7:24–25	70	16:4	39	4:14	161		
7:25	220 n.3	16:16	313	4:14–15	62, 294		
8:1	88	16:20	41, 313–14	4:15	233		
8:3	143	16:21	39	4:17	15, 38–9, 53 n.5, 77		
8:3–4	142			4:18	15, 299		
8:11	123	**1 Corinthians**		4:19	299		
8:18–21	137	1–4	14, 47–48, 300 n.36	4:21	300		
8:19	277	1:1	38	5–6	300 n.36, 301		
8:22–23	123	1:2	38–9	5:1	301		
8:25	151	1:3–9	149	5:1–2	177		
8:29	102	1:7–8	56	5:1–5	17–19, 24		
8:32	111, 133	1:7	277	5:2	299		
8:35	133	1:9	55	5:3–5	18		
8:36	266	1:10	220	5:5	62		
8:39	313	1:10–4:24	101	5:7	143		
9	264	1:11	299	5:9	49		
9:1	272	1:12	225	5:9–12	162		
9:3	220 n.3	1:13	220 n.3	6:6	102, 162		
9:4	167 n.65	1:18	24, 74, 101	6:7	169		
9:4–5	264	1:18–25	101	6:12	276		
9:7	264	1:20	101	6:13	87 n.20, 301		
9:22	152	1:26	218	6:18	301		
10:3	144	1:28	87 n.20	6:19	164		
10:6–8	96	1:28–29	235	7:2	301		
10:9	103	1:30	40, 168	7:12	102		
11:1	264	1:30–31	235	7:12–16	162 n.62		
11:13–16	137, 137 n.46	1:31	48, 235	7:13	102, 162		
11:22	152	2:1	247, 293	7:14	102		
11:25	43	2:1–5	225, 293	7:15	102, 162		
12:1	219–20	2:3	227	7:25	100		
12:2	38, 101	2:3–4	227	8–10	300 n.36		
12:9–21	153	2:5	227	8:1–11:1	48, 54 n.6, 162, 270		
12:11	153	2:6	87 n.20, 101				
12:16	174, 312	2:6–16	101	8:1	225, 299		
12:18	312	2:8	101	8:1–13	31		
13:12	154, 223	3:3	299	8:4	141		
13:13	299, 301	3:5	103, 220 n.3, 265	8:7	270		
14:7–9	135	3:6	236	8:9	218		
14:10	125	3:7	149	8:11	270		
14:15	133	3:8	266	8:13	270		
14:17	59	3:9	149	9:1–2	38		
15:4	151	3:13	236	9:1–12	251		
15:5	41, 151	3:15	254	9:1–14	295		

Index of Ancient Sources

1 Corinthians (*continued*)
9:1–27   31
9:3   298
9:3–14   23
9:12   251, 295
9:12–18   251
9:14   249, 252
9:15   251
9:15–18   73
9:16   72
9:18   251
9:22   270
10:1   43
10:1–11:1   31
10:11   101
10:13   55
10:14–22   162
10:18   218
10:23   225, 276
10:27   102, 162
10:32   39
11:23   111
11:24   134
11:25   79
11:28   308
12:1   43
12:3   103, 185
12:7   277
12:8   152, 190
12:9   190
12:12–26   62
12:20   53 n.5
12:26   62
13:2   152, 190
13:4   299
13:8   87, 87 n.20,
                  152, 190
13:10   87 n.20, 88
13:11   87 n.20
13:13   190
14   132
14:4   225
14:6   190
14:9   190
14:22   102, 162
14:23   102, 162
14:24   102, 162
14:33   299, 313
15   118, 120
15:1   185
15:3   134
15:9   39, 72, 100
15:10   149
15:21–23   120
15:24   87 n.20
15:24–28   102
15:26   87 n.20

15:30–31   112
15:31   155
15:32   43, 266
15:33   169
15:49   102
15:50–57   118 n.35,
                 121 n.38
15:51   137
15:51–57   118, 125
15:53–54   121
15:54   122
15:56   88
15:57   70
15:58   266
16   182
16:1   200
16:1–4   15, 181, 192
16:2   192
16:3–9   52–53
16:4   52
16:5–9   16–17, 19
16:6   52, 252, 293
16:9   64
16:10   38, 77, 218
16:10–11   15
16:15   201
16:20   313
16:21   220 n.3
16:23   314

2 Corinthians
1–7   26–32, 66,
                   291, 302
1–9   25–26, 29–30, 66,
                  214, 297, 302
1:1–2:13   28–29
1:1   9, 11, 35, 187, 201
1:2   10, 11, 36,
                  49 n.2, 186
1:1–2   3, 36–40
1:1–11   35
1:3   10, 11, 36, 58,
                170–71, 174, 313
1:3–4   173
1:3–7   37, 40–42, 109
1:3–11   3, 36, 41, 66, 100
1:4   151, 170, 312
1:5   35, 170
1:6   35, 50, 110, 170, 312
1:7   170
1:8   3, 37, 151, 186,
                    266, 312
1:8–11   37, 41, 43–44, 109
1:9   3, 10, 35, 37, 41,
                58, 113, 123, 174
1:9–10   266
1:10   10

1:12   10, 48–49,
              49 n.2, 58, 60,
             75–76, 100, 243
1:12–13   64
1:12–14   4, 46–48, 52,
                     61, 131
1:12–2:13   3, 4, 26, 31,
                  45–46, 63,
                    179, 213
1:12–7:16   3, 5, 6, 45,
              179, 180 n.1,
                   213, 310
1:12–13:10   35
1:13   155
1:13–14   49–50
1:14   170, 177
1:15   16, 49 n.2, 58, 79
1:15–16   17
1:15–17   52–54
1:15–22   4, 49, 50–52,
                     65, 171
1:15–2:13   51, 171
1:17   57
1:18–22   54–57
1:18   10, 41, 174
1:19   16, 39, 40, 59
1:19–20   11
1:20   41, 167 n.65
1:21–22 10–11, 13, 41, 174
1:22   12, 51, 65, 123,
                    306, 314
1:23–24   58–59
1:23–2:4   4, 46, 54,
                  57–58, 171
1:24   13, 50–51, 62,
              103, 177, 222,
             234, 257–58, 308
2:1   15–16, 155, 227, 293
2:1–4   59–60, 294 n.34
2:2   51
2:2–4   172–73, 175
2:3   18, 59, 312
2:3–4   49, 53 n.5, 226
2:4   15, 18, 24–25,
           64–65, 151, 155,
          176, 251, 294 n.34
2:5   17, 57
2:5–8   24, 61–62
2:5–11   4, 15, 17–18, 31,
              60–61, 169, 171,
                 174, 176, 301
2:7   57
2:9   18, 60, 65, 172–73,
                175–77, 191, 226
2:9–11   62–63
2:11   243
2:12   11, 64, 101

Index of Ancient Sources

2:12–13	4, 26, 46, 63–64, 67–68, 70, 171, 173, 297	3:12–18	56, 78, 90, 99, 101	4:16	14, 98, 108, 114–15, 119–20, 122
2:13	5, 45, 64–65, 171–72, 177, 202	3:13	87 n.20, 88	4:16–17	119–20
2:14	10, 41, 49 n.2, 70–74, 99–100, 102, 152, 169, 174, 196, 223–24, 248	3:14	87 n.20	4:16–18	10, 42, 105–6, 112–14, 119, 122
		3:14–15	93–95, 102	4:16–5:5	114
		3:14–16	100	4:16–5:10	106, 114
		3:16	12, 89, 95	4:17	151
		3:16–17	123	4:17–18	115–16
		3:17	12, 96–97	4:18	119, 122, 124
2:14–3:6	68–70, 82, 84, 98–99, 103 n.26, 105, 126	3:18	11–12, 96–97, 99, 102, 114, 116, 124	5	137 n.46
				5:1	10, 108, 120–21, 14, 114, 122
2:14–4:6	4, 66, 103 n.26, 156	4:1	108	5:1–5	124
		4:1–2	99–100		
		4:1–6	31, 68, 84–85, 97–99	5:1–10	42, 105–6, 113, 116–19, 123 n.41
2:14–7:4	2, 4, 19, 26–31, 45–46, 64, 65–68, 171, 173, 179, 213, 219 n.2, 310	4:2	76–77, 131, 150, 230–31, 243, 288, 296, 298	5:2	123 n.42
				5:2–4	121–22
				5:4	123 n.42
2:15	42, 99, 101, 109	4:2–3	75, 309	5:5	10, 12, 56, 122–24
2:15–16	11, 74	4:3	74, 90, 109		
2:16	78, 84	4:3–4	49, 100–102, 124	5:6	11
2:17	6, 23, 74–75, 98, 100, 214, 220 n.3, 171, 298	4:4	11–12, 40, 63, 84, 96–97, 108, 124, 162, 224	5:6–7	152–53
				5:6–8	124–25
3–4	42 n.6	4:5	11–12, 103, 111–13	5:8	11
3:1	6, 23, 30, 75–76, 99–100, 131, 150, 160, 214, 220 n.3, 230–31, 288	4:5–6	109 n.28	5:9–10	125–26, 129
		4:6	10–11, 13, 108, 152, 224, 248	5:10	11–12, 113, 122, 129–30, 254, 298
		4:7	10, 14, 107–8, 119–20, 125, 156	5:11	31, 100, 125, 168
3:1–3	56, 79, 195, 225			5:11–12	314
3:2	23, 77, 99, 161, 177, 235, 288	4:7–12	14, 151, 155, 173	5:11–13	127, 130–32, 145, 160
		4:7–15	105–7, 114–15, 119, 122		
3:3	10–12, 77–78, 80, 84, 87, 161, 164, 174	4:7–18	114	5:11–21	127–29, 137, 145, 147
		4:7–5:10	4, 66, 97, 100, 105, 107, 126, 156, 170	5:11–6:10	5, 66, 126–27, 156
3:4–5	78–79			5:11–6:11	156
3:4–6	56, 98	4:8	41, 43, 114, 249 n.21	5:12	6–7, 23, 47, 50, 61, 76, 147, 150–51, 156, 177, 214, 220 n.3, 230–31, 288, 299
3:5	10, 74, 288	4:8–9	14, 108–9, 114–15		
3:5–6	13	4:8–11	41		
3:6	9, 12, 74, 78–82, 84, 86, 94, 100, 108, 139, 141, 150, 154, 177, 265	4:8–12	265		
		4:10	3, 12, 14, 24, 74, 108, 249 n.21, 307	5:13	31, 275
				5:14	140 n.51, 313
3:7	87 n.20, 88			5:14–15	132–35, 144
3:7–8	86–88			5:14–17	127, 137, 145
3:7–11	10, 56, 74, 78, 85–86, 99	4:10–11	109 n.28, 115, 119	5:14–21	127, 150
		4:10–12	109–112, 122	5:15	11
3:7–18	68, 82–85, 99	4:11	12, 108, 135, 266–67	5:16	11, 54
3:8	12–13, 139			5:16–17	132, 135–37
3:9	13, 42 n.6, 139, 150, 254	4:12	309	5:17	10, 13, 115, 145
		4:13–14	112–13	5:18	10, 83, 147, 149–50, 174
3:9–10	88–89	4:14	10, 12, 44, 119–20, 122, 125	5:18–19	11, 41, 137–41
3:11	13, 87 n.20, 88–90, 92, 139			5:18–21	40, 127, 145–46
3:12	170	4:15	10, 42 n.6, 49 n.2, 113	5:19	10, 138 n.46, 255, 313–14
3:12–13	90–93				

2 Corinthians (*continued*)		7:5	67, 109, 171, 175	8:6	49 n.2, 64, 179, 181, 181 n.3, 184, 190
5:20	9–11, 13, 62, 127, 147, 149, 177, 302	7:5–6	26, 173–74		
		7:5–7	67	8:6–15	180
		7:5–16	5–6, 17, 26, 28–31, 45, 50, 54, 64, 67–68, 147, 169, 171, 172–73, 179, 188, 191, 213–14, 297, 310	8:7	42 n.6, 49 n.2, 181, 181 n.3, 184, 185 n.7, 196, 234
5:20–21	138, 141–45				
5:21	11, 14, 40, 89, 134, 154, 191			8:7–9	190–91
				8:7–15	6, 32, 180, 188–90, 205
6:1	13, 49 n.2, 160, 300, 302	7:6	10, 31, 59, 64–65, 81, 179		
				8:8	196
6:1–2	127, 141, 149–50, 156	7:6–7	70, 170	8:9	6, 11, 14, 49 n.2, 156, 181 n.3, 184, 186, 222
6:1–10	145–49	7:6–18	67		
6:1–7:4	31	7:7	65, 156, 174–76, 185, 312	8:10	5, 178–79, 182, 185, 213, 197
6:3	197				
6:3–4	127, 150–51, 156	7:8	18–19, 24–25, 60, 294 n.34	8:10–11	15
6:3–10	127, 160			8:11	188
6:4	13, 41, 76–77, 83, 160, 177, 230–31, 265, 288–89			8:11–12	201
		7:8–9	175	8:13	151
		7:8–11	31, 175	8:13–14	208
		7:8–13	61, 226, 302	8:13–15	192–93
		7:9	156, 312	8:14	181
6:4–5	151–52, 156	7:9–13	17	8:16	49 n.2, 64, 179, 181 n.3, 184, 190
6:4–10	14, 41, 107, 109, 127, 131, 151, 173, 265, 269, 289	7:10–11	175–76		
		7:11	18, 171, 196, 288, 302	8:16–17	6, 27, 32, 177, 195–96, 180, 194–95, 199–200, 202–3, 213
6:5	266, 269	7:12	15, 17–19, 24, 60, 61, 81, 169, 176, 196, 301		
6:6	224, 248				
6:6–7	156			8:16–9:5	182, 188, 203, 211, 297
6:7	89, 223, 309	7:12–13	175–77		
6:7–8	153–54, 156	7:13	64, 156, 179, 312	8:17	187, 203
6:8–10	154–56	7:13–15	188	8:18	101
6:9–10	186	7:14	50, 64, 81, 296	8:18–19	196–98
6:10	312	7:16	156, 171, 178–79, 185, 214, 302, 312	8:18–23	76
6:11–13	27, 31–32, 141, 160–62, 168, 302			8:19	11, 49 n.2, 181, 181 n.3, 184
		8–9	2, 5–6, 26–32, 30, 42 n.6, 45, 51, 66, 173, 178, 179 n.1, 181–82, 184, 186–87, 193, 200, 210, 213–14, 291, 310		
6:11–7:4	5, 6, 30, 32, 50, 66, 147, 213–14			8:20	181
				8:20–21	197–98
6:11–7:5	142			8:21	11
6:12	168			8:22	197–98, 199 n.10, 203
6:14	162				
6:14–16	162–64	8	27–28, 32, 200	8:23	64, 179, 202
6:14–18	31	8:1	49 n.2, 181 n.3, 185–86, 195, 210, 312	8:23–34	198–99
6:14–7:1	2, 13, 26–30, 32, 40, 302			8:24	50, 203
				9	27–28, 32, 200
6:15	63	8:1–2	156	9:1	27, 181, 209
6:16	10, 78	8:1–4	81	9:1–2	201–2
6:16–18	164–67	8:1–5	180, 201	9:1–5	6, 32, 180, 192, 195, 199–201, 203
6:17	10	8:1–6	6, 32, 180, 184–85		
6:18	10	8:1–15	210		
7:1	31, 130, 167–68	8:2	151, 181, 190, 207, 42 n.6, 47	9:2	179, 192, 199
7:1–16	50			9:3	27, 32, 50, 181
7:2	243, 296	8:2–4	186–87	9:3–4	202–3
7:2–4	27, 31–32, 141, 168–70, 302	8:3	196	9:4	181, 185, 201
		8:4	181, 181 n.3, 201, 209, 49 n.2	9:5	181, 203
7:3	88, 161			9:6–7	205–6
7:4	50, 151, 174, 177–78	8:5	11, 38	9:6–9	6, 32, 204–5
		8:5–6	187–88	9:6–10	204

Index of Ancient Sources

9:6–15	180, 188, 204, 211	10:13	10, 226	11:16–21	254–56
9:8	42 n.6, 49 n.2, 181, 181 n.3, 184, 208	10:13–14	252	11:17	11, 237, 241, 256–57, 287
9:8–9	205–6	10:13–16	231–35, 252	11:18	54, 272
9:10–11	207–8	10:13–18	23	11:18–20	257–58
9:10–15	32, 204, 206–7	10:14–16	225	11:19	237, 240–41
9:11	47, 181	10:14	11, 23, 101	11:20	22, 240
9:11–13	10	10:15	76, 234, 266	11:21	227 n.10, 230, 237, 240–41, 258–59, 262–63, 310
9:11–15	204	10:16	226		
9:12	42 n.6, 181	10:17	48, 226, 237, 239, 256, 278, 304	11:21–29	259–62
9:12–14	187, 208–10	10:17–18	235–37	11:21–33	14
9:13	11, 47, 101, 181	10:18	76–77, 131, 231, 288	11:21–12:10	7, 238, 256
9:13–14	183	11:1	237, 256, 262, 285–86	11:22	22, 263 n.25
9:14	49 n.2, 181 n.3, 184			11:22–23	257, 263–64
9:15	49 n.2, 181 n.3, 184, 210–11	11:1–2	240–42	11:23	22, 83, 89, 225, 254, 265–67, 269
		11:1–4	239–40, 255–56		
10–13	5, 19, 25–31, 48, 54, 65–66, 74, 147, 160, 179 n.1, 214, 218, 220 n.5, 283, 287, 294 n.34, 297 302 308	11:1–21	7, 238, 255, 259, 261	11:23–29	41, 151–52
		11:1–12:13	7, 22, 214–16, 230–31, 237, 290–91	11:23–33	107, 265
				11:24–25	267–68
				11:26	268–69
		11:2	11	11:27	266, 269
10:1	220, 263, 300, 310	11:2–3	22, 152	11:28	269–70
10:1–2	219–23, 226, 230	11:3	47, 63, 169, 224, 296	11:29	227 n.10, 258, 270–71
10:1–11	21, 214, 216–19, 290	11:3–4	226, 242–44	11:30	15, 227, 256, 258–59, 272, 274–75, 281, 284, 304
10:1–18	7, 214–15, 235–37, 290–91	11:4	12, 22, 101, 240		
		11:4–15	15		
10:1–12:21	2	11:5	20–22, 47, 216, 225, 287, 291		
10:1–13:10	6, 45, 213–14, 219 n.2, 238, 290, 310	11:5–6	246–48	11:30–33	261, 271–72
		11:5–11	239, 293, 244–46, 255, 294	11:31	10, 58, 272
10:2	21, 54, 79, 229, 262–63, 291, 310			11:32–33	273
		11:6	227	12	132
		11:6–12:10	247	12:1	11, 272, 276–77
10:2–3	135	11:7	23, 101, 222, 258, 290	12:1–10	132, 261, 274–76
10:3	54			12:1–13:4	59
10:3–4	223	11:7–11	2, 248–52	12:2–4	277–81
10:3–6	250	11:7–15	49, 238 n.15, 287	12:3	59
10:4	154, 226, 310	11:8–9	258	12:5	48, 227, 258, 272, 278, 284
10:4–5	258	11:9	290	12:5–6	281–82
10:4–6	223–25	11:10	60, 202, 252, 294–95	12:6	58, 237–38, 241, 287
10:5	248				
10:7	21, 229, 239	11:12	248	12:7	63, 277
10:7–8	225–26	11:12–15	249, 252–54	12:7–9	282–84
10:8	11, 229, 231, 298, 304, 310	11:13	226, 247, 272	12:7–10	304
		11:13–15	22, 265	12:8	11
10:9–11	226–28	11:14	63	12:8–9	277
10:10	49, 216, 239, 247	11:14–15	162	12:9	15, 23, 42, 49 n.2, 227, 256, 258–59, 272, 288
10:10–11	21	11:15	22, 63, 83, 89, 126, 144, 243, 247		
10:11	239, 291, 310			12:9–10	284–86
10:12	22, 76–77, 130–31, 262–63, 288	11:15–21	239	12:10	14, 41, 131, 151, 227, 227 n.10, 237, 255, 258, 261, 265, 272
		11:16	237, 241, 256, 272, 287		
10:12–18	15, 21, 214, 216, 228–30, 246, 252, 291				
		11:16–17	241		

2 Corinthians (*continued*)		13:5–6	236, 308–9	5:16	98
12:11	20–22, 47, 214,	13:5–9	291	5:19	301
	216, 230–31, 237,	13:7–9	309–10	5:19–21	299, 301
	241, 246, 256,	13:8	155	5:20	299
	281–82, 287–88,	13:9	156, 227,	5:22	59, 152–53,
	291		227 n.10, 312		155, 186, 190
12:11–12	288–90	13:10	11, 216, 226,	5:23	221
12:11–13	7, 237–38, 247,		291, 298, 310	6:1	62
	286–87	13:11	10, 41, 156,	6:7	254
12:11–18	251		312–13	6:14	48
12:12	151, 306	13:11–13	35, 310–12	6:15	115, 136–37
12:12–13:10	287	13:13	11, 49 n.2, 133,	6:15–16	233
12:13	220, 237, 249,		186, 314	6:16	264
	290, 292–94	13:14	56	6:18	314
12:13–18	49, 238 n.15				
12:14–13:10	7, 58,	**Galatians**		**Ephesians**	
	215–16, 218,	1:1	38	1:1	38
	290–91, 311	1:4	38, 134	1:3	40
12:14	16, 59, 237,	1:7	244	1:3–14	40
	238 n.15, 250,	1:10	103, 130, 198	1:9	38
	291, 294 n.34,	1:11	185	1:13	56, 153
	303–5	1:11–2:14	265	1:14	56
12:14–15	258, 293–95	1:12	277	1:21	101
12:14–18	238 n.15,	1:13	39	1:22	39 n.3
	287, 291	1:15	149	2:7	152
12:14–21	291–93, 302,	1:15–17	38	2:11–22	137, 138 n.46
	304	1:16	96, 104, 136	2:15	87 n.20, 115, 137
12:15	60, 251	1:17	273	2:16	138 n.46
12:16	100, 243, 251	1:20	58, 272	3:1	220 n.3, 266
12:16–18	155, 195, 258,	2:1	64	3:7	210
	296–97	2:3	64	3:16	115
12:18	64	2:4	257, 268	4:1	219, 266
12:19	7, 58, 75, 168,	2:9	232, 247	4:2	221
	216, 225, 272	2:10	181	4:7	210
12:19–21	291, 297–302	2:16	88	4:12	39 n.3
12:19–13:10	15, 219 n.2	2:19–20	134	4:19	301
12:20	53 n.5, 306, 312	2:20	125, 134, 285	4:22	115
12:20–21	59, 214	3	264	4:24	115, 137
12:21	13, 31, 50, 160,	3:1	161	4:30	56
	162, 306, 312	3:1–6	88	4:31	299
13:1	59, 238 n.15,	3:5	289	4:32	62
	291–92, 294 n.34	3:13	134, 191	5:2	73
13:1–2	16, 31, 191,	3:13–14	142	5:3	301
	214, 216	3:16	264, 167 n.65	5:8	163
13:1–3	305–6	3:17	87, 87 n.20	5:10	125
13:1–4	291, 302	3:21	88, 167 n.65	5:15	218
13:1–10	291, 302–5	4:13–16	283	5:25–27	242
13:1–14	40	4:19	161	6:5	177
13:2	13, 50, 58, 58 n.10,	4:19–20	270	6:11–17	225
	293, 310	4:20	109	6:13–17	154
13:3	227 n.10, 258	4:21–31	96		
13:3–4	309	5:1	96	**Philippians**	
13:4	10–11, 14, 111, 186,	5:2	220	1:1	39, 103
	227 n.10, 258,	5:4	87 n.20	1:13	266
	272, 285, 307–8	5:11	87, 87 n.20	1:15	299
13:5	234	5:15	218, 258	1:17	299

Index of Ancient Sources

1:18	155	4:3	63–64	6:4	299
1:23	124	4:10	266		
1:29–30	186	4:12	38	**2 Timothy**	
2:2	312			1:1	38
2:3	299	**1 Thessalonians**		1:8	266
2:5–11	191, 191 n.8, 222	1:3	151	2:3	39
2:7	103	1:5	289	2:17	283
2:7–9	307	1:6	59, 186	2:20	108
2:8	249	2:3	301	4:6	39
2:11	40, 98, 103	2:4	236	4:14	254, 283
2:12	177	2:5	58		
2:15	141	2:7	161	**Titus**	
2:17	155, 209, 295	2:9	60, 266, 269	3:4	152
2:18	155	2:10	58	3:9	299
2:28	155	2:11	161	**Philemon**	
2:30	209	2:14	186	1	266
3:1	155, 253, 312	2:16	254	9	220 n.3, 266
3:2	218	2:18	102, 220 n.3	19	220 n.3
3:4–5	263	2:19	50	25	314
3:5	263 n.25, 264	3:1–5	270	**Hebrews**	
3:7	264	3:2	39	1:3	102
3:8	100	3:3–4	186	2:14	87
3:9	144	3:5	266	4:15	143 n.52
3:16	233	4:1	98, 219, 312	8:8	79
4:2	312	4:3	38, 168, 301	9:15	79
4:4	155	4:7	301	12:10	47
4:5	221	4:13	43	12:24	79
4:8	312	4:17	43, 280	13:20	313
4:9	313	5:5	163	13:20	79
4:10	155	5:8	154		
4:10–13	209	5:13	312	**James**	
4:15	161	5:16–22	312	1:9	174
4:15–17	250	5:18	38	3:17	221
4:18	73	5:23	41, 313	5:12	51
4:23	314	5:24	55		
		5:26	313	**1 Peter**	
Colossians		5:28	314	1:3	40
1:1	38			1:3–12	40
1:7	265	**2 Thessalonians**		1:11	42
1:15	153	2:8	87 n.20	1:17	130
1:15–20	102	3:1	312	2:22	143 n.52
1:15–23	137, 138 n.46	3:3	55	3:18	143 n.52
1:18	39 n.3	3:5	151	3:20	152, 283
1:20	138 n.46	3:8	60, 266, 269	5:14	313
1:22	242 n.17	3:16	41		
1:23	220 n.3	3:17	220 n.3	**2 Peter**	
1:24	39 n.3			1:13–14	120
1:28	242 n.17	**1 Timothy**		3:13	136
2:8	218	1:2	39	3:15	152
2:11	117	1:10	87 n.20		
2:15	72	1:13–16	100	**1 John**	
3:5	301	1:16	152	3:5	143 n.52
3:9	115	2:6	134		
3:10	115	2:14	243, 243 n.18	**Revelation**	
3:12	221	3:3	221	21:2	242
3:13	62	4:6	265	21:3	285
				21:9	242

SEPTUAGINT AND APOCRYPHA

Genesis
2:8 — 280

Exodus
4:10 — 74
34:30 — 91 n.22
34:34 — 95

Leviticus
26:11–12 — 165–66

Numbers
33:55 — 282

Job
37:15 — 104

Psalms
15:10 — 109
30:13 — 108
87:16 — 43
111:4 — 104
111:9 — 206
114 — 112 n.32
114:3 — 112
114:8 — 112
115 — 112, 112 n.32
115:8 — 112

Proverbs
3:4 — 198
11:24 — 205
22:8 — 205

Isaiah
1:22 — 75
9:1 — 104
49:8 — 150
49:13 — 173
52:11 — 166

Jeremiah
9:22–23 — 235
38:33 — 78–79
39:40 — 79, 79 n.15

Ezekiel
20:34 — 166
28:24 — 282
37:26–27 — 165–66

Hosea
2:6 — 282
10:12 — 208

Sirach/Ecclesiasticus
1:12 — 130
2:10 — 109
42:9–10 — 241
43:19 — 282

1 Kingdoms
16:7 — 131

2 Kingdoms
2:14 — 167

1 Maccabees
8:9–10 — 223

2 Maccabees
1:5 — 138
5:20 — 139
7:33 — 139
10:4 — 221

Wisdom of Solomon
7:25 — 102
7:26 — 102
9:15 — 120
12:18 — 221

PSEUDEPIGRAPHA

1 Enoch
71:5 — 280

2 Enoch
1:1–10 — 179
8:1 — 280 n.30
22 — 280

The Life of Adam and Eve
9–11 — 243
9:1 — 253
37:5 — 280 n.30
40:1–2 — 280 n.30

Martyrdom and Ascension of Isaiah
7–11 — 280

Testament of Abraham
8:1–3 — 279

Apocalypse of Abraham
23 — 243

Testament of Levi
3 — 280

Testament of Ruben
5:6 — 253

DEAD SEA SCROLLS

Damascus Document (CD)
6:19 — 79
8:21 — 79

JOSEPHUS

Jewish Antiquities
3.315 — 139 n.48
6.144–56 — 139 n.48

Jewish War
5.415 — 139 n.48
7.116–62 — 71

GRECO-ROMAN LITERATURE

Plato

Republic
10 — 279

EARLY CHRISTIAN LITERATURE

Apostolic Fathers

1 Clement
5:6 — 266
30:8 — 221

Diognetus
7:4 — 221

Patristic Literature

John Chrysostom

Homilies on 2 Corinthians
1:2 — 38
1:3 — 41
4:1 — 57
4:5 — 61–62
5:1 — 65, 72
6:2 — 77
7:2 — 86
11:5 — 143
12:1 — 149
13 — 171
23:2 — 246
26:2 — 283
28:2 — 300
29:1 — 305

INDEX OF AUTHORS

Allo, E. B., 16 n.3, 53 n.5, 59, 60, 64, 73, 107, 115, 115 n.34, 118 n.35, 135, 140, 140 n.51, 143, 149, 188–89, 191, 193, 197, 200, 237, 247 n.19, 256, 275, 283 n.33, 305
Amador, J. D. H., 29 n.24

Barnett, P., 29 n.24, 38 n.2, 62, 107, 130, 185 n.7, 187–88, 196, 206, 214, 225, 227, 237 n.19, 254
Barrett, C. K., 18, 18 n.5, 28 n.20, 54, 69, 73, 92, 107, 114, 141, 196, 197, 214, 218, 221, 226, 237, 247–48, 305, 305–6, 309, 313
Belleville, L. L., 83, 84 n.18, 90, 91 n.21, 92, 94
Betz, H. D., 25 n.15, 28 n.23, 115 n. 34, 180 n.2, 183, 195–97, 200, 200 n.11, 205–6, 276
Beyer, H. W., 233 n.13
Bieringer, R., 20 n.8, 24, 24 n.11, 27, 30 n.25, 50 n.4, 138 n.47, 140 nn.49–50, 159 n.60
Bleek, F., 24, 24 n.12
Bornkamm, G., 28, 64
Brenton, L. C. L., 95, 104, 166, 173, 198, 205, 208
Bruce, F. F., 28 n.20, 314
Bultmann, R., 28, 41–42, 64, 69, 107, 117, 130, 132, 143, 144 n.55, 152, 228, 237, 239, 247 n.19, 254, 271, 305, 309

Calvin, J., 57, 61, 71, 121, 140, 143, 144 n.55, 283, 300
Chrysostom, J., 38, 41, 57, 61–62, 65, 72, 77, 86, 140, 143, 149, 161, 169, 193, 246, 283, 300, 305
Collange, J. F., 28 n.23, 107, 120 n.37, 140

Dahl, N. A., 159 n.60
Danker, F. W., 29 n.24, 257
Dauzenberg, 72
Delling, G., 283 n.32
De Lorenzi, L., 84 n.18

Duff, P. B., 71 n.14
Dunn, J. D. G., 95 n.23, 191 n.8

Ellington, J., 311
Ewald, H., 25, 25 n.13

Fallon, F., 28 n.23
Fee, G. D., 55, 57 n.9
Fitzgerald, J. T., 47 n.1, 107, 109 n.28, 147 n.58
Fitzmyer, J. A., 91 n. 21, 138 n. 47, 145 n.57, 159 n. 60
Ford, D. F., 29 n.24, 41 n.5, 42 n.6, 181 n.4
Furnish, V. P., 16 n.3, 18 n.4, 28 n.20, 51, 59, 64, 84, 92, 104, 107–8, 114, 118 n.35, 119, 120 n.37, 130, 132, 135, 140, 140 n.50, 159, 169 n.66, 174, 178, 189, 192, 196, 200, 203–5, 214, 222, 237, 245, 247 n.19, 266, 271–72, 275, 283 n.33, 288, 313

Garland, D. E., 29 n.24, 214, 218, 222 n.7, 237, 247 n.19, 270, 276, 288, 305
Georgi, D., 21 n.9, 182 n.5
Gillman, J., 118 n.35, 121, n.38

Hafemann, S. J., 29 n.24, 71 nn.13–14, 75, 84 n.18, 87 n.20, 90, 91 n.21, 107, 112, 167 n.65, 185 n.7, 203, 214, 233, 233 n.14
Harvey, A. E., 43 n.7, 120 n.37
Hausrath, A., 25, 25 n.16, 53 n.5, 214
Heinrici, C. F. G., 247
Héring, J., 57
Hester, D. A., 29 n.24
Hock, R. F., 249 n.21
Hughes, P. E., 74, 107, 197, 271–72
Hyldahl, N., 294 n.34

Jeremias, J., 280 n.31
Judge, E. A., 271

Kennedy, J. H., 25 n.17, 53 n.7, 214
Kim, S., 104 n.27

Kraftchick, S. J., 24, 24 n.10, 111 n.30
Kreitzer, L., 20 n.8, 159 n.60

Lambrecht, J., 20 n.8, 29 n.24, 50 n.4, 51, 54 n.6, 64, 68, 68 n.11, 92, 106, 113 n.33, 114, 122 n.40, 125, 130, 132, 138 n.47, 146, 148 n.59, 159 n.60, 170 n.67, 180 n.2, 200, 200 n.11, 204, 206, 210, 214, 218, 219 n.2, 220, 225, 247 n.19, 272–73, 277, 308–9
Lang, F. G., 118 n.35
Lewis, T. J., 163 n.63

Malherbe, A., 224
Marshall, P., 250, 250 n.22
Martin, R. P., 28 n.20, 40 n.4, 54, 63–64, 69, 138 n.47, 169 n.66, 200, 214, 218, 225, 237, 247, 266, 271–72, 275, 288
Martyn, J. L., 101 n.25, 135 n.44, 136 n.45
McCant, J. W., 29 n.24, 214, 238, 271, 275
McKnight, S., 183 n.6
Merkel, H., 138 n.47
Metzger, B., 117
Mitchell, M. M., 182 n.5, 296 n.35
Munck, J., 183 n.6
Murphy-O'Connor, J., 28 n.20, 113 n.33

Nickle, K. F., 182 n.5

O'Mahony, K. J., 180 n.2, 185 n.7
Omanson, R. L., 311

Peterson, B. K., 219 n.1, 248 n.20
Plummer, A., 28 n.21, 58 n.10, 62–63, 107, 125, 135, 146, 153, 197–97, 214, 228, 237, 274, 278 n.28, 283, 283 n.33, 287, 305, 308

Savage, T. B., 110 n.29, 111 n.31
Schmithals, W., 28
Scott, J. M., 29 n.24, 48, 67, 71 n.14, 101, 167 n.65, 214, 232, 232 n.11
Semler, J. S., 25, 25 n.14, 214
Spicq, C., 221 n.6
Stockhausen, C. K., 80, 80 n.16, 81, 84 n.18, 85, 91 n.21
Stowers, S. K., 200 n.11

Thrall, M., 16 n.1, 20 n.8, 28 n.20, 36, 51, 53 n.5, 59, 63–64, 68–69, 71 n.14, 72, 92, 95 n.23, 97–98, 97 n.24, 100, 107, 114, 117, 118 n.35, 132, 134–35, 140 nn.49–50, 144 n.54, 146, 148, 169, 178, 184, 186, 192–94, 197, 200, 205, 209, 214, 218, 222, 237, 247 n.19, 252 n.23, 263 n.25, 266–67, 271–73, 278–79, 283 n.33, 292, 314
Traub, H., 280 n.31

Vanhoye, A., 84 n.19, 85,

Wedderburn, A. J. M., 182 n.5
Williamson, L., 71 n.14
Windisch, H., 91, 143, 144 n.55, 228, 247 n.19, 271, 284
Witherington III, B., 29 n.24

Young, F., 29 n.24, 41 n.5, 42 n.6, 181 n.4

INDEX OF SUBJECTS

abundance. *See* God: and the economy of abundance
Achaia
  and the collection, 182, 183, 192, 199, 201–3, 202 n.12
  and the preaching of the gospel, 235, 268
  and the recipients of 2 Corinthians, 5, 37, 39, 52
  regions of, 244, 251
Adam and Eve, 280
affliction. *See* Paul: afflictions of
ambassador of Christ. *See* Paul: ambassador of Christ
angel of Satan, 283, 284
  See also thorn for the flesh
anointing. *See* Spirit: anointing of
anxiety. *See* Paul: anxiety of
apostle(s)
  at Jerusalem, 21, 247
  false, 22, 226, 247, 253, 259, 265, 268, 271, 291
  intruding, 22, 23, 24, 28, 30, 31, 32, 47, 50, 54, 66, 67, 74, 76, 83, 89, 101, 126, 131, 132, 144, 147, 154, 179 n.1, 213–15, 216, 220, 220 n.3, 222, 224, 226, 229, 231, 232, 234, 236, 237, 238, 240, 241, 242, 243, 244, 246, 247, 249, 250, 251, 252, 254, 255, 256, 265, 270, 276, 287, 290, 291, 294, 296, 300, 302
  signs of an, 287, 288, 290, 306
  See also super-apostles
Aretas, king, 273
authority. *See* Paul: authority of

Beliar, 63, 163, 163 n.63
  See also Satan; serpent
benediction, prayer of thanksgiving, 40–42
blessing(s)
  and the collection for Jerusalem, 200, 201, 203, 204, 206
  God's blessing, 208, 311–12, 314
  spiritual blessings, 193, 209

boasting
  as merely human, 257
  in Christ or the Lord, 229, 231, 256
  in oneself, 229, 230, 231
  in visions and revelations, 274–86
  in weakness, 271–73, 284–86, 299
  of Paul in the Corinthians, 48, 49, 50, 173, 177, 201, 202
  of the Corinthians in Paul, 48, 49, 50, 61, 66, 131, 151
  of the intruders in Paul's work, 23, 234
  Paul's foolish boasting, 7, 22, 214–15, 216, 220, 226, 230, 231, 237–89
  vocabulary of in 2 Corinthians, 48
  within limits, 235, 236
body
  a tent, 117, 119, 120, 121, 124, 126
  an earthen vessel, 14, 107–9, 109 n.28, 111 n.30, 115, 119, 120, 122, 125, 126
  nakedness apart from, 118 n.35, 121, 122
  present transformation of, 113–16
  the resurrection body, a building from God, 10, 118, 120, 121
Bornkamm-Schmithals hypothesis. *See* partition theories
brothers, unnamed, 194–99, 202, 296–97
burden. *See* Paul: not a financial burden to the Corinthians

Christ
  agent of salvation and reconciliation, 56, 138 n.46, 139–40, 143
  became sin, 11, 14, 40, 89, 134, 141, 142–44, 154, 191
  crucified by reason of weakness, 307–8
  died for all, 5, 11, 12, 111, 127, 132–35, 137, 144, 314
  face of, 13, 15, 99, 103, 104, 105, 108, 152, 248
  faithfulness of, 4, 46, 52, 54–55, 65
  fragrance of, 73
  image of God, 2, 11, 12, 97, 99, 102, 104, 105

Index of Subjects

Christ (*continued*)
  judgment seat of, 2, 11–12, 105, 113, 119, 125–26, 129, 130, 132, 254, 298, 254
  Lord, 11–12, 40
  love of, 132–33, 313
  messiah, 11
  preexistence of, 191, 191 n.8, 191 n.9
  sinless, 10, 11, 142, 143–44, 143 n.52, 144
  Son of God, 11, 12, 55, 55 n.7, 56, 104, 191
  sufferings of, 3, 35, 42, 50
  See also Jesus
church. *See* community, Corinthian
clemency. *See* Paul: meekness and clemency of
collection for Jerusalem
  appeal to complete, 189–93, 205–6
  background of, 181–83
  delegation sent to prepare for, 195–99, 201–3
  generosity of the Macedonians to, 185–88
  relationship between chapters 8 and 9, 200–1
  theological significance of, 207–11
  vocabulary for, 181
commendation
  before God and conscience, 66, 77, 98–99, 99–100, 131, 288, 296, 298
  by the Lord, 230, 235, 236, 304
  Corinthians ought to commend Paul, 7, 47, 131, 235, 256, 287, 288, 289
  Paul accused of self-commendation, 31, 132, 288
  self-commendation, 22, 75, 131, 150, 156, 229–31, 236
  theme of, 76, 230–31, 235
community, Corinthian
  a chaste virgin espoused to Christ, 11, 240–42, 259
  a letter of Christ, 11, 13, 77, 79, 80
  and avoiding defilement, 162–68
  building up of, 225, 226, 277, 298, 304–05, 310
  of a new covenant, 13–14
  Paul's letter of recommendation, 23, 56, 66, 70, 75–78, 79, 80, 99, 161, 225, 235, 288
  the temple of God, 40, 163–4, 169, 226,
conscience. *See* Paul: conscience of
consolation from God, 3, 35, 40–42, 109, 174
  See also God: of all consolation
Corinth
  crisis at, 15–19, 20–24
  disorders at, 297–302, 305–6
  opposition to Paul at, 20–24
    See also apostles: intruding; super-apostles
  See also immorality, problem of
Corinthians
  disobedience of, 224
  need for self-examination, 308–9

obedience of, 62, 63, 176, 177, 209, 210
partial knowledge of Paul, 49–50
repentance of, 6, 17, 19, 30, 31, 54, 171, 172–73, 175–76, 312
the church of God, 39
the temple of God, 13, 32, 40, 78, 158, 160, 162–65, 167–67, 226
Corinthians, Second
  and the church today, 1–3
  literary integrity of, 24–32
  literary plural, 37, 48, 78, 97, 103 n.26, 105–6, 135, 144, 196, 220, 220 n.5, 307
  occasion for writing, 15–20
  outline of, 8–9
  partition theories. *See* partition theories
  purpose, 7, 32, 298–99, 310
  ring patterns, 29, 31, 32, 68, 84, 98, 99, 158, 171, 173, 235, 255, 256
  summary of, 3–7
  theme of, 46, 47–50
  theology of Christ, 11–12
    See also Christ
  theology of God, 10–11
    See also God
  theology of ministry, 13
    See also ministry
  theology of the church, 13–14
    See also community
  theology of the gospel, 14–15
    See also gospel
  theology of the Spirit, 12
    See also Spirit
covenant
  new, 2, 4, 7, 9, 10, 12, 13–15, 21, 66–68, 76, 77, 78–82, 84–90, 90–97, 99–100, 101, 105, 107–8, 112, 116, 123–24, 126, 139, 164, 167
  old, 4, 10, 12, 13, 83, 85, 86, 87, 88, 89–90, 92, 93–94
coworker
  of God, 146, 149
  of Paul, 39, 59, 64,
creation, new, 2, 5, 10, 13, 15, 115, 128, 135, 135 n.44, 136–37, 136 n.45, 138, 139, 145, 150
crisis. *See* Corinth: crisis at

Damascus, escape from, 238, 271–73
dangers. *See* Paul: dangers endured
death
  and resurrection, 120–26
  at work in Paul, 109–12
  of Christ, 11, 14, 15, 73, 74, 127, 129, 132–35, 137–139, 141, 142, 144, 144 n.53, 145
  See also ministry: of death and condemnation

Index of Subjects

deceitful workers, 22, 247, 253
  See also super-apostles
deuteropauline letters, 39 n.3, 137 n.46
disobedience. *See* Corinthians: disobedience of

earnestness
  of the Macedonians, 180, 191, 196
  of the Corinthians, 176, 190, 196, 302
  of Titus, 190, 195–196
earthen vessels. *See* body: an earthen vessel
Ephesus
  affliction at, 43, 266
  harsh letter written from, 4, 20, 59
  Paul's base of operations, 15, 17, 20, 20 n.7, 52, 53, 53 n.5
Eve, deceived by the serpent, 22, 63, 224, 242, 243, 243 n.18, 254, 259, 296
  See also Adam and Eve

faith
  in the God who raises the dead, 43, 112–13
  of the Corinthians, 58, 59, 62, 190, 210, 227, 234–35, 257, 303, 308–9
false apostles. *See* apostles
fear of the Lord, 66, 125, 129, 130, 132, 298
financial support
  accepted by others, 22, 246, 248, 252, 288, 290
  and patronage, 23, 246, 250
  and the Corinthians, 49 n.3
  Paul's refusal of, 6, 7, 15, 169, 222, 246, 250, 251–52, 255–56, 290, 291, 293, 295
  See also patronage
first installment. *See* Spirit: first installment of
flesh
  according to the, 135, 229, 255
  as mortal, 108, 110, 111, 116, 119, 126
  realm of the, 143, 168, 216, 217, 218, 223
  sinful, 143
  walking according to, 217, 218, 222, 229
forgiveness
  and reconciliation, 140, 141
  extended to the offender, 4, 17, 18, 46, 61–63, 171
fragrance. *See* Christ: fragrance of
freedom,
  and the Lord, 96
  freedom in giving, 187
  of Paul, 73, 252

generosity
  an appeal for, 188–93, 204–6
  God the source of, 206–11
  of the Macedonians, 184–88
Gentiles
  and the blessings of Abraham, 142
  and the collection, 181, 182, 183, 193

and Jerusalem, 197, 209, 232
and Paul, 267, 268, 167
as unbelievers, 162
glory
  and apostolic suffering, 67, 105
  and the gospel, 99, 102, 103, 104
  and transformation, 11, 12, 15, 95–97, 114–16
  of God seen by believers, 4, 12, 13, 15, 96–97
  of Moses' ministry, 82–90
  of Paul's ministry, 82–90
  on the face Christ, 10, 13, 15, 99, 103, 104, 105, 248
God
  and the economy of abundance, 42 n.6
  comforts the downcast, 10, 31–31, 65, 173, 174
  enlightens believers, 103–5
  faithfulness of, 52, 54–55, 65, 144
  Father of Jesus Christ, 3, 10, 11, 40, 41, 173, 186, 271
  knowledge of, 10, 69, 70, 73, 75, 98, 99, 102, 152, 217, 224, 248, 258
  of all consolation, 10, 41, 44, 109, 171, 173, 174, 313
  of hope, 41
  of love and peace, 41, 310, 311, 313
  power of, 14, 24, 74, 108, 111, 153, 154, 156, 227, 237, 272, 285, 289, 307, 308
  promises of, 11
  the Father of mercies, 10, 41, 171, 313
  the living, 10, 12, 13, 32, 56, 66, 69, 75, 76, 77, 78, 80, 158, 160, 161, 162, 164
  triumphal procession of, 71–73
  who raises the dead, 11, 14, 15, 35, 36, 37, 41, 42, 43, 44, 58, 66, 112, 113, 123, 174
  word of, 6, 69, 74–75, 98, 99, 100, 214, 296, 298
  See also Corinthians, Second: theology of God
gospel
  glorious, 12, 98, 102
  light of the, 63, 98, 104, 108, 224
  of Christ, 11, 12, 39, 98, 101, 102, 209, 251
  of God, 269
  paradoxes of, 14–15
  veiled, 30–31, 49, 68, 74, 84–85, 99, 100–101, 101 n.25, 103, 104, 105
grace
  and peace, 37, 40
  and the collection, 181, 184–88
  of God, 115, 147, 149–50, 180, 185–88, 196, 208, 209, 210
  of the Lord Jesus Christ, 191
grief
  of Paul, 58, 59, 60, 62, 64, 155

grief *(continued)*
  of the Corinthians, 61, 173, 175
  of the offender, 61, 62

hardness of heart. *See* heart: hardness of
hardship lists, 41, 107–13, 147–57, 261–71, 286
harsh letter, 4, 5, 7, 17, 18–20, 25, 26, 27, 28, 29, 30, 59–60, 62, 64, 65, 175–77, 178 191, 192, 294 n.34, 297, 302, 308
Hausrath-Kennedy hypothesis. *See* partition theories
heart
  hardness of, 94
  law written on the, 78, 79–80, 82, 88, 89–90
  of flesh, human, 69, 77, 80, 81
  of stone, 80
  sign of affection, 5, 12, 31, 32, 127, 158, 159–62, 168, 169, 302
  veil over, 12, 90, 95
heaven(s)
  and paradise, 277, 278, 278, 280, 280 n.30
  number of, 280
  vision of, 277–81
holy kiss. *See* kiss, holy
hope
  of Paul, 36, 47–48, 49, 90, 119, 119 n.36, 122, 124, 125, 131, 151, 234, 308
  of resurrection, 42, 122, 124, 125
humility. *See* Paul: humility of

image
  of Christ, God's Son, 2, 97, 102
  of God, 2, 11, 12, 96, 97, 99, 102, 104, 105
immorality, problem of, 1–2, 6, 15, 19, 20, 30, 31, 50, 59, 160, 165, 215, 300 n.36, 301–2, 306, 312
imprisonment. *See* Paul: imprisonments of
inner person. *See* person: inner
Israel
  and a new covenant, 79–82
  and unbelief, 93–96
  of God, 264
  restoration of, 81

Jesus
  another, 22, 24, 101, 240, 242, 242, 244, 246, 252, 259
  dying of, 3, 14, 24, 107, 109–12, 113, 126, 155, 307
  life of, 3, 14, 24, 106, 107, 109–12, 109 n.28, 116, 126, 155, 307
  See also Christ
  judgment, 125–26
  See also Christ: judgment seat of

kiss, holy, 313
knowledge of God. *See* God: knowledge of

labors. *See* Paul: labors of
letter and the Spirit, 80–82
letter written in tears. *See* harsh letter
letters of recommendation, 6, 23, 30, 75–78, 75, 150, 160, 182, 195, 214, 225, 247, 288, 298
life. *See* Jesus: life of
love
  for the offender, 18, 62
  fruit of the Spirit, 153, 190
  Paul's love for the Corinthians, 18, 19, 46, 60, 64, 65, 175, 176, 177, 249, 250, 251, 295
  See also Christ: love of; God: of love and peace

Macedonia
  and Paul's travel plans, 16–17, 20 n.7, 52–53, 53 n.5
  and the collection, 182–83, 185–88, 201–3
  2 Corinthians written from, 20, 174, 313
  Paul meets Titus at, 20, 26, 64, 65, 67, 109, 169, 171, 173–74
meekness. *See* Paul: meekness and clemency of
minister(s)
  of a new covenant. *See* Paul: minister of a new covenant
  of Christ, 22, 89, 225, 254, 263, 265, 270
  of Satan, 243, 247, 253, 254
  See also super-apostles
ministry
  and apostolic hardships, 105–6, 107–13, 114–16, 173–74, 265–71, 289–90
  and reconciliation, 10, 127, 129, 137–45, 147, 148, 149, 150, 156
  of a new covenant, 13, 78–82
  of death and condemnation, 86–90
  of the Spirit and righteousness, 86–90
  wages for, 250
  See also financial support, and patronage
Moses
  ministry of, 86–90
  veil of, 87, 90–93

nakedness. *See* body: nakedness apart from
new covenant. *See* covenant: new

obedience. *See* Corinthians: obedience of
offender, the, 17–18, 19, 20, 24, 20, 31, 59, 60–63, 169, 171, 172, 175, 176, 177
old covenant. *See* covenant: old
outer person. *See* person: outer

painful visit. *See* visits to Corinth by Paul
partition theories
  Bornkamm-Schmithals hypothesis, 28–29

Index of Subjects

Hausrath-Kennedy hypothesis, 28–29
Semler-Windisch hypothesis, 27–28
Weiss-Bultmann hypothesis, 28–29
partnership
   and the collection, 181, 209, 210
   in the gospel, 250, 252
   with immorality, 163
patronage
   accepted by intruding apostles, 6, 22, 246, 249, 259
   refused by Paul, 2, 7, 23, 47, 238, 246, 249, 250
   See also financial support
Paul
   a fool, 7, 237–38, 241, 256, 259, 261, 281, 287–88
   a powerful warrior, 223–25, 226
   accused of being cunning, 100, 243, 296–97
   affliction in Asia, 43–44
   afflictions of, 3, 14, 14, 24, 32, 35–36, 40–42, 50, 59, 65, 66–68, 105, 107, 109–10, 115–16, 119, 151–52, 153, 155, 156, 173–74, 174–75
   ambassador of Christ, 5, 9, 13, 62, 66, 72, 126–27, 129, 141–42, 145, 147, 149–50, 156, 160
   anxiety of, 26, 63–65, 171, 174, 240, 262, 269–270, 297
   apostolic sufferings. *See* hardship lists
   approved and tested, 231, 236, 308–10
   authority of, 7, 18, 19, 58, 62, 75, 177, 198, 218, 219, 222, 225–26, 235, 298, 304, 306, 309–10
   beatings endured, 151–52, 261–62, 266
   bodily presence of, 219–23, 226–28, 290
   boldness of, 90, 218–28
   call and conversion of, 103–4
   change of travel plans, 52–54, 53 n.5, 57–60
   conscience of, 47–49, 58, 76
   contrasted with the many, 74–75
   courageous and open, 99–100
   criticism of his in speech, 226–27, 247–48
   dangers endured, 10, 44, 260, 261, 262, 268–69, 270–71
   despaired of life, 43–44
   endurance of, 148, 151, 152, 272, 273, 289
   fragrance of God's knowledge, 73–74
   humility of, 222–23
   imprisonments of, 148, 151, 259, 261, 262, 266
   integrity of, 2, 48–49, 98–105, 130–32, 219–28
   Jewish pedigree, 263–64
   labors of, 152, 262, 262, 266
   meekness and clemency of, 219–22
   minister of a new covenant, 10, 26, 66, 70, 74, 77, 78–82, 105, 108, 112, 126, 170
   missionary assignment, 23, 228, 231–37, 232 n.12, 246
   not a financial burden to the Corinthians, 7, 23, 49, 249, 250, 251, 258, 259, 287, 290, 291, 292–96
   not inferior to the super-apostles, 7, 238, 246–54, 259, 277, 282, 288
   openness of, 78
   opponents of, 20–24
      See also apostle(s): intruding; super-apostles
   persecutions of, 286
   preaches free of charge, 248–52, 293–95
   prisoner of God, 10, 11, 71–73, 100, 105, 223
   qualification for ministry, 68–82
   refuses financial support, 6, 7, 23, 222, 248–52, 290, 293–95
   See also financial support; patronage
   reliability of, 52–54, 54–56
   the aroma of Christ, 11, 70–71, 73, 74
   visions and revelations of, 274–81
   weapons of his warfare, 218, 223–25
   See also boasting; ministry; visits to Corinth by Paul
person
   inner, 113–16
   outer, 113–16
pledge. *See* Spirit: pledge of
poverty
   of Jesus Christ, 5–6, 191
   of the Macedonians, 5–6, 186
prayer, 305, 309–10
presence. *See* Paul: bodily presence of
promises. *See* God: promises of

qualification. *See* Paul: qualification for ministry

reconciliation
   between God and humanity, 137–45
   between Paul and the Corinthians, 170–78
   call to, 149–50, 156–70
repentance. *See* Corinthians: repentance of
resurrection
   body, 5, 10, 116–26, 42, 105
   of believers, 12
   of Christ, 113
   present experience of, 42, 68, 74, 105, 107, 110–112, 113, 126
   See also hope: of resurrection
revelations. *See* Paul: visions and revelations of
righteousness
   ministers of, 22, 63, 89, 245–46, 253–54, 265
   ministry of, 85–89, 139, 144, 150, 154, 254
   of God, 11, 40, 89, 129, 134, 141–144, 154, 191

righteousness (*continued*)
  weapons of, 89, 147, 148, 153–54, 223
ring pattern. *See* Corinthians, Second: ring patterns

salvation,
  and affliction, 42
  Christ, the agent of, 11–12, 56, 139
  day of, 150
  economy of, 314
  the Spirit, the pledge of, 12
Satan, 17, 18, 22, 46, 61–63, 99, 101–2, 158, 162, 243, 247, 253–54, 283–84
  See also Beliar; serpent
Scripture
  use of in 2 Cor 6:16–18, 164–67
  use of Jeremiah and Ezekiel, 77–82
seal. *See* Spirit: seal of
Second Corinthians. *See* Corinthians, Second
Semler-Windisch hypothesis. *See* Partition theories
serpent, the, 22, 63, 224, 242, 259, 296
  See also Beliar; Satan
severe letter. *See* harsh letter
Silvanus, 37, 38, 39, 55, 59
sin, 11, 14, 40, 80, 88, 89, 96, 102, 115, 134, 141, 142–44, 144 n.53, 154, 191, 222, 249, 290, 293
Son of God. *See* Christ: Son of God
Spirit
  and letter, 80–82, 86
  and the Lord, 96
  anointing of, 10, 11, 13, 41, 55–56, 58, 174
  fellowship of, 7, 56, 312, 314
  first installment of, 56, 123, 174, 314
  of the living God. *See* God: the living
  pledge of, 11, 13, 117, 119, 123 n.43, 125
  removes the veil, 12, 95–96
  seal of, 56
suffering(s). *See* Christ: sufferings of
super-apostles, 20–24, 47, 54, 58, 61, 246–54, 257, 258, 262, 262 n.24, 270–71, 287–88, 290, 296
  See also apostle(s); Paul: opponents of

temple of God. *See* community: the temple of God; Corinthians: the temple of God
thorn for the flesh, 63, 262, 272, 275, 277, 282–84, 286

Timothy, 1, 15, 18, 19, 37–39, 40, 53 n.5, 55, 59, 76, 203 n.12, 265
Titus
  and the collection, 6, 32, 194–99
  bearer of the harsh letter, 4, 17, 20
  Paul's search for, 63–65
  report of, 20, 170–78
  visits to Corinth, 178, 188, 297
  See also earnestness: of Titus
Trinity, 56, 310, 314
triumphal procession. *See* God: triumphal procession of
Troas, Paul's anxiety at, 26, 63–65, 171, 173, 174, 177

unbelievers,
  blinded by the god of this age, 63, 99, 102
  separation from, 13, 26–27, 40, 159–68

veil, *See* Moses: veil of
vices, lists of, 299, 301
virgin, 241
  See also community: a chaste virgin espoused to Christ
visits to Corinth by Paul
  first visit, 39, 293
  painful visit, 4, 5, 6, 30, 16–17, 58–59, 192, 222 n.8, 293, 301, 302, 305
  third visit, 58–59, 293–96, 305–6

wages. *See* ministry: wages for
  See also financial support; patronage
weakness
  boasting in, 256, 271–73, 276, 277, 281–82, 284–86
  of Christ, 285, 304, 307
  See also boasting
Weiss-Bultmann hypothesis. *See* partition theories
witness
  of God, 58
  of Paul's conscience, 47, 58, 76, 100
  of two or three, 305–6
word of God. *See* God: word of
world, the
  god of this age, 103
  reconciled to God, 5, 10, 11, 12, 13, 15, 66, 137–41, 314

www.ingramcontent.com/pod-product-compliance
Lightning Source LLC
Chambersburg PA
CBHW032026290426
44110CB00012B/682